Four
in the
Corps

FOUR
IN THE
CORPS

From Boot Camp to
Baghdad—One Grunt's Enlistment

Richard C. Meyer
SGT/USMC
G. Co., 2/5
2000–2004

iUniverse, Inc.
New York Lincoln Shanghai

Four in the Corps

From Boot Camp to Baghdad—One Grunt's Enlistment

iUniverse books may be ordered through booksellers or by contacting:

iUniverse
2021 Pine Lake Road, Suite 100
Lincoln, NE 68512
www.iuniverse.com
1-800-Authors (1-800-288-4677)

ISBN-13: 978-0-595-35076-6 (pbk)
ISBN-13: 978-0-595-79780-6 (ebk)
ISBN-10: 0-595-35076-3 (pbk)
ISBN-10: 0-595-79780-6 (ebk)

Printed in the United States of America

CONTENTS

▼

"Tragedy is me getting a teeny, tiny little splinter in my pinky fin-ger. Comedy is you walking down the street, you fall down an open man-hole and die."

—Mel Brooks

BOOT

The only way that a guy can know what it's like to be a pretty girl is to walk into a recruiter's office. All eyes are on you, chairs are pulled out and promises are made. Security with a hint of adventure is offered. Who could turn that down?

My father was an Air Force officer who spent most of his career as a navigator on refueling planes. I grew up loving the military. There were ten miles of farmland between my house and the base where my father worked, Offutt AFB in Bellevue, Nebraska. In the days before the huge annual air show, I would get a free preview as the pilots practiced their maneuvers over the cornfields. It was the 80's; the time of G.I.Joe, Rambo and Top Gun.

During my senior year of high school, Iraq invaded Kuwait. The upcoming war occupied my thoughts and I was dying to go, but just a year too young. I watched the war on CNN, marveling at the technological omnipotence the U.S. had over Iraq. I felt that it was the great war of my generation and I had missed it by one semester.

I graduated from high school and drifted through life, hitting the trifecta of post-high school loserdom—a job at McDonald's, no girlfriend and getting kicked out of college for bad grades. I dreamt of being a cartoonist, but I didn't have the talent, wasting half of my twenties before I realized it was not to be. After a bad break up, I finally got my first real job, working at Dell Computers. For the first time, I didn't feel like a complete failure. I was good at my job, made friends and was working at an amazingly successful company. The work was temp-to-hire, with a promise of permanent employment.

Things were going fine until I got into a fight outside of work. I ended up getting arrested three times for the same fight. It turns out that telling someone you're going to beat them up, going to beat them up and actually beating them up are three separate crimes, an interesting legal tid-bit it cost $5,000 to learn. I was fired from Dell until my trial seven months later. When my charges were reduced to Disorderly Conduct, I was re-hired at Dell, only to be laid off at the end of the fiscal quarter a few weeks later.

Once the new quarter started, the geniuses at Dell realized that they couldn't keep up production with just 30% of their workforce, so they rehired all their old temps. My heart sunk when I learned that, though I had worked at Dell for almost two years, I was starting over at Square One since I had been laid off and re-hired.

Like anyone with a miserable existence, I had a rich fantasy life. I loved comics, movies and books about war. My favorite was "Black Hawk Down", which was just becoming a best seller. The book was like an action movie, only real. I decided that I wanted to do three things: shoot machineguns, fly around in helicopters and go to war.

The army vets from nearby Fort Hood that worked at Dell were quite enthusiastic when I told them I was going to go into the Army. I briefly mentioned checking out the Marines, but that was my fallback plan. My only knowledge of the Marines was that they were a Department of the Navy and that they had an infinitesimal budget. I had family in the Air Force, Army and Navy, but none in the Marines. Marines were abnormal, stupid, brainwashed robots. They got the worst of everything and if it was good, they got it last. My Army friends concurred; the Army was the only way to go.

My visit to the Army recruiter was not the highlight of their year. When I told them that I had some legal trouble from the fight, they lost almost all interest. They said that it would be extremely hard for me to even get into the Army and that there would be numerous hoops to jump through. The earliest they could get me in was about six months—maybe. I had no intention on wasting another six months in my aimless $7-an-hour existence.

I walked across the parking lot to the Marine recruiter since they were the only other service that had infantry. It started to bother me how the Army had just brushed me aside. The Army recruiters were in their early thirties and didn't look like anything special. I was mid-twenties, in decent shape, and never had a drug in my life. Why wouldn't they want me?

Marine recruiters are under enormous pressure to get "bodies" every month. The other services are pickier about whom they grab, but the Marines really don't care. The Marine philosophy is, they *will* make a Marine out of you, no matter what kind of pathetic piece of cookie dough they are given.

As I opened the door to their office, an early twenties, football player-type with a blond flat-top who looked like he stepped out of the recruitment poster rose to shake my hand. When I told him about my legal troubles, he actually perked up. "You didn't kill anyone, did you?" No, I just got into a fight. Did you win? Yeah. Well, good to go, here's a pen, let's start filling out some forms. My sordid story didn't even make him blink. Everything was doable. Every rule had an exception. They could get me in the Corps in a week if I passed the physical.

I started the voluminous form-filling process and was introduced to my recruiter, Sgt. Schofield. He had been in the Reserves for six years; then gone straight into Active Duty as a recruiter, which was rare. He was the hot recruiter in the office, the one who pulled in the high numbers every month. Taking charity cases like me must have been his cross to bear.

The ASVAB test and Physical would be taken at the San Antonio MEPS (Military Entry Point Sub-station). They put us up in a motel by the highway, gave us some vouchers for the diner next door, and told us we had a 4:00AM wake-up call.

At the MEPS, I took the self-paced ASVAB (Armed Services Vocational Aptitude Battery) in a computer lab with about twenty other people. I felt like I was doing well until about halfway through the allotted time when people started finishing and leaving. More and more people left until it was just three others and I, with twenty minutes left to go. My confidence disappeared; I must be a moron to take so much time. I was the last one to finish and I dejectedly walked up to the proctor. I was shortly informed of my score—a 95 out of 99, the highest in the class. The guy who walked out first with a cocky smile on his face got a 38. The recruiters were ecstatic with my grade.

Back at the hotel, I spoke with my roommate, who was going into the Air Force. He had a guaranteed bonus and a shorter enlistment. Even better than that, he had a calm, confident and optimistic air about him—he had a bright future and he knew it. He didn't say anything about my choice, but you could tell what he was thinking: why would anyone join the Marines? I started to doubt my choice; I was going into the Marines, for Christ's sake. I considered backing out, but then I thought about how much extra work my recruiter had done to get me in. And what else would I do? Deliver pizzas? I was tired of being an almost-artist and a sort of-student. I wanted to be something real, even if it was difficult.

The next day, I went through the hours-long physical and got to experience all the joys of standing in a cold room with a dozen men in their underwear. It would not be the last time. I was sweating the exam since I have scoliosis and flat feet, but the doctors didn't even bat an eye and I passed with flying colors. There were some guys in there to which the description "mutant" would be charitable, but they made it through as well. The military isn't exactly Harvard.

We were taken into a small, court-like room and given the Oath of Enlistment, by a cute female Air Force officer. While taking the Oath might literally be a matter of life or death, all that occurred to me was that after I took it, I could no longer ask that cute chick out.

I returned home and quit my job. I had enough money to coast into boot camp, so I decided to relax for the next month. Between enlistment and going to boot camp, an enlistee is in the Delayed Entry Program. You're supposed to go to DEP functions on the weekends, where they PT you very lightly and try to keep you pumped up for boot camp. Being in the DEP is a heady, but silly time; you walk around wearing your "Marines" T-shirt with your head held high, bragging to everyone how you're going to be in the Marines, but you haven't done anything yet; you haven't earned it. You're sure you will; you'll be the best and it will all be easy.

I thought it would be fun to watch every movie that remotely had to do with Marines. "Full Metal Jacket" is great—and I would learn later, highly accurate—but after you see that there's a sharp cliff, a long drop and then you're watching flicks like "The Walking Dead" and "The Punisher" with Dolph Lundgren.

During one DEP function, we ran through an obstacle course at the nearby Army National Guard camp. Every military movie has an obstacle course scene in it and it always looks like great fun. It's one of those "They get paid to do that!" scenes that make someone want to join. By the time I got a fifth of the way through the course, I was totally exhausted; the rest of it was a blur of stumbling rubber-limbed around pieces of wood and metal poles and having one strange obstacle explained to me several times before I even understood how to get through it. One girl fell off a rope ladder about fifteen feet off the ground and had to get medical attention. We thought it was a big deal, but to the recruiters, it was just another day at the office. This sure wasn't Dell.

After the obstacle course, they took us to the armory. "Kid in a candy store" does not even begin to describe it. They let us fondle the weapons and ask any dumb question we could think of. The Marine Corps could teach a class in the art of seduction; if I was ever on the fence, this sealed the deal.

I still had to figure out what I wanted to do in the Marines though. Since I had such a high ASVAB score, they tried to steer me toward a technical MOS, but I had read too many G.I.Joe comics as a kid—I wanted something combat-related. I've never seen a Schwarzenegger movie where he played a really bad-ass radar technician whose equipment is always in perfect working order. I tried to figure out which MOS was technical, but still had some cool Rambo-like aspects. In my heart, I knew that I just wanted to fire machineguns from the hip, but that doesn't exactly transfer well to the civilian world. I finally narrowed it down to combat engineer or field communications. The catch was that I couldn't pick a specific job, just a broad field. When I saw that one of the jobs in the combat engineer field was "seamstress", I knew that with my bad luck, that would the job I would get put in. I decided to go into comm. Maybe I'd work with satellites. They have satellites in James Bond movies, don't they?

As Boot Camp approached, I became apprehensive. I was about to go to what was basically a prison for the next twelve weeks, so I tried to cram as much fun into my remaining days of freedom. When my recruiter told me that my departure date had been pushed back a week, I wasn't exactly heartbroken. I couldn't sleep the night before I left, so I stayed up all night, flipping through comics and watching "Shakespeare in Love" on TV.

The recruiter picked me up and took me to the MEPS for final processing. As I was going through some final paperwork, I told the sergeant on duty something that had been gnawing at me: I wanted to go into the infantry. The sergeant had to make some last-minute calls to make this happen. He put me on the phone with a colonel, who told me that there was no going back after I switched. I told him I understood.

After a very long day on lock-down in the MEPS watching "The Matrix" and "Rush Hour" and eating stale sandwiches, we were bused to the airport, where we would take a short flight to San Diego. I had been to San Diego several times, so I knew that the Marine Corps Recruit Depot shared a common fence with the airport flightline. When we got to San Diego, we were told to wait in the USO for several hours until the drill instructors picked us up that night. It was a beautiful day and I wanted to see the water one more time. The others got wide-eyed when I told them that I was going to the shore. When they told me that they didn't think we were allowed, I reminded them that no one said we couldn't, so it was alright. Throughout my enlistment, I took every opportunity to assert my independence so that I didn't feel like property. Even if it wasn't a big deal, I always felt the need to do such things. Just as often, I got the wide-eyed look of fear from my peers.

The walk took longer than I thought. I didn't get to see the ocean, just a part of the bay, but it was still worth it. I got back to the USO with plenty of time, after downing every bit of junk food I could afford. I had less than ten bucks to my name. Though the USO was filled with about 60 enlistees, no one spoke. The History Channel had an hour-long special on Marine Corps boot camp. It was quite an experience to watch it, knowing that I would be hitting those famed "yellow foot prints" within the hour. Just as the show was about to end, the DIs showed up to grab us. Apropos, but creepy.

We filed out into several buses and vans. Everyone was quiet, including the surprisingly low-key DIs, since we were still in view of civilians. My bus was driven by a tomboy-ish female Marine who swore and gave us withering glares of disgust.

Though the Recruit Depot was right next to the airport, we had to take a circuitous route to get there. The approach to MCRD is very ominous; you have to go under the highway and through a drainage tunnel-looking underpass before you emerge at the front gate. When the bus stopped, a DI jumped on board. If you ever saw a boot camp movie, you know exactly what he said. We were ushered out and told to step into a pair of the 60-or-so yellow footprints that were painted on the ground. The Marine Corps has something called "Barney-style", after the kids TV show. It used to be "Mr. Potato Head"-style, but that's too old-fashioned. Our first order was to stand in formation and the Marine Corps had dumbed it down enough that no one should have been confused as to where to stand.

The yelling started as they made us read some Articles of the Uniform Code of Military Justice which were written on the wall, which all boiled down to: "You are property. We own you." We were shoved into the adjacent building, where we were stripped of all contraband. Somehow I was able to keep my watch, which was expressly forbidden.

We were squeezed into a tiny room with one barber who had fifteen minutes to give as many of us haircuts as possible. A wiry Puerto Rican DI started yelling at us to move back, but there was nowhere to go. The DI pushed the recruit in front of me so hard that he fell onto me and we both fell backward, mosh-pit style, onto a bed of bodies. This was quite a shock. It might seem minor, but imagine that you were at work and your boss ran up to you, yelling and spitting in your face, and then pushed you onto the floor.

When we changed into our cammies, I was shocked at how prevalent skid-marks were with my fellow recruits. Putting the uniform on for the first time should have been a proud moment, but I just felt like a sucker. We were told to put on our "go-fasters"—sneakers—and we learned that the Marine Corps has a stupid name for everything. A pen is an "inkstick", a flashlight is a "moonbeam", a hat is a "cover." The point is, you are not in your old life, you are in the Marine Corps. *Everything* is different.

It was already late when we learned that our day had only just begun. There would be no sleep that night. We were ushered into a room with a huge eagle, globe and anchor on the wall. There were no chairs, so we had to kneel on the floor, which caused extreme pain after a few short minutes. We kneeled there for almost two hours as we signed away the remaining bits of control over our lives.

Reception lasts from a couple days to a week, which sucks because you don't start your 12 weeks of hell until you get to your training platoon. Reception is a comedy of errors in which relatively low-key reception DIs teach you the most elementary skills to keep you from getting choked out Homer Simpson-style by your training DIs. It's also your first taste of having to do things exactly right or facing the consequences. Something as simple as filling out a one-page form can take an hour because you have to be micro-managed, which is known as "going by the numbers." It seems silly until you realize that you are dealing with a wide breadth of humanity from all over the country, some of whom are dumber than dog shit. You find yourself fucking up the simplest things simply because you are nervous. Our first piss test was like a Monty Python routine. Pissing in a cup, writing your initials on a sticker and putting a sticker on the cup became a feat of herculean difficulty. Half of the recruits couldn't pee under pressure, several of them spilled piss everywhere and almost everyone fucked up the sticker.

By some weird quirk of fate, I was allowed to keep my goatee until my third day. When we were finally allowed to buy toiletries, we got our first "fuck you" from the Corps. Although every other service gives their recruits their first issue of uniforms, the Marine Corps makes their recruits buy everything, which means that the average single recruit comes out of boot camp with less than $1000 for three months' work.

Though in my next four years, I would be shoved and choked out by my seniors and shot at by Iraqis, the only people who I will never forgive are the members of the Italian family that ran the barber shop at MCRD. I recognized their faces from the pages of a fifteen year-old boot camp scrap book I flipped through at my recruiter's office. Three generations manned the barber chairs and inflicted more pain than I have ever experienced in war or peace. They knew that we could not say one word to them, since the DIs were glaring at us, so they would grind their dull clippers into our scalps, not caring as we winced in pain as chunks of flesh disappeared into the rusty blades. I fantasized about coming back after I graduated and beating all of their asses.

Our two days at medical were among the worst days I ever had in the Corps. The total degradation and condescension we experienced, contrasted with the relative dignity of being a civilian just a few days earlier, was almost unbearable. Being looked down upon by a Marine DI was one thing, but even the Navy personnel who did something as glory-free as running the eye test treated us like absolute scum.

A corpsman ripped my vein when he took my blood, but I was so busy trying to get to the next station without getting yelled at that I didn't even notice the trail of blood I was leaving. While standing ramrod-straight, eyes forward, in the line for the hearing test, one brave recruit tapped me on the shoulder and pointed out my bleeding arm. I started to feel like I was going to pass out. When I asked a DI if I could sit down, he smiled and told me that I was in the perfect place to fall down. Any damage I did to myself could quickly be repaired.

I had to wear the military-issue BP glasses, much to my chagrin. "BP" stood for "birth control", since no woman would fuck a guy who wore them. Not only was I going to miserable for the next 12 weeks, I was going to looking like a nerd as well.

I'm not going to spend much time describing Marine Corps boot camp, since it's an American institution that's already been exhaustively described. Go rent "Full Metal Jacket"—that's exactly how it is. The Marine Corps doesn't change anything unless it has to. We're the only service that wears the same exact dress uniform we had during World War 2. Although movies and books make Boot Camp look like the end-all, be-all of military existence, it isn't. At best, it's 1/16th of your enlistment. It's rare to spend the majority of your enlistment with more than one of your fellow recruits. After graduation, you will split to the four corners of the world and rarely see each other.

When I graduated from boot camp, I spent my ten days of "boot leave" dreading going to SOI—the School of Infantry. Boot Camp had been difficult for me and the things that gave me the most problems were the grunt activities like running and hiking. I spent Boot Leave at my Uncle's condo in San Diego. He was a chaplain at Marine Corps Air Station, Miramar, which is the most beautiful Marine base for one reason and one reason only—it was built by the Navy. The Top Gun school was located there until the base was switched to the Marine Corps in the early 1990s. I spent a lot of time at Miramar, enjoying the high standard of living and kicking myself for joining the infantry. I was stupid enough to pick Infantry, even though I had never been athletic and was eight years older than the average recruit. I cursed every G.I.Joe comic and Rambo movie that made the infantry sound like a good idea.

The seed of an idea formed in my head: I should switch to the air wing. My uncle was a high-ranking officer; maybe he could pull some strings. He had been suggesting that I try to switch since it was a "waste" for someone who scored as high as I did on the ASVABs to be slogging it out in the grunts.

I reported for duty at the School of Infantry, Camp Pendleton, CA, which was the ugliest and saddest military installation I'd ever seen. Alcoholism wasn't invented at Pendleton, but it sure was perfected there. I went into the receiving barracks and saw a few people I knew in boot camp, which wasn't a great comfort since they were all people that I didn't like—further evidence to me that I wasn't meant for the grunts. Receiving was where they chose what specific MOS you would have. Everyone wanted to be an LAV crewman since they didn't hike. The rumor went around that the higher your ASVAB score was, the better job you would get. I was singled out for having the highest GT score—a sub-set of the ASVAB—in the entire class. A reservist who heard that was incredulous, sputtering, "But…but…he reads comic books!?!"

We had to wait two weeks until we would find out our MOS. In the interim, we would pull Camp Guard while we waited for the next training cycle to begin. The guard force was supervised by a bunch of burn-outs who had been dumped from their units in The Fleet. They were pissed at being professional baby-sitters, so they took it out on us. A simple barracks clean-up would last all night. When you were relived from your four-hour guard shift, if you didn't say, "Good Afternoon, Sergeant. This Marine reports that Post 6 is all secure; nothing unusual to report at this time" word-for-word, you would be rewarded by being kept on that post for another four hours.

While standing watch at a remote guard post a mile from SOI, it got bitterly cold, so my buddy and I took decided to take refuge inside a shack. We'd peek out every couple minutes to make sure that no one was sneaking up on us. When our shift was almost over, I came out and laughed about how we had gotten away with sleeping and chilling out during our entire shift.

"Is that right?" One of the nutso sergeants had walked the long way through the brush just to spy on me. Instead of chewing us out, he just turned around and headed back to the barracks. I thought I had dodged a bullet until I realized he had canceled the van that was to bring our relief. We stood there for five more hours until the van drove up. We were told that every one on every post was not being relieved for twelve hours because of our indiscretion. While that was bad, we had at least been outside and able to walk around. A buddy of mine spent all 12 hours standing in a 3-foot-by-3-foot area next to an armory door, with nothing to look at but bare cinder-block walls. When they came to relieve him, he was hallucinating and he didn't believe that the guys who came to relieve him were real.

The only good deal on guard was being a Rover, in which you and three others would wander around the camp and check on the poor suckers stuck at posts. Usually you were given, a walkie-talkie so the NCOs could check up on you, but if you were smart you would check out and head out to rove before they gave it to you.

Sherman, a lanky Nordic kid from Orange County, became one of my best friends. Though only eighteen, he acted like he was in his early forties and nothing seemed to fluster him. I was chosen to lead the Rover patrol, so I dutifully took the squad from one post to the next, nearly running the whole way.

"What's your hurry, Meyer?" Sherman asked.

"Got to hit all the points. Keep everyone from getting in trouble."

"Look, no matter how much you check on everyone, someone's going to fall asleep right after you leave their post." Which was true.

"This is my first time as squad leader and this is how I was shown to do it."

"Let me guess; Meder was squad leader last time."

"How'd you know?"

"Meder's a good guy, but he tries too hard,; he's going to wear himself out. You're running around like a maniac because you've been Meder-trained; once you're Sherman-trained, you'll be a lot happier."

Sherman-training consisted of us hitting all the posts once and then sleeping in the bushes for three hours. Sherman then woke us five minutes before our shift ended and we walked back to the squad bay. Our groggy just-woken-up faces looked a lot like tired-from-hiking faces, but the impressions of twigs and leaves we each had on one side of our face gave us away.

I lucked out when we were "dropped" to "Chilling Charlie", the easiest training company. The worst was "Broken Bravo" which drove their Marines so hard that they had 40 people on light-duty. My MOS would be 0351 Anti-Tank Assaultman. I would be walking, but I bucked up when I heard that 51s were trained in two different anti-tank rocket launchers along with plastic explosives. It was considered a "smart" MOS. The general consensus was that dumb guys were either made riflemen or machine-gunners.

At this point, I thought it was all over for me. I wanted out of the grunts in the worst way. My uncle had one of the gunnies he worked with speak with me. He told me that I "only" had to do three years as a grunt and then I could switch to the air wing. Thanks, gunny!

My heart sank when we met our squad instructor, Sgt. Norris. While on guard, I had accidentally called him "corporal" and when he found out that I was going to his training company, he vowed to make me miserable. Though he remembered the incident, he couldn't remember my face, so he asked us who called him corporal. I raised my hand and he nodded warily, promising to deal with me later.

Once we got settled into our new squad bay, I was called into the hallway by Sgt. Norris. He shocked me by telling me that I was the squad leader, saying that he picked me because I had shown integrity by raising my hand. He had just re-enlisted in the Marines, after being out for a year and working as a cop. Since he needed to brush up on his knowledge, I would be in charge of the squad most of the time. This had an immediate and positive affect on me. I now had the eighteen Marines under my care, so I didn't have time to worry about myself. This was right after boot camp, when everyone was still brain-washed. Any kind of authority was followed without question, even if it was just a fellow student who was a squad leader.

I came to love being a squad leader, especially since the perks included being exempt from pulling firewatch at night or duty on the weekends. People came to me with their problems and I was actually able to help them. The other squad leaders had a problem with me because I was not the "yell and scream" type, but I pointed out to them I was the only squad leader that did not have any UAs or discipline problems in my squad.

The only really bad part of SOI was the first 9 days, in which we did not get one day off. After that, we had weekends off and a couple of free hours at night. The only really strenuous part were the range runs, in which we would speed-walk with full packs to a range a mile or so away. The rest of SOI kicked ass; it was the G.I.Joe/Rambo shit that I had always wanted to do. Every few days, we were shooting a new cool weapon and the instructors kept the atmosphere relaxed, so that people actually learned. There were a few boot camp fuck-fuck games, but they were rare. I made great friends and have great memories. I loved SOI.

Anyone who enlists west of the Mississippi becomes a West Coast Marine, so Deep South or New York accents are quite rare. Our platoon guide, Furnari, had joined while going to college in the MidWest, but he was a New Yorker to his bones. Mature beyond his years, he was a great guy, but his accent was so thick that it was almost impenetrable. He also used East Coast slang we didn't understand. After an exhausting day of training, the night NCO allowed us to order pizzas.

"Hey Furnari, what kind of pizza do you want?"

"I dunno—just regular."

"How do you want it?"

"Regular."

"Medium?"

"No, Large."

"OK, Large. How do you want it?"

"Regular! Regular!"

"What the hell do you mean by 'regular'?"

"Just cheese!" Furnari said, sounding like Vinnie Barbarino.

The riflemen graduated after thirty days at Charlie Company, but those with "Weapons" MOS'—machinegunners, mortarmen, anti-task assaultmen, and TOW gunners—did an additional three weeks in Weapons Company. I fell in love with the SMAW (Shoulder-mounted Anti-tank Weapon) rocket launcher as soon as I touched it, carrying it around like a new-born baby. After lunch though, they called the entire company into the squad bay. For some reason, they randomly changed everyone's MOS'. I was now an 0331—machinegunner—the "dumb guy" MOS. What the hell? As soon as I held the 240 Golf medium machinegun though, I forgot all about my old MOS. I defy anyone to hold a machinegun for one second and not instantly spring an oak-hard woody. By all modest estimates, I have seen 18 million movies and TV shows with guys shooting machine guns. I was hooked.

Our instructor, Sgt. Post, looked exactly like the main character from the movie "Office Space." He was one of the funniest guys I ever met, along with being a fantastic Marine and great teacher. The Marine Corps is notoriously poor and it has very little money to send people to extra training, so jump wings and scuba insignia are very rare. Somehow, Sgt. Post had jump wings and had been to Ranger school, which was almost unheard of for a Marine. He told us that at one of their staff meetings, they were told that there was a quota to send one instructor to jump school and then to Ranger school. Sgt. Post's buddy, who was a PT stud, raised his hand immediately. To make himself look good, Sgt. Post also raised his hand, knowing that his buddy would be picked. Ranger School is a grueling three months in which the average student loses 30 pounds, so no one else wanted to go. Sgt. Post's buddy was just about to head off to Ft. Benning when he injured his leg. With one day's notice, Sgt. Post was sent off to take his buddy's place. Though he said that Jump School was fairly easy, Ranger School almost killed him. Marines aren't even allowed to wear the coveted "Ranger" tab on their uniforms; he said that all he got out of it was a chronic cough and messed-up knees.

Sgt. Post was a victim of a phenomenon that I would become all too familiar with years later. Once a Marine gets to the rank of sergeant, he gets in-depth performance reviews called Fit/Reps. One bad Fit/Rep can kill your career, even if all your other Fit/Reps are glowing. Sgt. Post had been a sergeant for almost five years and had been continually passed over for promotion even though he had completed Airborne and Ranger school, which is incredibly prestigious in the grunt community. After banging his head against a wall for half a decade, he applied to the Officer Commissioning Program and got accepted.

Sgt. Post had a peculiar teaching assistant, a little Lego Man named "Machinegun Bob." In the good cop/bad cop equation, Machinegun Bob was as bad as it gets. Sgt. Post would never punish or thrash us, he would simply make us try to live up to the example set by Machinegun Bob. Putting Machinegun Bob in the push-up position, he would tell us to hold that position as long as he did. Machinegun Bob always won. The little fucker.

My fellow students took the concept of seniority to ridiculous lengths. When we got to Weapons Company, the class ahead of us tried to lord it over us because they had been in the Marine Corps *two weeks* longer than us. The sad thing was that we were so brain-washed at the time that most of us actually let them do it. Mostly it would just be high school bullshit, like yelling at us if we went in their squad bay without permission, but one little guy seemed to make it his personal mission to psyche me out. He kept trying to scare me about the final hike, in which we would carry the .50 cal.

"Yeah, most of you aren't going to make it. It's pure hell, man."

"Well, it can't be that bad. I mean, you made it," I replied.

His boys started laughing, thinking I was trying to clown on him, but I was just stating the obvious. There's nothing in the Marines that is impossible; no matter how hard they make anything, most people pass. He screwed up his face as he leaned in.

"Oh yeah, keep talking. You'll see. I can see it in your eyes—you're going to fucking die."

I *was* afraid of the hike. The .50 cal. is a beast. The 26-pound barrel was the lightest component in the system, which made it as heavy as the 240, which was the heaviest thing we carried on the last hike. The box-shaped receiver was sixty pounds and the tripod was forty-four. I had to do something to help me make this hike.

Getting psyched-out on a hike was the biggest danger. If you start worrying or doubting yourself, you breathe quicker, waste energy and lose focus. On past hikes, the weapon kept slipping off the top of my pack where I carried it. The energy needed to lift the gun back onto my pack was energy that I didn't have to spare. When I used both hands to keep the gun on top of my back, in a crucifixion-like pose, my arms would lose circulation. I needed a way to keep my arms down, so I could swing them and use the momentum, but also keep the part of the gun system from falling off of my pack. During a 240 shoot, we threw away dozens of cloth ammo bandoliers. Looking at the bag of bandoliers, I realized that I could loop the straps of them around either side of the .50 cal. receiver; I could hold my arms down and swing them, while still making sure the receiver stayed tight on the top of my pack. I passed the idea to my squad, but they got worried about looking different, thinking we would get in trouble. I showed them how the bandoliers could come off in a second if the squad instructors complained about them.

My plan worked just fine, though it was probably unnecessary. In SOI, it is almost impossible to fall out of a hike. At one point, our platoon stretched out over a mile, but none of the squad instructors failed us. My scheme had helped alleviate my fears and prevented me from psyching myself out though.

I had to go on emergency leave for a week, so when I returned my buddies had graduated and I was with the junior class. It was the second time I had returned to Pendleton after ten days of freedom and it got harder each time. Out of rebellion and to feel like I still had some control over my life, I grew a goatee over leave. I was determined to keep it as long as possible, so I told myself I'd shave it in the restroom at the San Diego airport. When I got there though, I thought I'd look like a homeless person doing it there, so I decided to do it in the private restroom on the Coaster train to Oceanside. I was so depressed on the train that I forgot to shave and I didn't remember until the bus was pulling up to the front gate of Pendleton. The MP who came on the bus to check everyone's IDs would chew me out and rat me out to my command if he spotted my facial hair. As the MP walked down the aisle, I put my hand over my goatee, looking like Rodin's "The Thinker", and held my ID card up with the other hand. The MP walked right by, not batting an eye at me. After he left, two other Marines started making loud comments about my goatee, but I didn't say anything to them since they were "Fleet Marines" and I was still in SOI. When I got to my squad bay at SOI, I made a bee-line to the head to shave my goatee. Miller, a fellow Texan in the junior class who hadn't met me yet, later told me that when he saw me in there he assumed that I was an instructor because of my age.

On graduation day a bus pulled up to take me and some of my buddies to our first duty station—the Fighting Fifth Marines at Camp San Mateo, a whopping three miles away. I had wanted to go to a unit in Hawaii, but because of the cost of re-locating families, they were only sending single guys there. We would be shown to our new unit by Master Sergeant Stafford, who rates a book himself. He was a lifer who had survived the bombing in Beirut in 1982 who was known for having no outside life and being freakishly dedicated to the Corps. During his free-time, he would jog with his gas mask on, frequently passing out and falling into the road. On holiday weekends, he would grab a couple of MREs and head on up to the hills. He wore boot camp issue BCs and lived for free in the barracks, even though he had several hundred thousand dollars saved up. He wore his cammies until they were almost bleached white by the sun and he bragged about getting by on less than $20 a month. He uncharacteristically splurged on a new car, which he never drove, just washing and waxing it every weekend. Every few months he would get a girlfriend; he didn't have a problem getting first dates, but when he took the women to the chow hall to eat and or put a pack on their back and made them hike the foothills of Camp Pendleton, he had little luck getting a second date.

We were going to "The Fleet"—the main body of the Marine Corps that trains, deploys and fights. Though that was exciting, we were all dreading the first year-and-a-half, in which we would be considered "boots." Being a boot is like being a freshman, the new kid in school and a pledge in a particularly brutal frat, all at the same time.

San Mateo looked like an abandoned water treatment plant in the middle of the Ozarks. Maybe three buildings out of fifty were less than forty years old. The architectural style was "cinder block" and the only attempts at making it remotely hospitable to humans was the same coat of scummy yellow paint that had been applied to all surfaces. Several of the "buildings" were actually barns made of corrugated tin. Half of the buildings didn't even have bathrooms, so there were Porta-Johns every block or so. If a building did have a bathroom, it looked like a set from "The Exorcist." Forget about toilet paper, paper towels or soap. You were lucky to have a stall door. San Mateo was known as "San Ma-ghetto" and the phrase fit—it was as bad as the worst ghetto I had ever seen.

Even worse than the conditions of San Mateo was the isolation. It was located at the far northern edge of Camp Pendleton. All of the quality-of-life/recreational programs, such as the base shopping center, movie theater, bowling alley, and fishing lake, were all at Mainside, 30 miles away. The bus ride from Mateo to Mainside took three hours since you had to take such a circuitous route, switching buses in Oceanside.

Camp Pendleton is located midway between San Diego and Los Angeles. San Clemente borders it on the north and the Jewel of the California coastline, Oceanside, sits to the south. In the immortal words of Old Ben Kenobi, "You will never find a more loathsome hive of scum and villainy." Oceanside is so sleazy that it's actually "TV sleazy"—things happen there that I've only seen on TV. Hookers follow you on the sidewalk, trying to solicit you. You're never farther than 30 feet from a drug dealer. The downtown is nothing but cheap bars, bad restaurants and DNA-stained hotel rooms. San Clemente is a rich person's pond with a small scum of surfer trash floating on the surface. Most of the town is out of the price range for Marines and the part that is affordable is Oceanside-sleazy. The only real options are for a Marine are to go an hour south to San Diego, two hours north to LA or 5 minutes to the PX into a bottle.

As we got divided up into the different companies, I prayed to be sent to Weapons Company, which rolled in Humvees. When I found the gunny with the roster though, he told me that I was going to Golf Company, whatever the hell that was. The Golf Company police sergeant—whose dramatic title covers up fact that his job revolves around handing out sheets and pillowcases and making sure the parking lot is swept—showed us to our rooms, which looked like prison cells. I asked him what kind of company Golf was and he proudly answered that it was a helo company. When I asked him if Humvees could fit in helos, he just laughed.

Our "senior Marines" were at a Division Schools for another week, so we got spared the initial hazing as we checked into the unit and got our gear. The Marine Corps had just adopted the MOLLE gear system and we were among the first Marines to get it. Though the MOLLE gear was light-years above the decades-old ALICE gear we used in SOI, it would be so maligned by the grunts who used it that the entire system would be deemed a failure within two years. The main "design flaw" was a plastic pack frame that could snap, but in my experience it only broke when people mis-used it by doing things like throwing a 100-pound pack, ten feet down onto concrete. When the plastic frame snapped, they would declare that the entire "MOLLE" system "fucking sucked dude." The Marine Corps had developed the MOLLE system in-house after spending millions in R & D and it disappointed me that they would drop the system so soon, even after the Army adopted it after putting it through exhaustive testing.

While getting our gear at Supply, the machinegun section leader, Cpl. Washbourne, took me aside and leaned in close, hissing that if I didn't make my fellow boots hurry up, he would make us wish we had never been born. This was nothing like the respectful and trusting work relationship I had with Sgt. Norris. I didn't think much of it at the time, thinking it was just an anomaly.

After work that night, Washbourne took us aside to give us some advice. Tall and thin, with a shaved head, he looked like a cross between Clint Eastwood and Lee Van Cleef. He was a strange mix; highly-intelligent with a razor-sharp wit, he was one of the toughest men I ever met, though he didn't look like anything special. He was into punk and thrash metal, but he was also Old Corps like Chesty Puller. He would defend you to the higher-ups and then thrash you within an inch of your life after they left. He was an unapologetic bully, but also a surprisingly wise and caring human being. No one was ever on the fence when it came to Washbourne—you either loved him or hated him. Later on, I would find that almost all of the seniors befriended him as a form of supplication, since they feared him so much. I hero-worshiped the guy from day one, but I was ecstatic when he left. People said that he crossed the line and I agreed, but one thing about him over-rode anything else: I knew that he would keep me alive in combat. I had no doubt that he could lead me through the most harrowing,

D-Day-like combat without getting a scratch on me. I'm not saying that he was the devil, but every time the devil had a family reunion, Washbourne went on leave.

Washbourne lounged in front on the barracks in his Adidas track suit, which he was so brazen as to wear during the work day. No one corrected him on it. He told us what time the PX closed, since the worst thing to happen to a grunt was to realize he was too late to buy that night's booze. His beer coolee had a picture of a morbidly obese and unfortunately nude woman. When he noticed us looking at it, he advised us to start liking fat chicks because that was all most grunts could get. He espoused the merits of fucking fat chicks at length and then retired to his room.

As he spoke, his two squad leaders appeared, beers in hand, glowering at us. Marr had a shaved head, blue eyes, and a wrestler's body while Chuck looked like a less-attractive version of Super Mario. These two salty lances knew the gun well, but they both had tempers which undermined their effectiveness. They were "salty" since they had gone to Okinawa and had been on ship. We were boots until we had done so as well.

The only other senior Marine around was Cpl. Herrera, who was getting out in a month and couldn't have been happier. He picked up corporal only a few weeks earlier, since he had spent half of his enlistment on light-duty. We thought he was cool because he gave us insider info on how to make things easier for ourselves in The Fleet, but when the other seniors got back, he ratted us out every chance he got. I learned my first lesson: Never believe that someone who outranks you is your friend.

Sgt. Faamaligi was our acting platoon sergeant since most of the staff sergeants were at the Staff NCO Academy. He was a big Samoan guy(if that isn't redundant) who knew the Marine Corps inside and out, but his personal life always kept him from getting ahead. Even though he had been in for eight years, he was still a sergeant. Usually during a Marine's second enlistment, he works in a "B" billet—drill instructor, recruiter or embassy security guard—to further his career. Sgt. Fam, as he was known, took me aside and gave me some advice. He spun me up on the horrors of being a married grunt, which is rarely a good combination. He was quite open and honest, admitting that he hadn't picked up staff sergeant because he had "stepped on his dick", while working as an instructor at SOI, by putting hands on a student. He got "bad paper", which quashed his hopes of becoming a drill instructor, thus retarding his career. Lesson number 2: Don't step on your dick. Easy enough to remember.

Sgt. Fam told us boots that he was re-establishing the "platoon fund" in which everyone chipped in five bucks each paycheck. This wasn't mandatory technically, but pretty much anything a huge, Samoan sergeant says *becomes* mandatory. He told us that the money would be used for platoon parties and as a fund to help out Marines in need, but it still sounded fishy to me. I coughed up the money a couple of times and then got deeply suspicious of the whole deal, so I made myself scarce the next few pay days and avoided "donating." A few months later, Sgt. Fam transferred out of the unit left with several hundred dollars of "platoon fund" money. Maybe he held a party in our honor with the cash.

When our seniors returned to the company, they were able to devote all of their energy to the primary mission of every "saltdog": making us realize we were scum. They especially loved any demeaning or lowly work, and if we had to be on our hands and knees to do it, all the better. We would scrub the sidewalk with bleach and water for hours to get their dip spit stains out. We had zero control over our lives. Meals were deducted from our paychecks, but we were rarely allowed to go to breakfast or dinner. The senior Marines were afraid that if they let us go to meals, they might suddenly be told that they needed to get us for something and then they would look "bad." I failed to see how saying "Sir, the Marines are at chow, they'll be back in a half hour" was so awful, but I hadn't been in that long. I hadn't yet learned that fear ran the Corps. Our seniors would were so afraid of making the wrong decision that they would make no decision at all.

Since I was married, but hadn't moved my family out yet, I lived in the "Crack Houses"—crumbling one-story barracks that were built during the Eisenhower administration. The Marine Corps is under-funded, but there was really no excuse for these kind of living conditions. The week after I moved in, USA Today had a cover story about abysmal military housing, with a picture of one of our "crack houses" on the front page. My first night in the room, it was so cold inside that I had to sleep in my sleeping bag. I spent an hour looking for the furnace controls, until I realized that there weren't any. To save money, they had it set so that the furnace came on for one half-hour every three hours. It would heat the room to about 95 degrees, then cut off—so it was either too hot or freezing cold. If I lived in a tenement, I could have gotten a judge to order the landlord to keep the heat on.

My roommate was a salty lance who had been a problem child since he enlisted. A big, friendly country boy from Texas, Stanwood never met a job he wouldn't try to weasel out of. When he returned from being UA for two weeks, he simply stated that he had "gone fishing." His excuse was so crazy that I think it bought him some points for originality. He was confined to quarters while the CO decided what to do with him.

Stanbo, as he was known, was more than happy to pass all of his shit-bird knowledge down to me. I got confused when he told me he was a "skater", since he wore cowboy hats and Wranglers, but he explained that a skater was someone who skated out of work. His basic philosophy was that the Corps would take everything it could from you, so it was your duty to take as much back for yourself. I took that to heart, with reservations. I wanted to succeed and become an NCO, but I could already see how people let the Corps into too much of their lives. Being afraid to go to chow that you paid for was stupid and it didn't jibe with my vision of a fearless Marine. I would do my job, but I would also guard myself from letting the Corps infect every cell in my body.

Another personal issue developed back home, but I didn't want to bring it up since I had just gone on emergency leave a month earlier. I confided my problem to Stanbo while out drinking and the next day Washbourne called me over. He was pissed that I hadn't confided in him, and he sent me to the first sergeant to arrange my emergency leave.

If Master Sergeant Stafford deserves his own book, then First Sergeant Bell deserves his own television series or movie. He was known as "The Terminator" for two reasons: the first was that he had an accent that sounded vaguely like Schwarzenegger's, but the main reason was that he was absolutely indestructible. He had spent the majority of his career in Force Recon—the baddest motherfuckers in the Corps. Force Recon isn't very famous in the civilian community, mainly because they are not part of SOCOM, which includes the Navy SEALs, Delta Force, the Rangers and Air Force Para-Rescue. That doesn't mean that Force Recon lacks any skills that the aforementioned units possess, it's just that Charlie Sheen has never played a Force Recon operator.

First Sergeant Bell was beloved, admired and feared by everyone in the company. It wasn't just because he could beat all of our asses—individually or all at once—it was because he was the best the Marine Corps had to offer. He knew everything about the grunts, but he wasn't cocky or condescending. He was a career staff NCO, but he didn't have the stupid lifer habit of making minor things like field day the entire focus of your life; he was all about libbo and getting us off early on Fridays. He was in charge of disciplining any recalcitrant Marine, but he didn't hold grudges. Washbourne would keep me alive in combat, but First Sergeant Bell could lead me through the gates of Hell without fear in my heart.

I wanted to go on leave, but I knew that this was a bad way to start off in the company. First Sergeant Bell called me in and explained that family business was important, but when I came back it was time to train. He made it clear that they didn't *have* to let me go, but the "Skipper"—as he called our CO, Captain Gerst—was allowing it. For as many complaints as I have about the Marines, whenever I needed time to attend to family matters, I was always given it without reservation.

When I returned from leave, we had some new boots in the Machinegun section, though I didn't try to befriend any of them. Another "escape plan" had formed in my mind—I wanted to try out for one of the officer commissioning programs. There were several different programs, but because of my age I only qualified for one. I ordered some correspondence courses and I planned to finish my degree in my free time, since I was only thirty credits shy of my bachelor's degree. That idea quickly ran headlong into reality when I realized that I would be spending every week in the field. The Corps pays full tuition for any class a Marine takes while on active-duty, but only POGs—Personnel Other than Grunts—have time to take them.

Like a dork, I happily assembled my MOLLE pack for my first field op in The Fleet, remembering my happy times in the field in SOI. It was now December and "Sunny California" was colder than Nebraska. I wore my Poly-Pro long underwear on the cold, early morning drive to our training area, but I was too much of a boot to know that you can overheat even in sub-zero temperatures. Before we had hiked half a mile, I was drenched in sweat and light-headed. Heat exhaustion is the main nemesis of grunts in training. I struggled to our first patrol stop and pulled my Poly-Pro off to the jeers of my senior Marines.

As we patrolled up and down the hills, my old fears resurfaced. I could barely keep up, which was further evidence that I was not meant for the grunts. I no longer had the distraction of leadership that helped me hike in SOI. I struggled to our Observation Post, where we would set up a defense and see if the other platoons could find us.

Hyatt and I would switch off manning the gun while the others slept. An hour isn't a long time to spend reading a book or talking on the phone, but an hour lying awake on the cold ground at night is an eternity. Dire consequences befell any boot who fell asleep on firewatch. Since we only had one-hour off between shifts, it was almost like getting no sleep at all. Right before dawn, I fell asleep behind the gun. Sgt. Fam snuck up, trying to catch me asleep, but somehow I woke up just as he approached. When he asked me if I was awake, I was able to given a semi-believable "yes." Hyatt didn't react as quickly when he was caught asleep on the next post and it was the first of many strikes against him.

We put our packs back on and hiked over to a shooting range. Though the pace was reasonable, I just couldn't keep up. Sgt. Fam grabbed me by the collar and dragged me like a rag doll. It was humiliating, but he didn't mean it to be; it was the only way to keep me up with the rest of the platoon. Sgt. Fam wasn't even mad; he had been in The Fleet long enough to understand that things like this just happened.

The company would run through an assault course in which we would sneak up on an enemy position and fire in a coordinated manner. We had done this sort of thing in SOI with little fuss, a high level of autonomy, and a lot of motivation, but now we couldn't be trusted. The seniors were tense about looking bad. More energy and vitriol was spent on making us "dumb boots" clean-up afterwards, than was put into making it good, motivating training. When the trucks finally came to take us back to Mateo, I couldn't have been happier. Three days of misery and humiliation were over. Only three and a half years to go.

The next week was a refresher course in patrolling for the rifle platoons. Weapons Platoon's only job was to look busy somewhere off to the side. It would be the worst three days in my enlistment. Ross would become my best friend in the Corps, but I had to hate him intensely first. The Marine Corps has an obsession with uniformity; everyone has to have the same gear, the same way. If one person is missing his boonie cover, than everyone has to wear their helmet. The coast was right across the highway and a bitter wind kicked up after sunset. We were told that we could wear our beanies if we all had them. When Ross sheepishly admitted that he had forgotten his, the senior Marines went off on him like he had killed Christ. It couldn't just be that everyone wore theirs and Ross was the dumb-ass with the cold head; no, it had to be a major issue. In their defense though, it had been about the third thing that Ross had forgotten to bring. Over the years, that story has been exaggerated to the point where people say that Ross showed up in his underwear with only a canteen cap in one hand, but he did have slightly more gear than that.

We spent most of the day running gun drills, in which we would run fifty feet, fling ourselves onto the ground and acquire a target. As Sgt. Post had told us, "Gun drills are legalized hazing." We got very good at it, but it became clear that proficiency wasn't the point of this exercise; we were being put in our places. When I confused the phrase "mortar section" with "motor section", Washbourne jumped on my chest and starting screaming at me like a maniac. As he raged at me, his voice drowned out and I wondered what had brought me to the point in my life where grown men sitting on my chest and yelling at me was a part of the job.

The senior Marines seemed to think that freaking out on us was their primary job and teaching was a distant second. To show us how pathetic we were, the senior Marines did a gun drill themselves, beating our best score by a few seconds. Our hatred towards them gave us the incentive to pour it on and beat them three rounds in a row. They finally edged us by a few seconds and "retired undefeated."

After dinner, Washbourne had a pow-wow with the boots to find out why we were "fucking up." This was the other side of Washbourne—the charming, casual, paternal side. The others gave canned answers meant to appease him, but I didn't even try. I was 27 and hadn't dealt with immaturity like this since the 4th grade. I wasn't even learning anything.

When I cursed under my breath after being put on firewatch, I was yelled at by a Harry Potter-looking dork named Williams, who told me that I didn't "rate" to complain. On watch that night, the bitter ocean wind cut through me. I put on every "warming layer" I had and was still freezing, so I pulled my sleeping bag over my body and walked around like a black nylon ghost, peeking through the zipper. None of the senior Marines pulled watch, so who would catch me?

As we waited for the trucks on the last day, I started to go through an MCI (a correspondence course from the Marine Correspondence Institute), which attracted the seniors' attention. MCIs range from military subjects to math and grammar and each class you complete adds points to your promotion score. My seniors were shocked that I had one and many commented that, after two years, they still hadn't done any. I could tell since most of them were still lances. I figured that getting promoted was the only way to end the indignity of being a boot, so I had a lot of incentive. I studied promotion regulations on my free time and found out that it was fairly simple to get promoted; it mainly involved having a high PFT, doing 5 MCIs and staying out of trouble, but that was something most grunts couldn't handle.

The weekend was a blessing and a curse. Two days without having your "boot" status shoved in your face, but also two days isolated in a far-off camp surrounded by drunken morons who can't get laid. Stanbo had been sentenced to CCU, but had come back early because of an ankle injury that was widely-believed to be faked. CCU (Correctional Custody Unit) was a chain-gang for recalcitrant Marines. It was meant to "re-motivate" young Marines who had fallen in with the wrong crowd, but still had time left in their enlistment to redeem themselves. They lived in tin shacks near SOI and got treated worse than recruits. During the day, they pounded big rocks into little rocks, just like in car-toons.

When Stanbo came back to Golf, he was in a state of limbo. He couldn't train or hold a weapon because of his punishment status, but he was also on light-duty, so they couldn't fuck with him. He was confined to his room and wasn't allowed to wear civvies, which was a curious punishment. Luckily, he had a fat girlfriend who treated him like he was a sheik. Stanbo wasn't exactly Brad Pitt—he looked more like Garth Brooks—but this girl was definitely trading up. She brought him fast food for every meal, spent hundreds of dollars buying him video games and model airplanes to occupy his time, and fucked him in his three-foot wide bed, which was quite feat for those two heifers. You had to admire Stanbo; he had more fun on restriction than most people do as free men.

During our last field op before Christmas leave, we would shoot the 240 for the first time in The Fleet. As the seniors set up a qual course, the tension rose. We spent a half-hour trying to prop up driftwood to staple our targets to. It seemed to me that having proper targets would be in the Marine Corps' best interest, but what did I know? Why did I think this was going to be fun? The love of shooting that everyone has when they leave SOI was instantly killed. The seniors acted like idiots; when it was your turn to shoot, they would slap your hel-met, throwing off your aim. Several boots failed and only Mohler, Miller and I qualed as first-class.

On our last day in the field, we shot from a support-by-fire position at a bun-ker while the riflemen assaulted uphill. Chuck said some things that were infor-mative and constructive, but he spewed so much bile that I just stopped listening to him. Another lesson learned—if you make someone hate you, they won't lis-ten to you later, even if you have something crucial to say.

During the down-time, I observed my senior Marines interacting with each other and I came to the conclusion that they were all gay. I had never seen a group of men that were so close. They spent every waking minute together and they were always grabbing each other and wrestling around. They'd go off to piss in the bushes together and sleep in a "spooning" style when it was cold. As I would get on in my enlistment, I would realize that they were just close because they spent more time together in one four-year enlistment than most married couples do in ten years. The spooning thing seems weird and gay until you have to sleep on a mountaintop at night in the winter and then it becomes the greatest idea in the history of the world.

After the boots ran the course several times, Washbourne took a turn on the gun. For all his excesses, he was an absolute artist with the 240. I swear that he could have written his name in bullet-holes on that bunker wall if he had wanted to.

We returned to the rear and got ready to go on leave. My senior Marines had been cool enough to let me go early to catch my flight. I went to get some of my gear out of Miller's room, where all the boots were watching a movie. When I told them I was leaving, they all gave me a hearty good-bye and wished me a Merry Christmas. I just stared at them like they were idiots—I hated them all. To me, they were nothing but my fellow prisoners—the worst they could do was get me in trouble, the best they could do was stay away from me. At that time, I still thought I could get by on my own, never needing to rely on anyone.

While on leave, I caught an episode of "JAG", a good-hearted but silly show about a Navy fighter pilot who becomes a JAG lawyer and then gets into a bunch of military-related adventures like he's "Magnum, PI." In that show, Marines came in two types: they were either murderous dirtbags or brain-washed lifer idiots who practically ask permission to breathe. Silva lamented having been a fan of the show, thinking it was an accurate depiction of military life when he enlisted.

The episode centered around the Osprey, a controversial new tilt-rotor airplane that could take off like a helicopter and fly like a plane. It was designed for the Corps to replace the fleet of forty-year old helicopters we flew in. As the saying go, "The history of Flight Safety is written in blood" and the Osprey had many high-profile crashes. It had also been the center of a controversy in which a high-ranking Marine Officer had falsified documents to get the aircraft approved. My first weekend in The Fleet I went up to Tracers, the sad, empty E-Club at Mateo, and saw a small shrine to a dozen Marines from my regiment who had died in an Osprey crash. I didn't know why they were trying to foist this seeming death-trap on us when the retro-fitted 46s we flew in were just fine. I vowed that I wouldn't let myself be shoved into an Osprey, but I would later learn that the Osprey had the shortest development life and one of the lowest fatality rates while in testing. With its increased range, it could be a life-saver in combat. Hopefully it would not be tossed away like the MOLLE system. After the war started, the Marine Times had a headline that stated "MOLLE: Failed in combat!" I would have loved for them to tell the whole story and had another story titled "Dumb-ass corporal kicks MOLLE pack down stairs out of laziness, fails to report small crack in frame; then bitches when it snaps eight months later."

Leave was good, but strange. At home I was a man with friends who respected me, but in Cali I was a dumb boot cleaning some corporal's toilet at two in the morning. I constantly bragged about being a Marine, yet I absolutely dreaded going back to my demeaning existence in Mateo.

To have a taste of freedom, dignity and peace is horrible when it all goes away. The ride from the airport in San Diego to Pendleton is like the ride to prison. Mass-transit filled with drunks and losers. A changeover in diseased Oceanside, then a dark and lonely ride through 30 miles of Pendleton to get back to Mateo. No one spoke on the bus full of jarheads; we all looked hollow-eyed, like ghosts.

Though the regs only stated that our hair had to be "graduated from 0-3 inches", it was grunt tradition that everyone would have a fresh haircut each Monday morning. Due to lack of funds and simple laziness, many people (the author included) found themselves frantically banging on a buddy's door at 5:57 in the AM hoping to get a "barracks cut" before formation. The best haircut I ever got was given to me by Silva when he was drunk. When he tried to do it sober the next week, he screwed it all up, so I dubbed him the Drunken Barber. Some Marines liked cutting hair, either to make a little spending money or just for pure aesthetics. As Lewis put it, "I love cutting a white boy's hair. White boy hair cut easy. I hate cuttin' a nigga's hair. Nigga's hair take an hour." One of the reasons so many Marines have shaved heads is that it's the easiest haircut to get in three minutes. Every Monday, a handful of Marines would show up with the classic "barracks cut"—uneven fade, patch of hair left behind, and a bloody ear. I joked that I should open a barber shop in Oceanside called "Barracks Cut" which would only be open from 5:00-6:00AM on Monday mornings.

Until we went to CAX in April, we would have a hike about every two weeks. They would start at twelve miles and progress all the way up to twenty-six, which sounded impossible. The fear of hiking becomes all-consuming; nothing can be enjoyed because it's constantly in your mind—"Five days until the next hike." The Marine Corps considers hikes to be the be-all, end-all measure of a Marine. First Class PFT, Rifle Expert, First class Machine Qual—none of that matters if you can't hike. Even though it counts against you if you do bad, it helps you in no way if you do good. Hiking as a means of travel in combat went out with Andrew Jackson chasing the Seminoles. A group of Marines are almost completely useless after a hike; they can barely move, let alone fight effectively. The higher-ups would always say, "Well, what if all of our trucks went down and we had to march and fight?" All of our trucks went down, like, all of them in the whole Marine Corps? What did them in—infected diesel fuel? Marines experienced serious and lasting injuries for little benefit. The excuse would be that this tested our mental toughness and it was co crucial, blah, blah, blah…As Keller—who had the high rifle score in the company—said, "You'd think it would matter more to the Marine Corps that we only get one week a year at the range and most of the fuckers here can't hit the broad side of a barn."

My senior Marines all popped Rip-Fuel—an Ephedra-based stimulant—so I decided to try it in the hope of actually doing well on a hike. I had popped No-Doz on hikes during SOI, which had helped a lot. I took the Rip-Fuel tablets about a half hour before the hike was supposed to start, hoping they would kick in as soon as the hike got hard. For some reason though, the hike was pushed back for another hour and a half, so I was peaking before the hike started.

On the first three-mile leg of the hike, I couldn't be stopped. I passed the first person in my platoon and ended up in the platoon ahead of ours. I was feeling great until we hit a steep hill; halfway up I lost all of my energy. I stumbled through another six miles on fumes and then crashed. On our last break, I was reeling and so dizzy that I couldn't even stand up. Once again, I was failing in front of my peers, even after trying this trick. I looked at the others in the back of the pack and was surprised to see Marr. He looked almost as bad as I did and he was usually a great hiker. I could read his expression—no matter all the great things he had done, no one would forget if he did badly.

When we started up again, a few senior Marines fell back to "encourage" us. When Devers—who was usually a bitter little fuck who never had a good thing to say to any boot—sidled up next to me, I expected the worst. To my surprise, he was supportive; he told me that everyone has a bad hike once in the Corps, even the champs who can hike two packs are going to blow one hike out of their ass. His encouragement really helped me; one of the big problems I had was the feeling that none of my senior Marines gave a fuck about me. I got some energy back and started to catch up. With two miles to go, Gunny Seese waddled back and ordered the last twenty Marines to put their packs in one of the Humvees so they could catch up. I was relieved and humiliated when I was picked. After dropping my pack. I was able to catch up. I didn't catch as much hell as my peers since I was almost a decade older than them, but it still hurt.

After the hike, Washbourne called all of the hike-drops together. I thought he was going to strangle me, but he just wanted to know what had made me fall back. I told him about the Rip-Fuel and he nodded understandingly. He said all that mattered was that I finished. This was what made Washbourne such a great leader—he could read people. I deserved an ass-chewing, but he could see that would just demoralize me further. I didn't need anyone telling me I did bad—I knew it.

That was the beginning of our "Work-up"—four months of intense pre-deployment training. The next two weeks were nothing but constant hiking, up and down hills, day and night. Military analysts have something called "The Christmas Tree Effect", in which every piece of gear some officer decides a grunt

must have is issued and hung on them. Look at the old combat pictures—
Marines took Iwo Jima with nothing but a rifle, bayonet, helmet, web-belt,
ammo and one canteen. For a three-day field up we would take the following:

> Rifle, NVGs, Bayonet and scabbard, Cleaning gear, Compass, Helmet, Gog-
> gles, Flak Jacket, Load-bearing Vest, 6 magazines, All-weather coveralls,
> Poly-pro long underwear, Two pairs of gloves, Two extra pairs of cammies,
> Three pairs of underwear and socks, Poncho, Poncho liner, 2 canteens,
> Hygiene gear, Iso-Mat, Camel-Bak, Entrenching tool, Two days worth of
> MREs, Sleeping bag, Beanie, Boonie cover.

A full pack weighs about sixty pounds. In addition, the Marines in Weapons
Platoon had to carry crew-served weapons which added another twenty pounds
per man.

Mohler was sick as a dog and the constant cold rain wasn't making him feel
any better. Washbourne got angry at Mohler's "whining" and when he caught
him sleeping while on watch, he woke Mohler up by kicking him in the jaw.
Barely a day went by where Washbourne didn't push, grab or threaten a boot,
but usually it was within reason. This just seemed gratuitous.

After two weeks of patrolling, we had a sixteen-mile night hike. It had been
raining all week and the route was flooded. The day of the hike, we got the military version of a cock-tease. Word got around that the hike would be canked
because the route was washed out. It seemed to be too good to be true, but right
before lunch our Platoon Commander, Lt. Matori, told us that as long as it was
still overcast after lunch, the hike would be canked.

We went into the chow hall, elated with our good luck. It had been raining
most of the last two weeks; it was sure to continue. As soon as we stepped outside
though, my heart sank. A beautiful blue clear sky that was so bright that I almost
expected cartoon birds out of a Disney movie to fly around my head.

Hiking in the daytime is bad, but when it gets tough, you can find a tree 100
meters ahead and tell yourself just to make it there. You can look back and see
your progress. There is none of that at night—it feels like you're walking forever,
but not getting anywhere. You can't even see two steps in front of you, so you're
expecting to turn an ankle and eat shit at any given time. With 80 pounds on
your back, a twisted ankle can be a major injury. Most of the trail was flooded
and it was basically a three-mile tightrope walk. Instead of having a break every
hour for ten minutes, the stops were totally random. We'd hike for an hour and a
half with no break and then go twenty-five minutes to the next break. The night
was so cold that I kind of wanted to just get going. I hiked with my Poly-Pro on,

which would have gotten me choked out by Washbourne if he saw it, but I had to wear it, it was just too cold.

People were dropping pretty steadily all along the route, but when we hit a long slow hill leading up to the half-way point there was a minor epidemic. Hiking is as much mental as physical and the slight incline just did some people in. It was really sad to see broken men lying on the ground in shame as people walked by and insulted them. It's a real "there but for the grace of God go I" moment—you're jealous of them because they don't have to hike anymore, but you're glad you don't have to deal with the shame.

The machine gun system breaks down into three parts—the gun (26 pounds), the tripod (16 pounds) and the ammo bag (18 pounds). Although the gun is the heaviest, it's the easiest to hike since you can just put it on your shoulders and it will stay there. Seniors didn't hike any part of the gun system, unless a boot fell out or couldn't handle the weight. The three parts were usually split between four boots, so one of them could rest during each leg of the hike.

I had not carried anything up the hill, so at the next rest break, Silva walked over in silence and set the gun down next to me. He would become one of my best friends later, but at that time I couldn't have hated him more. My age got to me sometimes, especially on hikes. I didn't see why this 200 pound, 18 year-old weightlifter couldn't carry the gun for another leg. That was self-pity talking though; I had to share the weight to be part of the team.

The line of Marines would slinky as people would bunch up and then run to catch up with the rest of the battalion. I felt guilty for not carrying my fair share and I was determined to hold onto the gun. I kept falling back and running to catch up, which totally screwed everyone behind me. I finally realized that I had to hand the gun off. Hyatt was short and chubby, but he could hike like he had a motor in his ass. I asked him if he could take the gun from me and he nodded like it wasn't even a big deal. It killed me to have to do this right in front of Washbourne, who I wanted to impress. With the gun off my shoulders, I was able to get my wind back.

We came around a bend and could see Mateo. This is the worst part of the hike—you can see the end, but it doesn't seem to get any closer. At this point, even if you've been sucking down water the entire time, your dehydrated muscles start to lock up. Even though this is the hardest part, almost no one ever falls out in the last leg of the hike. Falling out of a hike is the same if it's in the last ten feet or the first mile.

Sanchez only weighed about 110 pounds, but with the heavy mortar base plate strapped to his pack, his gear weighed more than he did. When he fell out, his section leader, Cpl. Dunn, took his pack and threw it on top of his own. Two packs plus a mortar base plate had to be at least 180 pounds, yet Dunn hiked it with no problem. I was crying for myself, yet Dunn who was smaller and skinnier than me was carrying twice as much.

Finishing a hike is an incomparable feeling. Pride in completing something so difficult, shame at not doing as good as others, and camaraderie from going though agony with your peers. Best of all, immediately after a hike is the most amount of time until your next hike.

We finished around 11:00PM, but we weren't able to go to sleep until "sight count"—a visual confirmation by the armorer that all weapons and optics have been turned in—was up. Everyone was jubilant and exhausted; we ordered pizzas and watched movies as we waited for hours for permission to sleep. While watching "BASEketball", we came up with the nickname for Chuck, our most hated senior Marine. He would be known ever after as "Squeak", a short, whiny character in the movie who never got laid. In this book though, I will continue to refer to him as "Chuck" since we ended up re-cycling the nickname "Squeak" for a staff NCO we had during the war. When the word came that we were off, we all just collapsed wherever we were.

With all of the pressure and degradation of being a boot, if you didn't have a good sense of humor you were going to lose your mind. Chuck's negative and condescending attitude was getting to me, so I walked into Ross' room to vent.

"I swear to god, I'm sick of that little Panamanian-Equadorian-Guatemalan-whatever-the-hell-he-is little fuck. Who the fuck does he think he is? I'm going to end up either kicking his ass or going UA."

Seeing that he needed to calm me down before I did something stupid, Ross pulled out the most effective de-fuser of any tense situation: The Happy Dance. Besides giving us the perfect nickname for Chuck, the under-rated classic "BASEketball" also introduced us to The Happy Dance—an idiotic dance that makes whoever is doing it completely unable of being anything but happy.

"Meyer, I'll tell you what you need to do. You need to do the Happy Dance."

"No, fuck you man, this is serious! I'm twenty-eight goddamn years old! I'm-"

"Look motherfucker, we got one rule around here: when you are told to do the Happy Dance, you will do the motherfucking Happy Dance."

"I ain't doing the fucking Happy Dance."

"Meyer…"

I'd do it just to humor him; then leave. Besides, the only thing that is more childish than doing the Happy Dance, is getting pissed off and refusing to do it.

The dance is pretty simple—you just sway in place while hitching your thumbs from side-to-side.

"Good. Now sing the song."

"I ain't singing the damn song."

"Sing the fucking song."

"Doin' the Happy Dance."

"Louder."

"Doin' the Happy Dance."

"OK, now sing it like you mean it."

"Doin' the Happy Dance…I'm doing the Happy Dance. The Happy Dance…The Happy Dance."

I couldn't help myself. I started laughing and temporarily forgot about my anger towards Chuck. Fuck Dr. Phil; talking about your feelings is for fags. All a grunt needs to get by is his gun and the Happy Dance.

The next week, instead of going out to the boonies, we set up camp in the half-mile area between Mateo and the mountains that bordered the ocean which was known as "The Backyard." During the SOTG Raid package, instructors from the Special Operations Training Group would train us in conducting helo raids. I was ecstatic that we would finally go on helos since riding helos was one of the three reasons I joined the Corps.

It was weird being "in the field" and yet able to see my room at the same time. It was extremely cold, so we drew straws to see which tents would get the two heaters in the company and Weapons Platoon lucked out.

Tension was high between the seniors and juniors. Fuck-fuck games were in full effect and we were getting thrashed constantly. As a result though, the boots got a lot closer. For some supposed infraction, we were taken into the bush and told to dig a fighting hole, which was forbidden in that part of Pendleton for environmental reasons. It started to rain and Chuck laughed, saying, "Now you're fucked." Once you're wet though, you can't get more wet, so I started to laugh and joke around while digging. This pissed the seniors off even more since we weren't being miserable on command.

We would be told to fall out of the tent and if we didn't do it fast enough, we would have to go back in and do it again. It was obvious they were just going to fuck with us regardless, so we just shuffled out while trying to look frantic. After one of the boots left their pistol unattended next to the seniors' unattended rifles, they punished us by putting three times as many people on firewatch as was nec-essary, so none of us got any sleep. I didn't see how this taught anyone anything—it was just our seniors fucking with us because their seniors fucked with them.

Washbourne was acting platoon sergeant and he was constantly past the red-line. When Silva got caught talking in formation, Washbourne rushed forward and kicked him in the chest, sending him flying into Vargas. Silva was a weight-lifter and a black-belt in Karate, but he was a quiet, soft-hearted guy. The Marine Corps is so exhausting that even when something fucked-up happens, you just want to move on with things. Over the next few days though, the boots started to talk about it. If they'll assault someone as harmless as Silva, they'd do it to anyone.

The strain of the last two weeks had taken a toll on my knees, which were in constant pain. I had to weigh how I was going to play this, since people got bad reps, sometimes undeserveably, for going to get medical help. Even if they didn't say you were malingering, they would act like you were. I finally got up the courage to bring it up with one of the corpsmen and I was surprised with his concerned reaction. Corpsmen are famous for being dismissive and sarcastic about grunts' injuries during training. Although docs are technically "POGs"—and god forbid, *Navy*—they are usually tougher than your average Marine. They have to do everything a grunt does, plus take care of the grunts when they get hurt. On hikes, a doc never stops moving; he hikes with his heavy medical bag on top of his pack and then he treats injured Marines during the breaks. Of the twenty or so corpsmen I knew, only one was a bad hiker and he was quickly chaptered out of the unit.

I was sent to the BAS (Battalion Aid Station), which caused many raised eyebrows from my seniors. Sarcastic comments were de rigeur, but I decided that I didn't care. The seniors didn't seem to give a fuck about the boots, so I would have to look out for myself. There are three types of Marines at any BAS: the hard-ass who gets his injury checked out long after he should have, the smart-guy trying to get a light-duty chit to get out of the hike on Friday, and the total shit-bird who is trying to get a medical separation for something bogus. The last group were the regulars at BAS and they knew all the corpsmen by name. Those guys were the reasons that docs—as the corpsmen were called—doubted Marines who were actually hurt. I've known some bullshit excuses for people getting out the Corps or going on permanent light duty. I didn't really care if someone was trying to fake or exaggerate an injury for one reason: if that guy doesn't want to fight, I don't want to fight next to him. Let him go home; that's fine with me. It does suck though when you're hurt and the doc is looking at you cock-eyed wondering if you're one of the con artists.

When I was seen, I immediately got the old stink-eye. The pain was real, but they couldn't find any inflammation, so they treated me like I was faking. One doc finally did listen to me and said that marching on the sides of hills had unevenly worn my ligaments, which were rubbing against my patella. It was a common injury, but there wasn't anything they could really do for me. Still, it was nice to be listened to and believed.

The up-side was that I got to take it easy for the next couple days; the down-side was that I would miss the first helo ride us boots would get. The helo mission occurred late one rainy night and was a complete cluster-fuck. Squads were set down in the wrong places and general confusion reigned. Cpl. Long-mire's team "eliminated" a machinegun crew and then used that gun against the remainder of the enemy. For his intrepid thinking, he was later awarded a NAM (Navy Achievement Medal), which surprised me since we were in such a lock-step environment.

At the end of the week, the SOTG instructors gave us a a final brief. Any time we had a meeting or a class, several boots would fall asleep, to dire consequences. The stuffy room made me groggy, but I kept myself awake. When I looked down at my paper though, the senior Marine behind me slapped me in the back of the head, accusing me of falling asleep. It's a testament to how brain-washed I was that I didn't even consider hitting him back. We were so lorded-over day and night that when we got hit or kicked or thrown onto the ground, we would try to figure out what *we* did wrong. I still regret not slugging any senior Marine that put their hands on me, but that is rewriting history. Every new generation of recruits comes out of boot camp with less self-respect than a beat dog. The mild belligerence I showed to my seniors when I got to Oki was considered outright rebellion by my peers, but I had to do it for my own self-respect. Before I went in the Marines, I was a "soft" civilian, but I didn't take shit from anybody. Now that I was a "hard" Marine grunt, I was jumping at my own shadow.

Although we did train, the majority of our time and energy was spent on cleaning the barracks. The weekly field day went way beyond any standard of hygiene and even someone suffering from OCD would have thought that we were going overboard. Not only would we clean our rooms like we were perform-ing surgery in them, but we would even clean under solid objects. I never under-stood why they made such a big deal about making people clean under their cabinets, which were flush to the ground, so that even dust couldn't get under them. The single Marines had to take every piece of furniture out of their rooms every week. It had nothing to do with cleanliness and everything to do with mak-ing us miserable. While the senior Marines were in their civvies and getting drunk, the boots would be up until two or three in the morning, missing chow, and spending hundreds of dollars a year on cleaning products for rooms that they didn't even have the freedom to put up posters in.

Many of the scenes that the seniors threw were related to field day. For some real or imagined slight, Chuck pulled us into one room and threatened us each in turn. It was quite interesting sociologically, because nearly everyone in that room could beat Chuck in a fair fight, yet we just stood there with our heads hung low and took it—simply because he was a senior Marine.

Williams had become a ghost in the company, but he would pop up on field day to feel big. Chuck at least trained and participated, so you respect him on that level; Williams was just a pussy. He could tell that we didn't respect him, so he yelled at us that he couldn't wait to get his cast off and start kicking some ass again, but we could see through him. If you're trying to look tough while yelling at someone, you shouldn't let tears appear in the corner of your eyes while doing so. I had to bite my lip to keep from laughing when I remembered how he had told me once that before he enlisted he had lived, "the rock-and-roll lifestyle."

Milligan's philosophy on field day reminded me of the old saying from the Vietnam War, "We had to destroy the village to save the village." During field day, he would use so much bleach in his room that your eyes would tear up, which I think was his strategy. Anyone inspecting his room would assume that the near-toxic levels of chlorine gas signified excessive cleanliness and they would quickly leave. Good plan, come to think of it.

The next week, we went high into the mountains. The machinegunners had a primo assignment—hike to the highest point and shoot down onto an assault range while the riflemen ran a mile-long assault course. When we got up there, a Humvee dropped off a four-foot-tall pallet of ammo. We thought we were just supposed to grab our share, but it was all for us. This was going to be fun.

One thing that kept me sane during my enlistment was that I never lost my moto. "Moto" is short for motivation, but it encapsulates much more than that—it means being excited about the real grunt work involved in the job. No matter how demeaning or miserable things got, I could always get excited about a helo ride, or fast-roping or shooting or some good, realistic MOUT training. Unfortunately, most of my peers weren't able to keep that moto. Their hatred of some parts of the grunt life extended to all parts. If you go through four years of hell and can't find some bright spots to enjoy, then you're going to be one miserable bastard. That's why most turn to drink, I suppose.

The shoot was an all-day event. The seniors had stopped harassing all the boots equally and started focusing on the problem children—Hyatt was number one on their list. Hyatt was a strange case; he did everything that you could do right and everything you could do wrong. He could out-hike anyone in the battalion, knew all his knowledge and generally displayed a happy, carefree attitude, but he would also fuck-up little things and draw unwanted attention. He was short and chubby, yet strong, and he looked like a cross between an elf and Snuggle, the fabric softener bear. What was unfair was that because of Hyatt's "bad rep", he was under constant scrutiny, so his mistakes—no matter how minor— were always noticed.

Hyatt was a fun guy with a quick wit, so when things were slow, the seniors would joke around with him and tease him in a friendly way which sent a mixed signal. He was a "dumb boot", but he was also good enough to joke around with when they were bored. Inevitably, he would go "too far"—which was usually just him getting a good comeback in after they insulted him—and we would then all get pulled aside and yelled at for thinking we "rated." They would swear that they were done "being cool" with us and that the games would start again. Within a few days though, they would get bored and start teasing Hyatt again and the whole cycle would start all over.

Even though I was excited about shooting, I also dreaded it because there were so many ways to mess up. We didn't shoot that much, so it was easy to get rusty. You are supposed to change barrels every 200 rounds, but they never got a chance to cool off since the same barrel would be back on the gun in five minutes. The team leader—who loads the gun and changes barrels in addition to keeping the gunner on target—has to really be on the ball or he's going to burn himself. I preferred to be the gunner—less pressure and more fun. I shot so many rounds that day that the barrel glowed red in direct sunlight, which I was inordinately proud of.

Marr showed off a lumpy burn on his hand that he got from grabbing a hot barrel when he was a boot. He said that one of us would get one too; it was sort of a badge of honor. Apparently, Ross was very honorable. After burning himself while changing barrels, he waited until the shooting was over to get himself looked at. His glove had almost melted to his hand and the pain increased as the initial shock wore off. We poured our canteen water on his hand as the seniors chuckled at this right of passage.

The day had been pleasant, but the night was bitterly cold. I had a rep for having a complete inability to retain the smallest bit of body heat; I was always the first person to put on warming layers and the last to take them off. This caused major problems when we would suddenly have to go on a long patrol with no notice. When the order was given to move, you never knew if you were going ten feet or four miles. If you still had your warming layers on, you were sure to over-heat.

As the temperature plummeted, it became clear that this was going to be one hellaciously cold night. I put on more and more warming layers until I topped out with my personal record—seven. Two Poly-Pro tops, one sweatshirt, one Woolie-pullie sweater, one Gore-Tex jacket, a second BDU blouse, and then my poncho liner blanket stuffed under my jacket. I was so puffed up with extra layers that I didn't even have to hold my head up, the clothing did it for me. I could barely move, but at least I was warm. Hot chow pulled up in a Humvee, but it finally got so cold that they canceled the shoot, to no one's disappointment.

The day you left the field was always high-stress time, since the seniors are so scared of looking bad that they have you running all over the place trying to clean up and look busy. Those ranges have been used for the last fifty years; every time you pick up one new brass shell you uncovered two old ones. None of the seniors could be bothered to help out and since they comprised half the company, that meant the job took twice as long as it should have. They would freak out if they found five shells on a range that was half-mile wide.

In my haste to get out of the field, I committed the ultimate grunt sin—I lost my rifle. Sitting down to eat chow, I leaned my rifle against a tree. When my seniors called me and a few other boots over, I wrongly assumed the other people that were eating would watch my weapon. When I returned, my rifle was gone. I knew I was in for it. For as much trifling bullshit that they over-reacted about, this really was a big deal and I didn't have a leg to stand on. What's worse, my platoon commander, Lt. Matori, had been the one who found it and he refused to release it to anyone but my team leader. Chuck glowered at me and threw my rifle at my chest. I really did feel like a dumb boot at that point. To this day, I still have dreams that I lost my rifle and am frantically looking for it.

The next week was a "maintenance stand-down," which meant that we would stay in the rear and take care of our gear and personal issues. We had been in the field every week for two months and we needed a break. Marr told us that they used to get one week in garrison for every week in the field.

We were scheduled to go to the rifle range, which meant a week of "snapping-in" at Mateo and then a week at Camp Margarita on the range. The Marine Corps may cheap out on a lot of things, but not when it comes to the rifle range. During the two weeks at the range in boot camp, the DIs are told to lay off of you and not stress you out. Before you even go to the range, you are given an entire week to snap-in with an unloaded rifle to perfect your shooting posture. There are only five different shooting positions, so after an hour you've done every one of them twenty times. By the afternoon, you're begging to go back to the field. Some people—especially seniors—would screw around instead of forcing themselves into the painful shooting positions, but I forced myself to keep dry-firing. I really wanted to pick up corporal and I knew that a high rifle score is crucial.

If you had been in JROTC in high school or had at least twenty hours of college, you could enlist as an E-2, Private First Class. I officially got promoted to PFC the last week of boot camp and I automatically got promoted to lance corporal six months later. I was still a boot, but it was a step up the ladder. Though it is officially considered hazing to be "pinned", it was common in the grunts. The seniors would try and scare us with tales of how painful being pinned was, but I found the idea exciting. I had joined the Marines because I was tired of a normal, boring life and this was like a gang initiation. After the official promotion ceremony in front of the company, a boot would be pinned by his seniors in private-voluntarily or not. You were supposed to get more respect if you didn't try to weasel your way out of it. As soon as I got my "crossed rifles", I dutifully reported to my seniors with a smile on my face. Like any initiation, after going through some pain and/or degradation you are considered a part of the group. At least that's the way it is supposed to work.

The seniors were gleeful with anticipation as they took me to the lockers at the back of Gimeno's room. Gimeno told me that this was a big step and that rank had its responsibilities as well as its privileges; that's what pinning symbolized. He warned me that it was going to hurt as he pushed me against the locker. I had taken the backings off of my rank insignia earlier and the two sharp points on each pin were already digging into my skin. I had adjusted my shirt so that the points were on my chest instead of on my collar bone where they naturally rested. Gimeno raised both fists and then slammed them down onto my rank insignia. The force of the blow hurt more than the pricks from the pins. The other seniors took their turns and I noticed a curious phenomenon. The wimpier and less-respected seniors were the ones who hit the hardest and enjoyed it the most. Badillo's face showed pure joy as he dug the rank insignias into my flesh with his thumbs in an excruciating circular motion.

Being pinned hurt, but it was nowhere near as painful as I had imagined. After each pinning, I pulled the rank out of my skin with a popping sound. A few seniors, like White and Devers, demurred when I offered to get pinned by them Though one side of my chest only showed two small pin-pricks, the other side bled like a stuck pig and I had a stain that was three inches wide. I proudly showed off the blood stain to everyone I passed, being careful not to let any staff or officers see it. A few of my peers had tried to avoid getting pinned and they were tracked down by the seniors later that night.

In the following weeks, I was disappointed that being pinned had no lasting effect on how the seniors treated me, but I was still glad I did it. I liked the tradition and hoped that it continues. I wouldn't want to go to war with anyone that was afraid of a little pain.

We left for Camp Margarita, at the southern part of Camp Pendleton, where the entire company would stay in one squad bay for the week, even the married people. Everyone was on lock-down for fear of, as Gunny Seese told us, "the one dumb-ass lance corporal who always shows up late on qual day."

Shooting started the minute the sun rose. While other services have computer-graded targets that rise and fall by remote control, we had paper targets stapled to large frames on a pulley system. Half the group would shoot and the others would be down in "the butts" pulling targets. You would pull the targets down and count the points; then paste the holes up and mark the score. It can be fairly hard to find tiny bullet holes on a six-by-eight-feet paper target; someone's promotion could be riding on their score. The shack in the middle of the pits is quick to yell at anyone who isn't giving fast or accurate "pit service." The senior Marines would sleep while we raced to pull the targets.

We were excited that there was an E-Club on Camp Margarita, imagining a joint filled with beer and man-hungry sluts. When we got there though, we discovered that all that was inside was a Subway sandwich shop and some video games. I was walking between the pool tables to go outside when a senior named Foster stepped in front of me. He was short and stubby with a perpetually grey face. He was the lowest-ranking senior since he was constantly in trouble.

"If you think I'm moving for your boot ass, you're crazy."

"That's fine. I'll just go around you."

"You think you're pretty smart, huh? Fucking boot…you think you rate? You ain't shit."

"I'm just trying to get by you."

"You ain't getting past shit. I'm gonna kick your ass."

Foster's buddies crowded around, seeing what I would do. I still had most of my brain-washing left from boot camp and my self-image had been almost obliterated since I got to The Fleet, but I was still a man. I had to play this carefully though. Foster was in terrible shape and drunk to boot, but there were ways he could beat me without using fists.

"If you're so tough, why don't you step outside? I'd like to see you qual tomorrow with a black eye," he snarled.

At that time, no boots had gotten into it with any seniors, not even verbally. He didn't realize the play he had given me. I could tell his tough-talk was all bluster. If I went out and he swung at me, no one could begrudge me defending myself. If he didn't, he would reveal that he was all talk.

Without saying a word, I walked outside to the porch. I turned around and looked at him, still inside by the pool tables. He seemed flustered and confused, but his cronies bucked him up and he went outside to meet me. I was really working without a net; there was no precedent for challenging a senior Marine like this. He charged up toward me and I braced to fight, but instead of hitting me, he just continued to berate me. It was clear that he wasn't going to fight, so the situation just defused. I took that as a moral victory, but I was still angry that the other seniors didn't stop that obviously drunk idiot from acting unprofessional.

McPoland got drunk for the first time and it was oddly entertaining to see his nerdy, robotic ass walk around and explain his state of inebriation in scientific terms to anyone who would listen. McPoland never made many friends, but after seeing him loosen up, people started to warm up to him, giving him the nickname, "Donny Binge."

Shooting on the range goes as follows—three days of practice, qual on Thursday and then a day of tactical shooting on Friday that doesn't count toward your score. It had been raining all week, which we were used to, but the POGs weren't. They got the brass to cancel the range on Wednesday, which pushed our qual shoot to Friday. That was a big problem since I had gotten permission to fly home early on Friday afternoon. I now had to hope I could finish in time to get to the airport before I lost $450 on a non-refundable ticket. When qual day came, I was all nerves; I felt that my promotion to corporal rested on getting another Rifle Expert Badge. I pulled targets in the morning, which took a lot longer than usual since they wanted to give everyone their best chance by giving them "alibis"—second chances for Marines who have legitimate rifle problems. By the time I was done pulling targets, it was noon. My plane left at 5:00PM which meant I had to be there by 4:30PM (this was before 9/11) and it was an hour to San Diego.

I quickly blew the shooting out of my ass. At the last course of fire—the 500 meter prone—I would have to hit 8 out of 10 to qual as expert. Most people hit about half of their shots at this distance. I looked at my watch—it was 3:00PM and I was just getting to the 500 meter line. I missed the first three shots and my heart sank. No Rifle Expert, which meant not being able to wear the Second

Award Badge under it. It would also probably take another couple months to make corporal now, in addition to being out $450.

The shooting ended and I ran to the parking lot. My officers let me hand my rifle off—which was a big deal—so I could leave early. One of the seniors even offered me a ride to the airport, which surprised me since he had a rep for being a real prick. I was too much of a boot to realize that by taking me to the airport, he got out of work early as well.

We jumped in Cpl. Dunn's Explorer and took off for the airport. Dunn was a strange one. He was built like a track runner, but was also amazingly strong; able to hike two packs. He had passed the grueling Sniper Indoc, but left the Sniper Platoon because he had "personality conflicts" with the other snipers. This was par for the course, as we would find out later that most of the senior Marines hated him. He was a chronic philanderer in addition to being a drunk. He ran his mortar section like a martinet and every one of his boots hated him, yet they would come to his house to drink with him on the weekends. I was cool with him since he was one of the few seniors who accorded me some respect because of my age. He had a sister in the Corps in Oki who he was very close to and they were trying to get stationed together. He was charming when he was sober, but a prick once one drop of alcohol hit his lips.

Nestled just outside the exits of Pendleton and Miramar like hemorrhoids were clusters of Pay Day loan centers. Even as a corporal, I found myself going to one every few months and I knew several lances who went to them almost every month; no sooner would they pay one outrageous loan back then they would taking another one out. I used to view these stores as vultures that "took advantage" of young enlisted Marines, but that was a load of bilge. With all of our benefits and pay, no one should have been a broke—hell, Moser managed to save $40,000 during his four-year enlistment. Sure there were a lot of rip-off joints aimed at boots, but the most serious problem was just simple bad financial planning. We spent so much time being lorded-over that when we did have freedom over some aspect of our lives we would often fail to take control.

The Navy/Marine Corps Society was a charity that gave 0% loans to deserving Marines, up to several thousand for needed car repairs. Repayments would be taken directly out of your paycheck. Before you would get the money, you would be interviewed by a counselor who would go over a budget with you, which I considered demeaning and insulting, even though it was just sensible. One counselor had a poster that said "Don't expect me to put more effort into your life than you do." That pissed me off at the time, but now I look back and realize how accurate it was. Though I had a much-deserved rep as a whiner, there was an air of self-pity around everyone I knew. We worked ungodly hours each week, but there was still plenty of dead-time in there to balance your checkbook, work on a correspondence course or work out that were not taken advantage of.

We would spend the next week at MOUT town, flying out on Tuesday and hiking back seventeen miles on Friday. I loved MOUT town, but the helo ride was what I was really looking forward to. Since we wouldn't be patrolling while at MOUT town, I loaded my pack down with a six-pack of Mountain Dews, a couple canned milkshakes and a bag full of candy. We waited for the helos in "sticks" of about sixteen men per bird. We would be flying in the 46s, which had been around since the Vietnam War-the *beginning* of the Vietnam War. I was a little nervous about flying something so rickety, but it's not like the birds were in any worse shape than anything else in the Marine Corps.

The birds approached and we were told to put on our packs. Several boxes of blanks had been added to my pack and when I went to put it on I found I could not lift it. As the others ran toward the birds, Stanbo looked back at me in disgust.

"Jesus Christ, Meyer, it's just a pack. Do I have to put it on for y—ugh!"

When he attempted to lift my pack with one hand he almost gave himself a hernia. It took both Mohler and Ross to get the pack onto my back and help me onto the waiting helo.

I ran through the hot prop wash and my heart started to beat harder. I kept reminding myself to have my rifle muzzle down when I entered the bird. We were told all kinds of horror stories about what crew chiefs do to dumbasses who come in muzzle up. I got on and sat down, beaming like an idiot. The seniors were blase and even the juniors who only had one ride were unenthused, but I loved it. It was so loud that it felt like I was in the engine.

The birds lifted off and Mateo shrank below us. We swung around in a wide arc and I got to see the other birds in tight formation. It reminded me of Star Wars with all the ships flying together on a mission and "Flight of the Valkyries" piped up in my imagination. I whipped out a disposable camera and took pictures. Seniors shook their heads at me for being such a tourist, but I was getting to do something I dreamed of and I wanted to remember it.

When we landed at MOUT town, I exited through the rear ramp and the ground sloped up sharply, bringing me closer to the rear horizontal blade. It made me think of the bald Nazi in "Raiders of the Lost Ark" who gets sliced through by the Flying Wing's propeller. I took a sharp left, but didn't get far. My pack had slid down the wet ramp alright, but once it hit the mud I could barely drag the damn thing. We were supposed to be making an assault on the town, but it was so muddy that people could barely get up and down the ditches surrounding the town. Even though I was barely moving at all, I wasn't much slower than the rest of the people. The whole assault kind of petered out.

The three days I spent in MOUT town during SOI was some of the best training I ever had. The instructors in SOI were professionals who actually wanted us to learn, while our senior Marines were playing fuck-fuck games because they were miserable and hated their lives. I learned almost nothing that entire week except that Mohler will fall asleep in any given situation.

We wasted two days while the NCOs taught us we were dumb boots…in an urban environment. Once our corporals got done "teaching" us, the MOUT Instructors took over and we finally started to learn. The company was split into aggressors and defenders. My platoon holed up in a mock hotel to await being attacked after dark. I scanned the surrounding hills through my NVGs for hours until I saw the enemy creeping up on our building. I was Mohler's team leader and I knew he would fall asleep on watch, so I reached into my pack and gave him one of my Mountain Dews to keep him awake. He was shocked that I had them and asked me what else I had.

We were using blanks, so when we shot the approaching enemy they just kept coming. The blanks were making the 240 jam—which was a common problem—so Marr grabbed it and fixed it in the dark, impressing the hell out of me. As the enemy started to flood into the building, Marr shot the 240 from the hip; the sound was so loud that I thought I would go deaf, but it was still exciting. The best training is when forget that it is training and you just fight.

When it started raining the next day, most people saw that as just the capper to another miserable field op, but I decided to have fun with it. While assaulting a building, I slid through the mud like a hero in a John Woo movie; then combat-rolled to get behind some cover. I was breathing hard and having a blast; I looked up and saw some of my seniors staring at me like I was a weirdo. I didn't care; at least I was getting something out of it, instead of just being bitter like them.

The culmination of the training was a night assault on a block of buildings which were defended by the best of our senior Marines. Both sides would be firing "SIMs"—paintball rounds which were fired from modified M-16s. We wore protective face masks, but as we ran toward the building, my glasses fogged up so badly that I could barely see. By the time we were stormed up the stairway, I was effectively blind. When we stacked up to enter an occupied room, I told Mohler to stay in front of me since I couldn't see. Everyone who had stepped into the danger area had been killed, so people were wary to go in there. Mohler gathered up his courage, took one step into the room, yelped in pain and fell back onto me.

"My dick! My dick! They shot me in my dick, man! Owwwwwwwww…"

Smoke obscured the passageways so we didn't realize that the walls didn't connect to the roof. Marr scrambled over the wall, jumped into the contested room and killed the defender, impressing us all yet again.

Our last morning there, we prepared to step off on the 17-mile hike home. Gunny Seese gave us a surprise inspection to make sure no one was trying to sneak off with any blanks or smoke grenades. Just before, I had found a belt of blanks that I had forgotten about in my patrol pack and since it was too late to turn them in, I put them in Hyatt's sea bag since mine didn't have any room. I looked over as Gunny Seese pulled a five-foot-long belt of blanks out of Hyatt's seabag while Hyatt sputtered comically, trying to explain. I ran up and took the heat for him.

We stepped off on the hike in a positive mood. Most of it was a flat stretch along the highway, so there would be something to watch besides the heels of the Marine in front of you. Half-way through, we took a strange detour that took us under the highway onto the road to a public beach, which was weird since I hadn't seen when we left the base. When civilians drove by us on the winding beach road, the staff NCOs screamed at them to slow down, like we were still on base. After five hours of hiking, we were within three miles of Mateo, as the crow flies. The hike hadn't been that bad.

Although it only should have taken 45 minutes to get home, it ended up taking two hours at full-speed with no break. Rain had flooded the tomato patches we usually hiked through, so we just wandered in the dark, trying to find a way around the water. When Marr started to complain, I knew it was a difficult hike. The last mile was the worst hiking experience I've ever had. We then heard the impossible—Washbourne had fallen out. It seemed unbelievable until I remembered that Washbourne had severely twisted his ankle while carrying two packs.

Everyone was in excruciating pain and completely dehydrated. Even the toughest hikers had to trade the gun off every 100 feet. We finally realized that it took more energy to constantly switch the gun off, so Ross kept the gun and we helped him along.

We finally arrived at the basketball court by our barracks. Dropping my pack felt like being released from prison. The hike had been a wringer—physically and mentally. I heard sobbing and looked back to see Boyd crying after Dunn yelled at him. I didn't like Boyd, but even I would admit that he was a tough motherfucker. No matter how tough you are though, a hike is going to reduce you and wear down your defenses.

Miller had come back early from MOUT town because of food poisoning and he earned our eternal enmity by bitching about having to sweep the basketball court while we were hiking. The final tally for the hike was almost 23 miles. I couldn't believe I had made it, even though I hadn't carried my share of the gun system yet again.

It incensed me that they made Washbourne get counseled for being a hike-drop and go to remedial PT the next day, considering that he had a legitimate excuse. After we got secured, Ross and I bought him a six-pack out of respect. Washbourne may have been the devil himself, but you had to respect him. He could out-hike anyone, but that didn't get him any leeway with the higher-ups. Washbourne understood that some people just weren't great hikers, even though he was. He never hesitated to carry the gear of a straggling boot. When Devers yelled at me for falling back, Washbourne told him to be quiet. He would defend us to anyone, no matter what their rank.

It seemed like we were on a never-ending grind of hikes and field ops, but things were coming to a close. After a few more weeks of training and the three-week CAX in April, we were done. We would have a month off before we went to Okinawa. When I broke it down like that, it didn't seem that bad.

Just as there started to be a light at the end of the tunnel training-wise, things finally gelled among the boot machinegunners. Mohler was the lanky and laid-back lightning-rod for all the seniors' ire. Hyatt was the mascot of the group, eternally optimistic and always pissing off the seniors. None of our seniors had any game, but Hyatt could pick up women at will; it wasn't even a thing for him. He looked a like a short, chubby teddy bear and women loved him. Several of the machinegun boots—Milligan, Silva and Mohler—were real lady-killers and that just drove the seniors crazy. As the seniors sat in front of their barracks room getting drunk on a Friday night, their "dumb boots" paraded a steady stream of women in front of them.

Everyone was changed to some extent, either from the boot camp brain-washing or simply from exposure to so many people from different cultures. Hyatt changed the most. He was from a small town in Northern Cali and was extremely religious. His church was big on "fellowship" and all of his friends came from church groups. In fact, everything in his life before the Marines came from church—he listened to Christian music, read Christian books and watched Christian TV shows. He was open about being a virgin and he was against pre-marital sex and pornography. By the time he left Golf Company a year and a half later, he was juggling three girlfriends and had the biggest porno stash in the battalion.

Though his descent began almost immediately, he denied it to the end. First, he would "peek" at the porno mags in other people's rooms, but only to corroborate that they were as bad as he had been taught. Then he would ask to "borrow" the mags, since he didn't want to bother the person by looking at them in their room. When I saw a stash of pornos in his dresser, I questioned him about them.

"Well, most of them aren't even mine."

"So some of them are."

"Yeah, but only a few."

"Hyatt, you bought your first porno. I'm so proud of you."

"Shhh, keep it down."

"Where'd you get them?"

"At that magazine store in Oceanside."

"Dude, I know what store you're talking about and it's not a magazine store. It's a porn store."

"No, they sell all kinds of magazines."

"They *have* all kinds of magazines, but the only ones that anyone actually buys are the pornos."

"The thing is that I didn't go in there to buy pornos, but after flipping through some regular magazines, I started to notice those *other* magazines."

"Yeah, I do the same thing. It's all those years in Catholic school. I always have to flip through Time magazine for twenty minutes before I work up the courage to go to the porn section."

"I started to wander around the store and suddenly I was in front of the pornos and then I found myself at the counter buying some."

"What, like you just blacked out and found yourself with an issue of 'Cherry' in your hand?"

"Actually it was 'Barely Legal' and one called 'Big Butts'. Heh-heh. The point is that I didn't *want* to buy the porn."

"But you did."

"Oh, hells yeah."

Milligan was and remains to this day the heart of the machinegun section. When he left, it sounded the downfall of the cohesiveness of our group. He was a from the Deep South and was so dark that when you took a picture of him all you saw were eyes and teeth. While looking at a group photo once, he couldn't find *himself* until someone else pointed him out. He was good-natured and solitary and chicks just loved him. His southern drawl was so thick that it was almost impenetrable. You would be two feet away from him and have to make him repeat himself three or four times just to understand. It got so bad that it became the first running joke in the section—Milligan language, which was similar to Snoop Dogg's "Fo schizzle my nizzle" language. Walking into a room, I would say something like, "Hey shama, how's your lama?" and the response would come "Not too fama."

Even three years later, I still see people not as individuals, but as the roommate pairs they were when we were boots. Hyatt and Milligan were a pair, and the next pair was Mohler and Showers. Mohler was a rich bean-pole from Mississippi. His dad owned his own business and the family even had their own lake. *Their own lake.* He knew that he was going to take over his father's business, so he had no worries about the future. He came from the 'Dirty Dirty" but he was a Cali kid at heart. He was a skater/surfer and a punk rock fan from way back. He was smart and personable and you really had to try to not like him. He had the same problem as Hyatt though, he was cool and funny, so sometimes the seniors would drop their guard around him; then get mad and pull back. He couldn't stay awake in the field to save his life, which brought him endless grief. From the beginning, he was pegged for leadership, so he got ridden harder than the rest, but I think there was a lot of jealousy among the seniors toward him as well.

Showers is my buddy, but just like Ross, I hated him before I liked him. Showers was tall blond kid from St. Louis, straight out of high school and already a dad. He was quiet and kind of a home-body, but revealed a sly sense of humor if you got to know him. He walked with a limp because his left foot was tilted inward at least 30 degrees off of what is normal. I loved the guy, but even he'll admit that the docs should have steered him away from the grunts. His condition kept him out of a lot of training, which engendered a lot of jealousy and bitterness among others. He was constantly accused of malingering even though anyone could look at his foot and tell he had a legitimate problem.

Silva was the player of the section and he was famous for having a three-some with two chicks from UCSD. Most of the seniors had trouble arranging a two-some. Even more impressive was that he got the chicks to do it in a nasty cinder-block barracks room in, what a friend would later describe as, "ManTown, U.S.A." One Monday morning, as we were sweeping the sidewalk, he told me about his weekend. Silva had gone down to TJ with some of the others and went to a whorehouse, which fascinated me because every war movie I'd ever seen had made it seem like grunts and whores went together like peanut butter and jelly. Since he was raised by women, he was a sensitive sort, so after he fucked the whore, he got into a deep, meaningful conversation with her. They parted ways and she told him that she would call him soon. The next day, he got a call and the girl on the other end of the line said that she wanted to come up and see him. When she finally got there though, it turned out to be another girl, just one with the same first name. She had called the Barracks phone directory and asked for a Carlos Silva that she had hooked up with earlier and got transferred to another Carlos Silva. They laughed about the mistake and started drinking together. Silva got drunk and horny, but he still had a rep to protect; the girl was fat and nasty, so he took her away from prying eyes. The "Million-Dollar Room", as it was called, was a sad and empty rec center with ten year-old video games and a broken wide-screen TV; no one ever went there. Silva took the chick into the restroom and they did the dirty next to an overflowing toilet. When he sobered up later on, he regretted telling me the story and tried to back-pedal, saying that he didn't have sex with her, they just made out. The detail about doing it with a nasty chick in a puddle of toilet water didn't change though.

While manning the phones at the company office, I received a call from Housing telling me that they had an open apartment on Mainside if I wanted it. My wife was still living in Texas since I hadn't been able to find an apartment in Cali. Not knowing southern California that well, I hadn't been able to find an affordable apartment in a good neighborhood, so I had her stay back home until we got some base housing.

Serra Mesa is quite possibly the shittiest base housing in the Marine Corps, not just because of the buildings, but also because of the people. It is the ghetto with camouflage. The average denizen of Serra Mesa is a boot-ass kid who married his high school girlfriend because they both got lonely after he went to Cali. You might ask why he doesn't just get a girlfriend in Cali; the answer is simple—people in Southern California hate Marines. Admitting to a girl that you're a Marine is the fastest way to talk yourself out of a piece of pussy. It's better to explain your haircut as being a result of a recent stint in prison or a mental hospital. Considering that Pendleton has been around since World War II, SoCal has had 60 years of bad experiences with jarheads and even the ones that depend on Marines for their livelihood hate them with a passion.

A boot from the Mid-West who always had farm-fresh snatch on tap back home finds himself to be a social leper in sunny California. The first time he goes back home, he marries whatever chick he knew best, even if their relationship was never meant to be anything but a high school fling. In fact, most grunt marriages have "high school" written all over them. Petty jealousies, hot and cold running emotions, all mixed with alcohol and shitty rap music coming out of speakers that are more expensive than their cars. And kids, because nothing spells success like having kids at the age of 19.

Base housing is still a barracks of a sort, so you can be inspected at any time or kicked out because of problems with your chain-of-command. What's more, you forfeit your sweet $1100 housing allowance if you move into base housing and there is no way that Serra Mesa is worth that much. You have to shave just to go and buy the paper at the store at the bottom of the hill. I once got chewed out in the library for walking in to return a book in work-out shorts. I thought I should have been commended for even going to the library. You have to check out of the library when you get out of the Corps and most of my friends didn't even know where it was.

The 26-mile hike was considered the culmination of our training; a marathon-length hike that had to completed in less than eight hours. The past three weeks were either good or bad deciding on how you wanted to look at it; the fifty-odd miles we had put on our boots had either gotten us in shape for the 26-miler or worn us out. I stuffed my ammo pouches with candy and PowerBars, not only for their energy boost but also just to have something to do; the hike would be a day-long event.

The hike was kept at a do-able pace, so I was able to hang in there, but just after the half-way mark I started to feel a sharp pain in my foot. Each mile it got worse and I realized it was going way past any earlier injury I got while hiking. To say that your feet hurt on a hike is like complaining about getting wet when swimming, but I knew this was not just pain, it was damage.

Though I was in misery, Hyatt looked like he was strolling through the park. He took the gun system from so many ailing or hurting Marines that our seniors actually ordered him *not* to help us anymore. He shrugged, taking that as good-naturedly as he took everything else. My foot was getting bad—either fractured or broken—but I didn't know what to do. I couldn't prove to my seniors or the corpsmen that my bones were literally cracking. Quitting was not an option; as Losey said, "If you're going to fall out of a 26-miler, fall out during the first hour." I was more than halfway done, but the extra 26-pounds of the gun was putting excruciating pain on my foot. I wanted to finish, but I needed help. I whispered to Hyatt that I thought my foot was broken and asked him if he could take the gun. He was more than happy to help, since the hike was so easy for him that he was bored.

We hit the tomato patches for our last hour of the hike. Marr berated me for not carrying my fair share of the gun system, but there was nothing I could say. I hoped that when I went to the BAS I could prove it was broken so they wouldn't think I was just being a bitch. By this time, I was pretty much hopping with one foot, only using my bad foot to make the smallest of steps and then taking loping strides with the good one. We finally got into camp and as we went downhill toward the football field, I looked over and saw Sgt. Fam skipping playfully, showing that the hike hadn't gotten to him. He had dragged Marines most of the hike, carrying their gun systems and he still had a smile on his face and a spring in his step. Remarkable.

I walked like Frankenstein to the armory to turn in my weapon, not able to move my knees. Though everyone was hurting, the younger guys had a much quicker recovery time. Though they might be nursing crotch rash or blisters, a half-hour after the hike they were fine. Recovering from a hike for me was an all-weekend event. In my dingy barracks room, I took off my boot with the finesse of someone disabling a bomb. Relief coursed through me as I saw my foot, which looked like a balloon. I wasn't a bitch, it really was broken, or at least fractured.

The next morning, I woke up late and went to the PX where I saw Mora looking weary.

"Hey Meyer, did you hear?"

"Hear what?"

"Salinas is in the hospital. Brain-dead."

"That's not funny."

"It's not supposed to be."

I had seen Salinas sitting down at the armory, looking out-of-it, but I was wrapped up in my own problems. I hobbled to the barracks to get more info. Salinas had collapsed on the way to BAS and they were not able to revive him. His condition was so bad that the Camp Pendleton hospital sent him to a civilian hospital. His family had been alerted and was en route. There were few people on base, but everyone that was around was going to the hospital for a vigil.

I went back to my room, switching into my Charlie short-sleeved dress uniform as ordered. We rarely wore anything other than cammies, so this signaled how bad off Salinas was. Our vigil would be a de facto wake. My foot had gotten even worse overnight; it was so big that my shoelaces on my dress shoes couldn't even cross each other so I could tie them.

The hospital was in San Juan Capistrano, a rich LA suburb, quite a far cry from Salinas' hometown of Brownsville, Texas. I had just recently gotten to know Salinas and he was a good guy, though a little difficult and proud. He didn't get along with the other 51s, who were very conspicuous by their absence. Sections are like families; they might fight within the unit, but they usually stick together. It was shocking that none of the 51s went to see him in the hospital or showed any extra concern.

We flocked to First Sergeant Bell when he came into the hospital lobby, hoping he would make sense of things. He had brought an attractive Asian woman to show us some female support, who we would later find out was his ex-wife. After he visited with the family, he let us in two at a time. It was strange to see my new friend in his hospital bed; he looked like he would wake up at any time. The situation was beyond hope; he was brain-dead after having an aneurysm and they were just waiting for his brother to arrive before they pulled the plug. I tried to tell his bereft family how good of a Marine he was, but they were inconsolable. They questioned everyone who came in about why he died, looking for any malfeasance.

I went back out, still upset, and rambled to First Sergeant Bell, while he listened with endless patience. He was a hard man—probably the hardest I'd ever meet—but like Washbourne he also had endless wells of compassion. We held the vigil until Salinas' brother arrived; then left, so his family could be with him away from prying eyes.

On Monday, the BAS was stuffed with more than 60 Marines who got injured on the hike. I sweated while they developed my X-ray. If my foot was simply swollen, I would never live it down. The technician came out and showed me the small faint crack in the X-ray and told me my foot was fractured. A clean break would have been better for me, reputation-wise, but a documented fracture was almost as good.

So many people were injured that they ran out of crutches, so they sent me to the main hospital, which gave me a choice between crutches and a cane. Spirits were low and I knew that everyone would get a good laugh at seeing "Grandpa" with a cane, so I chose a nice wooden one. Crutches are widely-reviled as being used by malingers to elicit sympathy. Light-duty commandoes are infamous for using their crutches all week and then dancing at a club on the weekends. I got shocked stares from my seniors when they saw me out in town actually using my cane, which was almost unprecedented.

An officer and two enlisted Marines were chosen to escort Salinas' body home and I asked to go, but they had already chosen the Marines. In the next few days, there was an investigation to see if there was any wrong-doing, but nothing was found. We lived a hard life; war was not the only way Marines died in uniform. Weeks later, Gunny Seese told us that it was revealed that Salinas was a "preemie", and thus more susceptible to heat-related brain injuries. It seemed odd and inappropriate, like they were trying to defend themselves, when they had done nothing wrong in the first place.

I had barely gotten my wife moved into base housing when it was time to take off to CAX. Spending 21 days in the desert seemed like such a huge deal back then—like we were going to war. The coastal region quickly melted into sand as we wound our way into the high desert. We arrived in the dark to what looked like the surface of the moon. All we could see were aluminum Quonset huts called K-Spans (although we thought they were called "Case bands"). The K-Spans looked like they were built to store broken lawnmowers and the light in ours didn't even work.

The next day, we woke to see where we were. This was not the rolling sand desert of the movies; it was rock, gravel and mountains as far as the eye could see. There was something scary about being there—there's so much death and misery associated with the desert—but something lasting happened to me there. I fell in love with the austere beauty of the desert. I would later fall in love with the ocean for the same reason—because they both share the same formless, yet infinite beauty. Esoteric sure, but that was one of the things I loved about the Corps; it took me to places I never would have gone and introduced me to people I never would have met.

The first three days were lazy so that we could acclimate ourselves. We were given some silly briefs about dead Marines being found dead in the desert with full canteens because they didn't hydrate properly. We got a brief about all the endangered flora and fauna of the desert and we were instructed not to shoot the large turtles that lived there, which made all of us want to really, *really* want to shoot those turtles.

We stayed at Camp Wilson, which in relation to our surroundings was a major metropolitan area. Another thing I gleaned from the Corps—everything is relative. Porta-Jons might be disgusting places most people think are just for construction workers, but all you have to do is spend two nights in the field shitting in the bushes and a Porta-Jon looks like a four-star hotel. I am not alone in achieving the ability to sleep while sitting in a porta-potty when the weather is bad enough.

Camp Wilson had a huge hangar-like chow hall, but it didn't have enough toilets to deal with the punishment that the food dealt to our insides. While on one of our hour-long PT runs, I could tell that the re-constituted eggs wanted out of me in the worst way. In the "no excuses" atmosphere of the grunts, having the shits is no reason to get out of a run. That sort of thing used to make me despise the Corps, but now I can look back and realize it was necessary. In combat, when the platoon is about to rush the enemy's fortress, no one is going to accommodate you because you've got a case of the mud-butt.

My only choice was to sprint ahead of the platoon, drop my silkies and try to be done before they got too far away. The only privacy to be had was behind a lone scraggly bush. As I squatted down like my Neanderthal forefathers, Sgt. Fam accused me of faking illness to get out of the run. As he rounded the bush, I splattered the desert and he jumped back in disgust With no other options, I grabbed a handful of sand and scoured my ass like an old steel pot.

When I pulled my pants up and started to sprint to catch up with the platoon, Sgt. Fam told me to slow down and pace myself. Sgt. Fam was as strong as a bull and he could hike straight up a mountain, but even he admitted that he was a weak runner. One thing that always bothered me was that people who were good at hiking would always say that hiking was really a mental challenge, not a physical one; so if you were a poor hiker, you were weak mentally. The same people would then do poorly at things I was good at, like swimming and running, and they would say that with activities like that, you were either naturally good at them or you weren't.

When Sgt. Fam fell back to "help" me, he was able to get a breather. No one would talk shit to him if he didn't finish with the rest of the pack, like they would with me, so I sprinted 500 meters and caught up with the platoon, to everyone's amazement. My victory was short-lived, as I soon felt a rumbling down below. Luckily, there was a Porta-Jon up ahead, but when I got to it, I saw that it said "Women Only." I knocked once and then jumped in, imagining some female gunny coming up and chewing my ass.

When I got out, the platoon was just a dot on the horizon, a half-mile away. I was able to catch back up, which surprised even me. I was still "Old Man Meyer", but I was no longer the weakest or the slowest. The time I had been putting in at the gym had paid off. Instead of chewing my ass, Washbourne was just curious about what was wrong with me.

"I did a bad thing to the desert, corporal."

Our first week was fairly easy and fun. We would hike a mile to some nice, automated ranges, shoot; then hike back and be off by 3:00PM. We could then go to the entertainment district of Camp Wilson, which was the PX and the laundromat. Let me tell you something though, that joint was jumping; you would have thought it was Studio 54. When the overweight female Marine is washing her clothes dressed in nothing but a t-shirt and her silky PT shorts—now that is sexy…if you're in the desert.

The easy training ended and we started on the Range 400 series, a set of huge mile-wide ranges set deep in a C-shaped canyon. This training would be much more realistic, with snipers, CAAT humvees and tanks working with us. The Range 400 series is the most realistic training the Marine Corps has.

The machinegun section was running smooth, but it was already the beginning of the end. We would soon get a member who would tear the section's reputation to shreds. Since support (which is what a weapons platoon is) is so critical to the survival of the rifle platoons, we were given six riflemen to fill out our under-manned section; three of them would stay. The other platoons screwed us by giving us their odd ducks and problem children. Sometimes you get someone like Elias, who was a great and tough Marine, who was just butting heads with his superiors. Sometimes you get someone like Reed. Later on, this book will seem like it's about nothing but Reed, but when we first got him he didn't seem that bad.

Three of the six—Elias, Reed and Weiche—were happy about the possibility of coming to Weapons Platoon since they were having problems in their old platoons. The hazing and fuck-fuck games were a little worse in the rifle platoons. Washbourne could be the devil himself, but you had to fuck up bad to catch his wrath. It wasn't that way in the rifle platoons; even if you were perfect you still caught heat. The other three weren't enthusiastic about being with us. You could see that they were embarrassed to be foisted off on another platoon since everyone knows that you don't give away your star players.

Weiche was more than happy to be with us; than again, Weiche was happy to be anywhere. He was short and hyper-caffeinated; a nice enough guy, but he tried a little too hard, which put people off. He was in a weird and untenable position since he had come from Security Forces, which sounds high-speed, but is basically permanent guard duty. After SOI, SF Marines go to another month of training out east before heading out to guard naval weapons sites, docks and foreign training areas. After a year or two of pulling guard duty, they come to The Fleet as a lance or corporal, but they get treated like boots. They have stripes on their collars, but no field experience to back them up. They end up in a grey area—not boots, but scorned by the salt dogs. The general consensus was that only two types of Marines came out of SF: locked-on moto-dogs or burn-outs.

Our seniors tried to make the Range 400-series sound like D-Day without the ambience, but it turned out to be extraordinarily exciting, realistic and motivating training. The only thing that was de-motivating was the continuing boot/salt-dog crap. When my peers and I became senior Marines we never called ourselves "salt dogs" and we pulled firewatch along with out boots. We even put "salty" lances on working parties along with the boots.

Washbourne always had a temper, but it was getting out of hand. Later on, I would find out from Jaramillo that he was taking some pretty heavy-duty supplements to get ready to take the Force Recon Indoc, some of which were known to increase aggression and anger problems. It was really grating to know that the better we became, the worse we got treated. We were *the* hot machinegun section in the battalion and we got no acknowledgment of that by our seniors. Once while doing gun drills, I got excited about beating my personal best time and I was instantly set upon by Chuck for being a fucked-up, loud-mouth, know-nothing boot. I consoled myself with the fact that, unlike Chuck, the chicks I fucked didn't look like Olive Oyl.

Losey went UA right before we went to 29 Palms. Even though he had been in for seven-and-a-half years, he was only a lance because he had been busted down as a corporal for drunk-driving a week before he picked up sergeant. In the grunts, you get respect for the miles you've hiked and the pumps you've been on, so he didn't get treated like a boot. He was an Old Corps-type, stocky and short with a little bit of a gut, but he could hike until his boots split. As the saying goes, he had forgotten more about the gun than most people knew. When he was denied leave to take care of some family problems, he went UA. He was an Indian and they couldn't touch him on the rez. It was a dumb move, since he was so short that he wasn't even going to Oki with us.

As many problems as I had with my seniors, I have to give them this—they always showed a united front. It would be almost a year until I found out that half of them hated each other. They would always back up each other in front of the boots. The time they spent putting us in our place when we got to The Fleet was completely unnecessary though. You come out of SOI wanting to learn and glad you're not a recruit or a student anymore. It's not like I got to the Fleet, looked at my seniors and said to myself that I knew more than they did—that would be stupid. They had been in their jobs almost two years longer than us, so of course we would listen to them, but they went so overboard with the salty/boot crap that we started to look for their weaknesses and see how we could exploit them.

Williams was the first senior to get de-valued in our eyes. On our first field op, he screwed up a really basic piece of machinegun knowledge and wouldn't admit he was wrong when I asked him about it. The next week, he fell out of a hike, which was unheard of for a senior Marine. Williams was so ashamed that he started crying, so Washbourne, who could be quite fatherly when he wasn't breathing hellfire, consoled him. Williams got broke and stayed broke. He was like a ghost in the company—not training, not leading, just sitting in his room and doing odd jobs for the company office. It was a sad fate, but there was always the strong suspicion that he could have made it if he really wanted to.

Stanbo had scammed as long as humanly possible until they put him back in training. He was a weird fit—not treated like a senior Marine, yet not a boot. He had earned Washbourne's ire and was kept on a short leash. For as many problems as he had and caused, Stanbo was a good field Marine. Washbourne used to say that Stanbo was gold in the field, but in garrison he would fuck up everything imaginable. He said that every time the company came out of the field, they should just leave Stanbo out there with enough rations to live until the next field op.

On the series 400 ranges, heavy guns and mortars would prep the area; then the machinegunners would sneak up the side of "Machinegun Hill" to provide cover fire for the riflemen as they assaulted through the objective. Each day began before dawn, when we would distribute thousands of rounds of ammo. The stress level was ratcheted up; the seniors would give indistinct orders like "grab that there" and if you grabbed the wrong box in the pitch blackness, they would absolutely lose it. We were loaded down with thirty pounds of ammo per man. Machinegun Hill was a break-off, but the good thing was that it was so steep that everyone ran half of it and then just walked the rest.

At that time, I was still one of the weakest boots in the platoon and it gnawed at me. My buddies realized that heavy lifting wasn't my forte, so they would be cool and help me out, with only gentle ribbing throw in. Even that started to wound my pride. I lost it and rushed around, yanking everyone's ammo off their shoulders.

"Fuck you! Fuck all y'all! I'm taking all the ammo!"

I had enough adrenaline to grab all of the ammo, but then quickly realized I was about to collapse. Chuck wisely ordered me to give it back and stop acting childish. The weight was intense and you had to really think about how you were going to carry it. Each lunch-box sized can of ammo carries two hundred rounds and weighs about fifteen pounds. With the weapon, gear and ammo, it felt like a huge, unseen hand was pushing you down into the dirt.

Before the attack kicked off, we waited on one side of a berm while the combat engineers simulated breaching a minefield with a bangalore torpedo on the other. They warned us about the blast and even had a count-down, but I didn't pay attention. I was talking to Silva when he suddenly turned into a bug-eyed, slack-jawed cartoon character. As I felt the pressure waves, I turned to see flame and debris shoot up in a column one hundred feet high. Bangalores ain't no joke.

We ran through the breech and toward Machinegun Hill. They wanted even more bang for their buck, so they had some SAW gunners augment our section. One of the SAW gunners was a senior Marine who had served a tour in the Navy. Like Losey, Salazar had been a week away from picking up sergeant when he was busted down to lance for drunk driving. After the attack, when the advisor/instructors called "coyotes" gave us some feedback, they made a comment about how the SAW gunners took forever to get into place. Salazar shrugged and snickered, not caring, and Washbourne snatched his fat ass up like a rag-doll and gave him a boot-style ass-chewing. It was quite shocking to see one senior unload on another, but also quite gratifying.

When we got into position and started firing, I was in my element. For as much as I hated the Corps, I loved this part and it never got old. Looking down the barrel of this absolutely fearsome killing machine and laying down rounds a mile away was awesome and I was getting paid for it. I never had a job I fit in as a civilian. Even at Dell, I didn't excel and I didn't care; I was a bored clock watcher. I loved this *and* I was good at it. Though I was on odd fit in the grunts, I still fit.

Mohler was my team leader and we got along great, even though he got tired of my whining. The proper prone shooting position for the 240 has the team leader laying on the gunner. Not only is it extremely gay, but since I was laying on a sharp incline, it made me slide down the hill. After many adjustments, we finally agree on a zero body-contact policy. When I said my elbow was hurting and I made him put a sandbag under it though; I think he just about lost it.

After the shooting finished, we got a glowing evaluation. I was so used to being told that I was a piece of shit that I had never really stopped to think that my buddies and I might be really good at our jobs. The coyote said that we were the best machinegun section he had seen in a while and he seemed genuinely impressed by our motivation. The coyote was the oldest Marine I had ever seen; he had to be at least sixty, but he still looked fit and happy. He was a gunner—a warrant officer rank only achieved by being an absolute master of every weapon that the Marine Corps uses. He had been in for about thirty years; after that much time, the Marine Corps is no longer your job, it's your life. The young Marines are like your grandkids, so he was much kinder than most career Marines.

The elation was short-lived. After a shoot, you have to clean-up the thousands of ejected brass rounds that are lying around, but you're never given a reasonable amount of time. We got five minutes and, sure enough, Washbourne and Chuck set upon us like a couple of rabid dogs to get the job done. After finishing, the boots climbed into the crowded rear of the humvee. I was pissed that we were getting treated like shit after being praised by the gunner, but the temp machine-gunners like Elias were loving it. They were being treated better than they had in their old platoons and didn't want to go back. Everything is relative.

Back at Camp Wilson, people started getting froggy. When grunts are bored, you know they're eventually going to start wrestling. None of the schools I ever went to taught wrestling, so I never really learned how to fight; which meant that in my late 20s, I still fought like a second-grader, with the attendant flailing arms, weird bird-like kicks and screeching. I would always lose to corn-fed motherfuckers who, if they were twins, probably would have wrestled the other fetus in their mother's womb. There are so many former high school wrestlers in the Marines that it's ridiculous and more than half of them say they went to state-level championships in high school.

Milligan challenged Washbourne and though he was respectful about it, there was a clear undercurrent of animosity. They fought for ten straight minutes, rolling around like a couple of cats in the dust. Eventually Washbourne pinned Milligan, but it was the closest he had ever come to being beaten. Washbourne patted Milligan on the back good-naturedly and it looked like the ill will between them had dissipated.

Things had been going downhill for Milligan. When we first got to The Fleet, he didn't screw up much, so the seniors didn't have much to hit him on. His accent and his penchant for large women made it fun to joke around with him. Milligan liked his girls "thick," as he put it. The hottest girls would hit on him and he would just want them as friends—his ideal woman was a chick whose legs were still together even when they were spread apart.

Sgt. Fam was back after being away for the last month dealing with personal issues. Sgt. Fam loved being in the grunts, hanging out with and bull-shitting with the boots. He didn't like fuck-fuck games; he was much more into encouraging people than demeaning them. One of the boots he took under his wing was McPoland, a mortarman and an all-together weird bird. He was a gun nut in a scary Columbine-like way and had a whole host of strange and opinionated views on everything. Needless to say, he was a virgin and very awkward socially. He looked like a nerd, but he was into every freaky death metal band in the world. He had a robotic, nasal monotone, starting every sentence with a long "ehhhhhh-hhhhhhh" like Steve Urkel.

By that time, the machinegunners were a tight group whose members' strengths and weaknesses balanced out quite well. The mortarmen were the complete opposite. They had four boots who were in amazing physical shape—Keller, Boyd, Vargas and Rodgar—and another four that were weak screw-ups. The problem with the all-stars was that, except for Rodgar, all they did was belittle and harass the non-hackers; which made them much weaker as a section. If you don't know what a mortar is, just try this: Remember the little green army men your mom got you at the drug store? Remember the one you *never* played with? That was the mortarman. The lame-ass loser kneeling down with a stupid tube pointing up in the air.

McPoland took constant abuse, so Sgt. Fam took him aside between some K-Spans. It looked like he was mugging McPoland and I went closer to see what was happening. Sgt. Fam was "bullying" McPoland, trying to get a reaction from him, but McPoland just shrugged it off. Sgt. Fam wanted to get McPoland to stand up for himself and started to show him how to fight. He could have just ordered Boyd, Vargas and Keller to back off, but that wouldn't have been the right thing to do. Those three were bullies, but they were *right;* McPoland and the others were dragging the whole section down and they weren't trying to improve themselves.

SSgt. Shores, our new permanent platoon sergeant, met us out at Camp Wilson, having spent the last several months at the Staff NCO academy. Though short and unimpressive-looking, SSgt. Shores was absolutely ferocious. He had a mellifluous and smooth, radio announcer voice, but his icy blue eyes could be terrifying when his mood slipped suddenly—as was his reputation. He wasn't afraid to go Old Corps on anyone, anywhere, if they got stupid. We had met him briefly in the field before CAX, when he was leading another platoon. He would sneak up on people and hit them in the head hard if didn't have their helmet on. Though he had a rep as a hard-ass, I found him very easy to get along with. As long as you didn't lie to him or lose your mind, you were golden. As Washbourne later said when he saw SSgt. Shores lifing the shit out of a corporal, "God, I fucking *love* that man."

Cpl. Darnell arrived from FAST company shortly before CAX. FAST stands for Fleet Anti-Terrorist Strike Team, which sounds like a Chuck Norris movie, but it's just Security Forces. Darnell was a good guy, with small lapses in judgment which always seemed to come back and bite him in the ass. Boyd lost his pistol and Darnell didn't tell SSgt. Shores about it, hoping to find it before they went anywhere. SSgt. Shores found out and called Darnell over. Before he went nuts, SSgt. Shores always had the same routine. He would lean in, acting like he hadn't heard what you said. Flashing his freaky blue eyes, he would then pounce on you like a lion. SSgt. Shores launched Darnell through the air in front of everyone. Though I got a nice surge of schadenfreude seeing a senior Marine get taken down a peg, it wasn't supposed to be the way that NCOs were treated in front of their boots. By the time I became an NCO, that type of behavior would be de rigeur.

The training was great; the only bad thing was the weather, which was bitterly cold in a way only found in the high desert. Next was the HAC (Helicopter Assault Course). We left in the single-rotor CH-53 Super Sea Stallions, which are about ten years younger than the 46s and more agile, but also more computer-dependent and thus, less reliable. We took off, flying low over the hard-scrabble surface of Twenty-Nine Palms. The bird was able to bank almost completely sideways as it went through a turn, so I would be looking out a side window straight down at the ground one minute and straight up in the sky the next. We were flying so close to the walls of the narrow canyons that it reminded me of the race scene from "The Phantom Menace." It was a little scary, but I just had to put my blind faith in the pilot. I usually do great on birds, but all the weaving around made me a little airsick. I felt like a pussy until I looked around and saw that the feeling was very mutual.

The company landed in several waves; then took off over the rough terrain. The way to our objective was less a mountain than a huge pile of oddly-shaped rocks. The going was rough and fast and Weiche fell so far back that First Sergeant Bell had to take the ammo bag from him—an unforgivable sin. His future as a machinegunner was shot. Weiche had already earned Washbourne's wrath; they had served together on the hard-duty base of Guantanamo Bay, but there was no shared bond. If anything, Washbourne was embarrassed by the connection and made sure that Weiche knew it, snatching him up by the collar in front of us.

The final approach was steep and treacherous. I only had one hand free to pull myself up, so I slowed down a bit. Marr had made it to the top and dropped his pack. He ran back, grabbed the gun from me and sped up to the gun line. At that point, as happens sometimes, common sense spontaneously sprung up without the sanction of an order and people started dropping their huge packs, since we would not need them for the final assault. When Mohler dropped his, it just kept rolling and rolling until it came to the edge of a precipice. It then hung there Warner Brother cartoon-style for split-second before plummeting 100 feet to the bottom of the ravine.

We got to the top and fired on the objective—a bunch of tires and wooden pallets 300 meters away. The Army would have had computer-aided targets that told how accurate the fire was. It seemed like a waste. When the shoot ended, we headed down into a canyon that would let us sneak up closer to our next objective. Since we were behind schedule, Washbourne grabbed the gun from me and sprinted ahead.

We hiked to a ridge that looked out on a huge expanse of flat desert floor, which would be our shooting gallery the next morning. We were told to dig fighting positions, which was a joke since there was nothing that resembled dirt or sand. The best you could do was gather rocks and form little forts as the temperature dropped like a stone. We spent hours making our position only to be told we were in the wrong place; we had to join the rest of the company on top of a mesa.

We set down on the summit and the cold got ten times worse, since we no longer had hills and ridge lines blocking the wind. The wind was like daggers; it seemed like it could reach in and pull every last bit of heat out of you. This went way past discomfort and got pretty damn close to "I want my mommy." Mohler, Weiche and I found a half-demolished fighting hole one and fortified it. We didn't even wait to be told to go to sleep—we just went. My former aversion to spooning no longer existed and we slept in a pile like newborn puppies. The only thing I didn't like about it was that both of them were skinny. Why couldn't I had gotten a nice fat guy like Hyatt to keep me warm? Firewatch that night had only the barest hint of professionalism. When woken for watch, I would just roll over two feet and get behind the gun, opening my sleeping bag just enough to see out of.

An hour after reveille, the XO walked up and asked why we were still in our bags. We played "lance corporal don't know" and he just moved on, obviously having gotten that a lot that morning. Two Apache attack helicopters flew in and strafed the target area. Unlike the bangalore, their hellfire missiles weren't much to look at. Again we were shooting at broken pallets, but I was thankful for the heat coming off of my gun's barrel.

We flew back to Camp Wilson; a couple more days of chilling out, one more big exercise and then we were done. Unfortunately, a major family crisis hit again. I was called in to see the chaplain and then the company XO. I was worried that leaving during such important training would make me look bad, so I wasn't going to ask for leave. I was surprised when they offered it without reservation. The XO spoke to my Platoon Commander, who vouched that I wasn't like other Marines who constantly used their personal problems to get out of training.

The Marine Corps might beat you worse than your dad did, but they look out for you even better than your momma had.

I hadn't spoken to Washbourne about this, which was big no-no since you were always supposed to go through the chain-of-command about everything. SSgt. Shores took me aside at breakfast and I asked him what he would do in my situation. He said if he was me, he'd already be at home. I told a few close friends what was up; the others just gleaned that "Old Man" Meyer was skating out of training again.

Situations like this created a rift between single and married Marines. Single Marines complained about married Marines getting more time off, going home early and getting to work late. Married Marines got more than a thousand dollars a month for housing, so to a single Marine, Married Marines were rich skaters. This was wrong for two reasons. As for the housing pay, that extra money was instantly eaten up by rent. A single guy had maybe a car payment and a phone bill, while I had to support three people on the same amount of basic pay. Our pay amounts would be posted in the company office, so I would constantly get people asking me for money since I was "rich." As for work, the shortest commute was thirty minutes and nice housing was at least 45 minutes away. Single guys could wake up at 6:05 and make the 6:15AM formation while I had to wake up at 4:30AM to make it. They were home as soon as the company was secured, while I wouldn't be home for an hour or more.

Being that I was a married Marine, I constantly had to crash in my single buddies' barracks rooms during the work day. Even my best friends would get tired of me from time-to-time and Ross came up with his own solution—the "Meyer-Unfriendly Room." He arranged his furniture in such a way, that his room became a maze and when I cracked the door to see if he was there, he could always hide behind a piece of furniture.

First Sergeant Bell drove me the three hours back to Pendleton, which was scary and enlightening. He had been a Force Recon operator for 14 years and was probably one of the toughest guys in the Corps, so I didn't want to say or do anything stupid. When he did normal things like get drive-thru tacos or listen to Madonna on the radio, it blew my mind.

I returned from ten days of leave to the usual slight resentment and silence, but things quickly got back to normal. Third time was the charm and Stanbo finally went UA for good. So did Pratt, a perpetually lost and befuddled mortarman who had dabbled in amateur porn in Oceanside. Pratt was known for his head being on a constant swivel and his perpetually quizzical expression. He was only confused about three things:

1. What we had been doing.

2. What we were doing at the time.

3. What we would be doing.

Besides that he was fine. His other odd affectation was that he had a small head, but an extra-large helmet which made him look like a penis when he wore it. Though he started as a rifleman, he had been shuttled through every section in Weapons before ending up as a mortarman. We barely noticed he was gone.

Another half-dozen boots in the company went UA as well, but the only that would really count—the one that would hurt—was Milligan. Though he had done great when we first got to The Fleet, he started to butt heads with the senior Marines, Washbourne especially. Some of it he brought on himself. He constantly fell asleep on watch. On one field op, it was almost a comedy routine. I woke him to replace me on watch and as I crawled into my sleeping bag, I warned him to stay awake for all our sakes. He nodded and assured me he would in his thick drawl and immediately fell asleep with his hand on his chin. I woke him up two more times in the next two minutes, then shrugged and went to sleep myself.

When Milligan got on the wrong side of Washbourne, his days were numbered. Unlike Losey and Stanbo though, Milligan could stand toe-to-toe with Washbourne. Things really came to a head when they started fucking with his free time. The seniors "volunteered" Milligan for every shitty work detail there was; even putting him on a two-week long working party in the field. After being caught leaving the base when he was supposed to field-daying, Washbourne made him hand over his keys. Milligan acquiesced and then went straight to his room, grabbed his other set of keys and drove off base.

The seniors fumed and started to plan all sorts of fuck-fuck games for him. Milligan came back later that night and chilled with a friend in another barracks. After the vengeful seniors stopped waiting up for him, he came back and told a few people he was going UA. They tried to talk him out of it, but when they saw that his mind was made up, they helped him pack and even loaned him a few bucks. The next day, when it was discovered that Milligan was UA, it caused quite a stir. We had a lot of UAs already, but they were all shit-birds. Milligan was different; he was good to go and what's more, he was the heart of the machinegun section. It would be downhill for the next two years before our rep recovered.

Milligan had a huge family and going to prison wasn't considered all that strange in his neighborhood, so his decision wasn't that scary to him. He had too much pride for the grunts. He couldn't laugh off the loss of freedom and dignity inherent in being a boot and who can blame him? Right before CAX, I had strongly considered going UA myself because of the constant degradation of the job, but I had to stick it out since I was married.

Milligan's roommate Hyatt got a notice for some bounced checks, which Milligan had forged. He wrote paltry checks up and down the coast and it was interesting and sad to see the mundane things he bought on his "crime spree." It was a real shame since I or any of the other machinegunners would have loaned or just given him the money if he would have just asked.

Though we all missed Milligan already, there was one way he could still help us out. We were all missing some gear and he had left all of his in his locker. Somehow, his locker popped open and several people were able to re-supply themselves. I needed an expensive sleeping bag to replace the one that I had left at Camp Margarita, so I asked Hyatt if I could come in and get Milligan's. Hyatt was pissed that people had been coming into his room without permission, so he said that he would sell it to me, to make up for the money that Milligan had stolen from him. I was bothered that he was trying to sell me someone else's gear, until I realized I didn't exactly have the moral high ground. I forked over 25 bucks for the sleeping bag, saving $200.

As we lost Milligan, we officially gained three others—Elias, Reed and Moramonroy. Elias was from El Salvador, but he had lived all over the country, as he let everyone within earshot know. Though a loudmouth, he was a good friend and a solid, stand-up guy, even if he did have a bit of a temper. He was a good addition to the team and I was glad to have him there. Moramonroy was a Mexican immigrant with an impenetrable accent that—PC be damned—made him sound like a caveman. He earned several nicknames: Eminem, Roy and Capitan Cavernicula ("Captain Caveman" in Spanish as Rodgar told us). Reed had a reputation as a whiner, but he seemed like a friendly enough guy. His violent temper and massive psychological problems would show themselves more over the next year.

Our work-up was nearly over; it had only been four months long, but considering how much time we spent in the field, it felt much longer. There's an adage that every year in the grunts ages you four years and my body seemed to agree.

Since we were a helo company, we had to qual in fast-roping and go to the helo dunker, which were both were scary and exciting. Fast-roping is Marine Corps simplicity at its finest—it's a rope you slide down really fast. There is no safety equipment, you just hold on with your hands and brake by grabbing the rope between your feet. If you let go or slip off you hurt yourself bad—so it's incentive-based training. We would train on the helo tower in The Backyard, a rickety grey-wood structure built about forty years ago. If it was a house it would be condemned, but this is the Marine Corps, where we use a structure until it falls down around us.

Peer pressure worked its magic and everyone, whether they were scared of heights or not, climbed up forty feet up and slid down the rope, each time wearing more gear until they maxed out with a full pack. The last trick was "Locking Out", in which you would kick your legs off the rope, then trap it between your feet to make yourself come to a sudden stop. When you kick your legs out, you are in a free-fall and I kept getting scared and not doing it right. My seniors made me do it over and over again until I did it right, which was the right thing to do. The fear of falling was nothing compared to the fear of shame of looking like a pussy, so I forced myself to do it.

My weakness was heights, but for most others its water. We trained on the HABD (Helicopter Air-Breathing Device), a soda can-sized underwater breathing apparatus. I was a little scared, but I took relief that I was the fourth guy in line. Surely the others would do fine and that would allay my fears. No such luck. Every guy in front of me, sputtered and freaked out underwater. It is unnatural to be underwater and tell your lungs to breathe in, but I seemed to have less problem doing it than anyone else.

Next we went to the Helo Dunker down at Miramar. During the brief, even the seniors who had already done this looked apprehensive. The dunker looked like an elaborate killing mechanism that a James Bond villain would design. Suspended over an indoor pool, the dunker was a twenty-foot long simplified version of a helo fuselage. It would be lowered down into the water and then flipped over to simulate how a top-heavy bird would react in a real crash.

When seeing films of people in Nazi Germany being led to their death, I never understood why one of them didn't fight back or jump for the Nazi's gun. They all just filed slowly into their mass grave. That's how it went in the dunker as well. I followed seven others into the dunker and fastened the simple waist belt. Surviving a helo crash goes as follows: first, don't freak out, you're not going to be able to leave the bird until it fills with water and the pressure equalizes. Second, it's going to be dark, so as soon as you know you're going down, get your hand on a reference point and map your way to the exit.

The first dip wasn't that bad. Strapped in and watching the water rise is freaky, but again, the fear of shame kept me—and I'm sure all the others—quiet. Grab your breath at the last moment, unfasten your seat belt loose and make your way to the exit.

The second time, the dunker turns upside-down underwater. When it starts turning, you'll think you're fully upside-down, but you see by the bubbles that you aren't even half-way there. You know you're upside-down when you feel the seat belt tight against your upper thighs as you hang there. When I unhooked my belt, I forgot to account for gravity; I sunk to the "bottom" of the bird—the top—and got disoriented, but I had a firm hold of my reference point, so I found the exit and pulled myself out.

The third time was the bitch of the bunch since we would be blind-folded. I sat in a queer way, with one hand on my reference point and the other held near my collarbone, so that as soon as my hand got wet, I would know to hold my breath. When the dunker stopped turning, I opened my eyes to find the exit and all I saw was black. I had closed my eyes every time I went underwater and was so intent on the exercise that I forgot I was wearing blacked-out goggles. In my confusion, I thought I had wedged myself under a seat. I kicked around, trying to swim free and felt myself mash someone in the face with my boot (White, I would later find out). I tried several different ways to escape and seemed to be altogether stuck.

The thought came calmly: I am going to drown. There were three times in the Marine Corps when I thought I was going to die and my response was always the same: calm resignation. "Well, I guess this is it." I put my hands together like I was praying, which was the signal for the scuba divers to rescue anyone trapped in the dunker. I imagined myself hopelessly stuck and didn't think that the diver could get me to the surface in time, but my hands hadn't been together for more than a split-second before a hand grabbed me in a strong grip and I felt myself being lifted up.

I got to the surface and took off my helmet and—oh yeah!—the blacked-out goggles. I thanked the diver, who nodded graciously, not thinking much of it. I was a little embarrassed about failing, but sudden pride in myself welled up. I had been certain I was about to die and I had handled it calmly. I had some doubts before about how I would react under such a situation and was glad that I handled it well.

I jumped out and got back in line. When I got back in the dunker, I grabbed the seat next to the exit, to make it easier on myself. I cheated a little by grabbing my reference point as soon as I got in, but hey, I wouldn't wait until the last minute in a crash, would I?

We still had some training, but they were quick-and-dirty one-day affairs, instead of the typical three days/two nights in the field grind. After spending so many field ops cursing how cold "Sunny" California could be, we did a quick helo raid and I got to experience the "microwave effect" of the coastal valleys in the late spring. After jogging a mile with the gun, I thought I was about to pass out; I knew it was bad when even the officers were dying.

For some reason, Roy was made my team leader and I got to see again how badly brain-washed we were when he put me in a horrible untenable gun position.

"Roy, what the hell are we doing? I can't see shit."

"I doan know, Moyers…Sheet…Corporal Washbourne gonna keel me."

"Did the shoot get cancelled? We're just sitting here."

"Ummm….Hey, dey're firing! Shoot! Shoot!"

"Roy, you see that fucking boulder three feet in front of my barrel? The one I pointed out to you when you put me in this fucked-up position?"

"Just shoot, man. We gonna get in trouble eef we doan get rid of our rounds."

"Try this on for size. 'No.' I'm not going to get a ricochet in the face because you're afraid of getting yelled at."

At one point, the training just ceased and we all sat on a dirt road, panting like dogs as we waited for more water to be brought up. Roy wasn't the only one making dumb mistakes that day. The heat must have been warping my brain because when we did a 360-degree perimeter defense around the helos, I pointed my gun inwards. I then felt the white hot glare of Washbourne's devil eyes (which I definitely deserved) and turned my ass around.

Washbourne went to First Platoon to become their acting platoon sergeant, to almost everyone's relief. He was getting to be a little much to bear, but in a firefight there's no one I would want next to me more. It's just that in peace time, he could be a little exhausting.

After spending so many nights in the field, any training that involved us being able to sleep in our beds was a god-send. The night-time helo raid we had planned was only supposed to take a few hours and I could go home afterwards. I was hyped up because the training sounded quick and exciting, so I started pushing my buddies playfully, like football players do before a big game. I was getting a little hyper and pissing them off, so they shoved me onto the ground. OK, I can take a hint. I laid down on my gear and waited for the birds to approach.

An hour later, I was wondering where the helos were when I suddenly felt like I was getting bitten by a large bug. I jumped up and realized that a cigarette that Silva had carelessly tossed over his shoulder had gone down my shirt. My anger toward him subsided when we were told that the raid had been canked. All we had to do was turn our weapons and ammo in and we'd be off in an hour.

The next day, we were supposed to be off by noon, but a problem arose. Gunny Seese found out that a SAW drum containing 200 live rounds had not been turned in the previous night. Everyone had just dumped their ammo on a pallet, so no one knew who did it. All of us junior Marines knew that it wasn't one of us—this had lazy-ass senior Marine written all over it. Seniors were notorious for tossing their ammo into the bushes or making their boots use it. They didn't want to fire the rounds since that would mean they would have to clean their weapons afterwards.

There was an unofficial policy of never returning from the field with any ammo. Our ammo budgets were so small that on most field ops, we didn't even have blanks. Grown men would be running around the hills of Camp Pendleton yelling "Bang! Bang! Bang!" When we did get live rounds, we would sometimes not be able to fire them all off properly in the time allotted. We would then be told to conduct a "Dump-Ex" in which we would quickly fire off the remainder of the rounds. It was a lot of paperwork to turn in half-empty boxes of ammo and all of the rounds had to be inspected to make sure they were not damaged. If we did not use all of the ammo we were budgeted for that fiscal year, the next year we would get even less.

Gunny gave us an hour for the culprit to turn himself in. In the meantime, every SAW gunner was pulled into First Sergeant Bell's office and interrogated. Rampone, like many innocent people who are accused of something they didn't do, looked guilty as hell. His bright red face was sweating profusely and his eyes darted around suspiciously, which made me laugh.

When no one stepped forward, the company was taken down to The Backyard; Gunny told us that we would not get off until every last round was found. If they were not found that day, we would work all weekend until they were. The seniors started yelling at us and driving us through the prickly bushes like hunting dogs. There were only four senior Marines that had SAWs, but instead of confronting their fellow seniors, they just took it out on us. The empty drum and half of the missing rounds were quickly found under a Porta-Jon along with two blocks of C-4 that had been there God knows how long. The mystery SAW gunner had broken the 200-round belt into 10-round increments and sprinkled them all over the hillside. After two hours, we had recovered all but fifty of the rounds, but when we went another hour without finding any more, it looked like it was going to be a long weekend.

The seniors huddled together to conspire and we hoped that they would finally confront their peers. A few of them snuck off to the barracks and when they came back—lo and behold!—they found a 50-round belt in a bush that we had searched at least a dozen times. Gunny knew that he was being played, but we did come up with 200 rounds, so he let us go on libbo. We found out later that Haberman, a grey-faced, alcoholic senior who was still a lance after three years, had tossed the rounds away. Several of the senior Marines had a few rounds stashed in their rooms, so they collected them up and strung them together. None of the seniors wanted to rat out one of their own, not even a shitbag like Haberman, but they did get their revenge. Hollingshead, the weird company clerk, purposefully screwed up Haberman's paperwork so that his promotion to corporal was pushed back several months.

Only one more field op before our month of pre-deployment leave. It was just one night in the field, with helo rides there and back, so it didn't sound that bad. They didn't even need all the machinegunners, so only about half of us went. Fuck it, one more night in the field couldn't hurt, especially with the weather being so nice.

As we flew South over the Pacific, I thought again about how lucky I was to get into a helo company, but as we descended, I started to have a bad feeling about the op. We flew low over the brush and I secretly hoped for a crash. A crash from ten feet is still a crash—you wouldn't die and I wouldn't have to do the field op. I confided this to Silva as we were pulling out the next day and he told me he had thought the same thing.

We headed east toward the mountains overlooking MOUT town, three miles as the crow flies. The way was long and circuitous with many switchbacks. The 240 seemed a lot easier to hike than usual; the training had built me up a little. What's more, one of my best buddies was hiking with me, which made it a lot easier psychologically.

We had been hiking for more than four hours when it became clear that we were lost. We would take longer and longer breaks, the officers speaking in hushed tones, huddled over maps. We finally got near the peak after six hours of hiking. When we sat down for a break, I thought we were stopping for the night, so I got out my poncho, laid down on the asphalt and went to sleep. An hour later, I woke up and saw Captain Gerst walking past me, cocking an eye at me quizzically, like he couldn't believe what he was seeing. I jumped up, stuffed my poncho in my patrol pack and caught up with the company.

On the rolling hills on the top of the ridge line, all patrol discipline broke down. People just raced through the high brush, not looking back to see if the guy behind them was following. I would briefly see a dark figure in the brush and head in that direction, hoping to not get lost. This went on for two more hours and it was obvious we were just wandering aimlessly.

Finally, we saw the dim lights of MOUT town. Marr told me to set the gun down in chest-high grass and fire on the town. I couldn't see two feet and there was at least thirty feet from my gun to the edge of the hill. I protested, but Marr didn't care and just wanted me to fire off the blanks and be done with it; the whole op was a cluster-fuck anyway. I fired my blanks into the grass; then rested on the buttstock of my gun. We did an "admin bivouac," sleeping along the road like hobos. There was supposed to be a firewatch, but no one cared; I sure didn't.

A few days later, we went on our thirty-day leave block in which we could go home or stay in the area and work minimal hours. I had very few leave days on the books because of all the emergency leave I had taken, so I worked through the leave block, trying to even out my leave deficit. During a leave block, work is almost a vacation anyway; we would usually be off by noon.

"I used to think it'd be cool to die young, with all this potential unfulfilled so I could be mythologized. But now I'm not young and I haven't done a God damn thing to be remembered for. My priorities have changed. I don't want to die anymore. Now I just want to be old and nasty and live alone and throw rocks at neighborhood dogs and just be a general burden on society. If society never set me up to be a hero, fuck 'em. They're gonna pay."

—The Filthy Critic

OKI/FAP

It was at March AFB that I would get my first glimpse of Reed's many problems. Hyatt and Reed started arguing over something petty and, out of nowhere, Reed wanted to fight him. I told myself it was just because of the tension of leaving the country, but it was only the beginning.

We flew on World Airlines, a quasi-civilian airline that only exists to shuttle the military from place to place. For some reason though, they don't want to admit that, so they'd thank you for flying, like you had a choice. Several hundred Marines on a flight has disaster written all over it, so they played it smart and constantly fed us.

The headphone jack at my seat didn't work, so I went to find a seat where it did. The Staff NCOs and officers had the front to themselves and only about half of the seats up there were taken; I heard pissed-off comments from higher-ups when they saw me slink in. I hadn't even been in my seat a minute when a staff NCO made me leave. I couldn't wait for that dumb lifer to get out of the Corps at the age of forty and have to work for a 25 year-old boss. Fucking loser.

I grew up in the Mid-West, so I thought I was an expert in heat, but I had never experienced humidity like that found in Okinawa; walking through the air felt like wading through water. To my delight, every vehicle on Okinawa looked like a newer version of my beloved but much-maligned "Battle Van."

We drove through densely-forested hills until we came to our new home, Camp Hanson. There was nothing special or unique about Camp Hanson, but I came to love it. It would be my best time in The Fleet. Work was light, field ops were few and libbo was abundant. There was a brand-new gym, a good library and two great chow halls all within a few blocks. Honestly—what more could you ask for?

As we came upon our barracks, some Marines from the unit we were replacing shouted, "Welcome to the Rock!" like this was some horrible place. We got our room assignments, but the seniors went up first to ransack the rooms for the best furniture. As soon as they let the boots go, I made a mad dash and was able to procure some good chairs and lamps for me and Reed's room.

Being around guys constantly led to weird behavior. Each room had large dresser/desks called secretaries which had a hole in the back for the plugs to go through. Elias was in the hall and I knew he would fall for the sick trick I had in mind. The secretary was in between the bed and the door, so if I kneeled on the bed, the hole was at the perfect height to stick my dick through. I got a buddy to tell Elias that there was something weird in the secretary. Instead of just opening the door and looking in, he stuck his entire head in before jumping back in fright.

The MSPF Marines were supposed to head to Guam the next day, but it got pushed back a day, which allowed us to settle in and get to know the camp. Four of us were chilling in Hyatt's room, when suddenly Reed got livid that Hyatt called him "stupid," which was silly since we called each other much worse things every day. Reed told Hyatt if he called him stupid again he'd kick his ass; a minute later, Hyatt did so and we laughed as Reed jumped on him, expecting a friendly fake-fight as happens so often in the grunts. I was shocked when Reed started trying to choke Hyatt for real. What the hell is wrong with this guy? I yelled for Reed to stop, trying to figure out what to do; I hadn't dealt with immaturity like this since grade school and maybe not even then. I told Reed to go back to his room, and he histrionically threatened that he was either "your best friend or your worst fucking enemy, swear to God!" Hyatt was hurt that Elias and I didn't immediately pull Reed off of him. I kept thinking it was just going to be a joke and Reed was just playing. How could anyone get fighting-mad over something so stupid?

An hour later, all four of us went out to eat together; I hoped we could all put it behind us. I tried to remember what it was like to be 18; that explained some of the over-aggression, but not all. Reed had been totally off-the-wall. The next morning, I brought it up subtly and Reed nodded when I told him it was not worth fighting over, but I could tell my advice didn't sink in.

The rest of the company arrived the next day and I jokingly held it over their heads that they were now "boot" to me. Ross and Silva were disappointed that they didn't get to go with us to Guam and didn't want to talk about it.

We headed back to the airfield the next day to board a C-17 Globemaster. I smiled, thinking that this was the kind of thing I had joined up for. I had flown in a KC-135 when my dad was in the Air Force, but this was much cooler. The plane was built for cargo and it was bigger than a basketball court inside. The crew handed out the in-flight meals which we dubbed "Air Force MREs"—huge boxes filled with two sodas, a sandwich and more candy than you could eat at one setting, which just blew our minds. When the plane took off, it felt like we were in a tilting building since there were no windows.

The forthcoming month in Guam would turn out to be not only the best time I had in the Marine Corps, but also the best time of my life. It was everything I wanted the Marines to be—exciting, realistic training with elite soldiers like Force Recon and Scout/Snipers, coupled with liberty in an exciting and exotic culture.

Anderson Air Force Base was built on land captured by Marines in World War II. After seeing how beautiful it was, it was immediately handed over to another service. It was spacious and empty, having much less personnel than it did in its heyday during the Cold War. We stayed in a huge, serpentine building near the beach. From a bird's eye view, it probably looked like a cross between an octopus and a swastika. It was at least a quarter-mile long, with endless twists, turns and stairwells. Originally built as a barracks, the rooms had been converted to every use imaginable; there were Air Force and civilian offices, a credit union, a library, barracks and an armory. It had an amazing view of the ocean and the land was lush and beautiful. Our rooms had no circulating air or windows, but it was something that I was used to. Marines were the red-headed step-children of the U.S. military and they always would be.

The chandeliers got my attention first. The chow hall was nicer than most of the restaurants I had been to, so I assumed it was for officers until I saw a couple of chicks with stripes. Food was made to order and you could take as much as you wanted. At Pendleton, you would get two pieces of rubbery, grey chicken and if you went up for seconds you'd get yelled at. Anderson's chow hall had little cards you could put on your table that said "Please do not clear my table, I will return shortly." Wait a minute—they clear your table for you?

Contrary to the myth of Marines being insular and arrogant, we were all very curious and talkative with the airmen. Their standard of living was so strange to us that we wanted to live through it vicariously as much as possible. We asked the airmen how bad their field days were and they just blinked, confused. There was no forced, weekly, all-night barracks clean-up—they were treated like adults. Each airman had his own large room and received hundred of dollars for COLA (Cost of Living Adjustment) since they lived outside the United States. Most of them used it to buy cars to tool around the island with in their ample free time. Times like this were a little tough because I felt stupid for not joining the Air Force, but no one makes movies about guys who fix airplane windshields.

We received our initial brief in a huge, ornately-appointed ballroom in the Officers' Club where they pulled a ruse that ended up tricking most of the Marines. They flashed a map of what was obviously Guam, but they renamed it as an enemy territory. They then launched into a brief of the terrorist activities on the supposedly nearby island and what our mission was be. It was a good piece of theater and a nice dramatic way to start the training, but I had to spend an inordinate amount of time explaining to my buddies that we weren't really going to war.

When the colonel asked Lt. Colombero, our dogged, but spacey platoon commander, what he did, he responded, "Uh…I work." Columbo, as he was called, was like a big puppy combined with every dumb-jock stereotype known to man.

He had risen to sergeant in the reserves and then went to officer training. He was eager and excited at all times, and just as often, completely lost. He had a reputation for being dumb, but as I got to know him I realized that he was just a little scatter-brained. He was highly motivated, but he seemed to focus on small points instead of the big picture. He had a couple of minor fuck-ups as a fresh lieutenant that became Golf Company lore, including losing his rifle in the field and forgetting to put all the parts back in after he cleaned it.

The Marines from Force Recon were the main effort—the door-kickers and room-clearers. We were outside security and the Snipers and Battalion Recon were the eyes and ears. Force Recon is the special ops branch of the Marine Corps, but it is not part of SOCOM—the inter-service Special Operations Command. The Marine Corps is paranoid about being seen as redundant and thus being reduced or eliminated, so when SOCOM was established in the mid-1980s. the Marines turned down a request for Force Recon to be a part of it. This cut Force Recon out of a huge piece of the defense budget, as well as keeping it from getting as many high-profile missions. Force Recon is easily as tough and capable as the Navy SEALs or Army Rangers, but they are always on the outside looking in. The up-side is that Force Recon is used as it is intended to be—as a recon unit that relays information to the commanders of a regular infantry division. Movies and books make it seem like Spec Ops units win every war themselves, but their main reason for being is intelligence-gathering. Since Force Recon is also a light and highly effective combat unit, they also get used for Direct Action missions such as ship takedowns and hostage rescue.

Force Recon had the latest technology and dressed in flight suits; nothing about them was standard-issue. They had to be prepared for any situation, so they carried odd tools like the hooligan, a medieval-looking crow bar; one even had a chain-saw built onto a aluminum backpack frame. They wore sunglasses, grew their hair long and were just plain cool, but what really set them apart was their intelligence. Sure, they were all amazing athletes—I even remember seeing one of them jogging at 12 miles per hour on the treadmill—but their real strength was their intelligence and maturity. I had dealt with so much egotism and pettiness from marginally-skilled people in the grunts, that when I met these demi-gods of military excellence, I was shocked at their humility. They had every right to look down at me, yet they were all friendly and enthusiastic. They performed at such a high-level that they knew that their strength came from being part of a team. There were no Boyds in Recon. They barely used rank and there was almost no schism between NCOs, Staff NCOs and officers.

After any training event, there would be a de-brief and weapons cleaning. The grunts would sit around, waiting for transpo, and sleep or talk on the ride back to the barracks; then sit around for hours, languidly cleaning weapons. We would then get word that the de-brief would be in an hour and once we were assembled, we'd waste the first five minutes with threats of being "fucked with all night" if anyone spoke out of turn. Force Recon had none of that nonsense; they worked hard and then went on libbo. They'd clean their weapons while waiting for the buses, then give the de-brief on the ride back to base. Once they arrived, *everyone* would help unload the gear—enlisted and officers—and they'd be in civvies and heading out on libbo within twenty minutes.

Every unit had to take turn cleaning the restrooms. When we had it, it was an all-day affair since none of the NCOs would help. Force Recon had half as many people as us, but they all participated in the clean-up. The commanding officer supervised personally and I saw staff NCOs cleaning toilets and showers alongside their corporals and sergeants. They were done in a half-hour and off on the town.

Training was held in an abandoned Air Force housing area, so we had every type of building to practice in. The program was taught by the SOTG(Special Operations Training Group). They were true professionals who spoke to you like you were a human being and—miracle of miracles—made you want to learn.

After a week of training, we finally got to go out on the town. We emerged from the thick island jungle into the beautiful main city of Tumon Bay which was every bit as nice as Honolulu, but less crowded. Of course, we headed straight for the strip bars. Guam is a part of the US, but it's also part of Asia which comes down to this: they like to get freaky. Unlike American strip clubs, the women were not crusty skanks who were either runaways or druggies. They were amazingly beautiful women of every color, who just loved to show off their bodies. Because of a classic Marine Corps fuck-up, we did not have access to our pay the entire month we were in Guam, so we weren't exactly high-rollers, but the women at the clubs treated us like kings, even though we tipped like bums. I once went out on the town with a budget of seven dollars and I was the richest guy from my unit. I was still able to afford three beers and two lap dances and they weren't the clinical, depressing lap dances of American clubs, those girls only off-limits area was their coochie and you only needed about two drops of charm to get that as well. Several side rooms existed in the clubs so guys and girls could go and discuss the Dewey decimal system, or at least that's how it was explained to me. Those girls gave it away like it was Halloween candy and God bless 'em for it.

Our favorite was Club USA, and not just because it was only one block from where we got dropped off at. With just one short catwalk and only one girl dancing at a time, it looked like it was going to be lame, but it turned out to be amazing. We settled down at the bar/stage and my buddies started getting lap dances, but I tried to be a good boy since I was married. The strippers actively encouraged you to feel them up, grab their tits and shove your face near their snatch—it was unbelievable. I saw that the other married guys were getting dances too, and an intense moral debate erupted in my head. Hot Rod made all my consternation moot by handing one girl some cash to give me a dance. Before I knew it, she put my hands on her perfect tits and started grinding away, talking casually the whole time. The girls knew we were broke, so she didn't press hard for more cash. Once that dance was done, I had crossed the threshold of being "bad," so I went whole hog, getting a dance from each chick. My favorite was a stunning Guamanian chick with short jet-black hair who showed off her skills by deep-throating my beer bottle and emptying it in a few quick chugs. I couldn't believe that they'd let you feel them up for a dollar or two, but I think it was their own form of advertising. Once they got you into one of the siderooms for some presumed sex, I'm sure the prices went up, but none of them did a hard sell. Even the waitresses would fondle your cock casually while you chatted with them.

Club USA became our home base, though Jesse did drag us out of there to actually see the island. Jesse quickly made friends with some locals who took us all over the island for free. We saw an amazing old cathedral and got to see some of the real, non-touristy side of Guam. The locals called their neighborhoods "villages" and they were fiercely proud of their heritage. There was a controversy in that some locals who owned beachfront property were selling it to foreign corporations, which offended sensibilities. Most of the tourists were from Japan, and the downtown area catered to them. Besides the strip bars on every block, the whole downtown area was rife with sex. Literally every store had porn and sex toys, even the department stores in the upscale mall.

We always ended up back at Club USA. The single Marines with game were getting in good with the dancers, though one made the mistake of actually licking some snatch on stage and he ended up with a sore on his tongue. Lewis had one girl wrapped around his finger; after he bought some expensive shots from her and realized his ATM card didn't work, she told him it was OK since she liked him. She was white and she loved Lewis, who was black; she said her roommate was black and preferred white guys, which I thought was fair.

Each girl would dance for two songs and some of them invited audience participation. One white stripper pulled Lewis on-stage, made him drop his drawers and started whipping his bare ass. For propriety's sake, the next stripper was black and she wanted a white guy to whip. Hyatt volunteered me and I went up on stage. The stripper unbuckled my pants and slipped my belt out in one smooth motion. She then started whipping my ass, which was probably fairly funny to her and the audience, but it hurt like hell. I had a cheap imitation leather belt made of plastic and the edges were cutting my skin; I had to figure out what to do. If I told her to stop, I would look like a wimp and ruin the good time everyone was having. On the other hand, this was more pain than I'd experienced in boot camp, even from the barbers. I gritted my teeth, expecting it to end some time soon, but she kept going. It got so bad that my defense instincts kicked in and I contemplated hitting her ass. Finally, it stopped and everyone looked aghast that I had taken so much pain. The next morning at the barracks, I went to change my underwear when I noticed that the blood had dried them to my ass. People jumped back as they saw the dozen bleeding wounds on my butt cheeks. Lewis had begged off earlier, so he wasn't as bad off. Nevertheless, we were both hurting and we joked about waiting until closing time at Club USA and then jumping the chicks who whipped us when they went outside.

We never had one full day off during the entire month and the few days we were allowed to go out into town, we never had more than a few hours. I had one buddy who managed to get completely staggering drunk, hook up with a French stripper and—he would later find out—contract a non-fatal STD—all in two hours. Now that's time-management.

We were led by a Staff Sergeant we nicknamed Doofy. He was nerdy, weird and condescending with a strong strain of incompetence. Force Recon operators are among the most patient people on the planet, but he exasperated them with his constant micro-management of every situation. In the war room, he would lean back too far in his chair and fall over, making us lose cool points in front of the other units. He was famous for once telling a corporal, "I can't wait to get home, sit in my favorite bean bag chair, pop a porno in the VCR and jerk off all over my chest."

The NCOs were already bristling under his command since he would yell at them in front of the juniors, thereby undermining their authority. When Doofy ordered us to buy compasses with our last few dollars, even though the Marine Corps was supposed to provide them for us, people had enough. We hoped that thought common sense would prevail and Doofy would realize we each had about six dollars, but he decided to make an issue of it. He told us that whoever did not spend the rest of his money on gear would not be allowed to go out in town, not realizing it was a moot point. If we did buy the compasses we wouldn't have the money to go out anyway. The NCOs huddled together to decide what to do. They were all of one mind except for Henio, a shy Navajo kid. He didn't want to make waves, which pissed off his fellow NCOs, who yelled at him in front of us.

Their planned mutiny excited me for two reasons. Doofy was going to get told off and if it went bad it would be on the NCOs, not us. Two of the NCOs with the best reps went to talk to him, but he didn't want to hear a word. He screamed at them for their audacity, but the issue about buying the gear did get dropped.

Though the island was beautiful, I was dying. A chest infection I caught three months earlier had steadily gotten worse. At times, it got so bad that I couldn't string three words together without erupting into a violent coughing fit. Before leaving Cali, I went to the BAS several times to get treated, but I was always blown off. By the time I got to Guam, I was hacking up cupfuls of mucus and coughing all day long, yet no one would acknowledge that it was anything worse than a cold.

I coughed so violently that I ripped a muscle in my chest. While training, I went to pick up the gun and I felt a stabbing pain. Anytime I coughed, my ribs would irritate the ripped muscle, making it even worse. The good news was that I finally had something physically wrong with me to show to a corpsman. When I told Doc Rowe that I thought I had ripped a muscle in my chest by coughing, he rolled his eyes, but when he felt the knot on my rib cage, his expression changed. He told me that he could get me an appointment at the Air Force hospital, but that he would have to run it by Doofy first. I knew that Doofy would hassle me if I wanted to get checked out. If I got a light-duty chit, they would probably just make me be gear guard in our windowless room and they would surely deny me libbo out of spite. I asked Doc if he could just prescribe me some antibiotics. He told me that it was better to let your body fight it off, since the antibiotics would weaken your immunity in the future. I thought he was just saying that so he wouldn't have to fill out the paperwork to get me the medicine. I repeatedly had to buy my own medicine, even though I had free medical coverage.

They were actually spending money on the training, which shocked me. Battalion Recon infiltrated the target area a few days before our op—just like they would in real-life—and sent us real-time photos of the objective. We even got access to DOD satellites for current photos. There was a a lot of play-acting; an Asian staff NCO played the rebel leader, which was great since we had an actual enemy to capture instead of just shooting blanks at a hill-side like we would do in Pendleton.

Every op got better and more involved than the last. We pulled a night insertion in helos, skimming low over the water before landing in "hostile territory." We got into vans that our in-country "allies" provided and rode toward the target building on the edge of the downtown Tumon Bay. Recon and Snipers had inserted a few days earlier in civilian clothes, their weapons hidden in gym bags, hiding out in a loft above a Chinese restaurant. They insisted that they had not broken cover and had stayed hidden the whole time, but I'm sure they went for take-out.

Not only were we traveling through town like gangsters, but the snipers were going to take a live shot at a dummy that had been set up in the target building as we pulled up. It blew me away that the local government approved that. We had a small run-in with the police on an earlier op when Chuck assumed that two police officers near our gun position were acting as the "enemy," so he wrestled one of them to the ground, not letting go until he saw the officer's badge and pistol. As much as I hated Chuck, he was a bad-ass little fighter.

Our departure date came at the perfect time, just when we all ran out of money. Although we had flown from Oki, we were returning by ship. The Marine Corps was testing out a program to transport troops and vehicles by high-speed civilian catamarans. The size of a small cruise ship, they could hit high speeds with their water jets. The ship seemed too good to be true; it was laid out like a first-class cruise ship with cushioned seats, brass railings and wood paneling. The Marine Corps managed to bring the niceness level down so we would be more comfortable. The first-class kitchen was only used by the crew to cook themselves steaks while we were fed cold hot dogs and warm soda. This was my first time in the open sea, so I got sea-sick. After I emptied my stomach. there wasn't much else to do, so I found a quiet, dark area in the back and slept for 24 hours straight.

When we got back, there was a noticeable tension between the Marines who had gone to Guam and those who had stayed in Oki and the topic of Guam quickly became a conversation-killer. It bothered me that my buddies couldn't just be happy for me. Not only had they missed out on the fun, but SSgt. Shores had been running them into the dirt every day. SSgt. Shores ran "Ultra-marathons" of more than 50 miles in his spare time and even hard-asses like Marr fell out of his thrash-runs. Luckily (for us anyway), SSgt. Shores injured his ankle fast-roping a few days after we returned, putting him out of commission for the remainder of the time we spent in Oki.

Field days in Oki were much worse than those in Cali, since the seniors had no incentive to make them any shorter. They weren't doing the work and they weren't going anywhere afterward, so they would just fuck with us all night long. Chuck would always spin his fellow seniors up and instigate problems. He would fly off the handle at any real-or-imagined slight. If we were down on our knees, scrubbing fifty-year-old linoleum and we were talking with each other, he would accuse us of "fucking around." He would then go to the seniors with the most easily-stoked tempers, like Marr, Devers and McCarty, and he would tell them that we were gaffing them off. Half in the bottle by that time, the seniors would get their revenge by making us re-do everything. While trying to scour out some scuff marks, I noticed that if I used my leg to move the scratch pad around, it would make the stain go away much faster than if I used my weaker arm muscles, but Chuck didn't want to see that. He insisted on me getting on my hands and knees while he stood over me, just to put me in my place.

By midnight, we had scrubbed, mopped, waxed and hand-buffed the 100-foot hallway six times. We realized that there was no way we could win, so we did start fucking around. Vargas could be a prick, but he had a good sense of humor. He started grabbing buckets of water and "accidentally" spilling them in front of the seniors' doors, flooding their rooms. When they came out to yell at him, he would make a whole production of earnestly trudging back from the washroom with two buckets of water, while exaggeratingly trying not to slip. He would then shoot both of his feet into the air and fall flat on his back while pathetically shouting, "Oh no! Not again!"

The seniors' plan back-fired and instead of pissing us off and making us turn against each other, the mood was jovial. We started singing "All night long" by Lionel Ritchie just to piss our seniors off. When the duty officer came by, the seniors hustled us into our rooms so that they wouldn't get in trouble for hazing. The field day was unofficially over, but my anger at Chuck had me so flush with adrenaline that I couldn't have gone to sleep if I wanted to. Ross and I decided that we would go on a PT run, just to show Chuck that he hadn't been able to wear us down. To make it even more annoying, I put a beach towel around my neck like a cape and started parading down the hallway, loudly proclaiming myself to be "SuperTowel." Gimeno got the joke, but Chuck went ballistic.

"What the fuck are you two doing?"

"Going out to the track, corporal. Gonna get a little motivating PT."

"Are you fucking joking?"

"No, we were just telling each other how good we felt and how much energy we had, so we thought we'd get some exercise. Is that a problem, corporal?"

"Yes, it's a problem! Get in your fucking rooms, right now! We have to get up in a fucking hour and a half!"

"Really, corporal? We hadn't noticed."

Fucking with Chuck like that was ten times more effective than outright belligerence and much more fun. Telling us to go to our rooms was a lawful order, so we had to do it, but we still declared a moral victory. No one bonds during good times; you never get the measure of a man when everything is going his way. It's times like this, where we were able to laugh at the misery of our situation, that made us so close.

We were going on ship in two and a half months, which I looked forward to and dreaded in equal measure. Our schedule was light until then, with only a few field ops and some short hikes. I quickly learned to love Camp Hansen and used it as best as I could. Instead of watching TV and drinking beer, I hit the gym and signed up for a full semester's worth of college classes. There was a good library and I read upwards of a hundred pages a day. First-run movies were shown daily and there were a bunch of good fast-food places at a food court called The Buck. It was kind of like a summer camp.

The Okinawans looked at Marines the same way that people did in Southern California; we were second-class citizens to be avoided at all costs. Countless movies and TV shows had taught me that Asian women went nuts at the sight of the American uniform, but that was not the case. I only knew two guys that dated local girls. Mohler quickly landed himself a girlfriend and all attached drama. Mohler was good friends with Cpl. Crouch, who was the Mohler of Force Recon. His Force Recon company was permanently stationed on Oki, so Crouch was able to introduce Mohler to some girls he knew in town. In America, girls usually go wild during college and then settle down in their late twenties, but that's when Japanese women start getting revved up. High school and college are so competitive in Japan that women that age barely have time to even think of guys. Many Japanese women find themselves in their late twenties and realize that, even though they have a career and money, they've never had any fun in their life. So they start hitting the clubs and sleeping around. Mohler was a big hit with the local girls since they saw him as a big, goofy cartoon character that they could fuck. Mohler's girl was so into him that she would drive onto base just to blow him in her car.

Mohler soon found out that his girl was still married to a lifer Force Recon staff sergeant. Though she had left her husband several months earlier, they were still legally married and her husband wanted her back. The staff sergeant thought that Crouch knew who was messing his wife, so he told him to meet him in a secluded spot off-base. Mohler went along and they were confronted by a hulking Force Recon operator with a baseball bat. The man told them to tell whoever was screwing his wife that he was coming for him. Crouch and Mohler promised to relay the message.

We loaded onto buses for my first field trip since the fifth grade. We headed to the heart of the island, where we received a surprisingly informative and evocative description of the horrific battle the Marines fought to take Okinawa. Almost sixty years later, there was still a palpable respect in the Marine Corps for the ferocity of the Japanese soldier. The tour guide told us that the Japanese would sneak up at night, killing everyone but the sleeping soldiers, who would wake up surrounded by their dead buddies. We joked that Milligan would have been the only one to survive. The tour was run by a young ex-Marine who had fallen in love with the island and stayed there after he got out.

After the guided tour, we headed to an underground fortress that had been turned into a museum. The entire mountain had been hollowed out like a base for a James Bond villain. Their island was literally a fortress. It made me realize why we thought we needed to drop the atom bomb to end the war. These people would spill a gallon of blood to defend a handful of soil.

We walked through the hallways which were carved out of rock and imagined how the Japanese felt when they were surrounded by Marines and the Navy; being bombarded by artillery twenty-four hours a day. We were shown rooms where the walls were pocked by grenade shrapnel. We were told that the Japanese wore grenades high on their uniform that they would pull just as the Americans closed in. I thought about getting captured by the enemy and the associated shame and fear. I decided that I would rather take myself and my attackers out then be captured alive.

In an adjacent building, there was a museum filled with war relics. It was awkward to gawk at the uniforms and swords and realize that the museum was half-filled with Japanese whose relatives had died on that very spot. Mora noticed Marines making insensitive comments around the Japanese and told them to show some respect.

As we drove to our last spot, I looked out the window and felt very lonely. The language was not the only barrier; the Japanese just didn't want to know us. I felt like a janitor or a groundskeeper—someone you walk by, but don't acknowledge.

The Japanese have a vending machine fetish and they will sell anything from them. On the sidewalks, I saw vending machines that sold magazines, toiletries, socks, flowers and even condoms. One of the most popular drinks was named Qoo and it was such a silly name that I couldn't stop saying it. Ross and I joked about moving to Oki after we got out of the Marines and getting jobs at the Qoo factory.

We stopped at a huge war memorial near the ocean. The land was shockingly beautiful and my friends and I took off to walk through the jungle to the beach. This is one of the brightest spots in my memory—I was in one of the most beautiful places on Earth with the best friends I would ever have. The Marine Corps had taken a lot from me—from all of us—but it had also give us this and I was grateful.

We brushed up on our fast-roping skills, since we would be doing it from helos in flight in a few days. I was dreading it, remembering the creaking, rotten-wood helo tower at Mateo. When I saw the helo tower at Hanson, I relaxed; solid concrete with a stairway instead of a rickety ladder, it was built like a bomb shelter. Things looked good until I realized that I had forgotten my gloves. I thought I was going to catch hell until Silva told me that he had forgotten his helmet, which was much more noticeable. I could borrow gloves surreptitiously and not got thrashed, but he was fucked.

Fast-roping is an acquired taste, but this tower helped me to love it. I was still afraid of heights, but I had some faith in myself and the seniors were acting like they cared if you did it right. Cpl. Gimeno had gone to HRST (Helicopter Rope Suspension Training), so he was running the show. He calmly stood next to a forty-foot drop, guiding person-after-person down the rope. I prayed I would never get sent to HRST school.

After a couple of slides down the rope—each time wearing progressively more gear—we started going down in sticks of ten Marines at a time, racing the other squads. Reed was absolutely fearless; he would run, jump and *then* grab onto the rope in mid-air, which was fool-hardy, but I couldn't help but admire his fearlessness and abandon. The machinegunners won the contest and a brief smile cracked SSgt. Shores' twisted face.

Silva dreaded going back, knowing he was going to get thrashed. Cpl. Elliot made Silva come into his room—door closed, of course—and thrashed him like a recruit. You weren't supposed to have to do things like that in the Fleet. You have the option of refusing, but if you do they'll just find five different *legal* ways to make your life miserable. Coupled with the abuse he took from Washbourne and the general degradation of being a boot, Silva's motivation for being a grunt was being killed. He was a black-belt in Karate, could bench-press several hundred pounds, was bright, personable, and amazingly mature for his age. He would be a perfect grunt, the kind of calm presence you would want on a battlefield, but a myriad cuts and insults had turned him off.

On the huge track field behind our barracks, three helos waited to take us up. A few days earlier, the same grounds had held a small carnival, but now we would have some more exciting rides to go on, and no tickets were required (luckily for Chuck, there was no height requirement either). Though I was nervous, the helo tower had bolstered my confidence. We started on the older, two-rotor 46s, which are a smooth ride. Once the bird got into a steady hover, you would crab-walk to the edge of the greasy rear ramp so that you didn't slip and fall, and grab the rope which was hooked to roof of the cabin. When the crew chief gave you the signal, you would kick off and slide. It was surprisingly easy and fun.

Next we would fast-rope from the 53, whose huge single-rotor kicked up an enormously powerful propwash that would knock you down when you hit the ground. They rushed us onto the bird, but the seat belts were all tangled up, so it was hard to tell which one went to what seat. Hyatt sat down next to me, but couldn't find the other half of his belt. I realized that I had hooked up to his belt, but since we had already given the thumbs-up to the crew chief, the bird was taking off. It was too late to fix things, so I told Hyatt to just play it off. Once we got to hover-level, the crew chief noticed Hyatt without a belt and lit into him. Chuck's beady eyes burned as he mouthed threats to Hyatt over the roar of the engine.

Instead of easing yourself in a sitting position to the edge, you would walk to the edge of the "hellhole", a trapdoor in the middle of the cabin, which was much more vertigo-inducing. I decided I would follow the advice of Wile. E. Coyote and not look down. I grabbed the rope with both hands in a death-grip. The crew-chief gave me the signal to go and I stepped off the edge. Wow! We were a lot higher than in the 46. On the descent, I had enough time to see the top of the four-story barracks we lived in, be proud I had done it, start to get scared, close my eyes, calm myself down, open my eyes and then notice that my hands were getting very hot. I remembered to let go of the rope when I was three feet from the ground, so I could spread my legs into a wider stance so that I wouldn't snap my ankles.

I landed solidly enough and started to run for the sidelines to make room for the next Marine. The prop-wash was incredible; I ran as fast as I could to keep from getting knocked over, but the current was just too strong and I flew ass-over-tea kettle onto the ground. I was embarrassed until I sat down and saw the next three Marines do the exact same thing.

As soon as the training was over, Chuck cornered Hyatt and really let him have it. I interrupted the harangue, telling Chuck it was my fault. That threw him for a second, but he was dead-set on yelling at Hyatt, even after I exculpated him. Chuck said that even if it wasn't Hyatt's fault, Hyatt had a habit of fucking up, so that's what he was catching hell for.

We sat in the grass in front of our barracks, languidly cleaning our weapons until the higher-ups said we could turn them in to the armory. When I took my gear up to my room, I left my helmet behind. Chuck started loudly bragging about how he would punish me, finally deciding on a thousand-word essay. I was sick of his negative attitude and told him that even if I did write it, he wouldn't be able to understand it. I was surprised when there was no immediate reprisal for my disrespect, since boots didn't talk to seniors like that. Right after that, Cpl. Solis went upstairs and forgot half of his gear and Chuck yelled at *Mohler* for not bringing it up. Classic.

Chuck didn't give me a specific topic, so I busted out a thousand words of totally non-sensical stream of consciousness. It was kind of fun and I handed it in, almost enjoying the whole incident. Chuck didn't get mad at first, just a little confused, but his buddy egged him on, saying that I was messing with him, so he doubled it to 2000 words. In the next essay, I wrote an elaborate allegory that had all of the machinegunners dying, but only the seniors were allowed into Heaven since they were the only ones that were worthy. The word that really rubbed Chuck the wrong way occurred in a line in which St. Peter said that only the senior Marines were allowed into Heaven since they had been in the Corps a "whopping" year and a half longer than us boots. There's something about the word "whopping" that really sets off little Ecuadorean guys who can't get laid.

I showed my latest tome around; the reaction from the boots was "this is really funny, and it was nice knowing you." A couple of my peers were wide-eyed with fear about how this would somehow impact on them. After showing it to all the boots, I ran into Cpl. Longmire from the top deck, where the rumor mill had already spread tales of my intransigence. He asked to see my essay and I shrugged, handing it to him. He laughed while he read it, saying he wanted to be there when I turned it in.

I left for lunch after giving the paper to Chuck and when I came back, I found the floor abuzz. Everyone wondered exactly how my ass had been handed to me. Nothing had happened yet, so I figured Chuck was probably just going to get pissed off like always. While I was gone, he had gotten all the seniors together and shown the essay to them. Cpl. Ivy—the "cool" senior—went to the boots' rooms, asking them if they thought my paper was funny or disrespectful. Most people said it was both. Reed told Cpl. Ivy that he thought it was wrong and that he told me he that I shouldn't turn it in like that. Although Reed was constantly causing problems, he had a huge daddy-complex and could be quite wheedling when trying to get in good with authority figures, so I expected him to do this. I was ten years older than the rest of them and it all seemed like a tempest in a teapot.

Ivy reported back to Chuck that the general consensus was that I had stuck it to him and gotten away with it. I was ordered to report to Chuck's room, where I expected to receive another red-faced bluster session, as I had become accustomed to. I entered the room to find Chuck and every other senior in the platoon crowded in that small room, glowering at me. Despite being vastly outnumbered, I was calm. Though a couple were beet-red mad, I could tell the others were just there to support Chuck and really didn't care. Chuck put me at parade rest and lit into me; vague threats followed, so I just tuned him out. When he picked up the essay though, he started waving it at me violently, acting like he was going to culminate his harangue by throwing it at my face. This wasn't boot camp and I was a few short months from being salty; I didn't have to put up with this. I had been hitting the weights pretty hard and was in the best shape of my life; I decided that if he threw those papers in my face, I would deck him.

Marr started casting aspersions on my performance as a grunt, which didn't hold as much weight since I had improved so much recently. Chuck said he would bring this up to SSgt. Shores, which gave me pause, since he could be one devilish motherfucker. When Chuck screamed for me to leave, I walked out casually and confidently just to piss him off.

When I got back to my room, Reed asked what happened; I told him a lot of steam was produced and not much else, sure that he would relay that back to the seniors after I left. He admitted he had sold me out, but I wasn't mad. I knew he would fold like a deck of cards and he did.

Later that day, I got called back into Chuck's room and saw that SSgt. Shores was there. I expected SSgt. to go into T-Rex mode right away, but instead he calmly told Chuck and I to explain our sides of the story. I told him that the situation had gotten out of hand and it was just supposed to be a funny essay. He asked me if I had been told to write a funny essay and I said the tone hadn't been specified. He started to read my essay and a smirk appeared on his face. He read a little more, laughed, and then put it down. He leaned in close and I got a good look at those icy-blue devil's eyes of his.

"Is it true that there are about half-a-million things that I could do to make your life a living Hell?"

"Yes, staff sergeant."

"Write the damn essay and save your comedy for the chow hall."

When I asked the topic, Chuck screeched out "respect!" This would be my third night with little sleep, since I hand to hand-write all these essays so that I didn't use a computer to "cheat," like there's some web site out there with an essay on not leaving your gear outside that I could copy from. I felt like I had made my point and gotten whatever small victory was to be had, but I still wanted to get a final dig in on Chuck. I wrote out one-sentence descriptions of why I respected everyone in the company, even including people like Stanbo, citing my respect for his "addiction to freedom." Somehow I forgot to write anything about respecting Chuck. Whoops. I continued trying to annoy Chuck, in more subtle ways. When he yelled at us for not having writing gear on us at all times, I went out and got a little notepad with a kitty cat on it, knowing it would piss him off every time he saw it.

While cleaning the outside stairwell, Mohler came up, more jittery than usual, and told me that he was going home the next day. I was shocked since no one was allowed to leave The Rock unless there was a death in the family. There was a death; it just wasn't in his family. Though he was a rich kid, Mohler ran in a druggie/dirtbag clique back home in Mississippi. One of his buddies who was the most far-gone bragged to him about killing someone, but Mohler thought it was just drug-talk. Right before he went to boot camp though, it was discovered that his buddy's girlfriend had been beaten to death. It took almost two years for the case to go to trial and by that time we were in Oki. The DA tracked Mohler down and got the First Sergeant to arrange to fly him back to Mississippi. As always, confusion reigned and the First Sergeant thought that Mohler was an accessory to the murder, until Mohler explained the entire story in detail.

The seniors were livid with jealousy, which made it all the better. Mohler left and came back two weeks later happy as a clam. Shortly after he got back to Mississippi, his buddy changed lawyers and the trial was pushed back six months. The Marine Corps and the state of Mississippi financed a two-week sex and beer spree for Mohler, which he admitted proudly to the First Sergeant upon his return.

The jungle in Oki was a lot more fun and interesting than the scrubby hills of Pendleton. I was excited when I heard we would do a helo Raid on a MOUT town, since those were my two favorite things in the grunts. It was kind of funny to fly there, since the mini-MOUT town they had at Camp Hanson was only about two miles away from our barracks.

I was Elias's team leader and I tried to treat him like I wanted to be treated when I was a gunner. After pushing a branch out of my way, I would hold it so Elias could go through, like I was opening a door for a lady at a restaurant. Whenever I would hike the gun, which takes two hands to hold, the jerk in front of me with the M-16 would always let the branch whip back and hit me in the face.

We stopped so the officers could check their maps and Elias set down in an bad shooting position. He couldn't see the area he was covering, but that didn't bother others who were doing the same thing. I flashed back to Guam, where Cpl. Ivy kept putting me in untenable shooting positions. I told Elias to get up where he could see. He grumbled, but he did it.

Once we got moving again, we found out that we were behind schedule, so we had to run to catch up. The oppressive heat quickly sapped our strength and the terrain was so steep that you could barely walk. This was William's first field op after being on light-duty for the last nine months. As we got to the bottom of a ravine, he re-injured his ankle in the same exact spot that he had injured it the last time they were in Oki. What were this kid's ankles made out of—crackers? By this time, Williams' rep was so bad that even the boots were allowed to mock him.

Since I had to keep both hands on the gun, I kept slipping down the hill. Captain Gerst appeared and told us we needed to hurry, so I chucked the gun a few feet forward, scrambled up the hill and then continued that process until I got to the top. We came out of the jungle on the back side of MOUT town. The rifle platoons were peeking around the edge of the building at a church that was being defended by aggressors. This wasn't the Army, so we didn't have that high-speed laser-tag MILES gear. Instead, we had staff NCOs and officers from another unit that would judge how we were performing and would relay that to our higher-ups.

We snuck through the open cellar window of a cinder-block building. I jumped down in the dark and hit the ground after falling much farther than I had expected. I ran up some stairs and kept a low-profile as I tried to get eyes on the enemy. I turned a corner and nearly put my face right into a nice, voluptuous cammie-clad ass. I looked up and saw a cute female sergeant standing there in her tight t-shirt, which was such an anachronism that my mind almost short-circuited. The blood returned to my head and I crawled out toward a patio that faced the street, telling myself that she was secretly very impressed with me.

One of the mortarmen kept trying to get my attention, but I didn't like him, so I kept ignoring him.

"Meyer!…Meyer!…Hey…old man."

"What?!"

"Here."

He handed me the tripod, which I had dropped when I jumped into the dark cellar. I felt guilty for losing it, but I felt even worse for treating this guy so badly when he could have buddy-fucked the hell out of me. I thanked him profusely and went outside.

By this time, the aggressors had been flanked and some were being taken prisoner. One aggressor pretended to be a belligerent POW and Cpl. Getz tackled him to the ground like it was real life. We holed up in the church while they tried to round-up the remaining aggressors; then we went into the chest-high weeds at the edge of town and set down. I noticed that Elias's face was strangely clean.

"Hey, where's your cammie paint?"

"I sweated it all off, stupid! I'm fucking dying out here!"

It had been so hot that we got to conduct the raid without flaks or helmets, but the temperature had spiked while we were out there. I took off my boonie cover and wiped my face off. I felt like my brain was cooking. Elias and I both started getting delirious from the heat, even though we had been hydrating the entire time.

We moved back to the LZ and got in the defense while we waited for the birds. By this time, I had sweated out every drop of water in my body and my canteens were dry. Though there was abundant shade, Chuck purposefully set us down on the hot asphalt, while he lounged under a tree. When I got up to move three feet forward into the shade, he yelled at me to get back. I missed Washbourne. As rough as he was, he was finely-attuned to the needs of his squad. He could tell when someone was being a bitch and when they really needed help. Chuck just didn't care.

Although buddy-fucking could be intentional, it was just as often completely accidental. While being counseled by Marr for not following an order, Ross brought up a precedent supposedly set by Mohler.

"I didn't think I had to do it if I didn't want to, corporal. Mohler told me that back in Cali, when you told him to do the same thing, he said he didn't want to and nothing happened."

"No, he said, 'Aye, Corporal' and went to go do it. Get Mohler's ass in here right now."

Mohler's version of the events was so exaggerated that we joked that he bragged about telling Marr to shove his chevrons up his ass and if he ever gave him another order he would slap his bald head so hard that it would start growing hair again. Thereafter, any time someone exaggerated or fabricated a story about them supposedly "punking out" a senior, it would be referred to as "pulling a Mohler." It was determined that the true test of any proper punking of a higher-up was if you flipped his desk over. No matter how badly you ranked him out, if you did not flip his desk over on your way out, it wasn't a true punking.

We were scheduled for a 6-mile night hike, which I and all the others laughed off. If I could finish a 26-miler with a fractured foot, I could do 6 miles in my sleep. As if I wasn't confident enough, I was also taking Cell-Tech, a creatine supplement. I blew up like a balloon after taking it for a week, so it seemed like a godsend. If it helped me with lifting weight, it should help with hiking too, right?

Before we left the staging area, I could tell that something was really wrong. I felt out-of-it, weak, and overheated, but didn't understand why. I thought the dark would be an advantage in that muggy climate, but the jungle held the day's heat near the ground and the breeze dwindled to next to nothing at night. Less than a half-mile into the hike, I was hurting. My helmet was so hot that I imagined that someone had put something in it—a hot coal or something—as a joke. I kept taking my helmet off to cool my head and got yelled at to put it back on.

When we hit the hills, I fell back and had to run to catch up. I caught up, but when we went around a bend my ammo bag—whose zipper was busted—started to spill all its contents onto the ground. I knelt down to find them, knowing that I would have to sprint to catch up. I whirled my hands around like a blind man as Chuck appeared out of the darkness, launching into his usual tirade.

"I'm looking for small black tools on a black tar road at night in the jungle. Yelling at me won't make me find them any faster," I said, not bothering to call him by his rank. He sputtered, temporarily apoplectic with rage, while I found the rest of the parts.

The company was a half-mile ahead of us, so Chuck wisely slipped into cheerleader mode. We sprinted and caught up with the tail end of Golf. I felt embarrassed and made sure to tell my buddies about the lost parts as I passed them. I wasn't the only one hurting that night; people started falling out in the first mile, which was unheard of in Pendleton. The heat was unbearable, but just as I was about to collapse, we caught up with my platoon. I was proud of myself, but also realized that I had used my last bit of energy. When I fell back, the seniors shouted threats at me, but no one helped. I slipped back to the rear of the company, staggering drunkenly.

We finally had our rest break; we had only gone three miles, but it had seemed even worse than the MCRESS. I stumbled over to my platoon as the seniors ridiculed me. I couldn't understand what I had done wrong—I was in the best shape of my life at that point. Most of the seniors just drank and watched TV in the barracks while I lifted weights, ran and swam everyday.

When the battalion turned around to head home, I could barely lift my feet over the tracks in the mud; keeping a straight path was impossible. We hit the asphalt and the battalion sped into the distance. Trailing behind were more than sixty walking wounded. I was ashamed to be one of them, but it was such a large amount of people that it showed that the hike was no joke.

I kept walking, telling myself I could at least salvage some respect by making it back on my own steam. An officer sidled up and I expected the worse, but he just good-naturedly asked me how I was doing. I muttered something unintelligible and he told me to sit down. I kept walking and then he ordered me to sit down. He asked me if I knew where we were at. What kind of a question was that? I wasn't a retard. I couldn't give him a more exact answer than "Japan", which made him laugh. He asked me what day it was and I was insulted by his conde-scension until I realized that I couldn't answer. I searched my muzzy mind and realized I had no idea what day it was.

There were two platoons worth of Marines left behind—an eight of the battal-ion. Miller was completely delirious. They drove us back to camp and the BAS filled up, so they put non-emergencies on the lawn. I took my gear off and saw that I was soaked like I had come out of the pool. A corpsman came around to check everyone out and I told him that I didn't understand why I had been a heat casualty since I was in good shape and had been hydrating all day. He asked me if I took any supplements and I told him that I was on Creatine and had even worked out and taken some that morning. He shook his head and explained that creatine draws water from your system into your muscles—that's why you get pumped up. I felt like a complete boot.

An hour later, we were given a ride back to the barracks. I rode with Colvin and McPoland, two notoriously bad hikers. As soon as we got out, Boyd and Var-gas instantly set upon their fellow mortarmen, belittling them. It was straight out of grade-school. McPoland—who usually just took it in stride—snapped and started swinging and cursing at Vargas, who put his hands up and speed-walked backwards to avoid McPoland's wrath. Boyd threw an ineffectual and girly slap at McPoland's head, scratching deep into his scalp with the sharp edge of his ring. The "fight" was broken up and all parties were sent to their rooms.

Though he was over six-feet tall and muscular, Vargas—by his own admis-sion—wasn't much of a fighter. He was less a bully than a comedian, but he did cross the line. Boyd, on the other hand, was an ass who constantly bragged about himself and his abilities. This ultimate bad-ass would later use the "medical con-dition" of in-grown beard hair to get out of the Corps just before we went to Iraq. I guess he was too tough to go to war.

I went up to my room, embarrassed at having failed, but to my surprise, peo-ple were being cool. I asked Ross if the seniors were talking shit about me and he said they were just surprised that I fell out since I had been working out so much lately.

The next day, McPoland, Boyd and Vargas had to talk to the First Sergeant, while the hike-drops from my platoon had to talk to SSgt. Shores, who launched into a drill sergeant-style lifing, gigging us on not reporting in to him in a military manner. He made us go out and come back in three more times until we got it right. He then made us drink two full canteens in a row; if he made us drink another, we'd be spewing all over the office, which would just be another embarrassment on top of falling out. Whatever get-out-of-jail-free card I had with SSgt. Shores worked again and I got off relatively easy. He was a lot harder on the others who were chronic offenders. Like my seniors, he was more curious than angry. At least I was establishing a good rep.

After another all-night field day, Cpl. McCarty gave Jesse an impossible task, telling him to wax and buff the hallway, *but not let anyone walk down it.* I suppose we were supposed to rappel out of our windows three stories to the ground. Jesse realized it was a moronic order, so he simply cleaned the hall as best he could and went to breakfast. When McCarty found out, he lit into Jesse way out of proportion to his "crime." McCarty got personal with his insults, so Jesse defended himself and the other seniors crowded around him; his back was literally to the wall.

Jesse was showing remarkable restraint, but when Cpl. Darnell threatened him, Jesse had enough and shoved the corporal away from him. The seniors shouted that he had just assaulted an NCO and that we were all going to pay. The juniors—who had been peeking out of their doors at the commotion—started walking toward the seniors to defend Jesse. It looked like there would be a rumble—I hoped there would—but the seniors backed off of Jesse and ordered us to our rooms while they decided what to do. Chuck ran up and down the halls, threatening any boot he saw.

The next day, Jesse got called into he First Sergeant Bell's office. As tough as Jesse was, no one walks into that office without fear in his heart. After the First Sergeant heard of the improprieties and childishness of the NCOs, any thought of charging Jesse was dropped.

SSgt. Shores held a pow-wow/gripe session with the boots to find out what the problem was, knowing that letting us blow off steam would help. A lot of the boots didn't want to make waves and gave bland, non-committal accounts. I was surprised when he admitted that the NCOs had acted unprofessionally. Afterwards, things did calm down slightly, but the high school atmosphere never changed. Jesse' punishment was to clean the floor of the lounge everyday for a month. I went to war still being shaky on basics like patrolling, but I was an expert on washing the same hallway for eight hours straight.

I didn't hear about the epilogue to this whole drama until much later, but I still shudder when I think about it—it was one of the great punk-outs in Marine Corps history. After things had apparently calmed down, Jesse went to "talk" to Darnell in his room. Darnell was a little surprised, but he wasn't worried—I mean, c'mon, he was a corporal, right? Jesse came in and locked the door behind him, which is never a good sign. He challenged Darnell to a fight, right then and there, but Darnell demurred, trying to tell Jesse it was nothing personal and that he thought Jesse was a good guy. Jesse was disgusted and told Darnell that he wanted him to try to push him like he did when there were eight seniors backing him, but Darnell just sat down, trying to defuse the situation. Jesse launched into a tirade, telling Darnell how much of a bitch he was and how he was sick of punk-asses like him hiding behind their rank. He told Darnell that he *hoped* that this humiliation would gnaw on him for years, so much so that he would track Jesse down to regain his honor—just so he could beat Darnell's ass.

Ironically, when we were away from our families, we got off work much earlier. In Cali, we would have a late Field Day on Monday, spend Tuesday and Wednesday night in the field, stay late at the Armory on Thursday night and get off around two in the afternoon on Friday. In Oki, we PTed at 5:00AM before the "black flag" was raised that signaled it was too hot to train. If we weren't in the field, there would rarely be any scheduled events in the mornings. We would be told to "study our MCIs," which translated to "sleep or watch TVs in your rooms with the doors closed, but have an open book near you unless SSgt. Shores comes around." We'd get our mail at 2:00PM and then be off for the day. People would stomp their feet and curse if we were still "working" at 2:30PM.

As much of a pain as he was, Reed was a great roommate, which was one of those things I held in his favor. He was clean, quiet and considerate and extremely honorable when it came to borrowing money. As soon as he got paid, he would come looking for me like I had said something about his momma, which was extremely rare in the grunts where everyone was always out of money and borrowing from each other. There was an inverse ratio in which the better of a friend the borrower was, the more likely he was to welsh on the bet or stretch paying you back 10 dollars over a four-month period.

One night, Reed woke me up to tell me that the US had been attacked; The World Trade Center and the Pentagon had been blown up. It sounded like a plot from a bad action movie, so I rolled over and went back to sleep. I woke early to hear commotion in the hallway. Opening my door, I realized that something was up. Maybe Reed hadn't been joking? I went into Showers' and Ross' room and they apprised me of the situation. There was none of the wailing or grief I heard about in other places. Our reaction was calm and inquisitive and—here's where it gets kind of sick and fucked-up—we were enthusiastic: We were sure to go to war over this.

Grunts pray for war like a farmer prays for rain. Although our training was exciting as well as exhausting, it wasn't real. The POG who fixed planes in the air wing could see them fly; he saw his work had some kind of effect. We didn't have that. All of our misery seemed pointless. War gave a meaning to all of our pain and degradation. There was also the heady feeling that, unlike some guy in his arm chair feeling impotent, we could do something about it. There was no fear; it was more like a pep-rally before a big game. After sitting on the benches for two years, we were finally going to get our cleats dirty.

Our next hike was cancelled and it's a testimony to how painful hiking is that war was considered a pleasant alternative. We sat in our rooms and talked excitedly like a bunch of teenagers about to lose their virginity. Rumors swirled, but there were few solid facts. At the chow hall, McPoland giggled at the sight of people jumping out of the towers in terror and a Hispanic sergeant with family from New York threatened to kick his ass. There were a lot of weird and disturbing things about McPoland; he seemed like the kind of guy who would walk into a McDonald's with an AK one day. Although many people picked on him, I was always nice to him; when he went on his rampage, I wanted him to remember me being cool to him and spare my life.

In contrast to our excitement was the absolute silence of the two biggest braggarts in the platoon—Boyd and Vargas—whose behavior had devolved to the point where all they did was brag about themselves and bully and belittle people. It was a selfish, corrosive type of humor that was the opposite of the kind you got from Jesse and Mohler. When it was put-up-or-shut-up time, they both got as quiet as church mice. A year and a half later, McPoland would be a combat vet who had been calm and diligent under fire, while Boyd would be a civilian who had used his in-grown hairs as an excuse to weasel out of the Corps two months before we went to Iraq.

Marr called us into his room and gave us the word: we would be going to war. Ships were leaving Sasebo in Northern mainland Japan to take us to Afghanistan. I was happier than I had ever been and so were my fellow boots. The seniors were dour, which I attributed to a lack of fighting spirit, but in retrospect was just a fear that a war would delay them getting out of the Corps. Stop-Loss would be put in effect and anyone nearing their EAS would have to stay in until the war was over.

I went Moto-overboard, buying two machetes and strapping them to my back like Blade. That night, my buddies and I posed for pictures wearing my new balaclava hood and machetes like a bunch of kids excited about going to Disneyland.

A few days later, we got the bad news: we would not be going to Afghanistan. We were told that 1/1 was going since they were stationed on ship and were already halfway there. When most grunt units go on their regularly-scheduled deployments, they are stationed on ships the entire time. Only a few battalions like us were stationed on Oki. We also heard that when the ships left Sasebo, they thought they were just going on a training float, so they didn't bring any ammo.

I went into a third-grade pouting fit and holed up in my room, only leaving to take long walks by myself. We were so close to glory, only to have it taken away. Those few days in which we thought we were going to war were the happiest in my enlistment. I thought I was going to go to combat and be a war hero. Even more than that, I thought all the misery of being a boot was finally going to pay some dividends.

I spent the next few weeks in a fugue state. The weather seemed to echo my mood as several tropical storms belted Okinawa. Training would cease if a storm was even remotely headed our way. We would be confined to our rooms, which was fine by me as long as I got enough time to go to the PX and stock up on pogey-bait. They would spot storms as far away as the Philippines, then extrapolate that they *might* hit us and we'd get four days off.

Captain Gerst announced that we would have a talent show and that the winning team would geta day off. Mohler worked up a routine that had him as a cocky Osama Bin Laden. The skit wasn't that memorable, since it mostly involved Mohler rolling around on the ground and speaking unintelligibly, but seeing his lanky ass in a fatigue jacket, a t-shirt on his head and a beard made out of paper towel tolls was one of the funniest things I ever saw. Mohler's team won handily, but they never got a day off. Then again, getting a day off in Oki would be like getting knocked out when you were already asleep.

When we were deployed to Okinawa, our battalion worked under the auspices of the 31st MEU (Marine Expeditionary Unit). By the time we went on ship, we had to be qualified as a MEU(SOC)—Special Operations Capable. The Special Operations aspect was displayed by the combined use of all of our parts. A self-contained MEU, with its fighter/bombers, helicopters, tanks, tracs, LAVs and grunts, all riding in a flotilla of three ships, could conduct almost any mission imaginable.

We would conduct our first SOC-EX on Ie Shima Island, where we would conduct a nighttime airfield seizure. As much as I loved flying in helos, going over open water always gave me pause. I made sure that I got in last, so I would be next to the open rear ramp in case our bird splashed down.

We landed on the runway and exited in confusion, having been dropped off a half-mile away from where we were supposed to be. Dust that was kicked up by the birds clouded our NVGs and Chuck vented his frustration on us until the dust settled and he saw where we were supposed to go. As we hit the high weeds, it became hard to spot the man in front of you and there were frequent stops to let people catch up. On one stop, Mohler's tripod slipped off his patrol pack and he didn't realize it was gone until they had moved 200 meters away. When Chuck found out, instead of being professional he threw a tantrum, yelling and swatting at Mohler. If it had been a real mission, Chuck would have given away the patrol's position. Even worse, he made Mohler look for the tripod with a white lens flashlight, which could be seen for miles.

Chuck gave priority to his tantrum and left me as a one-man gun team. I rushed forward in the chin-high grass, dropping to fire at the enemy, while trying to keep up with the rest of the platoon. The barrel was smoking hot and, since the 240 has no forward hand guards, I had one hand on the pistol grip and the other on the carrying handle. A dark figure brushed by me and I jerked the burning hot barrel upward so as to not burn whoever it was. The young lieutenant continued on, not knowing how close he came to looking like Freddy Krueger.

We settled into our bivouac spot and Chuck and Mohler caught up, having found the tripod. Chuck told me I was team leader now, which I wasn't happy about. I loved being a gunner. Since I was the team leader, I had to make our range card, which showed our field of fire and all landmarks within. I saw a water tower and tried to estimate its distance, which is always tricky at night.

"Hey Mohler, you see that water tower? How far do you think that is?"

"What do you think it is?"

"Motherfucker, that's what I just asked you! I dunno…like thirteen hundred meters?"

"Meyer, you old fuck, you are fucking high."

"Well, what is it then?"

"Eleven hundred meters."

I wrote that estimate down and turned in the card. In the morning, I woke to realize that the water tower was so close, I had to crane my neck up just to see all of it. It wasn't even three hundred meters away.

That wasn't the only mistake made that night. The mortarmen were acting as machinegunners on this op, which I dreaded. After having to hear how bad-ass they were at everything, I didn't feel like hearing them brag about how carrying the 240 "wasn't shit." I was surprised when Keller actually gave us props and said that it was surprisingly exhausting to patrol with the gun. While on watch, two figures approached in the dark and, in a familiar and friendly voice, casually asked Keller where the command post was. He politely pointed them in the right direction and they went on their merry way. In the morning, Keller found out that he had shown the enemy how to find our CP, which they overtook.

On the weekends, I would catch a bus to Camp Foster, which was the biggest camp on the island and had a mall. While there, some friends I ran into convinced me to join them "out in town," an activity which I had assiduously avoided since I was married. I was curious about the two main attractions that I had heard so much about—Whisper Alley and the Banana Show. We first went to one of the go-go/handjob clubs, where I got to see Silva work his magic. Though Silva was raised solely by women and could be quite feminine, he also had a misogynistic side. He was good-looking enough that the girls didn't want to talk to him just to get money, and he would show off his ability to manipulate them, alternating attention with disinterest until they were totally confused and compliant.

We then headed to Whisper Alley, which is as famous to most Marines as Iwo Jima. Since World War II, corn-fed young Marines have been losing their virginity to the whores of Whisper Alley. We walked into the dark alley, seeing vague forms flit across in the distance. As we walked slowly, short hisses came from the pathetic one-room shacks on both sides of the alley. It was quite eerie and I wished that I had my 240 with me. As we got closer, the hisses became whispers of women beckoning us over. We edged over and saw a soft female form back-lit by a lone candle. Though shapely, once you got within a few feet of her, you could tell that she was around sixty years old. We went around to some of the others and saw that she was the youngest "girl" there.

Rodgar took over as our tour guide, since he was used to this kind of scene. Rodgar (RodriguezGarcia) was raised in Mexico and had been working as a factory manager when he decided to join the Marines. When he got to The Fleet, his English was barely passable, and he would just nod and smile whenever he was told something, clearly not understanding. Though the boot mortarmen endured a lot of hazing under Dunn, Rodgar just shrugged it off good-naturedly. He was an amateur boxer and was naturally extremely muscular. He had grown up in the mean streets in Mexico, and even Boyd admitted that Rodgar was the one person he wouldn't want to tangle with. Though he was insanely tough, he was also very mature and easy to get along with. Once his English improved, he revealed an excellent sense of humor.

Rodgar went around "interviewing" the whores for prices and services, all the while teasing them and grabbing their tits like he was testing tomatoes at the grocery store. He found out that the going rate was $20 for everything. The single guys were on the fence, debating their level of horniness with their ability to not throw up while fucking those old fossils. Showers was half in the bag and I told him I'd pay for him to do it. Before common sense could cut through the inebriated haze in his mind, we hustled him into the sixty-year-old's shack. I got a quick glimpse of the inside, which was beyond sad. It wasn't even a building, just some kind of rattan shack with a few worn pieces of furniture, a washbowl and a disgusting mattress that probably had some of Chesty Puller's DNA on it. The curtain closed and we waited outside for Showers, giggling as we eavesdropped. Showers came out five minutes later, ashen-faced, and wanting to leave immediately. The whore smiled and waved like they had a very romantic first date, calling him "Superman" for his prowess.

That experience was disgusting and sad, but at least we could say we went to Whisper Alley. Next on the agenda was the Banana Show, which turned out to be only a block away. We walked in towards the end of the Show, which they did every few hours. At first I was disappointed, but I came to view that as a blessing. On the small stage, a fifty-five-year-old woman was straddling a Marine whose pants were pulled down, pretending like she was going to blow him. His dick was trying to retract fully into his body to avoid that nasty beast. Undaunted, the woman then squatted over his face, shoved a banana in her weathered vagina, and started plopping out bite-size portions into his mouth.

After the show, more old women went around soliciting lap dances and grabbing Marines' crotches surreptitiously. On the way in, I had seen an argument in the parking lot between an apparent streetwalker and a guy who I took to be her pimp. I headed out to check on her when Rodgar sidled up. Not only was he our tour guide, he was also our protector, making sure that no one got into any trouble by their self. The pimp and hooker were nowhere to be found, but we did see that "Boltar" had slipped out, saying he had to take a piss, and was *sprinting* toward Whisper Alley, trying to get in a good screw before we noticed that he was gone. We waited outside the hut that he had scrambled into and laughed when he came out less than two minutes later. He had chosen the oldest one, who seriously must have been almost seventy. "Boltar" jumped when he saw us; then hurriedly tried to distract us by reminding us that we needed to get back to Hanson before curfew.

We would be at sea for six weeks. I dreaded being on the ship, imagining it as a floating prison. The difference between boots and seniors would be exacerbated in such close quarters. When boxing up your belongings, you had to list everything you packed and I got perverse pleasure out of writing "Magazine, pornography, Asian—Quantity: 1" on my property list.

We traveled through the heart of Okinawa and got to see more of its lush beauty as we headed to the docks on the other side of the island. My dread of ship life lessened when I saw our flotilla. They didn't look like prisons; they looked mighty and glorious. We started loading our gear and I got to see the immense hangar bay, which looked like something out of "Star Wars." The hangar was as big as three basketball courts and filled with 46s, 53s, Cobra attack helicopters and even a couple of Harriers.

We were told to make our way up to the flight deck to assemble as a platoon and we got our first tour of the labyrinthine guts of the ship. Moving around the ship is a lot like playing old-school video games like "Super Mario Brothers." There is no direct way to get anywhere; to get to the flight deck you had to go through the hangar bay, along a twisting corridor, through the chow hall and several more turns, up two flights of stairs so steep they were practically ladders, through the gym, up another set of stairs and then up a ladder to the flight deck.

The flight deck was five stories above the water and view was incredible. On the deck, there were almost two dozen aircraft. After a roll call, we were allowed to mill around and check out the ship. We strolled around, taking pictures like tourists while the seniors went down to our berthing area to choose their bunks.

Berthing was the worst part of ship life; I can't understand how sailors can live there most of their tour without going crazy. The only personal space you have is your rack, which is smaller than a discount-rate coffin. Showers claimed a top bunk by putting some of his gear on it; then headed back up to the flight deck to get the rest of his stuff. After he left, Vargas sidled up and asked whose gear was on the top bunk. When I told him it belonged to Showers, he laughed derisively and tossed it onto the floor, taking the rack for himself. This was the kind of grade-school bullying technique that would be embarrassing from a ten year-old; yet here it was in the adult world. Another machinegunner and I had to make Vargas leave, which he finally did, huffing that he didn't even want to be with the "nasty" machinegunners anyway.

I ended up with a bottom bunk of the triple-stacked racks. Every time they called reveille, I would get out of my bunk, trying to keep from getting jumped on by those above me. Any time someone changed their clothes in the two-foot-wide alley between the stacks of bunks, their cock and balls would dangle inches from my pillow. I'll never forget the time I got out of bed quickly after waking and found my face inches from Hyatt's chubby ass.

In the bowels of the ship, we got a class on ship life. A ship at sea is like a tightly-knit village and thus is very familial. A E-2 can call a captain "shipmate", instead of "sir" when they pass in the tight quarters. Areas like the gym and the chow hall could only be used at certain times since there were almost two thousand people onboard. The air locks, which regulated pressure and were fire and flooding safety measures, were found every sixty feet or so. No matter what rank you were, you would get excoriated by a sailor if he saw you not using the air locks correctly.

The interaction between sailors and Marines was tense, but professional. The ship was their home and we were just visiting. They joke went that "Marine" stood for "My Ass Rides In Navy Equipment". Taking care of a ship is a constant duty and they had no time for Marines making their life more difficult. We ate in separate chow lines and worked out at different times in the gym. Professionally, we didn't work together—they had their jobs and we had sleep. There was a resentment because, to the sailors' eyes, we didn't do anything and that's because we didn't. At Pendleton, we got worked like rented mules until we prayed for death, but there's not much a grunt can do on ship, so we were free all day, every day. Reveille was called, but not enforced. The only time we had to be out of the berthing area was between 9:00 and 10:00 in the morning for daily inspection. After that, you could go right back in and go to sleep. Sleeping sixteen hours a day wasn't uncommon. Meals were plentiful and quite good, but the lines were very long. Only being awake eight hours a day, you didn't need many calories, so most people would just have two meals a day and sleep through the third.

The coolest thing was "General Quarters", which was called when the ship was under a simulated attack. The sailors would man their battle stations and the Marines would be ordered to the rack. None of our weapons would be effective against the missiles, torpedoes or airplanes that would be used to attack the ship, so the best thing we could do was stay out of the way. Being ordered to go to sleep when others are working is an order that is rarely disobeyed.

One of our few duties was guard duty or "fuck patrol." In the Lower V—the storage area below the hangar bay—three Marines were on guard at any one time. No one is going to steal a Humvee from a ship at sea; our real reason for being down there was to make sure there was no fucking in the dark and seclusion of the Lower V. The Essex had only started having female sailors stationed aboard a few years earlier and the policy was "No fucking at sea." You could fuck your brains out at port calls, but they weren't having it on the open waves. The policy was in direct contravention to basic human nature, but that's the climate nowadays. A five becomes a ten when you're at sea. The girls who joined the Navy were almost uniformly homely with some extreme examples on the high and low end. One "girl" looked like a swarthy Chris Farley with a mustache and even she had a boyfriend.

None of the Navy chicks were interested in the Marines, not even as flings. I decided that my buddies and I would each have one Navy "girlfriend." They weren't real girlfriends; it was just a game to play on ship. I chose a tall, thick Puerto Rican chick named Bolanos. Out of boredom, we would talk about each other's girlfriends and what they were doing that day. I would serenade my girlfriend by singing "B-B-B-Bolanos." I never had a conversation with her and only spoke to her once to ask where the laundry room was, but nonetheless, I still hold a special place in my heart for my Puerto Rican flower.

I still thank God for Ortega; her story was just too good to be true. She was on the average side of cute and the fat side of ass—the kind of girl you might glance at, but you wouldn't turn your head to check her out after you passed her. She had a high, girly voice and was a little off when you spoke to her. I like Hispanic chicks in general, so I would check her out, even assigning her to Silva as his "girlfriend." She was nothing special until we heard the ultimate rumor—she had done amateur porn before joining the Navy. She had been on ship about a year and had moved on with her life, until some jarhead recognized her getting double-teamed on a porno DVD. This news spread like wildfire through the ship, followed closely by the much-borrowed DVD. It could have been a case of mistaken identity, but no one had the balls to go up and ask her. We goaded one of our corpsmen into asking her if it was true—thinking she might confide in a fellow sailor—and she admitted it was her. She was immediately ostracized by all the sailors; the chow hall was always crowded, but somehow there would be three empty seats on either side of her. Horniness eventually beat out social stigma and, after a week, she had a following of guys and a new boyfriend (her old one having dumped her after he found out about her past). I want to thank Ortega, from the bottom of my heart, for making ship-life much more interesting and giving me about eight thousand wack-off fantasies.

Like he did everywhere else he went, Mohler got a girlfriend on ship and she was a hot one. She looked like a young Sharon Stone mixed with Meg Ryan topped off with some DD tits. She wasn't cute "for a female Marine", she was cute period, which engendered massive jealousy by all haters. You had to give Mohler props, he even found a way to foil the fuck patrol. He and his girl would go out to the catwalk at night and wait for the lone sentry to pass them. They knew it took fifteen minutes for the sentry to go all the way around the ship, so they would use that time to suck and fuck on that metal catwalk forty feet above the rolling waves.

I fell in love with the sea. All my life, I had hated boats, having known only my dad's shitty fiberglass fishing boat. This wasn't a boat though; it was a city. I would stand on the smoke deck and stare at the rolling waves for hours. The sea never ceased to amaze me; it was infinite, powerful and ever-changing. It seemed to have moods and emotions in an almost female way.

Once I got a small bout of seasickness out of the way, it was smooth sailing— no pun intended. Most people tried to sleep through the first major storm we went through, but I wanted to read, so I went up to the deserted gym. It looked like it was haunted; weights suddenly jumped off the end of the bar and rolled around on the floor. The punching bag hung at a thirty-degree angle. The Snickers bar in my stomach decided it was time to go elsewhere, so I ran outside to the catwalk on the side of the ship. It was quite dangerous to be out there, but I didn't have time to make it to the bathroom in our berthing area. I looked down sixty feet to the water and saw unbelievably huge waves—some as tall as 25 feet. After I puked, I went back inside, where a sailor gave me some friendly advice on how to deal with seasickness, before going on his merry little way. It was just another day at work for him.

Force Recon and Snipers held informal briefs to attract qualified Marines. To get into either one, you had to go through a grueling Indoc followed by even more hellish training. The braggarts found themselves in a quandary; if they didn't volunteer, they would lose their bad-ass reps, yet most knew that they couldn't make it. Several people made loud overtures about how they would like to join—and how it would be easy—but there was always some excuse at the last minute.

Snipers hiked too much and I didn't think I had the patience that was so crucial to their job. Even thinking I could get into Force Recon was ridiculous, but I still wanted to try. Working out daily had improved my fitness dramatically. In ten days on ship, I went from 11 pull-ups to 22, which is almost unheard of. I wanted to be in Force Recon, not just because they were high-speed, but because of the maturity level they had which just did not exist in the line companies.

The low-key Force Recon brief was held in the lower V. The staff sergeant running the show was my age and built like a football player, but many of the other Force Recon Marines were whippet-thin. He explained the Force Recon life in simple terms, but his enthusiasm was obvious. Force Recon was a community of like-minded, self-motivated Marines. No shitbirds, no braggarts, no light-duty commandos. They did things once, they did them very well and then they went on libbo. By taking the Indoc, I would be setting myself up for failure. I could just hear Vargas or Boyd's endless jibes. Then again, I would have the pride of knowing that I had tried. As soon as I volunteered to try out, I noticed people giving me more respect, which made me even more motivated.

We got word that we had a real mission: evacuating American citizens from Indonesia, which has more Muslims than any other country. An Abu Sayyaf terrorist leader was threatening action if the U.S. entered Afghanistan. They always told us that Marines on deployment were the "tip of the spear," and now we would prove it. Although the brass didn't make it out to be a major or dangerous operation, my buddies and I were quickly turning it into D-Day in our heads. I could practically see the Combat Action Ribbon on my chest.

It would take us a few days to get to Indonesia, but I had a problem that needed fixing. Even though I had held the billet of Gunner for the majority of my time in The Fleet, I still had a rifle as my personal weapon, since I was originally a team leader. Gunners are supposed to have 9mm pistols; it's ridiculous for someone to carry a 26-pound machinegun and a rifle. I brought up the issue to Cpl. Solis, who took me aside and told me to stop whining about it, promising me that I would get a pistol. Two days later, I still didn't have one. The idea of me fast-roping with a machinegun, rifle, and ammo for both weapons was not pleasant. Our seniors spent a lot of energy making sure we called them "corporal" and making us clean floors for hours, but they had almost no interest in training us or preparing us for battle.

I asked Marr if I could see what I could do about getting myself a pistol and he nodded, saying "Whatever." When I went to my buddy Miller, who had been transferred to the armory, and told him my story, he was disgusted with my seniors, saying that the armory had several 9 mils that weren't even being used. All my seniors had to do was fill out one simple form and I could have had my pistol. Half of the boot machinegunners had the wrong weapons for their billets and we had to trade with each other every time we left the armory, which was a big no-no. Miller gave me a weapons card and told me to get the captain to sign it.

I thought the problem was solved, but the next day I was called over by Marr. Veins bulged in his blood-red forehead as he asked me why a boot like me thought I could go to the armory and get himself a pistol? I tried to explain, but he kept cutting me off. Whenever I had asked my seniors about getting me a pistol, they always said that they had been talking to the armory and that the wheels were in motion, but when I asked the armorers about it, they said that they had never heard anything about it. Things got so heated that I thought he was going to challenge me to a fight, but it just trailed off into a litany of veiled and not-so-veiled threats. He told me I had ruined things for the boots and that the fuck-fuck games would begin again in earnest.

While I was gone, Chuck had spoken to Reed and Elias—the two most volatile boots—and told them that they needed to rough me up or it would bring trouble on the boots. Elias was a hot-head, but we were pretty good friends, so he just told me that I was being selfish by making waves. Reed, to my surprise, didn't cause any trouble and just apprized me of the situation. For all the problems I had with Reed, I was one of the few people in the platoon he never or hit threatened.

The next day, we found out that our mission in Indonesia was scrubbed. Tip of the spear, my ass. I found out that the indoc in December was for Battalion Recon, not Force. Battalion Recon was not as high-speed, but they were still elite. Either one would get me out of Golf, which was all I cared about.

Back at Camp Hansen, I could go somewhere whenever Reed got too annoying, but on ship I was stuck with him, which gave me a lot of time to try and figure him out. He had a huge inferiority complex and a constant need for approval. He could never overhear a conversation without butting in and trying to trump you, which was related to the strange and sad relationship he had with his dad. Through conversations with him, it was clear that his whole family detested him and had thrown him out of the house several times, yet he absolutely revered and worshiped his dad. He was constantly belittled at home, but it became a chicken-and-egg conundrum. Was Reed so messed up because of his dad's abuse or was Reed simply angering and offending his father the same way he did with us?

His worship of his dad reached comedic proportions. You couldn't mention any weapon without him saying his dad owned it. He would brag about things that, even if they were true, would impress no one. His signature line—which I often used to mock him—was, "My dad has a $500 belt buckle." He was so far gone that you could mock him to his face and he just wouldn't get it. If someone said their dad has a Desert Eagle, he would say his dad had two, one silver and one black—then you could say "Yeah, my dad has five" and he would get this look like, "Curses! I've been bested again!"

We were still boots, but we were getting closer to being salty and Reed, like the rest of us, was testing his boundaries. Most of his ire was directed at his fellow boots; almost always without provocation. He would eavesdrop on a conversation, correct you on something you weren't even wrong about, then flip out and want to fight you if you told him he was wrong. That, coupled with him being a notorious narc, made him absolutely detested. Back in Oki, the main hang-out was Ross and Showers' room. We had to establish a secret knock to keep Reed from being let in. Reed eventually figured this out and would just pound on the door, begging to be let in. Once, after banging on the door for ten minutes, he went through the adjoining room's shared bathroom, acting like we were "joking" by not letting him in. We all suddenly had someplace we had to go in the middle of the movie we were watching.

We would constantly give him chances to be cool and be one with the group, but he would always end up stabbing us in the back. Out of boredom, we started giving everyone silly nicknames. I was "Oldy Whine-a-lot", Ross was "Flat-chest, Round-head", Hyatt was "Chubby Bunny" and Silva was "Fruity Cumshot." Reed begged for us to give him a nickname, and we kept begging him off, telling him he couldn't take a joke. He continued to plead, so we relented. Mohler dubbed him "Dukes" since he always wanted fight, which I changed to "Dukes Yeah-but" since he had to jump into every conversations with "Yeah, but my dad…". Silva laughed at the nickname, commenting on how appropriate it was and Reed threatened to punch Silva if he called him "Dukes" again.

"You're stupid, dude. Do you hear yourself? You're saying that you're going to fight me if I don't stop saying you always want to fight someone."

"I don't care. If you don't stop saying that I'm going to punch you in the face!" That was another signature line, which he thought was fearsome, but really just sounded like something a five year-old would say.

We weren't supposed to wear boots in the rack because the black shoe polish would smudge up the white paint. After PT, when Mohler crawled into his rack with his tennis shoes on, Reed pulled his usual passive-aggressive narc routine in which he wouldn't actually tell on you, he would just "correct" you in a voice so loud that the senior two rows away would hear him, which was his way of showing "leadership."

"Hey, Mohler! Why do you have to wear shoes in the rack, Mohler?!" Reed would always say your name like it was an insult and put it at the beginning and end of every sentence. I suppose right now if he's reading this he's thinking,

"Hey, Meyer! Why do you have to point out my serious personality flaws and deep-seated mental illness, Meyer?!"

"The rule is 'no boots' in the rack, not 'no shoes', because they don't want shoe polish getting on the walls. How am I going to scuff up white paint with white shoes?" Mohler asked.

Reed turned eight shades of red as his mind short-circuited with rage. He sputtered "Footwear!" and stormed off.

My standing with the seniors was officially dubious and I was labeled a trouble-maker. The fuck-fuck games began again, but they had a limited scope, since they couldn't take me somewhere to thrash me. They tried to put me on every working party, but since I was taking so many college classes, almost every time they tried to give me some shit duty I would nod and say I'd love to, but I had to go to class.

The only detail they got me on was laundry, but that was a doozy. The laundry room was at the far end of the ship and five decks down. Every few days, one unlucky soul would have to wash an entire platoon's load of dirty clothes. Just getting everyone's laundry down there took five trips and then you would have to wait in a line behind all the other units scheduled that day. Since only a few machines were working, it took me twenty hours to do everyone's laundry. That is not a typo or an exaggeration—fourteen hours of waiting and six hours of cleaning. I felt like I deserved a medal after the job was done.

After two weeks at sea, we came to our first port call—Darwin, Australia. The port was industrial, but located just blocks from downtown. After numerous safety briefs, promotion ceremonies and assignment of working parties, we were allowed to change into our civvies and go out on the town. Although port calls are for R & R, they also have a more realistic reason—restocking the ship with fuel and food. Although I was targeted by the seniors, somehow I avoided getting picked for the first day-long working party, but they did get me by denying me an overnight pass. All NCOs and the older lances were supposed to be able to stay in town overnight, but somehow my name wasn't on the list.

Marines have to have a "libbo buddy" wherever they go; Darwin isn't exactly Saigon in '68, but there were still traps—financial, alcoholic and vaginal. Picking a libbo buddy was almost as stressful as asking someone to the prom. People jockeyed for the best "date" and tried to avoid getting asked out by an "ugly chick." I was worried that my buddies wouldn't want to be saddled with a married guy who didn't drink much, so I almost blushed when my Silva asked me to be his libbo buddy.

It was odd to see a hangar bay full of Marines and sailors in their civvies. The Staff NCOs had been in the military so long that they had forgotten how to dress themselves; they looked like little kids going to Grandma's house. The hangar bay was set up like a flea market, with civilians hawking phone cards and tour tickets and exchanging currency.

I didn't realize how huge the ship was until I got off of it. Counting the tower, it was at least 12 stories high and as long as four city blocks. While walking to the bus stop, I saw some aborigines camping near the water. I was shocked at how dark they were and the contrast between their stark condition and the affluence of the city. They seemed like they were ripped from a distant era.

We waited for a bus until we realized that the downtown area was only a five-minute walk. The downtown was modern and airy and even though we were in a modern, English-speaking culture, we acted like we were on Mars. The first time the Marines heard an Australian accent, they giggled like Japanese school girls. The stores were filled with typical tourist crap, as well as some truly amazing aboriginal art which I fell in love with. I'm sure the locals considered the painted boomerangs to be a gentrified and simplified version of their culture, but it still spoke to me.

My buddies didn't want to spend all day flipping through magazines and buying artwork, so we went to a bar called Lizard's, which was probably considered a tourist trap, but the grunts absolutely loved it. I was shocked to find out they served alligator and kangaroo meat; I was so used to hearing about every damn animal almost being extinct that I assumed kangaroos were on the endangered species list. They were so associated with Australian culture that I thought it would be like serving barbequed bald eagle in a restaurant two blocks away from the White House. After talking to some Aussies though, we found out that there was actually an over-population of kangaroos. It still didn't mean they tasted very good.

The Aussies lived up to all the stereotypes, but in a good way. Although we loved Darwin, they told us that it was considered the ass-end of Australia. They had a Sizzler, my favorite restaurant as a kid, so I begged my buddies to go there with me. They all ordered beers since the drinking age is 18 in Australia, even though we were ordered to go by the American drinking age. As I drank my Coke, I watched Silva suddenly freeze; I turned to see SSgt. Shores and Washbourne walk in on Shore Patrol. My buddies all shoved their drinks in front of me, like SSgt. Shores was going to believe that I was drinking four beers while they were all sharing one Coke. Shores and Washbourne sat down two tables away, ruining my buddies' appetites.

Since we were bored and getting on each others' nerves, we started playing childish games. A mutual friend of Silva's and mine would sometimes get on our nerves by telling long-winded, exaggerated stories, so we came up with a code. If he started to get annoying, apropos of nothing, one of us would blurt out, "Razzle Dazzle." If the other person concurred, he would wait and then say, "*Razzley* Dazzley." The funny thing was that even when we used those nonsense codes, the person would never question us, but it would make him end the conversation much more quickly.

"Yeah, so after I kicked that guy's ass, he avoided me from then on. Yeah. And his girl was all about me, yeah, she wanted the dick. Every time I saw her, she'd be all like-"

"Razzle dazzle."

"Uh…she'd be all like, 'Man, I want to get with you. My guy's such a loser. I should be with a real man like—'"

"*Razzley* Dazzley."

"Yeah so, I'm going to fuck her when I go back home. I gotta go."

Worked every time.

The next day, we racked our brains and came up with the brilliant idea of going to the mall. If I was smarter, I would have gone with Jesse and a few others, who went on a nature tour and came back with great memories and photographs of them jumping off a beautiful waterfall. The mall was like any you'd find in America, which made it all the more strange when you saw dirt-poor, shoeless Aborigines wandering through like ghosts. I couldn't tell if they were trying to evoke pity or they were really that bad off. Australia is about the same as America economically, but even the poorest bums in America at least have shoes and shirts.

In the food court (yeah, I know, "Join the Marines, travel to distant lands, and go to the food court") they had a small cart that sold meat pies like it was the Middle Ages. This might sound ridiculous, but those meat pies were the best thing that happened to me in Australia and I dream about them to this day.

While my buddies hit on high school chicks, I went to a bookstore. Usually the age difference didn't bother me, but when they would look at a 16 year-old chick and say how hot she was, I got a little uncomfortable. I headed to the military section and saw that they had many books on East Timor. The civil war in East Timor barely made the news in America, but it was huge in Australia, considering how close the islands are. East Timor was a typical Third World melange of failed communism, rising militant Islam and chronically corrupt officials. The country had imploded and Australia was the main force to quell the violence. I rifled through a book and came upon a picture of First Sergeant Bell in his high-speed Force Recon uniform looking like Schwarzenegger's tougher brother.

One of the corpsmen had a particular problem with the "women" in his life. Twice during the last pump and once during this one, he started to get busy with a girl that ended up being a dude. In the Philippines, when he freaked out at his continual chain of bad luck, the hooker he was with became so upset at not being accepted by him that he/she pulled out a razor blade and tried to slit his/her wrist. Once could be bad luck, twice could be coincidence, but three times is a "lifestyle choice."

The next day, I finally got put on a working party. I wanted to hurry up and get it done, but there was so much confusion that it didn't even start until almost ten. We would be loading food into the refrigerated cellar a couple decks down. No big deal, we had only been at sea for two weeks—how much food could we need? From the hangar bay, boxes of food had to be passed through 300 feet of twisting hallway and down five flights of stairs to a freezer as big as a ranch-style house.

With the Marine Corps, whenever you're working hard, you'll usually get a break every hour. When you don't get a break, it usually means that it the entire working party will be less than two hours. After three hours with no break, I got a bad feeling. A guy from the dock walked by and told us that we weren't even a third of the way through. I noticed a small drop of blood on one box, then another drop two boxes later. Each box had a bigger drop than the last. It turned out that Mohler had cut himself and was moving so quickly that he didn't even notice.

The people in the freezer had been in there for three hours with nothing but t-shirts on, so they moved them to the back of the line and we all moved forward. I now had to do everything that had been exhausting me before while balancing on a ladder. My calf burned as one leg supported me and the 30 pounds boxes that I had to hand down. After another hour of this torture, we started to hand down milk and I dropped a huge four-gallon bladder of milk down fifteen feet. It exploded everywhere and the Filipino petty officers got mad at me, but I couldn't care less. That working party was more exhausting than a 12-mile hike.

I moved into the freezer to stack boxes and I got the novelty of working next to a female sailor. She wasn't that good-looking, but like I said before, a 5 is a 10 on ship. Our hands would brush when I handed her a box, which was the most female contact I had since Guam. I finally had enough and cheesed off, saying that I had to go to the restroom. I hung out in my rack for a half hour until people started filing in. The working party was finally over; now to find a libbo buddy. The pickings were slim and I finally I went with Chaav, a guy I barely knew.

The next day we sailed north toward East Timor, which was one day's journey at leisurely pace. When I enlisted, I thought that the closest I would ever come to seeing action was a humanitarian mission like this. Only about a third of us would be going ashore, so I was surprised that I was picked. They needed radio operators and I was nominally trained on our squad radio, having completed a whopping day-and-a-half of training the previous January. Since machinegunners are attachments, we almost never use the radio, so I barely knew more than the average person, but I knew enough to fake the funk.

Ross was going also, which would have been great, but I was mad at him at the time. It was common knowledge that I hated the stuffy and smelly berthing area and would spend all of my free time reading in whatever abandoned passageway I could find. My seniors gave my buddies static about me being different, telling them that they needed to get me into line. My seniors would lie in their racks all days and get mad at me if I went to read in the library or work-out. Out of spite, my seniors decreed that I had to have a buddy whenever I left berthing—a rule that was not applied to anyone else. Not only was that ridiculous considering I was 27 at the time, but it was also an unlawful order, so I ignored it.

I hated seeing my buddies start to get infected with the same nameless dread of authority that my seniors had. The thought that they *might* get questioned about their actions led people to avoid making any decisions at all. Sticking your neck out might lead to it getting chopped off. I tried not to let my seniors see that the "buddy" punishment was embarrassing me, but it was. I caught Silva following me around the ship to keep tabs on me because he was afraid of getting in trouble for not knowing where I was. I spoke with Silva and Ross on the smoke deck one night and told them it was bothering me. It felt like they were prostrating themselves before the seniors and leaving me out to dry. They tried to impress upon me that my intransigence and independence were causing problems for them.

I was quite excited about going to East Timor and fixed my gear like I was going to war. I decided to wear the MOLLE bandolier since I had seen Force Recon wearing it on their leg, which allowed better access in the prone. Ross was a close second in the moto department, so I showed him how I was wearing the bandolier. He got worried and asked if I had asked permission to wear it. I hadn't since I knew that any corporal I asked would be scared of being different and would tell me not to wear it. It was ridiculous that I had to carry this piece of gear, be accountable for it and pay for it if I lost it, yet I couldn't use it.

The next morning, Ross sidled up and told me he had asked Cpl. Elliot if I could wear the bandolier and he said I couldn't. The Marine Corps had spent thousands of dollars equipping every Marine with this piece of gear and no one was using it because they didn't want to stand out. I was pissed at Ross for even mentioning it to one of our NCOs. Denying me over-night libbo in Darwin—fine. Making me take a libbo buddy everywhere I went on ship—whatever. But messing with my Moto was unforgivable. I was away from my family and being ordered around by idiots seven years younger than me; I needed something to look forward to. Ross tried to talk to me, but I stormed off.

We would be outfitted with the HABD breathing gear that we had trained with in Pendleton. I was surprised we got them since we hadn't used them in Oki when we flew to Ie Shima Island. I asked the crew chief then why we didn't have them and he said that he was told that they couldn't let us use them yet since the Marine Corps had not finished writing their manual on *how* to use them yet.

Though the civil war had ended the year before, East Timor still did not have anything resembling a functioning government, so it was still considered a war zone, which meant that we would get $150 of "danger pay" even if we were only there for an hour. I was excited about showing my Leave and Earning statement with "Danger Pay" written on it to my buddies back home.

The birds were parked on the edge of the flight deck and there was little margin for error. I usually finagled it so that I was the last person on a bird so I would be right near the exit if we went in to the water, but my plan back-fired and I ended up in the middle—the worst place to be. If I was up front I could swim out of the open doors that the crew chiefs shot the .50 cal's from. The bird took off with a lurch and the ship quickly shrunk in the distance. Giant hovercrafts known as LCACs (Landing Craft, Air-Cushioned) came out of the belly of the ship and followed us the short distance to the island.

The land was lush and mountainous, but what really got my attention was the biggest honking helicopter I've ever seen. It was almost as big as a 727, with an insanely huge single-rotor that drooped half-way to the ground when at rest. "UN" was painted in twenty-foot tall letters on the three-story-tall bird.

Our detachment was split into smaller groups to guard schools, power plants and hospitals. Ross, Cpl. Elliot and I would guard some Navy medical personnel who would work at a tuberculosis clinic. The land was beautiful, but the city had the basest poverty I had ever seen. Calling the corrugated tin shelters "shacks" was being charitable; they looked more like poorly-constructed dog houses. All around were people with nothing to do and no where to go. Basic amenities did not exist. Their gas station was a card table with jugs of gasoline on it.

Our seniors' one great claim-to-fame was visiting East Timor during their last deployment. Though they were not shot at, our seniors constantly held it over our heads that they had been in a "war zone." The one platoon in the company that had gone ashore saw no action. Those on the ship, *heard* shots being fired on land. That's it. The quickest way to turn a senior Marine apoplectic with rage was to sarcastically shout "Hoorah! Get some!" when they were talking about East Timor, as Jesse was wont to do.

We pulled into a horseshoe of buildings that comprised the tuberculosis clinic and tried to set up comm, but we couldn't get a signal because of the mountains. Cpl. Elliot made Ross and I climb up a tree with the radio like a couple of monkeys to get a better signal. I was hoping to inspire fear in the locals; now I just hoped they would stifle their laughter.

The people there were very happy to get to see the Navy medical personnel we brought to augment their clinic's staff. The Navy docs and corpsmen set up quickly and started seeing patients, though most had minor injuries or just wanted a check-up. The temperature spiked and it started to get pretty miserable in that dusty courtyard. The only thing to do was keep track of some mischievous kids who were climbing tree and chucking coconuts at us. Most of the kids were quite enamored of us. "You Rambo? Mister Rambo American?" We weren't supposed to feed them, for fear of starting a riot. The kids found a way around that policy by simply waiting until we threw our MRE trash away; then gleaning whatever goodies we left inside.

The men had a fairly typical Pacific Islander look, but the women were quite striking. Lithe and petite, with beautiful delicate features; they looked like a cross between an Indian and a Mexican woman. I blushed when I saw them breast-feed in public, but I got over it, taking furtive glances at some beautiful, golden-brown titties.

After awhile, the sailors in the clinic noticed us grunts wilting in the mid-day sun and started inviting us in. The female sailor was Indian, which surprised me, and when she offered me a Pop-Tart I was convinced that was a sign she wanted my body. I sat there quietly, feeling like a Neanderthal next to the highly-trained medical professionals. Like most docs, they were chatty and friendly and the picture of professionalism. I had nothing but great experiences with Navy personnel and my opinion of them would only get higher as time went by.

A colonel from the UN detachment came around to glad-hand the locals and see what was up. He was fatherly, but not condescending, which was the perfect tone for an officer. This wasn't his first assignment with the UN and he seemed to think that East Timor was doing better than most countries that received the

UN's help. Before we left, a little kid held up his hand and I gave him a high-five. I spent the next five days sick as a dog.

That night, I found out I was being replaced as radio operator for the next day because Cpl. Elliot thought it was unprofessional that I sat down on a bench in front of the people. I couldn't have been happier. Later, I found out that no one did more than one day in East Timor because they wanted to make sure everyone on ship went ashore so that they could qualify for the humanitarian medal.

We headed back to Darwin to refuel before making the trip back to Oki. I was still bothered with Ross and Silva, but libbo buddies make strange bedfellows and we ended up signing out together. I spied Reed coming up with his puppy dog eyes and I tried to scram, but Silva was a softie and we ended up getting saddled with Reed. To my surprise, Reed was actually cool. He was a complete freak and annoyance in uniform, but if you got him into civvies, he was a calm and friendly guy.

At Lizard's, Silva declared that the theme for the night was "no more hoes"; we would stay at Lizard's instead of wasting time and money chasing girls. After three hours, I told Silva that we needed to go somewhere else, but he refused. I couldn't believe it; I was being held hostage by my libbo buddy. I finally left, not caring if I got in trouble. Reed followed me outside and was actually the voice of reason, promising to try to coax Silva to leave, but I was still mad, so I took off. Though my senior Marines were everywhere, so were thousands of other Marines. Whenever a senior Marine asked me who my libbo buddy was, I just pointed to the nearest Marine.

Later that night, I returned to Lizard's and Silva was gone. Fucking perfect. First, he wouldn't budge; then he takes off. I ran into him a block away and he was pretty far gone. He started to needle me, trying to get my goat. His selfishness was really pissing me off and I considered punching him in the teeth. Although he was a black belt and a hard-core weightlifter, he was plastered, so I thought I could take him, but Reed came up and told us we were going to miss curfew.

Soon after getting back to my rack, I heard about our first libbo casualty. Dunn had come back on ship completely soused and had a run-in with First Sergeant Bell. Dunn was so damn drunk that he lost his mind and started to talk shit to The Terminator. You couldn't get me drunk enough to challenge that man; even Washbourne didn't want to tangle with him. Dunn swung at the First Sergeant and just got taken apart. The floor of the flight deck and hangar bay was coated with a substance called "Non-Skid." It looks like rubber, but it ripples in waves when it dries and the peak of each wave becomes a razor-sharp point. It keeps people from slipping and falling off the ship since it grips your boots like a vice. First Sergeant Bell grabbed Dunn by the collar and wiped his face along the Non-Skid.

When Dunn was taken to the BAS and chained to a rack, he refused medical treatment on his badly mangled chin. Silva had to pull guard duty on Dunn, which he ended up enjoying. It was quite an experience to be a boot and see one of your senior Marines trussed up like Hannibal Lecter with you in charge of him. Dunn ordered Silva to untie him, but Silva just laughed. Anyone knew that from then on, Dunn wasn't a corporal.

The next morning, Dunn was released and came back to the berthing area. He was sober, but the idiotic drunk in him was trying to turn his ass-beating into a victory. He proudly showed off his wound, which was beyond disgusting. His entire chin was ripped open; the skin was flapping in the breeze and it looked like a sideways vagina. He said he was looking forward to the scar, but it wouldn't have been just a simple scar; there was no way it would have healed properly by itself. The sergeant major came to talk to Dunn and ordered him to get his chin sewn up.

The boots were ecstatic about a corporal being brought low, especially a blowhard like Dunn. Even the seniors let it be known that they thought he should be busted down. His drinking problems had been an embarrassment and because of his superior stamina, he had always made them look like pikers on hikes. Dunn could be a overbearing alky jerk, but he had always been cool with me and there was a dedicated and hardy Marine under that alcoholic skin. I thought it was a shame to see him let himself be taken down by his addiction.

We had a few more days in Australia, but I was no longer speaking to Silva and Ross. Though I was great friends with Mohler, the age difference seemed more pronounced with him. Mohler asked me to be his wingman with a couple of Swedish chicks he met the previous night. Showers had failed in that billet, acting like a kid at his first dance; barely saying a word. Loudmouths like Boyd tried to sidle in, but his boorish attitude turned the girls off. Mohler said I was the only one that acted normal around his girlfriend when she visited in Cali, but I had to beg off—marriage and all.

Hyatt and I ended up being libbo buddies and we had a great time. I hoped we had cleared the tension between us from the incident in the helo and his feeling that I should have stood up for him more with Reed. He quickly got a girlfriend out in town, though she was a little dubious. Upon re-consideration, she might have even been homeless. It was endearing to see them fall for each other so quickly and then make starry-eyed plans on how they would stay in touch.

Like with Guam, we pulled anchor at the perfect time, just when we were all going broke. Our last obstacle before heading back to Oki was Wog Day, which is celebrated whenever a ship crosses the equator. Those that have never crossed the equator are Wogs and those that have are Shellbacks. It's "colorful" hazing, though the seniors made it sound like they could do anything, including hitting us, and it was all legal. They talked about all the things that had been done to them and the plans they had for us.

Jesse was attracting even more heat from the seniors than me; they tried to turn us against him by making us clean the berthing area for hours after he got in an argument with a senior. Though there were some that sided with the seniors, most of us saw that Jesse was just standing up for himself. Jesse let it be known that he would refuse to participate in Wog Day. If they put their hands on him, he'd lay them out. He didn't want to give them the satisfaction of having fun at his expense. The seniors feared that others would follow Jesse, so they enjoined us to "not be pussies" and go along with Wog Day. If it was as bad as they made it sound, I wasn't going to go through it, but I didn't want to abstain and find out it wasn't that bad. SSgt. Shores called Jesse out of formation and tried to intimidate him by leaning in and hissing in his ear, but Jesse stood firm.

The night before it was to begin, the seniors tried to start the "festivities" early. First Sergeant Bell walked in and got pissed when he saw seniors putting their hands on juniors. The NCOs were told in no uncertain terms that—Wog Day or not—they'd be tangling with the First Sergeant if they didn't cut the crap.

Early the next morning, the captain came over the PA and introduced "Davey Jones," who said in a cheesy, pirate voice that he had come on-board because he heard there were lots of nasty Wogs that needed to be put into shape. When I heard this grade school play-acting, I knew it would all be in good fun.

The seniors made each boot wear a Wog shirt, which was cut up and written on in a way to embarrass you. Some people got it hard and some got it easy. All of Silva's comments about the guys in the company who were in good shape came back to haunt him. He had to wear a shirt that said "Omigod, Sgt. Carroll is like super-buff," which was an actual quote of his that he was trying to live down. My shirt was pretty tame; almost complimentary. Since I had blown up from working out and my wife was pregnant I got dubbed "Buff Daddy."

The object of Wog Day was to shuttle the wogs through the passageways and up to the flight line, where the "King of the Sea" would watch their punishment and then turn them into Shellbacks. It started in berthing, where they made all the wogs get on the floor, "nuts-to-butts", and conga on our asses as we had shaving cream and water sprayed on us. I had to laugh; I thought I would be getting in fistfights with seniors and instead I was playing silly, pre-school games.

You could tell who the seniors' favorites were by who they focused on. They gave special attention to the lieutenants, who were wogs like us.

In the chow hall, we were ordered to eat green eggs and other nasty-looking slop. Most people blanched at the thought, but upon closer inspection, I saw that it was just perfectly normal food with food coloring on it. When I bit into a green sausage link, a corporal broke character and told me I didn't really have to eat it.

After another half-hour, we finally made it up to the flight deck, which looked like a church carnival. Wogs had to duck-walk everywhere since only the Shell-backs were allowed to stand. The Navy personnel were participating as well and my heart sank when I saw my "girlfriend" Bolanos and realized I was crawling around like a duck in front of her. When they made us duck-race and do duck push-ups, it started to get a little boring. The final test was a hose-down in front of a guy dressed like Neptune. I waddled my way in, got sprayed and emerged a ShellBack. All in all, it was a good fun. Our NCOs said that they enjoyed it more than the one they had gone through, which had been much more violent. The Staff NCOs had watched everything closely to make sure no one caught some knuckles while duck-walking their dignity away.

As we approached Oki, I felt like I was leaving home instead of going home. I took dozens of pictures of the ship and the sea and tried to get as much time on the flight deck as possible. I put my hands on the forward edge of the flight deck and did push-ups, looking down 80 feet to the crashing waves. A loudspeaker from the tower told me to get my dumb ass back. They had been threatening to make us do a hike on the flight deck in full gear—just doing laps for hours—but it never happened. Instead, they kept us busy with tests and classes. Gunny Shores took us to a tower above the flight deck where we had a Jeopardy-style quiz. The boots lost, but no one cared since it was so beautiful up there. As we were about to leave, we saw three Harriers swooping down to land. Harriers were the only VTOL (Vertical Take-off and Landing) planes the U.S. had at the time. The first jet slowed to a hover 100 feet above the flight-line. I thought that it would slowly descend to the deck; but it dropped like a rock. It bounced on its hydraulics twice; then the pilot popped the canopy and hopped out—just another day at the office.

The thought of doing poorly on another hike was dogging me, so I decided to do something about it. Everyday, I hiked on the treadmill at a speed much faster than we usually went. It looked pretty silly, but it was better than falling out of a hike and sitting on the side of the road like a bitch. When the Recon Indoc came in December, it would be time to put up or shut up. I made a work-out plan that detailed exactly how much faster and stronger I needed to get every day.

One day, our seniors got a bug up their collective asses and decided to put us in our place by springing a pop-PFT on us. Chuck was bleating about how lazy we all were and how much they were going to PT us when we got back to Oki. To their shock, half of the boots could do more than 20 pull-ups and we all did more than 15; none of the seniors could do more than 12. The "thrash session" petered out as each senior shuffled back to the racks to go to sleep.

SSgt. Shores had been promoted to Gunnery Sergeant and I accidentally called him by the wrong rank. He fixed me with an icy glare and glanced down toward the deck—wanting me to push to pay for my mistake. I did push-ups until told to stop, as was the custom, when Cpl. Smith from Snipers walked up and asked me what I was doing. I told him what I had done and he just looked at me and shook his head sympathetically. He told me that there was no regulation that said I had to push for calling someone by the wrong rank. I realized that no matter how independent I thought I was, I was still brainwashed to some extent.

Although ship life had been great, the tight quarters caused us to get on each others' nerves; I was no longer even talking to my two best buddies. Getting into Recon and moving on with my life was my main priority; being anti-social just gave me more time to work out. After we got back to Oki, I asked Gunny Shores if I could work out on my own instead of PTing with the platoon. He went me one better, insisting that I swim as well as run and work out every morning. From then on, I woke an hour before reveille and went to the pool, where I'd swim for 500 meters, jump out, walk across the street and run a mile as fast as I could. At nights, I would lift weights and run on the treadmill. My seniors tried to throw a monkey-wrench in the works by making me check out with them before my morning swim, but after a couple of days of me waking them up at 5:00AM, they let me do my own thing.

My biggest goal was to get my run-time down to six minutes per mile, which was considered "perfect" as far as the Marine Corps was concerned. I tried to shave 15 seconds off my one-mile each day. As I hit my goals, my confidence grew. I told myself that the faster I ran, the less time I would spend running. I would set the treadmill at 10 miles per hour—the needed pace—and see how long I could keep up. Halfway through, I realized that I had enough energy to keep that pace up the whole time. I was breathing heavy and my flat feet were beating on the treadmill like a seal's flippers, but I was doing it. As the last tenth of a mile approached, I bumped the speed up even more to see what I could han-dle. I hit a mile with six seconds to spare, knocking off more than a half-minute from my previous run. Hyatt was on the ski machine next to me and he was as shocked as I was, remembering me being tail-end Charlie in nearly every run and hike.

This was a watershed moment; I was never more proud of myself—not even when I graduated from boot camp. I was a skinny, nerdy momma's boy as a kid; [start playing sad music here] you're not going to have the greatest childhood if you suck at every sport imaginable. Sports humiliation was a major part of my childhood and it affected me so much that I retreated into books and art. It also affected me socially, in that I had few friends as a kid and I had enormous problems making friends in the adult world. I kept looking at the stats in my notebook to remind myself that they were real. I was the one to keep up with now, not the sorry-ass old man lagging at the back of the pack. It made me think that my pie-in-the-sky dream of joining Recon might become a reality.

Reed started telling everyone that he was going out for Snipers. In Weapons Platoon, only Vargas, Boyd and Reed were trying out for Snipers and they all had one thing in common—they were all loud-mouthed braggarts (though Vargas was cool if you spoke to him alone). Both Boyd and Vargas were in good enough shape to pass the Indoc, but Vargas had character and Boyd simply did not. I was sure that, right before the Indoc, Boyd would make some excuse why he didn't want to do it and Reed would do the same. Reed had a small, but naturally muscular wrestler's body, but he almost never worked out. He was in good enough shape to get through the daily rigors of grunt life, but he didn't push himself. Also, he just didn't have it mentally. He had been tasked to go through the Combat Swimmer's course and he DORed (Dropped On Request, i.e. quit) fifteen minutes into the class. Combat Swimmer's was a tough class, but it wasn't exactly SEAL training; it just weeded out people with fear of water or those that were seriously out of shape. Reed bragged for weeks about being picked for the course; he left for the first day of class at the same time I left for breakfast. By the time I got back, he had gone to the class, dropped out as soon as it got challenging, came back and changed back into his cammies—setting the land-speed record for being a bitch.

The biggest obstacle to Reed getting into Snipers was his personality. His emotional issues had continued to run rampant, with him picking fights on ship for trivial issues that would bother no normal person. His outbursts were almost a daily event and were getting more public. While marching to the armory, Reed got in a shouting match with Chuck and then got into a pushing match with Elias over nothing. Elias slipped on the wet pavement, which Reed made it into some kind of major victory. Now Reed was even getting lippy with seniors and Marr wanted to throttle his ass.

Mohler had a kind heart and tried to listen to Reed, which only back-fired on him. Several times, Mohler would listen to Reed's woes, only to have Reed try to pick a fight with him minutes later. Reed would later develop a near-homosexual obsession with Mohler, borne out of the fact that Mohler was the only one who would put up with him anymore.

Reed's attitude would not fly in a highly-professional unit like Snipers, and Reed knew it. They had no time for whiners, non-hackers or baby-sitting. Vargas would later get kicked out of Sniper school for pulling a simple prank. Reed had been kicked out of his own house by his father; then got kicked out of the recruiter's house he was staying in. In the Corps, he had been kicked out of 2nd Platoon and he was sure to be kicked out of Snipers. Physically, he might have been able to pass the Indoc, but mentally he wouldn't have lasted a week.

Two days before the Sniper Indoc, Boyd dropped out, saying he didn't need to take it since he was getting a medical discharge. Like many black Marines, Boyd had a problem with ingrown hairs. While on ship, the Sergeant Major had told him that he could get a medical separation for that since it was in-curable. That was an old regulation from the days of jungle fighting when ingrown beard hairs could get infected. Boyd was in no danger, but he saw a way to get out and he was going to ride it all the way back to civilian life. When Ross challenged Boyd about weaseling out of the Corps, Boyd snorted and said, "I did my time"—less than half of his enlistment.

The night before the Indoc, Reed told me that, even though he knew he could make it, he decided he was happier as a machinegunner and felt more at home with us. By this time, only Mohler gave him the time of day, so he must have known how much he was hated. The real reason he didn't leave was that he knew that no matter how badly he acted, we were stuck with him. We were a "family" that couldn't kick him out and "friends" that had to hang out with him.

Our last field op in Oki was a Squad Competition. Weapons Platoon operated by section and Ross and I were looking forward to putting the loudmouths in mortars into their place. I carried the typewriter-sized radio since I was nominally trained. All we had were our small patrol packs with a poncho and sleeping bag stuffed in them. Since my pack was filled with the radio, Ross and Silva had to carry my gear. Sweet.

The weather was nice and the jungle was beautiful as we headed off into the brush. This was what I loved and I stopped to appreciate it. Instead of being burdened with gear, we were traveling light and looked Vietnam-cool in our boonie covers. Ross and I were getting along great again and egging each other on as to who could be more moto. Even the seniors were being pretty cool.

As nice as it was though, the jungle will take it out of you and we got pretty drained. We set up a patrol base and listened as other squads went by, oblivious of our position. As radioman, I had to stick with Marr and Chuck, which separated me from my buddies, but it was nice to be around seniors and not get treated like an idiot. We had another close-call when a squad skirted our perimeter, so Marr sent some of us on a patrol to knock off some of the enemy.

The jungle was easy to get lost in, but you just had to stay in a straight line and eventually you'd hit a road. I was no great shakes at land nav; once, when we went on a land nav course, I not only did not find any of the points, but I also lost my protractor and my room keys to boot. As we approached the road, we heard people rustling through the high grass, clearly lost. Peacetime or not, I was taking this seriously, envisioning being in a similar situation in Afghanistan. I enjoyed the feeling of being a hunter, while also being acutely aware of how easily the tables could be turned.

The lost Marines started calling for help and I laughed when I realized they were McCarty and Boortz, two of the 51 seniors. McCarty wasn't that bad, he just had a case of little-man's-syndrome. Boortz was a lazy shitbird who was the same rank as us boots, but acted like he was too good to do any work. They stumbled out of the foliage onto the black tar road, bedraggled and discombobulated, even though they were only 100 meters from the company CP. Roy was across the road from me and I told him to aim in on them, but he refused. I pointing to them, but he just shook his head, not wanting to acquire any of the senior's wrath. Staying under the radar was his MO.

I called out the challenge and they looked around, not able to find me. I shouted "Bang! Bang!" so loud that Silva heard me back at our patrol base; then stood up and ambled up to them, smirking all the way. They were parched, so I offered them my water. McCarty started to make some excuse to save his pride, but they had left their map behind, lost their wits and gotten hopelessly lost. They had then gotten killed by a "boot" who had to take care of them and point them in the direction of home. It was a minor event in a field op, but it was major for me because I had beaten two seniors at their own game.

As it got dark, we left our patrol base since it had been compromised. The rain made the slimy ground even more treacherous. The land rolled like a roller coaster; if you lost your footing you'd slide twenty feet down into a creek. Marr had plotted a point much farther away on the map, but it got so dark that we couldn't see our hands in front of your faces, so he set us down for the night.

Setting up for the night usually involved designating fields of fire and assigning watch, but this wasn't a normal field op. All you could see were faint glimpses of stars between the canopy of trees. We set-up a nominal watch and the seniors crashed. When I stopped rustling around, I could hear everything in the whole valley. There was a POG unit making a ruckus to wake the dead, talking loudly like they were camping at Yellowstone. Cool breezes would occasionally spring up and the whole experience was wonderful. Strange, considering I was lying in mud in a foreign jungle.

Usually, the fear of a senior finding you asleep on watch keeps you awake, but they couldn't have found me even if was sleeping next to them, so I just went to sleep. The next morning had no semblance of military propriety. We woke after the sun rose and it was funny to see where everyone was. Sleeping on a muddy incline, I had slid twenty feet down the hill. Ross asked what happened with firewatch since I never woke him up and I told him that I wasn't tired, so I pulled his and Silva's watches. He laughed at my obvious lie.

As we patrolled through the thick vegetation, I kept getting my gear snagged on three-foot-tall stalks of grass. When I saw one standing up in the middle of the path, I reached out, grabbed it and instantly felt a sharp, cold pain. I looked down to see a strange sight: the grass, which was about a centimeter wide, went in one side of my right index finger, disappeared; then re-appeared on the other side. It took me a few seconds to realize that the stiff blade, with its serrated edge, had cut deep into my finger. This was my introduction to Sawgrass.

I pulled myself free and stared at the wound; it was deep, but no blood was showing. Ross asked me if I was OK, and I nodded. I held it up since it was starting to sting and kept walking. As we reached a steep hill, Marr's eyes went wide. I looked down and saw that my whole forearm was running with blood; a steady stream dripped off my elbow to the jungle floor. Ross bandaged me up, while Marr looked inordinately concerned.

I walked to the company CP to see the company corpsman, who blew me off without looking at it. Ten minutes later, he took the bandage off and jumped back, which is never reassuring from a medical professional. He opened the wound up; it went very deep at an angle almost parallel to the bone. It would need stitches, so it was my ticket out of the field. There was a storm coming in and I was looking forward to my nice, dry barracks room.

Walking into the Camp Hansen BAS, I was informed that I was way too ripe with jungle funk and needed to shower before I would be seen. I returned and had my finger looked at. The deceptively-deep cut surprised the corpsman, who couldn't believe a blade of grass could cut that bad. The MO looked at it, winced a little; then nodded to the corpsman. Since there was no meat in the finger, the anesthetic made it blow up like a balloon.

I was sent to the MO to get my light-duty chit, which would spell out what I could and couldn't do. There was a hike in a week; it would have been lame to ask him to write down "no hiking," so I just prayed fervently. My prayers were answered; I could hear Ross bitching already. The company was supposed to be in the field for two more nights and, as rotten as it was, I was glad they were out there. Nothing makes a warm, dry room more pleasurable than to know that all your closest friends are sleeping wet in jungle muck.

The next day, I was disappointed to find out that the weather was so bad that the company was being pulled out. Oh well, I still had the hike to console me. Everyone told me how rough the Squad Comp got after I left, where suddenly that ordinary field op turned into the landing at Omaha Beach. Ross was pissed that my finger was going to get me out of the hike, but he admitted that it was a legitimate and deep wound…and that I was skating-ass bitch.

I felt bad watching my buddies go off to hike, but Ross gave me enough jibes that I didn't feel *that* bad. Ross was one of those guys who never got a chance to skate ever. He went to every hike, field op and PT session in his four-year enlistment, while people like me seemed to be blessed by the gods of skating. During the hike, I was supposed to stay in the BAS and help the injured Marines that would inevitably be filing in. The other guys there were all permanent light-duty commandos; it was nice to get a break from training, but hanging with a bunch of non-hackers like them made me want to get back to training with a quickness.

Ten days of blissful light-duty followed, but the stitches had to go eventually. One of the five stitches came loose, so I had cut it and pulled it out on my own without pain. The corpsman that would be taking the remaining four out was the same one who put them in, so I trusted him. I know there exists a simple medical tool for cutting and removing stitches, but it must have been in the shop that day. That blankety-blank mother-effing corpsman grabbed some needle-nose pliers and just yanked the sons-of-bitches out. I was writhing around and stamping my fist in pain. I wondered if I was being a bitch, until I realized that what had just happened to me couldn't be done to a POW under the Geneva Convention.

I was sent to Humvee Driver's Course, which I was very excited about. In Pendleton, Humvee Driver's Course was two weeks long and took you through every terrain and situation imaginable, but in Oki, it was three days long and all you learned was how to drive on the left-hand side of the road. It was the ultimate crash course; the "final" was on the second day, with the driving section comprising a day-and-a-half. When you're in a school, you're considered detached from the company, so you don't have to deal with their bull-shit. Even though we had been there for five months, people were still getting stupid about field day. After dinner, I switched into civvies and started to head to the library to study. People asked me why I wasn't helping them clean and I told them I had one night to study for a final that had no re-tests and I was detached from the company. This started a minor shitstorm as all the boots tried to guilt me into staying. There was a lot to study and I knew they were going to pull their usual shit of dragging a one-hour clean-up over four hours. They got Badillo, a shit-bird senior, to try and tell me I couldn't leave, but I was the same rank as him, so I just left.

A third of the class failed and were immediately dropped from the course, including some who already had Humvee licenses already and were just re-qual-ing. I was excited as hell to be driving a humvee, not knowing that two years later I would be spending every day and night in one for three months. The driving section mostly consisted of us doing endless laps around the camp to eat up the mandatory eight hours of supervised driving.

The next week was the Recon Indoc; I was so motivated that I told anyone that if they didn't see me with a canteen in my hand (being that hydration is so important to proper training), they could dead-leg me to teach me a lesson. After a few people caught me, I asked Lewis to postpone giving me one since I was too sore.

My heart sunk when I found out that my seniors had put me on the rifle range the week of the Indoc, apparently to spite me. It looked like all my efforts to get in shape were in vain. I came up with an idea: if Reed could DOR from swim training, why couldn't I DOR from the range? I brought it up to the sergeant in charge of the rifle range, who shrugged and said it was fine with him; he didn't really care since I wasn't one of his boys. I headed back to the armory to turn my rifle in.

After about an hour of cleaning weapons, I got called to the armory window and told that Gunny Seese wanted to speak to me. I picked up the phone and he demanded to know why I was UA from the range. The Corps is anal-retentive about lists and I had fucked up his counts. I told him I had checked out with Sgt. Williams, but that wasn't what he wanted to hear. He told me to double-time to his office and speak to him and First Sergeant Bell. He used the First Sergeant's name the same way your mom did when she said, "Just wait until your father gets home."

I walked into the small main office and Hollingshead nodded toward the First Sergeant's door, his eyebrow cocked ruefully. No one went to the First Sergeant's office for a good reason—you were either in trouble or a member of your family had died. I knocked, asked permission to enter and reported in with the utmost respect and professionalism—so he wouldn't eat me alive. I quickly sensed that things were more calm than I had imagined. Gunny Seese lounged on a small couch as First Sergeant Bell went through some paperwork. First Sergeant told me to explain myself and I told him about training for the Recon Indoc. This got his attention and he turned to Gunny Seese, who shrugged and said he had no idea since none of my seniors had passed it up the chain. First Sergeant tested me on how hard I was training and when I told him I was running sub-six minute miles and could do 22 pull-ups, Gunny was noticeably impressed—something he rarely was. First Sergeant Bell seemed to perk up and started to reminisce about his days in Recon, telling me what to focus on.

The main bone of contention was that the Indoc was on Friday and I had to shoot on Friday, even though you actually qual on Thursday. Friday was just a fuck-off; you fire while wearing a gas mask, fire on the move and at moving targets, but it didn't count toward your score. Most people hated the last day because it was such a waste of time. I thought the First Sergeant could exempt me from it, but he said he couldn't. He told me that he knew everyone in Recon and when we got back to Cali, he could arrange a screening for me at any time. He ordered me to get a first class PFT that week and shoot expert on the rifle range. I told him I would.

Leaving his office, I had mixed emotions. I was angry at my seniors for fucking me over and pissed that I had to miss the indoc for the final, useless day of shooting, but I also had to be honest with myself and admit that I was relieved that the possibility of failing the indoc had been removed. At least I had the cache of not having backed out like Reed or Boyd.

I ended up getting Rifle Expert by a few points, much to my relief. Now I could take that embarrassing Sharpshooter Badge off of my Charlie uniform. My next challenge was the PFT, but there was an added spin. Though we weren't hanging out anymore, Silva and I were at least talking to each other and I bet him $50 that I could beat him at the PFT, which he gladly took. He had been working out even more than me, but he was topping out at only 18 pull-ups. Each pull-up was worth almost a minute of run-time, so if I got 20 pull-ups I could run two minutes slower than him and still beat him. He didn't see me as any sort of competition, even though I had gone through the same thing with an overly-cocky Ross in June and won.

For some reason, in the days before the PFT my pull-ups dropped down to 17. The night before the PFT, Silva had duty and got almost no sleep. I told him that if he wanted to nullify our bet, that would be alright. He seemed surprised at my offer, but he thought he was a shoe-in, so he wanted the bet to stand.

The next morning, I woke up an hour early just to hydrate properly. I wasn't cocky, but I felt like I had a good chance. When we filed outside, Silva looked bushed. The first event was the pull-ups, which would make or break me. I decided to go first so that Silva's score wouldn't psyche me out. By the time I hit 5, I knew I was going to make it. I got to 20 and just hung there, waiting for the grader to confirm my score. Silva got 18.

Crunches are a "gimme," in that everyone says the person they're counting for gets 100—no matter what. Gunny Seese knew this, so he made everyone count out loud so he could hear if they were skipping ahead. I started the crunches and was feeling pretty good, until I got about halfway through and heard Hyatt saying, "Forty-eight, forty-nine, fifty-two, fifty-four, fifty-five."

"What the hell are you doing?"

"Shhh, I'm hooking you up."

"I don't *want* to be hooked up. I've got a bet riding on this and I want it to be on the up-and-up."

"Oh."

"How many extra points did you give me?"

"I dunno. Ten or fifteen."

I counted from then on and hit 115, but there was still doubt in my mind that I had actually done 100.

On the run, the clock doesn't begin until the last man crosses the starting line, so I edged up front, looking back at Silva. The race started and I sprinted out in front of everyone. Sprinters burn themselves out, but I ran ahead to get a psychological edge. I made the first lap in 6:18. A light rain came down, which was just perfect, cooling me off as I ran. Everyone else running up front with me was almost ten years younger than me. Washbourne was acting as a ref at one corner of the track and the surprised look on his face when he saw "Old Man Meyer" in front made the whole race worthwhile.

I lost about twenty seconds on my second lap and was starting to feel the burn. I knew I had Silva beat points-wise, but I still wanted to beat him on the run and he was catching up. I also wanted to beat loudmouths like Boyd and Vargas who I could see gaining on me as well. I decided to slow down and walk up the last hill and then sprint the last half-mile. Hyatt caught up to me and admonished me for "giving up"; I didn't have the extra breath to explain my plan and his withering glare got the better of me, so I started running again.

The end was in sight when I started to feel like I was running on empty, but all I had to do was look back and see Boyd, Reed and Vargas and I got the incentive to keep going. I crossed the finish line at 20:10. Silva came in shortly after and congratulated me. I told him about the deal with the crunches and said that I would make it up to him. After work, I went to his room and did 100 crunches and Silva conceded defeat. He admitted he got cocky and didn't prepare, thinking he had it in the bag.

One of my best friends in boot camp and SOI turned into a complete shitbag when he hit The Fleet. He was a good guy, but he just "failed to adapt" as they say. Salazar was from Odessa, Texas and looked and sounded like a paunchy version of Bill Paxton. He was my age and generally laid-back, except for a temper that would flare at the oddest times over relatively innocuous things.

He started scamming as soon as he got to The Fleet and each lie was more audacious than the last. When he told Housing that he had to care for his dying grandmother and have space for her live-in nurse, he ended up getting a huge, three-bedroom apartment that was meant for sergeants or above. He exaggerated a simple knee injury in an attempt to get a medical separation, but he still ended up going with us to Oki. He was a horribly bad actor and I would watch as he would walk perfectly normal, turn a corner and see his seniors, and then start limping for all his worth. I wondered if he remembered to limp on the same leg every time.

We were on the honor system when it came to reporting our PFT scores, but when it was his turn, he gave an insanely high score—twenty-minute three-mile run, eighteen pull-ups, and 100 crunches. His seniors saw through him and made him re-do the PFT the next day, under close observation. There is a step a foot off the ground on the chin-up bars that is used so people can get a good grip on the bar and then hang there before starting. Salazar used the step to vault himself up, saying "one" as his chin barely crossed the bar. "Two" never came and his seniors thrashed him for lying.

His last scam was the piece di resistance of his shit-bird career. When we returned to Cali, he was denied extra leave. He then called the battalion duty officer, identified himself as a Red Cross worker, and said that "Lance Corporal Salazar's grandmother's doctor" (her again) had requested that Lcpl. Salazar be given immediate emergency leave since she was near death. Battalion actually bought it and they told his company to prepare the paperwork. He was almost on leave when his higher-ups got suspicious and called the Red Cross, who had no idea what they were talking about. Needless to say, Salazar did not get his leave.

His med sep was continually pushed back and he spent his last two years in the Corps getting fatter and sweeping the stairways.

One of the traditions of deployment is the float book, which is like a high school yearbook, only with no women and lots of pictures of drunk Marines hanging around shirtless in their barracks rooms. Each platoon got a few pages to put their own pictures in and ours would be would be arranged by the 51's section leader, Cpl. Gimeno. When we finally got the yearbook, our allotted pages were filled with nothing but—you guessed it—pictures of Gimeno and Monty, shirtless and drunk, in their barracks room.

There were parts of my job that I loved and I figured if I could just do those parts of it, and none of the bad parts, I would stay in the Corps for twenty years. Since no jobs like that existed, I had to invent some. "Undercover Marine" was my favorite. As an Undercover Marine, I would live as a civilian and not go to work or train, except when I wanted to. I would still receive all pay and benefits and even have my own small armory. They didn't want me getting a civilian job, since I needed to be on-call in case they needed me. I would remain ready, keeping my eye out for danger and protecting America from the safety of my own couch. I realized that the higher-ups might not go for that, so I invented a job that would keep me in uniform and on-base. As a "Comfortable Weather Commando," I would fight—and fight hard—as long as the temperature was between 60 and 80 degrees.

The MSG recruiters came around and there was a big push for volunteers. Marine Security Guard Duty is the most prestigious job in the Corps, since they guard the embassies. Usually only the best of the best get in and there are a dozen ways in which one could get dis-qualified, such as being married, having debts or even being ugly (seriously). The perks are insane: your own room that is cleaned by a maid, personal chef, chauffeured car, tax-free pay, automatic promotion, regular hours, and a stipend to buy yourself some suits. In your three-year tour, you would do one hard-ship tour in some shit-hole and one in a nice country.

After 9-11, they greatly expanded the number of needed MSG Marines and standards dropped precipitously. Literally everyone who applied got accepted, though some would be weeded out during MSG school. Unfortunately that meant that three of my best friends—Silva, Hyatt and Showers—would be leaving Golf. I hated seeing them go, but I had to admit that it was the best choice for them. Since Afghanistan didn't pan out, it looked like all they would miss would be another tedious and exhausting work-out.

I would have paid good money to get a FAP, and I lobbied unabashedly to get one. Whenever a battalion comes off deployment, about fifty Marines are

"FAP'ed out" to work at a variety of mundane, but necessary jobs. FAPs are considered 6-12 month vacations and almost everyone hopes to get them, even if they won't admit it. I had only lived with my wife three months out of the last two years, so I wanted one in the worst way; not to mention the fact that it would get me out of doing another work-up. Though many dropped subtle hints, I just went to Marr and blatantly asked for one. I mentioned it to Gunny Shores almost every time I saw him. Just before we left Oki, I found out I got one of the coveted spots.

Since the MSPF Marines got to Oki a few days earlier than the rest of the company, we got to leave earlier as well; we flew home the first week of January. Once you got back from Oki, you were no longer a boot—or so we had always been told. Mohler and I joked about calling our buddies remaining in OKi from Cali as "salt dogs" and ordering them to clean our catwalks. When we got back, we were still boots though; it's not like the NCOs were going to help us clean the laundry room. We would be boots until all our seniors left six months later.

By the time we left Okinawa, all we had left were our own uniforms and personal items. We were each allowed to take one duffel bag and one carry-on; anything else had to be mailed home or thrown away. The day before we left, Showers came to my room, sweating profusely.

"Meyer, man, thank God you're here. I need your help getting my TV to the post office before it closes."

"Oh, you mean the TV that I never watched? Why don't you get one of your 'good buddies' like Boyd or Ritchie to help?"

"They're all making excuses. I need your help, man."

"Let me get this straight—all of those guys who would hang out in your room every night, the same ones who would leave all of their trash when they left, the same ones who never liked you before you got the TV and who I constantly told you were taking advantage of you—none of those guys will help you?"

"God! Fuck it! I'm sorry I asked. I guess I'll have to just carry it there myself."

"Dude, it's too big. You'll drop it going down the stairs."

"Then what am I supposed to do?"

"Look, because I'm your buddy, if you can't find anyone else to help you—I will."

"Thanks, man."

"But first you need to go back to all of those free-loaders and tell them they have to help you. Ask Boyd first. Maybe you can get all the gear he used to steal from you every time he went in your room."

It really had been a shame how people had taken advantage of Showers and how he had let them. I became good friends with Showers in Oki, but not because of his TV. Once he got it, I stopped going to his room since it was always filled with assholes. Instead, I would invite him to play chess in my room. Showers did poorly on tests, but he was a savant at Chess. One of my great victories in life was playing him to a draw, which was as close as anyone ever came to beating him.

When I was gearing up for the Recon Indoc, I traded some M-16 mags to Reed for the Recon swim shorts he bought for the Combat Swimmer's Course he bitched out of. We were expressly told that since we were traveling on a civilian plane and going through customs we could not take anything related to firearms on-board. If anything was found, the flight would be grounded and all of our gear would be taken off the plane and inspected by hand, which would take all day. When we got to Alaska, they let us get off the plane to stretch our legs. When we got in the line to go through the metal detector before re-boarding, Reed sidled up to me with his little-kid-getting-away-with-something grin and bragged that he had the mags I gave him in his carry-on. I told him to throw them in the trash, but instead of putting them in any of the dozens of garbage cans throughout the airport, he tried to slip them in the trash can *right next to the metal detector*. Of course, he got caught and he immediately ratted me out for giving them to him, as if that had anything to do with him idiotically trying to brings the mags onto the plane. Luckily, the higher-ups were able to convince the inspectors that Reed was a lone idiot and they let us back on-board without incident.

We checked into 2/4's barracks. 2/4 had been out of the deployment rotation for two years and it showed. Their barracks were disgusting, which was especially galling since we had left our old barracks in Pendleton, and the ones in Oki better than we found him. Checking in was surprisingly informal; as soon as you got your room key and linen, you were free to go.

Everyone's gear and vehicles were still in storage, so there wasn't a TV or stereo to be found. I dreaded the thought of spending a night in a barren room, hearing drunk jarheads yell at each other. I invited Mohler to stay with me at the hotel I was getting in downtown San Diego. Getting there would be a trick; because of Mateo's isolation, it took two hours just to get to Oceanside by bus, which was just twenty minutes away by car. Somehow Oceanside had gotten even scummier in the previous six months. There was something incredibly mortifying about being in that shitty bus terminal again, after having literally been around the world.

Knowing from experience that hotels don't like to rent to groups of Marines, I pretended to be alone and got a room with no problem. After watching some good old American cable TV (which got old in about ten minutes), Mohler asked if I would buy him some beer. We walked around for an hour, trying to find a liquor store that was still open. We were an odd couple to say the least. He was a 19 year-old skater/stoner rich kid from Mississippi and I was a 28 year-old comic book nerd from Texas, but we got along really well. That was the best thing about the Marines—making great, lifelong friends with people I never would have met in normal life (normal life obviously ending the second I joined the Marine Corps).

The next day, Mohler went back to base early and I wandered around San Diego. After having dinner (at Sizzler, natch), I headed for the bus stop. The bus pulled up and the group of ten or so people crowded by the entrance, blocking the sidewalk. I was in the back of the pack and heard a harsh voice growl, "Get out of my way." I looked to my right and saw two large homeless guys walking straight toward the group of people on the sidewalk. They were homeless, but they weren't the pitiable type. Both were over six-two and built; they looked like they asked for change during the day and just took it at night. All they had to do to avoid the crowd was step two feet into the grass and walk by them, but the lead bum didn't want to do that. "Get the hell out of my way, I'm not joking," he said as he leaned forward to charge the crowd.

I looked around to see if anyone was acknowledging what was happening, but they all just focused on getting on the bus. I saw that the lead bum was intent on barreling through the remaining two people still blocking the sidewalk, a Mexican women about five-foot-nothing and her four-year-old daughter. I couldn't believe what was happening.

When he reached out to grab her shoulder, I grabbed his sleeve and spun him into the grass. "What the hell is wrong with you, you piece of shit?" I demanded. He looked at his buddy, who gave a noncommital shrug. I pointed down the street. "Get the fuck out of here!" He muttered vague threats and inaccurate insults (calling me a "nigger") and then they took off. I looked over and saw that everyone had gotten on the bus; the driver gave no sign that she had witnessed anything. A feeling of embarrassment came over me—did I make a big deal out of nothing? I was a little screechy, but he was going to knock the woman and her girl down out of pure meanness.

I got on the bus and everyone avoided eye contact. The message was clear: we're all going to pretend that it didn't happen. I ruminated on what had happened the entire journey back to base. I was proud of myself for doing something instead of just sitting there, but I was also very sad, in a naive way, about the whole situation.

On Monday, I told a few close friends about what had happened. Silva professed being proud of me. I couldn't understand the whole situation. Silva explained that in places where bad things happen every day, people stop fighting it and just try to get on with their lives. As boots, very little of what we went through was constructive or deserved, yet it was rare for someone to be openly defiant. I had been more of a tough guy back when I was a civilian. Back then, I could say whatever I wanted to anyone. Now I had to look at their collar and think if it was worth getting fucked with for a month, just to respond to one of their insults.

We couldn't go on post-deployment leave for another ten days. In the interim, we would draw new gear and test our guns and gas masks. The fuck-fuck games were pretty much gone, but we still pulled all the shit details. Three hours into another field day, Darnell came in and told me that the duty officer needed to talk to me—my wife was going into labor. My joy at being able to see my first-born son was almost equaled by my happiness at getting out of cleaning the common areas.

I ran a half-mile to Battalion HQ and waited for the duty officer, but after waiting for forty-five minutes, I took off to a payphone and called my dad. Afterwards, I headed back to the duty, who immediately dressed me down for not reporting in to him immediately. I explained that he wasn't there, which he dismissed with a grunt as he set about getting me my emergency leave papers.

I checked the Marine Corps website during leave and saw that I had made the cutting score for corporal. I would be a boot no more. I didn't work out once while on leave, spending all my time with my new son. I lost almost everything I had gained and I could no longer blame my seniors for me not getting into Recon. My Recon dream slowly petered out, ending with a whimper instead of a bang.

Several single guys I knew professed to getting bored and dis-illusioned on long leave breaks and even wanting to come back to base early, but I was never that way. I came back on the last flight possible and was always completely miserable. The longer I was on leave, the more of a civilian I became and the harder the transition back to Marine. I was always glad to see my buddies, but a rueful "Here we go again" expression was the common sight on these reunions.

At least I would be going to my FAP right away. FAPs ranged from mindless drudge work, to MP duty, to jobs so great that it was ridiculous. The dream FAP was Range Maintenance, in which all you did was drive out to ranges and check to see if they were clean. If they were dirty, *you* didn't clean them—Heaven forfend—you would just call whatever company was there last and tell them to fix it. During the initial FAP brief, we were all on pins and needles, waiting to find out what our job would be. I ended up with one of the lamer ones, S-4, the paper-pushers of the regiment. Not only was this a bad job, but the Regiment was leaving in three weeks to pull a six-week-long double-CAX.

I got my check-out sheet and dreamed of when I would be checking out of the company for good in two years. Though you could steam through it in two days, you were given a week to check out. Wouldn't you know it that it took the entire week? I spent most of that week watching "Buffy, The Vampire Slayer" with Silva, a cultural phenomenon I had heretofore been unfamiliar with until the American taxpayer paid me to watch it.

Those that got accepted into MSG were checking out as well. When saying my farewells to my departing friends, I was taken aback by how close we had gotten in little over a year, but I had to admit that they were going to have much better lives, so I kept my bitter jealousy to myself. Elias has been accepted into the program, but he wanted out of it since he would have to extend his enlistment to go into MSG. Elias was built like a mountain, but even he was nervous about getting counseled by First Sergeant Bell for dropping out of the program.

One day, Reed tagged along with Silva and Mohler while they took the much-traveled route from Mateo to the Carl's Jr. by I-5, driving down Cristianitos Road, the border between San Diego and Orange County. When Reed saw an Orange County Sheriff's cruiser, he told Mohler to slow down. Mohler told Reed that he didn't need to since they were still in San Diego County and the deputy was out of his jurisdiction. Since Reed's dad was The Greatest Cop in the History of the World and Reed was an expert in all aspects of law enforcement, Reed started yelling at Mohler, telling him how wrong he was. Reed had invited himself along and, before they had gotten two miles down the road, he was threatening the guy who was doing him a favor.

A car passed Mohler's, which set Reed off for some reason. He started yelling at the driver, who yelled back and then pulled off the road, wanting to fight. When Mohler pulled over, Reed asked him what the hell he was doing. The other driver cursed at Reed and motioned for him to step out of the car. Reed jiggled the door handle dramatically and then stated that he would love to kick the guy's ass, but the door wouldn't open.

Depression set in as soon as I checked-in to S-4; it was what the kind of stultifying, office atmosphere that made me enlist in the first place. I was the most junior Marine in the office; guess who would be emptying the garbage cans and cleaning the office every day? I asked if they were going to the double-CAX and I got an "oh, yeah" as an answer. Motherfucker. Since I was the boot of the bunch, I had to sit in the office and answer phones while everyone else went to eat. I saw a very long year ahead of me.

After lunch, I was called into Captain Irons office; he was in charge of Supply for the entire regiment—four battalions. He had a snarky, distant air about him and he asked me some questions, trying to get a feel for what I could handle. He let on that there was another job he could put me in, if I was right for it. It had to be better than this freshman shit I was doomed to. He perked up when he heard that I had worked at Dell. When he asked me what my ASVAB score was, I knew I had the job. He drove me down to the motor pool and explained that I would be the new Fiscal Clerk, paying the bills and managing the budget. It was classic Marine Corps thinking—put the guy who was fifty grand in debt and had five overdrawn credit cards in charge of the Regiment's money.

Even as the fiscal clerk, I would still be going to CAX, even though I had no real job to do there. The Marine Corps has this concept called "bodies", in which they'll decide they need 80 guys for a double-CAX and they will get them, no matter what fit. My job involved working with the Regimental Fiscal Clerk, Cpl. Ortiz, even though he would be working at mainside in 29 Palms and I would be in the boonies. Not only would I be in the dust for two months, I would just be standing by and pulling odd jobs to boot. They were sending me away from my family for two months after I just got back from Oki. Marines at Regiment never went to Oki, so the yearly double-CAX was their only "deployment" besides war. My friends agreed that I wasn't just being a whiner (which I had a rep for), but no one had a reasonable solution. I went to talk to the chaplain, but he was so busy that I left without speaking to him.

I decided to ask if I could get out of the FAP. There were so many people that were jealous of my FAP that I wouldn't have a problem finding a replacement. I told First Sergeant Bell that I wanted to stay. He was leaving that week, but he held more sway than anyone. He pushed it up the chain-of-command and the sergeant major denied it. Case closed.

My first impression of Supply was the same as everyone else's—they were some skating-ass bitches. In the grunts, you only see Supply once a year, so you get the feeling that they only work once a year; but their job is more complicated than that. Besides issuing everyone their personal gear (though that is now handled by a private, for-profit company), they also pay the bills, manage money, make contracts and generally make everything work. If it isn't a person or a part of the landscape, it got there because of Supply.

Staff Sergeant Pangelinan's jump wings, scuba bubble and Force Recon oar caught my eye instantly. I would spend the first month or so thinking he was a grunt until he laid it all out for me. He had gone to the Gulf War as soon as he got to The Fleet as a Supply POG, but as soon as the fighting started, he was loaned out to a line company as a provisional rifleman. He shot two Iraqis, which floored me. This was early in 2002 and, at that time, almost no one in the Marine Corps had actual combat experience. After three years at MCRD in San Diego, he got hooked up with a primo spot working I & I (Inspector/Instructor) which is considered the Holy Grail of sweet jobs in the Corps. Their job is to run the Reserve centers and train reservists on drill weekends, which means a lot of free time. They are given a lot more autonomy than in The Fleet and it's a non-deployable job.

Hawaii had one of the few Force Recon reservist units. They sent SSgt. Pangelinan to Jump School at Fort Benning and then gave him their own impromptu Scuba training. They didn't hand it to him either, making him take it three times before he passed. Force Recon is the highest-budgeted unit in the grunts, so they got to do some great training. Instead of shouting "butter-butter-jam" with unloaded weapons they would fly to the Philippines or Australia and work with allied armed forces.

SSgt. Pangelinan then went back to his old regiment, the Fifth Marines, where he quickly settled in. When I got there, it seemed like he knew everyone on the base, but he had only been back for six months. He was a schmoozer by nature, but he could chew ass when he needed to. He was from the "you catch more flies with honey" school of thought; there would be a lot of nodding and winking and "Don't worry about it, dawg", and then the problem would be solved, the missing gear would be replaced and you were off on libbo. SSgt. P (as he was known) was one of the rare Marines who was actually good with money. Though he had been hit by a nasty divorce early in his enlistment, he had bounced back, met a great woman and started another family. He had enough money to buy and rent out one house and live in a great house on base that had an ocean view. He was always up on the latest technology and was a libbo hound of the first order. He could out-run almost anyone in the company and knew the most minute Marine Corps knowledge like the back of his hand.

I was the first and last grunt to be FAPed out to Supply. No one was hostile, but I kept my eye out for any tricks. After a quiet, awkward morning, some of them started asking me questions in the afternoon. Garza was a big, Mexican kid from the Rio Grande Valley in Texas who had taken to the LA/Cali lifestyle wholeheartedly. He was friendly and humorous, but with an edge that made me think that we might get into a fight. He had the usual gripes about grunts which I laughed off; then he got a little more personal. There were some pugil sticks in the warehouse and he asked me if I knew how to use them. I said that I did and showed him a few basic moves, feeling embarrassed. To my surprise, they seemed genuinely impressed. One of them egged Garza on to fight me with them and he agreed, though he looked a little unsure of himself. He hadn't trained with them since boot camp, but he didn't know that I hadn't either. He easily had fifty pounds on me, but I felt like I was defending grunts everywhere, so I stood my ground.

I leapt at him with a very basic swing, caught him while he was off balance and knocked him into some boxes. He acquiesced nobly and I was happy that my bluff had worked and that the situation had been defused. Later on, he told me that he had needled me because he thought that I just rode around in Humvees and he didn't believe that I was from a helo company and actually humped the 240.

The thought of another two months away from my family was really eating at me; I found myself muttering to myself in the car about the injustice of it all. I tried to separate the legitimateness of my feelings from the whininess and ended in a dead heat. SSgt. P seemed like someone I could talk to, so I composed an outline of all the reasons I wanted to stay in my old company. I went through it a several times to edit out the self-pity. I asked to speak to him outside and managed to calmly delineate my reasons without sounded like a bitch, which seemed to impress him and surprise me. He told me he'd bring it up to the lieutenant immediately, but as long as he could get a replacement, he didn't see why there would be a problem.

Leaving work the first day, Cpl. Ortiz sidled up and invited me to his church. I begged off and that was the last time he was even remotely cool to me. Ortiz was a great athlete and smart as a whip, but he had a real superiority problem. We butted heads almost immediately because of his condescension and horrible teaching methods. The job was complicated enough without his constant jibes and insults. I was still a lance and he had a year on me in the Corps, so I deferred out of respect, but he just kept at it. For a complicated procedure with twenty or more steps in it, he would run through it in lightning speed and then wonder why I didn't get it exactly right the first time. His accent was almost impenetrable and I constantly had to have him repeat himself, but he was unclear in more way than one. He would tell me, "This is how you do this form and you always do it the exact same way. Always. Always! Except when it's different." I had put up with a lot of his shit, but the "always except when it's different line" blew me over the top and I started yelling at him. SSgt. P laughed when I blew my lid and he later let me in on an office secret—Ortiz was their golden boy, but he had been slipping lately.

Ortiz left for CAX early and I stared at the computer for three days without figuring anything out. At its simplest, my job was ordering gear and paying bills (i.e., shopping), but it was like shopping in a store where all the boxes were the same size and had no labels. A canteen wasn't a canteen, it was an M1877802540NC62048 and if you got one number or letter wrong you just bought a gross of tampons, non-returnable. There was no catalog and very little instruction.

Golf Company would not let me switch out with anyone, so I was stuck there. I confided in SSgt. P about my family problems and he brought me in to speak with the lieutenant. I told him I needed time to get settled into my new apartment and get my family moved in. He gave me two weeks, which was more than enough. I would still be going to CAX, but by the time I got there it would only be a month long.

In the interim, I got promoted to corporal, which was a great pay-off for all of my hard work in Oki. What made it even better was that I got promoted despite a mutual hatred between me and me seniors. Instead of kissing ass, I did an end-run around them and scored another stripe. Chuck picked up corporal with less than a year left on his contract, but I wasn't even at my halfway mark yet. Monty and Mora also picked up the same day and I noticed some resentment from Monty and Devers, who had showed up to pin him and Mora. Usually you can have whatever senior you were closest with pin you, but I hated all my seniors. I had gotten corporal on my own, despite and in spite of them.

Afterward, I ran into Marr and Chuck at the barracks and asked them if they wanted to pin me. Marr laughed embarrassedly and Chuck avoided eye contact, giving me a pallid handshake. Chuck espoused the opposite of the platitude expressed in "Bambi": If he didn't have anything bad to say, he didn't want to say anything at all.

On the day I was to leave for 29 Palms, Providence stepped in. Up until that day, I felt like I was the only one who saw through Ortiz. Though he was the golden boy of the office who picked up rank even faster than I had, he was also arrogant, deceptive, intransigent and disorganized. Garza told me that since Ortiz had gotten to the company, the higher-ups thought Ortiz "walked on water." Ortiz was a real my-way-or-the-highway type and he got into a tiff with the lieutenant out in 29 Palms. He had been living on Mainside in a barracks room and working in an air-conditioned office while the others slept in tin K-spans. He would commute to the camp every few days to check in with the lieutenant, but his work was slipping. The LT felt that Ortiz had too many distractions at Mainside and told him he would now stay with them in the sand. Ortiz told the LT that if that's how it was going to be, he refused to work. This blew my mind—I had never heard of anyone refusing to work in the Marines. Sure, everyone sand-bags and scams sometimes—you have to or you'll go nuts—but Ortiz just plain quit. I told SSgt. P that I didn't know it was possible to quit anything in the Marine Corps.

Lt. Chapell wanted to press charges, and SSgt. P wanted to wring Ortiz' neck. SSgt. P had covered for Ortiz many times and Ortiz had shown him no loyalty. Bad for Ortiz, but good for me. I would take Ortiz' spot living and working at Mainside while Ortiz pulled shit details in the middle of nowhere. This was Meyer Luck in full effect. My friends and I had noticed that I seemed to have a peculiar kind of luck that came in two forms—totally, undeservedly good, with great things just falling into my hands without me working for them or horribly, irreparably bad, in which even things that I specifically worked to keep from happening, happened twice as bad.

We had gotten a new sergeant the day before. Sgt. Pucci was on the edge of being chubby and deeply, proudly sleazy. He had been kicked out of his job as a recruiter after an "incident." He was a glad-hander who actually seemed to like coming to work, if only to perfect his latest scam. He had been a sergeant longer than I had been in the Corps, which was both good and bad. With the stain on his career from whatever he did as a recruiter, his career was pretty much done, but he was putting his nose to the grindstone, hoping for a little redemption. Since he was still checking-in, he didn't have to go to CAX, though he would be driving us out there.

Sgt. Pucci drew a van from the motor pool to drive ten of us out to 29 Palms. It quickly became clear that he wasn't your average Marine Corps sergeant—he seemed more like a used-car salesman. We took a lot longer than usual to get to 29 Palms and he started concocting an elaborate story to explain our lateness, which seemed unnecessary, since we had no specific time to be there. He spotted the Tactical Vehicle Entrance to 29 Palms, and hoped that he could use that as a short-cut to get to Camp Wilson. A tactical vehicle is a Humvee, tank or trac, but Sgt. Pucci insisted that "tactical" just meant "military"; since the van was owned by the Marine Corps, it would be alright. I tried to explain to him what "tactical" meant (a Ford Econoline van doesn't qualify) and that we were sure to get stuck, but I was the low man on the totem pole, so I said my piece and shut up. It wouldn't be my ass on the line if anything went wrong.

We quickly got stuck up to the axle and every plan to extricate the van only mad it sink deeper into the sand. When I saw the tires disappear below the ground, I hid my water bottle in my patrol pack. None of the other geniuses had brought any water and I knew that they would be begging me soon. I remembered the stories about people dying in the desert within a mile or two of civilization. We were about eight miles away from anything.

When it became clear that we were hopelessly stuck, Sgt. Pucci put on his best politician grin and trudged over to one of the local's dwellings to ask for help. To say it was a shack would be charitable; it looked like the wind had blown debris into a vaguely house-like shape. An annoyed desert rat got us out in less than five minutes. He did not have a high opinion of the Marines, having to do this about once a month. He told us about an eighteen-wheeler getting stuck so bad they had to get a crane out there to get it out of the stand. After the guy left, Sgt. Pucci was extremely proud of himself for "solving" the problem, which struck me as the perfect metaphor for the Marine Corps—getting into a problem through sheer stupidity, then taking credit when someone else bails you out.

No one cared that we got to the camp after dark, though Sgt. Pucci had added even more detail to our fake story and sworn us to secrecy. I checked into a K-Span, feeling awkward since I didn't know most of the people there. Ortiz strode in and you wouldn't have known how much trouble he was facing from how he acted. He was cocky and loud and started needling me right away. People had been boxing out of boredom and when someone noticed the tension between Ortiz and I, they suggested that we box. I asked Ortiz if he wanted to fight and he begged off with his usual weird smile.

Lt. Chapell came to our hut and asked me to take a walk with him. He gave me the lowdown on Ortiz, clearly steamed. He had gotten very dark in the two weeks he'd been out there and his white eyes seemed to be bugging out. Ortiz had been close to picking up sergeant, but that was all over now. Lt. Chapell told me I had a big job and asked if I felt I was up for it. I told him I was, still acting non-chalant, not wanting to queer the deal.

As I was packing to leave the next day, I noticed that Ortiz barely had any gear. Though he was told to pack everything, he had only taken what he'd need to live at Mainside. I asked him if he wanted to borrow my gear and he seemed surprised. Something about him told me it was a bad idea, but just like with Reed, even if someone bugs the hell out of me, I still want to help them.

On the ride to Mainside, the company gunny had to stop in the mountains to check on some training the company was doing. I got out to correct them on any deficiencies, but it turned out that their defenses were just fine. Those clerks, cooks and mechanics had almost as much field time as I did.

I hopped out of the dusty humvee and looked at my new home; it was the nicest Marine barracks I had ever seen. While I was unpacking, my new roommate came in and started to bitch under his breath about having a roommate. I'm usually pretty apologetic and deferential, but I wasn't in the mood, especially from a POG. I told him I'd barely be there and that I'd help him clean up on field day.

The next day, I was taken to a typical scuzzy-looking one story concrete-slab "flat-top" building. I imagined an open squad bay, rubbery linoleum floors and fifty-year old rusty metal desks, like every other Marine office I had seen. When I opened the door though, I was surprised to find that it had been remodeled to make it into a modern civilian office. I knew Ross would be blue in the face if he came off a 17-mile hike after four days in the field and found out my appointed place of duty was a computer desk. I could get used to this. I got a rough explanation of my job from Captain Irons before he took off.

The woman who ran that office (and pretty much the entire base) had the misfortune to have the same name as a woman who had recently drowned her kids and blamed it on a black man. Susan Smith had done four years in the Marine in the early 1980s, gotten out, married a gunny and gotten a civil service job on base. Her Civil Service rank was equivalent to that of a captain in the Marines Corps and it was funny to see dusty officers come in from the field and defer to her. She was one of the coolest people I met in my enlistment, absolutely masterful at her job, while still being fun and approachable.

Ortiz got driven in from the hinterlands. He languidly tried to show me what he had done, but I didn't pay attention. I didn't want to hear a thing from him; I would rather do it on my own. I spent the next few days staring mutely at my computer screen, before I buckled down and started systematically going through his records. His golden-boy reputation cracked almost instantly under closer inspection. His records were abysmally inaccurate and it took me a week to correct them. Even worse was his handling of money; he had basically stopped paying all bills four months earlier and his bill-paying had been sporadic at best since the beginning of the fiscal year. The regiment was thousands of dollars behind in their accounts.

The more I dug, the worse it got. In the Marine Corps purchasing system, if you don't spend your unit's money, it gets reabsorbed into a general fund. If you order something and it gets discontinued or lost, it is up to you to recover the funds, not whoever you paid. I leaned heavily on Susan for advice and eventually found that Ortiz—through malice or just laziness—had misplaced over $30,000.

Susan told me I could get it back, but it would be a lot of work. With only Ortiz' patch-work records to guide me, I would have to trace every order and see where the money went. The Marine Corps' proprietary financial program, SABRS, looked like an Atari video game, but by whittling down the garbage dump Ortiz had left me, I was able to recover the funds over the next month.

The Marine Corps, in its infinite wisdom, realized that if they didn't give 29 Palms a great standard of living, people would start losing their damn minds. Thus, this dusty base in the middle of nowhere had the best amenities of any Marine Corps installation—even the air stations. The chow hall had restaurant-quality food and you could eat as much as you want. They would stack the luncheon meat so high on your hoagie that you could barely fit it in your mouth.

During my time at 29 Palms, I would accomplish a lot while also being almost catatonically lazy. It took me about a week to figure out that—as long as I didn't lose my mind like Ortiz—I could get away with just about whatever I wanted. I ironed my cammies and shined my boots once a week and no one said anything. I'd show up to work around 8:30AM, which would have caused apoplexies of rage at Pendleton, but since I was pretty much my own boss, no one said a thing. I would tool around on the Internet for about an hour before getting in one hour of serious work. Then it would be a half-hour until lunch, so my mind would drift and I would chat with Susan or walk around the office. Returning from my two-hour lunch, guilt would kick in and I would get in another two hours of good, solid work. After another hour of Internet and chit-chat, I would leave at 4:30PM. At night, I'd catch a free movie at the base theater, work out for hours; then walk around in the cool desert air. I got my one-mile run back under six minutes and read several books a week. I wasn't allowed to leave on weekends, but it was almost as good as Oki. 29 Palms was a little taste of being a civilian in the middle of my enlistment.

I asked for the key to the building so I could "work late," but I really just wanted it to use the Internet to check out porn. I didn't know that the system would shut down every night at 10:00PM and anyone on it would get their password changed. When it went down, I thought that some shadowy government unit somewhere had seen what I was checking out and I was busted. The next morning, I frantically spent two hours trying to get back into my account before finally telling the computer tech that I was locked out. Without cocking an eyebrow, he hit a few keys and I was back in. I had another problem though. I had left one of the doors unlocked, which was a major security breach. I felt terrible and voluntarily turned my key back in.

Although there were about fifty Civil Service workers, there were only eight Marines and six of them were officers. Officers without men to lead are some of the most useless creatures on the planet and it was funny to see them buoy their spirits while they wasted their youth. In the Marine Officer Corps, nearly everyone volunteers for Infantry or Flight School, but those fill up fast and there are still a lot of glamour-free jobs that need filling. The officers there reminded me of frat guys who had graduated from college, but had not started working in the real world yet. They spent most of the day planning their next road trip to LA or Vegas. Since they enjoyed none of the perpetual exhaustion of being a grunt, they always had boundless amounts of energy to burn off on "extreme" sports on the weekends. They were like a bunch of puppy dogs. One officer that worked with me would constantly pepper me with questions about being a "real" Marine in The Fleet; he considered himself a side-lined quarterback.

Half of the Civil Service workers were former Marines and many were Nam vets. Contrary to the popular view, those Civil Service workers were highly competent and they really worked their tails off. Instead of the condescending and rude attitudes I usually received from civilians who worked with Marines, the people there were all highly patriotic and supportive of the Corps. Being the only grunt they worked with, they acted like I was Rambo and oohed and ahhed at all my stories about The Fleet that would have put any other grunt to sleep.

At the desk next to me was a PFC from Miami who called himself Jugo. Like me, his job involved going through someone else's files and fixing mistakes, but his work load was ten times what mine was. He didn't have the stripes or the "I'm just a grunt" excuse to fall back on, so he really had to put his nose to the grindstone. He was exceedingly bright and personable; so much so that it seemed like a waste for him to be in the Marines. Like most Marines, I needed something from the Corps—discipline, a feeling of accomplishment and pride. I could never tell what Jugo needed from the Corps; I'm still not really sure why he joined. No one normal joins the Marine Corps. Normal people go to college, get a lame job selling cell phones over the Internet and fade into oblivion.

Cpl. Fatty looked like a civilian dressing up like a Marine for Halloween. Once a Fleet Marine, he came out with his unit to CAX, did the job I was doing, met a local girl and got engaged. When it came time to re-enlist, he switched MOS' so that he stay in that job. Two years later, he was getting out on a med sep, but all he really needed to do was lose fifty pounds and he'd be fine. He didn't seem like a Marine—he seemed like a tall, fat guy who would work at Best Buy or something. Like Ortiz, he was arrogant and cocky. A Marine with a size 38 waist shouldn't be cocky about *anything*. Since he was checking out and rarely there, he would have been a dead issue to me except for the fact that he refused to recommend Jugo for lance corporal, because he thought Jugo was a smart-ass. Jugo's proficiency level was easily that of a corporal and though he could be a little "loose" (he once called me by my last name before I quickly disabused him of that notion) he was one of the most competent and professional Marines I had ever met. It seemed to me that Fatty was just hating on the young upstart. I constantly sang Jugo's praises to the officer in the office who always requested my grunt stories.

My buddies back in Mateo already thought I was a skater, but if they knew how I was rolling in 29 Palms, they would have disowned me. Not only did I have AC, my own desk and a computer, but I also had access to a golf cart to tool around base. It had the corny name of "Dingbat", which I could never remember correctly, so I just called it the "Doodlebug". For the first few weeks, I felt too guilty to use it, but as the temperature climbed, I gave in. I drove Jugo to the highest point on Mainside and turned the Doodlebug around, wanting to see how fast I could get it to go. Jugo was worried about getting in trouble if I wrecked it, so I told him I'd take the hit. We took off down the hill, burying the needle past 40 mph.

On May 9th, I hit the half-way mark and paused to reflect on my previous two years. Though Boot Camp was rough for me, I loved SOI. Being a boot sucked, but I still had a lot of good experiences and Oki was a blast. I didn't get to go to Afghanistan, but the rumblings about Iraq were promising. Even though this was the half-way point, I saw myself as being a lot closer to getting out. 29 Palms had been a vacation and I would be in a skate-ass FAP until next year. I'd return to Golf, train for a month; then go back to Oki. I'd be eligible for a school cut as soon as I got back from Oki. When I broke it down like that, it didn't seem bad at all.

Lt. Chapell was a year older than me and had been in the Marines for twelve years, starting as an enlisted Marine. He was stationed at 29 Palms during the Gulf War and told me about the huge parades and crowds that lined the highways for miles when the Marines came home. My favorite part was the women who supposedly flashed their tits in "support." He picked up sergeant in his first enlistment and then went into an officer program that paid him to go to school. He still had all military benefits and even picked up staff sergeant. After he got commissioned, he came to the Fifth Marines. With the pre-requisite divorce out of the way, his job was his life. A lot of people had problems with him, but that was mainly because they wouldn't put themselves in his shoes. As an officer, it was his job to make sure the rest of us didn't slip right off the edge into complete nastiness. The main problem I had with him was that since the job was his life, he seemed to assume it was ours as well. Whenever we would pull another fourteen-hour day, I would pray that he would get a girlfriend.

Iraq was just an inkling back then, but Lt. Chapell kept feeding me hope. I was making his life easier and finding money, so I was on his good side. When I told him about getting jerked around about Afghanistan, he told me I could put money on going to Iraq. I scoured the Internet constantly to find news that confirmed his assertions.

It still bothered me that Ortiz had just dropped his pack and quit. He had the brains for it, he just didn't have the heart. I asked if Ortiz was getting punished and Lt. Chapell just shook his head ruefully. The CO had turned down his request to punish Ortiz, assuming it was just a personal problem between the two of them. The company office was in disarray and they wanted Ortiz to go in and straighten it out. The company office is vital to the unit, but the junior enlisted that work there come in two types: malingering shitbags and super-moto lifers. Ortiz ended up pulling the same shit over there, but by the time they found out, he was processing out of the Corps.

Ortiz became a fixture of my thoughts. He wasn't an easy-to-understand jerk like Boyd; that would be easy to quantify and ignore. He was much more complex. He had come from Mexico as a kid and lived in an all-Mexican enclave in Northern California, so his accent was still quite thick. He was intensely religious and a tee-totaler, yet also a braggart and a jerk. I could never quite get a handle on him. Even when I was being bothered with him I still found myself helping him out by loaning him my gear.

Even though I had to stay at CAX a week longer than the rest of the company, I was going to be sad to go. Corny as it sounds, I was determined that the taxpayer's money not be wasted. I found it abhorrent that Ortiz just stopped giving a damn and lost so much of the regiment's money. I felt that the thirty grand I recovered for the regiment more than paid for my two hour lunches.

Although the POGs at 29 Palms never went to the field (the only gear most of them had was a Camel-Bak to use while PTing) they didn't go out on week nights either. The town outside of base was broken-down and sad, so it was better just to chill in your barracks room. Vegas, LA and San Diego were all about the same distance, so people would just chill on base during the work week and save money, then go on road trips on the weekend.

The base had more female Marines then I'd ever seen, so many that it wasn't even a novelty. Their looks varied the gamut from Average to Yikes and most seemed like they came from very poor families. Supposedly they got promoted more quickly because they used their feminine wiles with their superiors. While less than half of the guys in Golf had steady girlfriends, every female Marine had at least one boyfriend, no matter what she looked like. Female Marines can pick and choose through a huge catalog of available sex partners, while most grunts are happy to get lucky once with the fat chick that works at Spanky's Pizza in Oceanside (ask for Mandy). That causes resentment in the ranks that cannot be denied. Marine Corps history is filled with stories of POGs stepping up to the plate and acting as grunts in combat; I needed only look at SSgt. P to see an example of that. Most women aren't strong enough to handle the rigors of grunt life. They could for an afternoon or for one post, but they aren't built for pro-longed patrolling and close-combat. Most *men* have a hard time keep up in the grunts. The concept of "every Marine a rifleman" is the core concept of the Marines and, in that regard, women can't hold up their end of the bargain. Women work great in other services, but the grunt-based Marine Corps is a bad match for them. As I would tell my Marines when I was counseling them—we don't work at Wal-Mart; this is not the normal world. In the real world, any kind of discrimination is unconscionable, but I don't consider it discrimination to say that women can't hack it as grunts—it's just reality. Marines aren't normal people: they're trained attack dogs. The ferocity of Marines in combat is unbelievable and I don't think women are capable of that. Our secret is this: we get treated like shit and it makes us mean. Unless she's built like Chyna, she is not going to be able to carry me to safety if I get shot. With that said, seeing women in uniform never got old. It's just plain hot, what can I say?

I was proud that I was able to close-out the CAX account without a penny being wasted. Six weeks earlier, I came to 29 Palms completely ignorant of my responsibilities. I surpassed the accomplishments of someone who had been trained for the job and had three years' experience. I also met some great people and had not been treated like a piece of shit once. On my last day there, I walked around the base and took pictures, missing the place already. To any normal person, it would just have been six weeks of a boring job in a dusty town, but compared to the two previous years, it was a little piece of Heaven.

I returned to Pendleton the next week, much more assured of my job than when I had left. I wasn't thrilled about being back, since it meant a return to being a member of a group, instead of being on my own program. For the last two months, I hadn't gone to one formation, hike, or field op. The next eight months were strange and amorphous; I can't remember it the way I can my time in the grunts. Every field op in the grunts was unique; even four years later, my friends and I can remember the exact day a hike happened.

POGs are a hot-button issue with most grunts. To them, POGs are non-fighting, pencil-pushing Marines-in-name-only that work civilian hours, never hike and never go to the field. Most grunts have an irrational and emotional hatred of POGs, since they supposedly have such comparatively easy lives, but more often than not, that is not the case. I got to see how the grass is not always greener. While it is true that I only went to the field once, we had regular hikes that were just as hard of those in the grunts. We PTed and ran 3-5 miles every day. When a grunt isn't in the field or at the armory, he is usually sitting in his room either sleeping or playing PlayStation. There is no "stand by in your room" in the POGs since you have an actual work place. Some of the toughest Marines I met were the cooks, who had a job with zero glamour and even less appreciation. When I would thank a cook after he handed me my food, he would either give me a dirty look, thinking I was being sarcastic, or get so touched that he wanted me to marry his sister.

A POG office is called a "shop" and mine was filled with characters. Cpl. Delgado arrived a few weeks after I did, coming straight from a unit on Oki. He had used his time overseas wisely, picking up NCO, saving a lot of money and getting in great shape. Garza dismissed his puffed-up arms as being "club muscles," only good for impressing girls. He looked like Slater from "Saved by the Bell" (don't act like you're too cool to know who I'm talking about) and had a hyper, excited way of talking. He was a cool guy, but I held tight to my policy of not becoming friends with anyone who outranked me or was senior to me.

Brown looked vaguely like O.J. Simpson and was one of the most chronic liars I ever met and I mean that as a compliment. He was constantly telling wildly imaginative stories, but the funny thing was that the things he actually did were even more off-the-wall. He lived deep in the hood in LA and was quite a mystery man, seeming to be a lot older than his professed age of 23. He was an inveterate shirt-chaser and one of the friendliest guys I ever met; he could shmooze himself into anyone's confidence. He was extremely shady and constantly hinted that he could get you anything for the right price. He would do strange things like steal small personal items as a "joke." Though he was a confirmed POG, he didn't have the usual defensive snobbery towards grunts that most POGs have. He absolutely worshiped the grunt side of the Marines and was constantly asking me for more information. His grunt knowledge was pretty damn good and he was a great athlete to boot. I probably spent more time talking to him than anyone else, but I still never felt I got to know him. He had so many stories, cons, and lies that I don't know how he kept them all straight. He was one of the happiest people I've ever met; he could get enjoyment out of almost any situation and bad things just rolled right off him like water off a duck's back. He seemed more like a character from a movie than a real person. In Iraq, he lived up to all his stories and became highly-decorated.

His best buddy, Mundaca, was from deep in the mountains of Peru. He had grown up in abject poverty, but he wasn't bitter, just tough. He told me of the epidemic of kidnappings in his country. He told me if your family didn't pay the ransom, they'd cut off your head. The Indian names of the local villages fascinated me and I would have him repeatedly tell me them and coach me on my pronunciation. He had followed his brother to America and quickly became extraordinarily successful. Like Brown, he was in amazing shape and almost always in a good mood, though when he got angry you could see that he grew up in a harsh environment. He was smart as a whip and, like SSgt. P, great with his money. At the age of 22, he was a family man with a house he had signed for being built in Rancho Cucamonga, which I thought was just a fake town from the movie "Next Friday" until I found out it was real. Though he had calmed down after he got married, he was still Brown's partner-in-crime. Mundaca, Brown and Sgt. Pucci all had amazing constitutions; they could work a thirteen-hour day, drive down to Pacific Beach in San Diego, party until 3AM and then drive back and get two hours sleep before going to PT. Though one of the most junior Marines in the warehouse, he had eclipsed Brown to be put in charge of the warehouse until Sgt. Pucci got there. Even then, because of his maturity, he was the go-to man for any important job.

Garza was still a lance, even though he had only three months left in the Corps. He kept a countdown on the dry-erase board and I took vicarious thrill when he updated the count each morning. Garza professed no regrets in not picking up corporal, but I could tell it bothered him. Like Brown, he was quite the con artist and he was quite open about his plans to become a drug dealer when he returned to Texas. Garza liked to push peoples' buttons, especially if they were staff NCOs or officers. It seemed silly to jump on him for not polishing his boots or coming back from lunch two minutes late. Once, I had to take him outside to counsel him, which was embarrassing for both of us. I told him that it wasn't smart to make waves when he was so close to getting out.

Salazar was also from Texas and a smart-ass of the first order. Unlike Garza, he was whippet-thin and in excellent shape. Though he was very smart, he just didn't care and his area of responsibility was in constant disarray. He was fiercely Hispanic and would correct other Mexicans for saying Spanish words like "San Diego" or "Texas" in flat, Caucasian tones. He had been in Cali his first three years, which was strange, since most POGs do a year in Oki before coming to a stateside unit. He worked nights at the PX, which blew me away since grunts never had the free time to work a second job.

Black was a POG to the bone and proud of it. While the others could be made to feel guilty for not going to the field or missing a hike, Black let it be known that his place was behind a desk. He was good at his job, but he had an attitude which grated on Garza, who I had to stop from kicking Black's ass several time. Black was good at snapping on people and, though he wasn't very imposing physically, he never backed down when someone got pissed off at one of his cracks. Though he fell out of almost every PT run, he was a surprisingly good hiker. On one hike that was just killing me, I looked over to see him chatting amiably with the Marine marching behind him. He was one of those brothers to whom being black was almost his full-time job. If the president got killed right in front of him, he wouldn't bat an eye, but if Bernie Mac died, he'd be in mourning for a year.

Kim was the boot of the shop and the only one who I was technically in charge of. He was an Asian kid from the LA area who had just gotten out of his MOS school. His first PT session was pathetic and it was obvious he hadn't exercised since boot camp. Nonetheless, we all started with very positive attitudes toward him. Unfortunately, when I was at Mainside during CAX, I didn't see him for two months and he got corrupted by hanging out with senior Marines who didn't give a damn. While in formation, the call went up for bodies for a working party and I volunteered Kim, who calmly said that he didn't want to do it, like he had a choice. I whirled around and yelled at him in front of the others, a common occurrence in the grunts, but very shocking among POGs. This was my first real experience of being a senior Marine and I used what I had learned from my seniors while trying to leaven it with common sense and maturity. I didn't play fuck-fuck games or demean him, like what happened to me, but I was not his buddy either. I tried to follow the middle ground, but he just kept screwing up.

We had a regiment-wide field event with races, tug-of-war, etc. I volunteered to be in the squad "boots-and-utes" (utilities—i.e camouflage pants) race. There were few volunteers and they had to grab whoever they could find. I told them I had two Marines I could bring. I went and found Kim and a Filipino kid nicknamed Blets and told them to report for the race. Neither was happy about it, but they both said that they would be there. I told them what they needed for the race and we all headed off to grab our gear.

I returned with my gear and saw Blets talking to a staff NCO nearby. I went to the staging area and saw my machinegunner buddies from Golf. They were happy to see me, but I felt awkward—I was no longer one of them. Though I walked by their barracks several times a day, I avoided them for the most part since we had less and less to talk about as time went by. They were hiking up mountains and sleeping in the rain and I was typing on computers and going home every night.

After a while, it became clear that Blets and Kim were ditching me. Whatever vengeance I had planned would have to wait until after the race though. The race started and by the time I got to the first event, the obstacle course, I was far in front of everyone. Marines from Golf were acting as referees and I was quite happy to see the surprised look on Boyd's face when he saw that I was the fastest man in my squad. I ran the O-course twice and waited for the rest of my squad to catch up.

We headed to the pool, where there was a huge high-dive structure with three levels. We had to climb up a ladder and jump off the second deck, which was about twenty feet high. I wasn't crazy about heights, but all the fast-roping I had done had gotten me used to them. To my surprise, one of the staff sergeants got about eight feet up the ladder, got scared and then went back down and begged off. This would never have happened in the grunts. I climbed up and noticed that twenty feet seems a lot higher than it sounds. There were about eight people in front of me and the guy at the front was a beast—6 foot 5 and almost 250 pounds. I thought he was waiting for the command to jump until I saw he was frozen with fear. I knew if I waited in line I might start to psyche myself out like he had, so I walked past him and right off the edge.

The last leg was a long run up a ridge line and then down a rope. Another Marine and I finished the race and waited at the finish line for ten minutes like a couple dummies until we realized we'd have to go back and help the rest. The squad's final time was horrible, but I was proud of myself.

I went to the barracks and found Kim and Blets playing video games. I went off on a tirade before asking them what happened. Blets told me a staff NCO had ordered him to help out with another task, which did kind of fit what I had seen. For all I know, the staff NCO might have just asked Blets where the hot dogs were and then went on his merry, little way, but Blets had covered his ass well. Kim had no excuse and seemed to think if he just laid low I wouldn't notice. I promised Kim that he would be formally counseled and punished for being UA.

I spoke to SSgt. P about it and he told me to handle it however I saw fit. In the grunts, I would have fucked with Kim endlessly—but this wasn't the grunts. Instead, I made him write a 2,000-word essay about following orders. As we headed out of the office at the end of the day, Lt. Chapell pulled me aside. He told me that I was being too harsh on Kim and that I couldn't tell Kim to do his job or go UA, like I had. I wasn't allowed to give punishments like essays, only officers could. He cut the essay to 1,000 words and told me to go easier on Kim.

Things between Kim and I would get much worse before they got better. Garza left, but his effect on Kim didn't and Salazar was just as bad. Salazar still hadn't picked up corporal, even though he only had a year left. Though he was smart and capable, he didn't follow through on anything. Kim and Salazar were roommates and Kim got fed lessons in bad attitude almost 24 hours a day. What was worse was that Sgt. Pucci was hanging out with Kim and treating him like his little protege in sleaze. I started to do monthly counselings on Kim that were accurate, but harsh. I told him that he had been tainted by bad company and he was off to a terrible start in the Corps. I delineated each of his short-comings so that he would know exactly what he needed to fix.

Two months went by and Kim didn't get any better. I gave him another scathing review and then, somehow, he started to turn around. While he had started in pathetic shape, he apparently had been working out in his free time and became one of the best runners in the shop. On an hour-long race up a ridge line, Kim was the first to the top and I was the second. I gave him another cautiously positive approval with a strong hint to not get cocky. The following month his review was glowing and I told him he needed no further review.

Somehow, Kim had turned around and I liked to think I had been the main reason. Maybe he had gotten tough for the same reason I did as a boot—to shut his senior Marines up. I felt like I had followed a balanced route and I tried to hammer into him a real sense of responsibility. Ortiz had left the entire regiment in the lurch out of laziness and spite. I wasn't the fastest or the strongest Marine in the shop, but I felt like I had made a difference. This billet was low in glory, but absolutely crucial to the regiment. Kim seemed to understand.

Instead of building us up, the daily PT just wore us all down. Though I was running sub-six minutes miles at 29 Palms, a month after I got back I was lagging on every run. Since all I did was work, commute and sleep, I didn't see why I should put myself out for anyone. When the PFT approached though, I realized I needed to get back into shape. I had done good on my last two PFTs by having friendly wagers that motivated me, so I thought that would work again. Those times though, I had made the bets a month before the PFT, so I had time to prepare. This time, I only gave myself a week and I made the mistake of picking Mundaca, who had recently finished the Marine Corps marathon in less than four hours. Though I beat him on the pull-ups, he blew my doors off in the run. He seriously would have had enough time to shower and change clothes before I crossed the finish line. I paid him the $75, which was as much money as I had won on the last two PFTs put together.

Something bothered me about my run time. Even though I blew the run out of my ass, I only ran one minute slower than I had in Oki, when I was in the best shape of my life. More than 15 people had finished below 18 minutes, which was hard to believe. After work, I got in my van and drove the run course, expecting it to be around 2.8 miles, since I could tell it wasn't a full course. I followed the route exactly and when I got to the finish line, my odometer told me the run had only been 2.5 miles long. That was pretty damn scandalous, even for a scammer like me. I broached the subject subtly at work the next day and I was told that Marine Corps regulation allowed them to adjust the course by .2 miles to adjust for hills. Their excuse was bogus, but who was I to look a gift horse in the mouth?

Our long hours got even longer as summer began. I had rented an apartment in northern San Diego with the understanding that during my FAP I would come in at 6:30AM three times a week for PT and 7:30AM the other two days. Right after I got back from CAX though, the Regimental Commander ordered that we would have PT every day and hike every other week. He gave our com-manders a mandate to make sure we ran 15 miles per week and hiked 30 miles per month. That meant that I had to be at work at 6:00AM every day and 5:00AM on hike days. If that wasn't bad enough, Supply was having a once-every-four-years inspections from some officers from Headquarters Marine Corps in a month. Lt. Chapell told us that we would be working late every night and possibly weekends. For my "skate" FAP, I was waking at4:30AM and getting home at 8:30PM. After work, I only had enough energy to drive home, slam the door, and get in an argument with my wife before falling asleep in my cammies.

Though I had repaired most of Ortiz' damage, there were still some areas in which there were no records. The hierarchy of Supply was strange in that, even though I was the Regimental Fiscal Clerk, I worked for Headquarters Company Supply. Yet when I bought anything for regiment, it came out of HQ CO funds and then was supposed to be reimbursed by regiment. That meant that HQ CO was always broke and Regiment was fat with cash, which made the Regimental Supply Officer look great and made Lt. Chapell look like a piker. I compiled a list of everything I knew that HQ CO had bought for regiment, but I didn't have the whole paper trail and the Regimental Supply Officer, Lt. Hazen, balked at reim-bursing us.

Lt. Hazen joined as an officer in his late twenties and his pock-marked face made him look even older than his 32 years. He was dedicated and hard-working, but he had an extreme way of looking at situations—a person was either perfectly, eternally good in all fields of human endeavor or he was a purposefully ignorant and lazy demon who dreamed day and night of different ways to tear down his beloved Corps. I was introduced to Lt. Hazen by Ortiz my first week in the FAP. In the middle of the conversation, he stopped and began praising Ortiz so effusively it was almost homoerotic. When Ortiz' faults were exposed, Ortiz became the devil and I became the saint that saved the regiment from destruction. Although I enjoyed his praise, I took it with a grain of salt. When he liked you, he was so giving that it was awkward. When I was at 29 Palms, he once let me borrow his SUV just to save me from walking a few blocks in the heat. On the drive back to Pendleton, he bought me so much food that I thought I was going to have to put out. He tried to get me to apply for the officer program, saying that he would sponsor me. Like the officers at 29 Palms, he was a closet grunt and loved to talk about "real" Marine Corps topics.

Lt. Hazen tried to turn me against Lt. Chapell. Lt. Chapell bugged the hell out of me sometimes and I really wished he would get a girlfriend so he wouldn't want to be at work so much, but he was a good guy and had gone to bat for me on several occasions, both professional and personal. Lt. Hazen tried several subtle ways to get me to say that all the regiment's fiscal problems were because of Lt. Chapell's supposed incompetence, but I refused, for the simple fact that it just wasn't true. Hazen would cut us money in dribs and drabs, but when he finally gave us our "bulk" reimbursement, it was barely half of what we were owed. He refused to reimburse us for anything if we didn't have a receipt, even if we could show him what we bought by holding it in front of him. Once, when Lt. Hazen stormed in and demanded to see Lt. Chapell alone, I was sure that they were going to fight. Enlisted guys can fight all day long, that's fine, but when officers fight it's indicative of the whole system collapsing. In the end, because of his junior billet, Lt. Chapell just had to take it. Ortiz really should have paid for all the trouble he caused; Lt. Chapell trusted him too much and it cost him dearly.

The month before the inspection seemed like a year; perpetual exhaustion was the constant state. Our long hours went way past the bell curve of being useful; we were all so tired that we started making stupid mistakes. Tempers were flaring and even SSgt. P went drill instructor on us one day. The shop was almost in a state of mutiny when the inspection finally came. Instead of tearing us apart, they were there to calmly inspect and correct—it was very un-Marine Corps-like and surprising. The day before the inspection, Lt. Chapell told me that my section wasn't even being inspected. I was relieved in a way, but it quickly dawned on me that my last month of 80-hour work-weeks had been a total waste. Through the entire hellish month, Lt. Chapell had promised that we would be working fewer hours afterward, but that was not the case. After the inspection, we would stay late each day and practice marching or teach each other classes.

Though he was in the most inglorious of POG jobs, Brown was more moto than most grunts. He actually enjoyed going to the field and thought that hikes were fun, since he didn't do either often enough to get sick of them. After work, he would stick around to hear SSgt. P's stories about the Gulf War and his time in Force Recon. Brown often spoke of taking the Force Recon Indoc and re-enlisting as a grunt. When he heard that 1/5 was having a Sniper Indoc, he asked Lt. Chapell if he could go, but he was denied. The next day, he was working out at the gym and told the Regimental XO about the situation. POGs are much more relaxed about rank in social situations, so he was able to speak casually to that high-ranking officer. The Regimental XO was a grunt and he assured Brown that he would get him into the Indoc that weekend.

Sniper Indocs are always brutal—constant hiking, mind games and physical and mental abuse—but Brown's story of what happened was hard to believe. He told us that the evaluators made them low-crawl through sewage and pissed on them. The sewage story was dubious; I had never seen any sewage in the area he described, though there was a sewage treatment plant nearby. In Carlos Hathcock's book, the famed Marine Sniper described being pissed on while lying in wait for a Viet Cong officer and I think that might have been where Brown got the story from.

Out of eight applicants, only Brown and two others passed. I was quite proud of Brown and let him know it, but there was a pall over the festivities. Even though Lt. Chapell had been forced to let Brown take the Indoc, no one at the regimental level could make him give Brown up if they wouldn't give him a replacement. Replacements are divvied out by HQMC and Supply had already received three replacements that year. Brown wasn't going anywhere.

After Brown went over his head and took the Sniper Indoc, Lt. Chapell had it in for him. When Lt. Chapell went through the company family contact roster, he thought he found some ammunition. It appeared that Brown put a different woman's name down as his wife than he had previously. Lt. Chapell started questioning people about Brown's private life and everyone's story was different. Brown was so mysterioso; he was such a liar and a fantasist that, since nothing could be believed about him, *everything* could be believed. Someone brought up the theory that maybe Brown's wife decided to go by her middle name, but when SSgt. D's office records were checked, the new female name did not match the old middle name. I started to believe the lieutenant's theory. Though Brown lived in nearby LA, he only went home on weekends since it was "too far away."

Yet almost every night, he would drive all the way down to Pacific Beach in San Diego with Mundaca to party. I could see him having another wife down there.

When Lt. Chapell thought he had enough of a case, he went to the company office to bring it up to the CO. He returned twenty minutes later, looking dejected and embarrassed. The answer was deceptively simple—there was another Marine named Brown who had just joined the company. Brown had scored against Lt. Chapell for the second time in two weeks, without even know-ing it.

Iraq was in the news more and more and the battalions started preparing to deploy. My grunt skills were hopelessly rusty, so I started asking for time in the field, which was unheard of. Lt. Hazen told me about a training op which was supposed to be the largest heliborne operation since the Gulf War. I asked to go and he approved. Golf had gotten their new machinegunners and I would get to work with the boots for the first time. I loved helos and couldn't wait to get back on them. I told my friends that I would be going on the 9-day exercise with them. They seemed both proud of me and incredulous that I had asked to go to the field.

A few days before the op though, Lt. Chapell said he absolutely needed me to work that week. The dire emergency wasn't anything big, but an officer isn't any-thing without men to lead and he didn't want to lose me. It was the end of the fiscal year and I had repaired about as much as I could, though my work was suf-fering. My mind was on war and I no longer cared if PE matched RA funds. Lt. Hazen ordered me to work in his office at regiment so he could keep a closer eye on me, but I was managed to finagle my way out of that. War was looming and the only skills I had that were sharp were stapling and typing.

I kept subtly hinting to Lt. Chapell that I needed to go back to my unit before the war, but that didn't get anywhere. I became less and less subtle until I finally just blurted it out. He tried to avoid the subject, so I pressed him on it. I hadn't been to the field or shot a weapon in nine months. He told me with a straight face that we wouldn't land in the Middle East and go to war the next day; I could brush up on my knowledge on the flight over. Nice. In the last year, my buddies back in Golf had gone to Squad Leaders Course, Division Machinegunners School, Martial Arts Instructor Course, MOUT instructor, and Corporals Course. I had gone to Division Comptrollers Course. I was caught in a Catch-22; even when HQ CO got some spots in those schools, Lt. Chapell wouldn't send me because I "wasn't really" from HQ CO and it would be a "waste" of a billet. He even told me that I could only go to the rifle range after everyone else in the shop had gone, even the ones who weren't going to Iraq.

I figured that I'd go the Ortiz route and start screwing up and being lazy until Lt. Chapell got pissed and kicked me out of his shop. To that end, I almost stopped functioning entirely. I went two weeks without doing one constructive thing and I finally got thrown a bone—Lt. Chapell let me go to the field. The weather was beautiful; not only would I be in the field, but I would be the vehicle commander for a Humvee. Whenever there is a field op in a POG unit, the squads are cobbled together out of whoever they can find. I had a cook as my gunner and a mechanic as my driver. The fourth spot would be taken by the new company first sergeant, First Sergeant Booker.

Going to the field with a Humvee was strange for me. Getting the vehicle ready took half the day. Although the Marines in the company were supposed to rotate who went to the field, it inevitably ended up being the same guys each time. Those guys didn't really mind going; going to the field once a month was a nice vacation from work and family. They didn't do it enough to get sick of it. Since weight wouldn't be an issue, I loaded the vehicle down with pogeybait.

Cpl. McGrogan, the cook, ended up being a great guy. The only weird thing about him was his predilection for pissing on one of the rear tires. I would find out later that was tradition with Humvees, but I didn't think it was tradition to piss uphill. I laughed as I watched him realize his mistake too late and jump around, trying to shake the piss off of his boots. The cooks are the last vestiges of the Old Corps and—though they might seem to have a girly job—they are some hard motherfuckers. They work ridiculous hours and get no appreciation ever. I've worked in the food service industry before and I know to never piss off a cook—a booger is the nicest thing he'll put in your food. Cooks tend to be constantly on edge and it is still normal in the kitchen for an argument between any two ranks to turn into a behind-closed-doors, no-rank "discussion."

I switched places with McGrogan and manned the .50 cal. in the turret. I loved that weapon dearly, but hadn't fired it in since SOI. I always assumed that the turrets in humvees were automated, but it was only a hook on a handle that kept the turret in place. If you pulled the handle, you could swivel the turret 360 degrees. I couldn't help but smile like an idiot; this was the kind of thing I had enlisted for.

We drove deep into the hills and I found out the real mission of Headquarters Company: to constantly put up and tear down a small city worth of tents that the regiment would be commanded from. The main tent was almost a thousand square feet, had several rooms and was air-conditioned to protect the electronics inside. Putting up this mobile fortress was a herculean task and even the staff NCOs helped out. It was exhausting work, but it was impressive when, after an hour or so, a valley filled with buffalo chips was transformed into a command base for an entire Marine Corps infantry regiment.

Instead of patrolling all night like we would in the grunts, all we had to do was watch a road in our humvee. That sounded easy, but since First Sergeant Booker was our fourth man, we only had three people to man the turret. I was back to my old boot days of a maximum of two hours of sleep in a row in the field. We got a call that every vehicle had to give up one man to be an aggressor to probe the defenses. I must have explained to half the regiment that we only had three guys and taking one would mean that none of us got any sleep, but it fell on deaf ears. When the Marine Corps need bodies, they get them—no matter what.

I volunteered myself to be an aggressor, since it sounded like fun. They put six of us in a humvee and drove us out of the perimeter. They let us out within sight of the defenses. It looked to me like they were trying to set themselves up for a slam dunk and a pat on the back. Salazar was usually sarcastic with everyone, but since we were in my element, he deferred to me. Since I was a corporal, I got the better pair of NVGs (7 Bravos) and I quickly fell in love with them. When I was a boot I only got to use the monocular 14s and spent most of the time falling into ditches. With the binocular 7Bs on, I could walk as well at night as I could on a sunny street. I took Salazar on a long, meandering flanking movement to the blind side of their defenses. The others had given up and purposefully walked into the defenses so that they could go to sleep, but I had something to prove. Salazar was a marathon runner, but even he got winded following the steep course I took. I was happy to see that I hadn't lost my grunt skills. We made it within 30 feet of the command tent, which was well within grenade range.

Being a POG in the field was a lot different than being a grunt. There was no reason to bury myself under seven warming layers; when I got cold I just flipped on the heater. My boots barely touched the ground the entire field op. I got my first experience of sleeping on a warm hood in the field, which was like heaven. The only hard part was assembling and dis-assembling the huge tent-town every day. The second morning, my vehicle was chosen to ferry a major back to Mateo. I had already ravaged my pogeybait stash and was looking forward to a resupply. While driving down the road, the wind chill in the turret was painful, but the hot breakfast more than made up for it. As I walked through the chow hall, I was especially proud of my dirty face and faded cammies—the hallmark of any true grunt.

The three days in the field did me good, but it only made it worse when I got back to the office. Getting back to Golf Company seemed hopeless. I still had one option, though I had never known anyone who used it. The Marine Corps has a process called Request Mast, in which anyone of any rank can make a formal request to anyone of any superior rank. It is used when your immediate chain-of-command is not amenable to your needs and you want someone with more weight on their shoulder to listen to you. Going around the chain-of-command is a huge military faux pas for several reasons. First of all, it calls into the question the leadership of your immediate superiors, implying that they can't fix things on their own level. It is also a tacit way of saying they're wrong and that you are "telling" on them. The general feeling was that only whiners used request masts and it was usually done to get out of intense training like a hike or a CAX.

I ran my situation past the other guys in the shop and they agreed with me that Request Mast was my best choice. It was November then and everyone was sure that we were going to war, yet I was not being allowed to train as I would fight. I didn't even know the junior Marines I would be leading into combat. When I broached the idea of using a request mast, Sgt. Pucci got a devilish grin. He liked the idea of me doing an end-run around Lt. Chapell and sticking it to him. I still liked Lt. Chapell, but with war this close, I thought he was showing disregard for my life and those who would be under my command by not letting me train. When I told Lt. Chapell what I was going to do, he looked like he was going to have a snit. He then dismissed me, saying that other officers would not go against him. When I turned my Request Mast in to the company office, it caused a minor stir since barely anyone ever did that.

The next day, First Sergeant Booker called me in to his office. He was a career Force Recon operator and a true grunt who hated being in a POG company. He had been expecting a sob story, but his dour expression changed into excitement when he heard my reason for wanting to leaving HQ Company. He told me that a Request Mast was unnecessary since I had a legitimate complaint and he asked why I hadn't come straight to him. I said that I thought that since I brought it up to my lieutenant and he nixed it, that Request Mast was my only option. He shook his head and told me he'd get me in to see the company commander as soon as possible. A good first sergeant is more valuable than gold; by the time they hit that billet they know most of the powerful people on base and a few phone calls can solve almost anything.

Captain Cashman looked more like a banker than a Marine Corps Infantry officer, but looks can be deceiving. During his first PT session with us, I was shocked when he busted out 20 perfect pull-ups without even getting red in the face and then ran three miles in less than nineteen minutes. For reasons of bureaucracy, they had to eliminate my FAP to get me out of it. Approval for that would have to come from the Regimental XO. Luckily for me, the Regimental XO was the same moto dog that approved Brown to go for the sniper indoc.

The next day, Lt. Chapell glumly asked me how long I would need to turn everything over to Kim. Once I had Kim spun up, I could take off. In the POGs, they usually make a big deal whenever anyone leaves the shop, giving him a plaque or a gift, but I didn't want anything—I just wanted to go. I got word later that Lt. Chapell got me a unit coin, but I never went back to get it.

I had spent scant time with my grunt buddies over the last year, but I had come by enough to keep track of things. Silva and the others had left for MSG school in the spring, but Showers had come back to Golf. After 9/11, HQMC had briefly relaxed their rule against MSG Marines having any kids, but they then changed their mind and chaptered Shower out for that same reason. Showers was embarrassed to be back, especially since he was told that if he didn't make it through MSG school, he would be sent to another grunt unit. At least he came out of the whole ordeal with 60 days of free leave. They had made everyone who went MSG extend their enlistments by six to 15 months and Showers got his extension cancelled, which he was happy about.

Mohler had been the section leader while I was gone and he had functioned as a lightning rod for trouble. The new chain-of-command did not follow the old model, in which the NCOs were the backbone of the company, Before, when NCOs were counseled, it was done behind closed doors so as to not undermine their authority in front of their boots, but Mohler had been humiliated in front of the boots on several occasions for very minor reasons.

Just as I had predicted in Oki, what little bits of sanity Reed had left were tossed aside when he became a senior Marine and a corporal. Hardly a day went by when he didn't have a freak-out, blow-up or pick a fight over the stupidest thing imaginable. What's more, he would always pull his childishness in front of the boots. I remembered the united front my seniors projected and how it took me six months to figure out that half of them hated each other. I later asked Rager how long it took him to realize that there was something seriously wrong with Reed and he told me, "Two days." Like with Ortiz, the chain-of-command was completely oblivious, thinking Reed was a good Marine.

Rager was already well-established in life when he decided to enlist. His prize possession was a huge, white Ford truck. A month before Thanksgiving leave, Rager told someone that he would be leaving his truck at the barracks over the break, since he was flying home. Reed overheard that and asked Rager if he could use his truck while he was gone. Rager didn't want to give a corporal a hard "no", so he told Reed that he "probably" wouldn't let him borrow it.

A month later, the company was dismissed for Thanksgiving leave and everyone headed up to their rooms to change into civvies. Within a few minutes, Reed knocked on Rager's door, smiling cheerfully.

"Hey Rager, can I get the keys now? I want to beat traffic."

"Corporal?"

"Your keys. You said that you'd let me borrow your truck while you were gone. You know, since you won't be using it."

"I don't believe I said that, corporal."

"What?! You—I planned my whole leave on having your car! You're not just going to leave me stranded here!"

"Look, corporal, I wouldn't let my best friend borrow my truck for an entire week."

"But you said I could borrow your truck, Rager!"

"No, I said you *couldn't* borrow it."

"No, you didn't! You said I *probably* couldn't borrow it!"

During Seahorse Wind, he constantly harangued the boots, while refusing to help anyone out on the long hikes. After they completed a hike with gas masks on, Reed told Lt. Sprincin that he had thrown up in his gas mask; then had such incredible dedication that he ate the vomit and soldiered on, never missing a step. Moser had been next to Reed the entire time and knew that was a lie, but Sprincin believed Reed and wrote him up for an award, which showed how disconnected Sprincin was with his own platoon. One need only spend an hour with us to see that Reed was a constant thorn in our sides.

Nearly every training event had been ruined when Reed turned it into his own personal sideshow. He was completely out of control and bringing the entire section down. He had developed a strange obsession with Mohler. Mohler could make friends with a rock and, though he absolutely hated Reed, he still treated him like a human being, which Reed took complete advantage of. Reed and Mohler were roommates and, while Mohler had a huge and ever-growing group of friends, Reed couldn't buy a friend. Reed invited himself everywhere Mohler went and would show up unannounced at Mohler's girlfriend's house, sixty miles away, if he knew that Mohler was there. The strangest thing was that Reed picked more fights with Mohler than anyone else. Reed wanted to kill Mohler because he wouldn't chip in on the Playstation II, that Reed bought and then declared was "theirs." He just assumed that since they were roommates, they were married.

Back then, I would try to talk to Reed and get him to see that we needed to stick together, but no matter how much loyalty he was shown, there was no issue too small to send him into a fury. He walked into Miller from Third's room one day uninvited and plopped down on the couch. Miller was an easy-going guy and knew Reed had no friends, so he didn't make a fuss. Miller and a buddy were discussing a movie and Reed, who considered himself the ultimate expert on everything, butted in and corrected Miller on some bit of trivia. Miller argued the point in a conversational manner, and Reed decided to clarify his point by throwing Miller's expensive paintball gun off the second deck, breaking it. When Miller threatened to report Reed to the first sergeant so he could get reimbursement, Reed threatened to rat him out for having women in his room after hours. This was normal human interaction in Reedland.

I had numerous car problems while I was on FAP, often being stranded on base over-night, and Reed generously let me crash in his room whenever I needed. Even though he was a nut, he had been an excellent roommate and I told him that I wouldn't mind having him as a roommate again if we went back to Oki. I kept weighing him and coming up on the side of forgiveness. While I never got the feeling he had been physically abused, I knew he had been constantly belittled by his father and bullied by his peers. I could understand that, after he learned how to fight in high school, he would turn into a sad, minor bully himself. He had some good qualities: he was dedicated and enthusiastic about being a grunt. He was just raised poorly and I couldn't fault him for that, but he was an adult now and he needed to act like one.

While I was on FAP, Reed started having "brain problems" that I'm not entirely sure were fake. Often when he was in his barracks room with Mohler, he would suddenly drop to the ground "unconscious." Mohler got so used to these dramatics that he would just leave Reed where he lied, stepping over him when he needed to get to the microwave. Reed would "wake up" and ask for a corpsman, who would always check Reed and tell him that all of his vital signs were normal. Reed was able to convince the MO to get him an appointment to get an MRI, but he never went. I assumed that since he knew his fainting spells were fake, he didn't want to be found out. Looking back, I wished that he had gotten checked out. Reed was so strange, paranoid, delusional, self-hating, violent and needy that there might have been something physiologically wrong with his brain that could have been detected.

There was no end to the strange stories about Reed. Crozier told me—and his story was corroborated by several others—that shortly after the boots arrived, Reed had "accidentally" let it slip that it was his birthday. He then told the boots that there was a "company tradition" that people got one spanked on their birthdays, bemoaning that he would have to receive twenty-one spankings, one for each year. He got onto all fours and looked back at the boots, red-faced and excited, and told them to get to it.

There was no spanking tradition.

Reed was the third squad leader since none of the higher-ups knew of his tantrums and instability. Since we were under-manned, his squad was light and as soon as he heard I was coming back, he asked for me to be in his squad. I didn't mind at first, thinking that I could work with him better than anyone else.

Rivaling him as the biggest problem in the section was a boot named Carpenter. Carpenter would end up getting a separation for having mental problems two years later, but it only took me about ten minutes to figure out he was a whack-job. Carpenter never knew his father and was extremely awkward socially. Tall and gaunt, he was preternaturally strong, or as grunts more succinctly put it, he had "retard strength". He had gotten kicked out of the Army for failing to adapt. He slowness seemed to bespeak a learning disability, but he also showed the after-effects of being a heavy drug-user. He could astound you with trivia, and then appal you with his total lack of understanding of the simplest things. He constantly got his fellow boots in trouble, so they were sick of them, but he had recently done something to piss the entire platoon off.

Carpenter was absolutely in love with his trailer-trash hooker of a wife. They had met when she served him at a diner five years earlier. His "brother"—who we would find out later was his mentor in the "Big Brother/Big Sisters" program—encouraged him to ask her out, which was strange since they were on a road trip, hundreds of miles from home. That didn't stop Carpenter from exchanging numbers with her and starting a telephone relationship that lasted on and off for the next four years. They got married a month after he hit The Fleet, even though they had barely seen each other in real life. She was given the benefit of the doubt by us, but she managed to out-do anyone's worst prediction.

Ryan had let Carpenter crash at his house, which Carpy completely took advantage of, staying there for months and moving his wife in after the wedding. Carpenter was horrible with money and he and his wife were soon broke. He mentioned that to Monty, the acting platoon sergeant, who decided to have a platoon fund to help Carpenter out. They gave Carpenter more than a hundred dollars without asking for repayment. A week later, Carpenter was again complaining of being broke and Ryan let it be known that Carpenter's wife had spent the money on expensive booze and knick-knacks for the house. The whole platoon was pissed, but Reed lost his mind and pulled Carpenter into his room for some Old Corps action.

During most of the time I was on FAP, Montgomery was the acting platoon sergeant, since he was the senior NCO, having been promoted the same day as me and Mora, who went to MSG. Monty developed a rep as a self-serving and hypocritical prick, and was especially hated by the boots. He was notorious for milking a simple hand injury; using it to get out of PT, field ops and hikes. Monty's personality was somewhere between a game show host and a used car salesman and he had inveigled himself into the good graces of the higher-ups, much to the chagrin of the rest of the platoon.

Doughy and balding, Monty, like me, joined in his late twenties. To his credit, unlike me, he did not get brain-washed; he was confident and charming with his seniors, who treated him like an equal. He was gone for almost all of the work-up we did as boots, since he went on a month-long NBC school, followed by the Division Shooting Match. Thusly, he missed out on all of the degradation of being a boot. In Oki, Devers would excuse him from working parties and weekly field day so that they could hang-out together in his room. Though Monty was widely hated, he was also quite popular. Though he could be amazingly selfish, he could also be gregarious and funny. Also, since he was so hooked in to the power structure of the company, it was usually to your best interest to be on his good side.

My first time in formation back with the platoon was a mixed bag. Everyone was friendly and Mohler told me that he had missed my sense of humor, but I knew that none of the old problems had been solved and many were much worse. Boyd was gone, but Reed had more than taken up the slack. I was still glad to be back in the grunts, even though I knew it would be harder on me physically.

The first boot I had a run-in was with a kid nicknamed "Out-of-action" Jackson, who had gone on permanent light duty as soon as he got to The Fleet. He had learned how to play the system, successfully avoiding almost any work and getting a medical discharge that was dubious at best. Though he wasn't training, he was still on our roll and we were responsible for him. After the first few days, I noticed that he was always missing, which caused problems for Mohler. I found Jackson and told him that he still had to check in with us. He shrugged and told me he'd see what he could do. I locked him on immediately, which seemed to surprise him. Mohler had attempted to charge Jackson several times for being UA or disobeying orders, but every time he pushed the charges forward First Sergeant Young refused to pursue the charges. The fact that Jackson and the first sergeant were both black raised suspicions on why Jackson wasn't getting nailed to the wall.

Jackson didn't report in the next morning. I found him in the company office, where he told me he had been ordered to remain by the company gunny. He had me over a barrel until I could check with the gunny and confirm that order. When I did find the gunny, he told me that he *had* ordered Jackson to stay in the office at all times, but it was while ago and for a different situation. Jackson was already adept at playing mommy against daddy.

Later that day, I ordered Jackson to watch the phones at lunch so one of the Marines who actually trained wouldn't have to do it. While I was gone, Jackson left for a doctor's appointment and didn't even bother to find a replacement for him on the phones. That morning he had said he could never leave the office and now he couldn't stay. I wrote a formal counseling for him and gave it to him when he came back from the doctor. He read it slowly, shaking his head and smirking the entire time. I cocked my hand back to smack him, remembered I was in the company office, and then adjusted my swing, knocking the pen out of his hand. He denied smirking at me, which was even more punk-ass than actually doing it. I finished counseling and told him to get out of my sight, then turned around and saw that the CO had watched our exchange. The company commander smiled, tacitly approving the whole situation. The next day, Jackson was officially moved to HQ platoon.

I asked my buddies about our new platoon commander, Lt. Sprincin, and received a litany of complaints. By all accounts, he was an aloof and officious prick who never had a good word about anyone in his platoon. Even worse, he had singled out Reed as being an exemplary Marine for the "puking in the gas mask" episode. When he happened upon Reed arguing with Ross during one of Reed's daily tantrums, he counseled <u>Ross</u> for arguing with a fellow NCO. Though I believed my buddies' stories, I leavened their assessments with an understanding of the natural animosity NCOs had toward officers. I came from a family of officers, so I understood that much of the time, when an officer was "acting like a fucking asshole, dude", he was just enforcing necessary standards. I would give Lt. Sprincin the benefit of the doubt.

The first time I saw Lt. Sprincin was during an NCO's de-brief after the platoon had hiked out of the field. Just as my buddies had told me, he did not have one positive thing to say about an entire platoon of men who had hiked 17 miles in the rain with more than one hundred pounds on their backs. Officers aren't supposed to be cheerleaders, but a basic tenet of leadership is to buck your men up as much as you run them down. His attitude was so dismissive that there was a total disconnect between him and "his" platoon. He seemed more like an inspector sent by HQMC, than like a line company boot-tenant that would be fighting by our side.

After the meeting, we had a gear inspection. Ross let me lay out my gear on the spare bed in his room, since he was one of the lucky few who had a room to himself. The lock on his door didn't work, which he had repeatedly brought up to his higher-ups, to no effect. We were told to fall out for a formation, so I had a boot pass to Lt. Sprincin that I had to stay and guard my gear, which was unsecured. He passed back to me that I needed to be at the formation, regardless.

Fifteen minutes later, I returned to find that all of my warming layers had been stolen. Marines are notorious thieves and the first thing a boot is taught in SOI is the old Marine Corps adage, "Gear adrift is a Marine's gift", which means that it is almost a Marine's right to steal unsecured gear. I went straight to Lt. Sprincin and explained what had just happened. He responded that I could relax; I wasn't in trouble for "losing" my gear. I would have ample time to buy replacements. I re-explained that it was not my fault that the gear was stolen from a room whose lock was notorious for not working and that I wanted him to sign a missing gear statement that would let me replace the $40 of gear from Supply for free. He wouldn't hear of it and dismissed me outright. That would be the <u>best</u> interaction I ever had with him.

During night training, we practiced calling in MEDEVACs and CASEVACs (medical and casualty evacuations) from helos hovering over The Backyard. Knowing that my knowledge was rusty, I took voluminous notes, but when I looked up halfway through, I noticed that none of the boots had written anything down. I yelled at them and quizzed them on what we had been taught, but none of them could answer correctly. I told them that this wasn't something useless like a hike; this training could save someone's life. After the training ended, I decided to drive the point home. We were a quarter-mile from the barracks, but I would show them how far that could be. I wanted to thrash them, but I wanted to teach them as well. I told them that we would simulate what would happen if they couldn't get a bird for their buddy. I aimed my finger at Rager and "shot" him; they would now have to carry him back to the barracks. We patrolled in the dark, pretending we were in enemy territory. I made them speed up, slow down, and hide in the bushes—simulating battle conditions. I "shot" Fernandez and now half the squad was dragging their two wounded buddies. They were drenched in sweat and we had only gone about 300 meters in the cool night air.

People stared as my Marines carried each other onto the basketball court in front of the barracks. After letting them catch their breath, I told them that not learning how to save a fellow Marine's life is like saying you don't care whether he lives or dies. Victory in Iraq was assured, but the odds were that at least one person in the company was going to go down. Out there, all we would have was each other, so we had to take care of each other. I cut them loose and instead of them being five demoralized, bitter boots, they seemed to actually get it. Instead of getting away from me as soon as they could, several of them hung back to discuss training and the upcoming war.

Our next field op would be a truncated version of the SOTG Raid Package, since we needed time to prepare to go to Iraq. Although the order had not been given yet, we were updating our wills and getting our affairs in order. The raid would be textbook—we would fly out, patrol to an "enemy camp," engage, and then egress by chopper. Though Reed was a junior corporal to me, he still lead the squad; I didn't sweat it, since I knew I'd be picking up sergeant soon. I would be a team leader, with Rager as my gunner and Carpenter as my ammo man. Between Carpenter and Reed, it seemed like I was book-ended by defective human beings. I had been told good things about Rager, but he didn't make a big impression at first. All I knew was that he was the "old man" of the boots at the age of 26.

We drew our weapons and ammo and I handed two cans of blanks to Carpenter. Knowing his reputation for fucking up everything, I kept my words simple. "Carpenter. Here. These are yours." We put our weapons and ammo in the locker room and set up a guard over lunch time. When everyone came back from chow, they were supposed to grab their weapons and ammo and head down to the backyard where the helos would pick us up.

After lunch, I went down to the backyard and got in my designated stick. I made sure that my team was up and got my game face on. I wasn't a boot anymore, just looking at for myself, I was in charge of a team. When I asked Carpenter a question, he responded languidly without getting off his ass or even facing me, which is a big deal in the grunt world. I lit into him and he jumped up to parade rest. Ross was taken aback, never having seen me yell like that.

I realized that Carpenter didn't have his ammo. I asked him where it was and he gave me a blank look.

"The ammo! The ammo, motherfucker! Where is it?"

Blank stare; then a look of recognition.

"Oh, you mean those boxes?"

"Yes, Carpenter, the fucking 'boxes'—the fucking *ammo cans!*"

"I didn't know I was supposed to bring them, corporal. I just thought you wanted me to put them somewhere."

My mind almost short-circuited with rage. Where did we get this guy? He wasn't even messing with me—that was the sad thing. The Marine Corps never tries to complicate anything. They always make every instruction and job title as simple as can be. Carpenter's billet was Ammo Man. Can you guess what that job entails?

Reed was nonchalant about it, which didn't make sense since he flipped out about everything. I got the feeling he had told Carpenter not to bring the ammo, so that we wouldn't have to spend much time cleaning the weapons.

As the birds came in, a personal problem arose. I had made the mistake of drinking two Mountain Dews during lunch. I tried to keep my mind on the mission as my team got on the bird, but as soon as I tightened my seat belt over my distended bladder, I knew I was in trouble. This may sound like a ridiculous thing to worry about, but let me make an aside. Besides paying bills, not having potty problems is one of the few things that distinguishes adults from children. As silly as it sounds, constantly being in potty distress as an adult is endlessly mortifying. One of the things I hated most about being a 27-year-old boot was having to ask my 21-year-old senior if I could use the restroom and being told "no." A man in his late twenties doing the potty dance is not a pretty sight.

I put my ear plugs in before I even got on the bird. I used them whenever necessary, which always engendered derisive comments from some "tuff" guy. While in Oki, I heard Boyd say that he thought it was cool to not wear ear plugs when firing the mortar system until his ears started ringing constantly. Rock on, Boyd.

We were making good time and I guessed that we would be down in ten minutes. I could make it. When we got to the site though, they started making wide circles, trying to eat up time to simulate how long it would really take to get to an objective. We were flying over a residential section of Fallbrook; so many houses down there, so many toilets—it didn't seem fair. It was then that my grotesque grunt mind came up with the perfect solution. I knew from my Human Sexuality class that you couldn't piss when you had an erection, so I used my imagination to concoct an appropriate scenario. Since 99% of my mind still had to focus on not wetting my pants, I didn't have a lot of brainpower left over to come up with a plausible situation. I envisioned us landing and having a cute black chick with big tits come on the helo and start blowing me. It worked; whatever mechanism blocks that piss flow was in full effect.

The bird landed and I bid adieu to my Nubian princess. I had enough professionalism to get into a proper defense, but as soon as the birds took off, I rushed into the bushes and relieved myself. We patrolled to the enemy camp; this was my first time in the field in front of the boots and I wanted to show that I knew what I was doing. I patrolled by the book, constantly checking my surroundings in all directions and I noticed that most people were just walking like it was Sunday in the park. I didn't want to step on the other seniors' toes by correcting their boots, but some of the machinegunners were bunching up. They seemed surprised that I corrected them.

We went up a hill that was so steep at one point that the man in front had to pull the next man up. Whoever was in front of me buddy-fucked the hell out of me and just took off once he got to the top. I tried to climb up the slope, but every time I grabbed a clump of dirt, it broke off in my hand. Moser finally gave me a boost and I pulled him up in return.

At the top, we had to low-crawl to keep from being spotted. Most Marines hate low-crawling, but I love it since it's exactly the sort of G.I.Joe thing you do when you're six years old. I had to hurry to catch up to the elevens who had scouted the route. In combat, the guns go in first and set up in the best spot to provide supporting fire for the elevens who will sweep through the target and conduct the raid. The elevens are the movie stars and the machinegunners are the supporting actors, but one doesn't work without the other. We carry more shit than they do, but we don't have to go as far.

The raid went well, though I was envious of the elevens when they got to sweep and clear the village. After we patrolled to our exfiltration site, the elevens kept walking in front of my machinegun like the exercise was over, but we were still supposed to be tactical. We had a long wait in which I tactically looked at bugs and yelled at Carpenter for falling asleep.

Rager aggravated a foot injury and didn't go on the next raid, which I found out at the last minute. With a two-man gun team, I would have to carry the tripod, ammo bag and ammo, in addition to my M-16. It was a ridiculous load and Reed, though he was carrying nothing, didn't offer any help. I was told this was par for the course whenever he was in a leadership position. I put a sling on the tripod so that I could be hands-free to use my rifle, but that brilliant idea came back and bit me on the ass.

When we landed deep in the hills, we were told to execute a movement-to-contact, which is a much faster pace than a regular patrol. I was carrying more weight than anyone else and I hadn't patrolled in more than a year. To make matters worse, the ammo bag strap and the sling I put on the tripod worked together to give my neck what my DIs would have called an "outstanding blood choke." Reed saw the trouble I was having and didn't lift a hand.

We got to a steep hill and the elevens rushed up like little mice, but I was totally red-faced; getting choked out by my own gear. The hill was so steep you could barely stand and after struggling to get to one spot, I was told I had to move 50 meters to the left. To stay out of sight of the enemy, I had to go down on the steepest part and kept slipping down. Reed was nowhere to be found. I finally spotted him and yelled for help, but he pretended not to hear me. When I got close enough that he couldn't pretend any longer, he said that he had to go check on the other gun team.

I finally got into place, but the raid was a wash. The line was stretched too far back on the crest of the hill and they could barely see the target. My absence during the FAP showed itself again when someone yelled, "Australian Peel!" I sat there waiting for something to happen and then noticed that the entire company was staring at me, waiting for me to do something. Beltran, my buddy from MSPF who was now a sniper, told me it meant that since I was on the far right, I was supposed to go down the hill first. Oh, *that* Australian Peel.

Though I was spent, the rest of the company considered it a cake walk. Rampone helped me carry the gear since Reed refused. To make things even peachier, a seam in the crotch of my cammie pants split all the way down to my knee. Not only was I exhausted and being choked out by my own gear, but I was also showing more leg than a damn Rockette.

The helos came in low and it was quite a sensation to see the bottom of the bird whizzing fifteen feet above my head. After we landed at Mateo, I desperately wanted to go fix my pants, but Reed was afraid of getting in trouble for letting me go and told me to stay. I could have pulled seniority or just gaffed him off, but I wanted to show the united front that my seniors had shown.

The Christmas break was approaching and I knew I had some things I needed to work on. My knowledge was fairly good; but I needed to get in better shape, hiking-wise. They gave us a big send-off for Christmas, saying to expect it to be our last time with our families for awhile. For some reason, even though plenty of people lived in the area, they gave Ross duty right in the middle of the break. I told him that I'd take his duty, which earned me the eternal appreciation of his mother, so I'm told.

During the break, I constantly checked the Internet for news that President Bush had finally given the "go" order. I went to the gym, but after three days of running, a pain in my knee got so bad that I couldn't run anymore. I told myself I couldn't just quit, so I jumped back on and gritted my teeth through the pain, imagining having to run and fight with an injury in Iraq. Finally, it became clear that I was just going to injure myself further, so I stopped. Just like in the SOTG raid package two years earlier, the constant movement on the side of mountains had aggravated my knee.

When I returned to work after leave, it was the first time I had ever been happy to go back to Pendleton. President Bush had all but confirmed that we were invading Iraq and I was on Cloud Nine. I thought of the old Chinese curse, "May you live in interesting times." My last year in the Marines might be miserable, but it sure wouldn't be boring.

As soon as we got to work, we were told that there would be a battalion-wide meeting in the gym. Though they still wouldn't tell us what it was for, we all knew it would be the "Go to War" brief. The brief was the usual, cheapjack Marine Corps affair, with a presentation that was neither visible or audible. Through the wah-wah of the unintelligible voices, we gleaned some solid news—we would leave in two weeks.

We were scheduled for a week of MOUT training at an abandoned Air Force Base near Victorville, but we hoped it would we canked since we were leaving so soon. No such luck. I was of two minds; I would have liked more time at home, but I knew I needed the training. I'd rather live through the war than have one more week of watching "That 70's Show" reruns (though the margin was close).

I should have had my mind on preparing for war, but my main worry was Reed, who was completely out of control. While forming up to march one block to the armory, Reed had the section assemble right in the middle of a large puddle. Elias casually suggested that he have them form up ten feet to the left where it was dry, and Reed flipped out, mocking him and challenging him to fight in front of the boots.

We received our desert uniforms and boots and we were ordered to wear our new boots on a three-mile hike to the grenade range. Even a boot in SOI knows that you break a pair of boots in before hiking in them, but we weren't given that luxury. True to form, we lost half a platoon's worth of Marines on the way there. I kept up, but knew that I wouldn't make it back. Rager's foot was ripped up so badly that he bled through the leather of his boot, which I didn't even know was possible.

I've never been crazy about grenades for two reasons. The first is that they are disappointing as all get-out. I grew up watching action movies where one grenade could blow up a small house and the most powerful explosive in the world was one grenade thrown into a box of grenades. In reality, grenades can only kill in a five-meter radius and they don't do a damn thing to vehicles. They don't even make a big ball of flame, just a puff of dirt kicked up off the ground by the concussion. The other reason I'm not a fan of grenades is that I throw like a damn girl. While the tossing a practice grenade in SOI, I actually hit my own head with my hand and the grenade hit the dirt and rolled about ten feet before popping off. The instructor shook his head, very worried for the future of the Marine Corps.

My feet were killing me and simply walking to the grenade pit was agony. Since I was afraid of flubbing the throw, I threw the grenade from my shoulder like a shot put. My foot hurt worse than when I had fractured it on the 26-miler, but I didn't tell anyone since there was no point. They weren't letting Rager ride back in one of the humvees, even though he could barely stand. I would stay with the pack as long as I could, but I knew it was hopeless. I could only keep up so long.

A long, slow climb took us the first third of the way and my old talent for hills helped me keep up and even pass some people. Leaning forward to get up the hill took the pressure off my ripped-up heel. As soon as we hit the top though, I was done. Rager and I fell back, but no one harangued us. Everyone knew it was bogus to make us march in new boots.

SSgt. Melendez had just come to the company, straight from the drill field. Though he was the shortest staff NCO I'd ever seen, he didn't have a trace of the dreaded Little Man's Syndrome. His toughness came from the fact that he didn't feel the need to show it. He didn't act little, so he didn't get treated like a punk.

True to form, Reed sidled up and "helped" Rager and I. Reed was infamous for always falling back to "help" the stragglers, which let him walk as slow as possible while still getting plaudits for "looking out for his Devil Dogs." This wasn't the crazy, angry side of Reed, but it was a side that made people despise him just as much. He quickly told SSgt. Melendez about his award for puking in his gas mask and eating it. As Elias put it so well, "My dog eats his puke all the time and no one gave him an award." Reed would turn around every ten minutes ago and ask if we were OK to make himself look good.

We got to the barracks long after the rest of the company had gone to lunch. Rager hobbled to his room and I collapsed on my gear. It seemed like hiking would always be my downfall. I had finally gotten myself in shape to where I could hike well and now something stupid like new boots was making me look like a piker in front of the junior Marines. I went to Ross' room and slowly took my boots off. I was worried that the injury would turn out to be small and unremarkable and I would just be a bitch. After I peeled my sock off, a piece of skin as big as a potato chip separated from my heel. Scott walked by and I called him into the room. Scott was a good-hearted jock, but also a loud-mouth; if he saw that I had an actual injury, he would let everyone know. He jumped back when he saw the red pulp where the skin used to be. I could see in his face that he didn't think I was really hurt until he saw my heel. I spent the remainder of the lunch period showing off the hunk of skin and doing my Goldmember imper-sonation.

After lunch, we had a formation in which it was announced that I would be picking up sergeant at the beginning of February. The boots all seemed amazed at this "new" corporal picking up. Getting the news on the same day I had fallen out of a hike threw a pall on the excitement though.

The day we left for Victorville, I made my mark on Golf Company history. I was a bad hiker and "family problems" seemed to get me out of every field op (at least according to Ross and Moser it did), but I could come up with nicknames like Shakespeare. My piece de resistance—the crowning achievement of my nick-name-giving career—was "Swivelfoot" (actually the best nickname I ever came up with was "Cpl. Mommy combs my hair," but its only if you've seen a picture of the guy and I don't have one). Ross and I were getting moto since Victorville promised to be some kick-ass training, so we decided that everyone needed a cool G.I. Joe-style nickname. Mine became "Skidmark" because of the "shit-run" I had completed at CAX and Ross was "Swamp-ass" because of his penchant for not wearing underwear in the field. Showers was next to us, not bothering a soul in the world, when I gave my friend the appellation that will haunt him to his grave. My brother had a G.I. Joe with a loose knee joint that I called "Squeakyleg." I thought of how when you ran behind Showers during PT it made you dizzy because his foot would rotate almost all the way around every time he took a step. I called him "Swivelfoot" and peoples' eyes lit up. The greatest and most appro-priate nick-name in the history of Golf Company had been born.

While in Iraq, Levesque—that seedy French fuck—tried to re-write history and say that he came up with "Swivelfoot." It was only after coming up with sev-eral eye-witnesses that I was able to prove him wrong. Levesque was among a third wave of machinegunners that had been grabbed from the rifle platoons and sent to the Division Schools Machinegun Course along with the "real" 0331s. Jesse had somehow mutated Levesque's name to sound like "L'il Bitch" and Levesque took perverse pride in the nick-name. Levesque had a checkered his-tory. Levesque went UA right before we left for Oki and turned himself in while we were gone. Anyone who goes UA gets stuck with a shitbird rep for the rest of their life. He hadn't helped himself by being a drug pop twice. The funny thing was that he was a great grunt and one of the most moto machinegunners. He loved the gun and wouldn't give it up for anyone.

Staying at the barracks late one night, I was hanging out in Miller from Third's room when another friend of his brought in two young chicks, neither one especially good-looking. The chubbier one obviously knew Miller quite well and, after listening to her conversation for a few minutes, it was clear that she knew more about the company than the first sergeant. She used Marine jargon and dropped names like she had memorized the billet roster of the entire company. Miller wasn't exactly Brad Pitt, so I was surprised when he rebuffed her advances. I finally gleaned that she was Levesque's wife, though that is using the word "wife" loosely, much like she used her body. Often when my single Marine buddies would hear how much marriage pay I got, they would remark on how they should go out into town and marry some whore and then split the extra $1100 a month with her. To Levesque that wasn't just idle talk, it was a workable plan. He married a "Barracks whore"—a girl, usually plain or chubby, who jumps from Marine-to-Marine. They're easy to identify since they're the only women who can explain the difference between a company, a battalion and a regiment.

Miller asked her if she came to visit Levesque and she asked him why she would do that. She said she had to do her laundry and she was there to get her clothes. She then named five Marines and which pieces of clothing she left in each one's room.

While I was on FAP, the company office had wanted to bring Dart—the first of my generation to pick up sergeant—in to run the machinegun section because of perceived "leadership problems." None of us would deny that we were rough around the edges, but we were still the best machinegun section in the battalion. Dart was very short and so muscular that he was almost wider than he was tall. He was a go-getter and had earned his quick promotion, though many people grumbled about it. People said he had an attitude, but for as good as he was at almost everything, I found him remarkably humble. Nonetheless, I was glad when he wasn't chosen. It would have been a huge insult to the section for a rifleman to be made section leader.

If I had to fill The Corps with clones of just one Marine, I would have picked Moser. He had the most of the best qualities and the least of the worst. He was in great shape and sharp enough to pick up on any new skill taught to him, but plenty of people had that. There were few people who had those attributes in addition to the ones I valued the most—maturity and common sense. I never saw Moser get unduly angry or irrational. When I was section leader in Iraq, I gave him a disproportionate amount of responsibility and told him, "You fucked yourself by being reliable." He had been slow to pick up rank because of some minor infractions as a boot—"accidentally" flipping off the duty and refusing to remove a rebel flag he had hung in his barracks room after the sergeant major ordered him to take it down.

That brings me to another one of those things that you aren't supposed to talk about. Although almost no grunts are black, most of the high-ranking staff NCOs are. During my entire four years in Golf Company—in which I saw more than two hundred people come and go—there were four black Marines below the rank of corporal. In contrast, our regimental sergeant major, battalion sergeant major, three of our first sergeants and our master sergeant were all black. It seemed that there was a "glass ceiling" for non-black Marines. Half of the afore-mentioned black staff NCOs—including our regimental sergeant major, battalion sergeant major and first sergeant—were all POGs.

The funny thing was that the Marine Corps, at the lower enlisted ranks, was the most racially harmonious place I had ever seen. You didn't have a choice who you worked with, so it behooved you to get along with all types of people. There was no political correctness and the most vile things were said in jest on a daily basis, yet it was extremely rare for anyone to get offended. I never saw anyone refuse to work with someone or cause problems with another because of race.

Cpl. Chhav wasn't as good of a fit as Moser. He was in great shape and moti-vated, but he had one problem—he couldn't take a joke. In the politically-incor-rect environment of the grunts, you have to be able to laugh things off or you're going to go nuts. While nowhere as bad as Reed, he would either pick fights or walk off in a huff about mild comments that anyone else would just laugh off, like the time Ross threatened to blind-fold him with dental floss.

Victorville is like Barstow without the nightlife; half of the buildings are made of corrugated tin. We pulled into an old air force base and I got depressed when I realized that, even though it had been abandoned for ten years, it was still nicer than Pendleton. Though there were numerous empty barracks buildings, we ended up staying in an old ammo dump. As usual, our standard of living was as high as your average garden tool.

It took us all day to get there and all we had to eat was the one MRE we were given in the morning. I stood in formation, with a sharp headache, wondering why there was no food or water at the camp site. When someone asked Gunny Brouillet where they were, he derisively accused us of not filling our canteens or rationing our one MRE to last through the day, which pissed me off since the only duty of a company gunny is to provide water and food and when he failed on those two counts, he turned the blame on us.

That night, we went to the old commissary and received our MILES gear. MILES is the military version of Laser Tag—circa 1982 technology—but it was high-speed for us. The MILES company is privately run and we received the usual condescension we got from all civilians who worked with the military.

They crammed the entire company into a row of storage closets. I knew how nasty grunts could be, so I went outside to sleep by myself. I preferred to sleep in the cold than to be crammed in a parking space-sized concrete closet with fifteen burping and farting grunts who would probably piss in the corner instead of going outside.

After finding a gallon of tapioca pudding, God knows where, a 51 boot named Jolly bet that he could eat the entire can. When there is no television and you can't go anywhere, that sort of thing is highly entertaining. He ended up vomiting up a half-gallon of tapioca, but at least he gave it the old college try.

The next day, we were introduced to our evaluators and instructors. I shivered during the pre-dawn march to the base theater, remembering the bitter high-desert chill of the HAC during CAX. The training package was being run by the Warfighting lab, a tactical think-tank from the East Coast. While the other services are loaded with theoretical, forward-looking units like that, the Marine Corps is usually wistfully pining for the old days of the mounted cavalry.

They showed us a very disheartening movie in which our weapons were compared with the Soviet-style weapons that the Iraqis used. They had built several mock-up rooms in a field and hired a film crew to record them shooting the place to bits. Our rifles and SAWs used a small, 5.56mm round that has little penetrating power; smaller rounds are less likely to go through your enemy and into an innocent bystander. I had read in "Black Hawk Down" that the Rangers had to shoot the attacking Somalis five or six times just to stop them. The 7.62mm round our machineguns used would blow arms and heads off with a single round. This was the same round that *every* Iraqi rifle used. In the movie they showed us, the Iraqi rifle rounds would penetrate cinder block walls. One AK round went through a cinder-block wall, through two wooden interior walls and lodged itself in a metal office desk. In contrast, our rounds could barely go through *wood* and cinder-block walls might as well have been polished beryllium steel.

Communication within a squad is essential, especially in an urban environment, but all we had were hand-and-arm signals, which look really cool in movies, but basically all you can say with them is, "Stop," "Let's go," or "Get down." There's no hand-and-arm signal for "OK, we got shooters in the NW building, some spotters in the crowd and a suspicious truck." The PRRs (Personal Role Radio) that the Warfighter Lab provided us with were a god-send. PRRs looked like the radio headsets you'd see on a kid working the drive-thru at Burger King, but they were worth their weight in gold. Their range was about 250-500 meters and they were meant to be used as squad-level communicators.

After the usual Marine Corps scare tactics in which they told us how expensive the PRRs were and all the horrors that would befall anyone who lost or damaged theirs, we were cut loose in the parking lot to walk around and test them. Of course, someone immediately said, "We got a Black Hawk down!" which was kind of funny, but then you get idiots like Reed, who repeat it about twenty times. Even worse, Reed who would SHOUT EVERY THING HE SAID OVER THE PRRS! Reed would also interrupt every damn conversation and generally act like an idiot. He had perfected the art of ruining everything to such a high degree that he could actually pre-ruin things. Just knowing Reed would be involved in some future endeavor promised that it would suck. I made a mental not to never let him get a PRR when I was in charge.

Everyone needs a cool call sign, so I tried to get people to use the name of my childhood (and adulthood, let's face it) hero, "Snake-Eyes", but no one was biting. I ended up with "Grandpa". Afterward, I was pouting about people killing my moto when Ross reminded me that no one gets to nickname themselves. It's not like he wanted to be called "Dirty R." At least it wasn't something like "Ba-dildo".

The Warfighting Lab training package was usually two weeks long and they even had a 30-day version in which you acted like you were in a protracted city war, but we were doing a quick-and-dirty five-day version. We would train in the old base housing neighborhoods. After the base was decommissioned, a local woman bought the land and rented it out for training. She was also in the business of taking the houses that were salvageable, uprooting them entirely; then selling them God knows where. The buildings had been built in the fifties and Marines had been breaking windows and kicking down doors for the last few years, yet they were still nicer than the base housing in Pendleton.

The Marine Corps was really pulling out the stops. Several of the instructors were on exchange programs from ally armies; there were Australian and British Army and Royal Marines. I was taken aback the first time that one of the foreign soldiers yelled at us for goofing off; it was like your parents having the across-the-street neighbor spank you when you were bad.

Since we were training like we would fight, we received ten-pound, bullet-proof "Chicken Plates" for our Kevlar vests. Made of ceramic and covered in kevlar, they wouldn't stop an AK round, but they would protect us from shrapnel, which is just as deadly and more prevalent in battle. We had always complained on field ops when we had to wear our "heavy" flaks, but when we got our SAPI (Small Arms Protective Insert) plates we learned what heavy really was. Everyone seemed to get a few inches shorter when they put their flaks on, which were now twenty pounds heavier. We used to throw them on like jackets, but now we had to heave them onto ourselves like our backpacks.

At least I didn't have to wear any MOPP gear. MOPP stands for Mission Oriented Protective Posture, an awkward phrase that was used pejoratively to describe the heavy, charcoal-filled over-suits that were meant to protect us from Nuclear, Biological or Chemical attacks (NBC). After we realized that we only had enough training MOPP suits for half the platoon, the corporals decided that the boots would get the honors. Showers was the only senior Marine who had to wear one. While walking to our training area, I started to feel exhausted; then I looked over at Showers, who had a rifle, tripod, ammo bag, three cans of ammo and a MOPP suit, limping along with his crazy foot. Everyone always made fun of him, but he was carrying twice the weight of any other senior Marine and keeping up just fine.

When Weapons Platoon was given a clean, dry room in the HQ building, I knew it wouldn't last. Sure enough, as soon as we got settled in, a Gunny from HQ told First Sergeant Young that we needed to clear out. First Sergeant Bell would have given that Gunny a death-stare so frightening it would have turned him sterile, but First Sergeant Young just shuffled us out saying, "Don't worry. We'll leave, dog."

Our first day of training consisted of refresher courses in the morning followed by basic MOUT techniques in the afternoon. All of my buddies were MOUT instructors, so they were called away to teach classes. All that was left was Showers and I and a bunch of boots. My buddies taught MOUT basics, such as clearing rooms, and I got to see them as instructors for the first time. We really had come a long way. Two years ago we were dumb-ass boots who couldn't even bring the proper gear to the field; now we were the experts, training men for battle.

We learned several different breaching methods, using gear we didn't even know the Marine Corps had. We started by jumping over walls, which sounds simple, until you factor in the extra sixty pounds of gear. With all that weight, your vertical leap tops out at about two and a half inches, so you have to rely on your buddies to get you up and over. Exhaustion set in quickly. By the third time, it would have been hard to get over that wall if it had a damn escalator. Lemke's first impression will forever be branded in my memory. Running to get enough momentum to jump over a wall, he flapped his arms effeminately as he ran on his tippy-toes. Scott told me his nickname was "Terry the Fairy" and it seemed to fit. If Saddam could see us now.

The next event was the grappling hook, which I thought was just something you'd see on the Adam West Batman show, but it is actual military equipment.

The grappling hook is carried by the 51s since their job includes breaching. In combat, the grappling hook is thrown into an area with trip-wires and pulled across to detonate the explosives from a safe distance. Or you could use it to go after The Penguin and Catwoman.

Flinging the hook and catching it on the windowsill of an open window was surprisingly easy, but climbing was not. The success rate was about one in five. It's easy enough to climb the rope with your feet against the wall like Burt Ward, but when you get even with the windowsill, you have a problem. Once you let go with one hand to grab the sill, you're supporting your entire body weight plus sixty pounds of gear on the other hand. Even if you can grab the sill with both hands, pulling yourself up after you've exhausted yourself climbing is a herculean task. To my surprise, Carpenter was one of the few to make it into the second floor; he didn't even quit after he almost fell. I made sure to compliment him afterwards. If you jump on someone when they screw up, you should also compliment them when they succeed.

The next event involved a collapsible ladder, which was more realistic than climbing a rope. With a ladder, you could have one hand free to use a firearm to clear the room you're entering. Working in two-man teams, you could both be on the second floor in no time. My only problem was gear-related. The moto knife I bought when I thought I was going to Afghanistan kept falling out of its scabbard. Each time it hit the ground, some boot had to hand it to me, costing me cool points.

We were taught the combat glide, which is used when moving down hallways. You walk with your shoulders squared toward the enemy, taking little pigeon steps. The way you hold the weapon tight to your body utilizes some rarely used muscles and the 7-pound M-16 begins to feel like an anvil. I thought I was a bitch until I saw the shaky barrels of the other guys' rifles. Reloading with one hand without looking down at the weapon became inordinately difficult.

When we got back to our sleeping area, we found that we had to move to some even smaller sheds across the lot. This was our third move in two days. Our company motto was, "We go where we're kicked." I thought I was going to get stuck with McPoland, Colvin and Reed, but I got offered a spot in the "cool" machinegunners room. There was something horribly wrong with the door and when you opened or closed it, it made a horrific, metallic shriek that sounded like the gates of hell opening.

The next day, we were critiqued as we conducted room takedowns. While waiting, people would break windows for fun, which attracted the ire of the instructors. They told us the Marine Corps has to pay for any damage to the town, which was funny because the whole place looked like Beirut already. I wondered if we could sue the owner if we got hurt; the whole place was filled with broken glass and rusty nails stuck out of every wall.

By then, my buddies and I had known each other for three years and our conversation was an almost-unintelligible collection of in-jokes. Any new phrase that came along was gladly added to our lexicon. When Elias got mad at Ross for fooling around, he tried to put him in his place by telling him, "You're stupid twenty-four seven." When everybody laughed, Elias thought it was because he really got Ross good, not realizing we were laughing at his lame put-down.

When we were boots, I got along with everyone in Third, but when I came back, I got the cold shoulder. I could understand if they were a little bitter and jealous of me; it would have bothered me if I went to every hike and field op and then some guy came back from a year in a desk job and became a squad leader and a sergeant. The tension didn't bode well for the future since Third would be the platoon I would be attached to during combat.

After 9-11, a Guardian Angel program was established in which armed Marines watched out whenever we congregated. Those on Guardian Angel did not train and were separate from the company. Rager had pulled guard for the first two days and when it was time to switch out, Mohler volunteered Carpenter, who was also in Reed's squad. Reed went ballistic when he heard that and he went to confront Mohler. Though they were 50 meters away from the company formation, you could have heard Reed screaming twice as far away. Reed bumped chests with Mohler, trying to intimidate him. Mohler was and is the nicest guy in the world, but I could see he was getting hot when he cocked his helmet back like he was about the brain Reed. The entire company witnessed Reed embarrass our section for the umpteenth time. I looked over at Moser, who nodded and we both went over to subdue Reed. I was hoping that Reed would resist so we could pound him with justification, but as soon as he saw Moser and I heading his way, he backed off.

I had been deferring to Reed since he was still my squad leader and I hated dissension in the ranks, but he was totally out of hand. When he got back to the formation, I chastised him for being unprofessional. As an excuse, he blurted out that he was upset because his father had just been involved in a shoot-out. This took me by surprise and I instantly went from being disgusted with him to trying to figure out how I could help (I think I was an abused wife in a former life). I asked him if he had told anyone and he said he hadn't. I told him I would go to the lieutenant and see if I could get him out to see his dad, but he said he didn't want to make a big deal about it and wanted to drop it.

After we got cut loose, Elias went to the boots' room and surveyed their weapons. Apparently, a boot named Lopez gave him attitude, so Elias wanted to beat him up. Lopez was a big kid from the mean streets of Las Vegas. He wasn't a trouble-maker, but he had that Latin pride and he butted heads with several NCOs. Ross and the others decided that they would make the boots clean weapons all night long as punishment. This meant that we had to take shifts to go over and check on them. It seemed like fuck-fuck games, especially since I knew how Elias could be a bully sometimes, but I didn't know the boots well enough at the time to judge the situation.

There was noticeable tension between the boots and NCOs during PT the next morning. Reed accused one of the boots of ignoring the seniors, so he called him out, under the guise of teaching him wrestling. Reed knew more technique, but the kid was another hard-ass Mexican and they were pretty evenly matched. Reed finally got the upper hand and pinned him. Not being gracious as a winner, Reed "accidentally" slapped the kid in the face as he let go of him. The kid got mad and Reed pretended it was an accident, while also accusing the kid of being a whiner.

My feelings about "putting hands on someone" were pretty well set. We didn't work at Wal-Mart; we were training for war, and as long as you didn't injure the boot, I didn't think it was wrong for someone to catch an elbow or eat some dirt. In a worst-case scenario, we would be captured and tortured. You don't want the first time you get hit to be in wartime. Reed deemed himself the enforcer of the section. At the armory on my first morning back with the company, a kid named Ryan answered a casual question of mine in an informal manner, which set Reed off; he ran over and pushed Ryan to the ground. I had seen Ryan at BAS the previous day, speaking to Showers and some other seniors like they were buddies. I felt strongly that there should be a distance between the ranks. If I would have known how great a guy Ryan would turn out to be, I would have defended him.

The next day, we conducted a full mission. I was put in charge of a culled-together squad and went to get the brief. We used a mapping system that the British military devised in Northern Ireland, in which buildings are given codes instead of addresses, so if the enemy eavesdropped on our comm, he still wouldn't be able to pinpoint our location. I thought I was a genius when I came up with the idea of taping the map to my buttstock so I could see it while aiming my rifle, until I saw that half of the company had the same idea.

I knew Reed would endlessly question my orders and undermine my authority, but I had Elias to back me up. The boots seemed like a good lot, though I didn't know them well. We snaked our way between the houses as we made our way to our target. We came to a wide open space, an obvious danger area, so I halted the squad in a brick-walled carport as I peeked around the corner to look for snipers. The likeliest sniper nest was in a building to our right. While I tried to look for an alternate route, Reed started screaming about how we were all going to die. I imagined him doing the same in a battle. I ignored him and consulted with Elias about how we would get across. Elias and I would provide cover fire while the rest of them crossed. Reed kept crying, so I left him behind.

We had fallen behind the rifle platoon and it was unclear which building they were in. Finally, one of them whistled and we headed over. They had already cleared the house, but they needed us to shore up the defenses. I placed one gun facing out the north wall and the other out the south. Rager felt that his shooting position made him unnecessarily exposed. No matter how well covered and concealed, the gunner is always going to be the most exposed. I told his team leader, Scott, to move his gun where he saw fit. Scott found a good spot, then second-guessed himself, and asked me where I thought he should go. I told him that when he makes a decision, he needs to stick with it. He nodded and edged Rager into a better fighting position.

Enemy troops started to probes our lines and my boys started firing at figures darting out of bushes and around corners. I kept going from gun-to-gun, checking on the teams, but also keeping an eye on Reed, who was screaming like a maniac. Goggle-eyed and red faced, he kept shouting that everything was wrong—WE WERE ALL GOING TO DIE!!!—yet he had no realistic solutions.

The training was intense and, with the blanks and smoke, it felt like a real firefight. I told Elias about Reed freaking out and he nodded ruefully, saying that was how it always was. I did a double-take when I noticed that Showers was sitting in a bathtub with an embarrassed expression on his face. I asked him what the hell was going on and he said that there was no space for him in the room with the gun, so he got put in there. His rifle had been commandeered, so the best thing he could do was stay out of the way.

I went to check on Levesque's gun and found another Reed-created fiasco. Crozier was acting as team leader for Levesque and he had stashed an ammo can in a small closet next to the gun. For some reason, this set Reed off and to "teach Crozier a lesson," he started flinging the ammo all over the room. Levesque was yelling at Reed for being an idiot as I walked in. I rushed up to Reed and put my finger an inch from his eye. This has special meaning for Marines since that is how drill instructors put recruits in their place; there's something very demeaning and infuriating about it when you're on the receiving end. Reed started to argue and I screamed over the gunfire for him to shut the fuck up and quit freaking out; that I was in charge and he would do what I said. For some reason, instead of escalating the situation, it seemed to defuse it. Reed just kind of shut down and I resumed supervising the guns.

I saw one of the instructors with his "God Gun" that could kill or bring back to life anyone he saw fit. I wanted to ask him if I could take Reed out of the game, since in real life he would have been knocked out by one of us by then.

We moved to our final objective, which was bristling with enemy fire. People's sensors were going off right and left and I couldn't tell if it was mine or theirs. Elias and I covered our men and then saw that we had "near miss" on our indicators, which was sobering to say the least.

We got good news when we got into the last building—Reed was dead. It should have been terrible that everyone would be ecstatic to hear that, but he had more than earned their enmity. After we finished the assault, I saw that my sensor said I was dead.

The great training had been nearly ruined by Reed. There's a code of silence within the enlisted ranks—especially the lower ones—that you handled things at your own level and didn't rat people out. Reed wasn't being handled; he had only gotten worse. What he did with the ammo was inexcusable and, in a real-life situation, would have gotten him butt-stroked or shot by his own people. Reed wasn't changing; all of the fights he had gotten in and all of the calm attempts at listening to him had failed—there was just something basically wrong with the kid. "Kid" was the operative term; for whatever reason, at the age of five or so, he had stopped developing emotionally, psychologically and socially. It would have been deeply sad if it wasn't for the fact that he was endangering Marines' lives.

When I told Ross what happened, he gave me the same tired expression Elias had given me. Telling anyone that Reed was acting crazy wasn't exactly news. We couldn't fire Reed and there was no place to put him—we were stuck with him. That night, we got a temporary reprieve from his idiocy when Reed went to the BAS. He had a fever (appropriate for a hothead) and they decided to keep him for observation. For a day or two, he could infect the BAS instead of our section.

The news that Reed was gone spread through the platoon and raised everyone's mood. You wouldn't know that we'd all slept in rusty sheds in the desert from the smiles on our faces. With Reed gone, we could concentrate on learning new techniques from the British, who taught us innovative urban patrolling techniques that they developed in Northern Ireland. The British instructors didn't just try to meet a pre-designated minimum standard; they trained us until we got it right. We messed up the first few times, but with their advice we got very proficient in a short time. The British aren't free with compliments; soldiering is a stern and taxing profession for them. In the British Army, it's common for it to take ten years to pick up corporal, but their rank means more since it took so long to earn it. I'd rather listen to a British Corporal than one of our own captains.

With Reed gone, not only did the machinegun section get along better, all the sections did. With Boyd and Vargas gone, Keller toned down his junior-high antics and became a valued member of the platoon. He was tall and broad-shouldered, with a perpetual grin on a face that was still fighting off the oily ravages of adolescence. Keller did almost everything above average, yet he caught more shit than anyone, since he was always getting yelled at for goofing off. He had a penchant for always getting caught. He led squads professionally all day and as soon as he started screwing around, the instructor came by and chewed him out. He just couldn't catch a break.

Elias got posted from his squad leader billet after he got in an argument with an officer. Elias was my buddy, but his temper always got him in trouble. He wasn't wrong in the strictest sense—the officer told him to employ the guns in an improper manner—but he had no tact. As much as I rail against the inequities in the Corps, I felt that officer/enlisted relations should be kept formal. If that isn't maintained, all you're left with is a bunch of guys arguing over who's right.

As we ate dinner, each person remarked on how great the day had been with Reed gone. We were away from civilization, but we were happy because we were doing realistic, motivating training. Our contact with staff NCOs and officers had been limited, yet somehow the company did not fall apart in their absence. NCOs weren't getting treated like idiots, so they weren't acting like them. We worked hard, learned some useful knowledge and thoroughly enjoyed ourselves. It was a great day.

The latest addition to our platoon was Sgt. Quinn, who had been our senior Marines' senior Marine. He came back to Golf after having been at a different unit for three years, which didn't usually happen. We delighted in hearing him tell tales of our seniors when they were boots. Chuck had always bragged about standing up to one of his seniors and going toe-to-toe with him, but Sgt. Quinn told us that Chuck got laid out with a one-hitter-quitter. Quinn called the platoon together that night and chastised us for not visiting Reed in the BAS. We looked at each other quizzically until we realized that he wasn't joking. We didn't waste time explaining about Reed; he would find out soon enough.

The next day, we conducted a company-wide attack with a twist. Machinegunners are almost always parceled out—one squad of two guns per rifle platoon—but this time we would fight as a section. You weren't supposed to concentrate your assets like that, but it would be fun to fight along side my buddies. Ross would be the section leader and I would have my own squad. Moser was Ross' number two, carrying the radio. Throughout his time in the Corps, Moser realized that it was usually better to be second-in-command. The top spot was for people who needed their egos stroked, but when the section got in any trouble, the top man was always replaced. No matter who was in the top spot, they always relied heavily on Moser, so he was in more of a permanent leadership spot than anyone.

We sat in a house on the edge of the development and waited to go. The company commander and our platoon commander would be staying there, observing and calling in fire support, as they would in combat. I watched Sprincin struggle to climb onto the roof and cringed. How did this geek get in the Corps? He looked exactly like Waldo.

A blank round went off and I whirled around to see who did it. Crozier, in his excitement, had flipped his weapon off "safe" and accidentally squeezed the trigger. He looked mortified and all the seniors were livid. The other boots just had a "better him than me" expression on their face. We were in such close proximity that, if it was a real round, it probably would have killed one of us. I never feared going into combat, but the thought of accidentally shooting another Marine scared the hell out of me.

No one would have said it was wrong for me to smack Crozier in the head for what he did, but I saw in his eyes that nothing I could do would make him feel as bad as he was making himself feel. I took him outside and tersely counseled him while he hung his head in shame. I told him that I didn't know him that well, but I had already heard good things about him and I would consider this just a blip on the radar screen if he didn't do it again. I've found that mercy, in the right circumstances, is ten times more effective than punishment.

When I got back, Ross told me that one of the boots had told him that Reed had a negligent discharge on our last mission. Great. I had just admonished a junior Marine for something that a senior Marine had gotten away with. Double standards like that were common, but I tried to avoid them.

Ross led the way, which was great. For all of his "dirtiness," he hadn't missed one field op, hike, or school and it showed in his cool and casual command. We set up in one house and decided to try something new. Like Rager had brought up, the gunner is wide open when shooting, so we came up with a solution. We had recently been issued one pick-ax per squad, so we used ours to bust a hole in the outer wall. Within a few minutes, we had a hole big enough to shoot out of, but small enough that it would be hard to see from the enemy's point-of-view. We thought we were pretty damn clever until an evaluator saw the hole and yelled at us for de-valuing the property. The whole base was so trashed that our infraction was the equivalent of pissing on a turd.

There were snipers somewhere across the wide road that needed to be spotted before we could move. I walked into a room and a burst of machinegun fire went off so loudly that I started reeling. I had forgotten how loud a gun can be in a confined space—it was like a physical force.

A tank came up to cover us as we crossed a danger area. After my squad crossed safely, I sprinted across the wide alley into rippling waves of intense oven-like heat. In my moto excitement, I forgot that exhaust comes out of the back of a tank at almost 900 degrees. I stumbled out of the blast feeling raw. Later that day, I asked Elias why he didn't warn me and he said that everyone was shouting at me, but I didn't hear them. Often when someone gets busted down, they drop their pack and become belligerent with their replacement, but that wasn't the case with Elias. He seemed to have fun being a regular machinegunner again.

There is a peculiar effect that happens when a grunt gets something new: he wants to use it for every situation. There is so much repetition in training that anything out of the ordinary becomes fantastic. Elias had been given a smoke grenade that became his whole world. Throughout the planning and at each step of the mission, his solution to every problem involved the judicious use of his smoke grenade. I think he forgot about the machinegun entirely. He would have loved to have been told that he had just been made section leader of the new Smoke Grenade section.

We had been doing well until we got to sniper alley. The evaluators used their god guns to take out anyone they thought had exposed themselves to sniper fire. People were going down right and left and nobody could find the sniper. The sniper was finally spotted, but we would have to expose ourselves to shoot him. Each deck had a small wooden wall that bounded the porch; it wouldn't stop a bullet, but it was good concealment, which is all you can hope for sometimes. There was a small hole that Rager could shoot through and I told Scott to have him pour it on.

I went to go check on my other gun and saw that there was a room full of people just sitting and chatting. I was confused until I realized that they were all dead. Someone yelled that it was time to roll and I went to go get Rager and Scott. Scott was heading out the door, but Rager was still lying with the gun. I thought Rager hadn't gotten the word, so I went to give it to him when an evaluator shot me with his god gun. Rager was dead already; I had just died going to check on a dead man.

I sat in the room with the dead people. It wasn't just the shitbags and fuck-ups; there were several good Marines. Tardif and his squad came around the corner and he asked us why we were all just sitting there. When he was told that we were all dead he said, "You got to be kidding me." He looked like he was looking at the future ghosts of his friends.

Afterward, I took Rager and Scott aside to figure out what we did wrong. Rager realized that what got him killed there would get him killed in war and he was justifiably concerned. I had them brainstorm ideas that we could use to keep Rager alive. There wasn't much we could do; you have to expose yourself to fire to get the enemy in view. I wanted to show Rager that we would take every step necessary to minimize the danger he would face.

The next day, we conducted an attack that was small in scale, but much more intense. We would attack a small cluster of buildings that were filled with the Marines acting as the enemy. Both of my guns were undergoing repairs, so the elevens didn't really know what to do with us. We ended up getting stuck on trac security, which was fine by me. I was tired of running around and looked forward to an hour of chilling out while the others worked their asses off.

Five minutes after the platoon took off, the evaluator casually walked up and told me that the trac had just been blown up by a missile. Well, that was unexpected; I guess I wasn't trac security anymore. I wasn't keen on running two blocks in full gear, but once I got halfway there and heard the intense gunfire, I got moto. This would be cool. I'd get to do some run-and-gun eleven action. I was so into the make-believe that I didn't see the cross-beam of a fence I was sneaking through; I hit it so hard that I went completely off my feet and flipped up into the air. I hit the ground hard and when I got back up, I left my cool points on the ground where they belonged.

The elevens were so well-concealed that I ran past them and they had to call me over. We hustled into a house that looked out onto a U-shaped courtyard. There was a furious pitched battle going on in the courtyard and almost everyone that entered the courtyard got killed.

I grabbed Carpenter and Barney-styled the situation for him. He looked completely lost and nodded dumbly at my commands. I shook my head, knowing that I would be leading that mental midget into combat. I went through the door into the courtyard and attached myself to whoever was in the front of me, which turned out to be Kennel and a new corporal named Yoder. Blanks were going off non-stop and my blood was up. I caught myself smiling and having fun and had to remind myself to treat this like it was real.

The bulk of the fire was coming out of two windows on the left, but I was able to crawl under them and stay out of their sight. I popped up between two windows and smiled, feeling like a hero from a John Woo movie. I pulled a grenade and tossed it in. In reality, that would have killed anyone inside and deafened me, but the enemy acted like nothing had happened since the grenades didn't set off their sensors.

Though it was risky, Kennel decided to breach through the window. Yoder and Kennel jumped in and took cover in a closet, but when I tried to enter, my gear got caught on the windowsill. An enemy popped around the corner and I squeezed off five rounds at him as my sensor went off.

Kennel and Yoder emptied several mags down the hallway, while I sat down in some broken glass. Kennel told me that I should help them and I reminded him that I was out-of-play and that it wouldn't be fair. He pointed out that they had killed each enemy several times, and since they weren't playing fair, why should I?

I scrounged up some rounds from "dead" Marines and caught up with them. Kennel and Yoder had secured a foothold and were pushing down the hallway. When Carpenter finally appeared, I put him to work guarding an empty room, which was about his speed.

The exercise bogged down in the hallway. We were all officially "dead," so all we were doing was making each other deaf. One Marine threw a "blue-body" grenade down the hallway just as an evaluator stepped around a corner, hitting him in the face. The evaluator pointed his God Gun at the Marine, killing him. He was the only Marine that was killed by spite that day.

They gave us a good critique afterward, but it didn't sink in much. People would listen to the evaluator if he out-ranked them, but if he didn't, they would just argue and defend themselves.

The tracs pulled up and the crew said they could give us a ride back. I was excited, but the others were less enthused. Though not as cool or foreboding as a tank, a trac is still a fearsome-looking machine. It looked like the Jawas' Sand-Crawler from "Star Wars." The rear ramp dropped down, which seemed like the coolest thing in the world at the time. The amtrac is a quintessential Marine Corps vehicle, no other service has it, and it embodies the spirit of the land-sea warrior that is a Marine. As the ramp closed, it felt like a tomb sealing. We bumped around in the dark for much longer than it would have taken to walk back. When the ramp finally dropped on that rolling coffin, I couldn't get out fast enough.

Elias' family owned a pizza place in town—as he told any human within ear-shot—that could come out and cater. When the captain approved that, Elias was as proud as a new father. The pizzas arrived and transformed that barren, abandoned site into the happiest place on earth. Elias got bothered with everyone checking out his sister, but I was surprised he even let her come, considering the mobile sausage factory that is the United States Marine Corps. We had only been there a few days, but I had already had more experiences and memories than in my whole year on FAP. Contact with staff NCOs and officers had been kept to a minimum and somehow the whole system didn't fall apart, as the higher-ups tend to think. And Reed had been gone for days. Good times.

Our last event would be a company-wide attack utilizing all vehicles and assets. For some reason, I was leading the squad attached to Second Platoon, instead of Third. I tried to talk to Monroe, one of the leaders in the platoon, but all he would do was ask where Moser was. After several futile attempts to get him to be cool, I spoke with Budzynski. Bud was a quiet and down-to-earth guy who looked vaguely like David Duchovny. I hadn't known him that well when we were boots, but right before I came back to Golf, I saw him in the PX and he spoke to me like we were old friends. I asked him to spin me up and he did so without giving me any grief. Bud was really a cut above; he was in great shape and highly-skilled, yet he didn't have an attitude or ego. He was the kind of guy you'd want to marry your sister.

I cursed as I saw Reed ambling up the road. Reed sidled up and told me a dramatic tale of how the BAS had ordered him to stay, but he had demanded to train. Considering it turned out that all he had was a cold, I'm sure he was kicked out, but that wasn't the news in Reedland. He started acting like he was in charge, but I had gotten the brief and we were kicking off in ten minutes. Since Ross was the acting section leader, I asked him if Reed would act as squad leader.

"Fuck that. He just showed up. You're in charge."

When I told Reed that, his ego's self-defense mechanism instantly kicked in.

"Ok, so I'm like the co-squad leader, running things when you're not there."

"No, there's no such thing as a co-squad leader. You're the second team leader."

"Yeah, so I'm second in charge."

"No, that would be the first team leader. Miller."

"OK, so I'll just be running things when you're busy."

His self-delusion was more solid than the Rock of Gibraltar.

The last attack turned out to be much smaller than promised. While holed up in a room, we fired on the enemy with both guns; the sharp roar of the guns was painful, but we still did our job. Carpenter huddled in a fetal position against a wall, covering his ears with his hands, looking like a little kid that just wanted to go home. He wasn't providing rear security or distributing ammo, which was his job, he was just sitting against the wall with a woe-is-me expression. I had no sympathy for him being a pussy like that and I was glad when Reed jumped on him and started yelling at him. Maybe Reed could be useful after all.

The exercise was cut short and the evaluators called "Cease fire!" Like a little kid, Reed threw his last grenade and then tried to pretend like he didn't hear the cease fire when an evaluator yelled at him. Monroe shook his head, telling me I needed to get Reed under control. The same kid who wouldn't give me the time of day now wanted to tell me how to run my squad; I didn't want to hear it. Reed had come from their platoon; they hadn't been able to rein him in, so they dumped him on us.

I heard a high-pitched whine and looked down to see that my sensor showed that I was dead. This was the third event in a row that I had died in. A squad leader constantly has to go from gun-to-gun, so he will be exposed more than the others. I could reduce the danger, but I couldn't eliminate it.

The tanks pulled around and I asked Ross if he wanted to go take some moto pics. Anyone else would have said that I was acting like a boot, but this was what fueled me. I was very conscious that this was the last time we would take our pictures together before combat.

I had to return my PRR to the Warfighter Lab. I was sorry to see it go; it had served us incredibly well and was second only to our weapons as an effective weapon. I asked if we would have them for Iraq and I was given a vague, but encouraging response. A British instructor told me that every grunt in his unit received a PRR every time they drew their weapon from the armory.

As we waited for the buses to arrive, an event went down that will live in the history of Golf Company for all eternity. We saw something that, to us, would become the eighth wonder of the world: The Victorville Turd. As a grunt, I have spent more time in Porta-Jons than any ten construction workers. When compared to shitting in the woods, a porta-potty is like a suite at The Four Seasons. Elias exited a Porta-Jon and spoke animatedly to a small group of Marines, who then headed straight for the Porta-Jon he came from. Loud exclamations and laughter were heard, and the new disciples spread the word. Soon, half of the company was talking about the momentous discovery: a turd that as wide as a fist and at least 18 inches long. I thought they were joking or exaggerating and I was embarrassed at the commotion it caused. Then I realized I didn't have to anything better to do in that dirt lot for the next several hours. I shook my head; here I was at the age 29, about to go to war and I was going to look at some huge log.

I opened the door and stepped forward slowly, expecting the creature from "Alien" to jump out. It was even bigger because they said it was. Eighteen inches were visible before it disappeared under the cloudy, blue water. I went back and spread the word to the few who hadn't gone. Everyone wondered who did it. An obvious suspect was Elias, but my suspicion was Slater who had an insane metabolism that seriously led people to suspect he had a tapeworm; even though he ate constantly, he was rail-thin. He was one of the few who didn't check it out, which was suspicious.

That turd became part of our lore and it became a point of pride to have been there and seen it. Upon reflection, I don't think it was a single person's log. It was the same width as the vacuum hose that is used to suck out the shit. I think the hose got plugged up and the guy just shook out what was already in there, but I didn't tell any of them that. Why ruin a good story?

I was glad we had gone through that week's training, knowing that the lessons I had learned might save my life soon. Although we had been told previously that we were going to Kuwait, it was only to be "forward deployed." They coyly avoided saying there would be an invasion. We got the final go-ahead after dinner one night and I started squealing like I had just had my name called on "The Price is Right." Ross was happy too, but the general mood was more subdued. Sgt. Quinn said that it wasn't something one should be so happy about.

The next week was supposed to be our last in America, but instead of it being a mad dash, it was surprisingly relaxed. We were already packed and prepared; all we needed was a flight. New staff NCOs and MSG Marines had checked into the company while we had been at Victorville. When I went to the armory, I saw one of the new staff sergeants at the window. SSgt. Sikes was given the choice between two types of night optics and he seemed unsure as to which one he should choose. I gave him my advice and he told me he had just been on three years of MSG duty, which was "not even really the Marine Corps" as he put it. He seemed shy and quiet, like a nice guy who would just stay out of the way. Little did I know that, four months later, he would earn the Silver Star for combat gallantry.

SSgt. Pettigrew, our new section leader, looked like someone's son playing dress-up. He was five-feet-nothing, 100-and-nothing, with bad teeth; he looked like a blonde, less attractive brother of Michael J. Fox. He came out and introduced himself and then just stood there, listening as we bullshitted. Though he seemed innocuous at first, we would all come to hate him; so much so that we would resurrect the nickname for our previously most-hated senior Marine, "Squeak" and give it to him.

Our flight date kept getting pushed back until all of 7th Marines from 29 Palms had departed (or so the rumor mill told). With nothing to do, I had a lot of time to think and it was all on one subject: Reed. I had an overwhelming fear that I would be forced to shoot him while in combat. This may sound melodramatic, but it was a very real possibility. It made me sick to think of it, especially since there was a good side of him that I had seen in Oki, but his lack of control would have gotten people killed if any of the training events at Victorville had been real.

Machinegunners are support; we protect the elevens while they advance to finish off the enemy. Reed's tantrums would not only endanger his team, but also the eleven squads he was protecting. His problems had escalated over the last two years. Nothing was making him better. Nothing made him see the light. He seemed to have little grip on reality. The "shooting" his dad was supposedly involved in turned out to be nothing like he implied. His dad simply responded to a call of "shots fired," just like every other patrolman on duty that night. I had no fear of the Iraqis and no qualms about shooting them, but I saw the very real possibility that I would have to make a choice between Reed's life and the lives of other Marines. Scott thought I didn't know Reed, so he informed me that his tantrums were par for the course. A junior Marine should never have to say that about a senior.

The thought of having to shoot Reed caused me extreme distress. We weren't characters in a movie; I had lived with him in the same room for six months. The deadly seriousness of the situation was horrifying. I later confided in others and found that they had independently come to the same conclusion.

Whiling hanging out in Showers' room, I heard a loud argument in the parking lot. When I went out to see who it was, I was surprised to see that Master Sergeant Stafford and a gunnery sergeant were about to get into a fight. Since everyone had to empty out their rooms, the one small dumpster had filled up, so people were putting their trash next to it. Master Sergeant Stafford tasked Gunny Betancourt with getting the mess tidied up, so the gunny made some boots re-shape the mountains of trash in a somewhat military manner. That was not to Master Sergeant Stafford's liking though, so he started berating Gunny Betancourt in front of half the battalion. The highest-ranking Marines I had ever seen arguing before were a sergeant and a corporal and that was embarrassing to witness, but this was just disgusting. Master Sergeant Stafford was saying the vilest things, calling the gunny a bitch and a punk, threatening to kick his ass and begging for him to throw the first punch. I didn't like Gunny Betancourt—he was the type of lifer who would yell at you for stupid things like having your hands in your pockets—but I felt for the man; he was in a hell of a predicament. Master Sergeant Stafford had been in the Corps eight years longer and was a survivor of the Marine Barracks bombing in Beirut. Gunny Betancourt was so mad that he was shaking, but he stayed professional, calling the Master Sergeant by his rank and telling him to calm down. If he threw a punch at the Master Sergeant it would kill his career; all over a stupid argument over an over-flowing dumpster.

Though I would usually get some satisfaction out of higher-ups embarrassing themselves, this just made me sick and reinforced my belief that it was foolish to make a career out of being an enlisted man. I could break my back and ruin my marriage for the next ten years, only to be punked in a no-win situation in front of my men by someone who had just one more stripe than I.

"A good world is not found, a good world is made."

—Karl Zinsmeister

WAR

We spent the whole week in limbo, waiting for a flight. We were worried that we would be confined to base all weekend, but we were cut loose with the caveat that everyone would be available by phone at all times. Echo Company had been told at the last minute that they were leaving on Saturday, so they were not allowed to go home that night. The rumor mill had us leaving last, sometime in the next week, and I was glad to have one more weekend at home. The war would start at the same time whether we got there that week or the day before the invasion. On Saturday, we got the call to report to work before dawn on Sunday. I went on one more shopping expedition, buying a bunch of stuff I ended up forgetting on the kitchen table.

My last night at home was stressful and I ended up blowing up at my family several times. We still had to fulfill our obligation to deploy to Oki; we were told that we would probably be in Iraq until July, and then fly straight to Oki. I was looking at six months to a year away from home. I hadn't prepared as well as I should have and I was having trouble packing. It was a bad way to leave.

Several people were late on Sunday and Carpenter was totally incommunicado. Ryan had tried to contact him all weekend since they both lived in my old stomping grounds, Serra Mesa. I hoped that Carpenter had gone UA. I already had one psycho to watch out for; I didn't need another. Carpenter showed up around noon. Since his wife was with him, I didn't life him in front of her, but if I had known all the problems his wife would cause for us later, I would have lifed the both of them.

We went to the BAS to get the last of our series of anthrax shots. When I got inside, I got to see the comically embarrassing sight of Sprincin standing around with his shirt off. He was the only one who hadn't worn a scivvy shirt under his cammie blouse, so when they told everyone to take their blouses off to get their shots, he stood there like a jerk with his xylophone-like ribs showing to all the world. He counseled Carpenter for being late, while I stifled laughter at his ridiculous appearance. He was too dense to realize how futile it was to threaten someone who is going off to war. What could he threaten Carpenter with? Make him fight on the Iraqi side?

Miller asked the corpsman if the anthrax shot would leave a scar. When he heard that it did, he pouted, saying that he didn't want to be disfigured. For some reason that struck me as the funniest thing in the world, considering where we were heading.

We formed up to walk to the buses which, in the grand Marine Corps tradition, were parked a half-mile from the barracks. A small crowd of families wished us well, but I felt cold toward them. We were not going to be a part of their world for a very long time. I had more immediate concerns; our 100-pound, "everything and the kitchen sink" pack was a back-breaker.

As we drove by battalion HQ, we saw Jackson outside on one of his ubiquitous working parties. People slid their windows down and hurled abuse at him, calling him a bitch and a coward. Their invective was so strong that I started to feel sorry for him, and I didn't even like the guy.

We arrived at March AFB and set our gear in rows outside the hangar. Gunny Linton decided that our lines of packs weren't in perfectly-spaced ranks and threatened to start fucking with people if they weren't "straightened out in about five fucking seconds." Since I was the only one close enough to get it done before he blew his stack, I started picking packs up and throwing them the whopping three feet over to their designated spot. When I threw mine, I heard a crunch that didn't sound good.

I went to the small PX to buy my last bit of pogey-bait and realized I only had a few bucks. I had forgotten my money along with the last minute necessities I had laid out on my kitchen table. Thankfully, Showers loaned me some cash. Showers and I had become much better friends over time. I secretly worried about him, since his bad foot had kept him out of so much training. Part of the reason for my burgeoning friendship with Showers had been the slow realization that his medical problems were real.

That night, as we boarded the plane, I had no fear that I would be harmed—all those G.I.Joe comics and action movies had convinced me that I would live through anything—but I worried for my fellow Marines. I saw myself as the star in this movie and they were the supporting players. The odds alone foretold that some of us weren't coming back.

Upon entering the plane, we realized what a circus it would be. With only a quarter of the people aboard, all of the storage space was taken. Though our packs were in the belly of the plane, we boarded with 60 pounds of war gear and our weapons. We weren't allowed to put our bulky gear on or under our seats. Showers and I put our gear in the seat between us, making a pile four feet high. A stewardess told us that we had to move our gear. I tried to get her to look around and see the reality of the situation, but she just kept repeating her demand. I told her that until she gave me a better option, it wasn't moving.

The plane took off and I dug into my patrol pack to get the CD player I bought a few days earlier. I popped the Shakira CD in, hit "play" and nothing happened. I checked and re-checked the batteries and hit every combination of buttons. It had gotten broken when I had been ordered to move the packs for no good reason. I went red with anger; the CD player was my only connection to normal life. None of the staff NCOs cared that I hadn't been to a rifle range in over a year, but I got daily admonishments on my boots not being shined and my hat not being on exactly straight. Or calling my hat a "hat," instead of a "cover." Or any other ephemera that had nothing to do with being a grunt. but had everything to do with making me miserable and wanting to get the fuck out.

I ripped the cover off the CD player and started smashing it on the seat rest. Showers started tripping out since my tantrum seemed to come out of nowhere. I was going into war with a mental defective and a psycho in my squad. None of my best buddies were in my squad and my fellow NCOs in Third Platoon were resentful of my promotion. The one small comfort I had was ruined because of a staff NCO's whim. Showers tried to calm me down, but I was still hot. For no good reason, I snapped the Shakira CD in half and tossed it on the ground. There was nothing wrong with the CD and I came to regret breaking it.

When we stopped in Maine, they let us get off to stretch our legs. Mohler went to the gift shop and bought a moose hand-puppet. The sight of that lanky stoner in tan fatigues playing with a moose puppet was too funny. That was one of the things I loved about Mohler; he could make almost any shitty situation endurable.

Another quick stop in Germany and then the home stretch. I watched the monitor, which showed our progress toward Kuwait and I was surprised at how short of a flight it was from modern Europe to the Middle Ages. As we approached Kuwait City, I looked down and got a bad feeling in my stomach. What a wasteland. This wasn't like 29 Palms, where home was two hours away. We were going to be living in sand for months on end.

We landed in the dark and came out onto the wide expanse of the landing strip. Some tents had been erected, but it didn't seem like a major military operation was being launched. Simple things like where to piss hadn't been established, so after asking staff NCOs who had no clue, people just pissed on the tarmac. A guy drove by in a truck and yelled "Gas! Gas! Gas!" so we all scrambled to pull our masks on. After a few minutes, we were given the "all clear"—it was just a drill.

Unlike the flight to Oki, where they stuffed us to the gills, this time we were barely fed. Someone finally found some water and oranges and the staff NCOs acted like they were doing us a favor by giving them to us. I realized that while some of my war fantasies would come true, I was about to enter a new hell—day and night being lorded over by prick staff NCOs and officers. Boot Camp was only twelve weeks long; they had to feed you three times a day and give you at least seven hours of sleep. Even in The Fleet, you got weekends and nights off. This would be endless.

The buses arrived and suddenly, even though we had waited for them for hours, *we* were late. The atropine injectors we had just been issued on the tarmac fell out of our gas mask carriers as we were hustled around like recruits in the dark. To top it off, they made the NCOs clean up the cigarettes that the Kuwaiti drivers had tossed on the grounds. Cleaning up is almost always a job for the boots; it undermines the NCOs to make them clean the ground in front of their men. They were sending us a message—we were in Staff NCO country now.

After rushing onto the buses, we sat in them for an hour with the shades drawn. We were told that every convoy had been shot at so far and that the curtains were there to protect us, which turned out to be a lie. It was just another excuse to keep us in the dark—literally. No one spoke on the long, bumpy trip. During all of my fantasies of combat and glory, I had not stopped to consider the barren environs we would be living in. Two hours later, we stopped at our new camp, which consisted of a dozen half-erected circus tents and four porta-potties.

We were told to set up our pup tents by squad, which was confusing since I was technically a sergeant, but I hadn't been formally promoted yet. The senior man in the section is usually given control of First Squad, so I went over with them. Mohler was the current squad leader and he seemed weirded out that I was with them, but he didn't say anything. My best friends—Ross, Elias, Mohler and Showers—were all in First Squad, and I couldn't wait to take over. What's more, I wouldn't have to deal with Reed or Carpenter anymore once I officially took over First Squad.

Levesque and I put our pup tent together in the dark. Levesque was kind of slimy, but I liked that about him. The best grunts were the ones who were rough around the edges. I didn't want some guy who was an honor student in high school; I wanted the burn-out who used to beat up the honor students in the parking lot during lunch. Levesque was more of the instigator-type, egging people on to fight each other, but he was easy to talk to and, most importantly, he was very short. I loved Mohler, but I wouldn't want to share a tent with all six feet six inches of him. The one-man pup tents we put two Marines plus gear into were built for civilian campers, so they started ripping almost immediately. We had been re-united with our duffel bags and had a ridiculous amount of gear. In the middle of the night, I woke up to find Levesque and I tangled up like an old married couple.

In the morning, they asked for out-going mail and I hastily tossed off a letter. We had been given our deployed address before we left, but I didn't take advantage and mail myself anything or give the address to family and friends. I had already become obsessed with food, hoarding the remaining pogeybait in my patrol pack. I was depressed and angry with myself for not leaving my address. We were told that it would take two weeks for mail to go in either direction. That meant that I was getting another CD player and food in a month—maybe.

There was nothing to do but wonder about the future, so we constantly pestered anyone of higher rank for info. We didn't know then that no one knew anything more than we did, but people like Sprincin would allude to knowing the battle plan, saying that they were not allowed to share it with us.

A general came to speak to us on our second day there, so we had to march to the regimental camp three miles away to see him. The surroundings were so flat and featureless that it felt like we were on a treadmill and it seemed to take forever to go the short distance. The regimental camp seemed like a functioning base, instead of the hobo headquarters we were staying at. It was an awe-inspiring scene—thousands of Marines amassed fifteen miles from Iraq. We had to wait for the general for an hour and when he did give his speech, it was a huge buzz-kill. He spoke generally about attacking some enemy somewhere and would not commit to anything. He made it sound like we were training at CAX. The speech lasted all of five minutes and it bummed everyone out.

The hike back really took it out of us. The hardest part of the hike was to realize we weren't hiking *to* anything. There were about forty large tents that were being erected slowly by local contractors. The few that were up had no one living in them, yet we weren't allowed to go into them. It felt like this was the camp being built for the *next* war. The Marine POG camps and Army bases had PXs, fast food, phones, showers, internet and women. We had a rickety, wooden crates that you could set your toothpaste on while you brushed your teeth. It didn't really compare.

After two days at LSA-5 (Life Support Area—Fifth Regiment), we were told that we were moving out to a TAA (Tactical Assembly Area). Our BC didn't want us getting "soft," so he decided to take us two miles out into the sand and set up our own camp. Suddenly, the LSA didn't seem so bad. That morning, I was officially promoted to sergeant, but there was a catch. Mohler did not want to switch squads with me and end up with Reed and Carpenter, so he went to Squeak, who told me that the squads would stay the same, only their names would change. Third Squad was now First Squad, even though we were still attached to Third Platoon. I was mad at Mohler, but I couldn't blame him. No one wanted my squad because of the two bad apples. I would have traded my third stripe to get Mohler's squad.

Reed had made a good first impression on Squeak by yelling at Miller. When we were told to fall out, it took Miller five minutes just to get out of his tent. As he slowly ambled toward the formation, Reed went off on him and Squeak seconded that emotion.

I double-checked my gear, knowing that it would be bad hike, no matter how short it was. Walking in loose sand is twice as hard as walking on solid ground and we were carrying the biggest packs I'd ever seen. My jaw dropped when I saw Carpenter's pack. We were given the opportunity to store our duffelbags in a tent at the LSA, but Carpenter had apparently crammed everything from his duffelbag into his already-full pack. His pack looked like it was pregnant with triplets. It went a foot above his head and was more than three feet thick from back-to-front. I yelled at him for his stupidity and then took a picture of him so I could show him how idiotic he was later.

Since I was a squad leader, I didn't have to carry part of the gun system, but it was my job to drag anyone who couldn't make it. Shortly after we kicked off the hike, good hikers like Ryan and Lopez started falling back. After forty-five grueling minutes, we stopped for a break. I looked back and saw that we had only gone 3/4 of a mile. During the first leg, Miller had fallen to the back while I was distracted. I felt bad for losing him and told him to give me his tripod, but he had fastened it to his pack so securely that we didn't have time to get it free. I was surprised to see that First Sergeant Young had done well on the hike, since I was told he fell out of almost every hike back in Pendleton. I was told that he had put most of his gear in one of the humvees.

On the second leg, everything fell apart. Almost immediately, I was carrying Rager's gun and as soon as he took it back, I saw that Ryan needed help.

"Give me the gun, Ryan."

"I got it sergeant. I'm fine."

"You're obviously not fine. Give it to me."

"I got it. Don't worry."

"It ain't a fucking request, Ryan! Give me the damn gun!"

Ryan was a good hiker and even he was dying. I had put Miller in front of me, so I could see when he fell out, but somehow he slipped by me again. Gunny Brouillet asked me if I knew where Miller was and I said that I assumed he was still in front of me. He fixed me with a withering glare and told me that Miller was in the back of the pack on the ground. That was good for me, since I was about to fall out myself. I handed Ryan's gun back to him and went back for Miller. The XO was checking out Miller, who was delirious. We put him in a Humvee and I then found myself far behind the rest of the company. I jogged up and was able to catch the tail-end of the company, but was too spent to work my way up to my platoon. It was embarrassing to be in the back and I hoped people would understand I had fallen back to help someone. I saw Sgt. Dart scoot by like he had a motor in his ass and I secretly hated him very intensely for about a half-second. I then got over it and realized that Dart was doing fine because he had worked to become that fit. He wasn't born strong, he was born short—he had worked to make himself strong.

We stopped on a large plain while Miller got an IV drip. I was supposed to be mad at Miller, but I wasn't. He just wasn't a good hiker. After a few hours of setting down, moving twenty feet to the right, then moving again, we finally cemented our position. The battalion would be in a huge triangle with our lines facing the LSA.

The next day, after sitting around feeling sorry for myself all morning, I told my squad to work on their holes. I worked on mine for four hours before it was deep enough to kneel in, but Miller's team was kicking ass. Miller had a reputation for being lazy, but left to his own devices, he made the best fighting position in the whole battalion. Reed's team was not doing as good, but I was giving Reed a few days to be butt-hurt about being posted from squad leader before I confronted him on anything.

By the next day, Miller's hole was even better than the textbook example. It was so deep that they had to build stairs just so they could reach the gun. I had gotten my one-man hole deep enough to sit in, but Reed's hole was lagging. I went over and chatted casually with Rager, telling him that their hole was good, but they needed to catch up with Miller's. He nodded amiably and went back to work.

Reed had been in his tent with one of his "headaches" that always coincided with manual labor. He got livid when he heard my comments. As I walked back to my hole, he came out of his tent and started screaming and cursing at me in front of the boots, as was his habit. He told me that if I didn't like the hole, I should help them. This wasn't going to fly. I gave myself a minute to calm down and then I ordered him over. This talk was inevitable, but I didn't think it would come so soon. I sat down casually next to my hole, but made sure to have my shovel at arm's length, so I could swing it at his face if he tried to attack me.

He charged up, red in the face, and was about to start into one of his tirades when I cut him off. I told him that I knew how he had operated in the past and I wasn't going to put up with it. He wasn't going to embarrass us like he had before. He seemed surprised that I said that and started to argue that the dirt in his area, twenty feet away, was twice as hard as the rest of the dirt. I cut him off again, telling him that I had apprised Squeak about his temper and I had been given the power to bust him down to ammo man. If he persisted in being a problem, I would get him sent back to 2nd Platoon. That was a bluff, but it got his attention. No matter how badly he was hated in Weapons Platoon, he was hated twice as much in Second. I gave him two choices: get the hole dug or become a lance corporal. He sputtered that he didn't want to talk; he just wanted to go fix his hole. I let him walk off.

We had plenty of time to read and the first book to really hit home was "Bravo-Two-Zero," which told the story of a British SAS squad—operating in Iraq during the Gulf War—that was captured and tortured before escaping. The portrayal of the Iraqis opened my eyes. The tales of torture and degradation were all the more disconcerting because it showed how institutionalized torture was over there.

Even though we were living like pigs, we were still required to get haircuts every week or so. Many people shaved their heads so that they wouldn't have to deal with the grimy conditions or the niggling idiocies of the staff NCOs. When we got back from Oki, Miller suddenly got very image-conscious, so much so that he started dying his hair and sun-bathing nude in The Backyard. Male Marines are never allowed to change their hair color and Miller stopped doing so after he was corrected by staff NCOs. A year later, he was accused of having "out-of-regs" bleached hair and he was forced to get a haircut. Even after they cut an inch off his hair, the staff still accused him of having lightened hair and made him cut it again that day. The next day, they still complained about his hair. Miller and I both explained to them that we were in the desert and the sun was lightening his hair, not the bleach he put in it a year ago, but they wouldn't hear of it. Though his hair was only two inches long, it was then deemed "out-of-regs" for length, even though the regs said that it could be three inches. Miller and Moser both had thick heads of hair and small foreheads, so their hair always looked bushy. First Sergeant Young (who shaved his head) would always harass people by quoting the regs that said that hair could not be "eccentric." That's supposed to mean that people can't use excessive amounts of mousse or have fad haircuts, but it was used as another way to harass Marines. Reed was going around assaulting people and malingering and he was constantly given second chances, Meanwhile, Miller was getting his third haircut in two days.

During my first week at the TAA, my greatest fear was taking my first shit in Kuwait. There is just no way to maintain your dignity while shitting on the ground; I always felt sub-human. With all the gear and straps, it's quite a balancing act to avoid doing something wonderful like accidentally shitting on your gas mask. My other fear was akin to the fear that first-time mothers experience before they give birth; when you eat nothing but MREs, you don't shit for five or six days and when you do, it is large, bone-dry and painful. Every dump was followed by two large dollops of blood falling out of my ass. My first dump was an almost religious experience; I told my friends about it afterward. No one thought that was weird, since they each had their own epic shit stories they wanted to share.

After a week at the TAA, we started getting hot food delivered by truck for dinner and sometimes for breakfast. Cooks are the hardest working guys you'll meet and they get zero appreciation, so they're a bit sensitive. The food wasn't great, but they didn't have the best supplies, so I didn't really blame them. A lot of salt and you could keep almost anything down.

The Marine Corps has a tradition in which the lowest ranks eat first and are served by the higher-ups. Since I was a sergeant, I got my plastic gloves on and started to serve the Marines, which I enjoyed because I got to talk to people I didn't usually see. Everyone would try to get "the hook-up" and I would try to appease them as long as there was enough food. A staple of our diet was a long, thin tan-colored turkey hot dog that was dubbed "Camel dick".

The food never got better than barely edible, but at least it was mostly identifiable. A thick mucousy yellow gravy was another staple, so I was surprised to see some white gravy one night served along with some shoe leather…I mean steak. My teeth couldn't pierce the tough meat, so I grabbed one end between my teeth and the other with both hands and pulled as hard as I could. After struggling for about ten seconds, it finally snapped and the steak and my hand hit my plate, splashing me with white gravy that I found out later was actually supposed to be mashed potatoes.

The cooks were sensitive and didn't want to hear any negative comments, of which they were many. I was embarrassed about the rude comments that Marines made when they received their food, so I tried to smooth things over with the cooks. Miller didn't have the same air of diplomacy. After opening a tureen of unidentifiable goo, he turned to one of the cooks and said, "So what's this? Slop?" The head cook, a staff NCO, got so upset that tears started to form in the corners of his eyes.

"You want to make comments? Go! Get out of here. You don't get nothing."

"Let me get this straight…I'm being denied food in a time of war?"

The general consensus was that we would take Baghdad within three weeks of crossing the border. We imagined a month of occupation, a month staged in Kuwait standing by in case there was trouble and then we would go home. In the

Gulf War, the Marine units left three days after the fighting ended. The Marine Corps is a fighting machine; we don't have the resources or manpower for long-term occupation; that's what the Army is for.

Our feeling about the Iraqis echoed the crude sentiment stated by the Marine Corps colonel in Full Metal Jacket, "We are here to help the Vietnamese because inside every gook, there is an American trying to break free." I imagined a small resistance from Saddam's cronies, who knew they'd face jail time, along with small bands of men whose pride had been injured by seeing foreign troops in their homeland. We were sure that the entire Iraqi military was nothing but inept cowards, but more than that, we expected that every Iraqi chafed at the yoke of Saddam and—if given the chance—would gladly kill him and live in a free and democratic society.

After a few days at the TAA, most of the tents were in shreds. I was quite proud that I had the only remaining working zipper-door in the company. The only good thing that came out of the squad leader switcheroo that was pulled on me was that I ended up with the tent I had shared with Levesque. I was the only person below staff sergeant that had his own tent and I prized it like no other. Most people were cramped beyond belief.

Ross told me he woke up one night and asked his tent-mate, Mohler, why his sleeping bag was wet; Mohler told him he had spilled his water. Months later, Mohler admitted he had been pissing in a bottle since it was cold outside and he accidentally sprayed Ross's bag a little. Instead of being angry, Ross laughed and told him he had done the same thing to Mohler's sleeping bag a week earlier.

Fire-watch was set at 25%, which meant that the most sleep anyone below sergeant got was three hours in a row. We started doing "stand-to" every morning during the hour before dawn, which has traditionally been the most likely time for an enemy attack. It was a good practice in combat, but when it became part of the daily routine, it really started to grind people down. First Sergeant Young would come around, after getting his eight hours of beauty sleep, and give really helpful comments like, "Get your hands out of your pockets," while his hands were in his pockets.

It took time for me to get used to being sergeant. I pulled fire-watch until I realized that I was the only sergeant pulling it. The sergeants' job was to pull Sergeant of the Guard. I'd walk down the line and make sure people knew the "challenge and pass" and make sure they were awake. The attitudes of those kids were incredible. They were getting no sleep in freezing cold weather, yet they maintained their senses of humor. I never caught one person asleep.

As in boot camp, I went to church whenever times got bad, going as much for the time away from the company as for the actual service. We were promised a weekly service, but the priest didn't even show up after we waited for two hours. A couple days later, he showed up, like he was doing us a favor, and said that he *might* show up in two weeks or so. I went to the Baptist service from then on. Chaplains are absolutely crucial to a unit, yet often completely useless. Far from being the hippy tree-hugger priests I had in catholic school, these were hard men from an earlier day. I met a chaplain at the chow hall in SOI who spent the whole lunch period complaining that the only Marines who went to see him were "pussies" who just wanted to get out of the Corps. I went to the battalion chaplain as a boot—distraught at never seeing my wife—and the great advice he gave was to write letters to her and call her on the phone. Wow…thanks.

Gunny Brouillet and Squeak took the platoon to the low hills between the TAA and the LSA to train. Squeak had us low-crawl to shooting positions without being seen by the "enemy." After every squad finished, the other squads would critique their approach. I got good advice from my peers and took it in stride, but some others, like Elias and Chhav, took it personally.

As usual, Carpenter was lost in the sauce and had to be corrected constantly. While moving into position, he put the A-Bag on the wrong side of the gun, a simple mistake that he kept repeating. Reed jumped on top of him and started berating him. The next day, Squeak told me that Carpenter complained about being hazed. In couched terms, I told Reed that I condoned him getting Carpenter's attention by almost any means, but I wouldn't accept him kicking, punching or slapping Carpenter, which to my knowledge he had never done. Reed had crossed the line by telling Carpenter that he could shoot him in time of war if he was out of order, but I let that slide since I was thinking the same thing about Reed.

Chatting with Miller one day in his fighting hole, the XO walked past us to the shit trench 20 meters away, dropped the kids off at the pool; then walked back. He stopped and fixed us with an accusing glare as he passed us.

"Why didn't you Marines challenge me before I entered friendly lines?" he asked. Miller looked over at me and cocked an eyebrow.

"Are you serious, sir?" Miller asked.

"Security is a serious issue, Corporal."

"Sir, we watched you walk right past us, take a shit, and walk back. We knew it was you."

The XO squinted, started to say something, then turned away.

After two weeks at the TAA, the company was "allowed" to go back to our designated living area, the LSA, and use the showers that had just been installed. I didn't believe that the showers were up and, if they were, that they were any cleaner than living at the TAA. When the call went up for volunteers to stay back and guard the TAA, most people saw that as a sucker bet, but a few others and I realized that it was a great deal. Two days away from the company, and most importantly two days away from the staff NCOs and officers. I enjoyed the hell out of their absence, sleeping peacefully and listening to my Jewel CD on Miller's CD Player. Her first CD is like the poetry your girlfriend used to write in the ninth grade, but in that austere, all-male environment, it because sublimely beautiful.

When the company came back, I heard that Reed had been acting up in my absence. Though he had acted normal for the two weeks since I counseled him, his true nature was starting to show. On the truck to the LSA, someone offered the Charms from their MRE to whoever wanted it and Rager and Reed both raised their hands. When Rager was given the candy, Reed threw a fit and actually *ordered* Rager to hand over the Charms. Even when he wasn't doing something violent or crazy, he was being immature in a way that was almost unimaginable.

White re-enlisted at the TAA, which was surprising since he didn't exactly knock it out of the park in his first four years. He had recently married and acquired some step-children, so the $8000 re-enlistment bonus was very enticing. That sounds like a lot of money, until you find out that it isn't a lump sum. It is doled out over the next four years, which comes out to about $166 a month.

The Marines with expectant wives started getting shuttled to Camp Commando to make calls. When Jesse and Hot Rod were told that they were going, we all shoved money and long lists of food to buy at them. I had known both of them since we were boots, but I never got close to either one since we didn't work together much. Jesse was one of the funniest guys on the Earth, though his pride endlessly got him in trouble. The previous fall, Rager had gotten drunk and pissed off the catwalk, as Marines are wont to do. When Cpl. Dreyer started to yell at him, a 51 boot named Jones butted in and started arguing with the corporal. Jones looked like a English Lit grad student, but he was one of the most bad-ass street fighters I ever met—an intellectual dirtbag.

Dreyer reported both of them to the higher-ups. Rager got busted down and Jones got the first of many brushes with military justice. The next day, Jesse confronted Dreyer at the armory. Dreyer was correct by the letter of the law, but Jesse was steamed that Dreyer hadn't given him the professional courtesy of allowing him to discipline Jones without alerting the higher-ups. Jesse told Dreyer that he was going to hit him if he didn't get out of his face. Notice I didn't say "threatened"—Jesse never threatened anyone. Though freakishly strong, he was quite easy to get along. He wasn't like Reed, who was always telling people he was going to punch them in the face; if he said he was going to hit you—duck. Jesse got busted down to PFC for socking Dreyer in the mouth. He was out-ranked by almost all of his boots, but it didn't diminish the respect they had for him.

Rodriguez was much more laconic. He had been dubbed "Hot Rod" to differentiate him from Rodriguez-Garcia (a.k.a. RodGar). Like the rest of the 51s, he was not a great hiker, but he never fell out. He was older and more mature, though his roughneck, Heavy Metal days showed through at times. He was from Northern Cali and had a quick, clipped way of speaking which seemed strange coming out of such a large, lumbering guy. I joked that Hot Rod's motto was "Talk fast, move slow." When a fellow Mexican would try to speak to him in Spanish, he'd shrug and say, "I'm a coconut, dog." Brown on the outside, white on the inside. He got the job done and rarely attracted negative attention from his seniors, though I'm sure his size had something to do with that. It was a damn shame it took him so long to pick up corporal.

The weekend before we left, he had been cut from work early to take care of some family business, under the assumption that we weren't leaving until some time the next week. He showed up to work on Monday to an empty barracks. With his good rep, no ulterior motives were suggested and when he arrived in Kuwait, four days after we did, he showed no more distress than if he had simply missed a bus.

The engineers built a rudimentary range and we trudged out there to zero our guns (adjusting the sights to make sure the guns shoot straight). Since I had never done that before, I delegated it to Miller and Reed, who did a fine job. The task had put me on the spot and I realized that, because of my time away, I couldn't be the classic know-it-all sergeant. I decided that my strengths were looking out for my men and being moto about combat; I would to play to those strengths.

2/4 was in Oki at the time and we were due to replace them in July—maybe. We were told that we would either (A) go back to Cali in June and then fly to Oki in July, (B) stay in Iraq until July and fly straight to Oki, or (C) a reserve battalion would be called up to replace 2/4 or we would stay in Iraq indefinitely. Moore had a brother in another battalion who told him that they were scheduled to replace 2/4, which was a relief for me. That meant we would go home after the war was over, supposedly sometime in May.

During the night shoot, the XO told us to experiment with putting the PEQ-2 laser spotter on the gun. The gun has a rail on which you can attach a night scope, but after you start firing the gun, it shakes too much too look through the scope. With the team leader though, the gunner doesn't really need to see. The team leader gives the gunner adjustments to make on the Traversing and Elevation Mechanism (T&E) to get the gun on target. The squad leader will usually "laze" the target with his PEQ-2 to guide the team leaders. The PEQ-2 emits a "white" laser, which is invisible to the human eye and also safe—you can't blind anyone with it. With NVGs on, it shoots out a perfect straight line as far as the eye can see—it's truly amazing. While shooting, the gun-mounted PEQ-2's beam would jump all over the place, but the idea was still useful. The PEQ-2 would show you exactly where the gun was pointing before the trigger was pulled.

After the shoot, the XO ambled over to check on the experiment.

"So boys, how'd you like using the PEQ-2 on the gun?"

"Well, sir, it had some good poi-," I started.

"Worst idea ever, sir!" Reed answered cheerfully. No one *ever* asked Reed his opinion, so this was a rare treat. Also, he loved to run any idea down, especially good ones. He told the boots that it was "weak" to put a sling on the gun. I asked him what they should do if they were going up a steep hill and they needed both hands to get up. His response? "Worst idea ever!"

I got to know Squeak better at the TAA, though things quickly soured between us. He confided in me that he had gotten "bad paper" when he was an instructor at SOI when a student had a negligent discharge on the gun line while he was the range safety officer. He was blamed and his career was effectively killed. Though only 24, he was already a staff sergeant. He had spent most of his time outside of the grunts, working in the company office as a junior Marine, re-enlisting as a recruiter, and then being an instructor at SOI. He was scrawny and awkward and the other staff NCOs didn't take to him very well.

Squeak was catching heat for us pulling high crimes and misdemeanors like pissing without a helmet on. He started to harp on it and when we gaffed him off, he quickly turned against us. I had no ill will toward him (at that time any-way), but I knew how the Corps worked. As a sergeant, I had no power to make my Marines lives better, but I could keep them from being worse. My guys were miserable enough without me pestering them about useless rules I didn't even care about. It's not like we were in any danger. You could see all the way to the horizon in every direction. The only way to sneak up on us would be to burrow under the ground like the monsters in "Tremors."

Carpenter had what psychologists call "zero affect", which meant that he rarely displayed any overt emotion. He had a deep, sonorous monotone that made him sound vaguely like Richard Nixon. He was known for beginning every sentence with the word "well" and never being able to get to the point. Every story of his started with the Big Bang and moved forward from there. Once, when he came loping up to Martial Arts class five minutes late, I interrogated him.

"Carpenter, where the hell were you?"

"Well…Two weeks ago, Corporal Moser-"

"Are you fucking shitting me? Why were you late when I told you when and where you had to be and I reminded you ten minutes before it was time to leave?"

"Well…when we were at the LSA last week-"

"Motherfucker! Shut the fuck up! Stop acting like a goddamn retard. I don't want to hear about ancient fucking history!"

"Well, sergeant, I was trying to teach you-"

"Listen, Carpenter, I'm a fucking sergeant. You'd don't 'teach' me shit."

"Well, I was trying to *inform* you that Cpl. Moser-"

"Goddamnit!…Wait—you know what? Fuck it. The class isn't starting for ten minutes anyway. I'm going to fucking humor you, Carpenter. Go ahead; tell me your damn story that probably starts when the sperm met the egg in your fucking mom's snatch."

He looked at me, his dull eyes sensing a trap.

"Go ahead, Carpenter. It's your show."

"Well…as I was trying to tell you, sergeant. Two weeks ago, Cpl. Moser told me I needed to pack my gear better since it's always falling out. So when we were at the LSA, I dumped everything out and re-did it three times until I got it right, but when we got back here yesterday, I noticed that my right pack strap was coming loose. So I fixed it and then I sat down."

I glared at him, waiting for more.

"Is that it?"

"Well, yes, sergeant. As I was telling you-"

"What the fuck does that have to do with you being late for a class that is being held a whopping 200 feet away from your tent?!"

"Well, I was sitting next to my pack when I realized that I was late."

"Are you—Are you-….Fuck, I'm so mad that I can't even finish a sentence. Fuck it, Carpenter. Fuck it—you won. You blew my fucking mind. Your idiotic story—which by the way had *nothing* to do with you being late—just blew my mind. Go. Get out of here."

I paired up with Squeak and we started doing basic strikes and blocks. I didn't like sparring with someone who outranked me, so I pulled my punches. Nevertheless, when I tapped him in the chest, he flew back six feet like I was Superman. He got back up, rubbing his chest with an embarrassed smile. I had to give it to Squeak, I'd never met a scrawnier guy, but he still hung in there. He told me about getting his ass beat viciously as a boot and I believed him. The fact that he didn't go UA made me respect him; I'm sure it had been hard for him.

A few days later, we did "bull in the ring," in which people got paired up randomly to fight each other. Half of the guys were fair-to-good fighters, but I wasn't one of them. I went to Catholic school in Nebraska and I never even saw a fight until I moved to Texas my junior year of high school. My buddy Showers got paired up with me. Though not a great hiker, Showers had retard strength and was one of the better wrestlers in the platoon. I knew I couldn't win, but like Squeak, I could get points for not backing down. Four times, I attacked him and four times, Showers easily bested me. The last time, I didn't care if I got choked out, so I kept fighting him until I noticed that the ref had called the fight and Shower had stopped fighting me thirty seconds earlier.

The instructor of our class was Gunny Brouillet, who had been the company gunny until a senior gunny displaced him right before we left. Gunny was tall, with a full head of salt-and-pepper hair, a large nose and distinct French features. He looked like a guy who would be swinging a pike in the 100 Years War. Gunny was a warrior-scholar, but his real love was teaching hand-to-hand combat or "Wop-Bop-Chop" as First Sergeant Bell had called it.

While every action movie has the war hero Karate-chopping a hundred terrorists, in real life, the concept of hand-to-hand combat is ridiculous. The only situation I could imagine needing it was almost impossible. I and every one of my buddies would have to run out of ammo and lose our rifles, bayonets and grenades. Then the enemy would have to somehow lose all of their weapons as well and still want to fight us. Then, and only then, could I see us actually using hand-to-hand.

Mohler had attracted the ire of Gunny Brouillet early on. Back in Cali, while walking out to the PFT course, Mohler saw a dying bird on the side of the road, so he picked up a rock to put the bird out of its misery. When Gunny Brouillet saw Mohler throwing the rock, he went nuts, pulled Mohler aside, yelled at in front of his boots and threatened to post him from his job as section leader. It was typical of the situation in the company between staff NCOs and NCOs that he would embarrass Mohler over so minor an occurrence.

When Gunny called Mohler out to be a demonstrator, he knew he was in for some pain. Gunny put Mohler into a painful joint lock and threw him over his knee, but when Mohler cried out and started flopping around the ground, most of us thought he was joking. When he didn't get up though, it was clear that he was hurt badly. Mohler was checked out by a corpsman and then taken to Camp Doha, which was a permanent army base that had all the amenities of home. Mohler returned the next day, high as a kite on Demerol. He told us about sleeping in a real bed, watching TV, spending hours on the phone, and eating at KFC. The Army knew that everyone wanted to come to Doha, so they made a rule that you could only come there if you had a colonel sign a permission form. They couldn't handle the idea that they might step out of their air-conditioned rooms and find out that some damn Marines had eaten all the chicken at KFC.

Mohler was seriously injured and could bear no weight on his arm. It would take two months for him to get his full range of motion back. Mohler might have been a goof, but he knew his knowledge and was in great shape; he was a three-time rifle expert and a born leader. It was ridiculous to lose him, weeks before battle, for something as minor as martial arts. Gunny said that the injury was Mohler's fault since he didn't "execute a proper break-fall like he had been taught." If Gunny was such an expert, how come he couldn't show off the move without injuring him?

A controversy erupted after one of our frequent gas drills. Ross was nursing a bloody nose when a gas drill was sounded. A bleeding nose is a sign of exposure to chemical weapons and the lieutenant he was attached to thought that Ross was mocking the dangers of a gas attack. By the time the word got up to Sprincin, Ross was facing being charged and sent to another squad. Ross's squad had more rough edges than any of the others, but it was also the best squad in that they were the closest and watched each others' backs. Gunny Brouillet called their squad leader, Mohler, into his tent for a one-on-one. When he told Mohler that he was going to break up the squad, Mohler black-mailed him by saying that if he did, he would call his congressman and complain about Gunny injuring his arm. Gunny lost his cool demeanor and said that was just an accident.

Mohler's squad was assembled outside the tent and when Gunny went out, each one in turn said that they would request mast if the squad was broken up. Gunny seemed to admire their solidarity and the issue was dropped. This was another strike against Sprincin in everyone's book. He had not even spoken to Ross before he decided to charge him. He always assumed the worst of any one of us. This pattern would only get worse as time went by.

To our surprise, we received enough PRRs for all squad leaders and team leaders, which was a godsend. Though SSgt. D had three PRRs for my squad, I told him I only needed two. There was no way in hell that I was going let Reed have one. My eardrums ached just imagining that idiot's voice screaming through my headset day and night.

In addition to getting the PRRs, we also got a new and crucial weapon—the new M-16A4. It had a broom handle fore-grip, like a tommy gun, which helped when you drew it in tight in close urban environments. The biggest advantage though was the ACOG (Advanced Combat Optical Gunsight) scope, which could almost double the range in which a Marine could effectively hit a point target. In the British and Australian forces, almost every front-line combatant has a scope on their weapon, but the Marine Corps takes great pride in using "iron sights" as if using scopes was cheating. War isn't the damn SATs, let me cheat. The previous year though, the Marine Corps had established the Designated Marksman concept, in which every squad's best shooter would have a scoped weapon.

When the tracs we had been promised finally arrived, it was like Christmas morning. You can't make a grunt happier than by telling him that he doesn't have to walk. The trackers showed us their vehicles and let us crawl all over them like a bunch of kids. The AAV (Amphibious Assault Vehicle—commonly known as an amtrac or trac) was mainly a troop carrier, but with its turret, which was armed with a .50 cal. machinegun and a Mark 19 automatic grenade launcher, it packed a lot of firepower into a small space.

A few days later, we were told that we were going on a field op with the tracs. I didn't understand how you could go on a field op when you were already in the field, but hey, I didn't finish college, what did I know? I was excited since we were supposed to go within sight of the border. I didn't know that I was about to have the most miserable experience of my life.

We packed into the tracs, which was a tight fit with all our gear, weapons and ammo. The trac was designed for a single squad of Marines back when all you went to war with was a web belt with a canteen on it, so it was like playing Tetris trying to get us all in there. The ramp would drop, we'd pack twenty people inside and if the last few didn't make it in time, the ramp door would cram them in like a garbage compactor.

The two long top hatches were kept secured, even though they were supposed to be open so we could cover the blind left side of the trac with our machineguns. The crew didn't want to go through the hassle of unlatching the hatches. We drove for about an hour; then got out and set up a defense. With ten tracs, our lines stretched almost a mile and it took us a couple tries to fill all the gaps. I asked Squeak what the rest of the field op would entail, but he knew about as much as me. He thought that we would move to one more spot and then go home. That turned out to be true, but we had hell to pay before that.

We got back in the trac in a hurry and everyone was all jumbled together. My foot was twisted 90 degrees to the right, with no room to move and three people on top of it, and I didn't even have it the worst. I assumed that we had an hour ride at most and tried to get through it. Two hours went by, then three…four— this was getting ridiculous. I felt like I was in a mass grave. Others moaned in pain as their muscles started to cramp. I got my Mini Mag-Lite out, but the bulb was burned out, so all I had to see with was the light on my watch. Every bump we hit threw people into even worse positions. People started to wonder aloud what the hell was going on.

When the sixth hour rolled around, I started to get worried. My whole body was cramping and I was sure I would need to piss soon. I started to feel like I was going to freak out. I switched spots with Singh in the middle since I would be able to crouch and move my muscles a little. I was able to work some of the kinks out, but by the time I went to sit down, my sitting space had shrunk from a foot and a half to less than six inches. I had to squat on the tips of my toes while holding onto a latch on the roof.

Hour eight rolled around and I felt like I was starting to crack. This was like some kind of psychological torture—crammed in the dark, moving but never stopping, no break to piss, everyone out of water. I started to calculate how much gas the trac had; it had to be getting low. I *hoped* it was getting low. I passed a message to the Third Platoon Commander, Lt. Pettes, in the commander's hatch; he had his own seat and could see outside. He was a pretty good guy and he tried to get some info, but no one knew anything; they were just following the trac in front of them. I started to hate the crew. Why couldn't the hatches be opened? They were fucking with us on purpose. This was beyond initiation; I was starting to feel like I was going to go nuts. People started making weird moaning noises after hours of pain and I was one of them.

Hour 10 somehow made things easier. The worst had to be over. Somehow my body had shut down and I didn't need to piss, which had been a big worry. When we finally stopped, I almost started crying. How the hell could this have been such an emotionally exhausting experience? I wondered if I was weak for letting it get to me.

When the ramp dropped, I walked out slowly, trying to stay composed, not wanting to show how much the ride had gotten to me. I confided in Miller, who didn't look that bad.

"Jesus Christ man, there were a couple of times in there when I thought I was about to lose it and start screaming like a maniac," I said.

"I know, dude."

"No, I'm not kidding. I really thought I was going to go insane."

"I'm not kidding either, man. That was fucking horrific."

We were told that we could go to sleep, but it was only two and a half hours until reveille. I was tired, but I didn't want to sleep, since I was sure I'd have some fucked-up nightmares. When I told Miozza I'd take his watch so he could sleep, he looked like I just bought him a car.

We would go back to the LSA for a few days. Not only were all the showers up, but there was also supposed to be a visit from the mobile PX truck. We were ordered to fill our holes in before we left; I took a picture of mine and Miller's since I had spent so much time in them. As we were packing up to go to the LSA, I noticed that Ferguson was putting a Coke in his pack; he had been one of the lucky few who got to go to Doha. I offered him $20 for the can and he asked me if I was serious. I handed the bill over without regret and felt the can, which was still cold from the night air. I showed it off proudly to everyone, shocking them by how much I paid for it. I sipped it slowly over the next hour, savoring every drop. Ironically, that night at the LSA they handed out two Cokes with dinner for the first time. I went around buying people's second Cokes for five bucks a piece.

While waiting in the trac to go back to the LSA, Reed started loudly telling a long story about plucking turkey feathers on Thanksgiving to no one in particular. After five minutes, a guy nicknamed Chubby finally piped up and said that it was the most boring story he had ever heard. Everyone laughed and Reed jumped up and tried to start a fight with Chubby in the crowded trac. After realizing that he didn't have enough room to fight, Reed laid his head back and tried to go to sleep. Our corpsman was talking to one of the snipers about wrestling and he commented that Golf didn't seem to do a lot of wrestling training. Reed opened his eyes and started screaming at Doc, saying he'd wrestle him and beat his ass. I couldn't believe this kid; it was like going to war with a crazy person.

A half hour after we got to the LSA, the Mobile PX rolled up and the tents emptied. 400 people got in line for one small truck's worth of goods. By the time I got to the front four hours later, all that was left were razors and boxes upon boxes of tampons.

Though about a third of the company were dippers back in Cali, out of boredom, more than half dipped in Kuwait. The preferred type was "State-side" which aficionados of lip cancer felt was fresher than the dip produced overseas. Each dipper had an elaborate ritual that involved flipping the can downward while hitting it with their thumb, making a loud "thwock!" sound. Dip was so prized that people would save whatever remnants were left in their mouth after they were done sucking the juice out. When everyone ran out of fresh cans, they would bust into their "Re-dip" and try to siphon out whatever micro-grams of nicotine were left in them. I once saw a Marine who was so desperate that he bought someone else's re-dip.

Mail was coming in every day or two and I was the only one I knew who hadn't gotten any. Mohler said some POGs told him that the mail plane only went out when it got full. If it took a month to fill, then that's how long it would wait.

We went to the chow hall, expecting the same rubbery—grey chicken we got at the TAA, and I was shocked to see rib-eye steak, baked potatoes and rolls. Since there was a permanent camp guard, none of us had to pull watch and we all got an amazing eight hours of sleep. I pulled out the pictures of my family and looked at them right before I went to sleep, so that I would dream about them.

The next day, I got a pleasant surprise when I ran into ran into SSgt. P and Lt. Chapell. They smiled in shock and surprise at my sergeant stripes and congratulated me on picking up. I asked about Kim and they said that he was stepping up to the plate and doing a great job. I grilled SSgt. P on the rumors about the mail plane and he told me they were false. It was nice to talk to an officer and staff NCO that had common sense and didn't spent all their time on minutiae.

The copies of Star and Stripes that would trickle in were prized like no other. We read them for the "secret" messages—news of units moving or hints from President Bush that we were attacking soon. There was still a worry that the war would be called off and all of our misery would be for nothing. We heard rumors about Saddam's son being shot and Republican Guardsmen trying to assassinate Saddam.

I made sure that everyone who got a letter from Sprincin's class actually responded. I didn't want a couple kids to get left out and end up joining Al-Qaeda. My penpal was a tomboy who shot rifles in competitions and drew World War I bi-planes in her letter. Miller wanted me to trade me penpals since his kid was "lame." On the back of my letter, I drew a picture of myself in my gear that Miller deemed a little too idealized, but why dis-illusion the girl?

My first bad mark as a sergeant came from an incident so minor that I had to be reminded of it when I was counseled for it. During company PT, First Sergeant Young decided that we would PT "by the numbers", which meant that each exercise would be micro-managed Barney-style, which was how POGs PTed. After the First Sergeant formed us up like a bunch of recruits, he had us get double-arms interval from each other so that we would have enough room to thrash around in the sand without hitting the Marines next to us. The company stretched out over 200 meters, but instead of placing himself at the middle of the company, so we could all see and hear him, the First Sergeant stood at the front of First Platoon. He was so far away that he looked like an ant and we couldn't tell what the hell he was saying. People started laughing, since the whole situation was so ridiculous, and when he heard us laughing, he started shouting at us unintelligibly in the distance—which made it even funnier. For propriety's sake, since I was out in front of the platoon as acting platoon sergeant, I told them to lock it up. The platoon sergeants ahead of me got smart and started relaying the First Sergeant's orders so that we could follow along.

Several days later, Squeak told me he had to counsel me. I laughed since I thought he was joking, but he told me it was serious. Lt. Sprincin had ordered him to counsel me for losing control of the platoon by letting them laugh in formation. It was so petty that it didn't even bother me, but it embarrassed Squeak to have to write me up for it and he apologized for doing so. I thought that with a war pending, Sprinkles might have wanted to spend his energies on less petty pursuits, but pettiness was always prioritized by him.

Feb. 26th—We were under constant threat of being gassed by Saddam, since we were well within his missiles' ranges. The worst thing about getting gassed was that you couldn't fight it; you just had to sit there and hope your chemical suit, which was made by the lowest-bidder, protected you. I wondered how long I could live in my suit, pissing in it and drinking water through a tube while wondering if I was infected.

A British NBC squad had been attached to our battalion. Their Fox armored personnel carrier was fortified to operate in the most toxic environments imaginable for extended periods of time. All I cared about was that it had air-conditioning, though they tried to make it sound like that was a bad thing to make us feel better. The vehicle even had a robotic arm that could move around and test the environment to see if it was safe for them to come out. The British were professional, yet laid back. Once they were prepared to roll into Iraq, they chilled out and played soccer all day. Their MREs were much prized since they had canned meat and biscuits with Hershey bars and real tea—nothing was dehydrated or reconstituted. When they first got there, we had a big trading party with them, but they quickly got bored with us. Their gear and food was so much better than ours that we really didn't have much to offer.

Like the canaries that coal miners used to take with them down into the mines, the combat chicken (as he was called), was there as a first-warning against gas attack. Gas was probably the chicken's second biggest danger, as it was the only edible meat within thirty miles. We were told to put our gas masks on one day when the chicken was found dead, but it turned out to be a more ordinary cause. Sand had plugged up the chicken's nostrils, asphyxiating it.

The corporal in NBC was the unfortunate victim of a nickname which wasn't deserved in any way, but was funny enough that it stuck. Being that he had to keep track of the chicken—and that Marines are bored pervs—he was accused of having sex with the chicken's ass. Thus he was dubbed "Poopdick." Any time he came in sight, Jesse would yell out "Poopdick!"—or the shortened version, "Poopy"—and everyone would laugh. The corporal hated his nickname, but once you get stuck with one that funny, that's it; you have no recourse.

We could leave our rifle with a buddy, but we were supposed to take our gas mask everywhere. Showers and I were heading to the shower trailers when he asked me if we should take our gas masks. We had been told that we didn't have to wear our gas masks if we were PTing, so I figured that if you didn't have to wear it while exercising, you wouldn't have to take it with you to shower after exercising. I told Showers that since I was a sergeant, I'd take the hit if anyone made a stink.

As soon as we finished our showers, the gas drill siren went off. Nice. The NBC warrant officer was supposed to walk through all of the tents to inspect everyone before he turned the siren off; I didn't have a leg to stand on since I was a sergeant. When you get to that rank, there aren't any excuses anymore. I told Showers to hide in the shower stall until the siren ended. We sweated being found out for 45 minutes; all the while, Showers stood in the stall across from me, giving me dirty looks and mouthing, "I told you so." The "All clear" was called and we tried to slink back to the tent. Halfway there, we got caught by a staff sergeant. I had to step my game up if I was going to keep wearing my stripes.

Keller took center stage during the long hours we spent in the tent. With a captive audience, he was free to attack, in a humorous way, whoever came into sight. Roy, with his thick accent, sub-literate grunts and total lack of a sense of humor, was an easy target. Keller was reading a book about hunters in Africa, which described the hunting of a gazelle-like creature called a "yamsbach."

"Hey Roy, I bet you'd love to be with the guys in this book. Loincloth on, spear in hand, stalking the great yamsbach. It'd remind you of your first Brontosaurus hunt."

Keeping on the hunting theme, he would stalk around the tent, holding his knife by the blade. He would stop suddenly, point at the ground between someone's feet and say sternly, "Don't move! Deadly scorpion…" He would then throw the knife into the wooden floor with a sharp "thwock!"

"Don't bother to thank me, buddy. You'd a'done the same for me."

Of course, like any good thing, other Marines quickly ruined it. People started copying Keller and, soon enough, knives were bouncing off tent poles and skittering across the floor. Ross from Third ended up throwing a knife a half-inch into Ritchie's knee, almost keeping him out of the war.

We always assumed that the higher-ups knew more than they let on, but I learned that wasn't true. While working on some paperwork in the staff and officers' tent at the LSA, the griping and complaining I heard was the same as what I heard back in my tent. There was a growing fear that there would be no war and we would just sit out there on the border for months as a deterrent. Gunny Linton said it best when he griped that "they" should send us to Iraq or send us home. We had always referred to our staff and officers as "they," but there was several higher levels of "they" above them.

March 4th—Since I hadn't gotten any mail yet, Squeak hooked me up to go on the next run to Commando. We climbed into the back of a Humvee and debated whether a cigarette could set off the cans of diesel fuel we were sitting on. Halfway to Commando, Gunny Linton stopped our small convoy to let us check out detritus from the last war. We climbed a small berm and saw a huge elephant graveyard of destroyed Iraqi tanks. It was awesome to see the remnants of our last contact with the Iraqis and how decisive the victory had been.

We stopped at a US Air Force base so one of the boots could visit his wife who was stationed there. I was happy for the kid, but jealous at the same time, knowing he'd be doing a lot more than hugging her in his allotted twenty minutes.

As we rolled into Commando, we all got excited when we saw a scraggly bush, which was the first thing we had seen alive in the desert beside us. We had two hours in which we could either go to the PX trailer, which had an hour-long line, or to the phones; I chose the phones. We were told that this was a hook-up that the gunny had arranged, so we shouldn't cause problems with anyone since they could throw us out at any moment. I thought it was bullshit that a bunch of POGs with access to phones day and night would make us jump through hoops, but they were the only game in town.

After twenty tense minutes, I got ushered into the small tent. The phones were field phones and the procedure to dial them was quite elaborate; I tried and failed several times, before getting a dial tone. There was a delay on the line, so I felt like I was speaking to my wife from space. We only had five minutes and most of it was spent having the other person repeat themself, but it was well worth it.

The line at the PX was too long, but the chow hall was opening in ten minutes. We got in line with the POGs and I gawked at the female soldiers like a pervert. When I got into the tent, I almost cried. They had real food, catered and prepared by Indian contractors. I grabbed my tray of fresh food and headed for the dining tents, where there was ice cream, chocolate milk and salad dressing. I made an embarrassment of myself, getting seconds, thirds, and fourths. I eavesdropped on the POGs' conversations as they complained about the food and the "lousy living conditions."

When it was time to leave, I grabbed four ice cream sandwiches and headed outside. We sat in the afterglow by the humvees, as we waited for the people in the PX line to show up. I felt a little silly; I was 29 and about to go to war, yet I was ecstatic about eating an ice cream sandwich.

March 1st—We went back to the TAA and re-dug our old holes. I was glad I hadn't pissed in my hole before filling it up, as others had. The only thing I missed about the LSA were the porta-potties. At least I had privacy at the TAA. While unsuccessfully trying to jerk it in my tent, I saw someone's shadow appear on my tent wall.

"Meyer, you got mail."

"Shut the fuck up. Don't play with me."

"What?"

I should have recognized the small shadow—it was Squeak. I apologized and opened the tent to receive my first batch of mail. Those three letters were more appreciated than all the Christmas presents I received as a child put together. I read and re-read them; then lovingly crafted long response letters. In my optimism, I wrote that coming home in late May was not "an unreasonable hope."

After a month of constant, blowing sand, people started to get rifle problems. Many people stopped cleaning them altogether, deeming it pointless.

My rear take-down pin got clogged with sand, so I took it to the company armorer.

"Hey Yoder, I done broke my boom stick," I said, thinking that would get a laugh. Yoder looked over at Rampone, who shook his head ruefully.

"Gunny Linton said that the next person whose rifle got fucked up was getting charged. We've already have had to evac ten rifles to the division armorer," Yoder told me.

"Dude, just keep it to yourself. Gunny's gonna ream your ass. Wrap it in duct tape or something," Rampone advised me.

"Look, I'm not going into Iraq with a damn busted rifle. They can't fucking charge me for this. Here. Take it. I don't give a fuck what happens to me."

I was called back by the XO, who proceeded to blame me for the problem. He said that Golf was out of weapons and if they couldn't get me a replacement, I would go into battle without a rifle; which was the military equivalent of telling a kid that if he crosses his eyes they'll stay that way. Gunny Brouillet told the XO that he couldn't bust me since we weren't given guidance on the proper way to maintain a weapon in this extreme environment. The XO couldn't think of a plausible counter-argument; he just grumbled and told me to get a new rifle.

Spending all of our time together, we had nothing better to do than jibber-jabber all day long. I could make a detailed family tree for half the guys in my platoon. Two years with someone in the grunts is like six in the civilian world, considering you're with them so much, but no matter how long you know someone you would still miss out on giant swaths of their history, as Lewis demonstrated one day.

"Hey Meyer, oh hell old man, you *got* to hear my new system. [Here's where he says a bunch of stereo jargon I'm not familiar with mixed with hip-hop slang that I don't understand.]"

"Didn't you just get a new system like six months ago?"

"Yeah, guess I did."

"So what'd you do with the old one?"

"Oh, I put it next to the baby's crib."

"Baby? What baby?"

"Mine."

"You've got a kid?"

"Man, I got two kee-yids. One's two, the other's four."

"Motherfucker, I've known you for two years; how the hell do you know someone that long and never mention you have kids?"

"I'm sure I dropped it in there somewhere."

Two days after I went to Camp Commando, I heard a rumor that made me want to walk the twenty miles back there. At the LSA, there were only two shower trailers and they usually had one-hour waits, but at Camp Commando, they had so many that there was never a wait. At one trailer though, there was a line that stretched outside, so the MPs went to go investigate. They discovered two female Marines giving head in the showers for twenty dollars a pop. Supposedly, one of them was caught with $1200 dollars in her pocket. I have no idea if that was true, but the idea that it *might* have been true kept me warm many a night.

After weeks of endless "training," which consisted mostly of us sitting holes and shitting on the ground, we had a night shoot. As we hiked from the LSA to the make-shift range, a sandstorm sprung up, turning the moonlit landscape into an indecipherable blur. The whole way there, our head corpsman, Doc Winslow, babbled on to our arty officer. Though squat and doughy, Winslow could out-run and out-hike most of us. To the consternation of Gunny Linton, he always had a Stitch doll from "Lilo and Stitch" peeking out of his cargo pocket. While most people scratched out the shallowest fighting hole they could get away with, he went to town, making an underground Hobbit home that had stairs, two small rooms and a hallway. Doc Winslow must have been able to breathe through his ears because he could talk non-stop for hours. He would sidle up beside someone and launch into a two-hour soliloquy, never giving the other person a chance to talk. He would range from topic to topic, not caring if the other person was listening or if they even knew who he was. I think that's why he was so good at hiking; when his mouth was running, he could not notice all the miles we were covering. Since we moved in columns, he always had a captive audience. You couldn't shut him up either. A side effect of being able to breath through his ears was that he could not hear what the other person was saying while he was talking. There was no way to steer the conversation or make an excuse to leave. His mouth generated enough energy to keep those chubby little legs of his moving indefinitely.

By the time we started shooting, you could barely see twenty feet. It was unfortunate that the weather had been bad enough to curtail the training, since the five shooting stations actually simulated real battlefield conditions. When I got back to my tent, I found that the porn I had borrowed from Miller had been stolen. I suspected Monty—who had stayed back with a "medical" problem that popped up as soon as he heard about the range—but it could have been anyone who stayed back. I could have pulled rank and made people dump their packs, but I didn't want to be a jerk. It was a nasty french porno (nasty = good) and all we were left with was lame Maxim magazines. I would have preferred the bra section of the Sears catalog.

Staying in Tent City was good because it was more sanitary and comfortable, but tensions arose because of our close proximity. Although not even half the finished tents were occupied, we were given only one tent for two platoons. You had the length of your body, plus about a foot on either side, and that was it. We usually grouped together by sections, so I was surprised when Monty set down right in the middle of the 31 section. I asked him to switch with Showers and he refused me outright; then he took up twice as much room as anyone else—Classic Monty behavior. Showers had so little room that he couldn't even lie flat on the ground; he had to lay on his side and lean on the duffelbag next to him. I asked Monty to slide down and he blew me off, not even facing me to respond. I then ordered him, which was rare, but he was being just disgustingly selfish. We got into a pissing match and started shouting at each other. It got highly unprofessional and we both embarrassed ourselves. I went to his section leader, Sgt. Quinn, who ordered Monty to move, which made Monty speechless for the first time ever.

Since we were in the desert, we pounded down liters of water. That was fine during the day, but when it cooled down at night, your body suddenly had a huge surplus of water. Every night, I would wake up in the pitch-darkness and scramble for my Mag-lite, so I could put my boots on, grab my rifle and gas mask and stumble out toward the pissers. I had several photo finishes and it was more trouble than it was worth. Out of expediency, people starting pissing in water bottles when they woke up at night with a pounding bladder. Marines are all about simplification and realized that it was a lot easier to piss in a bottle than to put on all your gear and trudge out to a disgusting Porta-Jon. At first, people said they had to do it during the day because there was a sandstorm and then because it was noon and too hot. Eventually, most of the Marines pissed in bottles exclusively and left them wherever they pleased.

Every morning, when the lights were flicked on, there would be 80 bottles of piss throughout the tent. People would spill their bottles in the tent or toss them in the trash. I watched in horror as Hot Rod made a bottle of apple juice with the powder from our MREs and set it next to his piss bottle. As he listened to his CD player, he would grab the apple juice and drink from it without checking to see if he had the right bottle.

The situation got so bad that Sgt. Quinn made a direct order for the first time, saying that no one could use piss bottles anymore. His "good buddy" Monty gaffed him off and ended up spilling his piss bottle onto Doc Kali's Iso-Mat. Sgt. Quinn lost it and gave everyone five minutes to get their gear out of the tent. The tent did need to be emptied and cleaned, but I was a sergeant, so I wasn't going to be treated like a recruit. I would leave last along with Sgt. Quinn and Sgt. Williams. The corporals started yelling for people to hurry up, for fear that we would get "fucked with." Elias went by, yelling at people to hurry up and he accidentally kicked some of my stuff. I told him to watch out and he got mad, thinking I was purposefully being slow to get them in trouble. We started yelling at each other and I told him to report to Gunny Brouillet. There was a lot of resentment that I had picked up sergeant so quickly and it was coming out whenever I got into a small argument with another NCO. I was tired of the fighting and bickering and, most of all, the lack of professionalism. I took my gear out, set it down and marched Elias to the staff tent.

Elias had been my friend since we were boots and I was usually the one to defend him when others got sick of him. Elias' temper was like a boulder rolling down-hill. He would often get angry about mis-understandings or simple joking around, but you couldn't explain that to him. You just had to let him bluff and bluster, until the boulder got to the bottom of the hill and ran out of momentum; then he'd be a great guy again. He was a character—loud and out-sized—and that's what I liked about him, but things were breaking down. People couldn't have simple professionalism; everything turned into a shouting match. I didn't mind what anyone said to me one-one-one, but an image had to be maintained in front of the boots. If the seniors wouldn't listen to each other, then why should they? When we were boots, Marr noticed that we wouldn't correct each other when we knew the other person was wrong. He told us that we couldn't be afraid to give an order to a friend for fear that they would get mad at us; if they did, they weren't really your friend.

I brought Elias to Gunny Brouillet, who treated it like a recess argument. It bothered me that important issues constantly got under-played, but minor things would be over-blown. I was getting threatened by Squeak on a daily basis because of Miller's chin-strap, but huge problems like Reed were just swept under the rug.

Out of boredom, Reed took his Pocket Pussy out and started walking down the aisle, hitting people with it. Moser, who could have pounded Reed into paste, just shook his head when he got hit in the knee. It was disgusting, but Moser knew that if Reed failed to elicit a reaction and get attention, he would quickly quit. Apparently, Levesque didn't get the memo. When Reed hit Levesque in the leg with the Pocket Pussy, he immediately jumped up.

"What the fuck is wrong with you?" Levesque demanded.

We would only be there for seven months, so Reed really didn't have time to answer that question completely. Levesque's reaction was completely justified, but of course, Reed didn't see it that way. Reed went from what he considered "playful" to vengeful in an instant.

"Oh! Couldn't handle it, little baby? Little Bitch!" he shouted, red-faced, as he thrust the Pocket Pussy at Levesque.

"Keep that thing the fuck away from me!"

"Oh, this?" Reed asked as he hit Levesque in the face with it. When Levesque moved forward, Reed got wide-eyed like an animal and launched a vicious head-butt. If Levesque hadn't jumped back, he would have gotten a broken nose—and for what? Because he didn't want to get some of Reed's coagulated spooge on him? Often, I look back at incidents like this and wonder why I didn't jump in sooner. My thought process was always the same. I would see how Reed was acting and guess his next move, but then I would doubt myself. No normal human being would do what it looked like Reed was about to do. Yet, he would always do it—no matter how insane it was or how many witnesses there were. Levesque pushed Reed back, almost knocking him over and Sgt. Hashimoto jumped in between them.

After the drama died down, I thought about how I had just witnessed an unprovoked assault that would have gotten Reed arrested anywhere else in the world, but if I brought it up to the higher-ups, they would just dismiss it as "boys being boys." Sure enough, when I reported it later that week, they couldn't have cared less.

The day before we went back to the TAA, our embedded reporter arrived. I got excited when I heard the reporter was a chick, but when I saw her, I calmed down very quickly. Middle-age was tap-dancing all over face; she looked like a Hobbit with corn-rows. The next day, the company commander introduced her to the company. She worked for New York Newsday, which impressed almost everyone, but, since I had lived in New York City, I knew that it was bottom of the barrel. If the Times, The Post, The Wall Street Journal and The Village Voice were all sold-out; then you'd buy Newsday. I wondered how she was going to keep her privacy since there were no bathroom facilities. After a month at the TAA, a slit trench had been dug for us to shit in, but I was always worried I'd lose my balance and fall in, so I would still shit in the low dunes 200 meters away. They put up a lean-to with cammie-netting that offered her some degree of privacy.

After we got off the tracs back at the TAA, Schofield told everyone to stay in the area. Cammie netting had to be put over the trac and he needed lances to put it up and NCOs to supervise. I had to leave to speak with Squeak and all hell broke loose while I was gone. Reed tried to slip away, using the excuse that he needed to stash his tripod in his tent. Schofield called him back and Reed kept walking. When Schofield repeated his order, Reed turned, ran up to him and tried to pick a fight with him.

When I got back, Schofield and Sgt. Quinn came over and told me what happened, telling me I needed to do something about Reed; I promised them that I would. Reed had crossed the line; our entire point for being there was to support the elevens so that they could do their job. Reed had poisoned our already-strained relationship with them by picking fights with half of their platoon and threatening a sergeant over nothing.

While I apprised Squeak, SSgt. DeMalteris, Third Platoon Sergeant, started ripping Reed a new one, Drill Instructor-style, which was shocking coming from such a laid-back guy. I spent more than an hour telling Squeak of Reed's gradual descent and his many personal and emotional problems. Squeak seemed to believe me, but only up to a point. He went to speak to Reed and came back an hour later a wide-eyed believer. Squeak couldn't believe how far gone Reed was until he spoke to him. Reed was in complete denial and seemed to think that he was well-liked and a prominent leader in the company. Squeak walked the lines, randomly asking people about Reed, and got a litany of horror stories. Nearly everyone had a dozen stories of Reed's idiocy and immaturity and they were ecstatic to have someone to tell them to.

We took it to Gunny Brouillet, who listened patiently, but still seemed to think that Reed was just a little rambunctious; not a major problem. Squeak and I both envisioned a situation in combat in which Reed would start a fight while getting the gun up because one little thing went wrong. I told Squeak that I didn't want to bring Reed to Iraq; I would gladly carry his tripod and pull double-duty. I wanted Reed to get a psych eval at Doha. Squeak seemed to think that was pretty far afield, but he was onboard otherwise. He said that in a worst-case scenario, he would put Reed on trac security and he would never be with us on the battlefield. Since Reed liked to malinger about his headaches and the vomit that always evaporated before anyone saw it, so Squeak would get the machine-gunner corpsman, Chili, to deem Reed unfit for combat.

Gunny called all the squad leaders in the platoon together for a little pow-wow. Everyone agreed that Reed was a complete detriment to the platoon. Gunny seemed surprised, since it was almost impossible to get that many Marines to agree on anything. Gunny and Squeak had a sit-down talk with Reed. It made me sick to see that the whole platoon had stopped functioning that day to revolve around Reed. It was appalling to have to listen to two grown men tell another grown man why he couldn't hit someone with a used pocket pussy.

Reed was the brought to First Sergeant Young, who was of the opinion that Reed was a good Marine who just a few problems, though he did acknowledge the seriousness of his altercation with Sgt. Schofield. Reed was told—in no uncertain terms—that if he got into one more fight or argument, even with someone he outranked, he would be made an ammo man and busted down to lance corporal.

Five minutes later, he got in a fight with Bodine. Bodine was a happy-go-lucky joker who looked like a shorter version of Ben Affleck. He had passed the Sniper Indoc in Oki, but then decided to come back to the company, for which he endured endless ribbing, which he took good naturedly. He harmlessly chided Reed about his "headaches" that always coincided with PT or training and Reed tried to pick a fight with him. Unbeknownst to me at that time, Bodine was one of the best wrestlers in the company. Gunny Brouillet made the two of them fight it out to shut Reed up. Bodine had the upper hand throughout the fight, but not conclusively, so Gunny split them up. Gunny would wrestle Reed and Moser would wrestle Bodine. Gunny and Moser both beat their opponents and Reed *accidentally* ended up with a black eye. Reed was supposed to be busted down for the fight, but Gunny said that being wrestled into submission had made Reed learn his lesson.

Reed went into "excuse" mode, since his fragile pride could not handle the fact that he had been bested—him being The Greatest Wrestler Ever and all. Rager watched as Reed went to his fighting hole and started banging his head on the ground. Reed then laid down and called to Rager for help. Rager ignored him until Reed ordered him to go get a corpsman, which pissed Rager off because that meant that he had to walk 300 meters to Chili's position. Rager couldn't find Chili, but he did find Doc Cox, a great corpsman and a friend since Oki. Reed told Cox he had a concussion, which is a funny thing for someone with a concussion to say. Doc checked his vitals and his pupils and said there was no sign of a concussion. Reed crawled into his tent and stayed there for three days, nursing his pride. He finally emerged with a fading black eye, and a noticeably meeker attitude.

I spoke to the NCOs in Third Platoon about the Reed situation, assuring them that the next time Reed acted up, he would become a lance and an ammo man. I told them that they could count on our guns for support. Their reaction was bland and non-committal. They knew the current chain-of-command better than I and they knew that the higher-ups would not follow up on their threats against Reed.

Reed kept a low profile for the next week. When I returned to our pos after a meeting one day, he informed me that he wanted to charge Ryan for disrespect, saying that if he could get charged for it, then Ryan could as well. He gave me his hard-to-believe rendition, but after speaking to everyone in the squad, I got a clearer picture of what happened. In addition to carrying the gun, tripod, ammo and ammo bag full of tools, each team had to carry some squad gear. Miller's team carried the bulky NBC decon kit for the guns and Reed's carried the heavy can of thick gun lube. Before going out on a practice patrol, since Miller's team had been using the lube last, Reed told Ryan that he had to carry it. Ryan refused and Reed started yelling at him. As all NCOs do at least once, even if they won't admit it, when an argument erupts between an NCO and a lance, the NCO will at some point loudly state his own rank, which always sounds silly. Ryan correctly pointed out that Reed was a corporal in name only; he had never conducted himself as an NCO. I loved hearing that, since it proved that the boots felt free to treat Reed like the embarrassment that he was. They argued some more until Miller told Ryan to separate from Reed. It was the right call; even though Reed didn't deserve any respect, it was bad form to have a lance and a putative NCO arguing so openly.

I had spent so much time concentrating on Carpenter and Reed, that I had been ignoring the rest of my squad. A staff NCO once told me that the tragedy of leadership is that you spend 90% of your time on the worst 10% of your squad. Lopez was Miller's ammo man, which he resented. I could sugarcoat it, but Ammo Man is considered a bitch job. No one likes it, but sometimes you have to put good Marines in that billet. Lopez had been gone for most of the work-up because he had to take care of a family matter back home. After he came back, there was lingering resentment toward him from the other boots, so he kept to himself. Lopez had a sly sense of humor and would needle Carpenter when he was bored. Speaking elliptically one day, he said, to no one in particular, "I met an old gypsy woman once, who told me that one day I would meet a boy, not yet a man, who would wear the color green and his first words would be, 'Well...'" I laughed my ass off, but Carpenter—when he finally got the joke—wanted to fight Lopez over it. While they were on gun watch that night, they got into a loud argument over nothing and I had to yell at the both of them. Carpenter was an annoying weirdo who would run off on any tangent, but Lopez was just baiting him.

March 2nd—We received word that the invasion would launch on the 9th. The next day, We went back to the LSA and Chili told me that the Medical Officer was fighting for us stay there for health reasons. We had been shitting and pissing at the TAA for more than a month; there were clouds of flies everywhere. The MO bought us a few days, but the BC didn't want us to get "soft," so he sent us back.

It was now a week after our "deadline" of the 9th and I wondered if we would ever go. The TAA was truly rank and you had to keep moving or swarms of flies would crawl all over you. We started to get hiccups in our supply system; we missed meals and the water had a strong, bleach taste to it that made people sick. I counted the days until I got out of the Corps to pass the time. Though my EAS wasn't for 15 months, I could get a school cut in 12. People thought I would drive myself crazy, since my EAS was so far off, but I found it extremely comforting.

When we returned to the LSA for the last time, we heard about President Bush's Ultimatum to Saddam and his sons—leave in 48 hours or face invasion. We needed no preparation—we had been ready for the last month. Our higher-ups were much more concerned with major issues like chin-straps. We were wearing our helmets most of our waking hours and the rough chin-straps would get annoying, so people would hitch them up on the brim of their helmets "John Wayne" style. The CO started to get on Miller for his chin-strap and he put pressure on Squeak, who then put pressure on me. Wearing your chin-strap is important in combat, but less so in the chow-line. Miller could be a belligerent fuck, but he really did make an effort to follow the order. From time to time though, he would forget and the chain-of-command would go nuts. From their reaction, you might have thought that he had assaulted a fellow Marine after hitting him with a pocket pussy.

Squeak finally got sick of Miller wearing the chin-strap improperly, so he told Miller and me, his squad leader, that we had to wear our helmets at all times, even indoors. Not only was this an unlawful order, but it was the wrong way to discipline NCOs. By embarrassing us like this, Squeak was undermining our authority in front of our boots. Under that current chain-of-command though, that was par for the course. I wore the helmet like an idiot for an hour before it got to me. I took my rank insignia and threw them in the sand—a true movie moment. I then remembered that I had a family to support and I put them back on.

I decided to "go through channels" and speak to Gunny Brouillet. I told Miller that I was going to tell Gunny that if we had to be disciplined, it should be done properly by giving us a Pg.11 administrative punishments, not by frat pranks. Miller said that he would rather get fucked with than get "bad paper", which I thought was sad, but I understood. I found Gunny and explained the situation to him. He actually listened, but I did not get the desired reaction. He ignored my request to be Pg. 11'ed, but he did tell me that I did not have to wear my helmet all the time. I asked about Miller and he told me that the punishment still stood for him. I told Gunny if that was the case, then I would continue wearing it as a sign of solidarity. I went back to the tent and told Miller the same. He seemed to appreciate the thought, but he told me he really wouldn't mind if I took it off. Over the next several hours, he kept repeating that I should take it off and I finally followed his request at dinner time.

That night, a Pizza Hut vendor from Kuwait City came out and set up shop in a tent. Cutting in the four-hundred man line was so prevalent that people didn't even get mad. In fact, you'd get points for originality. I found one of my boots toward the front and I rushed forward with "an urgent message from the First Sergeant." I dragged the story out long enough to get a permanent spot in line. I ate an entire pizza by myself, gave another one away and spent the rest of the night sprinting from the tent to the shitters.

About three in the morning, SSgt. Sikes entered our tent and, in a calm but serious voice, told us that we had gotten the call to go to war. I got an adrenaline rush as I shoved my belongings into my pack. Within twenty minutes, our tents were empty, except for the piles of garbage. As a professional courtesy, you were supposed to let any boot's squad leader know if you needed to grab him for a working party. We had problems with this in the past, when Monty would unfairly assign the bulk of the working parties to boot machinegunners. I told one of Jesse's 51s to help clean and Miller told me that, as soon as I left, he went to Jesse to get out of it, "playing mommy against daddy." Miller was pissed and wanted to charge him, but I just wanted to talk to him. He was another tough Latino kid and I knew that an ass-chewing would just bounce off his skin. I explained to him that we were about to go to war and that the internecine disputes between the sections needed to stop. He seemed surprised at being spoken to like a human being and I never had a problem with him again.

Sergeant Major Davis became obsessed with the graffiti in the porta-jons; a small portion of which was racist, which he took as a personal insult. He told the battalion that he would ban us from using the shitters if he found any more graffiti; we would have to go shit in the dunes like we were still in the TAA. This order was counter-manded by the CO, thank God, but the sergeant major still made us put a 24-hour watch on the toilets with a roving guard and sergeant or above as SOG. Moser, who I always considered the most mature guy in our section, later admitted that he was one of the ones who wrote in the porta-jons. I asked him why and he said he did it just to piss off the sergeant major. I was happy that we were leaving, because I was supposed to be the crapper SOG that day.

We lined up by our tracs and were told the scheme of maneuvers. We weren't heading straight for Iraq; we would first move to a collection point, where we would draw our ammo and explosives; then we would move to a dispersal point, where we would prepare to move out en masse over the border. I had a sentimental last visit to my beloved Porta-Jon; then headed to my trac. People started taking moto pics of their squads. They were the kind of squad photos you see in every war book. I wondered if anyone in those old war pics had two psychos and three guys that they barely knew in their squad.

We moved out to the collection point, two miles past the TAA, which was just a bunch of crates of explosives and ammo in the middle of nowhere. It looked like a flea market, with people swarming around to grab their share of the rockets, grenades, flares, and C-4. Machinegunners usually don't get frags, but I wanted them to clear fighting holes and for the dead space in front of gun positions that the enemy can hide in. And because they were cool. I kept two and handed the team leaders one each. I debated whether I should give Reed one, but I decided that I didn't have a good enough reason not to give him one. I gave Lopez one, but didn't give one to Carpenter since he was an idiot.

As we sat around, Kennel complained about the new guys from Security Forces. I asked him why the NCOs in Third Platoon had such negative opinions of several Marines in their platoon who I thought were solid, though a little rough around the edges. He didn't really have a good answer, just saying that they were "nasty" sometimes. There was a condescending and egotistical attitude among the corporals in Third that did not exist, to such an extent, in the other platoons. The corporals in Third were good, no doubt, but ego is a detriment in battle. If you consider yourself to be an awesome Marine, you should be "awesome" enough to lift others up instead of running them down.

We arrived at our final staging area, the Dispersal Point. It was a pleasant day and everyone was in a good mood, chatting amiably. I got a G.I.Joe comic out of my moto stash in my pack and started to read it to get hyped up for battle. Miller thought that was hilarious, but everyone had something that got them excited about being a grunt, and that was what did it for me. People who join the grunts are romantics; they want to be the heroes they idolized in their childhood. It's not normal to seek out war. This isn't the Middle Ages; one can easily avoid any contact with combat their entire life. We had all sought this out and our dream was about to come true.

As we waited to board the tracs, I took out a pen to write some moto graffiti on my helmet. Though in all of the Vietnam movies I saw, everyone personalized their helmet covers, we were given express orders not to put anything on them, not even our initials. Uniformity was the watch-word. I assumed that was just a peace-time order and that once we entered Iraq, the higher-ups would be too busy to care what we scrawled on our helmets. Knowing that most people would write macho cliches like "Born to Kill" or "Ready to Die" I decided to go in the opposite direction. One line from Jewel's CD struck me for its girlish inno-cence—"Please be careful with me. I'm sensitive and I'd like to stay that way."

I thought it would be funny to go into war with that on my helmet. The right people would laugh at it and the wrong people would get pissed off by it, which was fine by me. During a leaders' brief though, no information got distributed since all the NCOs who walked up bugged their eyes out and told me that I had to cover up my graffiti before they all got in trouble. I couldn't believe that the staff and officers wouldn't have anything better to do, mere hours before we crossed the LOD (Line of Departure), but I was wrong. SSgt. Melendez stopped the brief to order me to cover it up, by any means necessary. I started drawing a skull over it, but the skull would have had to have been six inches high just to hide all of it. I cut a swatch from my pack cover and grabbed my sewing kit, which was part of the prescribed gear load. I had to have been the only person on the brink of war trying to thread a needle.

I took out some of my "Victory Pepsis" that I had planned on popping after we secured the GOSP, our first objective. I cursed when I saw that they were leaking, so I decided to polish them off. The thick, warm syrup was my last con-nection with the civilized world.

The Battalion Commander called us together and gave us a pretty good moto speech. In the movie that I was shooting in my head, this was a key scene—the warriors on the brink of battle. Lewis made a comment about the weight we were all carrying and Reed, out of nowhere, started shouting at him and asking if he was carrying an 18-pound ammo bag or 40 pounds of ammo. Reed wasn't even carrying that much weight; it was just another example of him ruining every good moment.

As we walked back to our holes, I heard Kennel giving his squad a moto speech, promising to buy them drinks in San Clemente when this was all over. Kennel's squad was tight and he started to pump them up, telling them that they were the best squad in the best platoon. I even heard him say they had the best machinegun squad attached to them. It surprised me he'd say that, especially since I knew that wasn't true. I had two nut cases that were occupying most of my energy at all times. Half of the squad actively hated the other and I knew things would only get worse.

Leaving just after dark, we would be the first major ground combat force entering Iraq. The gas siren went off as two faint streaks were seen in the sky—Scuds. They would overshoot us by dozens of miles, but regardless, we put our masks on and got in our holes.

A burst of automatic fire went off somewhere down the line and I tried to identify what type of weapon it was. It was so dark that our NVGs didn't even work. Too sharp to be a 240; it had to be a SAW. Were we being attacked? No, just a negligent discharge.

"All clear!"

We took our masks off and Reed showed me his.

"Hey Meyer, my damn strap snapped. I gotta go get it fixed."

"It's going to have to wait. We're loading up in five minutes."

"I'm gonna find the NBC officer and have him fix it. Fucking cheap piece of crap."

"It's pitch black out and his trac is at the other end of the column, Reed. There's no time."

"There's no time, huh? Just like there was no time to get the spring fixed either, Meyer?"

He seemed to think that I didn't know what he was building to, but I could see it a mile away. The tripod was missing its latch spring for the same reason that Reed's gas mask broke a strap—Reed never took care of his gear. Whenever he had a tantrum, he would toss his tripod or kick his gas mask across the tent. Every time we had a survey of gear to see what needed to be fixed, he always needed something done. Reed had knocked the tiny spring off the tripod three times in the last month. When I told him that I would get him another, he loudly proclaimed that he would get it—no problem. I checked with him several times and he always said he was on the case, but I forgot to check once we got the word to go. Both problems were easily fixable—the mask could still get a perfect seal by tightening the remaining five straps and the tripod would still lock out, even without the spring.

"Oh, you mean the spring you promised to fix, but never did?"

"You don't check on your men, Meyer! You don't care if I live or die!"

He had me on that last point.

"Get back in your hole and calm the fuck down."

He scrambled out of his hole and ran past me before I could stop him. I couldn't believe it. Rager shook his head in disgust. He was as sick of Reed as I was, probably more so, since he had to work under him.

"Rager, could you handle being a team leader and I'll make Carpenter your gunner?"

"Wouldn't be a problem at all, sergeant."

"Can you believe that shit? Was I out of hand? His shit's always broken because he's always chucking it all over the place."

"It's like going to war with my sister's kid."

I told Schofield what happened, since he was in charge of the count for our trac.

"I'm going to bust that piece of shit down. Fuck him. He'll be a damn ammo man til he EASs," I screeched.

"Whoa—slow down. It's too close to game time to change his job now. Your boys need to see you calm. Whatever problems you have with him can be solved later. You need to get your head in the game."

I was surprised at getting such clear-headed advice from Schofield, since we disagreed so much. He did have a point and I didn't want Carpenter as a gunner.

Someone in the distance asked what the problem was.

"Reed freaked the fuck out and ran off, that's what happened!" I yelled.

"Oh, I freaked out, huh?"

Reed emerged from the gloom and started charging at me, looking like he wanted a fight. Fine, fuck this piece of shit. I had been covering for that disloyal fuck for two years; he was a cancer in my squad. I might not have known how to wrestle like him, but I could sure as hell smash his skull in with my rifle butt. Before we crashed together, Schofield jumped between us.

"Get back on the damn line and quit causing problems like you always do, Reed!"

"I'm not going to get gassed because you're a shitty leader, Meyer!"

"Listen to me, you little motherfucker! Quit acting like acting like a bitch and a coward and get back in your damn fighting hole!"

I had just called him the two worst things one grunt could ever call another and he had no response. I was one of the least confrontational people in the platoon, but if Reed had called me what I called him, I probably would have shot him in the chest.

He sputtered more about dying and ran off again into the darkness. Fuck it. Leave him here; this could turn out in our favor. He can go to the brig for deserting during war and we could be rid of him. I went to the trac and told SSgt. D, "The idiot took off. He's gone." No clarification was needed.

The call went up to get on the tracs and I got the rest of Reed's team and his gear aboard. To my surprise, Reed sat down next to me with an amiable smile, as if nothing had happened. He told me that he found Lt. Sprincin, who "fixed" his mask. This kid was insane; there's no way that Sprincin could have taken off the entire head-strap harness and replaced it in that amount of time. I imagined he "fixed" it by looping the errant strap back through the buckle it was supposed to go through. Reed had completely lost his military bearing in front of his men, had been called a bitch and a coward by his squad leader, and was sure to be busted down to lance and posted to ammo man; yet he was acting like we just bumped into each other at the Jack in the Box in San Clemente. Even weirder was that as the ramp closed, he gave a seemingly sincere and Pollyanna-ish wish of good will to the rest of the trac as we embarked on this grand adventure.

We were sealed up in the darkness as the trac negotiated the rough terrain. As the ground invasion kicked off, the last berm was blown and we followed the tanks into Iraq. We strained to hear the radio traffic and the first word was of our foremost tanks engaging and destroying enemy tanks. There were some arty strikes ahead of us, but much more to our east, where RCT-1 was rolling toward Basra.

We were told that they would open the hatches as soon as we were firmly within the country. Schofield and Rohr had been bragging that they would take air watch when we crossed the border, so that they could take pictures. I didn't think that was fair; they never pulled air watch, yet they wanted to take that position only when it was cool to have it. The three that always took air watch were the SAW gunners, Miozza and Lovett, and me. I was obsessed with getting as much gun time as possible, imagining that there would be very little combat. I also got mildly claustrophobic in the trac.

The tracs stopped and the driver called for two elevens to get out and check a trench to our left. I overheard that one of our tanks had been hit, but there was confusion over whether arty, an enemy tank or simply overturning in a trench had taken it out of the game.

We never got along with that trac crew because, frankly, they were pricks. The driver was known as "The Trac Nazi" after "The Soup Nazi" from "Seinfeld". He was condescending and would never let us get on the trac until the last minute, so we would always have to rush on and get situated like a bunch of clowns. He never opened the hatches unless he had to and he never let us know what was going on.

The Trac Nazi popped into the troop compartment and started screeching about how this was "real", that we were in the shit and we needed to get our heads together. He told us he saw arty land ahead of us and saw one of our tanks blown apart and he accused one of the elevens who went out to clear the trench of lying down on the job. He thought he was laying down the law, but it just looked like he was getting scared and taking it out on the people locked in the dark in the back.

When they finally opened the hatch, the two designated SAW gunners popped up and took their spot. It had been decided that we would use their so-designated small machine guns over my 240 medium machinegun. The 240 had twice the range and stopping power of the SAWs and was thus deemed too valuable an asset to get knocked off the top of a trac. I wanted to go up too, just to get some air, but our trac commander—who I had dubbed "SSgt. No-Fun"— had yelled at us several times for having more than two people on air watch at a time. After twenty minutes of having the SAW gunners describe Iraq to me, I had to see it for myself.

Miozza let me take his spot. Tall and lanky, Miozza was the boot version of Mohler, for good and ill. One of the most sarcastic guys I ever met, he was surprisingly respectful when dealing with me, probably because I didn't treat him like a piece of shit like the rest of his seniors. On one of our long trac rides in Kuwait, he taught me the constellations to pass the time. Miozza and the rest of the boots were what I called the "9/11 generation." They had enlisted, knowing that they would go to combat. My fellow seniors and I had joined during a time of peace; we hoped for action, but never really thought we'd actually see it. Miozza and his ilk were all rough around the edges and I loved them for it.

I had imagined a huge armada, but all I saw was one lonely convoy in a vast wasteland. Lights and faint explosions were visible on the horizons toward RCT-1's area. Lovett was pointing at something and I turned to see two bright lights suspended in the sky. They were either missiles or shells and they were at the apex of their trajectory, so they seemed to be hanging in the air. On their descent though, they appeared to be heading straight for us. I got a sinking feeling in my stomach. This wasn't something I could shoot at; it was simple math whether it would hit us or not. After a few tense seconds, it became clear that it would overshoot us by thousands of meters; it was just an optical illusion that made it look like it was coming towards us.

My relief didn't last long. I looked to my right and saw one of our tanks blown apart. I hoped that it was simply a disabled and abandoned tank and that the crew had been picked up by another vehicle, but the blast marks on its hull told the tale. I couldn't believe that Iraq's joke of an army could take out even one of our tanks. There were real Americans in that tank who were dead—a simple fact, but hard to wrap my mind around.

After we secured the GOSP (Gas/Oil Separation Point), we would stand-by in case the Marines attacking Nasariyah needed reinforcements. For some insane reason, I convinced myself that there was a Pizza Hut in Nasariyah. I've always seen news stories about McDonald's in Communist China and Taco Bells in Moscow, so why couldn't they have a Pizza Hut in Nasariyah? Was that so much to ask?

Schofield's squad had been dubbed "Suicide Squad" since they were tasked with going into the GOSP and taking out any suicide bombers who might want to blow up the works. The entire GOSP complex was a bomb, so they didn't want to risk losing more than a squad if the place blew. I told Chubby that if they went in there, they should look for a break room so they could snag some snacks from the vending machines which I was sure they would have. He said my idea had one fatal flaw—we didn't have any Iraqi money. It took him for while to figure out why we laughed at his logic. Invading another country—sure, why not? But breaking into a vending machine? Whoa, you just crossed the line there, buddy.

A few hours later, the engine started to make weird sounds and my heart sunk—we would have to double-up. Our trac finally gave up the ghost and we filed outside. We had to squeeze our twenty-three Marines into the two other already-packed tracs in Third Platoon. I ran to take a piss, glad to be out of the trac for a second. The lack of piss breaks had put me in a real fear that I would wet myself while riding in the tracs. We would be wearing our MOPP suits for weeks on end and there were no spare suits to change into.

I hung back as the others tried to squeeze themselves into the other trac. Sene set his sniper his rifle against the ramp; when someone bumped against it, Sene looked like he was going to cry. A sniper rifle's "zero" (the fine-tuning of its sights) is what makes it so valuable. With its zero off, Sene couldn't be sure he would hit the mark. I had hoped to be the last one on, but as I stepped on the ramp, four people appeared at of nowhere, obviously having the same idea. When I finally got situated, all I had was about six inches of the middle row to sit on. This was going to be miserable.

As the trac lurched to a start, the precarious balancing act within completely collapsed. I looked over to see Rager's head almost completely disappear between Lovett's butt cheeks.

"Just because you outrank me doesn't mean you can sit on my damn head!",
Rager screamed while pulling himself free.

The weight of 35 people knocked me off my bench and I found myself sitting
sideways with hundreds of pounds on me. That was very painful and I didn't
know how long I could take it. I finally wiggled onto someone's knee, which gave
me a stable enough base to sit halfway up, but the strain on my back was incredible. We had no idea how long this torture would go on. I was surprised when we
stopped after only an hour and a half.

An idyllic scene greeted us when the ramp dropped. Instead of dead desert, we
emerged in a bright, warm land of slowly sloping hills and light vegetation. It
might have looked like a denuded landscape to anyone else, but it looked like a
rainforest to me. We laid down in the prone to provide security as they fixed the
trac. For an hour or so, I got an inordinate amount of enjoyment out of staring at
a few blades of grass on the berm in front of me. Waves of excitement rippled
through the convoy when someone spotted people on the horizon. With the sincere wish of a kid on Christmas morning, I hoped that they would shoot at us,
but no joy.

They got our trac running and it seemed relatively spacious compared to the
doubled-up trac. Though we had been in Iraq for twelve hours, we had only gone
about 20 miles. We had another forty miles to the GOSP. Surprisingly, we covered the remainder of the distance in just a few, short hours. When they told us
that we had five minutes before we dropped ramps at the GOSP, I was surprised
that I got nervous. The most dangerous part had been the breaching of the border; the GOSP was most likely abandoned. The Sunnis in the south had no love
for Saddam and it was unlikely that they'd stay to get slaughtered for him. Carpenter was asleep, treating the five-minute warning like some kind of snooze
alarm. I hit him in the helmet and yelled at him to wake up; then worried that
the others would think I sounded tense.

With no combat experience to flash back on, I thought of a scene from "Star
Wars." Princess Leia's blockade runner is about to be boarded by stormtroopers.
Her guards take up battle stations in the hallway as they watch the stormtroopers
cut a hole into their ship. That scene had a lot of resonance for me as a child
because, after watching it a few times, I realized that those soldiers *knew* they
would die, yet they still fought. It was the first time I considered the concept of
bravery.

I shook my head as I looked at the bland expressions around me. I was probably the only one thinking about "Star Wars" at that moment. The ramp dropped
and, as usual, the machinegunners didn't make it out in time. The ramp is only

kept open for ten seconds since it makes the inside of the trac extremely vulnerable to RPGs. Since the machinegunners were seen as a valuable asset, the riflemen always went out first. With our gun system and ammo cans, we got caught on every strap and bolt as we tried to make it out before the ramp closed. We never made the cool Hollywood exit, always having to use the small inset door like a bunch of jerks.

The whole area was completely deserted, so it felt kind of silly storming out of there, hell bent for leather. We got our guns in position and patted ourselves on the back for securing our part of the huge refinery. As I walked from Reed's gun to Miller's, a white truck started paralleling our line about 900 meters out. Though the gun's range is 1800 meters, realistically, you're not hitting anything more than about 600. Nevertheless, Reed told Rager to fire at the truck that wasn't doing anything hostile. I couldn't get twenty feet away from that kid without him doing something stupid.

After another hour, it became clear that nothing was happening, so people went looking for trouble. There was a small mortar pit about 300 meters away and a group of people went to go check it out. Reed jumped in on the search party and, by the time they returned, the whole mission was his idea and he did everything. They found a small cache of rusty AK-47s and some mortar shells, which seemed like a big deal at the time; we would soon find out that the entire country was one big ammo dump.

As many difference as we had, Reed and I were both glory-hogs; I felt that he had bested me by "capturing" the weapons. Twenty minutes later, Lt. Pettes called for a squad of elevens to go interdict a supposed Iraqi squad lurking on the southern perimeter. I immediately grabbed Miller's team and went and volunteered us for the mission. I yelled to Reed that we were going and he went red in the face, afraid that I would out-do him. "Employed in pairs!" he yelled in an effort to get me to stay. Employing in pairs is basic machinegun methodology, but he forgot about the trac right next to him that was covering his same sector of fire. He was temporarily losing a 240, but gaining a .50 cal. and a Mark 19. As we climbed into the trac, we all laughed at Reed's frustration. I told my guys to dump their ammo boxes and to wear the ammo belts Pancho Villa-style. That was frowned on officially—since the ammo supposedly glinted from the sun, giving away your position—but camouflage wouldn't be an issue here, considering we were wearing green MOPP suits.

The southern edge of the GOSP was filled with fighting holes and small bunkers, but it was obvious that no one was there. I held out hope for a straggler or two as we moved forward to investigate. The binos kept tangling around my neck, strangling me—that never happened to Rambo. I was struck by how professional the defenses were. If they had stood and fought, they could have held out for quite a while.

Despite the invasion, the civilians were still trying to go about their regular lives. We had to check all civilian vehicles using the two-lane highway. I was shocked by one truck, which looked like it could barely stand up without collapsing into a pile of rust, let alone drive. The men inside stepped out and squatted in that peculiar Third-world way, as if it was relaxing. The inside of the truck was a marvel of economy; all it had was a steering wheel, gas pedal and brake. I went to turn the engine off and realized that there was no key; they had to jury-rig the engine every time they wanted to go anywhere and then keep the engine on until they got there. The truck looked like it had been cobbled together out of parts found on the side of the road.

Back in my hole, we heard rumors that First Platoon had shot up some vehicles and SSgt. Sikes had cleared a trench, killing three hajis. I was insanely jealous. When another "mission" popped up, I jumped on it. People had been spotted at some crumbling buildings south of the perimeter. We patrolled over to a small park-like area with an old fountain and some trees. The Iraqi soldiers had stayed there before deserting, as evidenced by dozens of discarded army uniforms and gas masks, along with some cookies and dates. I wanted a souvenir, but this stuff was pretty raunchy-looking. I didn't want to touch those uniforms without boiling them first.

We found the soldiers' AKs in a fallen-down shack. The guns made me think about the joke about French rifles—Never Fired, Dropped Once. A be-draggled family was living in the old jalopy parked next to the hut. We used our translation cards to attempt to talk to them, more out of boredom than anything else. Sgt. Quinn offered a scared kid a Tootsie Roll, which the kid accepted after getting an approving nod from his father.

After dark, I was mesmerized by an uncapped oil well burning in the distance—a strangely beautiful sight. Even though it was 15 miles away, it made it bright enough to read a book at midnight. With shaded lenses on my binos, I could look straight at it and see the surface of the thick, roiling flame. I loved it. I slept like the dead and woke up feeling great. Miller asked me about the bomb—what bomb? I thought he was joking until I found out from others that a bomb had been dropped on the north side of the GOSP in the middle of the night. News to me.

We were being relieved by British forces, whose job was to hold the valuable southern oil fields and the port at Basra while we advanced to Baghdad. I drew a map to Saddam's gold on a piece of old paper and left it half-buried in the sand. The British rolled up like it was just a regular day. One of their corporals came up and spoke with us—or at least attempted to. His accent was nearly impenetrable and he had to repeat himself four or five times before we understood him. The British have a great rep for professionalism, which he exuded. We looked like a bunch of kids playing dress-up, but he looked like a rough, professional soldier. He was tall and ugly, with a thick-set body that would have probably gone to fat if he wasn't in the military. Though he was in his mid-thirties, he was still only a corporal. He looked like he wanted to puke when he heard that I picked up sergeant three months before my three-year mark. The British give out rank like the Corps used to—slowly and grudgingly. From what he told us though, they were paid quite well to compensate.

With little fanfare, we left the GOSP in British hands and continued North. We hit the main highway, which looked like I-5 on a Friday afternoon There were British, U.S Army and other Marine units clogging the highway as far as the eye could see. This was the huge support apparatus that allowed the grunts to fight, and they vastly out-numbered us.

Miller started yelling at a boot next to him in the air watch panel to give him room, but the boot wasn't able to comply. Miller got so mad at the kid that I thought he might hit him. I distracted Miller by telling him about the idea I got at the GOSP, about writing a book about the war. He loved the idea, especially the part about spilling the dirt on staff NCOs. I rode in Miller's trac since I was getting sick of Reed and Carpenter. Miller's Trac Commander was a laid-back guy I had nick-named Sgt. Fun. Unlike SSgt. No-Fun, he would pass us whatever info he had, joke around with us and let us do "crazy" things like take a piss if he knew we would be stopping for a few minutes.

After hours of in the traffic jam, I asked Sgt. Fun how far we were going that night. He told me that the plan was to keep rolling until we had gone 180 km, almost halfway to Baghdad. In the last three hours, we had only gone 30km. Luckily, the higher-ups realized that the highway was too congested, so we pulled off the highway for the night, setting down in a wide plain.

When we woke, we got our first dump of MREs since we left Kuwait. We also got a silly order that counter-manded a previous silly order. The day before we crossed the LOD, we were ordered to grow mustaches. Supposedly, some Iraqis had acquired coalition uniforms and were going to try to infiltrate our ranks. The higher-ups guessed that the Iraqis would probably shave their beards to blend in with us, but—aha!—the Iraqis didn't know that we would all have mustaches! The fact that half of the guys in the battalion couldn't grow a moustache in two weeks if the fate of the world hinged on it didn't sway our leaders one bit. While at the TAA, I had grown an insanely thick and out-of-regs mustache that looked like something Elliot Gould wore in 1971. That morning, we were ordered to shave our mustaches. The hair on mine was so long that it wasn't even bristly anymore; when I dragged my razor across it, it came off almost in one piece.

Kennel told me that he had some problems with my boys not moving quickly enough and not listening to him. He also felt like I wasn't riding them hard enough. Since he approached me professionally, I listened to him, but it was the same thing I had heard since SOI—if I wasn't yelling, I wasn't leading. He did have some valid points, and I told him I'd try to work with his squad better. He nodded and it seemed like everything had been taken care of between us.

The land changed for the worse when we entered the marshlands between of Southern Iraq and Baghdad. The word "marsh" conjures up the picture of a swamp with water and dense vegetation, but this marsh was more like mush—sickening, yellowish glop as far as the eye could see. The only civilization consisted of pathetic mud huts dotted along the half-constructed highway. We came to a long stretch of highway which had a bluff paralleling it on the right. Standard procedure was for the 240 to cover the trac's blind left side, but the bluff was a much more likely ambush site. You could see for twenty miles on the left, but there could be a whole division hidden past the lip of the mesa, so I turned the gun and covered the right. After a few minutes, Kennel started yelling at me like I was a recruit, telling me to cover the left. I knew everyone was tense from being in the trac all day and night, so I ignored his tone. I tried to explain why I was facing the right; we still had a SAW facing the left. "I swear to God, Meyer, if you don't point that gun in the right direction I'm going to see to it that you get busted down!" Kennel screamed. He had really crossed the line. I considered letting it go, but he had gone too far.

At the next stop, everyone was allowed to go stretch their legs and I went to find Kennel, who was talking to SSgt. D and some others. I walked by and growled to him to follow me. We got 30 feet away from the others and I pointed to the endless plains.

"What do you see over there?!"

"Nothing."

I pointed at the mesa.

"What do you see over there?!"

"A mountain."

"How about a likely ambush point?"

"You're supposed to cover the left side."

"And I have been, but in this situation I had to make a decision. And you don't fucking tell me what to do with my fucking guns, *corporal!*"

"I may be a corporal, but at least I earned it. You don't even deserve to be sergeant."

I went red and swung at his face, only getting a glancing blow before SSgt. D popped out of nowhere and got between us. The last time I saw SSgt. D., he was 30 feet away, but he must have seen us arguing and knew what was coming. He told us to separate and I went back to the trac, still fuming.

Even as I cursed Kennel in my head, I had to admit something to myself—he was right. I didn't deserve to be a sergeant; not a grunt sergeant at least. I had been promoted because of my rifle and PFT scores and my MCIs, not because I had been singled out for being an out-standing leader. My MOS knowledge was spotty and I was physically average. In my heart, I knew it and everyone else did as well; Kennel was just the only one to say it to my face. There's a saying in the Marines that goes, "Everyone gets promoted to their level of incompetence." If I worked at the Post Office and I was the greatest mail sorter ever—I loved sorting mail and I practiced on my free time—they wouldn't force me to become a letter carrier. I might have no talent for delivering mail and would spend all of my time wishing I was back in the sorting room. I *loved* being a gunner and I was good at it. I loved the gun so much that I even liked cleaning it; just being able to see it and touch it was a thrill. I would have been more than happy to stay a gunner for my entire enlistment, but you can't do that in the Marine Corps, where it's up or out. I had repeatedly asked to go to leadership schools and was always turned down, so I wasn't the only one to blame, but I could have made myself better. Quite frankly, even though I was busy as hell during my FAP, I still managed to watch three episodes of "That 70s Show" each night after work. Call me crazy, but I think I could have used my time more wisely.

That night, both of Third Platoon's tracs went down and we had to double-up with Second Platoon in pitch darkness. Two boots started arguing and trying to fight each other in the crowded confines, though they couldn't even move to get at each other. It felt like going into war in a damn clown car. An hour later, we stopped for the night. There was sporadic fire in the vicinity, but it was far enough away that no one cared. I got out my red-lens flashlight and searched for a rare spot of piss-free ground to sleep on. I laid down in my sleeping bag, hearing the trackers work on their vehicles. As rough as it was in the back of the trac, I still felt sorry for the trackers, who never seemed to get any sleep. They were awake every second that we were in the tracs and, when we stopped, they refueled and fixed their vehicles. To the trackers, their vehicle was their whole world and their boots rarely touched the ground. They even outdid us in nastiness, perfecting a way to shit inside their tracs by hovering above an open MRE bag and deftly dropping a turd inside.

Twenty minutes later, we were told to get back in the tracs. It would have been better to not even stop. I couldn't take being a sardine in a can, so I tried to get on top, which was frowned upon, but with 32 people on a trac, it was a simple reality. I squeezed my head through the crowded air watch hatch to find an open space on top; those on top insisted that there was no more room. I could have just pulled rank, but I wanted it to seem like I had a legitimate reason to go up there, so I pulled out my binos and said that I was coming up "to scan for enemy tanks." People laughed at my obvious ploy, but it was a good enough excuse to get me a spot up top.

The weather was cool, but my thick MOPP suit kept me warm. Compared to being inside, riding up top was like being in a limo. I had read "The Lord of the Rings—The Return of the King" at the TAA and the word that kept springing into my head was "Mordor." The land was vile, grey-yellow muck that seemed to exude misery and evil.

After a day in the marshes, we stopped among a confluence of several convoys to wait for our supply train. Our advance into Iraq was already being touted as the fastest in history and our supply lines could not keep up. I went to go talk with my buddies in First Platoon. One trac crew was listening to the BBC on a transistor radio and I got more clear information from that than from my own officers. The news was good; Iraq was folding like a lawn chair and coalition deaths were extremely low.

As I walked back to my spot, I saw Kennel walking toward me. After the adrenaline wore off the previous day, I got embarrassed by my behavior. Just because he took the low road didn't mean I had to as well. Yet I did what I had to do; in that atmosphere, in front of my boots, the only proper response to his insult was a physical one. I had to do it, but I still wasn't proud of it.

Kennel flashed a shy, embarrassed smile, which took me off guard. He apologized for the day before and said that the tension from constantly being in tracs had gotten to him and he had vented on me. I was amazed by his magnamity and told him that I was embarrassed how I had acted as well. We shook hands and never had another problem.

I needed to keep an eye on Reed, so I went back to riding in his trac. For once though, Reed's acting-up actually worked in my favor. After SSgt. No-fun caught Reed looking at a Playboy while on air watch, he made everyone in the trac switch to Sgt. Fun's trac.

Thick black storm clouds rolled in and by the time the sun went down, you couldn't even tell where the horizon was. We exited the tracs into glorpy mud so thick that it ripped peoples' boots off. We laid down behind our weapons in several inches of water. I had never been in such pitch darkness. We had to call out to each other to make sure that no one set up in anyone else's line of fire. We were told to have 25% on watch, but the concept of watch was ridiculous when you literally could not see your hand in front of your face. The wind and rain picked up and peoples' gear started blowing all over the place. Schofield's boys let his gear blow into a small stream. I was worried that someone's rifle would be buried in the mud and lost entirely. We were all dead tired, so I told my boys to just go to sleep. It was so dark that the NVGs didn't even work; the enemy would not be able to find us.

The next night, instead of setting down just off the highway like we had been, we pushed inland several hundred meters. The XO warned people to be careful around the tracs, since a staff NCO and officer in another battalion had their legs cleaved off when a trac ran over them while they were sleeping. Lt. Pettes tasked me with walking the tracs to the berm. I nervously called out for people to move out of the way as I led those huge machines forward. The guilt that I might lead the tracs over a sleeping Marine was almost paralyzing. The sky was clearer than the previous night and my NVGs were working fairly well; I was amazed at how the behemoths behind me could move so quietly. I kept having to turn around to make sure they were still there.

Carpenter got himself lost somehow. I walked the line back and forth four times, calling his name, worried that he might have been run over. When I found him and asked him why he didn't respond to me, he said that he didn't knew he had to. An answer like that would be insulting from anyone else, but it was par-for-the-course with Carpenter.

That night, an officer told us that approximately fifty Marines had been killed at a bridge up north. A striking feeling ran through me—it was as if I could see the Marines dying. Though I knew no one from the unit, every line company is the same. "Fifty Marines" wasn't just a line in a newspaper article, I could see each dead Marine in my mind, except they had my buddies' faces. It seemed impossible. I did not believe that any force could kill fifty Marines in open combat in one battle. We also heard that four Army soldiers had been executed on Iraqi television. The thought of that made me sick with rage: what human being could follow such an abhorrent order—to execute someone as spectacle? Then again, it seemed to fit. The Iraqis had no history of standing up to Saddam or refusing to follow any horrible order he issued—that's why we were there.

After the war, I was able to read about what happened and parse the truth from the rumors. I found out that those two rumors were based on truth and dove-tailed eerily. The "fifty dead Marines" rumor referred to Task Force Tarawa, which ran into fierce resistance on a bridge leading to Nasariyah, while attempting to rescue members of the 507th Maintenance Convoy, who had been ambushed and captured. Eighteen Marines were killed and fourteen were wounded securing the north bank of the river. Four captured U.S. soldiers were prominently displayed to the mass media, but none were publicly executed. Several of the dead soldiers left at the scene though were reported to have been shot in the head, execution-style.

The next morning, the air was brown and we were told that a vicious sandstorm was coming. Sand storms are one of those things that don't sound like a big deal until you go through them. We got a much-needed issue of chow and I was shocked to find a box of extra MREs that I was told I could have. My obsession with food had only gotten worse as it had gotten more scarce.

The next morning, instead of leaving at first light like usual, we sat around all morning. The storm grew to a gale and we huddled under our ponchos to keep the sand from filling our ears, eyes and noses. When it was time to go, Schofield asked me, in a professional manner, if I could light a fire in Carpenter's ass. Well, shucks, since you asked me nicely…I gave Carpenter five minutes to get ready and he still wasn't ready after fifteen, so I yelled at him and kicked his gear like a DI. Schofield nodded in approval, but I didn't like being that way. Reed and Carpenter were hopeless; all I would do by yelling would be to turn myself into a jerk as well.

I got into my usual spot on air watch and noticed that I couldn't even see the end of my gun. We closed the hatches and tried to wait out the storm, but after an hour they could tell it was going to go for awhile. They fired up the engines and we headed down the road with the hatches closed, hoping for the best.

After two more days of a declining sandstorm, we came upon an almost cartoonily beautiful landscape—a green field with grazing cows, a little farm house and a small stream. I became entranced by the beautiful, clear water and walked forward of the line a whopping two feet to check it out. Schofield started bitching about me crossing the line, though I was not in anyone's field of fire. I could have made a stink, but I decided to let it go. I thought it would be a little weird for two sergeants to start fighting in a war zone because one of them wanted to look at a pretty little stream.

Even though we were the first ground unit to enter Iraq, somehow dozens of units had gotten ahead of us. We heard there was actual enemy contact in this area. After passing hundreds of miles of open desert, they set us down in a mile-wide garbage dump just in front of an arty unit. I couldn't believe it. The other side of the road was clean sand, as it was on either side of the dump. Not only was it filthy, but if any enemy arty landed near us, all the metal on the ground around us would turn to shrapnel.

Our fighting holes had gotten pretty lax, so when I heard that the Battalion Gunner was going to check out each one, I rushed down the line to warn my buddies. As I went down the line, I realized my that my squad's position was a paradise compared to the others'. My squad was located on the edge of the dump, where there was just a single layer of trash above solid dirt. The rest of the company had been placed in rolling dunes of trash. Just ahead of First Platoon's lines were four dead bodies whose heads had been run over. I got the feeling that they were killed by locals thugs—probably Fedayeen—right before we got there.

We were in another "operational pause." Most people were eating their last bits of food. After a day in the dumps (literally), Lt. Pettes called the squad leaders together and gave us a "frag"—a short warning order. That was the first time we had been briefed since we left Kuwait. Back in Pendleton, we were given a complete briefing before every field op. Lt. Pettes told us that we would be pulling a feint while another unit went to secure the Han Tush Air Field. It didn't sound like much, but it was better than sitting in thirty year-old tins of vegetable oil.

We went fifteen miles up the road and our forward elements started taking small arms fire. In America, there's a phenomenon known as "Death by Cop", in which a person who wants to die purposefully provokes a cop into shooting him. It seemed that whoever was shooting us was committing "Death by Marine." Convoys move in a standard way—fast, light-armored LAVs at the front, followed by slower, but more powerful tanks. Thin-skinned, relatively weak AAVs and unarmored humvees and trucks followed in trace. Common ambush procedure is to let the armored vehicles pass and then attack the weakest links. Whoever was fighting us either didn't know that or didn't care. They would fire AKs at tanks, barely scratching the paint, and then get blasted off the face of the earth. My impression of those who fought us that day was that they were not jihadists or Saddam followers; just hardheads who didn't like seeing foreign troops in their country, no matter what the reason.

It was exciting to hear the shots popping off, but I was sure that any enemy would be dead by the time we got up there. After the shooting stopped, the convoy started moving again. When we came under an overpass though, we started to take fire from a walled compound off to the right. I got my first taste of combat—complete confusion. It took us at least a minute to spot the shooters and once we did, everyone started shooting at once. I couldn't leave the left unguarded, so I searched the area until I was sure that it was clear. I didn't want to miss out on the action. We had been in Iraq a week without firing a shot. I thought this might be our only firefight in the war.

The left side was clear; now it was my time to get in on the action. I peeked over my shoulder and saw Lovett firing his SAW. I yelled to him that I was going to turn around, but in my excitement I didn't wait for him to acknowledge me. I whirled around and found the barrel of Lovett's SAW six inches from my ear, just as he let off a six-round burst. I felt a blast of hot air in my ear and jumped back. I was resigned to the probability that I might lose hearing in that ear, but I would deal with that later.

About eighty feet away, three figures kept peeking over the edge of the compound's wall. Rohr started coolly blooping 203 rounds onto them as I aimed in. I fired off one shot and the gun jammed. I "sling-shotted" rounds one at a time by moving the bolt back by hand after each shot, until someone yelled at me to lube the gun. I cursed at myself for forgetting something as basic as that. We didn't keep the guns lubed up on the go because that would attract sand and foul the bolt. I got handed some rifle lube—which was thinner than the gun lube—and squirted it onto the bolt.

One of our Dragon Anti-Tank Men attached to us from Weapons Company was about five-foot-two and he had to make a pile of gear just to see out of the air watch panel. He dropped one hostile good with his rifle, but the pile of gear he was standing on started to fall apart and he slowly sunk out of the air watch hatch.

Lovett's SAW went down, just as mine ran out of ammo.

"Ammo!" I yelled. I looked over and saw Miller using his gun like a water hose, spraying the entire compound; I needed to get back in the game.

"Ammo!" I did a double-take when I saw Lovett calmly cleaning the bolt of his dis-assembled SAW, right in the middle of a firefight.

Still no ammo. I squatted down into the troop compartment and saw that Carpenter was sullenly staring at his feet, not even looking for the ammo. I kicked him hard in the chest hard, spinning him half-way around.

"Ammo, motherfucker!"

His eyes blinked back to consciousness, or as close to consciousness as he ever got. He didn't even know where the ammo was. I cursed at him while he scrambled for some ammo.

I stood back up and put my hand down inside the trac and shook it, waiting for Carpenter to hand me an ammo belt. I felt something strange in my hand and lifted it to see a Country Captain Chicken MRE. Someone had given me their damn trash to throw away in the middle of a firefight. I never got anyone to 'fess up to that one after the war.

Rager finally found Carpenter's ammo and handed it to me. The tracs moved forward slightly, blocking my line of sight to the enemy. The turret on the trac started to fire its .50 cal; displaced air hit my face and I could feel the reverberations deep in my chest—it felt good. I looked to the next trac and caught of glimpse of Miller flashing a proud smile and holding four fingers up. He had put down four belts—four hundred rounds.

We moved toward the middle of the complex, but I couldn't see any movement. The initial unemotional reaction to the shots wore off; I got intensely angry at whoever was shooting at us. What the hell was their problem? Sorry for trying to remove the damn dictator that you were too much of a punk to stand up to. We'll just turn around and leave.

One hut was being shot by about ten different weapons, so I joined in on the fun. After awhile, I started to feel stupid for shooting at dust and stopped firing. The convoy started up again and I noticed a black flag flying in front of the complex. I wondered if it meant something—I hadn't seen black flags on any other houses. I flipped back over to cover the left side and saw a couple hajis giving the same friendly wave we had gotten from everyone else. A flash of anger went through me. They knew about the ambush. I took my hand off the trigger and gave them the finger.

The convoy continued toward the air field. We would dismount at a farm suspected of hiding enemy combatants. As we approached, we were told there were incoming mortars, so they made us close the air watch hatches. When the ramp dropped, I followed the elevens toward the berm they were setting up on, assuming that Reed's team was behind me. Though Miller's team was already getting into place on another berm that was twice as far away, Reed's team hadn't even gotten out of the trac yet. When they finally trundled up, Rager got down in the prone and started to load his gun. Reed threw the tripod on the wrong side of the gun—after yelling at Carpenter so many times for doing the same thing—and he laid down to the left of Rager. Rager started to pull the charging handle to the rear to put a round in the chamber when Reed reached across the gun to grab the tripod. Instead of lifting the tripod with both hands, Reed lazily dragged it across the top of the gun. The tripod knocked Rager's hand off the charging handle, sending the bolt forward, making one round shoot off.

Reed dropped to the ground in the fetal position and grabbed his ears. He had to be joking. His head had been a foot and a half away from the end of the barrel, much farther than Lovett's SAW had been from my ear. Reed started moaning and rolling around on the ground in "pain."

"My ears! My ears! I can't hear! I can't hear!".

I didn't think that people who had just lost their hearing actually screamed "I can't hear." After rolling around like a bitch for about thirty seconds, Reed got onto his hands and knees and crawled toward Rager.

"You motherfucker! I'm fucking deaf because of you!"

"Corporal, I-"

"Shut the fuck up! I'm going to kick your fucking ass!"

This was classic Reed, he wants to be the victim *and* a tough guy. This scenario was playing out exactly like Squeak and I had imagined. Instead of getting his gun up, he was trying to pick a fight over a problem that he had caused. I yelled for him to get the damn gun up, but he didn't hear me over his tirade. SSgt. Melendez yelled at him as well, but we were in Reedland, so his tantrum continued.

I moved behind Reed and started to cock my rifle back to buttstroke him in the back of the head. That piece of shit more than deserved it. He had ruined the machinegun sections's rep, embarrassed himself and his Corps on a daily basis and now he was preventing the gun from being employed in a combat situation. As I was about to smash his skull, I stopped myself. This wasn't the movies— where you knock someone out and they're fine when they wake up—if I brained him with my buttstock, I could fuck him up for life. He was a piece of garbage and a complete failure as a Marine and a human being, but we were not taking shots. I would go to the brig and he would be given command of my squad if I assaulted him.

Rager finally had enough. His face mottled red with anger, he stopped considering Reed's rank and yelled at him like the little kid that he was.

"You shut your goddamn mouth, Reed! I'm tired of you fucking acting like a damn baby. Now stop your bullshit and help me get this gun up!"

Reed was taken aback for a moment, his mouth hanging open in disbelief.

"You're done, Rager. When this is all over—you're done."

"No, he's not," I said. Reed's shoulders slumped, realizing that no one was going to back him on this. Rager turned back and loaded the gun.

I went over to Miller's position and told him what happened. Miller shook his head, disgusted with Reed. It always bothered me how Reed got so many second-chances and yet guys like Miller got a bad rep because he wore his hair long and didn't shave every damn day.

A group of Iraqis were spotted about 400 meters away and Schofield told Sene to shoot them. Schofield was in charge of the attachments while they were riding in the trac, but not when they got outside. Sene ignored Schofield while his assistant B.B. got a closer look with their spotting scope. It was just some women and kids leaving the area, but Schofield called it up to higher on his radio, making the group sound ominous. He was given permission to shoot, which he relayed to Sene. Sene tried to use tact to tell Schofield he was wrong, but Schofield just kept screeching for him to shoot. Finally, Miller said the perfect thing:

"Schofield, just go away."

Schofield walked away, sulking. I could have kissed Miller at that moment.

The elevens searched the two farmhouses and found no signs of any enemy, just some farm animals that got blown apart by our mortars. To our relief, we were given permission to take off our heavy, awkward NBC rubber over-boots, which made our feet so hot that people were sweating through leather. Once the adrenaline from the firefight wore off, we all became aware of how little we had eaten in the last two days. Most people were completely out of food. Rager had rationed his food wisely and, in a show a kindness that shocked me, he gave half his food to Reed when he saw how pathetically Reed was eying his food. This was not a peace offering—none of us had any patience left for Reed—it was just common human decency.

"Why'd you call me a bitch, Rager?" Reed asked in a wheedling voice.

"Drop it," I ordered. I was tired of my squad revolving around Reed and his dramas twenty-four hours a day.

Although we were all out of our MREs, each trac had a few boxes of Humanitarian MREs. They had bright yellow wrappers and were about 50% bigger than regular MREs, since one of them was meant to be an entire day's worth of nutrition for one person, while our MREs were only a third of our daily requirement. We were given strict orders not to break into them, but I didn't see any civilians. I broached the subject to some of the other seniors in Third, but since they were lances and corporals, they didn't want to go out on a limb. I told them I'd take the rap if anyone gave them a problem.

I broke the box open and started distributing the MREs to the elevens, setting aside three MREs for my squad. When I turned to see if there were any other boxes of MREs, someone grabbed the three MREs I set behind myself. This wasn't a harmless, silly prank, some piece of shit had just stolen my squad's only chance at food. No one would admit taking the MREs. Though I rarely pulled rank, this time I had no problem doing it. I went around and taxed each team of elevens one MRE to replenish what their boys had robbed from my squad. I stopped once I got the three I lost, though I could have gotten more from them.

I was surprised when we turned around and went back to the dump. The "operational pause" was going on even longer since we were still low on almost everything, even water. I was still in the afterglow of my first firefight and quite cocky. Most people were inside the tracs during the fight, but I actually got to shoot. As cocky as I was, even I had to admit that I probably didn't hit anyone, and if I did, that they had already been shot about twenty times. Miller had brought a huge sniper scope and affixed it to his team's machinegun; while I was seeing vague shapes in the mist, he was seeing sweat on the guy's forehead. He shot one person and one vehicle. The person was Iraqi and the vehicle was American. While he was shooting, the turret next to him turned suddenly and he shot it at an oblique angle, the round skimming harmlessly off the surface. After the fight, SSgt. No-Fun spotted the mark and proudly told everyone that the enemy had almost got him.

Lt. Sprincin came around to get everyone's story. He didn't seem to believe anything we said, but he did have some news: Gunny Menusa—a platoon sergeant from our combat engineer attachment—had been killed in the firefight. This was our first death, and though I felt bad for him and his family, my sense of invulnerability was undiminished.

We spent the next two days in the dump and I had a lot of time to think. It was interesting to compare how movies and books showed combat with how it actually was. In movies, when the main character first gets an enemy in his sights, he pauses as he suddenly realizes that *gasp* it's another human being! He goes through some moral turmoil, pulls the trigger while half-turning away and then forces himself to look at what he did, horrified. When I aimed my gun, I wasn't looking at a man, I was looking at a target. We were more than happy to roll to Baghdad and back without firing a shot. That guy had brought it on himself.

I only knew one person who had the classic movie reaction. Ferguson was very religious and took care of his invalid mother when he wasn't deployed. Though he was a bright and cheery guy, he tried a little too hard, and he never really fit in. Before we left America, he bought a huge sniper scope and bipods to trick out his M-16. When we were ambushed, he coolly aimed in on one guy with his powerful scope and put him down with one shot. He then sat back down in the trac, apparently distraught. I heard a line once somewhere that stuck with me: "Lie to the whole world, lie to God, but don't lie to yourself." No one joins the Marines and volunteers for the grunts without wanting to go to war and shoot someone.

You can dress it up however you want, but there is a base part of yourself that wants to know how it feels to kill another man in combat. To say that doesn't exist in every warrior's heart is to lie. That blood-lust can coincide with patriotism and a sincere hope to liberate an oppressed people, but there is always that underlying reason. Ferguson didn't buy that scope to help him find orphans that really needed food. He wanted to kill and he wanted to see the man die with crystal clarity.

I was surprised by how confusing combat was. I spent most of the time trying to figure who was where and what was happening. Since it was not a movie and no one wanted a close-up, the enemy only showed themselves enough to see you and shoot at you.

One thing that was surprising by its absence was fear. I only considered the concept of fear once during the firefight, and that was only to think that I was vulnerable to incoming fire and a normal person would be scared, but I wasn't. Besides feeling like I was the main character in a movie who couldn't die, I also fooled myself with some bizarre logic. I told myself that a bullet is small and that there are a billion places it can go in the sky where it won't hit me, so the odds were on my side. The other thing that was on my side was the notoriously bad marksmanship skills of the Iraqis. They didn't use their sights; they would just "spray and pray."

I informed Squeak about Reed's tantrum and asked him if they were finally going to bust Reed down like they had promised. Squeak was noncommital on taking away Reed's rank, but he was livid and promised that Reed would not be a team leader any longer. Gunny Brouillet ambled up and wanted to know what happened. He listened calmly, as I vented like I was on the Oprah Winfrey Show; then he took me along to speak with several witnesses. We stopped near Reed's hole and he called him over. Reed ran over like a dutiful recruit, trying to earn brownie points. Reed gave his version of what happened, which was entertaining, to say the least. He said that there was a negligent discharge that went off for an unknown reason, he flinched, asked Rager what happened and then got the gun up. He said the whole thing took maybe twenty seconds.

"So what did you mean when you said, 'You're done.' to Rager?" Gunny asked.

"Oh, I just meant that he was done arguing and he needed to help me get the gun up."

He must have had that response prepared. It was a masterful play since the word "done" was ambiguous, but I and everyone there agreed on how he had used it—as a threat. Reed kept giving me an innocent "hey buddy" look like we were best friends. It was unreal.

Sgt. Quinn had been the first one to tell me that I needed to do something about Reed. When asked how long Reed's tantrum had kept the gun from getting up, Sgt. Quinn said the same thing I had said—two to three minutes. In combat, that is an eternity. Half of Third Platoon could have been wiped out in that time. SSgt. Melendez corroborated everything Sgt. Quinn and I said.

An hour later, Reed came up to my hole and sheepishly told me that he had been demoted to "Assistant Ammo Man"—a billet below our lowest billet that we invented for Reed. His self-delusion kicked in and he said that he would be our "squad advisor and tripod carrier." I told him that he needed to check in with Rager whenever he went anywhere and he nodded submissively. I knew what he was thinking; he was going to be contrite and suppress his natural nut-case reactions for a few weeks, until we forgave him and he got his job back. I let him walk away with his delusions.

With that taken care of, we had nothing to do but sit and think. We got our first issue of food and water in days and we ate ourselves sick. Unfortunately, this attracted clouds of flies so thick that when Ryan fell asleep, I watched as more than fifty flies landed and started crawling on his legs.

The next day, we were told that the mail was going out in five minutes. I grabbed a thin piece of cardboard from my MRE and scrawled out a quick cheery missive:

"In Iraq, doing fine. Had my first firefight yesterday. Think I got the guy good. I love you! Can't wait to see you!"

One thing that sucked about the constant movement was that, no matter how well you took care of your gear, every day something irreplaceable got broken and some vital piece of gear got lost. My dust goggles had gotten ripped off of my helmet since I had not secured them properly, so I had to resort to the amazingly uncool choice of using a pair of chemical goggles, like the ones you used in high school chemistry, that I found in the trac. I had made it known throughout Third Platoon that I needed a pair of goggles and would trade almost anything for them. As we prepared to leave the dump, Ross from Third came by and cheerfully asked me if I wanted a pair of goggles he had found. I was flabbergasted at this simple act of kindness, after all the strum-und-drang I had gone through with the rest of the guys in Third.

The land got greener as we moved further north, palm trees replacing scraggly bushes as the main type of foliage. We stopped in the most verdant place I'd seen in months. Third would take the right flank and we spent an hour moving from spot to spot to accommodate the rest of the company. Though we found a great position, we were ordered to move to a less defendable one. Kennel told Lt. Pettes that he refused to move his squad. We were being ordered to move so that the line would look straight and neat, not for tactical reasons. As many problems as I had with Kennel, I really respected him for sticking to his guns. Schofield did not support Kennel and he moved his squad along with the lieutenant's plan. Eventually, Kennel had to move his squad back to tie in with them.

After we set down, we drew up our range cards, which delineated our fields of fire. They needed someone to take the cards to the XO. Usually a boot would do a job like that, but I wanted to stretch my legs, so I volunteered. Since we always had to have a buddy wherever we went, I took Lopez. Before we had walked 300 meters, I found myself strangely exhausted. Just standing was an effort and I had to sit down halfway to the XO's trac. All the gear, no sleep, little food—I could barely walk. How was I supposed to fight?

The XO was with First Platoon at the left flank, which was only accessible by crossing a pipe over a ten-foot canal. Though I had no fear of being killed in combat, the thought of falling into that fetid, nasty water terrified me.

When I made it back to my squad, a back hoe rolled up to dig our holes for us. What was this—Beverly Hills? The back hoe belonged to the Regiment, which was staying right next to our company in an empty gas station. We got another issue of food which almost caught us up with our deficit. Slater's tapeworm served me well, as he traded me all of his snacks for my more-filling main meals.

Late that night, Lt. Pettes woke me and told me that a squad of enemy troops were probing our lines. I thought of how many things were wrong with what he said. If anyone was really out there, they would have gotten lit up like a Christmas tree. Both of my guns were already being manned; what was I supposed to do, wake up the rest of my squad from their three consecutive hours of sleep? As soon as the lieutenant left, I went back to sleep.

If I ever meet Tom Clancy, I'm going to kick him square in the balls. His movies and books led me to believe that our intelligence network was so great that it could spot the tits on a chick in a terrorist camp from space ("Patriot Games"). I assumed that wherever we went, some government agency was watching us by satellite and could tell us who was approaching us. That wasn't how it was; we rarely got any intel and when we did, it was ridiculous. We were once told that fifty tanks were heading for our position to attack us. Wow, fifty tanks?

OK, where are they? We don't know. OK, which direction are they coming from? We don't know. Then how do you know there's fifty of them?

The next day, I went to find my buddies from my FAP, over at regiment. I never found them, but I did see a French photographer chatting amiably with some grunts. The HQ trac was parked at a real-life oasis and Letta was perched on top of a trac, typing on her lap top. Yikes—can someone get that troll some make-up?

We moved south, and then east, trying to find our way to a parallel highway. We had to take a detour since some Air Force personnel were converting the highway into a landing strip. In stark contrast to us, with our MOPP suits and sixty pounds of gear, the airmen were in t-shirts and baseball caps; half of them weren't even armed. I briefly envied them, but then I thought about how our stories would differ. I could talk about combat and they would talk about setting up runway lights on an Iraqi highway.

Cutting across the country, we came upon many more units in "operational pauses." The LAV crews caught my attention; not only did they all have a surplus of MREs and much-prized bottled water, but they also had enough room in their empty troop compartments to store non-essentials, like lawn chairs and improvised shitters made out of ammo crates. Their four-man crews had much more autonomy than us; they waved at us in their t-shirts while sipping Kool-aid in their damn lawn chairs.

We stopped along that East-West road and set up a defense. Once again, phantom tanks were supposedly heading for us. Food was so low that 1st Platoon "found" some chickens and cooked them. The temperature dropped, so Lt. Pettes let us start up a much-appreciated fire. The land had almost nothing to burn, but we had plenty of MRE trash. I almost wept openly when I found a Tootsie Roll I had forgotten about in my patrol pack. Ferguson had been made the radio man, which meant that he went everywhere the lieutenant went. Lt. Pettes chatted amiably with Ferguson, but also took advantage of him by making him dig both of their fighting holes.

Higher-ups made us douse the fire, so I got up to walk around. Slater saw that I was bummed out and asked me what was wrong. I told him that the constant food shortages were really messing me with my head. Sleeping in ditches and getting shot at was fine, but don't take away my peanut butter and crackers.

There was an Iraqi armory nearby and, all afternoon, we had been told to get ready to secure it. As the sun set, we were told that we weren't going, so everyone relaxed. As soon as it got dark though, we were told that we were leaving in five minutes.

"Make sure your damn machinegunners are ready this time. I'm tired of waiting for them," Schofield told me.

"Just worry about your own boys," I responded.

The armory was abandoned, but we still stayed there for the night. I noticed that Kennel had a boot protege named DeWitt who was organizing our defenses. It seemed weird that he was chosen over several other senior lances and even corporals, but that was the way it was with Third—you were either in or you were out.

The next day, we rolled to an actual town. Telephone poles, intersecting streets and multi-story apartments—wow. We saw more Iraqis in five minutes than we had seen in the last ten days. Everyone was waving and kids came running up, cheering us on and asking for candy. We gave what little we had. As we came to the other side of the town, I saw a huge Babylonian fortress, just barely visible in the haze.

Whenever they dropped the ramp to disgorge the Marines inside, the machinegunners never made it out before the ramp closed back up. Since I was always on air watch, I thought I'd just scramble down the packs hanging over the side. When the convoy stopped, I crawled on top of the trac and slid down the packs which worked great until I got about two feet from the ground and stopped suddenly. My gear had gotten snagged on the rolled-up cammie netting and I was suspended in the air like a damn marionette. I didn't knew what hurt worse, my pride or my nuts, which were supporting the entire weight of my body. For such a spectacle, it was strange that no one noticed. I fell free a couple seconds later.

Ten minutes later, we got back on the tracs. We drove around aimlessly for hours, never going farther than three miles from the town; then set down in a field. We dismounted in the dark and I stormed off like it was D-Day, feeling very cool until I realized that I lost the ammo belt. Rager and I looked for the belt and I could tell he was bothered. I was starting to feel guilty for being a gun hog. I told myself that this was my last chance at war; Rager had more than two years left in his enlistment, he would have another chance. We found the ammo and set down for three hours of sleep.

Surprisingly enough, I felt well-rested when it was time to get up. As my boys packed up, I went to check if they left anything in the darkness. My foot brushed against something hard and I bent to pick it up—Ryan's NVGs. I walked up to Ryan and used a line one of my DIs used on me.

"You lost your mind, didn't you, Ryan?"

"Sergeant?"

"Just say you lost your damn mind."

"Um…I lost my mind. What's this about?"

I handed him the NVGs and walked off in a huff. I really wasn't that mad, knowing that mistakes were rare for him, but I had to rub it in and make him feel guilty, so he would remember next time.

For some reason, instead of going through the town, we took the tracs on some berms that were surrounded by canals on both sides. The berms were barely wider than the tracs and I worried about over-turning and drowning. I wondered if I could jump free or if the trac would still fall on me no matter how far I jumped.

We finally got onto a road and the tanks started firing at bunkers in some farm fields. We didn't seem to be taking any fire; they were shooting the bunkers as a pre-cautionary matter. The tankers were also taking pot-shots at every picture of Saddam with their .50 cals, so much so that it got passed over the radio that no one could shoot at pictures of Saddam anymore.

While trying to find a route to the river, we wheeled around in some farm fields. Several tracs got stuck, but they were able to be towed free. The two tanks that got stuck were too-heavy to tow. Our advance halted for a day, as they tried every method imaginable to get the tanks out. I was told that we would stay there until the tanks were free, no matter how long it took.

Jesse did a double-take and asked me if I was wearing cammie paint. I found a mirror and saw what he was talking about. I hadn't shaved in five days and had been sucking in exhaust twenty hours a day. Soot and sand had collected in my beard, making it look like a greasepaint beard you'd see in a Charlie Chaplin movie.

As I sat down in the mud, I saw a cylindrical object fly through the air. An AT-4 landed in the mud, thirty feet away from the trac that Sgt. Fun had thrown it from. Considering how calm he usually was, I wondered what had made him flip out. The trackers had a pet peeve about us leaving gear on the tracs, but we had little sympathy. Each one of them had their own seat and no one was crushing them when we rode. They also hung their packs on the inside of the trac in our already-crowded troop compartment, while our packs had to be strapped to the outside of the hull, where several of them had already come loose and been lost. Any gear that was left in the trac when we dismounted was likely to be thrown out, but Sgt. Fun had really crossed the line. He tossed a loaded anti-tank weapon as hard as he could, which is about as unsafe as you can get. Even though I liked him, he needed to burn for what he did, but since he was a Cool Kid, all SSgt. D did was tell him to calm down and it was never mentioned again.

There were a few farmhouses in our vicinity and on our second day there, a couple of locals walked up to our position. One of the men spoke good English and he was glad to be able to speak to some Americans. He told us that the people were very happy that we were getting rid of Saddam, telling us how Saddam's people had dumped chemicals up-river. He then started speaking, as if it was a foregone conclusion, about how we were going to take Iraq's oil as our just reward. It was sad to think he thought of us that way and we assured him that the U.S. had no plans on taking anything or staying there permanently. He seemed surprised and cautiously hopeful that what we said was true.

I'm still kicking myself for not buying the donkey he tried to sell to us. His asking price was only five bucks, but we turned him down since it seemed silly. A few days later, when we were all starving, I would have paid five hundred dollars for some donkey meat.

We finally got the tanks un-stuck and we headed off to find a way to cross the river. Though we enjoyed seeing the Iraqis, we were always wary of them getting to close to our tracs, where they could easily chuck a grenade into the air watch panel. An old lady got too close and the vehicle commander called for someone to check her out. I was so starved for action that I prayed that she was a suicide bomber. I leaned into the trac and told Rager to give me his pistol. He seemed bothered as he untied it from his gear. I hopped on top of the trac with the pistol in my hand like Magnum, P.I and looked over the edge, but the old lady was far down the road. I'd have to win the Medal of Honor some other day.

The first time I got a vanilla milkshake in my MRE was a momentous event. While I was on FAP, snacks such as Combos, milkshakes and hamburger patties had been added to the MRE menu. Any true grunt had the contents of all twenty-odd MREs memorized. Miller somehow had a shake with almost every meal and he showed me the perfect way to fix it. It tasted amazing and it actually raised my morale, as funny as that might sound.

An old woman (perhaps the same one I drew down on) walked up, smiling at us. We tried to communicate with her, to no avail. She nodded amiably and continued down the line. I worried that we were wrecking her small field and I cringed at how we were probably offending her family. These people didn't have much, and 120 Marines pissing, shitting and digging holes in their small farm wasn't exactly improving things. I made my boys piss down by the river, so that they wouldn't be exposing themselves in front of the females. I double-checked that we had policed up all of our MRE trash, which was the best that I could do.

We moved faster than any invading force in history, but the rivers constantly flummoxed us. RCT-5 was stopped cold at the Diyaliyah River, forty miles south of Baghdad. The rumor mill said that the bridge we were supposed to take had been blown by retreating Iraqi soldiers who wanted to fight in the confines of Baghdad, where they would have the advantage. The billowing black smoke and Cobra gunships in the distance seemed to confirm that. It galled me that we had spent days getting lost in farmlands; didn't they have satellite photos that could have shown us a quicker route to the bridge? Though our tracs were amphibious, the humvees, tanks and trucks were not. The engineers started erecting a pontoon bridge as my other gun team went in their trac across the river to secure the other bank.

If we did have to stay for a night, this was a great place. Rager asked where I wanted him to set the gun up and I told him that he was the team leader; it was his decision. Rager had taken to his team leader billet well, as I knew he would, but he still deferred to me too much. Reed had actually calmed down lately; the embarrassment of him being led by a PFC seemed to have gotten his attention.

I sat down on the bluff and lazily tossed pebbles into the water as others bathed in the river. It was a great view and the weather was clean and cool—a nice place to sit and reflect on what we had gone through. The last few weeks had been nasty and futile; we literally could have marched the 200 miles in less than a week. There hadn't been much glory or action—just a lot of mud and poverty.

An hour after sunset, I laid in my sleeping bag and listened as the XO walked up to Reed, who was manning the gun. The XO asked Reed why there weren't two people awake and Reed said that since there were only four people in the team and watch was at 25%, only one person needed to be awake. The XO looked to the right of the gun and counted eight people. Reed calmly explained to the XO that those extra four "Marines" were our packs.

After spending so much time trying to find a bridge and having our engineers begin building one, they finally found a perfectly good bridge just a few miles to the east that the Army had secured. I couldn't believe that our helos—that had been flying around the area the whole time—couldn't have spotted it any earlier. The town surrounding the bridge was the biggest we'd ever seen and the Army had it locked down; no locals were out. I was jealous of the soldiers, imagining that they had seen major action while securing the town. A rumor went around that a Marine had jumped off the bridge to commit suicide, but I didn't believe it. By that time, we had gotten so much bum scoop that I believed none of what I heard and only half of what I saw.

April 5th—We were finally within fifteen miles from Baghdad. It was thrilling to be so near our target, since Baghdad was supposed to be our ticket home. While driving through an industrial area we saw hundreds of Iraqis looting everything in sight. They didn't discriminate either; an object didn't need to be valuable or even identifiable to be looted. The battalions within the regiment took turns being the lead element and it was Fox Company's turn that day. I saw a tank that was so blackened by RPG fire that it was hard to tell what it was, but when we came close enough, I could tell it was one of ours.

We came into another farming community. After we set up our lines, SSgt. D called the squad leaders together. SSgt. D looked more serious than usual as he told us that Fox Company's First Sergeant Smith had been killed earlier that day. First Sergeant Young had been a friend of First Sergeant Smith and his death affected him greatly. First Sergeant Young gave the staff NCOs an ultimatum—if he caught anyone without their proper gear on, he would ruin the career of whatever staff NCO was in charge of that Marine. When I passed to my boys that they had to wear their gear constantly, they grumbled and I could tell that they were going to gaff the order off, but when I told them that SSgt. D's career depended on it, even the belligerent ones like Miller agreed, since no one wanted a cool guy like SSgt. D to get screwed.

This area had two-hundred-foot-tall telephone towers, but curiously, no wires. I guess that was on their long-range plan. Since one of our own had been killed in this area, we distrusted the locals. A haji would be dubbed "suspicious" if he walked by more than once. Lt. Pettes walked by my hole, taking a few Marines to check out a nearby farmhouse. I volunteered to go along, hoping for a little action. We didn't get to shoot anyone, but I did get a good view of a typical Iraqi farm house. Made of mud brick, it had solid metal doors with locks and metal grilles on the windows. I thought it was funny to have such strong security on a mud house. If I wanted to break in, all I had to do was pour water on the wall and shove my hand through. The family had apparently abandoned the house when we approached. They had different-colored flags flying from the roof that we were told were flown to celebrate some arcane holiday season. Lt. Pettes grabbed a few of the flags as dubious war trophies, but I didn't want to touch the mangy things.

When I got back, Reed ambled up with a conciliatory smile and asked to talk to me. He beat around the bush for awhile before getting to his point; he was humiliated by being made an assistant ammo man and wanted to know what he had to do to get his job back. He told me that he realized he had an anger problem and wanted to get some treatment for it when we got back to Cali. I was taken aback for a second, but then regained my senses. He was only willing to act normal to get his job back. I made him no promises and told him that he'd have to act better for more than eight days; it would take months before we trusted him again. He nodded submissively and walked off.

As the sun set, we got into our stand-to positions. I had my PRR on and I eavesdropped while Third Platoon's corporals bull-shitted with each other. They were obviously close and it made me envious, since all my close friends were attached to other platoons.

An hour or so later, the sky to our south lit up with explosions. It was just over the horizon, but I could feel it in my chest. This was how I imagined war would be; this was the all-powerful armada that would rain down death and destruction at will. The waves of bombs and artillery were relentless and I started to feel sorry for whoever was over there—they had no chance.

Before I went to sleep, I made sure to warn my boys to keep an eye out, not trusting the locals. There was a trench that cut through our lines that the enemy could use to infiltrate our pos if the guy on the SAW to our right wasn't watching closely. I wrapped the sling of my rifle around my hand so I could have it at a moment's notice if needed.

The next morning, the temperature spiked early on and as I sat leaning against the berm, I started to despair. My MOPP suit had not been much of a detriment up until then, since the temperatures had remained cool, but in even moderate heat it would quickly degrade my fighting ability. I didn't understand how I was supposed to run and gun when I felt like passing out just sitting on the ground.

Jeffords had a theory that there was a big map of Iraq somewhere and a monkey with a crayon. Wherever the monkey drew on the map was the route we would take and when his crayon broke, we'd stop for the night. The next spot where the crayon broke put us in a huge wheat field. It was strangely beautiful to see the tracs only half-visible above the wheat, looking like they were sailing through the fields. The site was pretty, but totally indefensible; a whole battalion could sneak up on us through the lush wheat fields. I was quite glad when we set down on flat ground on the edge of the fields. Since we were surrounded by friendly units, we were put on "Weapons Hold" for the first time, meaning that we couldn't shoot our machineguns for fear of hitting friendly troops.

My squad was put on a small farm road and told to make any locals who approached go back from where they came. Hopefully, they wouldn't tell us the same. A small, white truck approached and slowed but didn't stop. We didn't have a roadblock, so they might have just thought it was a checkpoint.

"Shoot them!" Reed screeched.

I saw what I thought was a woman at the wheel, so I stepped between Reed and the car. It turned out not to be a woman, just a confused old man wearing a head-dress. We went through the typical pidgin-Iraqi/charades style of communication. His attitude was patient and submissive, as it was with all of the other Iraqis we met. Being told what to do was nothing new to them.

Every time a vehicle came up, a couple of us would jump up to search it like we were about to earn medals of honor, but it quickly got old. Every truck was almost identical, with the same shoddy interior, homemade seats and—strangely enough—a single CD hanging from a string attached to the rear view mirror, but no CD player. The insides were nasty and I washed with hand sanitizer as soon as I got done searching each vehicle.

The blown-up tank near our pos became quite the tourist attraction. The tank were small and old and looked like it had been taken out by one shot. I found some old rancid tins of bread in a storage box and snagged an Iraqi ammo box as a keepsake. After making sure that no one had pissed inside the tank—always a distinct possibility when Marines are around—I climbed inside to see what it was like. It felt like a tomb. I wondered about the men who died in them; we were told that many Iraqi soldiers' families were held hostage to force them to fight. I imagined them sitting in these ancient tanks, knowing that they would die. Is it still bravery if you are forced? No, I thought, bravery would have been for them to stand up to Saddam and his regime.

Some trackers were playing with a machinegun they had pried off the Iraqi tank. Though it was a foreign gun, pretty much every gun works the same, so I assumed they would be able to handle it safely. Wrong. A shot range out and ricocheted off a rock. The order went out—we weren't allowed to go near any Iraqi vehicles or weapons.

When I headed down the road to the Command Post, I saw something on the side of the road that looked like a turd. As I got closer, I realized it was a mint chocolate MRE brownie. I couldn't believe it; this was like manna from heaven. I wondered how it got there, imagining a fat tank crewman tossing it away when he got bored with it. I picked it up to eat it, but stopped myself when I realized that I was acting like a homeless person. I then realized that I *was* a homeless person and wolfed it down in three bites.

The BC walked down the lines, giving the usual officer pep-talk, which was always awkward at best. I noticed that he was freshly scrubbed, with combed and washed hair, while we all looked like mud worms. He assured us that as soon as we secured Baghdad, we would head back to Kuwait. Rager asked him how we would get back down there since we had been told that as soon as we got to Baghdad, the tracs would leave since they were all on their last legs. Tracs were made to be launched off of ships, motor ten miles to shore and take Marines a maximum of fifty miles inland. We had already put almost 1000 miles on them. With a straight face, the BC told Rager that we might shuttle the battalion back in rented SUVs with Humvee escorts. I wondered if the BC was cruel enough to walk down the line, clowning people and messing with their heads. We were all tired of "The Mushroom Treatment"—being fed shit and kept in the dark.

The next day, we were told that we could take our MOPP suits off. We had been wearing them for eighteen days. Several people had lost their desert cammies when their packs were ripped off of the tracs, so there was a lot of horse-trading to make sure they each got a pair. Sgt. Fun had spent the last two weeks with half of his ass and most of one thigh showing through an ever-growing rip in his MOPP suit. The good times just kept on coming. An hour later, we got more chow than we could fit in our packs. As I gorged myself on a prized and rare hamburger MRE, we were told that mail had just arrived. What next, hookers?

I went to the CP to pick up my squad's mail and I saw some new-joins wearing the digital cammies that the Marine Corps had recently adopted. I was surprised that they were able to get us new guys since we were so far forward. I wondered how those kids felt. This wasn't Vietnam, where a kid left SOI and went straight to the front. That system had been fraught with problems. No one wanted to spend the adequate time to train new kids since they didn't know them and had nothing invested in them. Many died because they did not know simple things that every grunt was supposed to know. Nowadays, Marines train, deploy and fight as a unit. Many of the people I fought next to I had known for three years.

I was happy when I was told that none of them were machinegunners. I had enough problems with Carpenter and Reed. We had received two "diggies", Cortez and Acosta, at the TAA and they had been nothing but trouble. While I had at first asked for one to be assigned to my squad, I quickly changed my mind when I realized that one more person in my squad meant one more person in my trac. Cortez already had a horrible rep. At the GOSP, he had a negligent discharge that he lied about, even with the smoke coming from his rifle and a shell on the ground next to him. The night before, when he was woken for gun watch, he decided that he didn't want to do it, so he woke up Showers and told him it was his turn. Later on, he would claim that because of those two incidents, he had been pulled into a trac and beaten up. I didn't know if that was true, but if it was, I was glad.

While driving on steep berms over irrigated fields, the snipers' command humvee overturned and fell into a ditch. Those inside were unhurt and a squad from Third Platoon was sent to guard the vehicle while they sent for a wrecker. When the humvee was winched out of the muck though, the snipers discovered that they were missing a box of chows; Slater's tape worm had taken command of his body and he had snatched the chows in a moment of weakness. Slater returned them shame-faced, but we all knew how he felt. Several times, I had eyed an MRE peeking out of someone's gear and had considered stealing it, but I would have felt too guilty afterwards.

Military vehicles were parked on both sides of the road and there was a traffic jam up ahead. 150,000 coalition troops were trying to get to Baghdad and there were only two routes to take. We finally found an empty stretch on the right shoulder and our convoy pulled over. The Goose used his charm and got another unit to let us use their water bull, as long as we limited ourselves to one canteen per man.

Slater sidled up and asked me if I had any extra food. I told him I didn't, but I would share what I had left. He thanked me profusely, telling me that since he was in another trac than the rest of Third Platoon, Schofield and Williams often forgot to give him his chow. I went over to talk to Ross a few minutes later and he mentioned that he had given Slater food that night as well, though Slater hadn't mentioned that to me. I would have been bothered if it wasn't for the fact that I gave Slater the food that I deemed too nasty to eat.

There were so many units around us that we didn't even have to pull security; we just flopped down in the dirt and went to sleep. An hour or so later, a huge boom and a concussive wave of force woke me up. I looked straight up and saw almost a dozen glowing projectiles in the sky, all pointing right at our pos. My mind scrambled to make sense of what was happening; I figured that an incoming enemy artillery barrage had just missed us and that this was the corrected second wave. As when I was drowning in the helo dunker at Miramar, I was not afraid. I calmly realized that if that many arty shells were heading for us, we had no hope at all. I couldn't possibly get away in time and all I would do was look like a bitch. This all ran through my mind in less than three seconds. I looked up as the streaks got fainter and smaller and realized that they were heading away from us. I then remembered that there was an artillery battery on the other side of the road. My heart started beating again and I laid back down in my bag, immediately slipping into a deep and peaceful sleep.

We pulled off in a demolished neighborhood along side several other Marine units. I accidentally saw Letta taking a shit behind a low, crumbling wall, which I really could have done without. I looked away and saw a Marine riding a grey donkey like he was in a rodeo. We all got a good laugh until he got yelled at; I didn't know we had a rule against riding donkeys.

While loading up on our trac, I saw Sgt. Williams' high-speed, store-bought patrol pack on top, which was strange because he usually rode in Trac 15, the mortar trac. He was the Platoon Guide, an ephemeral job that reeks of boot camp and parade decks. In war, a guide has no real job. At the TAA, he never pulled SOG or any other duties, as far as I could see, spending all of his time sleeping or playing cards. It was a shame that he wasn't more involved, because he was an experienced sergeant and former sniper. Stop-Loss was keeping him with us until the combat phase was over, and he seemed to decide that he didn't have to contribute.

When Williams climbed aboard, I realized that Rohr had been successful in his plan to unseat Sgt. Schofield as squad leader. I looked over at Trac 15 and saw Schofield looking dejected. I didn't like Schofield—he did many stupid and/or annoying things—but his main problem was that he tried too hard. Williams was too cool to try at all. The switch highlighted my biggest problem with Third Platoon—the junior high school cattiness that prevailed. At least when Kennel had a problem with me, he had said it to my face; the other Cool Kids just sniped behind your back and complained about you to SSgt. D.

The closer we got to Baghdad, the more lush the land got. I was agog when I saw a house that had real glass in the windows and an actual air conditioner. People thronged the streets. Happy kids rushed forward, asking for candy. Their parents hung back, more restrained, but still smiling and waving. The kids were impressed with the Marines' tattoos, since they are forbidden by most sects of Islam. We tossed them candy and they sold us cigarettes. There wasn't one ounce of bad will on either side.

We came into the center of one of the suburbs. On one stretch of road, every car was a blackened hulk. I kept my eye out for snipers; in an urban environment, slow-moving vehicles are sitting ducks. A bus full of cute teenaged girls drove by, waving and smiling unabashedly. Someone said they were a bus full of hookers, but I thought that was a stretch. We were all enjoying the hell out of it, feeling like home-coming heroes. Rager pointed one old lady out.

"That old lady had one eye, sergeant!"

"She didn't have one eye, Rager, she was just winking at you."

The victory parade continued for hours. We came to a farm lane next to a levy on the outskirts of town. Some shots rang out in the distance, reminding us that we were still in a war, not the Rose Bowl Parade. After sitting on the road for an hour or so, we pulled into a farm field. As usual, we went back and forth until we got in the "right position", which inevitably looked like every other position. I saw the farmer watch us tear up his precious crops and I wanted to apologize personally. There were thousands of empty acres in this country; I didn't see why we needed to ruin his livelihood.

We settled in a fallow field with dirt as hard as rock. I was enthused from the positive reaction from the locals and I had a surplus of energy, so I told Rager I'd dig his hole for him. He squinted at me, suspecting a trap. I hacked at the ground for thirty minutes, made little progress, yet felt quite proud of myself.

After sunset, Rohr came by.

"We're sending a patrol about a klick out. You want to bring any of the guns?"

"Hell, no," I responded. Elevens had a philosophy: when in doubt, patrol. Machinegunners were all about chilling out. I didn't feel like going on a useless patrol just because they couldn't think of anything better to do. Rohr seemed to see the disregard in my eyes and he explained further.

"This is a no-shit mission. Supposedly there's a dozen armed men in those trees over there. We're going to patrol over and take them out."

"Holy fuck, are you shitting me? If that's the deal, then I definitely want in. What else do you know about it? I'm going to start getting my boys ready."

"That's all I know, I'm going to go see if Lt. Pettes has any more word."

One thought quickly dawned on me—I couldn't see through my NVGs when they were on my helmet mount. I usually held them with my one hand, which was fine when I was on a trac, but wouldn't work when I needed both hands free on a patrol. I kicked myself for not having fixed them in the past. This made things more dicey. I decided to shore up my confidence by getting more info from Lt. Pettes who, it turned out, knew less than Rohr did. The more I asked, the more it became clear that the patrol probably wasn't going to happen. We were told to get on the tracs and I thought we were about to rock and roll, but instead we were told we were leaving the area. What the hell? Talk about a cock tease. If there was really some enemy out there (which I strongly doubted) it would make us look weak to bug out.

I took my usual spot on top, racking a round into the chamber out of frustration. I wasn't going to sleep—fuck it—it wasn't even worth it. I was going to stay up until I got some goddamn action. That night went on forever. After about four hours, we ended up on the edges of a suburb; I saw the soft glow of television screens shining on the walls inside the houses. Men stood alone on their decks to smoke. It could have been a small town in America. We got onto a highway and came into a more built-up area. I had been awake for almost two days, but I refused to give up my spot on air watch, fearing that I would miss some action. It was just as well, since there weren't many volunteers to take my place. Rager was using my rifle and I was using his gun. In retrospect, it was pretty fucked up that I was such a gun hog, but I justified it to myself by saying that I was giving Rager time to rest.

By 4:30AM, I was nearly delirious. I looked through my NVGs at the other tracs and saw that everyone on top was asleep. We hadn't taken any fire in almost two weeks and I was about to pass out. I climbed on top of the trac, laid across the buttstock of the gun so that it wouldn't fall off the side and closed my eyes.

I woke up every fifteen minutes or so, but the small cat-naps helped a lot. Rager finally conked out as well, leaving Jeffords as the lone man awake. About 5:30AM, Jeffords gave me a subtle hint.

"Hey Meyer, maybe you want to be awake now?"

That idea was so crazy, that it just might work. I got back behind the gun, waking Rager, who looked like I felt—like shit. I had gotten to know Rager a lot better in the last few weeks. He had the patience of a saint when it came to dealing with Reed, who was now his subordinate. When I backed him over Reed at the Han Tush air field, I seemed to gain some respect from him. He was always the cornerstone of the squad—solid and dependable. It was a good thing that Jeffords woke us, because about two minutes later, tracer fire skipped through the sky.

"Hey Jeffords, did you see that too?"

"Yep."

"Are we being shot at?"

"Ummmm…."

Every time we got shot at, it went the same way. It never started abruptly; the enemy would always have to build their courage up. There would be one lone shot, followed by two or three rounds a couple seconds later, followed by a short burst, followed by the actual ambush.

A long burst arced through the night air.

"Yeah, we're being shot at."

The shots were coming parallel to our direction from the other side of the road. From the slow rate of fire, I could tell they weren't AK-47s; they were their big guns, the 15.5mms. Rounds that big would rip your flesh off with a near-miss. They seemed to be getting smarter, ambushing the rear of the convoy this time. I spoke to others in the front of the convoy later and they didn't even know their was an ambush that morning.

I scanned the left, but couldn't find any targets. The others were engaging targets on the right side. I wanted to switch around, but I couldn't leave our left side unguarded. I had done so on our first ambush and it was just selfish glory-hogging. When I saw a large painting of Saddam, I shot at it out of frustration.

When we came out the other side of the ambush, I turned to see Rager gripping my rifle, white-knuckled.

"How'd you do, Rager?"

"I got this one old boy right square in the chest, sergeant."

"That's fucking awesome, Rager. Feels pretty good, huh?"

"Yep…Can't stop my hands from shaking though."

He told me that the main ambush was on the right side, with shooters suicidally firing from twenty feet away. When he spotted a shooter, he fired, but missed by a wide margin. He walked his shots closer to the man and hit him with his fifth shot, watching through his NVGs as the glowing tracer sizzled into the guy's chest. He crumpled to the ground and was lost in the darkness.

Throughout the war, we had problems with idiots claiming impossible shots or ridiculous body counts. People even used the term "confirmed kill", which hadn't been used since Vietnam. "Confirmed kill" means that they sent you after a specific enemy and after you killed him, someone went out to the body and confirmed that you shot the right man, but people used it pejoratively as a way of saying that they definitely killed someone. There really was no way of knowing if that was true; our rifle rounds were weak and it sometimes took five rounds in the chest to put a guy down. Also, people aren't like in the movies, where they squirt blood like they're jelly donuts when they get shot. They might have just jerked suddenly and hit the ground because—hey!—someone is shooting at them. Rager's story was believable because of his maturity. I was surprised when he said he couldn't keep his hands from shaking afterwards. I thought it was some kind of sensitivity, but I later realized it was the after-effects of an adrenaline rush. I was on my own rush, being that I now had my second firefight under my belt. Most of the company still hadn't fired a shot in anger.

As the sun rose, we came to the suburbs of Baghdad. The snipers spotted Iraqis with AKs and called it up to higher. While before we could shoot anyone with a weapon, they now had to be directly shooting at us before we could engage. Most of the guys with AKs were either cops or people protecting their stores or homes from looters.

Thick black smoke billowed from burning Iraqi tanks. As much as seeing *our* tanks burning made me despair, seeing theirs burning made me ecstatic. Shells inside the tanks started to cook off and we were given the order to scoot down inside the trac. As we crept by, I peeked at the tank, not wanting to miss it.

We got reports of sniper fire and Sene scanned the area with his scope. The huge water tower ahead was a likely perch, but we couldn't spot any shooters. Suburbs were on either side of the road, as well as factories and empty army barracks. The convoy stopped and we saw Army humvees on the side of the road. They had gotten ambushed up ahead earlier and were waiting for our tanks to go up and clear the area. We followed our tanks up to where the highway hit its apex and a high berm went off to the right. When they couldn't spot anyone, the convoy started to turn around.

Shots rang out and, for the second time in four hours, we were being ambushed. As usual, it was almost impossible to see where the shots were coming from. Some civilians stood around, looking worried and lost. I searched for shooters, but didn't see any. There was a copse of trees on the left and I aimed in on it, but I was told by several people not to fire.

There was a strange old motorcycle with a sidecar parked in the intersection between the highway and the berm. One of the tanks shot the motorcycle and it burst into flame. What happened next is still a mystery. Something shot from the direction of the burning bike toward our trac. Reed yelled "RPG!" like we were in "Black Hawk Down." I was surprised to hear his voice, since I never let him on air watch. He must have snuck up.

The rocket appeared to be coming straight at me. "Oh well, I guess this is it," I thought. The idea that there were many places in the sky it could go and not hit me reassured me again. Another idea that popped into my head was that any normal person would duck in a situation like this, but my pride wouldn't let me. All these thoughts flashed through my head in less than two seconds.

The rocket flew over the front of our trac, hit the ground about sixty feet back, tumbled end-over-end and exploded right next to my buddy Ross' trac at the far end of the column. We still debate to this day what was actually shot at us. The sidecar on the bike seemed to have a recoilless rifle or a small rocket launcher; I thought that it had fired off when the bike burst into flames. Others maintain that an RPG had been fired from behind the bike and it just appeared to come from the bike. Either way, it was cool and exciting.

A mortar exploded six feet away from our trac and we were told to close the air watch hatches. I felt like a sitting duck in that darkened trac. I started hearing a pinging sound and wondered what it was. The trac made all sorts of sounds, but I had never heard a "ping" before. I was probably the last person in the trac to realize that the "pings" were AK rounds bouncing off the hull.

After ten minutes of sitting there like jerks, we were allowed to open the hatches. The convoy headed onto the berm to our right and we started receiving shots again. I gripped the gun tightly—this was a 360-degree shooting gallery. To our right was a walled suburb with a million places to shoot from. I scanned it, feeling like an RPG would hit us at any moment.

Enemy fire came from a nice-looking two-story farm house about 500 meters to our left. Everyone started shooting back, but my line of sight was blocked by an aluminum telephone pole. Perfect—a great firefight and I couldn't see half of the target. Fuck it, I thought, my 7.62 rounds would punch right through that pole. I started to rock-and-roll with the 240; when the 240 gets going, it's a truly awesome weapon. For some damn reason, Third Platoon had an unnatural fear of machineguns. From inside the trac, Gollum started squealing that one of my rounds was going to "bounce back and hit us!" I was shooting at a thin aluminum pole, not Superman's chest. At worst, the pole would deflect the rounds a degree or two to the right or left.

Sgt. Fun was shooting at the house, even though it was well within the trac turret's blind spot. The turret is only supposed to shoot at targets that are more than 800 meters away, because when it does, its guns will be safely elevated above the driver's and commander's hatches to its left. That was the reason to have the 240 cover its blind spot. It was always explained to us that the turret couldn't fire in its blind spot; that there was some mechanism to keep the guns from shooting if they were depressed below a certain point. That was not the case. I heard a sharp, horrific sound and looked over to see the turret's .50 cal. barrel an inch away from the driver's closed hatch, with an inch-wide hole drilled right through the thick armor. The inside of the trac instantly filled with smoke. I looked at Sene, whose face was ashen; there was no movement in the trac.

"He's got to be dead."

Sene nodded dully. After several tense seconds, we were told that the driver was alright. Luckily, the driver's M-16 had slipped from the bracket next to his chair and he had bent over to pick it up off the floor just before the turret fired through his hatch at point-blank range. I wouldn't have traded places with Sgt. Fun for all the money in the world at that point; the guilt must have been unbearable. The next time we stopped, the driver permanently switched tracs.

I spotted a guy walking casually away from the house and aimed in on him, but I knew I would get burned if I shot him. No innocent person walks calmly in the middle of a huge battle; he was obviously one of the shooters or an accomplice leaving the scene, but I had no proof. I regret not shooting him to this day.

When we left, I was quite full of myself. I was up to three firefights; that had to be the most of anyone in the whole company. The only thing that bothered me was that I didn't have any definite kills, just a hell of a lot of rounds shot off.

After every firefight, I collected up two of my spent shells. I kept them in my shirt pocket as a sign of my own growing personal mythology.

The convoy continued down the berm, turned right and drove through the neighborhood. We went through without incident and came out on the other side. When we came to a thick jungle on the edge of the neighborhood, we dismounted. I was hoping to stay on the trac on air watch, since it was getting hot, but no such luck. The jungle was so thick that when I got out of the trac, I wasn't walking on the ground, just a net of compressed bamboo and plants, pushed to the side by the trac. I threw my ammo belts on Pancho Villa-style, getting ready for action. I worshiped the movie "Platoon" and was shocked at how much this jungle looked like Vietnam. No one back home would believe me when I said that I patrolled through the jungle in Iraq.

Miller caught up with me, looking pissed, and told me he wanted to charge Ryan. I really didn't want to hear it; I had more problems from Miller than from Ryan. I told Miller to talk to me about it later. I was sure that it was just some minor tiff and that time would make it go away.

A flurry of shots rang out in the distance near 1st Platoon's position. The officers called a halt while they got info over the radio. I didn't know why we were being so skittish. Logic seemed to dictate that 1st Platoon could probably use some help; but what did I know? I didn't go to OCS.

We came out of the thick foliage onto a black tar road and followed it to the left. A couple meters down the road, I saw a pile of brass and links from a 240. My heart skipped and I got a sick feeling. We had gotten strange intel about this area. We were told that, hidden in this small jungle, there were a group of buildings in which Iraqi officers, dressed as civilians, were operating. We were "Weapons Free"—all targets were righteous.

A hundred meters down the road, a light blue compact car was riddled with bullet holes; I could see the grim expressions on those walking by it. When I came upon it, I saw a haunting and tragic tableau—a man in his forties and a woman in her late thirties, both dead, washing the road with their blood. The woman caught my eye; she was a little chubby, but still a natural Middle Eastern beauty, her hair died auburn and worn free. As with Salinas, there was something about the newly dead that made them much more disturbing. They still had the bloom of life on their cheeks; their clothes still looked clean and normal.

Out of respect for the dead, I made the sign of the cross as I passed them. Fifty feet ahead, Doc Cox was tending a wounded man. If that man could be saved—no matter by how small a margin—Cox would save him.

A small group of villagers watched us calmly from the other side of the street. My first reaction was to look away, but I felt that would be cowardly. I met their gazes and was shocked that there was no hatred or anger, just quiet acceptance. Our uniforms and vehicles were new to them, but the situation was not.

We came out of the jungle onto a winding lane bordering a beautiful blue river. Across the river was a lush, green park that could have been from any American city. A half mile away was a large tower, like the kind you'd see at a amusement park. The frisson of the tragic death behind us and the light-hearted fun ahead was stark.

I soon found myself supremely exhausted. I was traveling "light"—helmet, gas mask, flak and weapon—yet I felt like I had a full pack and machinegun on my back. Falling out with a lot of gear on was one thing, but falling out like this was unforgivable. I salvaged some pride by reminding myself that I had barely eaten for two days, but that was the same for everyone.

We got to a spot near the bridge to the amusement park and set down. Locals were trying to pass us to get to their homes, but we were told to make them stop. One family kept insisting that they had to go through because their baby was sick. That got everyone's attention and we sent some corpsmen over to find out what was wrong. It turned out that the baby just had a cold and they were using that as an excuse to skip ahead of everyone. Doc gave them some medicine and we told them they had to wait.

When we moved forward into the shade of the high wall around the park, I regained my strength. I saw some guys coming out of the park with a cart filled with sodas. I rushed forward and asked them how much; they gave me a blank face, waiting to see how much I had. I pulled out 12 bucks and, after a little hag-gling, I got five bottles of cold RC Cola. The XO caught me with the sodas and looked like he was about to admonish me, but something distracted him. I was almost home-free when Sprinkles saw me wearing my ammo belts Pancho Villa-style and he told me to take them off. As much as I grew to hate Sprincin, in retrospect, he was right. Wearing the belts across our chests made the links kink up and jam when you fired the gun. It was a small matter to clear the jam, but it was still a waste of time.

I realized that I had no way to open the sodas. Luckily, Levesque told me I could pry the top off with a bullet. It worked and I let him take a swig. Magana, from First Platoon, walked by and I interrogated him about the shooting. He shrugged, gave me a "couldn't be helped" look and walked off.

We were told to set our guns about six feet from the fence that edged a bluff overlooking the river. With the guns set back, anyone could have snuck up and lobbed grenades in on us. The higher-ups were getting tired and it was showing.

A building near 1st Platoon was loaded with candy, but the staff NCOs were keeping people out of it. We were given surprisingly free reign to roam the park and I took off in search of food. There was a restaurant on an island in an moat with a wide walkway leading to it. I walked inside and it looked like the set of a Doris Day movie. We didn't find any food in the kitchen, but there were crates of Pepsi. I grabbed twelve bottles and then tried to figure out how I would smuggle them back to my hole. My pockets quickly filled and I was forced to pull drastic measures. I sucked in my stomach and shoved four in my waistband, but still had four more. The only place left was my pant legs. I stuck them down the back of my leg and hoped that the elastic boot bands would keep them from falling out the bottom.

As I walked out, I ran into Rodgar and gave him a conspiratorial smile. I nodded him in the right direction and went on my merry way. I got to the end of the walkway and ran into Gunny Brouillet, who engaged me in some small talk. I looked guilty as hell; he must have known. I clinked when I walked, for Christ's sake. He let me go and I dropped all pretense, holding my pant legs as I walked.

I dumped my booty next to Rager's gun and his eyes lit up. I told him we'd share within his team, but everyone else was on their own. Since my pack was full of ammo, I borrowed his and headed back. The restaurant was a lot more crowded, but I was still able to fill my pack with Pepsis. I looked around the restaurant for some souvenirs. There were lots of glasses and plates, but they'd just end up breaking. I grabbed a fork and knife for practical reasons and a monogrammed napkin as a keepsake. I found a calculator behind the bar and justified taking it by telling myself that I'd use it to calculate defilade tables. There was a phone on the wall that Rodgar tried to get work, to no avail.

I ran into my buddy Miller from Third and we went up-stairs. The circular restaurant had floor-to-ceiling windows that looked down on the lagoon. Miller peeked down through a busted-out window and I could almost hear the thoughts bubbling up in his mind.

"Hey Meyer, do you dare me to fire a 203 round into the lagoon?"

"What are you—five? If you're going to do it, then do it."

"OK."

He pulled the trigger and I heard the distinct "bloop" of the grenade launcher. A geyser of water shot up, accompanied by an exaggerated "Boom!" Like a little kid, I high-tailed it out of there. Running down the stairs, I looked over my shoulder and saw Miller coming after me, confused at my hasty departure.

"Meyer, where you going? Wait up!"

I ran to the end of the concrete walkway before I turned around. I thought the grenade would detonate underwater with a muffled "whoomp", but it seemed to have exploded on contact with the water. Jokes were fine, but I was a sergeant and I couldn't be caught in the vicinity of such shenanigans. It was funny though.

As I got back to the tracs, I heard people muttering about a mortar landing by the CO's trac. Had Miller's 203 skipped over there somehow? No, that was impossible; he aimed straight down at the water; our tracs were two hundred meters away. I told myself that I had to be careful about who I told to "do it" in the future.

By the time I got back to my hole, word had gotten around that the staff NCOs weren't watching the door to the building with candy anymore. I tried to look casual as I stepped through a hole in a fence to get to the building. Showers had been told to guard the door, but so many people asked him to let them through that he finally gave in. I went inside and found a scene that was halfway between "Willy Wonka" and the LA Riots. The first room was already emptied but they other two were full of candy.

I ran into Chiariello for the first time since we crossed the LOD. I didn't know him well at the time, but I had heard he had some serious gun time already. He was a trigger-puller like me and we exchanged stories about our firefights. He seemed to be the only one who had more gun time than me.

Chiariello pointed me in the direction of the rest of the loot. The candy was all Iraqi-made, but several were recognizable rip-offs of American candy. I stuffed my pack like a criminal; then realized that there was no hurry. I started opening and tasting each brand, deciding how much to pick of each.

Lt. Pettes walked in and casually asked us which was the best candy. Cool, he was on our side. It wasn't like we were stealing gold from the Iraqi treasury; we hadn't eaten in days. First Sergeant Young walked in and started to admonish Lt. Pettes about allowing us to take the candy. Lt. Pettes strained for an explanation; then dropped all pretense and said that since we didn't have any food, we were simply re-supplying ourselves. I scooched by them with my full patrol pack before the First Sergeant turned his attentions toward me.

Rager's team was ecstatic when they saw my haul and I immediately sent them on "re-supply missions." By the time they got to the stash, it was almost entirely divested. We were still able to fill two sandbags full of soda and candy.

For hours, we gorged ourselves. I felt a rumble down below and I got up in a hurry. I ran like a crazy person around the camp, but every open spot was already occupied by Marines. I could tell I only had seconds left when I finally found an empty patch of dirt. I pulled my pants down and pissed out of my ass. After losing pretty much everything I ate over the last several hours, I pulled my pants up and saw that I was ten feet away from the engineers' sleeping area. Whoops.

As the sun set, I thought about how surreal the day had been—two firefights, tragic death, a sea of candy and then dumping my guts all over the nicest part of Iraq. It was the strangest day of my entire life.

The next morning, the CO had the remainder of the candy rounded up and distributed equally to each platoon. Rager's team and I now had three sand bags full of candy and soda. The higher-ups told us that we weren't looting, since we were leaving a receipt of what we took so that the owners could be reimbursed. *Right.*

Out of boredom, I explored the park. The tower seemed cool, but I avoided it since I was told that the Marines who went up the ten stories of stairs were celebrating by pissing over the edge. One brave soul even leaned out and took a shit. His ass got a better view of Baghdad than most of our spy planes.

I joined up with Miller from Third and we went to explore some offices. On the way there, we ran into some locals who were calmly looting the restaurant for furniture. We all nodded and waved to each other, enjoying the fine day. In several of the offices, there were strange, idealized paintings of western-looking children with blonde hair and blue eyes. I had seen the same thing in Japan. We weren't just "The Great Satan" to them, it appeared.

I re-supplied myself with some pens and notepads. Miller found a nice notebook with a map of the world—with Iraq in the center, natch—and a heavily air-brushed portrait of Saddam. I took some rolls of film, hoping there would be something cool on them. I found some brochures for the park that looked like they were made in the early eighties when the park was new. I laughed at first, but after thinking about it I got depressed. While this would be the lamest amusement park in America (the "attractions" were a bowling alley, a lake to row in and sodas) it was amazing to these people. I imagined that the privileged few who could afford to go there were probably Ba'ath party officials and high-ranking army officers. I imagined an Iraqi colonel giving the go-ahead to launch chemical weapons against the Kurds and then taking his daughter out for cotton candy the next day.

Later that day, we went on a vehicle patrol. Gunny Brouillet was standing in the air watch panel of another trac next to a pot-bellied sheik. It angered me to see an Iraqi in one of our vehicles, not realizing that was the height of irony, considering that we were in their country. Later, Gunny Brouillet told us that the sheik was a major player and he was pointing out Ba'ath party members in the crowd.

We spent an hour trying to negotiate our tracs down a berm on one side of a canal before they realized we were on the wrong side. We had to back the entire convoy up and turn it around on a crowded street, making us look like idiots in front of the Iraqis. We got to the opposite side of the canal and the foliage was so thick that several packs got ripped off the trac, including mine. Luckily, Reed jumped out and grabbed my pack. We stopped a hundred meters from a neighborhood that our snipers had been pulling missions in. The Sniper Platoon Sergeant had shot half-a-dozen Iraqis that night. BB informed us that Sene had bagged one at over 500 meters. True to Sene's mature nature, he hadn't bragged about it.

I first met Sene when I returned to SOI from emergency leave. He didn't pull any of the usual high school crap; he introduced himself and showed me around. Sene was a big guy with a deep scar on the side of his head with huge stitch marks that gave him a Frankenstein vibe. His arms were covered in tattoos, some of which he had done himself. We were both artists; at the TAA, he'd show me his sketchbook and borrow comics. He was one of the ringleaders of "Shotgun Willie's"—the gambling ring in our tent at the TAA—yet he didn't grate on me like Monty did. Sene was a member of the "Cool Kids Club"—as I had dubbed them—but he was different in that he was the only one I got along with. We spent hundred of hours next to each other air watch, sucking in the exhaust from the pipe two feet away. I was glad that I had already fathered a child because I was in serious doubt that I would be able to after breathing in that much exhaust

His assistant was a straight-laced eagle-scout type kid nicknamed "BB." There was nothing wrong with BB—obviously so since he made it into the Sniper Platoon so soon after joining the Corps—but he was still a PFC. Though he was a sniper, he hadn't gone to Sniper School yet. It bothered me that he got treated like a senior Marine, palling around with sergeants like it was cool.

Though there were usually five people on air watch, I was consistently the only one who faced left—the way we were supposed to. It was more comfortable to put your feet on the right wall and lean against the middle, facing right. Those that faced to the left had to stand on their tippy-toes on an MRE box and lean against the exposed bolts on top of the trac. Every time I turned to the right to stretch my back or get some relief, the "cool kids" would start muttering about me. Sgt. Williams asked me to watch the left more closely. Technically, he was right to do so, but the fact that he didn't do the same, or tell his buddies to do so, grated on me.

When we got back to the park, I sat down in my hole and ate the Iraqi candy slowly, hoping to give my system time to accept it. When I heard a whistling sound, I yelled "Incoming!" and jumped into my fighting hole. When there was no explosion, I sheepishly peeked over the edge while White sarcastically chided me for confusing the whine of a trac engine with the sound of an incoming mortar.

After two days at "Disneyland", it was time to hit the main prize—Baghdad. SSgt. D told us about the Army's "Thunder Run," in which a convoy of Army tanks had rolled into downtown Baghdad with impunity. We all agreed that this meant that there was no support for Saddam's regime and that the war was over. A year later, I would read more about the Thunder Run and discovered that—though it was successful—the Iraqis had hotly contested the incursion.

It only took us an hour to get into Baghdad at our typical speed of 15 miles per hour. The streets were filled with happy, waving people. I was waving so much that I had to switch arms when they got too tired. We got to the inner part of the city and came upon a mosque that was as big as an American shopping mall—ornate, gilded and absolutely beautiful. We had strict orders not to engage anyone who shot at us from mosques. The mosques had been there for hundreds of years; if we shot at them, our bullet marks would remain forever, constantly stirring up hatred of Americans.

We rolled into a residential area and promptly got lost. As it got dark, I scanned the rooftops much more closely. My heart jumped when I thought I saw a sniper, but it was just some detritus on a roof. Although the crowds were overwhelmingly friendly, it was impossible that everyone was welcoming us with open arms. The invasion had emasculated every man in the country. For the oppressed, it showed how small of a force was needed to de-throne Saddam. For the former rulers, it showed how brittle their grasp of the country really had been. If I was an Iraqi, I would hate any invaders, even if I simultaneously hated Saddam. Our opinions of the Iraqi people were benevolent, but condescending. We didn't hate them, but we damn sure didn't respect them.

We pulled into a small college on the east side of town. We were told that we couldn't dismount because the ground was laced with mines, which was silly because we could see people walking around in the supposed mine field. After the higher-ups figured out that it was safe, I went to look around the college. Right there on the grounds was a twenty foot-long missile on its launcher, partially camouflaged. Iraqi kids kept popping their heads over the compound wall to sell us cigarettes.

At dawn, we went on a foot patrol through downtown Baghdad to show the flag—no enemy contact was expected. Garbage was piled everywhere and the cloying, sickening smell of eggs and cooking oil hung in the air. Arabs usually rise early to take advantage of the cool morning air, but the only people we saw were store owners who were guarding their stores against looters.

We wound our way through a marketplace and a neighborhood of well-kept town homes before coming came to a large concrete soccer stadium. As we entered it, we heard several shots and ducked for cover. Kennel shook his head and told us that the shots were obviously too far away. There were dozens of abandoned army uniforms, boots and berets, but no weapons. I wondered what their commanders thought when their troops reported in to fight to the death, yet everyone brought a spare set of civvies. I wanted to grab some uniforms as souvenirs, but they looked rancid. I didn't even like stepping on them.

We set up our guns on the top seats, looking down over the edge. The city was cool and quiet, except for sporadic shots which rang out in the distance. It was all very nice, except for my growling stomach. Across the street, a family peeked out of their front door. After awhile, two men in civvies pulled up in an Iraqi army vehicle. They went into the house, got some thin, watery white paint and started slapping it on the vehicle. It took me awhile to figure out what they were doing. I finally realized that they had stolen a vehicle from the obviously crumbling regime and were trying to disguise it as their own.

After an hour, we patrolled a few miles to the river. On our way out of the stadium, Williams found a bunch of Iraqi flags. I grabbed one and added it to my war trophy stash, which also included some AK mags and an ammo pouch. We hit the street and started bounding from block to block, as if we were taking heavy fire. I had to piss urgently, but by that time we were in a nice residential area, so I had no choice but to piss on someone's wall like a dirty dog. We hit a major thoroughfare and headed right, toward the river. As I came around a corner, I instinctively pointed my rifle down a side street and some Iraqis who happened to come into my view instantly put their hands in the air. It was funny at first and then sad—did they think I'd shoot them for no reason?

We got into another commercial area and, to our surprise, we saw several black Iraqis.

"This must be the Compton section of Baghdad," SSgt. Melendez quipped.

The locals in the next neighborhood were more talkative and inquisitive, several going out of their way to show off their English skills. They asked the

Marines ahead of me where they were from, but the Iraqis had never heard of places like Oklahoma or Michigan. When I told them I was from Texas, they all let out a whoop and started chattering excitedly. Feeling I had the crowd in my hand, I cheesed things up by adding loudly, "Where the cowboys are!" This delighted them and they all started clapping. I left on a high note.

Unfortunately, someone upstaged me. Ahead of me, a large crowd was proudly following an Indian kid named Singh who they confused for an Arab. I thought Singh was a scammer who used his small stature to get away with things. In the trac, he had the worst habit of falling asleep and leaning against my legs, slobbering all over them. Carpenter had the same problem and I had no problem with kneeing him in the skull to made him back up, but Singh just wouldn't take a hint. I had to keep nudging him and nudging him until I lost it and shoved him back with my leg. Even after that, five minutes later he would be making sweet love to my pant leg all over again.

We finally got to the river, where we sat under the bridge and waited for something to happen. In the base of the bridge, there was a small alcove where I found a dozen three-feet-long artillery shells. I pulled one out and stood it on end for Lt. Pettes to see. He nodded and went to call it in, knocking the huge explosive over as he turned away. As it fell to the ground, my heart stopped, certain I was about to be blown up. The shell hit the ground with a terrible sound, but didn't explode. Lt. Pettes just said "whoops" and went back to talking on the radio.

A large man who I took for the neighborhood bully came up and started chatting with us. Though he was friendly, he was not very forthcoming. He was more than happy to give us directions and any kind of public knowledge, but he refused to direct us to hidden Ba'ath officials or Saddam loyalists, saying to do so "would be like a betrayal." Although it bothered me, I had to respect the guy. At least he wasn't rolling over and offering up his ass like everyone else in the country.

One of his buddies excitedly motioned for me to follow him down the bank.

He was a little weird, so I was wary, but I had a gun, so I relaxed. He took me twenty feet away down the bank to a little strip of grass over-looking the river.

"OK, well, there's green grass—that's surprising. Is this what you wanted to show me?"

He started to pantomime wildly, like he was playing a musical instrument, pretending he was having a good old time, laughing and carousing with some buddies.

"Did you take me down here just to show me where you used to party?"

"Party! Yes! Party! Party!"

"Well, good for you, pal. I'm glad you have some grass to party on."

The platoon split up; one squad would go to secure a local hospital from loot-ers and the other would go and guard a weapons cache that had just been discov-ered. I went with Rager's team to keep an eye on Reed. I noticed something strange about Carpenter; for the first time ever, he seemed to be lagging on a patrol. Carpenter had a lot of faults, but being weak wasn't one. His Camelbak back pack looked like it had a bowling ball in it.

"Carpy, what the hell do you have in there?" Rager asked.

"Well, I have my pictures."

"I've got pictures too, Carpenter. They don't weigh shit."

"Well, I have my writing gear and pens."

"Everyone's got that stuff too. What else do you got?"

"Well, I have my bibles."

"Damn, Carpenter, I've got a bible too."

"Well, I have *five* bibles."

Rager was speechless and Carpenter's "five bibles" line became a part of Golf Company humor. Several times since we left America, different chaplains had offered us bibles. Carpenter had taken one each time until he maxed out with five, but that wasn't what was really holding him back. Rager went through Car-penter's small pack and found it stuffed with thirty pounds of arcade tokens that Carpenter seemed to think were valuable. I think he saw the movie "Three Kings" too many times. The tokens weren't even cool-looking, they just had the word "Sinbad" written in plain English on one side. We all got a good laugh off of that and continued to tease him about it for months.

We came to a two-story elementary school which was walled off, like most of the buildings and houses were. In the courtyard of the school, the Iraqi army had cached a half-dozen light artillery pieces and hundreds of huge shells, like the ones I had found under the bridge. The stories about Iraqis hiding weapons in schools and hospitals turned out to be true. The courtyard had a perfect line of sight to the bridge and the guns could have decimated any convoy crossing it. If we would have bombed the place, they would have cleared out the weapons and gotten the ruined school on Al-Jazeera.

The rooms were stark and sad, decorated solely by the omni-present portraits of Saddam. I had jokingly said to a buddy a a few days earlier, "You know, now that I see Saddam's pictures so much, I'm starting to like him. He seems like a nice guy." Saddam knew the power of propaganda and he was quite a fashion plate. There were pictures of him in a suit, others had him in his famous beret and a few even had him in a traditional headdress and robe. He was almost always smiling paternally and, though a little jowly, he always looked good. There were pictures of him shooting a rifle with one hand, to show potence and vigor, but there were also pictures of him hugging children. The Saddam projected in the propaganda was a strong, protective and caring father. His portraits were snapped up quickly, but I was able to snag a poster of him wearing a fur hat like a Cossack.

The neighborhood started to wake up and kids peeked over the wall, grinning shyly. The Marines were glad to see children, since it was a reminder of normalcy. They showed their weapons and gear to the kids, letting the kids try on their helmets. The adults hung back, nodding paternally, but still wary.

There were stashes of Orange Crush and RC cola throughout the building. I wondered why a school had so much soda and then realized that it was for the soldiers that had been garrisoned there. I went to hang with Miller, who was guarding one corner of the building with Lovett. One person would watch as the others rested. Lovett pulled a porn out of his flak jacket, where it had been nestled next to his chicken plate. I asked if I could "borrow" it and he handed it over, giving me a conspiratorial smile.

I went to the shoddy principal's office around the corner. As I looked for a rag, I heard breathing and I turned to see a mangy dog in the corner. I kicked him out and got down to business. I hadn't had any release for a month. It was nasty to be doing it in a principal's office, but—fuck it—this was war. Desperate times call for desperate measures.

By the time I came out, a full-fledged block party had erupted. Men from the neighborhoods had come over and were fixing us sweet tea. That was great, but we needed something solid in our bellies. Luckily, they brought us a plain-looking pita bread that turned out to be absolutely delicious and very filling. I briefly wondered if it was poisoned, but the good will of the people was obvious. We thanked them profusely.

Rager was a big hit, setting his country twang to "11." Carpenter launched into a twenty-minute soliloquy to one local about why his name was Carpenter. At the end of the story, he told the guy that he was adopted, so he wasn't really a Carpenter. The Iraqi turned to me, completely perplexed. All I could do was shrug in sympathy.

One of the locals stood out. In his late forties, lean and wiry in a bantam-rooster type of way, he looked like an Iraqi Robert DeNiro. It was clear that he was in charge; he continually sent people to get more pita bread and tea for us. He said that he was an instructor at the military academy and that he had fought in the Iran/Iraq War and the Gulf War. We avoided asking him why he wasn't fighting us—it would have been awkward.

Gunny Linton pulled up and distributed one MRE per man. The company gunny is the mom of the company, making sure everyone has food and water. Since it wasn't a tactical fighting job, him and his two NCOs were seen as being separate from the company, since they didn't do "real grunt shit." While we were rarely ambushed in our armored convoy, his two-humvee convoy was shot at almost every time they went out.

The Iraqi trainer was curious about what was in our MREs so we handed him some of the pound cake. He chewed it deliberately, making a disgusted face. "It is like food for the baby," he said and he was right; MREs are mostly candy and carbs. He told us that the bread he gave us was all that his soldiers took into battle with them in Iran and that it "made you strong." I believed him; I always felt sickly after eating MREs, but after a few pieces of that pita bread I felt nourished and energetic.

He was quite funny, showing us little tricks you'd do to impress your niece. He'd pop the top of a soda can with a bullet—silly things that at the time were highly entertaining. Before he went to speak to another group, he leaned in close and told me something I will never forget. "You know why we are not fighting you today? Because you came in quietly. Not shooting up the place. No bombs everywhere. The British we kill, but you we like." There was a strong lingering hatred of the British because of their "meddling" in Iraq during the last two centuries.

After he left, I pulled out the fork I snagged at Disneyland and started to comb my hair with it. I hadn't been able to wash my hair for more than three weeks and there was a thick layer of grime coating my entire scalp. I felt like a dirty ape in the zoo, but getting that crap out of my hair was almost orgasmic.

Across the street, on the second floor of a house, a teenage girl took furtive peeks at us. I suddenly realized that even though the schoolyard was filled with kids, none of them were girls. When Miller waved at her, she giggled and jumped back inside. A couple minutes later, she gained the courage to wave again and was quickly admonished by an older female inside the house. Miller kept waving for her to come over, which was funny at first; then got progressively creepier until I told him to stop.

I laid down to sleep and awoke with a start about an hour later as the whole world seemed to be exploding. I had gone to sleep with my flak and helmet off, but when I woke I put them back on so quickly that I looked like I was in a speeded-up scene in a "Laurel and Hardy" movie. A huge plume of black smoke and debris shot 100 feet into the air and I could see busted-out windows on all the surrounding buildings. As my senses came back to me, I realized that it wasn't incoming arty or mortar fire, but must have been some set-off explosive. On the other side of the school building, away from the blast, the shockwave had shattered the Orange Crush bottle in Gollum's hand. Later on, we were told that engineers had found a weapons cache and decided to blow it in the open field next to the school, not thinking it was necessary to warn us or the locals. An Iraqi came up and asked me who would pay for his shattered windows. All I could do was shrug.

We left as dusk approached. Rager told me that Reed had taken off without permission earlier, when they needed some volunteers to go to the Turkish Embassy. It was fucked up that he left without telling me, but it was nice to not have to deal with him for an afternoon. Reed returned right before it was time to go. We set off in the dark and I was sucking wind the entire time. I was more worried about looking bad in front of the Iraqis than my boys. Since it was cool outside, the locals were out on the sidewalks and porches, but since the electricity was out, all I could see was the glow of their cigarettes.

When we got back to the college, Reed rushed up to brag about his day. Iraqis had been walking into the unguarded Turkish embassy at will and pulling petty crimes like stealing food from their kitchen. The Turkish Embassy staff asked for some Marines to come and guard them and Lt. McDowell—the arty officer attached to our company—asked for volunteers. Guessing that it would be a sweet deal, Sgt. Quinn and Reed jumped on it. Instead of repelling assaulting hordes, Reed told me they ate chicken, drank soda and watched Turkish music videos all day; he even got to take a shower. He went on effusively on how beautiful the Turkish women were in the videos and how he was going to Turkey to get married after he got out. Yeah, that's a realistic plan, Reed. I'm sure they'll think you're a great catch.

While we had a pretty interesting day in Baghdad, I would find out later that First Platoon saw some incredible things that they would never forget, though some of them wished they could. Ross told me that they checked out a military headquarters where someone found a horrific book that made those who looked at it sick. It was filled with pictures of Iraqis that had been tortured or experimented upon. Ross got the feeling that it was a book that the higher-ups would show to each other to get their jollies off. There were horrific pictures of children mutated by exposure to chemical weapons. One picture showed a woman who had been exposed to chemicals that prevented her from giving birth; she had been pregnant for almost two years and the child took up most of her abdomen, slowly killing her. Ross told me that those pictures would be seared in their memories forever. I think of this when I hear people say that the war wasn't worth it.

They then moved to a bridge where they saw a curious site. At the foot of the bridge on the opposite bank, there was a small storage area just like the one on this side where I had found the shells. A group of Iraqis pulled up in a pick-up truck and went into the storage room, pulling boxes of RPG rockets out and putting them in the truck. Jaramillo sighted in on them with his ACOG, but they didn't have permission to shoot. The Iraqis were eying the Marine across the wide river, but when they saw they wouldn't be shot at, they figured they were safe. Just then, one of the rockets fell out of the box and hit the ground, blowing the nearest guy into a pink mist. The Iraqis ran for cover and Ross asked if anyone else saw that, since it seemed too incredible. Chiariello confirmed he had seen it as well. The Iraqis came out after the dust cleared, grabbed the remaining rockets and sped off.

The next day, we packed up to leave Baghdad. It was widely understood that the war was over. We hadn't seen a lot of action, but I had three small firefights under my belt that I could brag about, so I was happy. We drove south to the area of our last ambush and pulled off the highway. We were told that we were stationing ourselves as a reserve force for Echo Company, which was heading to the east to rescue some POWs. With all of the bad intel throughout the war though, I doubted if there even was a POW camp. And if there was, why would they send a slow-moving line company when you could get Rangers or SEALs out there a lot faster?

We drove to the outskirts of town and pulled the convoy off the highway. All of the Iraqis who had left Baghdad expecting there to be massive warfare in the city were now returning to their homes. The road into Baghdad was backed up for miles. Everyone was waving at us and someone pointed out a funny phenomenon. A huge truck or bus would have three people in it, but a little sedan would be packed with ten people inside and four on top.

First Platoon left in their tracs to do a route recon. It was a completely pedestrian mission, but they all waved like they were in the Rose Bowl Parade as they left. I envied the guys in First Platoon; they had a tight bond and actually worked well together. More guys in First had big egos than in Third, but they could put them aside and work together.

We were not supposed to stay on top of the tracs when they were parked, but I was sick of sitting in the dirt, so I stayed up there. With my rank, there were few people who could tell me to get down. I snacked on my remaining Iraqi chocolates slowly so they would stay down. With nowhere to go and nothing to do, I stretched a simple shave over an hour.

I laid down on top of the trac to sleep. The radio intercom inside the squad compartment below my head, crackled to life. There was significant static garbling the transmission but—just like in the movies—I was able to glean the key words—"multiple RPGs" and "ambush." Someone had to be fucking around on the radios out of boredom. First Platoon had take a random road through an obscure hamlet ten miles outside of Baghdad. If we saw no significant resistance in Baghdad, who would attack well-armed grunts in an out-of-the-way place like that? It was suicide. I looked around to see if anyone else was reacting, but all I saw was people lying around, smoking and chatting.

Suddenly the word went up that we were leaving in five minutes. Knowing how short most ambushes were, I was sure that it would be long over by the time we got there. RPGs really stepped it up a notch though. Multiple RPGs took out the tank I saw the day that First Sergeant Smith got killed, so they could easily destroy a lighter-armored trac.

The tracs fired up their engines; the convoy turned around, went 200 meters up the road…and stopped…for twenty minutes. We were told that the higher-ups were trying to get more info on the situation before we took off. I thought that even if we didn't have all the info, we still had the responsibility to rush in there for our buddies.

When we finally got moving again, the convoy went 100 meters, stopped for a couple minutes, moved another 100 meters, turned around again and stopped almost where we had started. If you ever read "The Family Circus", they have this thing they do on Sundays where they draw little Billy running all over a park, chasing frogs or going down the slide or whatever, crossing and re-crossing his own path. That's what I felt like.

After First Platoon had been fighting for almost forty-five minutes, we finally headed toward them. We took a right off the highway onto a country road and headed toward the village a few miles away. The town was a lot nicer that any other I'd been to—ornate, multi-story houses with AC and TV antennas—pretty hoity-toity for Iraq. Although I didn't realize it at the time, upon reflection, the streets were absolutely empty.

The street suddenly became very narrow and one of our tracs crushed a parked car like a monster truck. The road became a jungle trail and the foliage became so thick that almost all of the packs on the left side were ripped off. Luckily, mine was on the right.

We were almost to First Platoon's pos when Trac 15—the mortar trac—went into a ditch. Our trac stopped as they went to check on Trac 15, which had nearly rolled over. When we saw that everyone was fine and that they could defend their trac, we left them there and headed to the rescue.

We turned left and suddenly had a clear view of a pontoon bridge, one hundred feet away, and the buildings on the other side. The higher-ups were being unusually tentative, making us stop and put people out on security. The jungle was so thick that when they opened the inset door in the rear ramp, they had to push the bamboo out of the way just to get out.

After the higher-ups argued about what to do over the radio, SSgt. D told us to mount back up. The simple task of loading on the trac had become a recurrent problem. Though it was Sgt. Williams' job to make sure everyone was in "his" trac, he was usually too cool to do so. Since I was always on air watch, I was the closest one to SSgt. D in the commander's hatch, so he would ask me if everyone was in. I would yell down into the troop compartment for them to give me a sign when everyone was safely in. Almost always, no one would respond and I'd have to squat back down inside and visually check that the door was shut.

"Is everyone in?" I asked.

Silence.

"Are we up?"

Silence.

"Hey!"

"God! We're fucking 'up', OK?"

I gave SSgt. D a thumbs up. The trac started to back up and I suddenly saw sunlight coming in through the still-open inset door and heard people yelling Reed's name. I turned around and yelled for the driver to stop. He moved back another couple feet—which could have been fatal—before he heard the message and stopped. I peeked inside and saw Reed—wide-eyed and red-faced—being pulled in as he cursed the driver. Several emotions coursed through me—I was mad at whoever said we were up when we obviously weren't, I was angry at myself for not visually checking, and I was bothered with Williams for not doing it himself. Even though I hated Reed, no one deserved to die like that.

The tracs rolled up to the edge of the bridge. My view of the battle field was partially blocked by the FST trac, which held the CO, Arty Officer and Sprinkles. The first thing that struck me was the noise. The gunfire was so thick and close together that it felt like a wall of sound. I had never heard that much shooting in my life. Across the river, there were two building to the left and few shacks and a three-story building farther down the bank to the right. Behind them was a thick palm forest where the fighting was going down.

The Marine Corps never strains their brain rethinking the wheel; they do everything as simply as possible. We had been told before the war that—just like how the battalions within a regiment took turns being the lead element—we would rotate which platoon was the lead element, but that's not how it went. First Platoon was always sent first, Second Platoon always followed them and Third brought up the rear. Third Platoon should have been called Last Platoon, since that's what we always were.

This was obviously a lot different than the tiny ambushes we had been through. I thought about Showers, Ross and Mohler, my best buddies, who were all in First Platoon. The firefight was raging like a storm. I spotted some Marines on the far bank—so far away I couldn't even make out their faces—and my jaw literally dropped open. A squad of Marines—which I correctly deduced was Tardif's—was moving to the right across an open field. The movie "The Patriot" flashed into my head, not only for the unflinching bravery of Tardif's squad, but also for the flat ground they were fighting over. There was no chance of cover; it reminded me of the way they fought during the Revolutionary War. They were moving and firing as calmly as if they were walking in the park.

I couldn't be with them, but I could still help. I led a steady stream of suppressive fire in front of them like a protective curtain as they moved toward a small hut. Ryan was firing on the same hut—using Miller's personal sniper scope that he had attached to the gun—and coordinated his rounds by sight, which was quite innovative, if you're into the specifics of machinegunnery. Tardif's squad was getting closer to my line of fire, which was almost perpendicular to them. In training. we never shot this close to our buddies, but I knew how close I could cut it. I was worried that there might be friendlies in the trees to the left of them, but I realized that Tardif's squad was the lead squad. I stopped shooting when they got within twenty feet of my rounds.

I got off the gun and looked up to see the trac officer in the FST trac ahead of us looking at SSgt. D and telling him to take care of me. I didn't know what he was crying about; I was shooting fifteen feet to the right of him. Other people in the trac were doing the same, my gun just made the most noise.

Sene was next to me scanning for the enemy.

"I got some movement…Two hajis by the house over there-" Sene told his assistant.

"Just make sure they aren't friendly," Rohr chimed in.

"You guys can see silhouettes. I can make out, like, facial features."

The arty officer in the FST trac started waving wildly at Sene.

"Don't shoot! I think he's a landowner!"

"God! Is anyone else going to tell me how to do my job?"

I couldn't help but laugh at Lt. McDowell's assertion. How did he know the guy was a landowner? Did he see a deed in the guy's hand? Was he collecting rent? I think he meant to say a "local" or a "civilian" and but the word "landowner" just made me laugh.

I thought I heard someone say they were going to fire a rocket, so I turned to the others.

"Get down! We're firing an AT-4!"

I noticed Rohr looking at me like I was crazy.

"What are you talking about?"

"I, uh…I thought I heard someone say they were going to fire an AT-4."

"Where do you get your information?

We were told that we would go across the bridge to get a wounded Marine. I couldn't believe that a pontoon bridge could support a 20-ton vehicle. The driver seemed to share that belief, so he sped across the bridge as fast as he could. We stopped at a one-room building just to the left of the bridge. Exhausted Marines were leaning against it, smoking and squinting into the distance.

I could hear more fire in the jungle to the front right. I was desperate to get into the action; I knew that this was "the big one" and it looked like I was missing out. I wanted to take my gun team out, but I knew that since I wasn't one of the "cool kids", SSgt. D would ignore me. I leaned in close to Sene—the only cool kid I was friends with—and asked him to ask SSgt. D if I could take my gun team out into the thick of things. He looked at me like I was nuts and turned away. He was right; that wasn't how the Marine Corps worked. Teams stayed with their squad, squads stayed with their platoon and so on.

After the war, I read an article about Custer's Last Stand that said that one of the reasons that the Indians beat Custer that day was that they fought in units for the first time. Previously, they fought as individuals, everyone trying to out-do the other in bravery and prowess. They never worked together—no concerted attacks, no defenses—just a bunch of guys swinging their dicks. I was pretty damn impressed with myself back then; always grabbing the gun from Rager. Squeak would later get on me for that and—though I didn't listen at the time— eventually I realized he was right. This war wasn't being fought for my own personal aggrandizement; it didn't revolve around me. My job was to be squad leader. I should have always had the squad on my mind instead of perfecting my own personal mythology.

When they loaded Taylor—a trac driver from First Platoon—onto the trac, I knew my last shot at glory was fleeting. I turned to Sgt. Williams, who was in charge of everyone in the trac.

"Let me take my guns out and support them over here."

"What?"

"I want to dismount my squad."

"The other half of your squad is over there."

I looked over his shoulder and damn if he wasn't right. I thought both tracs had come over, but it had just been ours. Miller's team was still on the other side.

We turned around and sped back over the bridge, just as fast as we came. The ramps dropped and we all filed out. As I ducked down into the trac to head out, I saw Taylor with a long, deep gash in his left thigh. As Singh ran out of the trac, he put his knee full-force into Taylor's gash. I wanted to punch his ass for that.

When we got out, I had to find Miller's team, since I was the only squad leader whose squad was split between two tracs. After I got eyes on Miller, I tried to direct Rager where to put the gun, but the SAW gunners kept taking the obvious machinegun spots. Rohr got pissed that I was taking so long, not taking into account the luxury he had of always having his team with him.

Sene crawled on top of a shack to get a better firing position as I went into the bushes to the left of the bridge to check on Miller's team. Ryan had been laying down some serious fire as we were evacing Taylor. Jesse looked like he was having fun, directing SMAW shots at the same building Ryan was firing at.

We heard over the radio that Keller had been shot in the leg, which made me extremely jealous. Why did he get all of the good luck? I would have loved to have a cool, non-life-threatening injury like that. After I got over myself, I became angry at whoever was fighting us. Keller could joke around too much, but he was a good guy. What were these hajis fighting for? To keep a dictator who had pocked their land with mass graves of its own citizens? If they were jihadists coming from other countries to support their "fellow Muslims", what kind of Muslim was Saddam, who invaded and killed hundreds of thousands of Muslims in Iran and Kuwait? Fuck them.

I found Lt. Pettes and asked him when we were crossing the bridge to fight. He told me we would go in five minutes, which sounded good to me. I saw Sprincin in the FST trac and cringed. Did he have to look like such a geek? He was yelling in his nerdy screech over the radio, trying to line up fire support. Why wasn't this guy behind some computer desk where he belonged?

Feeling antsy, I again asked Lt. Pettes when we were going over and he told me it would be ten minutes. What? Oh well, just ten more minutes. I went to my trac and had the crew chief throw me my gas mask that I had "forgotten" when I first got out. I heard shouts and saw people pointing to the sky. A Marine Corps F-18 was flying so high above us that it looked like it was in space. I saw a dark speck separate from the plane and heard the officers yell "Incoming!" This was going to be cool. The guided bomb hit the side of the building Ryan had been shooting at. It burst into flame and the plane flew away. That was it? Just one bomb? Cheap-ass Marine Corps.

The third time I asked Lt. Pettes when we were going, he told me that Captain Hammond had decided to have Third Platoon stay back and guard the FST trac, so that the officers inside could co-ordinate close air support and call in arty strikes. It was the right call—the FST trac's location was perfect for observing the entire battlefield—but I didn't have to like it.

I paced back-and-forth at the edge of the bridge, concocting a childish fantasy: I would run across the bridge, find my buddies and then help them win the battle. I could see it like a scene in a movie. My idea was stupid on several different levels; most of all because it involved me leaving my squad to go be a glory-hog. Reed was next to me and I could tell he had the same idea. He started muttering that he wanted to run over the bridge, but Walton talked some sense into him, telling him that before he got twenty feet away, he'd be tackled and hauled back. He wasn't special—everyone else wanted to be in the thick of it as well—but this wasn't a movie, it was real-life. Rear security wasn't glamorous and it didn't win you any medals, but it was still important. Walton was right—my place was with my squad, not selfishly running after glory.

Two CAAT vehicles from Weapons Company pulled up and my buddy Rutledge got out. I made quite an impression on Rutledge when we met in boot camp, where I was in the class ahead of him. While cleaning the company office windows next to his squad bay, I told him all about the baseball game we went to at Padres stadium, which he excitedly passed to his platoon. Weeks later, when they hadn't gone, he asked a DI when they were going; the DI bellowed that they didn't go to baseball games in that company and thrashed Rutledge for even asking. I knew him vaguely in SOI, but I got to know him a lot better in Oki, since we were the only married guys who weren't out getting handjobs in town. We'd run into each other in boring places like the library and the PX and hang out. After Oki, we both went on FAP together. Before I left my FAP, I heard that I was going to be sent to Weapons Company, since they were light on bodies. I would have missed my buddies in Golf and I loved helos even more than humvees, so I begged off. Rutledge went straight from a year on FAP to being the leader of his own two-vehicle CAAT team. He was there to ferry the wounded back to a helicopter MEDEVAC near the highway. Like us though, he wasn't allowed to cross the bridge, so we just chatted amiably, like we weren't 500 meters from one of the most intense battles of the war. A trac raced across the bridge and Tardif was pulled out. He had caught some shrapnel in his calf and was unconscious from blood loss. Rutledge's humvees took him to a MEDEVAC helo waiting by the highway.

While the XO was briefing the CO, the trac he rode over on went back to the fight without him.

"Now that I've seen Cpl. Tardif escorted to his MEDEVAC, I'm going to catch a ride back to the fight, sir."

"What ride?"

The XO turned around and did a hysterical double-take when he realized that the trac was gone. Even though he was the XO, he was now stuck on this side just like the rest of us. He joined Reed and I, pacing by the end of the bridge. Having nothing better to do, I sat down and changed my socks. I felt like a piece of shit; I was changing my damn socks and my buddies were living my "Black Hawk Down" fantasy.

With little fanfare, we were told to hop back on our tracs and prepare to go. I saw First and Second Platoon's tracs speed back over the bridge and I tried to catch glimpses of my buddies to see if they were OK. Inside the trac, I heard Gollum complaining about my shooting again and telling Williams he needed to "take care" of me. At first I was going to let it go, but I was tired of the catty atmosphere and decided to confront Williams about it. I called Sgt. Williams' name several times before he turned to acknowledge me. When I finally got eye contact, I asked him in a casual voice if he had anything he wanted to talk to me about. He seemed surprised that I said that and looked away, quietly saying "no".

As we pulled away, I looked into my ammo bag and saw that somehow, my last packet of MRE peanut butter had exploded all over my ammo. One thing that had always bothered me about the story of The Bridge was how Ross' gun "went down" and they weren't able to get it back up. Ross was the pre-eminent machinegunner and I couldn't believe that he couldn't fix whatever malfunction or stoppage was affecting the gun. A year and a half later, he confided in me the real reason. After we left Disneyland in Baghdad, his team had their own stash of looted chocolate which they stored on top of their ammo. After they fired off a few cans of ammo, they found the rest to be hopelessly gunked up with Iraqi chocolate.

A huge plume of black smoke rose from the far side of the river as we drove away. As we passed back through the town, we looked for our missing packs, but they had all been spirited away during the battle. Now that the fighting was over, the people were out cheering and waving at us. They were playing both sides against the middle, waiting to see who came out on top.

We stopped at the highway and waited for about twenty minutes. Two tricked-out two Army humvees drove past us, speeding toward the battle site. From their high-speed gear and Marlboro Man looks, I could tell they weren't line company grunts—probably Special Forces. We all looked like shit, but those guys were all ready for a Hollywood screen test. I envied them on several different levels simultaneously.

To my surprise, we went back to the college. It was the same thing that happened after our first firefight near the Han Tush airfield. It's like they wanted to go back to familiar settings after people were mean to us. As soon as the tracs stopped, I jumped off and headed over to see my buddies in First to see that they were alive and unharmed. As I walked through Second Platoon's area, I saw Scott stomp up to Acosta and yell at him. Though he was more than a foot taller than Scott, Acosta just stood there and took the abuse. Scott punched him in the head, but he was so short that he had to jump to do it. Acosta crumpled into a ball on the ground, hoping that Scott would show some mercy. The Goose waddled up and broke them up. The Goose told Acosta that he would prosecute Scott if Acosta felt he had been assaulted, but Acosta demurred.

In the distance, I saw Mohler's familiar lanky form striding toward me, his arms in the air. He was singing some silly song out of pure joy of still being alive. I asked him how he was and he gave me a quick run-down of what happened. This guy who I had known for three years suddenly became a character out of an action movie in my eyes. I told him how happy I was to see him alive and then went to go find Showers and Ross.

There was no chest-thumping in First Platoon; all I saw was numb expressions of exhaustion. I found Showers and I asked him if it was as rough as it sounded. Showers didn't give me any tough guy platitudes, he admitted that he was still shaken and very much glad to be alive. There had been a lot of mis-communication. They had heard that Carpenter had been shot, and we had heard that Keller was—both were untrue. I got to talk with Ross briefly before First Platoon was called over by their platoon commander, Lt. Maurer.

Lt. Maurer looked like your typical smirky frat guy and it was only much later that I would learn that he was actually pretty cool. He said he didn't like giving speeches or getting all touchy-feely, but he wanted to commend the entire platoon on what they did. I felt like I didn't belong there; it was gathering of heroes and I just didn't rate, but I was too fascinated to leave. They all looked wrecked, like they had been up for a week straight. Lt. Maurer singled out Martinez and Tardif for special recognition. We hadn't had haircuts in weeks, so everyone had shag hair-dos that made them look like David Bowie in the Seventies. Martinez' face really got to me. He didn't look like a battle-hardened vet or a cold-hearted killer, he looked like a lost, sad, little boy. More than just being physically draining, it had obviously been an emotional wringer.

When I went back to my pos, Rager told me that Squeak needed to see me. It took me about a half-hour to find him and when I did, he launched into a tirade. He told me that I was not allowed to shoot the gun anymore, since he got word that I was being unsafe. Williams had gone behind my back and complained to Squeak. He told him that the trac officer said that I almost shot him and he also mentioned the telephone pole. He accused me of being unsafe by exiting the trac with the gun in Condition 1. "Condition 1" means that your weapon is loaded and ready to fire, but on safe. Every rifleman and SAW gunner had done the same. Though there had been both SAW and M-16 negligent discharges so far, there had been none from the 240s. Squeak was not a machinegunner and his lack of knowledge was showing. The other thing that was showing was his career-ism. He had made a decision before he even spoke to me.

My mutual enemies were joining together. My relationship with Squeak had been poisoned when he pulled the crap with Miller about his chin-strap. Third Platoon's "cool kids" and I hadn't gotten along since we were in Oki. None of their accusations held merit. Later in the war, I found out that Walton was in the trac with the officer who said I almost shot him. He told me that he remembered quite clearly seeing me shooting and that there was no danger to anyone in the trac. Squeak accused me of not hitting anything, but Ryan told me he could see the impacts of my rounds on the hut at the bridge. Rohr had finagled it that Schofield got posted and I was next on his list.

Later in the war, when there was more time to talk, I would mention my problems with Third to others. I was shocked to find out I was not the only one who had problems with them. No one wanted to be attached to Third because of the catty, high school atmosphere that existed in that platoon. Ryan, Rager, Miller and I had put more rounds down range effectively than all of Third put together, but that didn't matter. All that mattered was which corporal was in tight with what staff NCO.

A couple of hours later, Gunny Brouillet spoke to the platoon informally. He acknowledged the battle, but tried to keep people from getting big heads. He alluded obliquely to Acosta, while reminding us how little training the diggies had. The theft of the chickens by First Platoon, two weeks earlier, still bothered him. He was deadly serious when he said he would find out which Marines did it and would punish them. To lighten the mood, I chimed in, "Those allegations are completely delicious…I mean false." Chiariello got a kick out of that.

Though we had not noticed her absence, Gunny told us that Letta left quietly while we were at Disneyland. The reasons we didn't notice her absence was that she spent almost no time with the bulk of the company; the only people she spoke to were the Marines in her own trac, which I felt was journalistically lazy. Gunny gave the impression that she left before she was kicked out by Captain Hammond, who was entirely within his right to do. Gunny referred to her not by name, but only as "The Bitch."

No one expects a middle-aged newspaper reporter from New York City to be a fan of the military, but she was obviously looking for dirt. He gave an example of how she had led one of our arty attachments into saying some racial epithets. As you have probably noticed from this book, I'm not afraid of telling the nasty parts of grunt life, but from the time we arrived in the region until the time we left, the only names I ever heard used for Arabs was "haji." It wasn't accurate—it referred only to Muslims who had completed the required once-in-a-lifetime journey or "haj" to Mecca—but it was not derogatory. She asked one kid what we called the locals and he gave innocuous terms like "haji", so she kept pumping him until he gave terms like "camel jockey" or "sand nigger", which I hadn't heard since the Gulf War.

As I laid down to sleep on the concrete to go to sleep, I overheard Williams bitching that I had been "shooting up the place like 'Desperado'." That was meant as an insult, but I took it as the highest compliment. "Desperado" with Antonio Banderas was one of my favorite movies. It was an American cousin to the Chinese John Woo movies that I loved, with their two-gun carrying heroes shooting while sliding down bannisters, jumping through the air and doing back-flips. They were heavy on stylish gunplay and light on plot—just the way I like them.

I never shot at an illegitimate target, yet I was always second-guessed by the Cool Kids and their hangers-on, which had nothing to do with my shooting and everything to do with petty high-school bullshit. Sgt. Fun had shot his own driver's hatch. Another cool kid had left his weapon on the ground and had to tell the driver to stop so he could go back and get it. Several times while on air watch, I had to grab a cool kid's unattended rifle before it clattered off the air watch panel onto the ground. None of those incidents were ever mentioned again, but they would never drop the fact that *some* of my rounds hit an aluminum telephone pole thirty feet from the trac. Third Platoon seem to have no understanding of suppression fire, in which an automatic weapon is used to keep the enemy buttoned up.

The next morning, First Sergeant Young informed us that Tardif was probably going home. Taylor was solid, but Gardner, who had been shot in the chest, was probably going to die. I felt bad that I didn't even know what Gardner looked like, considering the price he had paid for all of us.

We got a dump of mail and more food. Kids were still selling cigarettes, but some more interesting vendors appeared outside the gate. Looking back, I was surprised at how relaxed we were, considering how viciously we had been attacked not fifteen miles away. The general feeling was that we had been attacked by Ba'ath officers and foreign jihadists, not your common Iraqi citizen. Marines were mingling among the friendly crowd. Kids were selling 24-can packs of soda and I snapped one up for ten dollars, attracting much attention as I went to secure it in my pack. I returned to the street and bought some homemade cookies, which were plain but good. I imagined a woman in one of the nearby houses baking the cookies for her son to sell to us. It could not have been a more pleasant, pastoral scene.

A pimp appeared with two cute chicks he was trying to rent or sell; he didn't make it clear. From all the movies I had seen about war, combat was always followed by hookers, but this was my first sight of any. The girls looked willing, but time was fleeting and there really wasn't anywhere to take them to. Like in Oki, I was going to pay for one of my single buddies to do the deed and I would live through him vicariously, but it was not to be. It was time to go and there was no time for hoes.

By the time we left Baghdad, we were jaded about combat. We got lost trying to find the right highway out of town and when we pulled over to the side of the road in a residential neighborhood, I heard over the radio that there was a sniper in the area. Another voice languidly asked where the sniper was and the response was "200 meters away." No one reacted—200 meters, who cares? All of our engagements had been within 100 meters and the Iraqis were notoriously bad shots.

We headed to Samarra, an hour north of Baghdad. Turkey had stalled on letting US troops deploy from their land, but they were showing signs of cooperation. We were told that we might move north to the border, securing towns along the way and then fly out from Turkey. We also might go east and catch some ships at the gulf. Returning to Kuwait was seen as unlikely since no one thought our tracs could make it all the way back there.

As we approached the city, the word changed. We would go to Samarra as a show of force, just for the day. We would then turn south and slowly head back to Kuwait over the next week or two, hitting small towns to show the flag. The Marine Corps was a fighting force, not a force of occupation. The better-equipped Army would conduct the long-term occupation, we were told.

We came up on the west of the city, near a beautiful river with ornate houses built along its cliff. We paused on the bridge leading into town, since a local warned us of an ambush. It turned out to be false and we went into the town. Samarra was large, but nowhere near the size of Baghdad. We went onto the first street and turned right. Another Marine unit was already there and had identified a Ba'ath headquarters for us to check out.

A car came around a corner and crept toward us. Two men in uniforms got out, one with a pistol on his belt. I aimed at them and they stopped. The older one was co-operative, but I could tell that he was used to being the one with the authority. It turned out they were cops. In this military state, even the cops dressed like soldiers.

We went to a two-story building and stacked up by its huge wooden front door. I would have paid good money for a firefight, so I maneuvered to the front of the pack. The door was knocked open and we swarmed inside. Every door was kicked in and every room searched, but no one was there. Once we got inside, it was clear that it was a courthouse; not the Ba'ath HQ.

After twenty minutes, someone who went to college figured out it that the Ba'ath HQ was the next building over. A little embarrassed about our earlier mistake, we just walked into it—no drama this time. The large building sat on a prominent spot at a traffic circle and had a great view of the city, which is famous for its ancient Babylonian towers. We weren't given much instruction; we were just told to set up a defense. That meant that the lances manned the guns and the NCOs looked for cool shit to grab. An actual toilet was found and everyone used it, not worrying that it didn't actually flush. Though the downstairs was ransacked by the time I got there, I found a small dark office upstairs that was unmolested. There were thousands of ID cards that I dubbed my "Iraqi Pokemon" cards. I grabbed a couple dozen of them as well as my real prize—a set of 12 medals I found in a desk drawer.

We chilled in there for two hours and then went back to the tracs. Though there was a good amount of people in the streets, it wasn't as many as should have been out there on a normal day. I was surprised to see a huge weightlifter; I didn't think that anyone in this country had enough extra food to bulk up like that. A more pleasant sight was a cute, slightly chunky woman in her mid-twenties walking by in a knee-length skirt, her henna-dyed hair blowing in the breeze. I noticed that she purposefully walked right by us, instead of walking on the other side of the street like most of the locals had. It was nice to see a pretty young women who wasn't covered head-to-toe, but that good feeling quickly dissipated when I saw the looks of the local men and the barely-disguised hate in their eyes. I got the feeling that they were acting casual since we were there, but that they would not forgive the woman for "flaunting" herself in front of us. I thought that they were going to beat her down as soon as we left.

I showed two locals the ID cards I got from the Ba'ath HQ and they told me that they were cards that showed who was allowed to carry a gun. They really perked up when I showed them the medals. I assumed that they were just pins denoting membership in the Ba'ath party, but I was told that they were actually "Mother of All Battles" medals for veterans of the Gulf War. I got the feeling that before we invaded, they tried to stir up some patriotic fervor by handing out long-delayed medals to their vets.

A couple of reporters were talking casually with some Marines and I noticed that they were letting people call home on their satellite phones. Since I was one of the first to notice this, I calmly walked over trying to not incite a riot. The journalists were straight from central casting, with deep tans and blonde-tinged hair, to whom this war was just another story. They weren't interviewing anyone, just finishing up an assignment before they split. They said that since the combat phase had ended, they were heading out of the county. Most embedded reporters had already detached from whatever unit they were with. They asked if I had seen anything recently and I started to tell them about The Bridge, but they didn't seem interested. They had heard so many combat stories that I think the only that would have perked their ears up would have been some kind of scandal.

They handed me their phone, but all I got was an answering machine. I wasn't that bummed though since we were being told "unofficially" that we'd be home in about a month. I left that message on the machine and handed the phone back just as we were told to get back on the tracs.

I stared wistfully at Samarra as we got back on the road and turned south. This was the farthest north we would ever go and it was the end of the combat phase. I hadn't gotten to top The Bridge, but I had some good fights under my belt and I was ready to go home.

We traveled about twenty miles south and set down next to the highway. I wondered why we stopped so early and I was told that we were awaiting our plan for our withdrawal. Good to go. I had food and water and the weather was nice; I could stay there for a week.

I went over to find Ross, feeling weird when I got among First Platoon. They had been through hell together and they were a lot tighter because of it. I just didn't fit. No one made me feel that way; I did it to myself. Magana jokingly asked me if I wanted to join First Platoon and I thought, Oh God yes, but only if I could have been with you all two days earlier.

Rager had often told me how Reed couldn't open an MRE with having a temper tantrum, but I thought he was exaggerating. I had always avoided eating near Reed, but for some reason I found myself next to him when he broke out an MRE. He read the contents aloud, to no one in particular; then expounded loudly on why he hated that MRE for several minutes, while no one listened. As he grasped the end of the MRE bag to pull it open, he muttered to himself, "I always have trouble with this…", which would become another catch-phrase in the section. While trying try to open it the wrong way, he screeched and grunted; then threw it on the ground and stomped on it. Finally, he ripped a tiny hole in it and pried into it like a rat, all the while muttering that if he ever met the person that "invented MREs" he was going to "punch him in the face!" He did not say that jokingly, he was actually serious. He then pulled the meal pouches out the small hole he had gnawed in the bag and proceeded to open each pouch and spill the contents on himself, while cursing. When it was all over, I realized that I had just watched a grown man get out-smarted by an MRE for ten minutes. I apologized to Rager for ever doubting him.

The next day, after sitting and reading for hours, I got called over to SSgt. D's trac for a leaders brief. He looked like someone had just run over his dog, After some soft-pedaling, he hit us with the news: we were going to a town south of Baghdad called Samawah where we would camp outside the city and train for 60-90 days. If you would have kicked me in the stomach right then, I wouldn't have noticed. During the entire war, we had been promised a flight home as soon as Baghdad was secured. We were told that we were fighters, not occupiers—that was the Army's job. The Goose left the Gulf War three days after the fighting ended. All of our gear was in shreds—those of us that still *had* gear—and now they were going to take us to some shithole to train? That was like taking the winners of the Super Bowl and telling them, fuck going to Disneyland, we're practicing twice a day all summer.

I went back to my hole and passed the bad news to my squad. They took it well, but I was crushed. I sat and pouted for hours. I decided I had to take my mind off my current situation before I went nuts. I pulled out the notebook that I cadged at Disneyland and I wrote down all my plans in life, short-, medium— and long-term. I then started fleshing out a story I had gotten an idea for. Anything to keep from thinking about wasting away in that hellhole for three more months.

People were on edge and the boots were catching the brunt of their ire. Miozza—my fellow air watch champ—was a great guy, but he would fall asleep in a burning plane. After catching him asleep on watch dozens of times, Rohr told Miozza that he'd finally had it—he was going to send him to CCU when we got back. I had told Carpenter the same thing, after he repeatedly fucked up, much to Rager's approval. Carpenter needed to go to CCU; nothing I or anyone else had done had gotten him to get his head out of his ass. He was going to become a senior Marine and be a total drain on the entire platoon. Miozza didn't deserve to go though. Like Mohler, he was tough and smart—a natural leader. Rohr should have just kicked him in the head when he caught him asleep. I told Miozza that if Rohr was still talking about sending him to CCU when we got back, I would go to bat for him and make sure he didn't go.

We stopped on our way south in an idyllic pasture; I walked along the bank of the thin stream and took in the sights. With the green grass, well-kept house and spotted cows, it could have been a farm in Indiana. When I walked through Second Platoon's area to get to my buddies in First Platoon, I saw that every third man was standing and had a cardboard sign hanging around his neck that said, "I am on watch." This really made me angry, since I assumed it was just another example of The Goose unnecessarily fucking with his platoon. Those kids had been in the thick of the battle of The Bridge just days earlier and now they were being demeaned. It was one of the reasons I hated The Goose. It wouldn't be until I was almost out of the Corps that Moser corrected me. The Goose *had* made them do it, but not to humiliate them. He was trying to stick it to the XO, who he felt was being stupid when said that he couldn't tell who was on guard. That might have been so, but the PFCs and lances who were wearing the signs had looked pissed and embarrassed and didn't seem to be in on the joke.

I have almost no memories of covering the several hundred miles from Samarra to Samawah. I think I spent the entire journey in a fugue state. My next memory is of us stopping on the highway, just outside of Samawah. Though I was depressed about being stuck in Iraq, I was quite happy that it was our last day in the tracs. I had experienced more misery in those tracs than in the rest of my whole life put together. I had inhaled so much exhaust, that I seriously wondered if I had brain damage. I wondered if I would feel diminished if I had gotten stupider or if I wouldn't notice because I couldn't remember what I had lost.

The outskirts of Samawah were promising, with several multi-story houses with beautifully-intricate Arab architecture. Though I came away quite disgusted with their culture in general, I fell in love with their ornate style of architecture, just as I had fallen in love with the aboriginal art in Australia. There were Airborne soldiers perched on the roofs, looking casual and well taken care of. I wouldn't have envied them if I had known that they would still be in Iraq five months after I left.

On the right there was a large soccer stadium with the seats flipped up to spell "WELCOEM USA." Something as simple as that really meant something and I wondered who organized it and how the people who made it happen felt. We crossed a bridge and entered the downtown area, which was a fairly run-down. I was happy that we would stay in place for awhile and maybe even get to know some of the people there. I perked up when I saw some Army soldiers buying sodas from a bodega.

On the incline of an overpass at the south edge of town, a crumpled and burned Black Hawk helicopter sat on the ground. Seeing one of our vehicles like that always made me sick. The people in town seemed friendly, maybe it was just a mechanical failure that made it crash. I would have liked to believe that.

We headed to a huge railroad yard a mile off the highway. I was looking forward to being in a solid building, but instead of going inside, we set down in the dirt a few hundred meters away. When we were told that this barren stretch of dirt would be our home for the next 90 days, I wanted to cry. Thankfully, ten minutes later, they told us the word had changed. We would just stay there for the night and relieve an army unit the next day. Thank God.

As I wrote the watch schedule, the boots pulled their usual shenanigans. When we were told to go to 25%, that meant that one person in each four-man hole had to be awake at any one time. In Weapons though, we had either two or three-man holes, so it would be unfair to have one person up in each hole. We were allowed to join one machinegun hole with a neighboring SMAW hole as long as someone was awake and manning the gun. By the end of the combat phase, one of the riflemens' four-man holes had been added to our conglomeration, which meant that, between the nine of them, they would each only pull one hour of watch. I had started pulling the first watch each night, since I was feeling guilty about not contributing. Rank does have its privileges, but my boots—with the exception of Carpenter—had really impressed me and I wanted to let them get more sleep. No other sergeants pulled watch for their Marines. I would find out much later that, though the corporals were supposed to pull watch, many of them pulled rank and made the lances pull their watch, meaning the boots hardly got any sleep.

Third Platoon had an epidemic of people falling asleep on watch, not just boots, but corporals as well. Schofield even got caught asleep while on radio watch, lamely saying that he was just lying down with his eyes closed, but wasn't actually asleep. One night, Kennel caught every single member of his squad asleep on watch at least once. Every night, at least four people, and sometimes as much as half the platoon, was caught asleep. During the entire war, only one member of my squad was ever caught asleep.

An hour before reveille, the XO came around and found one of my boys on the gun, groggy, but awake. When he continued down the line though, he didn't find another person awake until he got to Second Platoon. *Everyone* in Third was asleep. After stand-to, SSgt. D called the squad leaders together. SSgt. D wasn't fuming, but he had obviously gotten his ass chewed. He started talking vaguely about "changes being made" and leaders dropping the ball. Williams and Schofield stood over his shoulder, glaring at the rest of us, like they were some-how separate and above the rest of the platoon. It reminded me of Monty and the piss bottle. When the "cool kids" fucked up, they wouldn't get singled out; it would be referred to as a group problem.

Later that morning, we drove back into town. We passed some Army humvees and a cute chick jumped up and waved to us. The girl was fresh-faced and blonde, quite a shock after months in the desert. The Army guys with her didn't look happy that she was waving to us, but I think they took some satisfaction in the knowledge that we could see for thirty seconds, but they had all-day, every-day to try and get in her pants.

We pulled up to a small fort and were told to get everything off the tracs as fast as possible; the tracs were detaching from the company permanently. Vague plans were made to have a party with the trackers at their base on the coast at Del Mar when we got back, but I knew it wouldn't happen. They were leaving Iraq as soon as they could get their vehicles back to Kuwait, but we would be here for months.

A couple of Army guys were inside the fort chatting with some Marines over the wall. Though there is supposed to be a rivalry between the Army and the Marines, I never saw it. On both sides, they were just glad to have new people to talk to. Though the town was peaceful, there had been heavy fighting to clear out the Ba'ath officials and Fedayeen, which was evidenced by the bullet holes in many of the buildings along the highway. This company from the 82nd Airborne had stayed at the fort for the last two weeks, but there had been no excitement since then. I assumed that since we were taking over for them that they were going home, but they told us they were heading to a city in Northern Iraq for their permanent assignment.

They warned us to watch where we stepped, since we had unknowingly set down in their designated shitting spot. Miozza got the word too late and his boot broke through a thin crust of dry sand and sunk into Airborne waste product.

When we were told to enter the fort, everyone scrambled over the low wall to get a good spot before they were all taken. Though we were relieving the Airborne, there was no formal hand-over; we just took over. The "airborne" patch was impressive was hell and so were their weapons, which were all stripped-down and collapsible to fit in their jump packs. I noticed that the airborne guys all looked like kids compared to the Marines of the same age and they seemed shy and deferential. I tried to pin down what was different about them and then I figured it out—they were nerds. Not all of them, but a vast majority. Whenever I'm among a group of Marines, I always think a bar fight is going to break out. With the Airborne guys, a round of Dungeons and Dragons was much more likely.

I took a gun team down to replace some Airborne kids who were checking the vehicles that would pass by the fort. Their specialized SAW caught my eye; with its collapsible stock and shortened barrel, it packed a lot of firepower into a small package. The soldier was more than happy to let me check it out and I was shocked at how heavy it was. Though it was smaller than our SAW, they put so many attachments on it—scope, laser spotter, flashlight—that it weighed more than ours.

When a long convoy of semis approached, I held my hand up and the lead truck stopped grudgingly. I went to the driver's side to see why this haji would think that he didn't have to stop and—lo and behold—it was a American contract driver. I was shocked that they were operating this far in-country already. When he told me that he was carrying mail, I let him through gladly. Though it was quite lucrative for these truckers to work in Iraq, I got the feeling that a sense of patriotism was as much of an enticement as the cash. Almost every trucker threw us cigarettes and told us how proud they were of us. I was shocked when I saw a husband-and-wife team operating freely in this Arab country.

Of the five buildings in our fort, one was taken by each platoon, another for headquarters and one was appropriated for the "cool kids." Not only had we been cut loose from the tracs, but our connection to Third Platoon was slackened as well. We had to be co-located, but we didn't have to be in the same room. I placed my squad on a large ledge on the second floor of Third Platoon's building.

It was the first time in a month that I had a solid place to sleep and I woke up the next morning, feeling terrific. I heard some crunching as I sat up and I looked down to see that I had been sleeping on broken glass and hypodermic needles. Instead of being worried, I just laughed—it would make a good story. I didn't feel like I was cut or punctured anywhere. Later, I casually asked one of the corpsmen if he that thought someone could *hypothetically* catch something if they *might* have come in contact with—oh, I don't know—let's say a hypodermic needle. He told me the intense heat would have cooked any virus in the syringe and that I shouldn't worry.

While the elevens conducted foot patrols, the machinegunners manned their guns to defend the fort. As long as we had one guy on the gun, we were golden. I laid on the ledge for hours, contemplating the future and enjoying the hell out of being rid of the tracs. After awhile though, I got bored and horny. On the far side of Third's building, there was a small closet-like room. A legend was born—the First Wack Shack. I was quite proud of my discovery and went to tell me buddies in First Platoon, who told me they had their own Wack Shack, but since theirs smelled and had no lock, it was inferior to ours.

I thought I was hallucinating when I saw two humvees pull up, filled to the top with the distinctive orange mail sacks. The whole company was abuzz; all the mail that had been sitting in Kuwait for the last month was now being trucked in. There were dozens of boxes and hundreds of letters; nearly everyone got enough mail to fill both hands. We had been starving in Baghdad just a week earlier, but now we were now rolling in more food than we knew what to do with. We spent the day leafing through magazines, showing off pictures of our families, listening to new CDs and gorging ourselves. Luckily, several guys got porno in the mail, so the Wack Shack was up and running, though not yet so busy that you needed an appointment. Over the next three days, we got enough mail to fill five humvees. We also got so many MREs that people were using the twelve-pack boxes as furniture. No one was wanting for food, mail, batteries, or CDs; and the beef jerky flowed like wine, baby!

Each platoon received a large goodwill kit, which was filled with packets of toiletries. Since we were attached to Third, we had to get our share from them, which I knew would turn into a hassle. I went down to Third's little dungeon and found that they had unilaterally decided that they would horde the toiletries. When I told them that I wanted my squad's fair share, they started bitching about how the good will kit had to last until we got re-supplied. Third was under-sized; their attachments—machinegunners, SMAW gunners, and snipers—had almost as many men as they did, but they always treated us like an afterthought. I could have pulled rank and made a big stink, but I was tired of their high school bullshit. With all of the mail we had gotten, the only person wanting for toiletries in my squad was Lopez. I grabbed enough razors for him and left, disgusted with their pettiness.

Even though Miller had a bad rep, when left to his own devices, he was an absolute workhorse. Using scrap wood and broken furniture, they built their own little fort on the roof that was a kid's dream. It had a desk inside, a concealed shooting position, cabinets filled with candy and a place to sleep in the shade. It was so great that I knew its days were numbered. Sure enough, Miller was ordered to tear it down the next day. Since the higher-ups couldn't see what was going on inside it, they decided that it had to go. I realized the danger of whoever was inside falling asleep while on watch, so I had checked it frequently, but I never caught anyone asleep. There were usually two other Marines in the little fort, reading magazines and talking, so they kept the gunner awake. It was the perfect set-up.

Kids started appearing at the walls, selling sodas, smokes and even whiskey. I cornered the market on the sodas, even scheduling resupplies. Far from being poor little third-world urchins, these kids knew just how to sell and got us for all we were worth. An Army disbursing unit came to our fort and I was able to draw $200 of "Split Pay" from my account, which I used to jumpstart the Iraqi economy.

I awoke that night to the sound of people whooping and hollering; the whiskey was taking affect. Elias and some other loudmouths used Rager's birthday as an excuse to get drunk. Rager just wanted to sleep, but in the grand Marine Corps tradition of "mandatory fun", they dragged him off to their building to "celebrate."

I had to provide two bodies for a working party, so I told Ryan to grab Lopez and report in. Ryan came back ten minutes later, saying that Lopez refused to go. Lopez said that the last thing he was told by me was that he was off for the next four hours. This was known as "playing mommy against daddy", in which a boot would play different orders from his NCOs off each other as a way to get out of work. I had done it myself quite effectively when I was a boot, but Lopez was playing me against me! I told Ryan to tell Lopez to get his ass on the working party immediately. I would deal with him later.

I had been gaffed off, but Lopez was usually as reliable as the sun rising. He had always been a quiet, strong presence in the squad. He didn't have many close friends, but he was a good guy—just a little stand-offish and defensive of his pride. I could do the classic yell-and-punish routine and all the staff NCOs would say I was a good leader, but all it would do was make Lopez feel more distant and get his defenses up. I believe in loyalty and giving people the benefit of the doubt. Lopez walked up, his eyes pre-glazed for an ass-chewing that he would just ignore. Instead, I casually asked him what was happening with him lately. He tried to play it cool, but after some prodding, I got him to admit that he was having problems with Miller and Ryan and he just wanted some time alone. That was understandable, considering he had spent the last three months within ten feet of them at all times. I recounted the events that had led to me counseling him and I told him that I knew what he was pulling; he was just getting an informal counseling this time, but next time, the gloves were off.

After five days at the fort, we got word that me might have a mission. I didn't believe that it would happen, since we no longer had any vehicles, but then—like a bad dream—our old tracs pulled up. I thought that they were long gone, but they had actually been holed up in the railroad yard, awaiting orders. After all of Third Platoon was caught asleep on our first night in Samawah, the squad leaders had been shuffled. My good buddy Lewis came up and told me that I was with his squad. I was happy that he had made squad leader—he deserved it. I could tell that I had been foisted on him, but I wasn't bothered. He was one of the few guys in Third that I could stand.

We would head to a remote spot to capture some wanted men, which was more information than we had gotten for any other mission. We took a meandering route through the hinterlands until dawn. It was supposed to be a surprise raid, but with a convoy of twelve tracs, we kicked up enough dust to be seen for twenty miles. When we got within a hundred feet of the target building, a little kid got spooked and turned to run. He took two steps, caught his foot on the ground and "ate shit", as we used to say. For some reason, I couldn't stop laughing. It was like getting spooked by a glacier.

We rounded up some craggy-looking adults for the interpreter, Al-Shameree, to question. Al-Shameree was an Iraqi-American kid I went to SOI with. Somehow, he had graduated from SOI even though he was "broke" and didn't go on any of the three mandatory hikes. He got to The Fleet and, over the next three years, stayed broke, barely trained, got even fatter, and worked a desk job. Then, when the war approached, he suddenly became the most important person in the battalion, even getting an article about him in "People" magazine. With his "elevated" status as the battalion interpreter, he walked around like he was a staff NCO, even though he was still a lance. When Lovett casually told some kids to stay back, Al-Shameree started yelling at him for being too "rough." I wondered how Al-Shameree even knew what "rough" was.

If whoever we were after was ever there, he was long gone. Out of nowhere, a CIA field officer appeared in his nice khaki pants and sunglasses to speak with our officers. I wondered where he came from; he hadn't come with us. Had he been living off the land and spying on the huts, waiting for one of the most-wanted to show up? No. His clothes were too clean. Once again, Tom Clancy had let me down.

We sat in a culvert while the officers yammered on. In times like this, Jesse—with his ability to squeeze fun out of the most miserable situations—was a god-send. He started doing a play-by-play for a dung beetle who was rolling a ball of goat shit up a sand dune back to his hidey-hole. For some reason, the dung beetle's struggle became utterly fascinating. The drama escalated when another dung beetle appeared and tried to jack the first one. The first dung beetle wasn't about to lose his shit—literally—after he spent all that energy pushing it uphill, so he whupped that other dung beetle's sorry ass. Jesse loved "Rocky" movies and he made the battle of the dung beetles into a pay-per-view event.

There had been a rumor that Golf would move to the train station with the rest of the battalion. No one liked that idea; our life at the fort was easy and we assumed that's how the rest of our stay would be. The only bad thing about the fort was the flies. Our shitter was a wooden box with two holes cut in it set over two large metal buckets. The bowls of shit would get burned by some unlucky junior Marines each morning, but as soon as the fire died down, the shit would once again attract thick clouds of flies. Shitting ten inches away from another man in plain view was bad, but having the flies that had been in the shit crawl all over you while doing so was much worse. I once had a fly jump off a turd in the bucket (not mine) and fly straight into my mouth. People started getting horribly sick from the flies. The corpsmen got it the worst, since they had to go around and speak to everyone that had the shits. Chili was in the fetal position, puking all over himself. Luckily, we got hand sanitizer in the goodwill packs and when people started using it, the sickness died down.

A huge explosion went off about a mile away and people started saying we were being attacked. When I told Miller that it was probably just a weapons cache being blown, he scoffed at me. As rounds and shells cooked off, a few RPG rockets sailed through the air, landing in the field between us and the cache. The call went up for everyone to get into one of the thick-walled buildings, but I stayed on the roof, excited by the danger. We found out later that it had been caused by a fire at an ammo collection point that the Army had assembled.

I visited Ross in First Platoon's building, still feeling quite awkward about being around them. Now that we had some down-time and people had time to think, they realized how big of a battle it had actually been and just how close they all came to dying. They also realized that since not all of us were in the thick of it, that they were "better" than us. Thus, The Cult of The Bridge was born. In front of their building, they had made a sign on the ground with rocks spelling out "The Bridge—First Platoon—April 12th, 2003." Any time you mentioned something that happened in the war, it would be greeted with an disgusted grunt and it would be made clear that *nothing* was as big as The Bridge. The fact that not one person on our side died in a battle which had no real effect on the outcome of the war was not factored in.

None of my friends who were at The Bridge rubbed it in. People who risked the most, like Tardif and Martinez, almost never spoke of it. It was the pricks who made it the end-all, be-all of Marine Corps existence that made it insufferable. Ross and I were able to joke about it, with him adapting a faux-dismissive attitude, but it was all in fun. In retrospect, most of those who were in the battle didn't lose their minds about it. It's like with cellphones—you only notice the ones who are acting like assholes.

Ross and I had both received dozens of comics in the mail. After a rainstorm almost ruined my comics, which were stored at my squad's exposed position on the ledge, I decided to put them in Ross' building to keep them safe. I felt kind of silly that I was in a war zone and my biggest worry was having my comics get ruined, so as a dumb in-joke, I wrote "The first rule of comics club is that you don't talk about comics club" on the MRE box I put them in. That box would end up haunting Ross for the rest of his enlistment. The other cool kids in First Platoon, Magana and Doc Bunstone especially, teased him endlessly about the "comics club."

Just like at the TAA, when the pace gets too slow, the staff and officers start getting bored and issuing arbitrary rules to make themselves feel useful. After a Marine in another platoon was caught on watch without his helmet on, we were told that we had to wear all of our war gear every time we were on post. Since our mag pouches and canteens were strapped to our flaks, we assumed that we didn't have to wear our LBVs (Load-Bearing Vests), it would be like wearing a belt and suspenders. Nevertheless, when the CO saw that Miller didn't have his LBV, Miller got his ass chewed.

One night, I got up to piss and saw that The Goose had his entire platoon in formation at two in the morning, just so he could yell at them. If someone in that platoon had committed a major fuck-up, it was almost understandable, but this was how he reacted to everything. With guys like Bud, Reyna and Dart, Second Platoon was a well-run crew. The Goose wasn't making his platoon better, but he was making them bitter. Even though his squad was co-located with Second Platoon, Moser had successfully finagled his boys out of those fuck-fuck games by telling The Goose that they were only attached to them for missions, not while in the fort. Smart move.

Cooped up in the fort, people started to get on each others' nerves, even guys like Doc Cox, one of the coolest and most laid-back guys I ever met. Putting their big bellies, long hair and side-burns aside, the Navy is the most professional military service there is. That's what they hang their pride on. Before the war started, we got several augmentee docs that they had pulled from desk jobs and hospitals. One of them made the mistake of telling Cox how to do his job and he got laid out. You can call a corpsman's mother a whore to his face or say that he's a fat fuck and he'll just laugh, but you never impugn his professionalism.

Mangy dogs were coming in to eat our trash and Wylie, a kid from Third, started befriending them. Dogs in Iraq are like wild wolves and they are vicious sacks of disease and germs. The higher-ups ordered that the dogs were to be carried out of the fort whenever they came in. When Picas, a mortarman, threw a dog out the front gate, it tried to run back in and he kicked it. Wylie went nuts and threw a crazy kick at Picas' head, sending the Skittles in Picas' hand flying everywhere.

Miller's girlfriend was crazy about him and he set the record for receiving the most mail, with Rager being a close second. Miller's team had gotten some huge lockers onto the four-foot wide ledge they lived on and Miller stuffed them with a small PX' worth of food. He would spend his whole day proudly arranging and cataloguing his lockers of goodies.

An opportunity came up that seemed to good to be true. 2/4 had been in Oki since January and they were due to be relieved in the summertime. We were told that, in all likelihood, 1/5 would be leaving Iraq within two weeks. They would go back to Cali, get thirty days leave and then head to Oki. They asked for volunteers to "cross-deck" over to 1/5, since they would be losing many of their senior Marines who were due to EAS soon. I couldn't think of a better deal. Even as a boot, Oki was a six-month vacation. Going to 1/5 would get me out of Iraq 2-3 months early. The thought of staying in Iraq was interminable. We had already squeezed whatever few drops of combat there were out of the country; I didn't feel like being a cop in a Third-World town.

Most people thought it was a terrible deal, since it meant spending almost the rest of the year overseas, but I was looking at quality of life. In Oki, I could get back in shape, call home every few days and save money. By the time I returned to Cali the following January, I would be eligible to get out early on a school-cut. I was able to convince a few buddies to put their names down as well—I would need people to hang out with, right? When the roster of volunteers was compiled, I triple-checked that my name was on it.

After several weeks of waiting, we got word from a gunny in 1/5 that no one was going anywhere. 1/5 was staying in Iraq and 2/4 would remain in Oki through the summer, until they were relieved by reservists. I was crushed, but at least the hope had gotten me through the initial shock of finding out that we were staying in Iraq indefinitely.

The chaplain came and performed a church service, though only about eight of us showed up. He brought a corporal from HQ who supposedly had a "life-changing experience." The corporal launched into a long and embarrassing story about how he used to live a "wicked" life until he "saw the light" during the combat phase. The only light I saw back then were the tracers coming out of my machinegun—Ooo-rah! He was very vague about what happened and I was glad when his story was over. Weeks later, I would find out what the big deal was. On the second day in Iraq, the corporal had spotted some hajis 600 meters away from the convoy. Though they were not acting hostile, he started shooting at them. Though no one saw anyone go down, he started saying that he had "a confirmed kill." From then on, he told everyone that the "death" he caused had profoundly changed him. The only thing he ever killed was a conversation.

Though the CO had put up a valiant fight, the BC decided that we would move to the train station. We were give one-hour's notice and Schofield started saying that we could only take one box of mail per man. My boys started frantically deciding what they would keep. Our families and friends had spent hundreds of dollars mailing this stuff to us. If we couldn't fit it all on the truck, then they could make another trip. I told my squad to bring as much as they wanted.

The train station was huge, with a dozen hangar-size buildings, train trestles and 60 foot-high cranes. Third Platoon had to report for battalion guard immediately in a different building, so Kennel told me to make sure that I saved a good spot for Third. Sure, because they were always so cool to us, right? I grabbed the best spot for Weapons Platoon and by the time that Third Platoon got back from guard duty, they were down-wind from the shitters.

Our building was as big as a football field and 60 feet high. It had a railroad track running down the center with a train engine and two cars on it. I was ecstatic to have a real roof and a clean place to live. After much thought, I picked a spot in the middle, which would give us maximum distance from the higher-ups who would stay up front, while also keeping us away from the blowing sand that would be coming through the open bay doors at both ends of the building.

In the next building over, there was a ransacked store room that was filled with dozens of shelves and usable junk. Miller and I hauled some shelves to our area; then sprinted back to get more before people snapped it all up. We ended up with two wall shelves to store our personal effects and two more shelves more that we put on their sides in an L-shape to make a cubicle for our squad. I made a chair out of engine parts and we turned a train window into a glass table. To decorate our happy little home, I took the four-feet long cardboard sleeve out of an MRE box and drew a 240 on it. Martha Stewart and Oscar the Grouch would have been proud.

The guys from Supply had gone to Kuwait to get supplies—appropriately enough—and they bought enough goodies to open a mini-PX for one day. HQ Company Marines were always assumed to have more info than line company grunts, so I pumped my buddy in Supply for information. He told me that the rumor mill had us leaving in mid-June, six weeks away.

I had screwed myself by putting the glass table right next to my rack, since it became a little hang-out where Kelting and some boots from First bull-shitted late into the night. After awhile, I noticed that they were talking funny and I realized that they were playing a drinking game. After an hour of trying to go to sleep, I started to like the idea of getting drunk, so I joined them. With his bright red hair and minute stature, Kelting looked like a leprechaun, but he spoke in a deep, gravelly voice and swaggered like John Wayne. Though he was scrawny, he never fell out of hikes or runs and he was one of the black belt instructors. I didn't like him—I thought he was a kiss-ass to the seniors when we were boots— but I had to respect him.

They were playing a drinking game in which the penalty for messing up was getting punched. They passed around a sharp, biting whiskey that was probably half-filled with Iraqi urine, but I didn't care. It smelled like turpentine and knocked me on my ass, so it did the job. After taking a swig, you would pass it around and have a chaser made with MRE beverage powder. I was stone drunk in about three rounds. These guys weren't my friends and they were among the worst of the braggarts of The Bridge, but I didn't care, I just wanted to be drunk and numb. Kelting meted out several punches to those who messed up. I purposefully made mistakes, but no one punched me.

I had originally stayed awake to make sure that they didn't piss on any of my stuff. It was an eighty-foot walk to the established pissing area and a fifteen-foot walk to the alley between the buildings, but I knew that at least one Marine would deem either way much too far. Just as I predicted, Levesque's nasty ass walked over to Second Platoon's area and pissed next to one guy's sleeping bag. Classy.

When the CO appeared out of the dark, I thought we were done, but all he wanted to do was engage in the usual awkward officer-enlisted banter. I got the feeling that he knew we were drinking, but he realized that we needed to blown off some steam. He disappeared back into the darkness and everyone else went to their racks, not wanting to press their luck. I found myself on all fours, crawling around and giggling like an idiot. This war hadn't been what I expected, but it had been an experience. It was about to get much worse.

The next day, when a call went up for everyone with humvee driver's license, I bolted up to the front—this had to be good. Squeak told me that we had just received four humvees from a Marine unit that was leaving the country. The humvees were parked in the alley between the buildings. I found the two that were in the best shape and claimed them for my squad, while Moser grumbled.

Golf Machinegun Section thus became Golf CAAT (Combined Anti-Armor Team). "CAAT" usually refers to the humvees in Weapons Company that have TOW missiles and .50 cals., but the term was also used pejoratively to refer to any armed humvees. We would no longer be attached out the line platoons. Instead, we would operate as a section, escorting patrols out in town. I fantasized about using the vehicles at my discretion to ferret out whatever resistance was left in the town, nick-naming my squad "The Instigators." We grabbed some mortarmen and riflemen as drivers, since I was the only machinegunner with a license. Squeak told me that I would still be a squad leader for admin purposes, but in the field I would be a driver, which was fine by me. Reed was traded to the 41s for Keller, who had a license, but also because Squeak didn't trust Reed out in town. I was glad to be rid of him.

Walton, the company clerk, was very happy to be detached from HQ platoon to drive for us. Eternally optimistic, he had a sly sense of humor and the ability to get enjoyment out of almost any situation. White was the complete opposite. After a year in the Old Corps at Guantanamo, where hazing and fuck-fuck games were de rigeur, he joined Golf in February of 2001—not a boot, but not a senior Marine either. He was in sorry shape and quickly got a bad rep, hanging out with Badillo and Dunn and developing a serious drinking problem. Though I had only been in Golf three months longer than him, I still thought of him as a "new guy." While he was technically senior to me by one year, he had picked up corporal about the time I picked up sergeant. With bright red hair, a grinch-like face and a serious hunchback, he was an ungainly sight. Considering what bad shape he was in, his snarky, dismissive attitude was especially galling.

Now that we had a place to stay and some wheels, it was time for a real priority—establishing another Wack Shack. Conveniently enough, there was a large room, half the size of a basketball court, right next to where we parked our humvees. Though we would end up having four Wack Shacks before we finally went home, Wack Shack II was the best because it was the only one that had a locking door.

They opened a kitchen and we started getting tray rats—horrible concoctions which were much worse than MREs. Come to think of it, if it would have been an actual rat on a tray, it would have been better than what they were serving. As I ladled out the slop, a boot named Jones told me he had some news for me. Jones was famous for two things: having been a carny before he enlisted and missing several teeth. While at the TAA, he had developed a bad rep for milking a foot injury. The rumor mill said that he had been bragging that it would keep him from crossing the LOD. After he was given a clean bill of health, he could suddenly walk just fine without his omni-present crutch. After fighting through the battle of The Bridge, he walked around with a cocky swagger, all five-foot-four of him.

"Boy, I wish I was a sergeant; then I'd be going home tomorrow too."

"What are you talking about?"

"You're on the list to go home, along with Sgt. Quinn and Sgt. Williams."

"Where are you getting this information?"

"I saw the list, sergeant."

"You're sure you saw my name? Meyer?"

"Yeah, I'm sure."

"This isn't the type of thing you should joke about."

"I'm not joking, sergeant."

I had to keep the line moving; I'd catch up with him later. I barely knew him, why would he want to fuck with me like that? After I finished serving the "food", I went to find Jones, but he was already gone. I rushed back to our building, my mind racing. Why would I be going? I had heard that they needed one sergeant to go home on advance party to help set things up. Quinn and Williams were leaving because Stop-Loss had been rescinded now that the combat phase was over. Yoder told me that Jones's platoon was stationed in another building since they were the Quick Reaction Force. Yoder said he had heard that if anyone was going home early, it would be Sgt. Hashimoto.

I rushed over to the QRF building, getting very anxious. This city was safe, so it wouldn't be like I was abandoning my comrades, but I knew they'd hold it against me. When I found Sgt. Hashimoto, he told me that I should "never listen to that kid. He's always passing bum scoop." I finally located Jones and I realized something was wrong when he was totally surprised that I wanted to talk to him.

"Tell me more about what you said about me going home."

"Oh yeah—you're going home tomorrow sergeant."

"Where the hell did you hear that?"

"Well…aren't all of the sergeants leaving? I mean, Sgt. Quinn and Sgt. Williams are leaving and I heard Sgt. Hash was going home soon, so I just assumed all of the sergeants were leaving."

"Goddamnit, Jones, use your head, They're not going to send every Marine of one rank home at the same time."

"Oh."

I had to get out of there before I hit the kid. On my way out, he cheerily tried to sell me a Pepsi. Fucker. It took two months before I could see Jones without having my blood pressure spike through the roof.

With so many MREs lying around, people started rat-fucking them for the goodies. While my squad might have had fifty MREs, they were all stripped of the M&Ms, chocolate chip cookies, and shake mixes. Miller was the worst offender in my squad, but everyone did it to some extent, even me. Walton told me that during the combat phase, when MREs were scarce, he caught First Sergeant Young rat-fucking several MREs just to get the rare picante sauce. I considered that a war crime.

MRE boxes were the most popular choice for chairs since when they were on their side they were the perfect height and they had just enough give in them to make them comfortable. A few times, I had to break into someone's card game and take their seat because I needed the Peanut Butter and crackers inside. Once a boxed was opened, it was ruined as furniture and became rat-fucking bait.

The engineers had dumped large mounds of dirt in a slalom on the road that led from the train station to the highway. They were supposed to deter suicide bombers, but the only cars it would keep out would be ones without steering wheels. While driving toward them, Ryan issued a challenge.

"No ball to hit one of those mounds, sergeant," Ryan dared me.

In the grunts, being "no-ballsed" is legally-binding, so I had to do it. I hit the mound at thirty miles per hour, sending my right tires flying into the air, as Levesque held on for dear life. Levesque wasn't done getting fucked with though. When I turned left onto the highway, I pulled the pin that kept the turret in place, and the centrifugal force made Levesque spin completely around.

Though we were from very different backgrounds, Ryan and I were both born scammers, so we bonded on that level. Ryan would always see through my bullshit when I tried to bluff him. He had been told that a building with a blue door was the local whorehouse, so on our way back from a patrol, we took a round-about way back to the base so he could find it. Ryan and I were both married, but I was sure that Levesque's nasty ass would take it for the team. We finally found it, but it was way too exposed; someone would have spotted our hummer parked there and gone to investigate. Damn this politically correct war. I wanted to hear how "Suckee, fuckee, smoke cigarette in the pussy" sounded in Arabic.

A package of sports equipment, which included some boxing gloves, arrived. I've always had a dilettante's interest in boxing, even going so far as to sign up for some open matches in Oki, before they got cancelled because of September 11th. I grabbed two pairs of gloves and asked my buddy Showers if he wanted to play around with them. As we walked the length of the building, people saw our gloves and started to follow us. By the time we got outside, we had attracted a crowd of twenty people. Showers and I looked at each other and shook our heads; with a crowd like this, we couldn't puss out and just tap each other. Before I knew it, Sgt. Hashimoto had dubbed himself the ref and Miozza, an amateur boxer, started giving me some pointers.

I leavened my lack of experience with aggression, throwing several wild punches at Showers. Showers let me tire myself out and then sent a crushing right into my head. Showers had a bad rep since he couldn't hike and didn't work out, but he had what we called "retard strength." It felt like someone had hit me with a bag of softballs. My head was knocked down below my waist and every time I lifted it, he just knocked it right back down. After five solid hits, I got smart enough to step back before standing up. I got a look at Showers, cursed and launched myself at him…and caught five more to the head. I was losing, but I could salvage some respect from the crowd by sticking it out, just like in the strip bar in Guam. When Showers hit me in the eye though, my entire field of vision jumped. I thought he had torn my cornea, so I raised my hands to call "time."

Miozza stepped over to check me out and Sgt. Hash called the match.

"You'll be OK. Good job, sergeant," Miozza said.

"You don't have to say that just because I'm a sergeant. I know I got my ass kicked."

"No, you got a few good shots in."

All I remembered was getting one glancing blow against Shower's stomach while I was hunched over. Showers looked like he felt bad for beating my ass.

"Good job, Showers. You really rung my bell."

"You got mad for real. After I backed up, you looked up at me and said, 'Motherfucker!' I was like, 'Oh shit, I better put this guy down quick.'"

I laughed, barely remembered cursing at him.

I had a serious black eye, which others made a big deal about, but I laughed it off. Somehow, getting hit made me feel better about being stuck in that shithole. The next day, when I blew my nose, my whole cheek and eye socket blew up like a balloon. I thought I had a cracked cheekbone that was letting air out of my sinuses, so I went to the BAS. When I got inside, I almost went into shock—the BAS had AC! The large room was divided between the Navy Seabees and the corpsmen, with absolutely every square inch accounted for. All eyes were on me as everyone checked to make sure that I wasn't just coming in to hang out in the cool air. With all the people who lived in there, the AC barely counter-acted their body heat; they couldn't handle any extra bodies. It pissed me off that these people were giving me the evil eye, when they lived in relative luxury.

The corpsmen did their usual excellent job. Not only were they knowledgeable and professional, but they also acted like normal human beings, with none of the pettiness that occurred among grunts. They had that among each other, I would find out later, but they were always great with me.

Our interpreter during the combat phase had separated from us in Samarra, going farther north to reunite with the family he hadn't seen in fifteen years. In Samawah, we received two new interpreters—one Shiite and one Sunni—who would go on patrols with us. They were quite a pair, one bald and fat, the other tall and thin, both in their late thirties, polite and intellectual. I wondered how they had survived in this bully-dominated culture. I was told to put them in my hummer and take them to Battalion, where we would link up with some other vehicles. While we waited in the hummer in front of battalion, the interpreters sold Ryan and Lopez little lamps and mirrors they brought along. One of the interpreters spied a porno mag peeking out of Levesque's pack in the back of the hummer. They started flipping through it like little kids, holding it low on their laps so that no one could see them. After a few minutes, they put the porn back. I grabbed a book and went to sit against the wall of Battalion HQ and read in the shade.

Twenty minutes later, I looked up to see Gunny Brouillet chewing Ryan and Lopez out. I went up and asked what was wrong and he dismissed them, telling them there would be hell to pay. He told me that a major "from division" walked by the humvee and saw the interpreters, who had taken the porn out again after I left, flipping through the mag. The major yanked the porn out of their hands like they were little kids; then told Ryan and Lopez to follow to him inside. Not only did he start reading them the riot act, but he even yelled at them for leaving their vehicle unattended with the interpreters inside after he ordered them out of it.

Gunny wasn't a screamer by nature, but I could tell he was going to make a big deal out of this. The patrol got cancelled and we went back to the company area.

Ryan and Lopez got called up to speak with Gunny and they came back looking grey. They were told that they would most likely both be busted down for their infraction. In the interim, they would pull every shit detail from then on. Ryan had a wife and Lopez had a kid, so their families would both be hurt financially if they got busted down. Though they both had rough edges, they always got the job done. It was alright for them to see the insides of a real woman blown across a black tar road, but it wasn't acceptable for them to see a picture of the outside of a woman in a damn magazine? Ryan and Lopez were like family and they were getting fucked for political correctness and to protect staff NCO and officer careers.

I told Ryan and Lopez that I was going to go to Gunny and tell him that whatever he was going to do to them, he needed to do to me as well. Ryan asked me not to do it, since I had a family to support, but I wouldn't be worth my stripes if I just sat there and did nothing. I told Gunny Brouillet that I knew that Ryan and Lopez had the porn and I thought it was ridiculous that they were being crucified over this; I wanted to share their fate, whatever it was. Gunny had a pretty good poker-face, but it seemed to crack a little. He nodded dully and said to expect more news.

The next time Ryan and Lopez were spoken to, being demoted was no longer mentioned. I didn't know if it was because I had gone out on a limb for them or if the higher-ups had calmed down enough to realize they were being too harsh. Nevertheless, Ryan and Lopez still ended up with every shit detail for the next several days. The next day, I noticed my name wasn't on the patrol schedule. With an embarrassed look, Squeak told me that I had been posted as a driver. I asked him if I still was a squad leader and got a vague "yes." He told me not to worry; I would get my job back soon.

For the next four days, all I did was sit around and read. If this was punishment, give me a court-martial. It looked like the party was over though, when I was told that I would be sent to Building Guard. Though there was already a camp guard, Golf was the only company that also had a *building* guard. Gunny Brouillet's only job was to oversee the building guard, so he inspected the Marines like they were West Point cadets before they went on their four-hour shifts in the blinding sun with all of their war gear on. The boots' morale dropped into the basement. They were being over-worked in a redundant and worthless post and, since every day at least one of them fell asleep on duty in the oppressive heat, all of them were constantly getting fucked with. The mortar and 51 NCOs had it much easier; all they had to do was stand-by in the building and walk around and check the posts once a shift. Monty really got on my nerves by acting like a martinet with the boots. He was lucky that he had some weight on his collar because all of the boots were getting sick of him. The bigger ones, like Doty and Jolly, looked like they wanted to squeeze him into a ball and roll him down a hill.

Coming back from Club Chaos one night, I saw that the whole section was running around like ants from a kicked-over anthill. We were hustled outside into formation and Squeak appeared before us, seething. He started chewing us out, assuming that we all knew what he was talking about, which we did not. We were finally able to glean that Cortez had ratted out Levesque for supposedly taking his unattended rifle and putting it in the dumpster that we used to burn garbage. Squeak was in career-saving mode and doing his level best to launch as many accusations at us as he could, even after we proved that Cortez' rifle was not in the burn pile. Levesque had put it behind the drawing that I did of a 240 to teach Cortez a lesson since he was continually walking away from his rifle.

To put us in our place, Squeak ordered us up against the wall to do the "Electric Chair," a thrash exercise from Boot Camp that is murder on the thighs if you do it correctly. It was dark enough that most of us could just cheese-dick it, but that wasn't the point—you weren't supposed to treat Fleet Marines like that and you certainly weren't supposed to treat combat vets like that. I debated whether I should tell Squeak what he was doing was unlawful, but I decided to just let it go. As I told Krout, if he could get through The Bridge, he could get through this.

Gunny Brouillet came out to investigate, so Squeak called us back into formation. Roy complained that we were being hazed and Elias seconded that emotion. Squeak demanded to know who had taken Cortez' rifle and Ross took the hit, just to save the rest of us. Squeak was on a tirade though, so he kept going, yelling at us for not knowing where Miller was. He had us run around the camp like recruits, promising to fuck with us all night if we didn't find him. As I rounded a corner, SSgt. D casually asked me what all the yelling about; he was surprised to find out that it was Squeak who was doing the yelling. Squeak had no friends of his own rank and he spent all his time hanging out near our vehicles, chatting with White. Just like his predecessor, Chuck, whenever he felt that we were gaffing him off, he would threaten us to stop "being cool" with us. A day later, he would be lonely again since none of the other staff NCOs wanted to hang with him and he'd be back chatting with us by the Hummers.

After we found Miller, Squeak started marching us around, which doesn't sound that bad until you stop to realize that it was the middle of the night, we had been patrolling all day and that even though we were combat vets, we were being treated like recruits. Luckily, Ross and I were scheduled for a patrol at that time and we made sure that it lasted as long as possible. Returning two hours later, we were shocked to see that they were still being screwed with. Luckily, by the time that we parked the car, Squeak finally let them hit the rack.

My driver's license saved my hash though and I was back on CAAT the next day. After returning from a patrol, Squeak called Ross and I over and tried to scare us. He had started walking around with his little chest puffed out and his face screwed up in a poor attempt to look tough. I cracked Miller up by saying that, when we got back to Cali, I was going to make him a t-shirt that said, "It ain't easy being the toughest man in the world." Squeak asked us what we did on our patrol earlier that morning, clearly intimating that we had done something wrong. Though we had only been patrolling for two weeks, it had already gotten so monotonous that I could barely remember anything from the patrol I just finished, let alone the one I did that morning. We assured Squeak that nothing untoward had occurred. He have us a "tough" squint and then left to get more information.

Squeak had confused the patrol Ross and I had pulled earlier with the one that White and Mohler had been on. Mohler and DeWitt, the golden-boy boot from Third, had been caught doing drugs while on patrol out in town. Mohler was a known and enthusiastic druggie, so I wasn't surprised, but I was disappointed that a great fighter and leader like Mohler would put himself on the line for a temporary high. Mohler didn't just do drugs, he *loved* drugs and he could wax rhapsodic about his drug adventures for hours. I had never done a drug in my life, but I found that my best buddies were all big potheads before they got in the Corps. I was surprised that DeWitt would risk his bright future, considering that he was already being treated like a senior Marine and an NCO by Kennel. I had forgotten about how, when we were at the fort, he asked to have my Iraqi gas mask to use as a bong when he got home.

I was told to go to Battalion HQ to guard the druggies before they got interrogated. Mohler looked calm; he had a brother who had done time for drugs, so he knew how the system worked, but DeWitt was a mess. I was surprised to see White and Ross from Third waiting to be interrogated, since they didn't seem like druggies. Mohler had gotten some drugs from a local and smoked it with

DeWitt in the back of the humvee. White was the driver and when he saw what they were doing, he turned them in. Ross corroborated White's story. I could care less what happened to DeWitt (though I had to admit it was nice to see an "uppity" boot catch some hell), but I had known the other three for years. Some officers gave me dirty looks for chatting amiably with Mohler and one pulled me aside to tell me not to talk to him. Yeah, he was my friend, and yeah, I did think he was guilty, but I wasn't going to turn on him like a cur dog. Mohler had been a good friend through thick and thin and he was one of the heroes of The Bridge. I felt that he should be judged for his conduct throughout his enlistment, not just one incident.

Mohler wisely kept his mouth shut, but DeWitt spilled his guts. Not only did he rat Mohler out, but he named ten *other* Marines from Golf that had supposedly done drugs as well. The next day, all of the suspected druggies were called up to the front of our building and made to turn in their weapons and optics. They were taken to Battalion, where they would stay from then on. Military justice is Napoleonic, so they were assumed guilty and would be treated as such. Mohler, Ryan and Levesque were no surprise, but I was shocked that golden boys like Reyna and Monroe were among the accused.

We then entered the worst part of my entire enlistment—an intense regime of micro-management and tension between the higher-ups and the grunts. It built until I openly wished for the deaths of some of my leaders. The first issue was over our uniforms and it tore away the last bits of loyalty and respect we had for Squeak. The Marine Corps has always taken pride in its appearance, using it as a bell-weather of their superiority over the other services. Whereas the Army would travel around town in flaks and t-shirts, we weren't even allowed to roll up our sleeves in the 120+ degree heat. An edict came down from First Sergeant Young—that since some people were getting "nasty," we had to wear our long-sleeve blouses from five in the morning until lights out, even inside the non-air-conditioned building. That killed our last bit of morale. First Sergeant Young never left the camp and the only time he left the building was to go to meetings in the air-conditioned battalion HQ. I can't think of a better way to ensure mutiny than to tell men who patrol sewage-flooded streets in full gear during the summer in the fucking Middle East that they can't even take their sweat and salt-drenched cammie shirts off when they get back from patrol.

We went along with this new rule for a day, assuming it was just a fit of pique and would soon be rescinded. When the order remained, we all got openly belligerent. Since we were on a twenty-four hour schedule, patrolling day and night, we slept whenever we could. I thought that common sense would leaven the order, but Squeak's career was obviously being threatened, so he started waking people who had patrolled all night to tell them to put their blouses back on. Moser looked down at his sweat-soaked rack and squinted at Squeak like he wanted to kill him. Squeak gave one of his "scary" looks and threatened to fuck with the entire section until he complied.

When it came to NCO belligerence, Miller and I were the champs. Squeak openly hated us and we returned the favor. The only time you were allowed to be in t-shirt and shorts was when you PT'ed, so Miller and I simply PT'ed all day long. My "work-out" schedule consisted of me doing a set of push-ups or crunches once every ten minutes. Squeak pissed and moaned, but he didn't have a way to gig us since we had many witnesses that we were PTing. Squeak closed the loophole by saying that we could only PT from 6:00-8:00AM. To get my mind off of my shitty life, I had been running around the base in the morning and had gotten my one-mile run down near six minutes again, but the bullshit in the company got me down and I quit running.

Though the food was horrible, it was the only thing to look forward to, but for some reason, the staff NCOs decided to ruin that as well. You could only get your food at once specific time during each meal, even though there was usually no line. Much worse was that they made you march to chow by platoon, which we hadn't done since boot camp. It was humiliating to be an adult, a sergeant and a combat vet and not being given the trust to walk the two blocks to the chow hall on my own. I would often miss the established chow times since I was on patrol and would then have to run a gauntlet of staff NCOs who interrogated me about why I wasn't going at the designated times.

We got another dump of new joins and I got a new machinegunner. Arellano was a half-white, half-Mexican kid from who-knows-where. The reason I never found out where he was from was because I never had any reason to talk to him. From the time he got to Golf until the day I left, he was eerily perfect. I used to joke that I imagined he went to Tijuana and killed whores on the weekends, because no one could be as perfect as he seemed. It was strange to have a kid who was straight out of SOI get to The Fleet and do almost everything right. I can only remember him fucking up two times and one was in a grey area. He had the worst case of helmet burn I ever saw. Wearing helmets as much as we did caused some people to get little bald spots on the sides of their heads. Usually their hair would grow back after a couple of days, but Arellano had a quarter-sized bald spot on each side of his head. It looked like antennae might sprout from them at any moment.

While I was at the Battalion HQ, a Humvee pulled up and five female soldiers got out with their luggage—not packs, civilian luggage. They worked for the Civil Affairs unit, which sounded like Public Affairs, so I thought they were just there to make everything nice for the journalists, but the more I found out about Civil Affairs, the more impressed I was with them. Grunts turn a country into a battlefield and Civil Affairs turns it back into a country. As Colin Powell put it, when you invade a country—no matter what the reason—you assume steward-ship for it. Everything that was wrong with the country before you invaded it is now your fault. Before the war, we assumed that once the combat phase was over we would be able to fly in enough engineers, architects, and construction workers to transform their benighted country; then they would love us. It didn't quite work out that way, but not for lack of trying. The Iraqis' amazing lack of initia-tive and inability to stand up to bullies in their ranks continually flummoxed any progress. One of the Civil Affairs soldiers told me why the city still had electricity problems three months after we got there. When Saddam's troops abandoned their post, the locals looted everything they could find, even if they didn't know what it was. Valuable pieces of the town's generators were stolen to be sold as scrap metal. Our Civil Affairs soldiers would order replacement parts from Den-mark and when they arrived weeks later, they would go out with some Seabees and make sure the part was installed. A few nights later, a bully from the neigh-borhood would walk right past the night watchman and steal the crucial new part just to scrape the brass off of it. Then the locals would blame us for not having a 24-hour guard on the power station, even though they knew, but refused to iden-tify, who stole the part. This process would repeat itself endlessly.

We shared the camp with several different units: Army National Guard MPs, Naval Reserve SeaBees, Army Reserve Civil Affairs as well as a Psy-Ops detach-ment. The MPs, who lived in the building next to ours, pulled the same basic mission as us; yet it was like we were on completely different planets. There was no interaction between our groups; no friendships, no fights. Though we had no interaction, we still had some influence on them. When we started doing martial arts training, they did so as well, to comic effect. One of their staff NCOs would demonstrate a move and the few soldiers who showed up for the optional training (imagine that) just did their own riffs on the demonstrated move. If the instruc-tor demonstrated a move-block-strike combo, the first soldier would do a block and kick, the second would do a punch and kick and the third would do three quick punches, a kick and finish off with a little spin.

While heading to chow, we saw an Army staff NCO standing over three pros-trate soldiers. While thrashing is common in the Corps, soldiers stop doing it after boot camp. The soldiers looked confused, like they were expecting the staff NCO to say he was kidding at any moment.

I cannot say enough great things about the Seabees, but I'll try. Their job was to repair the infrastructure of the town, but they didn't stop there. They turned our shithole train station into a liveable environment. They built shitters, a shower tent, and picnic tables for the chow hall, but their piece di resistance was "Club Chaos," which was the only place where they had air-conditioning for all. It had a pool table, a TV with a DVD and another with a Playstation 2. Every night, one of the SeaBees would show two scheduled movies. I got a bad rep for always being there when I wasn't on patrol, but it was better than sweating in long-sleeves in our building and getting yelled at because one of my boot laces had come undone.

Our camp was like a little town and the un-official mayor was The Barber. The Seabees had turned a room that used to hold a generator into a barber shop and he would work there everyday, giving haircuts for free. This situation was quite unique because he and his unit were in no way beholden to do so; they did it simply as a service to the Marines. The Barber was almost fifty, lean and bald with a great hook-nose; he seemed like a character out of a movie to me. No matter how hot or miserable it was, he could always be found inside, greeting everyone as if they were long-time friends. His barber shop was the only place of normalcy in the whole camp. He took great pride in the shop, making sure it was a pleasant place to be by decorating it with mail from home and mentions in the papers back in Massachusetts, where the Seabee unit was from. He was so social and disarming that people would instantly confide in him as if he were their favorite uncle; he could get anyone to open up. One wall was filled with Maxim centerfolds; while perusing the pictures, he asked me which girl I liked the most. I scanned past the bimbos to a Jewish-looking girl with thick, wavy hair and a sweet smile which revealed some nice, but large teeth.

"Good choice, she looks like a nice girl. Wouldn't want to put my corn cob between those chompers though."

Towards the end of our stay, one of the Army National Guard officers set up a massage table inside the barber shop, offering free massages to anyone. Surprisingly, she had almost no takers. She wasn't a knock-out, but that wasn't the real reason people avoided her. It would be too awkward, too intense and too personal. We had gone without physical contact for seven months; to get a little bit of it in that inhuman environment would be too much, too painful. If she massaged my shoulders for two minutes, I'd probably bust a nut and propose marriage.

The showers, another gift from our beloved SeaBees, were much-appreciated, but it was tricky finding the right time to go. The water was stored in a large, plastic sphere and between 9:00AM and midnight, it was too hot to endure. I usually took my shower as soon as I woke up, when the shower tents were empty and the water was comfortably cool.

People in the showers got much too comfortable around each other. About half of the Marines went to the showers every day in little groups. These "shower buddies" seemed to enjoy each other's company a little too much. Knowing that grunts had declared all of Iraq a Free-Pissing Zone, I didn't want to be within splattering range of anyone.

The floors were treated plywood and were quite slippery. Every other day, someone would slip and fall, which was both horrifying and hilarious. They would always fall like cartoon characters; their feet shooting out from under them so quickly that, for a split-second, they would seem to be levitating horizontally above the floor, before finally landing with a resounding "thud".

Women were allotted three separate hours a day in which to shower. Being that there were only twelve women and more than six hundred men, that ratio seemed a little skewed. I had considered "accidentally" staying in the showers when it went from the men's to the women's time, but I decided that was better as a jerk-off fantasy than as an actual plan.

Several times, staff NCOs would life someone in the showers for breaking the rules, such as shaving or wasting water. I wondered how sad my life would have to become before I would even consider lifing a naked man. Even if I burst into flames, that still would not be a good enough excuse to look at me in the showers, as far as I was concerned.

While sitting in my humvee, waiting to go out on another patrol, Ross and I were surprised to see Tardif walk by. Everyone assumed he was either in Cali or Germany, since we hadn't heard from him in three weeks. When we asked how he got back, he gave us the vaguest answer possible, just saying that he wanted to be with his boys. Since he came back to Golf, I assumed he had just been in a field hospital in one of the nearby cities. It took two months for anyone but his closest friends to find out what really happened.

Tardif had taken shrapnel in his calf and kept fighting until he passed out from loss of blood. He eventually ended up in Germany, where he was operated on and rehabilitated. After about two weeks, he was told that he was being sent to Cali to convalesce, but he told the doctors that he wanted to go back to his squad. He had to write a formal request to the officer-in-charge of the hospital to receive permission to return to Golf. They told him he could go, but he would have to find his own way to Samawah, a city he had never been to. Before he left, he called and told his fiancee that he had been ordered to return to Golf, so she wouldn't be mad at him. Tardif hitched a ride to the nearest air force base and waited for the next plane to Kuwait. In Kuwait, he found a flight into Iraq after "commandeering" some gear from a boot, since all he had were the clothes he was wearing. He then hitched rides from camp-to-camp across Iraq until he got to Samawah. I was in awe of this man who showed selflessness that would be hard to believe in a comic book, let alone in real life. His maturity and modesty was in stark contrast to some of the boots in First who had put up a sign that read, "What side of The Bridge were you on?" before they were ordered to take it down.

Returning from a patrol just after dusk, I saw that the whole company was abuzz, getting ready to conduct a raid. Though we hadn't fired a shot in anger in more than a month, it sounded like there might be some action on this op. I asked Squeak what my role would be and he told me that the roster had been made while I was out, so I wasn't on it. First I miss out on most of the action at The Bridge and now I was going to miss the only chance for some combat in this sleepy town. I tried umpteen ways to get on the roster, but he refused, needing to concentrate on preparing the vehicles. I went into the building and sulked as the company left.

The company returned a few hours later with as much ammo as they left with; the mission having been predicated on faulty intel. Perhaps to vent, Squeak called me over and started berating me for being "unprofessional" by trying to jump in on the mission. I couldn't believe I was getting yelled at for trying to go on a mission, but he did have some valid points. I had been a horrible gun-hog during the combat phase and my rep had suffered accordingly.

"I'm starting to wonder if you really want to be a squad leader, Sgt. Meyer."

"If it's for a real mission, I do, but if it's for the baby-sitting duties we pull around here, I'd rather not, honestly."

Just as I couldn't believe Squeak would be mad that I wanted to go on a mission, he couldn't believe that I would openly admit to not wanting my leadership position. It was so shocking that he abruptly ended the harangue, the fun of yelling at me having diminished.

Though I would get defensive and self-righteous whenever Squeak posted me from a job, I would later reflect on my short-comings. I could have been in better shape and maintained my MOS knowledge if I had applied myself during my FAP, instead of feeling sorry for myself. I had been immature by neglecting my duties as squad leader to hog Rager's gun. To my credit, I was the first one to tackle the Reed issue and I had gotten what little I could out of Carpenter's use-less ass.

Squeak could find fault with anyone, even flawless Marines like Moser and Walton. Like Sprincin, Squeak would turn on anyone without even hearing their side of the story, if it would protect his precious career. Walton smashed the front of his humvee when he hit a divider on the highway and Squeak immediately posted him and started talking shit about him. Not once did he stop to consider that Walton, as well as the other drivers, were so over-worked that they were fatigued past the point of being able to drive safely. Several times, the other driv-ers and I had considered requesting mast to get the higher-ups to let people with-out humvee driver's licenses drive. Each one of us was running on empty and it was only a matter of time before someone wrecked their humvee. Even in a sim-ple roll-over, the gunner in the exposed turret would be crushed and killed. Regardless, since there were so few drivers, even when Squeak posted Walton or Picas or me, he ended up reinstating us a day or two later. I once got posted as driver and was put back on the schedule the same day.

I did get in on the next raid though. In my excitement, I slapped on some camo paint, much to the amusement of smart-asses like White. We were raiding the fort that we had stayed at in town where, supposedly, some locals were run-ning guns. We rolled up with our lights off and I executed a cool "Dukes of Haz-zard" skid. My humvee escorted the first sergeant, so once again, I was on the periphery. I watched through my NVGs as the rifle squads flowed into the fort like ghosts. It was an awesome sight, but the raid was a total bust. There were no guns and our informants turned out to be a spiteful rival family that wanted the fort for themselves, so they concocted a story about the family that was living there.

Though Reed wasn't in CAAT, I was still his squad leader and therefore responsible for him. While chilling out in Ross' train car, he asked me about Reed.

"So how's Reed's dumb ass been acting lately?"

"You know what? He hasn't been that bad. I think he's on his best behavior, trying to get his job back."

"Don't tell me you're actually thinking of letting him become a team leader again?"

"Well, y'know, he does have some good qualities. He's motivated and he knows his knowledge."

"Oh, fucking Christ, Meyer. You always do this. He acts like a complete embarrassment and endangers your team in combat; then he acts 'normal' for a few days and you want to forgive him."

"No, dude. I think he's changed. He almost reminds me of how he was back in Oki, when he was, y'know, almost normal."

"Meyer, I don't know if you've noticed this, but Reed is not 'normal'—he's a fucking nut. He's going to stab you in the back and embarrass you for trusting him, like he's done to all of us dozens of times."

"Everybody deserves a second chance."

"Yeah, exactly. They deserve *one* second chance. Which he has gotten—several times."

"Y'know, Miller's been saying the same thing. He reminded me of, like, four other times I've said Reed's changed and he always ending up making me regret it."

"Well, far be it from me to ever agree with Miller, but he's right. Trust me, man. It's only a matter of time.

"Only a matter of time" turned out to be the next day. What Reed did made me cut ties with him forever and finally realize that he would never change. On the face of it, what he did was just kind of silly and sad, but when you look at the fact that he was a corporal in the infantry during a war—it's pathetic and unforgivable. The staff and officers were fucking with us twenty-four hours a day and morale was in the toilet. Anything that helped get your mind off the heat and misery was a god-send. Lopez had received a soccer ball in the mail, which everybody loved. He was still on Gunny's shit-list, so he was pulling constant work details like burning the shitters. While playing cards, he was bitching about all of the shit details he had to pull and Reed went off on him. I don't know why Reed thought he had any authority, since he was still an assistant ammo man serving under a PFC. Reed yelled at Lopez for being a whiner and Lopez started yelling back. Reed took his childishness to new depth by grabbing Lopez' soccer ball and threatening to pop it with his Ka-Bar. When Lopez refused to apologize, Reed popped the soccer ball.

During the entire episode, I had been hanging out with Ross in his train car. Moser came over, looking weary.

"Hey Meyer, just wanted you to know that your boy's acting up again."

"That isn't exactly news, Moser. I'll deal with it later, whatever it is."

Moser shrugged and left. By this time, I was so exhausted by all of Reed's dramas that there was very little that would surprise me. I assumed he was just getting into another argument.

Lopez told Reed to step outside and Reed demurred, saying that he wanted "to take the high road." Miller told Lopez to go outside and cool out; that Reed wasn't worth getting busted down for. Moser was disgusted by Reed, so he put his mind into action. Seeing that Reed wouldn't go out and face Lopez like a man, Moser tricked Reed into going outside by telling him that Squeak was out there and wanted to see him. Reed went outside and was surprised to see Lopez waiting for him. Lopez challenged Reed again, but Reed—the Greatest Wrestler in the History of Michigan—refused to fight, knowing that none of us would jump in to help him, no matter how badly Lopez beat him. Lopez begged Reed to hit him, while Reed quaked in his boots. Moser and Ross finally told Lopez that he had won; if Reed was too chicken to fight, then he had the moral victory. Lopez walked away, still fuming.

Just as Lopez left, Squeak appeared and Reed tried to salvage some pride. Squeak was the only person that Reed was bigger than, so when Squeak tried to chastise Reed for popping the soccer ball, Reed started to give him attitude. I let Reed go, hoping he would let out enough rope to hang himself. I was ecstatic when Squeak told Reed that, as soon as we got back to Cali, he would be dealt with. No one cared when Reed was making our lives miserable, but when he pissed off a lifer, the wheels would finally start turning.

A few days later, the call went up for volunteers to detach from the company to go work in Kuwait. They would live at one of the hooked-up bases that had phones, AC and fast food and their job would be to pack up gear for departing units. The down side was that they would be stuck there until the last Marine unit left, which would be September or later. At the time, we were still under the assumption that we would be home before the Fourth of July, so most people thought it was a bad deal. The only ones who liked it were the boots on Building Guard who were constantly being harassed. When Reed was chosen to go, we couldn't have been happier.

Mohler and the other suspects were really getting fucked with—working sixteen-hour days and pulling the worst duties imaginable. When it was discovered that some of the mechanics had shit on some rocks next to their building, Mohler and company had to go pick it up with trash bags over their hands. At night though, they would get a few hours off and we would run into them at Club Chaos and exchange rumors about when we were going home. Mohler was watching TV by himself when Reed silently walked up, sat down right next to him and put his arm around his shoulders. I sat a few rows back, wishing I had a camera to record this weird scene for posterity. After ten minutes of awkward silence, Reed stood up and tried to have some sort of emotional farewell before he left for Kuwait, to which Mohler replied, "OK, dude."

Golf was attracting notice, both good and bad. On one hand, we were the druggies, but we were also acknowledged as having seen the most action in the battalion. My good friend Sherman, from Weapons Company, told me that we were referred to as "The Cowboys", for our supposed shoot-first-ask-questions-later attitude. Tardif and Martinez were both getting Bronze Stars and Martinez was getting a combat promotion to sergeant. I thought that combat promotions went out of style shortly after the Battle of the Bulge, but it was nice to see one go to someone who deserved it as much as him. Martinez and Tardif were flown to Kuwait City, where they would receive their awards in front of the press. Jealousy sprung up in a few hearts, which was ugly to see. There's nothing more disgusting than hearing a person whine about how they deserved a medal for just doing their job. Not only did Tardif and Martinez both go above and beyond the call of duty, but they remained humble as well. You couldn't pay Martinez to talk about what happened. His story was incredible. After his squad leader, Tardif, was taken out of the fight, Martinez got pissed. When his rifle jammed, he picked up an Iraqi RPG and taught himself how to use it. After several mis-fires, he finally figured out how to get it to work and he shot it at a building holding five enemy fighters. He then ran up, got his rifle working again and cleared the room by himself, finishing off the survivors. Martinez and Tardif returned a few days later, telling amazing tales of going on libbo in civvies in Kuwait City and sleeping in a four-star hotel. Then they went back to work like everyone else, without holding their medals over other people's heads like lesser Marines would have done. Not only were they selflessly brave and humble, but they made people want to be better than what they were—a trait of a true hero.

The rumor mill was going strong and I was the worst offender. We had been told that the Dutch would take over from us, then the British, then the Polish who, it was pointed out, hadn't deployed their military since the Crusades. We finally saw something solid when a small group of Dutch officers came and stayed with us for a week, seeing how we were running things. It was late-May and the idea that this advance command group could get an entire battalion here to replace us by the middle of June was looking more and more unlikely.

I drove in the convoy that escorted them to Tallil Air Base, so they could fly home and report their findings. This was a primo assignment since Tallil was run by the Air Force and it had a huge PX and a phone center. I tried to make small talk with the Dutch officers and a distinct officious and condescending air was all

I got in return. Oh well, fuck 'em, at least I would get some potato chips outs of this run.

We drove them to the flight line at Tallil, feeling very superior to all the Air Force guys who would avoid eye contact when they saw that we were Marines. After beating around the bush, I finally asked the head Dutch officer when he thought they would be back to replace us. He looked at me coldly and said, "I am not here to bring you hope." Fucking Dutch bastard; Dr. Evil was right. If I knew anything about Dutch history, I would have been able to come up with some kind of cutting retort.

The phone center had a several-hour wait, but we were told that there was a comm unit that had a phone that they sometimes let people use. The comm unit was on the edge of base, in an expanse of powdery sand. They were more than cool and said we could use their phones. One female airmen was apparently so flustered with being able to speak to Marines that she walked straight into barb-wire, fell down and got entangled in it. As we helped her up, I wondered what hurt the most, the barb-wire or her pride. Not wanting to push our luck, we agreed to limit our calls to five minutes. Miller walked off and came back when it was his turn. He talked much longer than anyone else and seriously cut into Arellano's time. Only afterward did find out that he had already gotten to use another phone for twenty minutes while he was waiting for his turn with the phone. It was a really shitty and selfish thing to do and it pissed everyone off.

The PX was housed in this old Iraqi air base's basketball court. They had to regulate access, so they made us sit in the bleachers, letting us in two at a time. The Air Force personnel were generally doughy and older-looking and they seemed to give us a wide berth. There were some Korean soldiers with some sweet plastic rifles walking around in their shorts. One airman griped that the Koreans had more holidays than work days. Every time they needed them to help out, the Koreans would claim that it was some religious or national holiday.

When I got in, I promptly lost my mind, grabbing everything I saw. There was some stuff that was just weird, like a cane with a sword in it. We couldn't even bring Iraqi bayonets home, so who would buy that? I ended up with more than a hundred dollars worth of soda, chips and candy.

While my boys cycled through the PX, I spied a barber shop in a trailer next to the PX. I would have payed good money just to sit in that intense AC, but I needed a haircut as well. Like in Japan, these Indian contract workers made a simple haircut into a major Hollywood production. I don't know what the deal is with other cultures, but they all seem to think that slapping the scalp promotes hair growth, but I got my head slapped in AC, so it was all good.

As we left the huge base, there were vendors every ten feet selling Iraqi bayonets, sodas, and kefis. A kid with a huge brass sword straight out of "The Arabian Knights" caught our eye.

"How much?" Miller asked.

"For you—twenty."

The price was great and the sword was sweet, but we were under express orders not to buy anything from the locals, not even sodas.

"Should I get it?" Miller asked me.

"How are you going to get it home?"

"Maybe I could mail it the next time we come here. They got a real post office."

"I think they check all of the boxes...It is sweet though."

"Fuck yeah, I'd put it over my fireplace."

"Motherfucker, you don't have a fireplace."

"When I get one."

"I'm not going to rat you out, but if you get caught, it's on you."

"That's fine. It's only twenty bucks. If I can't find a way to get it home, I'll just bury it somewhere."

The Tallil run was Miller's first patrol in a while, since he had been off the patrol schedule for two weeks because of a lagging sickness. He had gotten used to chilling out all day, so when he was told that he had to go on a patrol during the hottest part of the day, he slammed his knife into a wooden table out of anger. Unfortunately, his hand slipped past the hilt and slid down the blade. Not thinking much of it, Miller bandaged it and went about his business.

Over the next few days though, it became clear that his injury was more than a simple cut. The Battalion Medical Officer said that it was bad enough to have him seen by the Division hand specialist. When the specialist saw Miller a few days later, I thought he'd just get another few weeks of light-duty. Miller returned a half-hour later and started packing his gear. I asked him what was up and he told me that he was going home. I laughed and asked what the doctor had really said, but it was the truth. The tendon in his forefinger had almost been severed and he had to go have surgery in Germany.

I was of two minds about Miller leaving. On one hand, he had been a friend for years and had served me excellently throughout the combat phase. Like me, he had a bad rep, but he loved the machinegun. Once the combat phase was over though, he became a real pill, as my mom would say. Every damn morning, he was the last person to get out of the rack, even though all of the higher-ups had to walk past his cot to get to the shaving table. I caught so much hell for him it wasn't even funny. I would have to tell him to shave three times every morning and when he finally did it, he would be the only person to shave indoors. Petty stuff, but enough of a constant irritant that it wore on our friendship.

The next morning, Miller realized that there was no way he could get that huge sword through customs, so went to toss it in the dumpster. Gunny Brouillet caught him and he brought it up to First Sergeant Young, who told Miller that he would be busted down for the sword as soon as we got back to Cali.

While patrolling in town, we got word of a running firefight between two tribes along the highway. Finally, there might be some action in this sleepy town. People would shoot into the air to celebrate weddings and births on an almost daily basis, since nearly every household had an AK-47. A half-remembered insult from a wedding party fifteen years ago was all it took to get someone riled up enough to walk down the block and shoot a guy in the chest.

As soon as we got within a half-mile of the two groups, the BC ordered us to pull to the side of the road. We were told that since this was a tribal matter, we would stay out of it while they called the Iraqi police to handle it. After a few minutes, the fighters realized that we weren't going to stop them, so they continued fighting as they moved out of sight. If I didn't hate the BC already, that cemented it. The BC was constantly volunteering us to stay longer, but he squelched almost every chance for us to see combat.

As I stepped out of the driver's seat, I looked up and saw Arellano standing stock-still in the turret, eyes locked on the target zone, his hands gripping the handles of the Mark 19 so tightly that his knuckles were white. I laughed when I realized that this was his first sight of people shooting at each other. It was a big deal to him, but it was nothing to us.

It was widely rumored that we were still in Iraq only because the BC continually volunteered us to stay. We heard from Marines that worked at Division that we were originally scheduled to leave the country in May, but another unit went home in our place. This was deemed unforgivable and I was livid at him for his supposed selfishness. This was before the insurgency brewed up in late summer, so there was no action anywhere. We were wasting our lives out there, just so he could pick up full-bird colonel. In the heat of that environment and under the pressure from the staff NCOs, our hatred grew to unprecedented levels.

When Gen. Mattis had a meeting with all of the battalion commanders that were still in Iraq; a rumor spread that filled my warped heart with glee. Supposedly, our BC had interrupted the general, who went off on him. In the Army, ranks are sometimes referred to pejoratively—a Sergeant, Staff Sergeant and Sergeant First Class will all be called "sergeant". That is never the case in the

Marines—a lance corporal is never called a corporal; a staff sergeant is never called a sergeant. We were told that the BC referred to himself as a colonel when he volunteered us to stay for the third time. Gen. Mattis reportedly barked at him, "First of all, *lieutenant* colonel, I am a general and I will not be interrupted. I have a plan for 2/5 and it does not involve them staying in Iraq."

While the rifle platoons were on a four-day schedule—two days of camp guard, one day of patrolling and one day off—CAAT patrolled day and night, every day, without rest. For all of Squeak's faults, he was a master at scheduling and logistical matters and he managed to get us as much free time as was humanly possible, which was usually just half a day, once a week or so. Though when we first started patrolling, we just went wherever we wanted to, we now had a regular route. Our first stop would be the police station, where we would pick up some police to accompany our rifle squad. After we swung by the western power station, we would drop the elevens and police off to patrol on foot. While they were winding through the back alleys and getting chased by wild dogs, we would swing by the hospital and then cruise randomly through the city. An hour or so later, we would pick up the elevens, hit the southern power station and then head home. The whole thing took one to two hours.

Samawah was a peaceful southern Sunni town of 100,000 people. They had no love for Saddam, who had almost completely cut them off after the Gulf War. They caused no problems for us and we weren't shot at once the entire time we were there. Our relationship was stand-offish; the kids loved us(our rather our candy), but the adults would just nod and smile from a distance.

Once, while patrolling the filthy Western edge of town, we passed an old woman, her daughter and her grandchild. They all nodded and smiled and we waved in return. It was a nice friendly exchange until I hit a pothole filled with sewage and splattered the nice old woman from head to toe in watery shit. I felt horrible, but there was nothing I could do. That small incident struck me as being very symbolic—no matter how much you want to help, eventually you're going to cover someone in shit.

One thing that bothered me about the Iraqis was how little effort they put into their own lives. There were constant problems with the sewage system in town, so people would just shit and piss in a bucket and then dump it out right on their front step. They wouldn't have the wherewithal to walk to the empty lot across the street and dig a hole to pour their shit into. They wouldn't clean their own streets or even their own yards. A beautiful house would have with an empty dumpster on its side in the front yard, with trash scattered all around it. Later, when I went to Nasariyah, we were told that the only way the British could get the people to clean up their own streets was to pay them to do it.

The city was filled with wild dogs. Now when I say "dog" you think "Lassie", but you should think "Cujo." The dogs there were huge, but rail thin, with filthy, matted grey hair; they were absolutely feral and vicious. More than once, I had to gun the engine as they tried to jump through the open windows of my moving hummer.

Later in this book, I will go on at length about how disgustingly Arab society treats their women, but I have to admit that they actually let their little girls be little girls. Pink dresses and bows in their hair and the whole bit. When we first got to Samawah, the kids would sell us sodas (always wanting the valuable glass bottles back when we were done) and we would give them candy. The order quickly came down that we weren't allowed to buy anything out in town, supposedly because our greenbacks were messing up their economy. We continued handing out candy to the kids, which raised spirits on both ends.

After a couple dozen patrols, personalities started to emerge among the kids. Ross started an in-joke in which the kids would use reverse-psychology on us, telling us they hated "chocolotay", as they called it. We decided that all of the distinct personalities that had emerged were a part of the "He-Man Chocolatay— Haters Club", after the "He-man Woman-Haters Club" from *The L'il Rascals*.

The leader was The Dancing/Karate Kid. No play on Broadway or karate dojo in Japan has seen such a master. "Multi-talented" doesn't begin to describe this kid. While parked on the street, a kid noticed Ross and I and—apparently trying to impress us—started dancing for no reason. The funny thing was that he kept acting like he just felt like dancing, as if he hadn't noticed us at all and had no interest in our "chocolotay." He kept peeking over his shoulder, waiting for us to get impressed. When the dancing didn't do the trick, he started doing wild Karate moves on his brother. When that didn't do it, he started mixing dancing with Karate, while peeking at us, waiting for a wave of candy. You had to give it to him, he was giving it his all. But he was trying too hard and, frankly, he was kind of annoying.

The next kid was a master of disguise, a camouflage expert, and basic all-around pimp. Not to be racist, but all Iraqis look alike. No seriously, they do. Maybe 1% look a little different. This kid had bright red hair like Richie Cunningham. He seemed not to realize that though. He would appear on one side of our humvee, say "Chocolatay?" and we would tell him to go away. He would then appear on the other side, with his collar flipped up, trying to pass himself off as another kid. Many kids tried this, but none of them had bright red hair. Thus he was dubbed The Red-Headed Iraqi Kid (a.k.a. The Master of Disguise, a.k.a The Man of a Thousand Faces and One Hair-do).

The next kid was an Iraqi superhero. While rolling through some trashed-filled alleys, we noticed one kid running along side us and flashing us a smile, like "Hey, look at me, I'm keeping up with y'all." It would have been more impressive if we had been driving faster than eight miles per hour. He wore a multi-colored track suit that was straight out of the 1984 Olympics. The Jump-suit Kid (a.k.a. The Flash, a.k.a. The Fastest Kid Alive) only made one appearance, but then again, maybe he made several, but he was just too fast for the human eye to see.

Speaking of invisibility, The Disappearing Ninja was the next kid to appear, or rather…disappear? While on the outskirts of town, tracking down reports of some shooting, we noticed a kid following us. Every time we would turn to try and get a good look at him, he would disappear. The only flaw in his power was that he would always hide behind something that was thinner or shorter than he was.

Rounding out the inner circle of the "He-Man Chocolatay Haters" club was The Pop-Up Kid, a.k.a. the Non-Ishta-able Kid. "Ishta" and "Imshi" were two ways of telling people to go away, as we often had to do when kids would swarm the vehicle. If you said it with enough bass in your voice, they'd usually jump back, but one kid was simply non-Ishta-able. If you Ishta'ed him on one side of the vehicle, he'd just pop back up on the other. Ishta him again, he's back on the side he started on.

One kid was memorable, but didn't quite have what it took to get into the club. While sitting behind the wheel at the police station, I heard "Chocolatay" and when I turned to see who said it, I almost jumped—this kid looked weird. He had a weak, receding chin, bug-eyes and a huge head made even more bulbous by a shaggy haircut.

"Hey Moser, do you see this freaking kid?"

"Damn, what's wrong with him?"

"I dunno. I'm going to mess with him."

"Don't be a jerk."

"I won't. I'll be teaching him English."

I leaned in close and he stepped toward me.

"Hey, kid. Say 'I.'"

"I".

"Say 'look'."

"Loog."

"Like".
"Lige…"
"Tweety."
"Tweedy."
"Bird."
"Bur."
"Good, now put it all together. 'I look'…"
"I loog…."
"Like Tweety Bird."
"Lige Tweedee Burrr."

I took out pen and paper and the kid got excited. The kids would often ask to see their names in English; then they would show us what ours looked like in Arabic. I drew a caricature of his bug-eyed balloon head and innocently handed it to him. He saw the pic, realized I was making fun of him; then crumbled it up and threw it on the ground. Good clean fun. He probably joined Al-Qaeda because of my mockery. Sorry, America.

If I died and was given the choice to be re-incarnated in Iraq as a woman or a donkey, I would pick "donkey" without hesitation. The way that women were treated was beyond deplorable, and that was just the things that we saw in public; I don't even want to think about what happened behind closed doors. We would always see married couples walking along the dusty roads; the man, clean and calm, walking with his hands behind his back; the woman, a step behind him, with a huge bundle balanced on her head or in her arms. The man would never even consider helping the woman. Once, I got so sick of this situation that when I saw an old woman carrying a huge bundle of sticks by herself, I pulled over and motioned to her that we would help her. The stark terror in her eyes shocked me and when I realized why she was afraid, I sped out of there so as to not endanger her further. Though we were all armed to the teeth and "infidels" to boot, she was not afraid of us, but she was terrified of what would happen to her if her husband or brother was told that someone saw her "consorting" with us. She would be beaten within an inch of her life and the blame would always be on her; never on the guy who stayed in the shade while she worked like a beast of burden.

As I said before, they did let little girls be little girls, but once a girl even started getting "womanly," she was behind closed doors until she was married and had kids. Middle Eastern women are incomparable beauties, yet when they are at their prime, they are cloistered. Once the man gets a few kids and a prized son out of her, and her beauty has withered from over-work and abuse, she will be allowed to go outside again. The withering of their beauty was the most shocking thing. Those "old hags" you see in the news; many of them are about 39. Those women are worked, all day in the sun until their looks are just destroyed.

A range was set up on an abandoned army base ten miles away. Getting there was a stressful ordeal as the "trail" was only a barely-seen set of tire tracks in the bleached-white rubble. What made it worse was that while I would have my eyes glued on the "road" to make sure I didn't drive us into a ditch, the vehicle commander would give me directions like "Go there", but he wouldn't point or nod or give any other indication where "there" was. When I would go the wrong way, I would get great clarifications like, "Not there!…There!"

Our first trip to the range turned out to be pretty cool, in that we actually shot like we would fight—from the turret in the humvee. We would race the humvee forward, jump up a berm, slam the brakes, skid to the right, and then fire on a target. I was a bit taken aback by the guns, having not shot them since we were in combat. I felt pity for the people we had shot at. Even a medium machinegun like the 240 is a terrifying weapon. It doesn't just put holes in people; it disassembles them.

While some people were turning to drugs, or dropping their packs, others actually improved. White shocked the hell out of me by becoming one of the better Marines in CAAT. White had a shitty rep, but two things had changed him and turned him around. The first was that he had gotten married to a cute chick (which surprised me, since he looked like a cross between The Grinch and The Hunchback of Notre Dame). She had kids from a previous relationship so the twin responsibilities of husband and father really improved him. The other reason was that his drinking buddies, like Dunn and Badillo, had gotten out of the Corps and he had started to dry out. Sober and married, White was almost likable. He was still snide and the kind of guy who would watch me as I was going to back up into something, not warn me, and then laugh after I hit it, but besides that he was great guy. He was responsible and diligent and I even found myself willingly having conversations with him. Another wonder of war.

Everyone loathed the Salman/Mass Grave site trip we had to do twice a week. Salman was straight out of the Middle Ages. Outside of Samawah, all the vegetation disappeared and it looked like the surface of the moon. It was so bright out there that everything looked white and I had to slap myself just to stay awake. The only landmarks were bombed-out military vehicles every twenty miles or so.

Salman, which was set down in a valley, was an oasis of soft green farms and blue streams. The ridge was dominated by the wall of an ancient fort. We tried to find our way to the fort, but we could never find a trail through the low fields and dikes. We met some of the local leaders, who seemed happy just to have someone new to talk to. The town had been skipped by the war, as it had been by every development since the invention of the alphabet. It was clear that Saddam had never done a thing for them. My old delusion about Nasariyah came back and for some insane reason, I kept looking for a Pizza Hut.

The mass grave site was in the middle of nowhere, several miles off the two-lane highway. I wondered how they ever found the place. When we were first tasked with guarding it, they made First Platoon live out there for several days before they realized that we could just come out there twice a week and check on it. They were worried that Saddam loyalists would dig up the bodies and remove them in an effort to eliminate evidence of Saddam's atrocities. The first time I went there, I got out to stretch my legs and I tried to find the grave. I looked for some part of the ground that looked different than the rest, but it all looked uniform. I then realized that I was looking too closely. I stepped back and widened my field of vision and realized that the entire area was the mass grave.

If I didn't hate Saddam already, that did it. This book isn't a polemic because I don't believe anyone gets their mind changed; people believe what they want and find evidence to support their beliefs. I realized that I was walking over the bones of dozens, if not hundreds, of people. I wondered how they had gotten out there. The hole was so big that they probably had to help dig it. Did any of them fight back? Was that even possible? The worst part was that this wasn't even abnormal. This was just one of the hundreds of mass graves that pock-marked this once-great country. I didn't understand how anyone could think that taking out a dictator who had done things like this, was in some kind of grey area.

Since we were so far away from camp, Squeak was given a satellite phone to call for help if we needed it. He always let us use it out there, as long as we kept it on the down low. It was strange to call and talk with my family while standing in a place that had brought so much grief to so many families.

On one of our many trips to the mass grave site, my tire popped. Humvees are made to drive while damaged and I knew from my Humvee Driver's Course that it could drive 25 miles at 25 miles per hour with a popped tire. I told Squeak that we could at least get back to the highway and a few miles toward Samawah before it crapped out, which was better than staying at the mass grave site.

The hummer made it a good ten miles down the road before I wore the wheel down to a ragged rim. Squeak called battalion to get them to send Motor T, but it would be several hours until they got to us. While Squeak let us make some more calls, huge nasty desert dogs started circling us. They started getting closer and Squeak gave us the OK to shoot them. We opened up, scaring them away and killing one. Sgt. Ali Baba shot at them with the grenade launcher, missed by a mile and then tried to make some excuse why it was not his fault. I slept on the hood, enjoying the cool night air. When Motor T arrived, they realized they brought the wrong size tire, but they were somehow able to jam it anyway.

By this time, the Wack Shack II had been up and running for a month and a half. About half the guys used it daily and many of them used it several times a day, including me. On average, it was getting used about 100 times a day, which brought the grand total to 4500 loads. There wasn't any drain to let the bad stuff go away. It started to reek after a couple of weeks, but you could still pretend the smell was something else. After a month though, the stench was wretched. I really could have lived my entire life without knowing what several thousand loads curdling in the desert heat smelled like. The stench became so bad that it started creeping out of the Wack Shack and into our CAAT team area. The worst part was that no matter how bad it was, it was your only option for some relief. The same people who would mock those who would still enter that bio-hazard were the same ones who would creep in to use it after the sun went down.

I sat in my idling humvee while the eleven squad mounted up on their five-ton truck, zonked out of my mind. The constant patrolling, along with my massive and uncontrolled weight loss, made me feel groggy and out-of it most of the time. The Goose suddenly appeared in my window and started threatening me to keep my speed down. The 5-ton drivers had been complaining to the higher-ups that we sometimes left them behind instead of escorting them closely. When I drove, I would often zone out and then realize that I was a few hundred meters in front of the slower-moving trucks. The Goose told me that he would be watching the speedometer in the truck and if I went above the battalion-directed speed limit of 35 mph, he would have my ass.

As we exited the camp onto the mile-long road that led to the highway, I tried to keep my eye on the speedometer, which was barely legible at night. After squinting at it and nearly hitting one of the slaloms, I said "fuck it" and told Moser just to tell me when it felt like I was going too fast. The Goose had the truck driver speed up to pace us and he started yelling at me like a recruit to slow down. I looked down at the gauge and saw that I was going 42mph—not exactly breaking the land-speed record. I looked over at Moser, whose weary expression told me that this was par for the course when it came to dealing with The Goose.

We hit the highway and I decided to fuck with The Goose. He wanted me to slow down? I could go real slow. As the lead vehicle, I slowed down to 18 miles per hour on the highway, making us look like the Rose Bowl Parade. Moser got a kick out of my belligerence. After a mile at that pace, The Goose blew his top and made the driver pass us as they roared off to the first stop. The Goose was known for his pettiness and childishness, but by having a tantrum and speeding off, he was taking his boys away from their armed escort.

I caught up and passed him as we headed to the police station. I got out to stretch my legs and turned to see The Goose barreling straight at me. This was an old drill instructor routine in which they would run at you to make you jump out of the way, but I decided that I wouldn't move an inch. I was sick of staff NCOs in general and this guy in particular. I wasn't going to give him the satisfaction of seeing me jump back. When he saw that I wasn't going to move, he stopped six inches from my face and started yelling at me. As his harangue went on, my alleged speed kept increasing. At first I was "endangering" his men by going 45 miles per hour; then it was fifty; then fifty-five. When he accused me of going sixty, I reminded him that humvees can't even go sixty miles per hour.

Usually an ass-chewing is considered suitable punishment, but he told Moser and I to find him after we got back to camp. As we got back in the humvee, Moser turned to me with a smile.

"If you were trying not to piss him off, you weren't trying very hard."

I didn't care, I was sick of the pettiness of staff NCOs. I was proud of having stood up to him, but I was still pissed. By the time we got back to camp an hour later, I was ready to fight. Moser knew The Goose well and said that he had rarely seen him this angry. The way that The Goose told us to meet him, I thought he might try some Old Corps shit, which was fine with me. If he put one finger on me, I could hit him back and claim self-defense. I took my helmet and flak off, not wanting to be encumbered if I got in a fight.

Moser and I went up front to find The Goose, who told us to go outside, around the corner. We would be in the dark and away from witnesses, so I sensed that he was going to mess with us. We went outside and waited. The Goose came around the corner and barreled right at me. I started cocking my hand back subtly when he stopped a foot away from us and spoke in a soft and casual voice. He told us that he just wanted to clarify the speed issue, while I waited to get sucker-punched. I looked over at Moser, who looked just as confused as I imagined I did. The Goose closed by telling me that I was a good sergeant and he knew we'd work together well in the future. I couldn't believe it.

We had to escort the CO to Nasariyah, a city an hour east of us which was famous for being where Jessica Lynch was held. Before we left though, a minor controversy had erupted. About half of the guys in CAAT chose to sleep out by our vehicles, since it was so hot in the building. A large tarp supported by two-by-fours had been erected to protect people from the sun. During the night, the wind kicked up and knocked it down. One of the beams hit the table where people kept their stuff. In the morning, Chiariello found that his prized sunglasses that he left on the table had been smashed. When he looked closer though, he realized that they weren't his pair, but a similar model that belonged to Sgt. Ali Baba. It looked like Sgt. Ali Baba woke up, found that his sunglasses had been smashed, and decided to switch them with Chiariello's. Chiariello was pissed, but he couldn't prove anything. He vowed to get passive-aggressive revenge on Sgt. Ali Baba, but I told him I'd handle it.

I was in a sticky situation. Sgt. Ali Baba had been in for almost eight years and had been a mountain warfare instructor when the war was brewing. He had gotten permission to leave that cushy job and come out and fight, which was very admirable. He got attached to Golf a few days before The Bridge and he served with Second Platoon before getting shunted to us. He was a good enough guy, I guess, just a little weird. He had this thing where he would do a "funny" gay voice almost constantly. Now everyone can do a a "gay" voice, it's a staple of comedy, but this guy did it almost every other sentence. It went beyond "doing" a voice and made it seem like it was his real voice.

Nasariyah was the same size as Samawah. The buildings were nicer, but the streets were much nastier. Turning down an alley, we found ourselves driving through watery brown sewage a foot deep. Luckily, humvees are 18 inches off the ground.

We got to see the hospital Jessica Lynch had been rescued from, which was the exact same model as the one in Samawah. Jessica Lynch was a lightning rod for all sorts of negative emotions among us. To us, she was the symbol of Army weakness, political correctness getting in the way of fighting ability, cushy POGs out of their element and women not being able to hack it. Our views were harsh mainly out of bitterness and jealousy. When we heard the initial report of her abduction—which involved her dropping a half-dozen Iraqis with her M-16 and only being taken down after she ran out of ammo—we correctly guessed that account was over-blown and inaccurate. It also bothered us that she got so much press. She was known around the world and the only coverage we got were blurbs in the sixth most-popular newspaper in New York City. After I got out of the Corps, I read Jessica Lynch's authorized biography and my harsh views melted away. The Rambo version of her story was not true, but that did nothing to diminish the bravery she had shown under extreme conditions. It wasn't her fault that she had been used by the media. The truth that eventually came out revealed her to be a poised and good-hearted young woman who dealt with circumstances much bigger than herself with dignity and honor.

The Marine camp in Nasariyah was quite different than ours, being situated in a museum in the middle of town. Security was lax; people walked around in their T-shirts within sight of several likely sniper spots. They obviously felt very safe there, though they told us there had been a rocket attack and armed men had probed their lines a few nights before. The museum had most of its artifacts still intact and a corpsman showed me that his "desk" was really a mummy in a glass case with a blanket over it.

The reservists were from New York and showed the same mature and energetic mood that I saw in our Naval Reserve Seabees. They hadn't been activated long enough to hate it and they seemed to enjoy working together. They had arrived in mid-May, after the shooting was over, and they were already getting ready to be relieved by Italian forces. They had stenciled images of the Twin Towers and their motto, "Never Forget", on all of their vehicles. Even back then, I thought the connection between Iraq and Al-Qaeda was tenuous at best, but I didn't care. Saddam had started the Iran/Iraq War and the Gulf War, had fired Scuds at Israel, subsidized Palestinian suicide bombers, gassed thousands of Kurds and had littered his land with mass graves of his own people. We had more than enough reasons to take him out.

Even though he had no responsibility for us, their CO made sure that we got food and water, which was more than our commanders had done. Later, I would read his name in the news when he was blamed for prisoner abuse that allegedly occurred at his camp. That didn't jibe with the friendly, positive and professional attitude I saw from everyone on that camp.

As we drove back to Samawah, I thought about how I would deal with "Sgt. Ali Baba", as the boots called him ("Ali Baba" being the term that locals used for "thief"). Though he was the same rank as me, he had twice as much time in the Corps. I knew that if he got in trouble, it could ruin his career or at least forestall his promotion for several years. A minor misstep could fuck you for years, as I had seen with Sgt. Post. Another worry of mine was more simple and realistic. I was a walking skeleton, having lost twice as much weight as any other person, and I easily could have gotten my ass kicked for accusing him of stealing the glasses. As sleazy as he was, Chiariello was a good Marine and I wouldn't be worth my stripes if I didn't deal with the situation.

My worries ended up being all for naught. When we got back to camp, I took Sgt. Ali Baba aside and told him that it looked like he stole the sunglasses and that people weren't going to let this drop. Before I got any further, he started flailing his arms and yelling that he wanted to speak to Squeak about it. Though I didn't know it at the time, Squeak wasn't crazy about Sgt. Ali Baba either and he was looking for a way to get rid of him. The next day, Sgt. Ali Baba walked up to Chiariello and casually handed him the glasses. He didn't admit guilt, alluding to the whole situation having been a conspiracy to get him in trouble. He was transferred to the company office and went back to his job as an instructor as soon as we got back to Cali. I later found out that they were only ten-dollar shades. A lot of the younger Marines were very materialistic and had $100 shades, so I assumed Chiariello's were as well, since he was making such a big deal about them. I was a little pissed that I risked getting my ass beat for some sunglasses you could buy at 7-11.

All the time in the sun was starting to bake our brains. First, we gave personalities to the kids we didn't even know, as evidenced by the He-Man Chocolotay Haters Club; then we gave personalities to insects. After swatting the same fly away from his re-constituted eggs for the fifth time, Ross addressed it politely, "Hey fly, I know you want my eggs. I have to admit that they're both nutritious and delicious, but I kind of need the nutrients since I got a damn eight-hour patrol to Salman today. Tell you what, catch me at dinner and I'll see if I can hook you up, OK?" After six months together, there was very little to talk about; which made it all the more interesting when Ross' napkin flew off the table and he called after it, "Hey napkin, where you going, buddy? If you want to leave, just tell me. I'll take you wherever you want to go."

Working parties would pop up throughout the day and it was understood that the diggies would pull most of them. Though the lances like Crozier and Rager were still junior Marines, they were combat vets now, so we provided them as many privileges as possible. Sometimes the non-diggie junior Marines were forced to go on working parties when the diggies were busy or they needed more than three bodies.

We were told to provide one body for a working party and Arellano, seeing that he was the only diggie around, got up without being told.

"Hey Arellano, sit down. You're good," I told him.

I looked around; there weren't many choices.

"Chiariello, head on up to the front and help them out."

"Send Arellano. That fuck's just sitting there."

"He's already been on eight working parties today. You're going."

"This is bullshit."

"Are we having a problem?"

I could see him weighing the benefits of telling me off versus my rank. He turned and headed to the front, shooting Arellano a dirty look as he passed him. I knew Chiariello would hold a grudge, but he would have to get over it. Acosta and Cortez were problem children, but Arellano was flawless. It bothered me that the diggies were being treated like slaves. I pulled working parties until I picked up corporal. The next day, I made a joke and Chiariello started to laugh; then stopped, still mad about the working party. I kidded him for living up to his Italian heritage by holding a grudge. Chiariello was still very high on himself for being at The Bridge and he would not concede one bit of merit in Arellano's character. He was offended that I picked him over Arellano, who got to Iraq after the combat phase was over. He didn't speak to me for three days.

Everyone handled their depression in different ways and Chili, the machine-gun section corpsman, dealt with it by disappearing. As soon as we got to the train station, he hopped in the engineer's compartment of the train engine in our building, claiming it as his own. The cab got blazingly hot and I didn't see how he could stand it. He said that he liked it because it was private and he could whack off in there in peace, but I think the main reason he liked it was because we couldn't tell if he was in there or not. While he had been cool before the war and had served honorably in combat, when we got to Samawah he seemed to decide that he didn't have to work anymore. As soon as we left Iraq, he was heading to a Navy base in Italy and he was just counting the days. When the machine-gunners came to him with real medical problems, he would blow them off and tell them that they were whiners. Corpsmen are very territorial and if one corpsman treats another corpsman's Marines without informing him, it's not unusual for them to come to blows. Professional pride is very high in the Navy. Chili just didn't care and the mortar corpsman, Doc Kalinauskas, voluntarily took up the slack. At Pendleton, Doc Kali was the proto-typical fat Navy POG, but when we got to Iraq he was "born-again hard." Forty pounds melted off his frame and his jaw line appeared for the first time.

Chili spent most of his time with a pretty, little Army chick who worked for Civil Affairs. There were less than a dozen females on the whole camp and most were average-looking, so they liked the attention they got, but Chili's girl didn't. She was legitimately pretty and married, so she avoided most men, which got her a reputation for being stuck-up and rude, when she was really just being professional. Chili was constantly by her side, which made the rumor mill go wild. Out of jealousy, people started a widely-believed rumor that she sold blow jobs for $20. Most people were childish and rude when speaking to Chili about her, but I was just curious, so he confided in me. While Marines deploy for six to seven months at a time, the minimum deployment for the Army is a year. She got news that her husband was blatantly cheating on her back home and she was distraught. She couldn't confide in her fellow women, since they were jealous of her, and she just needed a friend. Their friendship was platonic, but touching, if you could just get the jealousy out of your heart.

His friend got sick enough to be evaced. I asked him if he thought she was going home and he said he didn't think they'd let her. The Army is not as harsh as the Marines, but they have much longer deployments and they don't let their people go easily. We drove her to Tallil and dropped her off at the medical tent. We all got excited when a two cute medics sashayed over…and told us we weren't allowed to park there. Oh well, at least we could get some good food.

The chow hall had several signs that said that only people from that base could eat there. I slipped into line, feeling like a second-class citizen. One of the head cooks spied us and told us that we couldn't eat there, which was bullshit. The Marine Corps has the smallest budget of any service and anyone who came to our camp could eat at our chow hall. I considered making a stink, but I saw that they were serving the same nasty T-rats we had back in Samawah. Rutledge was loud about his disgust as he left. The head cook followed us outside and I thought he was going to start shit, but he actually came out to apologize, explaining that he was forced to kick us out and his superior would have done so if he hadn't. He looked like he felt really bad.

I always enjoyed Rutledge's company, not only for the conversation, but also to live through him vicariously. He came back from his FAP and was made a CAAT vehicle commander. Instead of traveling in a cramped trac during the combat phase, he rolled in style in his own humvee. The only contact he had with staff NCOs or officers was when he checked in with them by radio. When we got to Samawah, his life got even sweeter. His CAAT team's mission was to escort supply convoys from Kuwait and occasionally ferry officers to Baghdad. He would be away from camp four days out of five. Every other week, they would make a run down to Kuwait and live the high life. Even when they had to stay in Iraq, they would still get to hit up the nicer camps that had PXs, so they always had a cooler full of ice and sodas wherever they went.

Once, when they went down to Kuwait they called back to Samawah and said that "mechanical problems" kept them from returning. They milked that for all it was worth, getting a week's worth of AC and fast food out of it. Finally, they were told, in no uncertain terms, that they would be back the next day or they would not be allowed to go to Kuwait again. Suddenly, their humvees worked just fine.

Words cannot convey what it's like to live with the constant, oppressive heat. When someone told me that it was 130 degrees out, I told them that they were stupid: I didn't think that the human body could even survive at that temperature. When they showed me the thermometer that read 130 degrees *in the shade*, I couldn't believe my eyes. Dealing with the heat became my full-time job. Anytime between 11 and 4:00PM was murder. Every morning, before it got too hot, I would go out to the pisser and force myself to take a leak. I was pounding down six liters of water a day and almost never had the urge to piss. The piss stream was so weak that if I didn't thrust my pelvis forward, the few sad drops would dribble out onto my boots. More than once, I left the building to walk sixty feet to the pissers and had to turn back; the heat went beyond discomfort—it was pain. After a noon patrol, I headed to cool off at Club Chaos, two blocks away. A windstorm kicked up, only making things worse. It felt like a blast furnace. I wanted to turn back, but I was already half-way there. I pushed on, gritting my teeth and groaning like an animal. I hated the land and all the people who lived there. Why didn't they just leave? Ironically, our interpreter told us that the locals considered the heat a blessing, since it killed disease. As low as the standard of living was, I had to admit that the people were unusually healthy, so their belief about the heat seemed to have some credence.

Though Doc Kali tried to help, I was still sick as a dog and was losing pounds daily. At breakfast one day, I tried to force myself to eat, but I had no appetite. Slater was eating with me and he was always good company. Though he was one of the toughest men I had ever met, he had none of the egotism common to Third Platoon. He was an outdoorsman and survival expert, having spent much of his youth in the mountains of Colorado. He told me to throw salt on everything I ate, surmising that my problems came from a hydration imbalance. I took his advice and within two days my appetite was back and I was feeling better than I had in months.

A rumor went around that sounded too good to be true. One company from 2/5 was going to Kuwait to be the camp guard at one of the LSAs and they would probably stay there until it was time to go home. It was mid-way through June and it was obvious we weren't leaving any time before August. Supposedly, Golf was in the running to get picked, but I didn't see how. We had a half platoon of drug pops living in the battalion HQ, but supposedly Sergeant Major Davis went to bat for us. Squeak called us together and told us the we were leaving the next day. Everyone was ecstatic, except for Ross who said we would definitely be coming back in a few weeks. It pissed me off that he was ruining it. He even got into a shouting match with Cpl. Shaddock for his gloomy prediction.

The Army MP unit was excited that they could move into our building, which was much bigger than theirs, but they didn't know about the Wack Shack. A couple of their officers and two women rattled the door of the Wack Shack while

I was making my last, emotional trip. I calmly fired my last round and walked out past the soldiers with a flushed face. A few hours later, I asked Moser if they were going to make the boots clean the Wack Shack before we left and he smiled, saying that they already had. A couple of boots went in there with garbage bags on their hands and cleaned out thousands of wads of spunked-up toilet paper. Now that deserves a Silver Star.

We were going to drive to Kuwait at night to avoid the heat. I tried to grab some shut-eye, knowing I'd be driving all night, but they kept having formations. We had to throw away anything we couldn't fit in our vehicles, which included our much-used and much-repaired foam coolers. First Sergeant Young was assigned to my humvee and I noticed he had grabbed one of the good plastic coolers from the chow hall for himself. Since there wasn't enough space to take the foam coolers, people were dumping their ice on the ground, which offended my sensibilities. Ice was more valuable than gold in the desert. I opened the First Sergeant's cooler and saw that, though it was half-filled with ice and cokes, it still had about eight inches of room left in it. I put the ice I salvaged in his cooler. First Sergeant Young came up with twice as much gear as any other Marine and started loading it in, pushing our gear aside.

"Hey, First Sergeant, you mind if I put some of my Cokes in your cooler?"

"Ain't no room, Dawg. Ain't no room."

I looked over at Ross, who cocked an eyebrow.

"Well, actually, First Sergeant, I opened it and added about eight inches of ice and there was still room."

After sputtering in frustration, he said something that became another machinegunner in-joke.

"OK…but don't be confusing your Cokes with mine".

If that wasn't bad enough, as soon as he got into the back seat, he wrinkled his nose in disgusted.

"It smell like ass in here".

"It's probably just sweat, First Sergeant. We've had people running patrols in these vehicles, day and night, since we got here."

"Naw, it ain't that. It's someone's ass. Someone smell *sour*."

It took a long time for our convoy to get rolling and by the time we were half-way to Kuwait, I was loopy. I kept slapping myself in the face and trying to jump-start conversations with Ross to keep myself awake, but after five months together, we had all run out of things to talk about. Ross and I were both comics geeks, so we at least had that much in common, but I still had my limits.

"So, if you could be any of the X-Men, which one would you be?" Ross asked.

"Y'know, I didn't think it was possible, but you actually out-geeked me. There is no way I'm continuing this conversation. If I go any farther, I'm going to have to beat myself up."

Thirty miles later.

"I'd be Gambit."

Even without tracs, it took us six hours to go 200 miles. We crossed through the surprisingly weakly-guarded border in the dark. We had twice as many people guarding the gate to our camp in Samawah. Any normal person would have considered Kuwait's main highway lonely and foreboding, but I loved it. A lighted highway might as well have been midtown Manhattan.

We came to LSA-5, which had been the regimental HQ before the war, and got into our tents with a minimum of fuss. I awoke in the middle of the night with a shocking feeling—I was cold. I smiled to myself and grabbed my sleeping bag out of my pack. This was a problem I was glad to have.

I was the only one who woke to go to breakfast. I was disgustingly weak and sickly and I was looking forward to putting some weight back on. When I got to the chow tent, I almost cried—real food and plenty of it. I went nuts, profusely thanking each of the Indian contract workers for every scoop of food. Real eggs, real sausage, pancakes and syrup, milk and cereal—it was too good to be true. I went back for seconds and then started planning my next meal.

I went to the air-conditioned shower trailers in the afternoon, while most people were avoiding the extreme heat by sleeping in their tents. When I pulled off my shirt, I saw my reflection in the mirror and stopped—frozen. I knew I had lost much more weight than anyone else, but I didn't know I was this bad. In Samawah, people were constantly telling me how skinny I was, but I never saw myself all at once. I was a mess. My cheeks were sunken and my eye sockets looked hollow. My neck was a joke, barely big enough to hold up my head. I could see all of my ribs and when I turned to the side, my chest was no more than nine inches deep. I looked like I was dying. I didn't feel like I had caught anything or I had it any worse than anybody else, but my body was just not dealing with the heat. The good news was that, with the huge helpings at the chow hall, I would be able to put some weight back on in no time.

The call went up for the senior NCO in each platoon to report to The Goose, who was acting company gunny since Gunny Linton had left to get surgery. The Goose told us that Kid Rock was giving a concert at Doha that night and each platoon was getting six tickets. Half the Marines in the company were Kid Rock fans and supposedly his girlfriend at the time, Pam Anderson, was there as well.

Kid Rock had come to LSA-5 to sign autographs in an unnamed tent earlier that day, but most of us had been gorging ourselves at Camp Commando at the time.

I walked back to the tent, knowing that no matter how I divvied the tickets up, someone would be butt-hurt. Chili sidled up to me and hinted very strongly that he should go since the other platoons would probably ignore their corpsman when handing out their tickets. That seemed like a good rationale, so I told him he could go, not really thinking it through. To make things simpler, I decided to give two tickets to each section. Of course, Monty snagged one ticket for himself and gave the other to his favorite boot. His selfishness was appalling and I considered taking his tickets back, but I knew that would create a huge stink. Monty already had a terrible rep for selfishness. He would find a way to finagle himself a ticket no matter what.

I wrote all of the machinegunners' names on slips of paper and put them in a hat. I had to tell Chili that his spot wasn't guaranteed anymore, but his name was in there. The first name I picked was the biggest turd in the bunch—Cortez. The next was Elias, who probably didn't know who Kid Rock was, but by the time he got back he would be his biggest fan. I went to give their names to The Goose, but when I came back to the tent, I heard Moser and Elias talking about what they would do at the concert. I asked Moser what was up and he launched into some backwoods, Southern lawyer shuck-and-jive about how they had to redo the raffle because of some vague discrepancy and—lo and behold!—his name had been drawn. I could tell what was going on, but he had already gone through Squeak, so it was a done deal. It was sheisty, but I would have rather had a great Marine like Moser get rewarded than a fuck-up like Cortez.

The phone center was owned and operated by a Kuwaiti company and they were making money hand over fist. The phones only worked if you used their phone cards, which were a dollar a minute. With my combat and family separation pay, I was pulling down $3000 a month and I ended up dropping $400 in there in two weeks.

The door in our tent that lead to the shitters, chow hall and phone center was on Third Platoon's side, so when we opened the door flap, a blast of hot air would rush in. Third kept complaining and finally Schofield stood up and tried to tell Weapons Platoon that only Third Platoon could use the door on their side. Third only had about twenty Marines and Weapons had more than sixty, so it was ridiculous to tell the majority that we had to go the long way around. I was sick of the childishness from Third in general and Schofield in particular. I hated countermanding another sergeant's order, especially a senior sergeant, but he hadn't had the courtesy to run this order by me. I told Weapons that I was giving them authority to ignore Schofield and that they were free to use whatever door they chose. Schofield went to SSgt. D, who passed down an order reinforcing his, but it was a moot point. Later that same day, Third was moved to another tent when the guard schedule was established. Schofield didn't pull guard duty, so he stayed in his cot by the door. I made it a point to throw the flap wide open every time I went out.

My humvee driver's license saved my ass for the umpteenth time. It was decided that a two-team CAAT squad would not pull guard duty and would remain on stand-by until we were needed to escort convoys. This deal was sweet beyond belief. The only convoys were the buses that took out-going companies to the airport every week or so. Only half of the machinegunners got to stay in the reduced-size CAAT; even Squeak had to leave and pull sergeant of the guard, to the disappointment of no one. We kept a low-profile and got to skate like few people had in the history of war.

After a week of sleeping and eating, we were tasked with escorting a Marine unit to the airport. As we drove, I stared forlornly at the lights of Kuwait City. There was no connection between us and the Kuwaitis, no libbo in town and certainly no relationships with Kuwaiti women. Kuwaiti had many American stores and restaurants, but this was still a Muslim country. Though we could fight for them, there was no way they would allow us to mix in their culture.

As we got near the air base, one of the flatbed trucks carrying the departing company's quad-cons—closet-sized storage units—ran out of gas. The buses went into the camp and we stayed back to guard the flatbed. We siphoned some of our fuel into the truck, but the engine was so dry that it still took forty-five minutes to get the engine to turn over. In the interim, we all ganged up on Ross and tried to peer pressure him into letting us use the satellite phone he had been given in case of emergency. While at first it looked like he was going to go along with it, he quickly realized that, even though the phone's log showed that the staff NCOs had been calling home whenever they felt like it, if we used it and got busted *he* would be the one to catch hell for it. That would endanger the sweet deal we had in CAAT. As a dig, I told him, "It's OK to be scared." The look in his eyes told me that I had gone too far and Moser had to pull him away to keep him from punching me. The funny thing was that we had just used the satellite phones that day on base with permission and we had a phone center I used daily. I really didn't have anything much to say.

The Master Gunnery Sergeant in charge of getting units out of the country drove up in his civilian SUV. He told us he had contacted our unit and told them that, since it was almost midnight, it would be better for us to just stay out there for the night and drive back the next day. This was beyond cool since it let us get two good meals and check out the chicks. He took us onto the base, which was very well-defended, almost cartoonishly so. They had one fighting position that looked like a medieval fighting tower crossed with an Incan pyramid. I imagined some POG in there stroking his mint-condition M-60 and fantasizing about holding off an entire invading Iraqi force from his twenty-foot-tall, sand-bag battle tower.

The Master Guns got us a tent to sleep in and pointed us in the direction of the chow hall. The tent city was a mile across and looked like a something out of "MASH" or "Platoon." There were tents of all sizes—phone centers, chapels, men's and women's showers, gyms, and internet cafes. Every tent was air-conditioned and people walked around in civvies when they were off-duty. Although the gate was well-guarded, I noticed that almost no one inside had weapons, not even pistols.

The chow hall was bigger than three basketball courts put together. Since this base was on a 24-hour schedule, they had what they called "mids"—a light meal served at midnight. We lined up outside and saw that people from dozens of different units had scrawled moto graffiti onto the wooden fence. They were mostly from POG units and said things like, "472nd Medical Supply Unit out of Fort Stockton—stone cold pimps, hooah!" I proudly scrawled, "Golf CAAT—Three hours of work, every four days", which was absolutely true.

As we washed up in the sinks by the entrance, I noticed a soldier eying us nervously.

"Hey there guys, you new here?"

"Yeah."

"So, uh, what are you planning on doing with those long barrels?"

It took us a a few seconds to figure out that he was talking about our rifles. "Long barrels"? What is this—the Revolutionary War?

"We're going to carry them with us like we have every day for the last four months."

"I don't know if y'all noticed, but you aren't allowed to take weapons into the chow hall…Sorry."

"You know there's a war on."

"I know, but we've had several negligent discharges recently."

There seems to be a perception among POGs that guns "just go off." They think that if a firearm is dropped or nudged it might fire on it's own; which is a bit like saying that if you bump into a type writer, it will write a letter to Santy Claus. I had lived and slept with a loaded rifle—as had everyone else in my company—every day for the last four months. In that time, we had two NDs, both of which were caused by stupidity, not by the guns.

"Do you have any place we can check our weapons?"

"Well, no."

"Alright then, we're going to take them in."

"Ok, but could you please have them barrels down?"

When I stepped into the chow hall, everyone turned and stared at me like I was Doc Holliday. I got in line, feeling like a real roughneck. I was bone-thin and dark from the sun, wearing faded and filthy cammies. I moved to the front and saw some civilian contractors running the biggest grill I ever saw. It turned out that the food was the same as what we had at LSA-5. The only real exception was the soda fountain, which I abused way beyond the point of reason. The others were making fools of themselves at the ice cream machine, so I wasn't the only one.

There were about fifty chicks in the chow hall—many in small, approachable groups of two or three—but the guys that I came with didn't sit near any of them. Luckily, as I walked up, a lone Airborne chick sat down about eight feet away from them. Chiariello cocked an eyebrow when I sat down midway between them and the chick, instead of sitting with the group. I started riffing and cracking jokes like crazy, hoping she would start eavesdropping. When I heard her laughing at some of my jokes, I knew I was in like Flynn. I turned and "casually" asked her a question about the base and then launched into a twenty-minute conversation with her. The guys didn't even pretend not to stare and I even heard murmurs of approval from Moser and the others about "Old Man" Meyer laying the mack down. I wasn't trying to get into her pants (there wasn't time, man!), but I enjoyed the hell out of talking to a normal American girl while also raising my standing among my peers.

After several unsubtle hints that it was time to go, they finally just got up and left. I said good-bye, knowing that I was in for some junior high shit when I got back to the vehicles. When I came within sight of them, I started getting hoots and cat-calls and threats to rat me out to my wife. On the way back, I gave Krout, AKA Nintendo Thumbs, a point-by-point lesson on laying the mack down, using my behavior from that night as a prime example.

I slept on the hood of the humvee instead of in the stuffy tent. I looked at the control tower for the airport and thought of those flying home. I finally admitted to myself that we wouldn't be going home any time soon. I somehow knew that things were going to get a lot worse before they got better.

I woke at first light—already sweating—and rushed over to get some breakfast. Most grunts sleep through breakfast and I knew that my buddies would want to leave as soon as they woke. During my leisurely breakfast, I learned more about the war from watching CNN than I had by actually being in it. It was late-June and the insurgency was just beginning. I had trouble reconciling the images of guerilla attacks with my opinion of the Iraqi fighters as cowardly and inept. I assumed that it was just a blip on the radar screen and not the beginnings of a trend. I looked at my watch and realized I had been eating and watching TV for an hour and a half. I could already hear White bitching. I went back and caught some flak as they rushed me into my humvee.

Lying in my rack that afternoon, Schofield walked up with his usual constipated expression.

"Where were you at 7:00 this morning?"

"What the fuck is it to you? I was wherever the hell I wanted to be."

He got a sad, awkward look, scratched his neck, and then pouted.

"I was just trying to make conversation."

Huh?!? What was this guy—a robot? I thought he was trying to rat me out for missing morning PT, but after seeing his dejected face when I yelled at him, I realized that he *really* was just trying to make conversation. Schofield wasn't a bad guy, he just had no social skills whatsoever.

CAAT was the perfect job to scam in since any problem with the vehicles required us to go to Camp Commando for repairs. Ross didn't want to push our luck though, so I usually just took the mini-bus that went there daily. The first time I went to Commando after returning from Iraq, I went completely insane, having a pizza, two Burger King cheeseburgers and a Subway sandwich all in the same sitting. I didn't see how people could sit outside in the heat and eat hot pizza. Subway had an air-conditioned trailer in which I ate all of their competitors' food.

After getting back to the LSA, Rager asked me if I heard what happened to Carpenter. I groaned and he told me that Carpenter had been calling his wife in the phone tent at Commando and he left his rifle there when he left. An Army sergeant had to go after him and chew him out, telling Carpenter that he wouldn't give him his rifle back until his squad leader claimed it. When they couldn't find me, the army sergeant finally gave it back to Carpenter in disgust. Not only had he lost his rifle—which was unforgivable—but if the higher-ups would have found out, we all probably would have been banned from going to Commando. Worst of all, an *Army* sergeant had to correct him. I cringed when I thought of that sergeant telling everyone he knew about the fucked-up Marine he had to correct.

Rager chewed Carpenter out like a recruit and then I lit into him as well. After the ass-chewing though, I asked him why he was even using that shitty phone tent when we had a good one right at the LSA. He said that he had not been able to take out any split-pay from the bursar, so he had to use the collect phones at Commando. He seemed to be taken aback when I switched gears from belittling him to figuring out a way to take care of his finance problems, but that was my job.

I was an expert on the split-pay system, having abused the hell out of it. Before we left, we had to choose how much "split-pay" we could get in cash each month. Most people chose $50 or $100, but I knew I would be obsessed with food, so I chose $200. By June, I had already used my accrued $800 of split-pay. The Marine bursar would check your account on computer to see if you had passed your limit, but the Army just took down your social security number and docked your pay later. I ended up taking an additional $800.

Late one night, I heard a familiar laugh and went out to see Mohler standing by the smoke pit. As always, it was great to see him and we joked like it was old times. They had brought him and DeWitt down to stand trial and supposedly they were not letting them go home until the trial was over, which might be months away. Mohler called his dad and told him to contact their senator, who was a family friend. There had been some improprieties with Mohler's piss test that he was trying to use to exculpate himself. The next day he moved to Camp Commando; I wish I could have gotten punished like that.

Ross and I had a very strange friendship in that we were constantly getting on each other's nerves and vowing not to speak to each other, but we were the only two guys who were into comics, so he was forced to bury the hatchet anytime he wanted ask me if the Hulk could beat The Thing (By the way, the Hulk wins by a land-slide). Doty had found some comics sent by Operation: Comix Relief that were much-appreciated. Ross and I got into a silly argument over who the comics belonged to, which sadly enough does not even make it into the Top Ten of stupid arguments I've seen grunts get into.

Out of boredom, I started needling Ross about something and we started arguing. Since Showers was bored as well, he told us we should just fight it out. Talk like this is common and usually leads to nothing.

"You want to go, motherfucker?" I asked Ross.

"Cool with me."

Usually at this point both Marines will get up and act like they're going to fight, but then just wrestle playfully. The problem was that things between Ross and I were tense already, so I wasn't sure that he knew or cared that I was joking. We walked over to a clear spot in the tent and squared off. It looked to me like Ross thought this was a real fight. If I said, "Just joking, man" and he was just joking too, that would be fine, but if he was mad for real, I would look like a pussy by trying to weasel out. I got into a fighting stance and threw what I considered to be an obviously fake punch. Ross didn't see it that way and used a martial arts move he just learned from Moser to take me down.

Ross got up, having proved his point and went back to reading his book. I was fine, but my pride was hurt, so I whined that it wasn't fair for Ross to use a move he just learned, before going to my cot to sulk. A year and a half later, I brought the situation up to Ross and he revealed that he had thought the whole thing was real, especially when I threw a punch at his head.

With nothing but time on my hands, I spent hours lying on my cot, staring up at the tent roof as it whipped in the wind. My mind always returned to the same thoughts—the unparalleled excitement of combat. In my mind, I would stare down the barrel of my gun at an enemy down the road, watching the rounds from my gun as they arced slowly through the air, Matrix-style, before slamming into the enemy's body. His arm would fly off at the shoulder, two rounds would stitch across his chest, shattering his ribs, sending him flying through the air before crumpling to the ground. Coming out of my reverie, I would notice that my heart was racing and my whole body was tense—what the hell was wrong with me? What kind of person fantasizes about destroying other human beings so graphically? I calmed myself down. I wasn't a murderer. Hell, I didn't even think I actually hit any of the people I shot at. The firefights had been so damn exciting...so addictive...but they were never enough—I wanted more. The others didn't speak about such things, though Chiariello, who had been in the most intense combat we saw, admitted to having similar feelings.

So what was I—some kind of mercenary? No, I wasn't some piece of shit killing farmers in the Congo for a warlord. This cause was righteous. I had questioned everything I had been told and still saw with my own eyes how evil Saddam's regime was. So how was I better than they were? Well, first of all, I only shot at combatants. My aggression level had been ratcheted up far beyond that of a normal person, but that was what my job required. Normal people didn't seek out death and destruction; that had to be inculcated into me to make me a grunt. I came to the conclusion that if something *had* to be done, than there was nothing wrong with enjoying it. America would be a horrible place if everyone was like me, but it would be a much worse place if no one was like me.

After a few blissful days, we heard a rumor that we might be going back to Samawah. The insurgency was building and supposedly Echo Company was going up towards Baghdad and we would take over their section of town. When a week went by without any more news, we assumed we were safe. I was lying on my cot, reading a book, when Sgt. Hashimoto came by with a plastered-on smile and asked me if I had heard the news. I somehow knew what it was, but I made him say it anyway: we were going back. I went on rumor patrol, looking for any wisp of hope, but there was none. The only thing in doubt was when the trucks would get to Kuwait to take the company back. When the trucks didn't come the next day, we got a reprieve, though all I did was pout the whole day.

A Humvee we found at the LSA was deemed abandoned by our higher-ups, so we took it with us back to Iraq. It was strange to know that a $50,000 vehicle would just be left like that, but my time in Supply helped me figure out what happened. I remembered the problems we had with Lt. Hazen reimbursing us; even if we could show him what we bought, if we didn't have the paperwork, that piece of gear didn't exist. What probably happened was that a departing unit went to turn their gear and vehicles in, and saw on the manifest that the humvee wasn't on the list. If they tried to turn it in, it would then be on them to prove it was their humvee and that would be next to impossible. If they left it in the desert to rot though, no one would be the wiser.

I got sick when I saw Samawah again; I had made such a big deal of being done with that shithole. We settled into Echo's old building, an insanely huge covered repair yard. The good news was that we finally had a leave date, though there was some drama attached. The Dutch government finally approved a troop deployment and their advance party was arriving the next day. The main body would come in waves over the next few weeks. There was a possibility that we might go north to fight the insurgency after the Dutch relieved us.

The Wack Shack III was established in a non-working bathroom. It lost some points for not having a locking door, which always added an unneeded element of drama to every wack-off.

We patrolled Echo Company's old stomping grounds in the affluent northern part of town (affluent meaning that their toilets actually flushed). We made frequent stops at the northern police sub-station, in a tree-shaded road just north of the river. A new crop of kids tried to fleece us for candy, but one kid had something different to offer. It took awhile for him to get his message across, but through pigeon-English and rude hand gestures he was able to tell us that he supposedly had two hoes he could hook us up with. Some guys from Weapons Company had gone to a local whorehouse before getting ratted out by jealous locals, but I wasn't sure that this kid was hooked into the local pimp-ho power structure.

The pimp-kid motioned that if I gave him money, he would bring the women to us. Slow down, buddy…you're not the first twelve-year-old pimp who's tried to trick me like that. For the next two weeks, he always had an excuse why the hoes weren't there.

"Where the hell are these women you keep promising us?"

"Uh…school, yes."

"School? Are they students or teachers."

"Lady. Lady, yes."

"Well that's good to know. How old are they?"

"First one…fifty."

"Fifty?! Jesus Christ. How old is the second one?"

"Thirty."

"Well that doesn't sound so bad in comparison to the first one."

"Yes, very pretty…yes."

The kid started miming putting on make-up and sashaying.

"Yeah, that's not helping, kid."

I was bummed out when I heard that we had to still patrol our old sector as well. By this time, I had been at that damn police station over a hundred times and I was about to lose it. Whatever officer was with us would go inside, bullshit in the shade and drink sweet tea while we baked in the street. It was common for us to take our helmets off when we parked. Samawah was nasty, but it was safer than most American towns. All the protective gear was doing was making me a heat casualty. When I opened my flak and put my legs up on the seat in front of me, Moser cocked an eyebrow, then shrugged. Of course, that had to be the time that The Goose drove by. I knew I was in for it when I got back, but I barely cared.

Back at camp, I stepped out of my vehicle, drenched in sweat. When I walked past Squeak's rack, he stopped me, trying to be sly.

"How'd the patrol go, Sergeant Meyer?"

"Good as it ever does, staff sergeant."

"Anything you want to tell me about?"

"No." And that was the truth.

"Why'd you have your gear off?"

Wow, this guy is like Perry Mason! I had no idea that he knew! I often found that when a higher-up thought they had you backed into a corner, you could confound them with the truth.

"I took my gear off because it was over a hundred degrees out and we had been sitting outside the police station for over an hour. I only had my helmet off for a few minutes. Since we've been here for three months and haven't been shot at once, I didn't think it was a big risk."

He almost said, "Footwear", but instead he simply dismissed me with a defeated look on his face. Of course, I got posted as a driver, but I would get my job back two days later. Squeak had come to Golf straight from SOI where, like in boot camp, it was common to switch leadership billets willy-nilly almost every day as a way of keeping people on their toes. While that was only slightly childish in SOI, it was totally unacceptable in The Fleet, especially during war. NCOs need to be backed up or the whole system breaks down. For the rest of the month, Ross and I were switched back and forth as CAAT leader every few days, so no one knew who was in charge from day-to-day. Why should the boots follow an NCO who gets posted for stupid things like forgetting a shave or having a shaggy haircut?

The next day, Squeak called me over and asked me if I wanted to go to Kuwait. What this a trap? I expected him to start laughing when I said "yes", but he didn't. A convoy was going down to Kuwait and they needed bodies. Since I wasn't doing anything, he asked me if I wanted to go. I packed quickly, only telling Ross where I was going, since I knew that the others would get butt-hurt.

I ran over to where the convoy was parked before I could get replaced. I found a truck and asked the driver if he was excited. When he said it was no big deal, I could tell I had gotten bum scoop. The driver told me that we weren't going to Kuwait; we were going to get food for the locals from a dock a few miles from the border. This was disappointing, but I was still getting off-base and seeing new sights, so I was happy.

Instead of driving at night, we traveled during the hottest part of the day. Once we hit the highway, there were no wind-breaks, and the searing hot wind blew through the open cab of the truck. It went beyond discomfort to pain and I found myself covering my face and hunching over as I gritted my teeth. I kept myself busy by tossing trash out of the window. Drivers live in their trucks, so the cab was filled with water bottles and MRE trash. For some reason, I found littering in Iraq to be extremely pleasurable.

Within view of the border, we came upon an Army MP lazily guarding a checkpoint that led to the town of Umm-Qasr, Iraq's main port. The sand-choked sky obscured my view of the ocean. The languid waves seemed like they belonged in a land-locked pond. I hoped to stretch our time at the port to get out of the heat, but within ten minutes, all eight trucks were loaded with several tons of grain and we were ready to go. It might not have been exciting, but delivering free food to the locals was one of our major missions. I never saw one article that reported on the great miracle of the war—that although the Iraqis' established government disappeared overnight, not one person went hungry.

We got back in the trucks, but instead of heading back to Samawah, we headed to the nearby U.S. Army base, Camp Bucca. To our delight, the base had a double-wide PX trailer parked in the dust. It looked closed, but when we got closer we saw that we had five minutes left. The Army guys running the place didn't seem happy to see a bunch of grungy Marines, but I could care less. I rushed down the aisle like I was in one if those game shows where you can keep as much as you can grab in five minutes. I made it just under the wire and they closed the register right after I made my purchase. As we waited in the trucks, I watched the soldiers in the camp. These reservists were beyond laid-back; they looked like a bunch of civilians holding the camp until the real soldiers showed up. I was speechless when I saw a pot-bellied reservist with no shirt and blue shorts driving a Humvee with one leg hanging out of the open door.

It was late enough that we got permission to stay the night. Someone found a chaplain who was cool enough to tell us where all the goodies were. Once I started walking through the camp, I found that the reservists were surprisingly easy to talk to. I found the guys I came with playing cards with some MPs they had just met. The MPs seemed very happy to see some new faces and they let us roam their tent freely. They lived better out there than many people do in America. They had a huge cooler full of ice AND a full-size refrigerator. They had their own phone and a computer with an Internet connection. Their large tent only had eight enlisted men and one officer living in it.

Camp Bucca was so close to Kuwait that you could see the light poles on the highway in Kuwait. Most of the soldiers there were reservists and their job was to run a huge POW/terrorist camp. They told me they had about 1000 prisoners at that time, but during the combat phase they had more than 10,000, with only a skeleton crew to guard them. They told me that sometimes it would be one MP guarding 200 prisoners in a field with only barb wire as a barrier.

One soldier offered to let me use his phone card, but I couldn't get anyone on the line. I mentioned that I'd like to use their computer, but their lieutenant was using it at the time, so one of them took me to the command tent. Even though this was the nerve center of the camp, no one made any big deal when I came in—this sure wasn't the Marines. I spoke with an older guy whose flak obscured his rank, but since he spoke to me like a normal person, I assumed he was just an old reservist of equivalent rank. I used the Internet for an hour and no one hassled me. On my way out, I thanked the guy for showing me how to use the computer and I asked him what he did. He told me he was the colonel. Whoops!

I downed a warm, thick Mountain Dew and went to sleep on the hood of the huge truck. The next morning, I woke and went hunting for their chow hall. If they had a double-wide PX, I knew they would have a great chow hall and I was right. I was in hog-heaven as I stuffed myself with omelettes and pancakes, while I eavesdropped on soldiers complaining about the "lousy" food.

I went to "relieve" myself in the shitters and heard several girlish voices. I peeked through an air vent and saw several Army chicks chatting in their PT gear. One had huge jiggling boobs and I just couldn't help myself. I left the shitter with flushed cheeks and a guilty conscience. After another trip to the PX, we headed back to Samawah.

Sgt. Shitbag was a broke-down, hang-dog, ex-Army soldier who shuffled when he walked. He had spent almost twelve years in the Army before switching over to the Marines, presumably because his career had stalled and he was about to be kicked out in the "Up or Out" program, in which you are either promoted or are forced out. Soon after he got to 2/5, Sgt. Shitbag went on permanent light-duty. When we went to Oki, his only job was to make sure the battalion HQ was clean. Every morning, he would get a four-man working party to do his bidding. He didn't seem like a prick at first; he would tell the boots that once they buffed the hallways and cleaned the three bathrooms, they were off for the day. Hearing this, the boots would quickly meet all of their requirements. After finishing though, they would then have to waste an hour looking for the sergeant's lazy ass, before inevitably finding him asleep in a storage room. He would then go into a bathroom, find some evidence of it having been used during the hour that the boots were looking for him and would tell the boots to re-clean it. At the time, I thought he was either too stupid or too afraid of displeasing the officers to realize that the bathrooms are going to be used all day long. It's not like we could tell a captain to hold his water until we got a sergeant to inspect the head. This idiocy continued until the staff left for the night. Looking back, I realize that even if he would have secured us early, he would have had to stay there all day, so he kept us there for company and to have people to lord it over.

It wouldn't be until we got to Iraq that we got our revenge. While manning the turret of a humvee that would be escorting the BC's convoy, Sgt. Shitbag had a negligent discharge with the Mark 19 automatic grenade launcher. Though the grenade sailed harmlessly out of the complex, he was a corporal almost before it hit the ground. After having to show him the proper courtesy for the last two years, Moser took special pleasure in saying," What's up, *corporal?*" every time he saw him.

Generals would come by every week or two to "meet the troops" and it would always end up just depressing the hell out of us. All we wanted to hear was when we were going home, but they would never give us any info. The one guy who did raise everyone's morale was Gunny R. Lee Ermey, better known as the DI from "Full Metal Jacket" and the host of the hit cable show, "Mail Call." Packed into Club Chaos, the two AC units did little to counteract the body heat of more than 500 people. Gunny Ermey stormed into the club in character and launched into his most famous speech from "Full Metal Jacket." We shouted, "Sir, yes, sir!" at the appropriate times and everyone was laughing and relaxed. He broke character and spoke as himself, which was still over-the-top, but fun. He explained that he had convinced his network to pay for him to come out to Iraq by telling them they owed him for giving them their best-rated show. He then riffed on other celebrities who only met the troops in the safety of Kuwait, while he was flying in the same helicopters that probably ferried him around when he was in Vietnam.

He handled our questions with aplomb, though he did get a little flustered when someone asked him about "Saving Silverman." In that movie, a favorite of ours, he played a homicidal high school coach who reveals he is gay and kisses Jack Black at the end of the movie. Someone asked him why he did it, and he said with a smile that anyone there would kiss a guy too if they were offered several hundred thousand dollars to do so. He told us about the positive support we had back home and promised that a bunch of war heroes like us would have no trouble getting pussy when we got back in the States. After he said that, he noticed that there were two women in the crowd and he amended his statement by saying that "most of you" wouldn't have trouble getting some.

He had a civilian cameraman with him who kept signaling him to wrap it up; they had to hit several more camps that day. Everyone wanted pictures with him and he promised to get as many as possible. Gunny Ermey is, hands down, the most famous Marine in history and everywhere you go in the Corps, some jarhead has a moto pic with him. We all gaggled around him, jockeying for a shot. His cameraman kept getting louder and louder about him needing to leave, until Gunny Ermey finally told him that he wouldn't leave until everyone got their photos. You could see the affection he had for the Marines and it was more than reciprocated. I got a photo with him just before he took off, which I will always treasure.

The AC at Club Chaos was my salvation and I spent as much time there as possible. The second week of July though, they kicked people out of Club Chaos during the daytime so they could hold Corporal's Course in there. This was not good. In Kuwait, I had put on about ten pounds in two weeks, but I was still thirty pounds underweight. The AC was the only thing keeping me from sweating those ten pounds off. I had never gone to Corporal's Course and I was still foggy on a lot of things like marching, paperwork, and sword manual that I was supposed to be an expert in. Even worse, when they asked for volunteers for a Sergeant's Course to be held when we got back to Cali, Squeak told me that I couldn't go since I had less than one year left. They didn't like how I led, but they refused to let me go to any leadership classes.

I asked Squeak if I could audit Corporal's Course, sitting in on classes when I wasn't on patrol. He said that was fine as long as I pulled my fair share. Ross saw it as another one of my scams, which was only partially true. I pulled all the early and late patrols to make up for the patrols I missed during the worst heat of the day (funny how that worked out). I learned a lot about counseling Marines and the Uniform Code of Military Justice(UCMJ), which would have been crucial in charging Reed.

During the breaks, I would catch up with my buddy Sherman about the current rumors. Though more and more Dutch arrived every few days and the main body was arriving soon, there was still some doubt that we were going home. The sergeant major said that if the insurgency continued to grow, we might join Echo up north and stay for a few more months.

There was another problem I needed to question Sherman on.

"Have you noticed the shit people have been scrawling on the tables?"

"Not really."

"On every table—Hell, on every legible surface—there are dozens upon dozens of drawings of dicks."

"Heh, yeah, I guess you're right, now that I think about it."

"Poorly-drawn dicks, I might add."

"Well, people get bored in the classes."

"I realize this, but of all the things to draw—why a dick? I can see a guy drawing a picture of a dick going into a vagina or a girl's mouth, or anywhere near a girl, but why this compulsive need among a great many Marines to draw pictures of dicks?"

"Marines just like to draw dicks. What can I say?"

By this time, the heat was insane and whenever I wasn't at Camp Chaos, I was in my little hidey-hole in our building. In the middle of the huge structure was a small set of rooms with a hallway in-between. In that dark hallway, the temperature was about twenty degrees cooler than the rest of the building, so I would spend all my time in there, reading a book while pacing back and forth to cool off. People thought I was a nut, but I thought they were crazy for sitting in the heat and, even worse, napping in it. There's something basically wrong about seeing someone sweating profusely while they're sleeping. Most people could endure the temperature better than me. I would see them sit in that stifling heat all day in their shorts, playing cards or flipping through magazines. Lemke worked out constantly and barely ate; he was so ripped that he looked like The Illustrated Man. He had hollows underneath his shoulder blades that were so deep that you could have hidden oranges in them.

We now had radio phones at Battalion HQ that we could use daily. They were very difficult to operate and the calls had to be re-routed through so many sub-stations that there was a three-second delay, so you would spend most of the call talking over the other person. The phones were a blessing as well as a curse since people were getting news about cheating wives, emptied bank accounts and the like. Carpenter's wife was the worst, but Carpenter still defended "Princess Jen" like she was an angel. She had been a recreational druggie before, but after we left and she had full access to Carpenter's bank account, she became a full-fledged junkie. He called her once while she was stoned and when the phone went silent, he thought that she had OD'ed. He had a nervous breakdown, staring into space for hours.

Carpenter was so out of it that he couldn't even answer simple questions, so Rager went to go get Princess Jen's address out of Carpenter's notebook. Gunny Linton—who was convalescing back in Cali after knee surgery—wanted her address so he could drive out and check on her. When Rager opened the notebook, he found it filled with weird, sexual poetry, with lines like, "I fucked her ass so hard, like that time in the bushes, in her parent's yard." Other poems dwelt on his estrangement from the others and his underlying rage. The best was "My anger is like a raging inferno!" Imagining Carpenter saying that in his stentorian monotone cracked us all up. The craziest part was a poem on how to suck cock that Carpenter wrote in the second-person perspective, "You take the cock into your mouth." This was too weird to confront Carpenter about directly, but Chiariello couldn't help but shout quotes from the notebook every time Carpenter came into view.

We returned to the range, but this time Sprinkles tagged along and ruined it. Even though we never did gun drills in combat, he made us do them all afternoon like we were in SOI. He would make vague changes to the gun drills and then act disgusted when we misunderstood him.

"Why didn't you go with them up to the gun line, Sgt. Meyer?"

"You told me to hang back and let them do it by themselves, sir."

"You're still supposed to go with them, sergeant."

I was supposed to go with them, but not *be* with them. That's like some kind of Zen koan.

Squeak was going off on me non-stop since Sprinkles was going off on him and I let myself fall into the same trap. When Ryan complained about having too much ammo, I screamed at him to stop complaining. After the gun drill, I felt shitty for yelling at Ryan and I apologized. What I said was legitimate, but there was no need to belittle him.

The Salman trips were so miserable that I did everything in my power to avoid them. When Ross walked up, with a clipboard in his hand, I went off.

"Hey man, I got to make up the roster for this trip to Salman and I-"

"No! No! Fuck that! You always do that, Ross! You're not gonna fuck me like this! I just went to Salman two fucking days ago!"

"If you would have let me finish, *asshole*, you would have heard me say, 'I'm making this roster for Salman and I need to borrow a pen.' But since you want to be a bitch about it, you're on the roster now."

We had gotten a new CO and the initial consensus was good. Captain Kenney had missed the combat phase, having been an instructor at OCS. He accompanied us on a trip to Salman, where we noticed activity at one of the ancient forts. We drove up and saw 13 year-olds wearing police uniforms and milling around out front along with two adult officers. We had brought our interpreter along with us and, for once, he earned his pay. They told him that this had been one of the worst gulags when Saddam reigned, but now it was just the local police station. Things seemed peaceful until we saw a small mob heading up the rocky hill toward us. They wanted answers about relatives that were being held in the fort. A fat policeman got in a scuffle with one of them, which was the most excitement we'd had since April 12th. The drama dissipated and we left after the CO made some vague promises to the crowd.

When we drove up out of the deep valley and hit the highway, some older men waved us over and told us they had just been car-jacked. There are only about five different types of cars in Iraq and almost all of them are white, so finding their car was hopeless. I felt bad for not being able to help them, but it reminded me of a similar incident that happened back in Samawah. We were parked at the courthouse when an Iraqi came up and started telling us that some guy stole his truck. I asked an officer if we could help, but he said it was out of our jurisdiction.

"Sorry, buddy, we can't help you," I told the Iraqi.

"Then what am I to do?"

"You said you've seen this guy and you know where he lives?" Miller asked.

"Yes. I know his neighborhood."

"Then why don't you go and get it back yourself?"

"Oh no, I cannot do that."

"Why the hell not? You're like six-foot-four."

"Because he might revenge on me."

"Well fuck, that's life. Are you going to let him drive around in your own car and do nothing?"

"What can I do?"

"If I was you I'd get about five of my buddies and go wait in his neighborhood until you see him drive by. Then you pull him out of the car and beat his ass."

"But what if he has a gun?"

"Goddamnit, man, you *all* have guns here. Have some fucking balls."

Miller couldn't believe how cowardly this guy was, but it was quite common. After so many years of a brutal dictatorship, they were like children. It was a bully culture—one guy with balls could rule his whole neighborhood.

The insurgency was growing, but it hadn't reached Samawah. Rumor had it that outsiders were going to come there and start trouble, but it never happened. The worst thing that happened was kids throwing rocks at our humvee. It sounds silly, but it enraged me when it happened. I didn't throw rocks at cop cars when I was a kid and none of the cop cars in Papillion, Nebraska had 40mm grenade launchers on them. The parents saw it happen and did nothing.

I went to Club Chaos to sit in on Corporal's Course when I noticed a boot from First named Siler looking strange. I hadn't known Siler at all until we went to Kuwait, where his cot was near mine. Siler was a big ol' good-hearted country boy with a bushy hair-do that made him look like an Ewok. He was easy-going, but he had a rep for being weird. His name had been awkwardly stretched into the nickname "Insane A-siler". As a nickname-giving expert, that was a D—at best.

The sergeant major called me over and told me to escort Siler back to our building. Kind of weird, but no big deal. I went outside and found Siler in an alcove, hunched over and sobbing. I tried to ask him what was wrong, but he was inconsolable. He started spouting off about God and the Devil like a crazy homeless person. I tried to listen to him and show some compassion—thinking that was what he needed—but it had little effect. The more I talked with him, the crazier he got. He had gone up to the sergeant major and tried to convert him to some weird religion he had created in his head. He kept talking about getting taken over by the devil, making allusions to it being connected to the way we obey orders without question (in theory, anyway).

I asked him what had happened, imagining some inciting incident like a death in the family, but it seemed like he had just cracked. Being nice had failed and, while I wasn't going to be a prick, I needed to get him to the building. Siler was big, broad-shouldered and strong; even worse, he had just finished the Martial Arts instructor class in Kuwait. My third stripe was about to get my ass-kicked, but I had to try and move him. I grabbed his arm, expecting him to go crazy and start fighting me, but the exact opposite happened. He went absolutely limp, like a kid who doesn't want to go to bed. I tried to pick him up, but he was like a bag of cement.

I went into Club Chaos and dragged Rodgar and Hot Rod out of their class, which they didn't seem to mind. I gave them the low-down, but each wanted to try his best to talk some sense into Siler. Rodgar had a good approach, but he couldn't get through. Hot Rod was the bad cop; he told Siler he could walk like a man or get carried like a baby. Carrying Siler was easier said than done. Rodgar and I were unable to lift him together. I assumed I was the weak link, but when Hot Rod took my place, the best they could do was drag Siler's leaden body a few feet.

Tardif and Birdsong came over and said they'd take care of him. They were all in First Platoon, which was like a cult; if anyone could get through to him, they could. When I got back to our building, I told Chiariello about the whole incident and I was surprised at how concerned he was. Chiariello was snarky and sarcastic, but he was very loyal to his friends. Though he had promised not to tell anyone what Siler had confided in him recently, when I told him of the craziness that Siler was spewing, a look of recognition came into his eyes.

SSgt. Sikes was able to get Siler walking and he was taken to the BAS to be looked at, but he snuck out when they were distracted. They found him in one of the humvees and Doc Cox had to wrestle him out of there. He was taken back to the building and tied to his rack. He ranted and raved and then slept, pissing himself. The next day, he was gone.

Though weird, Siler was a good guy who had fought honorably and no one doubted that his problems were real. It was sad that he was brought low within two weeks of leaving. While speaking to his close friends though, it became clear that something like this would have happened eventually, whether in war or peace.

Besides being enthusiastic, hard-working and professional, the Seabees were the most motivated unit I'd ever seen. Though most were in their forties, they were the only unit that PTed every day. They didn't just go through the motions; while they ran their 5 miles a day, they would shout cadences just like in the movies. Bald spots and pot-bellies abounded in their unit, but underneath they were hard.

A small percentage of their cadences were "blue"; but nothing worse than you'd overhear in the chow line. Nevertheless, a few low-ranking Army chicks got "offended" and complained to Sergeant Major Davis, the highest-ranking staff NCO on the camp. These were the same chicks we caught dry-humping dudes in plain view at night and tanning topless behind the train cars. The Seabees' Master Chief, their senior staff NCO, would get a career-killing formal reprimand if his people did any more dirty cadences.

Everything was fine for a few days, but the day before the Seabees left, they did an extra-long PT session and a few expletives were inserted into their chants. Sure enough, the Army bitches complained. The next day, the BC held a battalion-wide formation to honor the Seabees and thank them for their service. I noticed that they all looked pretty glum, considering they were going home; when the formation ended, I found out why. The sergeant major made good on his threat, counseling their Master Chief and, even worse, making the Seabees walk in formation to the Army building and formally apologize to the half-dozen women who had been "offended." This sickened me; the Seabees I served with were the finest people I ever met while in the military and they had to prostrate themselves in front of a handful of skanks who treated the war like a personal dating service.

The Dutch main party was starting to arrive, so we had to move and give them our prime location. We shuffled over to Weapons Company's building, which was the largest. As soon as we got there, we found out that Cortez, Acosta and Carpenter had reported most of the machinegun section for hazing them. Though Cortez was the ring-leader, he had gotten encouragement from Lopez. Many NCOs in Echo, like McKee, had gotten busted down for hazing—entirely on the words of the boots accusing them. Squeak confirmed that we were being investigated, but he smirked, saying it would blow over.

The First Sergeant had a meeting with the NCOs in which he tried to hash things out with us, to no avail. "There seems to be a consensus in the section that

Cortez is a liar, Carpenter is an idiot and Acosta is a coward." When we all nodded, he sputtered in frustration. He was trying to make a point, not get us to agree with him. We all had a lot of problems with First Sergeant Young, but what he said next hit the nail on the head, even if we couldn't admit it to ourselves back then.

"You know, it's real easy to look at someone who's fucked-up and say it's all on him, but as NCOs, it's your job to guide those Marines. Now I heard some shit about Acosta, most of which I believe, but you got to ask yourself—How much training has he had? Y'all have been training for the last three years, but that boy is almost straight out of boot camp. Not everyone has the same qualities; he might not be the most bad-ass motherfucker, but he's a hard worker. The reaction he had was the normal human reaction; he hasn't been in the Corps long enough to be able to just shrug shit like that off. You can pat yourselves on the back and nothing can get better or you can make those kids into good Marines."

Cortez and Carpy were garbage, but Acosta was salvageable. Acosta was 26 and had been a video game-tester before he enlisted. Though he was over six feet four, he was very simple and child-like. His main problem was that he was under Cortez' sway and Cortez was a piece of shit. As a super-boot diggie, Cortez had been the only person that Acosta could hang out with, but now we had a great new diggie in Arellano. If I could just get them to be friends, some of Arellano's perfection might rub off on Acosta.

We were told to stay away from Cortez, Acosta, and Carpenter to prevent further problems, but they still had to earn their keep. They had been at Battalion HQ all day writing their statements and had missed all of the patrols, so I put them on the night runs. I went up to Battalion to tell them so and they seemed surprised that I would talk to them since they were "protected." Cortez looked cocky and Carpenter looked catatonic, but Acosta looked embarrassed. He kept looking at Cortez to see how he was reacting. I told them that they had time to finish their reports on the computers, but they still had to work. They agreed sheepishly.

I believe that I caused Cortez to rally the others to rat us out, since I had recently messed with him for fun and embarrassed him. Cortez was a notorious liar; each lie was more unbelievable than the last. He claimed a wife that no one had ever met; the picture he showed off of her was the same one he had told others was a picture of his sister. He had a rich fantasy life, telling us that he was a professional salsa dancer before he enlisted, once pulling down $10,000 in a salsa contest. He told us that the first time he had ever been in the continental United States was when he had flown to boot camp, which contradicted his earlier stories of being on a prize-winning high school band in Texas and being a professional dancer in Florida. My favorite lie was about how he got his car from Puerto Rico to LAX. I called him over to grill him on that one.

"Yes, sergeant?"

"Tell me again how you got your car to Cali."

"I had it flown there, sergeant."

"You had it flown…in a plane…" I said, giving him a chance to rescind his lie.

"Yes, sergeant."

"How much did it cost?"

"Oh, about two grand, sergeant."

"So how did you get the car? Did they deliver it to you?"

"No, I just picked it up."

"How'd you get it out of the airport?"

"I just drove it down the runway."

I actually started to have fun. I could see that Cortez was one of those guys who lied so much that he started to believe his own lies. He kept to his fanciful story and I let him go. Apparently, he got pretty steamed and started concocting revenge almost immediately.

Lopez' involvement was a surprise. He was solid as a rock, tough and smart, but he had never really fit in. A few weeks before, he had gotten into a shouting match with Fielder, who he thought was demeaning Acosta. Fielder had gotten close to crossing the line, but had not stepped over. Lopez just didn't like seeing people get picked on, especially when rank prevented them from truly being able to defend themselves. Lopez had been promoted to Team Leader when Miller went home and Ryan got accused. When the charges against Ryan were dropped, Ryan returned to the company and wanted the team leader billet, since he was senior to Lopez. I didn't like playing musical chairs with billets like Squeak had, so I kept Lopez as team leader. This decision was highly controversial with my peers and both Ross and Moser told me that I should take the team leader billet away from Lopez. Even though they were my buddies and I trusted their judgement, I told them that, even though I wasn't happy with Lopez for what he did, he had been a good team leader, so he was staying. The way I saw it, Lopez did the wrong thing for the right reason.

Captain Yagee was an air wing officer attached to 2/5 to co-ordinate close-air support during the combat phase. He didn't have a thing to do in Samawah, so he was assigned to conduct the investigation. Those with the most charges against them—like Elias and Chiariello—had been questioned repeatedly and at length at Battalion. Yagee then came to our building to interrogate the rest of us. He set up shop in a storage room full of broken glass and machine parts and he started calling us in one at a time. All of his questions were very leading, being variations on the old damning yes-or-no question "Have you stopped beating your wife yet?" Most people declined to talk, but others tried to be "tricky" by partially answering some questions. I told them that anything they said could be used against someone else and if two stories didn't match, then both of the Marines would be considered liars. The best thing to do was refuse to say anything and ask to see a JAG lawyer.

I was quite looking forward to being investigated. I had been told that Carpenter had reported me for kicking him in the chest during our first firefight. It was completely justified, but I knew they would not see it that way. When I went inside and sat down in front of Captain Yagee, I was thought it was going to be some kind of big Oscar-winning scene, but it was fairly anti-climactic. He asked me if I knew why I was there and I responded that I knew that the machinegun section was being investigated for "alleged" acts of hazing. I was disappointed as hell when he said that I wasn't being charged with anything—what do I have to do to Carpenter, shoot him? He handed me a paper to sign and started to explain it to me, but I was light-headed and dopey and I couldn't concentrate. As he droned on, I just tripped out while looking at his arms. I had lost a lot of weight, but Captain Yagee looked like he had AIDS. When he finally stopped, I went to sign, thinking that it just said that I had been read my rights; I then stopped and forced myself to read it again. The legalese was insane, full of double and triple negatives. It stopped just short of saying "Are you not unguilty?" and "Isn't it false that it is a lie that you didn't hit him?" I told him that I refused to say anything. There was a rumor that anyone who didn't talk would be stuck in Kuwait until the trial, which could be months away. I asked him if that was true and he gave a non-committal answer. I walked out, quite proud of myself for standing up to "The Man".

A new building meant a new Wack Shack and I remember Number 4 quite fondly. It lost points for not having a lock, but it did have a heavy wooden beam you could use to block the door. Unfortunately, this bathroom had urinals that people insisted on pissing in, even though looters had stolen the brass pipes that connected them to the sewer lines. The piss would just fall through the bottom of the pisser onto the floor. I noticed an increase in a weird phenomenon that I had first seen in Wack Shack II—some people had a weird urge to piss on, come on, or rip into shreds, the porno they had just wacked off to. I didn't know if it was just spite for the next guy or some kind of intense Catholic guilt that would pop up immediately after ejaculation, but someone had issues.

When I was told that Squeak wanted to speak to me, I assumed my usual defensive posture. When I rounded the corner though, I saw him sitting on his rack with a shy, casual smile on his face. After beating around the bush (or "going around the bush," as Elias would say) Squeak told me that he was putting me back in as section leader and CAAT leader. He said that, after much thought, he realized that his problems with my leadership probably came from me being thrown into the rank of sergeant with no training or mentoring. I got the feeling that Gunny Brouillet had put him up to this, or at least suggested it. The flip-flopping of leadership jobs stopped as well.

I then entered the busiest period of my Marine Corps career, holding five billets simultaneously: Driver, Squad Leader, Section Leader, CAAT Leader and Platoon Guide. I had never heard of any Marine holding more than two billets at once. It was exhausting, but it made the time move much faster.

Like any group of people who just entered a Third—World country, the Dutch all got violently ill and some of the Marines caught sick as well. This meant that my already over-tasked CAAT Marines now had to fill in for sick elevens on guard duty. We had already lost Showers, Miller, Reed, Scott and Mohler, and now I had to send half of my boots to the guard force. In addition to our six daily scheduled patrols, we also had to pick the interpreters up in the morning and drive them home at dinner time. Invariably, the CO would want to go somewhere once or twice a day, and there were also trips to Salman and other odd missions here and there. Now that I was in charge, I had to make the CAAT patrol rosters. There was no way to make anyone happy since we were so over-tasked. Once, Rager came off of two days of guard, got two hours of sleep and then had to go on a night patrol. After three more hours of sleep, he had to head out to godforsaken Salman. Rager was not a complainer, but I could see that he was getting on edge. I explained to him that I had no choice, but that was little comfort. We were so busy that I would have corporals as gunners on one patrol and lances as vehicle commanders on the next. I had to grab whoever was there and just shove them in the vehicles. More than once, I would return from a patrol and realize that I had to go on the patrol that was leaving in ten minutes because there weren't enough people.

Roy would always accuse me of favoring the others. He was such a whiner that I stopped even putting him on the schedule. I had to put him on a patrol one day since there weren't enough people and he got pissed when I woke him up at the crack of three in the afternoon.

"Roy, get up. I need you to go out in town."

"What the fuck, Meyer?"

"What do you mean 'What the fuck?' Get your fucking gear on."

"Oh yeah, you never ask your buddies like Elias or Moser."

"Actually, those guys are both on their second patrol today."

"Fucking buddy-fucker, man."

"You know what, Roy? I don't want to hear any of your shit. I haven't even put you on the schedule for two days since you always bitch like this. You want me to show you the last week's schedule? The only time you wake up is to piss and grab a sandwich."

Roy was a weird combination of good Marine and total shitbird. He was one of the fastest runners in the battalion, yet he had a huge potbelly. His uniform was always immaculate, yet he never knew what was going on. He would catch me being sheisty and lecture me about being professional, then he would sleep for three days straight. I saw him check the schedule and make a disgusted sound.

"What the hell are you muttering about?"

"Fucking patrol schedule, man. Look how many times you put Fielder and Fernandez on today. You got no troop welfares."

"First of all, the word is 'welfare', not 'welfares.' Let me break it down for you, since you don't know what the fuck you're talking about, as usual. We have 21 guys in CAAT, six of which just got pulled for guard. Each patrol takes two vehicles and six Marines. I give the boots as much rest as I can. Fuck—I put myself on three patrols today. Now you take this fucking pen and give me your fucking divine wisdom and make a better schedule."

"No troop welfares," he muttered as he walked away.

I had no ego as a sergeant—a good idea was good if it came from a lance corporal or a general—but he had nothing to offer. That was the worst part of being a leader. People are always second-guessing you and complaining, but they have no realistic alternative. They don't know the right way to run things, but they know your way is wrong.

People were so exhausted that even good Marines started pulling tricks to get out of patrols. They would pull their cots outside at night and purposefully sleep in hard to find areas, so that I couldn't grab them to put them on patrols. I had to make them to put chem-lights under their cots so they could be found. People would purposefully not check the prominently-displayed schedule, so they could profess ignorance. The schedule changed frequently, but I would always find one person per vehicle and update them. The boots—who professed wanting to be given more responsibility—would know that they had to go on patrol, but if the NCOs didn't come and get them, they would play "lance corporal don't know." I told them that responsibility flowed in both directions. Every person was in charge of making the others aware it was time to go, no matter the rank.

When I left for a dawn patrol, I told Roy that he had the next run, which was supposed to leave just as I was coming back. When I returned two hours later, I saw Lt. Chittick waiting next to an empty vehicle. Roy was dressing groggily, having just woken up. I hustled him and his team outside, practically dressing them. I chewed Roy out in front of his men, which I usually didn't do to NCOs, but he deserved it. He didn't have a leg to stand on and he knew it, so he looked down and shuffled his feet like a little kid. After their patrol, I pulled Rager to the side.

"You might be wondering while I just yelled at Roy for a couple seconds, but I'm taking you aside to counsel you. I judge people on their abilities. With Roy, I have minimum expectations. If he wakes up and puts his uniform on correctly, I'm happy. Fuck, I'm ecstatic. You, on the other hand, get held to the highest standard because I constantly see you operate above the level of other Marines."

With good Marines, guilt works better than an ass-chewing.

When we did a gear check, we found that my squad was missing a T&E, the part of the gun system that adjusts the gun's aim when it is mounted. With so many patrols, people would grab whatever gun was closest and put it on the turret. Though the guns would always be taken down after every patrol, we sometimes left the T&E on the gun mount and it was assumed that someone from another company stole one of ours while it was unattended. Squeak saw the missing T&E causing another stain on his career, so he made us completely empty each vehicle after every patrol, even if they were going back out in twenty minutes. As usual, I tried to insulate those under me from the heat, but Squeak was relentless. I would get my ass chewed if he found a bottle cap under a seat.

While returning from a patrol, I spent the last five minutes stressing to Ross how much pressure Squeak was putting on me and that the vehicle had to be spotless before he went inside. Sure enough, by the time I had turned the engine off and stepped out of the vehicle, he and the gunner were gone. There wasn't much trash in the vehicle, but I had been spending ten minutes after every patrol cleaning up the vehicles and I was sick of it. I was getting my ass chewed for my men and they weren't returning the favor by keeping me out of the line of fire.

I went inside and found Ross in the Weapons Platoon Cool NCO's room.

"Hey, you gotta go back and empty the vehicle like I was talking about."

"Are you serious? There's like an apple core and a dip can in there."

"There's some rat-fucked MREs, cigarette butts, *your* empty dip can that I specifically pointed out to you before you left."

"You're actually going to make me go back for that?"

"I have to."

Ross grumbled as he left and Moser waited until he got out of earshot.

"Dude," Moser said, quite eloquently.

"What? I had to do that! You know how bad Squeak is riding me over this shit?"

"Would it have been that big of a deal to pick it up yourself?"

"Yes! I'm a fucking sergeant and I'm cleaning up after lances every day. Besides, I explicitly told Ross to clean the vehicle, even pointing out specific pieces of trash."

"You should have just grabbed the pieces of trash and then counseled Ross about it afterward."

"So you think I should have cleaned it myself?"

"Look, I'm not busting your balls. I'm just saying that—in this situation—I disagree with the way you handled it. That's all."

I was floored. I was used to every difference of opinion between NCOs devolving into shouting matches, pushing matches and fistfights—often in front of their boots. To have Moser calmly explain why he disagreed with me was shocking. Neither of us convinced the other, but I came away even more impressed with Moser.

During my hundred of patrols, I got to compare the different styles of the patrol leaders. Though each patrol had one staff NCO or officer present, it was the young corporal that ran the show. As many problems as I had with these two guys, I felt that Kennel and Monty were the best patrol leaders. Kennel knew the sewage-filled back alleys and garbage-strewn empty lots like he had grown up there. He once took us so deep into the worst ghetto in town that I didn't think he'd be able to find the way out. Monty did not pull near as many patrols, since he was the SOG for the building guard the majority of the time we were there, but he more than made up for it. Instead of just hitting the same five points and taking the major roads like most of the other patrol leaders, he would take us on intricate paths through each neighborhood, sometimes doubling back on our trail to see if any trouble brewed up after we left.

After six months together, everyone had heard each other's stories a dozen times, so new topics of conversation were desperately needed. I had purposefully set my rack next to Chiariello's instead of near my fellow NCOs, since I could corner him for good conversation. Though a complete and proud dirtbag, Chiariello had also been a Teacher's Assistant in college, which meant that I could have conversations with him that didn't revolve around chewing tobacco or "this dude in high school that I totally kicked his ass." Not that our conversations were that lofty; most of them revolved around various activities we had engaged in with women that were probably still illegal in Tennessee.

Apropos of nothing, I decided that we would have a "trial" in which we would decide which one of us, if the occasion arose, would have the best shot at getting Angelina Jolie into bed. For the next hour, we each plead our case on the methods we would use to woo Ms. Jolie. I acted as both plaintiff and judge, delineating what methods would be allowed. Lying, of course, was allowed, but drugs or blackmail were not. Chiariello had some good lines, all completely shameless, but even I had to admit that they would work like gang-busters. After over-ruling Chiariello's objection that it was a conflict of interest for me to be the judge of a contest that I was in, I rendered my verdict. Though I believed we would both be able to get her into the sack, only I could sustain a relationship with her for more than two weeks. Chiariello conceded on that point, adding that he wouldn't want to stay with any woman for more than two weeks. He also made the good point that it would be better to move on, since he would then find himself in a much higher strata of women. No woman could say that she was too hot for him after Angelina Jolie fucked him. In fact, many women would want to sleep with him just for the cache of being able to say that had sex with a guy who laid Angelina Jolie.

Chiariello got endless amusement out of watching me sew up my cot every day. The only sign that our stay in Iraq was anything more than a two-day field op was when we were issued cots. My cot was the closest thing to a home I had; it wasn't like the Vietnam movies where people had as much room as a they would in a college dorm. My cot with all my gear stuffed under it was the only personal space I had. By this time, most people's cots had burst at the seams; they would droop to the floor when someone laid down on them. Between patrols I would spend hours trying to salvage the torn scraps of my cot, only to have the stitches pop as soon as I sat down.

Every night, I would take my cot outside and sleep as far away from the others as possible. I found a spot next to a dead garden, in which I had a whopping thirty feet around me with no other people. The only downside was that I was near two generators and, when the wind died down, the fumes were quite heavy. I wondered if I was getting brain damage. I told myself that if I survived all of the exhaust I inhaled while riding on the tracs, I was immune to almost anything; and as long as I was outdoors, the fumes couldn't get thick enough to asphyxiate me.

Chiariello was extremely astute when it came to judging people and he hit the nail on the head when describing Carpenter. "People always make excuses for him. They'll say, 'Yeah, he fucks up a lot and gets us in trouble, but he a a good person' and you know what? He isn't. He's a bad person. He is all about himself. He will see what needs to be done to make things better for the group and he will always choose the way that's best for him. Not only that, but he takes no control over his own life, knowing that we'll be there to pick up the pieces for him." When we went to the swim tank in boot camp, they taught us that when saving a drowning person, you never draw them in tight. In their terror, if they get too close to you, they will grab onto you and drag you down with them. That was Carpenter in a nutshell.

The last obstacle that could have delayed our return home was removed when it was confirmed that we were not going North to battle the burgeoning insurgency. The Dutch main party arrived and started making the camp their own. I was impressed by their vehicles and gear, which were all brand-new and modular, as if Ikea had become arms dealers. They had the same cammies as us and similar weapons, but instead of a SAW, they had a fully-automatic M-16 that had a 100-round drum on it—very cool.

The force consisted of Dutch soldiers and Dutch Marines and we found that their relationship was the same as the one between us and our soldiers—the Dutch Marines were the more elite force and looked down on the Dutch soldiers. True to the stereotype, the Dutch were all huge. The average height was probably six foot two with many topping six-six. I laughed when I saw Squeak standing among Dutch Marines that looked like Redwoods compared to him.

The Dutch were almost civilian-like, they were so casual. They could roll their sleeves up (horrors!), they could wear civvies when off-duty, and they could even grow beards as long as they kept them trimmed. I stopped in mid-stride when I saw one of their black soldiers playing basketball, his shoulder-length dreads whipping around his head.

We were glad that the Dutch were there, not only because they were replacing us, but also because they were new people to talk to. There were several fair-to-cute women among them that the guys hit on, all to no success. I couldn't blame the girls, we all looked like concentration camp prisoners and the Dutch soldiers looked like Mr. Universe contestants. Even worse was the awkwardness that came from not speaking to women for seven months.

Maya, one of the junior 51s, bragged about "macking" on a Dutch girl. I cringed when I heard the pick-up line he used, which would have been too cheesy to get into an episode of "Three's Company." He told me he grabbed a hunk of ice out of a cooler, walked up to a Dutch chick and dropped it at her feet.

"Now that we've broken the ice, why don't we get to know each other?"

I spent almost twenty minutes trying to explain to him how bad of a line that was; I almost got to the point of getting graphs and charts and setting up an impromptu trial to explain to him how lame that line was.

Maya wasn't the only who was making an ass out of himself. Colvin cornered a few Dutch Marines and started bragging of his exploits during the war, which he blew so far out of proportion that a five year-old wouldn't have been believed him. When he told the Dutch that he had "73 confirmed kills", one of them walked over to us, pointed at Colvin and asked us to "make that one go away."

They were building their own base out of pre-fab materials in the plains out-side of the train station because they had detected unsafe levels of asbestos and depleted uranium in and around the train station. Dart tried to get more info on this from the MO, who comically refused any validity to their findings.

"Sir, I heard that they found asbestos throughout the station."

"'Through-out' is an exaggeration. They only found them near the trains."

"Sir, there are trains everywhere. It's a train station."

"Yes, but they only found asbestos on the trains' brake pads. You'd have to be right next to them to breathe in anything unsafe."

"You mean like the trains that we all sleep next to every night?"

"Well, yes, but they'd have to do something to stir the particles up to get you to ingest them."

"Sir, they make the boots sweep next to the trains everyday."

In the weeks before our replacements arrived, we had trouble keeping it straight whether they were Belgian or Dutch or Danes. Once it was confirmed that they were Dutch, which country were they from? Holland, the Netherlands, Denmark? The trick I finally came up with to keep things straight was to remember "Austin Powers." Dr. Evil was Belgian and Goldmember was Dutch. We were constantly making jokes about the "Dutch Bastards" and using Dr. Evil's line, "I don't speak freaky-deaky Dutch." They put safety signs that would say crazy things like, "Flarven! Klarfenstruegel!" with a little lighting bolt next to it, to which I responded, "Oh, of course…*klar*fenstruegel."

While most of the Dutch were cool, some had serious attitudes. Keller was talking with a couple of them when one made a disparaging remark about our unit. Keller laid into the guy, belittling the "grand and glorious" history of the Dutch Marines and pointing out that, though the whole world knew about the US Marines, he hadn't even *heard* of the Dutch marines until they rolled into town. He told them that we had fought the war and they were just cleaning up after us.

In the line for chow one day, I noticed the Dutch soldier in front of me had his rifle on "fire." I considered myself the most laid-back sergeant in the history of the Marine Corps—I didn't give a fuck about haircuts, clean uniforms, shaves or shined boots—but I did care about safety. I made it a habit to constantly check other people's weapons, as well as my own. I tapped the guy on the shoulder and casually told him his weapon was on "fire." He looked over at his buddy, rolled his eyes, and then tried to tell me that in the Dutch Army, if there was no magazine in your rifle, you didn't have to have it on "safe." This was stupid for two reasons. There could still be a round in the chamber even if the magazine was out and secondly, how damn hard was it to flick the selector lever to "safe?" I told him even if that was their policy(which I doubted), we hadn't handed them control of the camp yet so they were still beholden to our rules. They had already had four NDs in the few short days they'd been there, one with a .50 cal. for Christ's sake. He looked at his buddy and then flicked his weapon on "safe" with a huff.

Those problems were the exception and, as our leave date approached, we integrated the Dutch into our patrols. I particularly liked their patrol vehicles, which looked a cross between a dune buggy and a pick-up truck. They were topped off with a turret that looked like something out of "Star Wars"; I asked one of them if I could climb into the turret and he nodded coolly. I set my rifle next to the wheel of their vehicle and climbed into the turret, spinning it around and pretending I was Han Solo in the Millennium Falcon. When it was time to go, I jumped down and got into my Humvee. When Moser asked whose rifle was leaning against the Dutch vehicle, my heart almost stopped. I jumped out and grabbed it before anyone but Moser saw that it was mine.

Forgetting your weapon is second only to shooting a fellow Marine in the list of grunt sins. I told Moser I was going to report myself to Squeak and he told me to calm down and just realize that I lost some cool points. As I started the engine, he tried to crack a joke and totally screwed it up, losing some cool points himself. I proposed that our mutual loss of cool points had negated each other and he agreed. When we returned after the patrol, my foot got caught on my rifle sling and I tripped as I got out of the vehicle. Moser laughed and reminded me that we were no longer even.

During our last two weeks, we were worried that trouble would flare up and our departure would be cancelled. When we first got to Samawah, if we heard shots five blocks away we would peel out and speed over to the scene of the crime like "Starsky and Hutch", but it was a different story now. While driving over a bridge, some shots rang out a couple blocks away.

"Did you just hear nothing?" Ross from Third asked. "'Cause I just heard nothing."

"I just heard a whole lot of nothing," I replied.

On our last patrol, we stopped by the river to take some pictures. Samawah had been hot, disgusting and boring—with no glory or action—but like anywhere you spend any significant time, you couldn't help but have some fond memories.

As the sun set on my last day in Iraq, I walked to the north edge of the train station and stared at Samawah, a mile away. It seemed unreal—we were really going home. As happy as I was, I had to admit to myself that I was a little afraid of going home. My life had been so different. I had to adapt to this inhuman environment and I worried about not being able to change back. For months, I had lived below the standard of living of a homeless person. The attitudes of the staff NCOs and officers had made me bitter and hateful. My aggression level had spiked through the roof and I still fantasized daily about the death and destruction of combat. But I had other dreams—normal dreams—and I meant to make them come true.

I got posted as driver since the First Sergeant remembered me having to slap myself in the face to keep myself awake the last time we went to Kuwait. This bothered me because I had always imagined driving out of that hell hole on my own steam. Right before we left, the First Sergeant gave me the job back, saying he'd yank me if I started nodding off. I made it within ten miles of the border before I had to let Ross take the wheel, since I was "bobbing for cock" too much.

I had been hoping to hold onto our humvees for a couple days so we could make some runs to Camp Commando, but they wanted the vehicles emptied and cleaned so we could turn them in the next day. The following morning, we turned them in to Motor T. I got my camera out to take a picture of the humvees I had spent so much time in, but then I changed my mind—I was glad to be rid of them.

With the vehicles gone, all we had to do was pack up our gear and heavy weapons and get a couple of out-briefs. One tent had rudimentary exercise equipment and it became quite popular with some of the men. Elias was the king of the gym and he worked out all day long. He was a real social butterfly and he would latch on to whoever came into the gym and shadow them on their workout. When that person left, he would grab the next person who came in and work out with them. I joked with Moser that Elias's daily work out was "chest, legs, triceps, biceps, quad, triceps, legs, chest, chest again, traps, lats, stomach, forearms…" Moser pointed out that though Elias was one of the strongest guys in the company, he could have worked one-tenth as much and been just as strong.

The missing T & E never turned up and Squeak was frantic. He tried pulling his old "Toughest Man in the World" act, but I couldn't care have cared less. It's great to say "Find it!" over and over, but it's not like I can drive down to Habib's House of Machinegun Accessories and buy another one. Besides, there were only five T&Es on our official count since we got one off-the-books right before the war started to replace one that was missing from Mohler's squad. Sprincin knew we had used to have six though and he would be inspecting us the next day.

I went to my buddies in other companies and asked if anyone could hook me up. Shaheen thought he might have been able to help me, but that didn't pan out. When it became clear that diplomacy wasn't working, I called my two juvenile delinquents, Ryan and Lopez, and gave them a black ops mission—get me a T&E by any means necessary. Those two criminals were more than happy to do it and they huddled together to conspire on the heist. They confidently promised me a T&E by the morning.

Morning came and no T & E. It was almost endearing to see Ryan and Lopez ashamed because they *couldn't* steal something. All of the other companies had their gear locked up already, but the sergeant major had a humvee in front of his tent with a T & E on top, just asking to be stolen. Every time, Ryan and Lopez approached the vehicle though, someone would pop out of a nearby tent to smoke or use a sat-phone. I patted them on the shoulder, bucking them up by reminding how many things there would be to steal back in America.

Sprinkles came in and told us to lay all of the gun systems out on-line and have each weapon's gunner stand behind their system. As he went down the list of parts in the gun system, he would call each part out and the gunners were supposed to pull it out of the gun bag and show it to him. Luckily though, he did it one system at a time. The others were watching out for us and, after a gun in first squad got inspected, they hustled their T & E over to Rager. Sprinkles didn't discover our subterfuge and we thought we were scot-free.

The next day, Ryan and Rager came up to me and said that Sprincin had just re-inspected the weapons. I got worried, but they gave me reassuring, conspiratorial smiles. Perhaps feeling something was amiss, Sprinkles decided to reinspect the gun systems in his tent. This time though, he only had one representative per squad. Sprinkles could see all six guns at once, so no one could hand off a T&E like last time. Under pressure, Rager and Ryan cooked up a plan that would be hard to believe in a Tom and Jerry cartoon, but somehow it worked. When

Sprincin told Rager to show him the T&E for Gun 5, Rager coolly pulled the T&E out of Gun 6 and Sprincin checked it off, not noticing he had been scammed. Rager and Ryan knew that they had pulled off the crime of the century and were quite proud of themselves. I was in awe of them. After the inspection, Sprinkles signed off on the loading invoice, which meant that if anything was found missing from then on, it was on him.

There was little left to do after we packed and palletized our weapons systems. After company PT, our days were free. Carrasquillo finally came back to Golf, after missing the entire war. He had not gone into Iraq with us since he had successfully exaggerated a case of heat stroke into some kind of heart condition. A few weeks after we crossed the LOD, the doctors confirmed that there was nothing wrong with him. The only thing that prevented him from catching up with us was lack of transportation. In May, Yoder and Gunny Linton had made a run down to Kuwait to pick up our sea bags. Yoder ran into Carrasquillo at Camp Commando, where he had been chilling while we were living like pigs. Yoder told Carrasquillo to get his stuff and meet them, but Carrasquillo ditched them and they had to leave without him.

As we ran around the LSA, Carrasquillo's lanky arms flailed as he gasped for air. Being a war-dodging coward was one thing, but the fact that he couldn't keep up with us, after he had all that time to work out and eat well, just disgusted us. As he fell back, people started hurling well-deserved insults at him. His own boots were running up and knocking him into the sand with impunity. His rank meant nothing anymore and even the first sergeant joined in on belittling him.

Though we had mini-buses that took us on daily runs to Camp Commando, the higher-ups also wrangled some large touring buses to take us to a huge permanent Army base near Kuwait City which was supposed to have a swimming pool. The first time I had the opportunity to go, I stayed at the LSA, imagining a nasty, third-world pool with algae on it. The people that went that day told me that it was amazing, so I went the next day.

The base was just as good as they said it was, which was weird since Marines exaggerate everything. It had a huge gym, two food courts, two PXs, and an immense chow hall—all air-conditioned. The soldiers stationed there lived in real barracks and drove to work. There were lots of girls, but most were plain-looking and those that weren't already had boyfriends on-base. Voeller was the only one of us who didn't look like a concentration camp survivor, so he had a better chance than most. He reminded me of "The Beast" from the X-Men comics. He was a big, stocky half-Samoan who was one of the best wrestlers in the company. He was also an acrobat who could walk on his hands as well as his feet, which was apropos since his squat thickly-muscled body was almost simian. He was the one guy in the company who was never in a bad mood. He was so happy that it was almost a mental defect.

By the time we had been at the pool for an hour, Voeller had an Army chick rubbing lotion onto his back. A few hours later, as we were waiting near the buses, we saw Voeller amble up with a shit-eating grin. Several people had seen him abscond with the Army chick into an abandoned tent and we all wanted to hear what happened. He told us that she had sucked him off and then they fucked, which was such a strange concept to us at the time that it may as well have been science-fiction. Since neither of them had condoms, he pulled out and blew his load on her chest. She wasn't bothered, but she did point out that she had to go back to work and she couldn't show up smelling like Samoan nut juice. Being a nasty grunt, he traded t-shirts to keep her out of trouble. To prove it, he lifted his cammie blouse up to show the stains on the brown army t-shirt he was wearing. Groans of disgust were mixed with murmurs of appreciation for a job well done.

The Warfighter Lab that had trained us at Victorville came out to the LSA to collect our opinions on how our new gear had fared in combat. When you ask a Marine for his opinion, you might as well say, "Start complaining now." Most comments were not constructive. I said that we needed forward hand grips on the 240s (known as "heat shields") since our gunners sometimes had to shoot from the hip, like Fernandez had when he fired the gun on his tippy-toes in tall grass at The Bridge.

After they heard our complaints, they started asking us ridiculous questions about future weapons and gear. They would say things like, "What would you think about a rifle that was half as big as the one you have now, twice as powerful and used caseless ammo which never jammed?" That was like saying, "Would you like a flying car with a machine in it that creates nymphomaniacs that shoot money out of their ass when they come?" I got the feeling that they were throwing in slam-dunk questions like that so they could pump up their report. We left scratching our heads.

Afterwards, Sprinkles came into our tent to do his own version of the Warfighter lab. He also wanted to speak to each of us individually. I thought he was going to have something big to say, since he almost never spoke to anyone in his own platoon. When I sat down with him, he spoke slowly like he was talking to a three-year-old. He told me that when we got back home, we couldn't act like we did out there. I sat agog as this kid who was six years younger then me told me, with a straight-face, that I couldn't pick my nose in public or pull off to the side of the highway when I needed to piss. These pearls of wisdom reminded me of the one time he spoke to the platoon before the war, when he told us, apropos of nothing, that he would prosecute us if we raped anyone.

We had very little to show for all the time we spent away from our families. We were forbidden from taking home any cool war trophies; we couldn't even take empty AK-47 magazines or Iraqi bayonets. Few people had taken many pictures; my camera had busted early in the war. Even when it did work, I was afraid I'd take some cool shot and then turn around and see my whole squad got killed while I was snapping pics. Luckily, we got a chance to buy some crap before we left. In one of the many empty tents, they allowed some locals to sell their wares. Bootleg DVDs and Gameboy games abounded, but there was some really nice stuff too. Jesse bought an ornate marble chess board that was absolutely beautiful. He always tried to get the most out of our travels and I laughed whenever I remembered him buying a didgeridoo in Australia and teaching himself how to play it on ship. The vendors were hilarious, using out-dated slang they must have gotten off of old episodes of "The Fresh Prince of Bel Air."

"What's up, my dog? Buy some nice bling-bling for your boo back in the hood, yo."

It was really time to go home; we were getting way too familiar with each other. While filing out for PT one morning, several people still had morning wood that they didn't even try to conceal. Still dazed with sleep, Elias looked down, plucked at the fabric on his silky Richard Simmons shorts and said, to no one in particular, "I got boner."

The customs check would be held at the LSA. We heard horror stories about a Marine who tried to get some contraband through customs and got his company's flight canceled so that everyone could be re-inspected. We could not take anything that was even remotely related to weaponry. I spoke to one MP who told me about all the crazy things Marines had tried to sneak home. One Marine had taken a pistol that was a family heirloom. His grandfather had taken it to World War II and his father had taken it to Vietnam, but when he was caught with it, the MPs had to confiscate and destroy it. An LAV crew had hidden parts for AKs in the gas tank of their vehicle and a graves registration unit had tried to hide a blown-off Iraqi arm in one of their quad cons. I took all of these stories with a grain of salt.

The staff NCOs did three separate "health and comfort" inspections during our last two days, in which they made us dump everything we had so they could sift through it. SSgt. Melendez went around making humorous assessments of the idiosyncratic things people kept deep in their seabags, like the G.I.Joes I had from my childhood that I had brought along for luck.

As we waited for out customs inspection, Carpenter walked up and stared dully at me.

"Carpenter, what the fuck are you doing?"

"Well…Rager and Chiariello said that you wanted to see me, sergeant."

"Carpenter, I almost *never* want to see you. Get away from me."

Rager and Chiariello busted out laughing at their prank. They were the boots that I had been closest to, but that was coming to an end. We had been closer than family for months, in miserable situations and harrowing circumstances, but when we got back to America they would just be some guys I worked with.

We were ushered ten-at-a-time into the customs tent and shown the ten-foot-by-ten-foot squares where our gear would be inspected. The inspection was nothing like we had been told. It would take too long to check everyone thoroughly, so all they did was check the top of each pack or sea bag and then move on. One MP got bothered when I dumped my sea bag out since that meant it would take longer for me to re-pack and get out of there to make room for the next Marine. They wanted to get this over with as much as we did.

The dream finally came true when I stepped onto the freedom bus. When we got to the airport, we were hustled through several stations in adjoining tents where we would be given briefs on customs, last chances for amnesty and a final gear inspection. Ross asked to cut in with me, but I knew that the ten people behind him would follow, so I said "no." He got pissed and we didn't talk again until we got back to America, but that was how we always were. We were constantly getting in little tiffs, not talking for a couple days (or months) and then hanging out with each other all-day, everyday.

I saved two shells from each firefight and I prized them above all else. We had been told that expended brass was not allowed. I plead my case to Sprincin and since he could see how much they meant to me, he let me keep them, but the army inspectors would have the final say. After they heard my story, the Army MPs were cool enough to let me keep them. They advised me to keep them in the bottom of my patrol pack until I got back to the States.

After we passed through customs, we were quarantined in one tent until it was time to leave. Carpenter had gotten into it with McKee right before we left the LSA and he got into another argument with him at the airport. McKee could be a prick, but he showed Carpenter more compassion than most. Rager told me that Carpenter was having a breakdown because of all the bad news he had gotten from home. His bank account was empty and his wife was a complete junkie, cheating on him with her drug dealer, for Christ's sake. Rager and Moser tried to give him some good advice, but it just wasn't sinking it. Carpenter just wasn't cut out for the adult world.

I made a point of watching Kuwait recede into the distance through the triple-paned airplane window. So much time spent in that region, yet we left with nothing. No ties to the land or the people, no friends or wives. It all went away with no more evidence than is left by a bad dream.

When we landed in Maine, Jones' family met him at the gate and handed him his contacts, so he could take off his BCDs. Behind them was a small crowd of local churchgoers and Vietnam vets who made it a point to find out when returning units were passing through so they could welcome them back to America. Though I hadn't cared about parades or seeing yellow ribbons on trees, it was very touching. When an old lady hugged me, I imagined her remembering welcoming her husband or brother home from an earlier war. A crusty old Vietnam vet in his VFW hat shook my hand with a vise grip and called me "sarge", a term which was so out-moded that it made me smile. I felt embarrassed that he was congratulating me, knowing that he probably saw much more intense and sustained combat.

As we milled around the shops, the greeters provided us with free cell phones to call home. After I bought some gifts for my family, I went to the diner and got a real American grilled cheese sandwich, which tasted like heaven. I remembered being there seven months earlier and seeing Mohler in the diner showing off his moose puppet and making everyone laugh. He was such a great guy; he had been in the most intense combat we saw, but his future didn't look bright, at least where the Corps was concerned. He wasn't even going to be able to go home on our leave block since he was on legal hold.

I watched the American landscape turn from green to brown and I knew we were almost home. As we circled over March AFB, I looked down at the dusty sheds and irrigated fields of the desert town. We had been through so much, but it was over now.

After we got off the plane, a working party was called to load our packs into some semi-trailers. Though we could not leave until the job was done, all of the boots tried to avoid loading the truck. I had seen this problem coming. In Samawah, I was always very light on the boots when it came to discipline, not wanting to harass them over trifles when they were already working so hard. Any man who has to stir burning human shit shouldn't get fucked with because his hair is too long. When we got back to Cali though, they would have plenty of free time to blow off steam, so I expected them to be more obedient. Since no one volunteered, I told Fielder and Fernandez to get on it. It wasn't considered cool to pick both of them for the working party—they were in the same squad and we usually tried to spread the work among squads—but they were the only machine-gun boots I could find. Though they were good Marines, they were also the most sarcastic boots, so I knew one of them would have something to say. Sure enough, when I told them to help pack the truck, Fernandez groaned and mumbled something under his breath and then Fielder said, "Fuck that!" I went red with rage, leapt over the bags and started screaming at Fielder, making quite a scene. He tried to explain himself, but I didn't want to hear it.

Since they were both in Moser's squad, I told him about it and he agreed that they were getting too loose and that he'd back me in whatever I wanted to do with them. Though I was still angry, I felt bad; Fielder had only been on American soil for five minutes and he had already gotten lifed in front of his friends. After they packed the truck, I called Fielder over and asked him to explain himself. He said that he was trying to tell me that he didn't say, "Fuck that" to me, he said it to Fernandez who had told him to climb up in the hot and stuffy truck. I wondered if he was trying to play me, but Fielder reminded me that he was usually the most belligerent boot and he had no problem with telling senior Marines what he thought. It was a curious defense, but it was accurate. I apologized for yelling at him, and he accepted.

My little roundelay with Fielder had prevented me from taking a badly-needed piss before the two-hour bus ride. I couldn't believe that I had dreamed of coming home for seven months and now all I wanted was a damn bathroom. It seemed that half of my memories of being in the Corps were related to being trapped in vehicles with no bathrooms. I flashed back to grade-school and used every trick I knew to keep from pissing myself. After an hour, we hit the south gate of Pendleton, but we still had an hour to go. I looked up at the nasty female bus driver. Would she see me if I pissed in a bottle in this aisle seat? I felt like a little kid having to worry about that. I asked Moore if I could switch seats with him to be near the window. He had no problem with having a grown man piss in a water bottle right next to him, but he'd be damned if he'd give up his sweet window seat.

When we crested the hill and Mateo came into view, I didn't see home and family, I saw a place with about two hundred toilets. Signs and banners had been put up by families and girlfriends, but all I cared about was the beautiful blue water in the bottom of a Porta-potty. We had been told that we weren't supposed to go to our families when we got off; we had to turn our weapons in to the armory first and then have a quick formation. As we drove by our barracks, we saw our families on both sides of the roads and lots of titties. When the buses stopped at the armory, everyone scrambled out and I saw several piss bottles on the ground.

I ran to the Porta-Jon near the guard shack, giving the guard a frantic nod. If all I got to do was piss and then go back to Iraq, I wouldn't have cared. After I finished, I stepped out and looked at the guard. He was from 2/4, the battalion that had been in Oki while we were in Iraq. I wondered how he felt about us— resentful or proud?

After a very quick formation, we were cut loose to our families. I had to walk through the crowd three times before I found mine. People were so happy to be with their loved ones that guys I barely knew introduced me to their families, as if they wanted my confirmation that they were real. My son didn't recognize me; I was familiar, but he didn't know how. I had expected this reaction, so it didn't hurt as much.

We would have a four-day weekend, come back to work for a couple days and then go on our month-long post-deployment leave. Besides reconnecting with my family, I had one mission: to put weight back on. My wife started crying when she saw me changing out of my desert cammies, I looked so sickly and weak. Two days after I got back, I started hitting the weights hard and eating everything I saw. By the end of the leave block, I had put on thirty pounds and finally looked like a normal human being again.

I contracted a near-fatal case of Short-Timers' Disease and every second of every day was spent on planning my hoped-for school cut. Most of my peers had their EAS' in June of the next year, but mine was in May. I had started research-ing how to get a school cut when I was in Oki and I could quote the regs from memory.

The first few weeks back were very easy, but eventually we got back to training and my old nemesis—hiking. Though I dreaded it, the fear was diminished. Before we left, a hike was considered your measure as a man, but after being in a real shooting war, I didn't feel like I had anything to prove to anyone.

The hike was supposed to be short and easy, but before we even made it out of the camp, I felt like I was losing steam. When we stopped at the main road to wait for the medical humvees to catch up, Jesse commented on how he was worn out already. Others agreed and it was nice to know I wasn't the only one who thought that the pace was excessive.

When we stopped at the half-way point, I knew I was in trouble. Pushing Rager and Arellano half the way there had sapped my strength. I was surprised that the hike was kicking Arellano's ass, since he was so great at everything. I had forgotten that this was his first hike in The Fleet. I flashed back three years and remembered the shock to the system I received on my first hike with Golf Company.

I had to shuffle on the way back since my feet hurt too badly to use the loping stride usually used on hikes. When Rager fell back, I went back to "help him." Unfortunately (for me, anyway), he got his second wind and rushed forward to catch up. Luckily, Showers saved my bacon by falling to the rear of the company. Before the war, Showers had been approved for a discharge because of his feet. The paperwork didn't go through fast enough though, so he ended up going to Iraq with us. I gave Showers words of encouragement, secretly hoping that he wouldn't take them. Ross had fallen back to help another Marine and he was haranguing Showers to keep up. I tried to get Showers to drink from my canteen, but he waved it away, saying he couldn't drink and walk, which made me laugh. Showers got steamed at Ross for yelling at him, but Ross wasn't saying anything that wasn't true.

The medical humvee picked up Showers and the Marine Ross was escorting, which completely screwed Ross and I. We were now a half-mile behind the company with no excuse to be back there. Our new XO was a gung-ho football-type and he good-naturedly encouraged Ross and I to catch up. I trotted to make it look like I was running, which seemed to make him happy. I realized that, though I was holding my rifle and somebody's tripod, Ross wasn't holding anything.

"Hey, Ross. Take this tripod."

"You gotta be kidding. I've been carrying two rifles and an ammo bag the whole time. I just put them in the humvee two seconds ago."

"Exactly. You 'had' been carrying a lot, but you ain't got shit now."

"Fuck…Gimme the damn tripod."

"Hey, we'll laugh about this later."

"I'm gonna kick your ass later."

I caught up with the company, which had paused at the main road. It had been a short hike, but a bad one, and several people were lying on the ground in pain or disoriented. To my surprise, Squeak had passed out and they had driven him to the BAS, which made me the acting platoon sergeant. It took me twenty minutes to sort out all of the mis-matched and missing gear to Gunny Linton's satisfaction.

After I got the count right, I congratulated Cortez and Acosta for doing so well on the hike. I always felt that if you're going to chew someone's ass when they fuck up, you should praise them when they do good. I still haven't forgiven them for their treachery, but I looked at the whole picture. Cortez had done well under pressure at The Bridge, even though he was straight out of SOI. Acosta just had a moment of weakness; he was actually a pretty good guy and his rep and confidence grew later when he got out from under Cortez' sway.

Chhav called my name and motioned me over. There were several other machinegunners right next to him, so I wondered why he wanted me. He was a weird guy, so I thought he had a trick planned. He told me that he had strained his back and needed help putting his pack back on, which surprised me since Chhav was usually in great shape. I bent at the knees and braced myself to lift a heavy weight, but when I pulled upwards, I almost threw his pack ten feet into the air. It felt like it was filled with Styro-foam packing peanuts.

Reed still hadn't returned, to no one's dismay. Just as we had theorized, when he was absent from the section, everyone got along better. The bad rep that the machinegun section had gotten because of him had almost totally been repaired since he left. Even better, Reed's working party in Kuwait had supposedly been extended to January, when the last Marine unit was supposed to leave. If everything went as planned, I would spend most of January on leave and get out the first week of February, so I wouldn't have to deal with that idiot. I was still angry about everything he had pulled during the war and I had promised Rager and Ryan that I would do everything in my power to make sure that he got busted-down like the staff NCOs had promised.

Scott was in the same working party and he called a buddy and told him they'd be in the next day. I was determined not to let Reed ruin our section again. We had heard that when he was in Kuwait he had bragged to anyone that would listen that he had saved his entire section during the war. The only way that would be possible was if his cowardly screams and tantrums had scared away the enemy.

Reed appeared in formation the next day, with his "Hey guys, no hard feeling, right?" look. Squeak looked liked he was going to be sick when he spotted Reed. After the formation, I reminded Squeak about how he and Gunny Brouillet had promised that Reed would be demoted as soon as he got back. Though Squeak had repeated that threat several times in Iraq, he gave me a wishy-washy answer and walked off. Reed left for thirty days leave a few days later and I vowed to bring the charges forward myself if the staff NCOs didn't.

Carpenter's slut-whore-wife had done every rotten thing we predicted and more. She got him kicked out of his base housing when the MPs found drugs in their house. When I heard that, I was over-joyed that she would be getting arrested for having drugs. When Carpenter told me that all the MPs did was write her a ticket, I told him that he must be confused. Sure enough, he showed me the ticket and when I spoke with to some MPs, they confirmed that she was not being arrested. She was banned from base, but she still had all other rights and benefits until Carpenter divorced her. We had finally gotten Carpenter to give up his unrealistic view of "Princess Jen" and see reality, in all of its over-weight, drugged-up glory.

Carpenter ended up having another nervous breakdown and being sent to the nut hut down at the Naval Hospital San Diego. When Ross went to check on him, he found out that Siler was living there as well, though he was out on libbo at the time. Siler had his own room, could wear civvies all day and was still getting paid. The wing was co-ed and Ross asked the girl in the room next to Siler's about him.

"He's crazy. The first night he was here he asked if he could shower with me."

"Doesn't sound too crazy to me."

Third Platoon was being sent to the Miramar Air Show to represent the grunts and I was tasked with assigning Marines from Weapons to go along with them. I put myself on the roster along with the best boots in the section. Not only would the Air Show be fun and moto, but it would also get us out of a field op and a hike that week.

The Corps had provided a bus to take the Marines to San Diego, even though everyone had cars—nice ones too. With no bills and no families to support, the average single grunt came back from Iraq with twelve grand burning a hole in his pocket. Lances were driving Lexus' and half of the company had rims. Martinez got spinners on his car and I always wondered if his spare tire had a spinner on it too. The staff NCOs made us fill the bus anyway, so all of the boots had to ride down to the hotel in San Diego in the bus; then they had to bum rides back to base that night to get their cars.

Since Miramar was in the air wing, instead of staying in a sheds or tents, we had rooms in a four-star hotel in La Jolla. Monty and I got assigned to share a room, which he wasn't happy about, but he was ecstatic when I told him that he'd have it to himself. I lived five minutes away from Miramar, so SSgt. D let me drive to work like a normal person.

Chiariello had come down to be our resident armorer, but they didn't end up needing him, so he got to chill all week. Chiariello had been seconded to the armory after we returned from leave. It was good to have an ally in the armory, but he was missed in the section. I like his viciousness in battle, and his sleaziness in general.

Since I was the senior man for the weapons attachments, I went to the key leaders' meeting the first day. It was held in a huge building that looked like something you'd find on the local UCSD campus; much nicer than anything I'd ever seen in the Corps. The room was filled with fighter pilots and recon operators; most were way above my pay-grade. The colonel talked flight windows and angles of approach, while I wondered where the snack machine was. Though it was nice to be in a cordial and professional atmosphere, it was still the Marine Corps, as I realized when the colonel reamed two lieutenants for talking during the brief.

As I pulled into the parking circle in front of the hotel for the morning formation, I looked up at the over-hanging balconies. I hit the gas and peeled out, deciding to park in the covered garage. If I had learned nothing else in the Marine Corps, I had learned this: Grunts + Balconies = Pissing. Sure enough, as my boys came out into the lobby, they couldn't wait to tell me how funny it was that Rager had pissed off of the balcony the previous night. I told Rager that if it wasn't for his compulsion to piss off of high places, he could probably be Sergeant Major of the Marine Corps one day.

For the four-day Air Show, we would conduct one helo raid for the crowd each day and run a static display showing off our weapons. All of the elevens were needed to fill the two birds, but only half of the weapons attachments were required. Those that didn't fly would interact with the crowd. To no one's surprise, Monty took the easy job out and put himself on the static display every day. I wanted my boys to be able to chill and talk to the girls in the crowd, so I put myself on two of the flights.

When the Air Show started, traffic was backed up for a mile outside of the gates, but we had special passes that let us cut to the front like rock stars. We had more than enough people to man the display, so I set up a schedule that allowed everyone ample time to wander the grounds that were filled with cool military vehicles of every kind. I was able to go home until my shift started, though I didn't enjoy it much. Chiariello tried to tag along, asking me if I wanted to go bowling. Chiariello and I would definitely have been friends if we were both boots, and though I treaded that line, I still believed it was disastrous to cross it. I begged off, not wanting to insult him, saying that I was just going home to sleep.

While manning the static display, the crowd was friendly and inquisitive and I felt very proud to be in uniform. I joked that this was the one time that the career planner could come along and get me to re-enlist. Though it probably broke about twenty state and federal laws, I let the civilians hold the unloaded weapons as long as a Marine was watching them closely. Some really cute chicks—all damnably too young for me—would come by and flirt with the younger Marines.

The Marines who went on the helo raid finally came by, looking like hell. The raid had gone well, but afterward they had to jog in formation in front of the crowd as a "pass-and-review." The small Recon team in front of them sprinted the entire way in their light gear and the over-burdened line company grunts could barely keep up.

Some guys in the crowd would try to show off their shaky or inaccurate weapons knowledge, which was always funny. One guy who had said that he had been in the Reserves was trying to impress his girlfriend. He pointed at the 240—mis-identifying it as an M-60—and bragged about how great he was at disassembling and reassembling it. Just to mess with him, Fielder told the guy he could "dis and ass" it if he wanted to. The guy proceeded to completely embarrass himself in front of his girl, to Fielder's amusement. Rager and Chiariello were laughing at two old, crusty, and fat bachelors whose stained t-shirts stretched over their beer bellies. I told Rager and Chiariello that was them in twenty years.

The kids loved the display and it was a breath of fresh air to see their unfettered excitement. I remembered coming to shows like this when I was a kid and I wondered if I was seeing any future Marines in the crowd. I was worried by the total lack of respect some of the kids had for firearms though. It seemed as if their parents had never taught them gun safety. I was shocked when one little black kid put a pistol right against a little girl's head. I grabbed it from him and admonished him, but I didn't think it sunk in. I had always loved guns and it bothered me how they got a bad rap for being dangerous. As Chris Tucker said in my favorite comedy, *Money Talks*, "Guns don't kill people—stupid motherfuckers with guns kill people."

The next day, the LT told us to conduct some dry-runs of exiting the birds. The elevens launched into their routine and those of us in Weapons—who had been at the static display the previous day—had to guess what their next move was. When we inevitably made a mistake, I heard the familiar refrain from Gollum and the others, "Fucking Weapons messed it up again." Luckily, Slater came over and explained the scheme of maneuver. When I complained to Slater about the negative atmosphere in Third Platoon, he agreed with me. Slater was an amazing Marine, but he had been completely mis-used in Iraq. When Schofield came back to Third from his FAP, right before we deployed, Slater got posted from his leadership role. Schofield's reign was so de-motivating that Slater stopped giving a damn. When the option was given for Slater to step into the lowly position of trac security, he took it gladly. It was a damn shame, considering how freakishly tough Slater was. During the war, I had secretly wanted to see Slater get surrounded by twenty enemy fighters, just so I could stand there and watch him take them all out.

I handed my camera to a buddy to take some final moto pics since this was probably the last time I would do something in the Marines that was cool enough to warrant taking a picture. I traded my rifle for Ryan's 240, and slipped my beloved SAW sling on to it. As I hung it on my chest, I felt like the ultimate bad-ass. When we climbed on-board, I couldn't help smiling like a kid. I wasn't with my old buddies—Ross, Silva, Hyatt Mohler, and Showers—but it reminded me of the old days, when everything was new and exciting. We had been blessed with an amazing crop of boots who would carry on when we left. A better bunch of guys I couldn't have hoped for.

We flew figure-eights over the hills of Mira Mesa as we waited for our flight window. After twenty minutes, I started to feel a little queasy and I almost never got air-sick. Rager was greener than his cammies. When he took his helmet off to barf in, the crew chief called Rager over and let him throw up out the side hatch. I had to take a picture. I had put myself on the schedule for another flight, but I decided that this was my last. I loved riding helos, but there was nothing more I could get from them. It was better to give my seat to someone like Rager who needed more time getting used to the birds.

When we straightened out and headed for the flight-line, I got a little bit of stage fright. I never had to be a grunt in front of an audience, and there were several thousand spectators crowded into bleachers that extended a quarter-mile down the flight line. As we descended, I worried about slipping down the greasy rear ramp in front of the crowd. When the bird landed, Rager's feet went out from under him and he tumbled down the ramp onto the flight-line. Later on, I told Rager that every bad thing that I worried would happen to me, happened to him.

We moved from the flightline to a small strip of grass which was filled with pyrotechnics. When we got within 100 meters of the stands, we set down on-line and aimed at the crowd. A few months earlier we were killing Muslim extremists with these weapons and now we were pointing them at a crowd of typical Americans.

For the finale, F-18 Hornets would fly by and a huge gasoline explosion would be detonated on the grass behind us to simulate a bombing run. We had been told it would be big, which was the understatement of the year. When I heard and felt the explosion, I broke character and looked back at it. A wall of flame sixty feet high and 200 meters long erupted on the flight line. If only they could have done something like that at The Bridge.

We got up and moved within a few feet of the crowd to do our "victory lap." Recon had been told to slow it down, so they kept a reasonable pace. The crowd was friendly and enthusiastic, some shouting their appreciation for our sacrifices. I didn't join for accolades, but this was nice. It was a long run, but I didn't mind; it was great to feel that popular support.

I watched the Marines interact with the large crowd our static display had attracted. My harsh opinion of Monty softened when I saw him with the crowd. He was great with everyone, especially the kids, and he was a great advertisement for the Marine Corps. I realized that most of my problems with him were personal and that when it came down to it, he was a good Marine. His MOS knowledge was superb and he had fought more than honorably throughout the war. He was a selfish scammer, but then again, so was I. When the chips were down though, he got rounds down range—what more could I want?

The next week would be eaten up by TEMP/TAP, the transition-to-civilian life class all Marines must take before they get out. Going there had been a dream of mine since I saw my seniors do it two years earlier. The company office told us that the class was held in the base theater, but when I got there all I found was an empty parking lot. I called the company office and got Keller on the line. I explained that they had given me the wrong address and I needed him to find out where it was. Just to fuck with me, he yelled out loudly, "Sgt. Meyer doesn't know where he is or where he needs to be." Derisive laughter in the background. Nice. I had to drive around Mainside and ask random Marines where the class was.

Our instructor was a grunt from Vietnam who looked like and had the personality of Santa Claus. Unfortunately, the five-day class had been truncated to three days. The good news was that if our company office was so clueless that they didn't know where the class was even held, they wouldn't know it had been shortened. Everyone from Golf agreed to not return to work until the next week, which would work as long as none of us cracked or squealed.

Santa worked for the Unemployment Office and he told us that we all qualified for Unemployment after we got out, which surprised me. He told us what states paid the most and that we could apply for benefits in those states without even living there. Someone asked him if he considered that scamming the government and he said that all it was doing was getting your rightful entitlements. Thank you, Democratic Party!

We learned about qualifying for disability, which was a point of contention for me and a lot of other Marines. Wall supposedly had an allergy to leather that he had only discovered after joining the Marines. The "problem" was a pre-existing condition, but he was supposedly getting a stipend for the rest of his life since the military exacerbated his "affliction." I even heard that Boyd's worthless ass was getting money for his in-grown hairs, yet we were told that hearing loss— which almost all of us grunts had to one degree or another—was not eligible unless you were almost completely stone deaf in both ears. The scar that I got on my finger from the saw grass in Oki got me qualified as "disabled", but since it didn't impair me, the level was set at 0%, which was different than not being disabled. Being qualified as being disabled supposedly got me points toward any state or federal job. I figured if things went bad I could stand on the side of the highway with a cardboard sign that read "Disabled Vet" and it wouldn't be a lie.

Santa had us role-play going through interviews and dealing with common workplaces occurrences. He reminded us that while threatening or pushing someone was acceptable in the Marines, it would get your fired or arrested in the civilian world. I was surprised to see Jones, the carny kid from First Platoon, in the class. When I asked him why he was there, he proudly told me that he was a drug pop and he was being kicked out. He was young, dumb, and married—never a good combination. He would go back to his old life and remember why he enlisted in the first place and his bad-conduct discharge would dog him for the rest of his life.

We got kicked out of our conference room the last day and had to conduct the final briefs in the base church across the street. We were threatened with dire consequences if we cursed or acted up in the church. They tried to shove three days' worth of briefs into one day and by noon, we were all near-catatonic. I went outside to get some fresh air, which few other people did since we weren't expressly told that we could. TEMP/TAP was all about shaking off that slave-mentality, but I soon saw evidence that some people didn't want to let it go.

By the afternoon, people were falling asleep right and left in the stuffy church. When one young Marine laid down on a pew and went to sleep, a female staff NCO starting hissing at him. When he didn't wake up, she walked over and started yelling at him like a drill sergeant, right there in church. When the guy woke up and asked her what her problem is, she went into a tirade, cursing and threatening him. She never identified herself, asked him who he was, or tried to counsel him in a professional manner. When we got a break, she ordered him outside, put him at parade rest (in his civvies, no less), and lifed him in front of everyone. This class was supposed to teach you how to be a civilian again. She had been awake the whole time, but she had missed the most crucial part of the class.

I wasn't able to enjoy my pilfered leave for fear of getting caught and my heart jumped when I saw someone from work had left a message on my phone. I called the company office and Sgt. Hashimoto told me, in his usual jovial tone, that he apologized for calling me away from TEMP and TAP, but that they had to have me come in and take the PFT the next day or (the usual threat) the company would not be secured. I explained about my family situation, which prevented me from getting to work before 8:00AM, and he told me they'd have a staff NCO there to administrate the PFT for me.

When I arrived the next morning, there was no one around to give me the PFT. Even worse, the company was being released after returning from the PFT, so my trip up to Mateo had been a waste. I spied Meeks, the training NCO in charge of records, and I sidled up to him and explained my situation. He congratulated me on my eighteen pull-ups, twenty-two minute run-time and 100 crunches. I was heading south on I-5 within ten minutes.

The next week, I spoke with Lt. Chittick, our new platoon commander, in his broom closet office. He asked me if I got my PFT score in and I said that I had, which wasn't a lie. He cocked his eye, suspicious of me.

"So, you got your score to the training NCO, Sgt. Meyer?"

"Yessir."

"I don't remember seeing you at the PFT."

Damn.

"Uh, yeah, about that sir. The thing is—Oh, I almost forgot! Did Carpenter tell you about his problem with his wife? That freaking guy…I'll go get him right now."

I sped out of the office before he could question me further, sending Carpenter to him with his latest problem. I laid low for the rest of the day and Lt. Chittick never questioned me about the PFT again. I don't know if he forgot about it or if he just gave me points for creativity and let it drop.

A new era had begun in Golf Company, which I dubbed "The Revenge of the War Dogs." The War Dogs were the new staff NCOs and officers in the company, who had either not been in the war at all or had gotten there after the combat phase was long over. Many of them projected a dismissive and condescending attitude towards us to make up for their feelings of inferiority. Capt. Kenney was the worst, coming off like an elitist prick. Though he had been training boot officers at Quantico during the combat phase, he constantly intimated that what we had been through wasn't "real" war and that we had just been lucky. That was like a senior in high school who was still a virgin telling a freshman who got laid every weekend that he didn't know how to get pussy. In training, we still practiced the same out-moded battle tactics that were used in Vietnam. It was like we had won the Super Bowl and now we had to go play Pop Warner football. Motivation sunk to an all-time low and people started doing selfish, self-destructive things, like doing drugs, fighting and going UA.

The condescension of the War Dogs led to a breakdown in discipline. The general feeling was: if we could go through a war and win every battle we were in; then come home and get treated like recruits by guys who weren't even in the war, then why should we even try?

Every day during PT, the Marines were getting run into the dirt. By Wednesday, one junior Marine noted that they had already run fifteen miles that week. We knew that in combat you never ran more than 10 meters from one covered position to another, but there was another reason for making us run so much. The War Dogs had spent the last three years at desk jobs, where they had ample time to get into shape. Feeling inferior because of their lack of combat experience, they tried to put us in our places by out-doing us on the runs.

In addition to running five miles a day, every Monday there would be a ruck run, in which the Marines ran the ridge-line wearing their war gear. The XO wanted to "spice up" the training and told Sgt. Dart to design a more challenging ruck run.

"Sir, what are we going to do with people who gaff it off or just plain quit?"

"I don't see that happening, Sgt. Dart. They're all Marines and will handle themselves accordingly."

Dart was right and during the next ruck run—which was augmented with stations in which Marines would do calisthenics and be quizzed on their MOS knowledge—three of the 51s gaffed it off, walking most of the way. When Dart ordered them to participate, McKee, Jones and SweetPea flat-out refused. Dart charged the three of them and they all had to line up outside of the First Sergeant's hatch to get read their rights. McKee was getting out in a few months as a lance, so he didn't give a damn, but the other two still had two more years and one more deployment. Jones and SweetPea were both tough and smart and would make great NCOs one day, but with McKee leading them down the garden path, they would be lances for a very long time.

The condescension of the War Dogs was inescapable. Even infallible Marines like Budzynski were not immune. Bud picked up sergeant and, after the promotion ceremony, Captain Kenney put his hand on Bud's shoulder and told the assembled company how exemplary a Marine he was. Later that day, the sergeants waited in the company office for the company gunny. Every day, there would be three platoon sergeant meetings with the company gunny. We would be excoriated if we were late, but we would still wait an average of twenty minutes for the gunny to show up to his own meeting. After waiting for forty-five minutes, Bud decided to do something useful with his time. He pulled a book on applying for jobs out of his patrol pack and started to read it. Captain Kenney walked up behind him and started shaking his head. He then walking off, sighing disgustedly.

After the captain got out of earshot, Bud turned to the rest of us.

"What the hell was that? It's not like I was looking at porn. I'm getting out in two months; shouldn't I be reading stuff like this?"

"He's like that with everyone."

"If I had been sitting here, staring at the table like a dumb-ass, that would have been fine. But I read a book to help me prepare to get on in life and suddenly I'm a piece of shit?"

We had several great sergeants like Bud, Slater and Martinez. All of them had wanted to be lifers earlier in their enlistment, but the constant unwarranted condescension had turned them off of re-enlisting. It was always expressed the same way. No one ever said they wanted to "get out"; they always used the phrase "get the fuck out."

Squeak was supposed to go to the Staff NCO academy until December, so SSgt. Greer, a.k.a. The Goose, was put in his place. The Goose had been the platoon sergeant while I was on FAP and he had a rep for being a prick, but something must have happened to him when he got back to America to cool him out. He was gone a lot since he was moving into a new house, so Ross, Rodgar and I split the duties of platoon sergeant. The Goose actually let us make decisions and he gave us a measure of independence and we returned the favor by acting responsibly.

A day after he got back from his post-deployment leave, Reed was back to causing trouble. On his first day back, he had to take a PFT to make up for the one we took while he was on leave. When reveille was called the next day, he **refused to come out for formation.** Moser sent Crozier up to get him and Reed told him that he was worn out from the PFT the day before and wouldn't go to PT with us. This was the same the guy who bragged every day that he was the toughest man in the world. A PFT is less strenuous than a regular PT session since it is entirely self-paced. Moser sent Crozier back up to get him and Reed finally trotted his ass out during the middle of the company formation, making us all look bad.

When Lt. Chittick questioned Reed about being late, Reed lied and said that no one told him we had PT that morning. When Moser heard what Reed told the lieutenant, he reported Reed for lying. Even a boot knew that we had PT every damn day. When Reed was called in to the platoon commander's office, he started his innocent act, which we had forewarned Lt. Chittick about. Lt. Chittick told Reed that he had a drawer full of counseling sheets from Squeak on him and he could bust him down at will. Reed left, noticeably humbled.

Chittick was a short, unassuming type who I wished I would have gotten to know better before I left. Though he had to toe the line as an officer, he wasn't afraid to tell us when he thought something that came from on-high was fucked. He was from Georgia and had enlisted in the Reserves before he became an officer. I first saw him at Victorville; I had gone to Second Platoon's area to find Elias when I saw a young, unfamiliar face. Since the kid had no rank on his Gore-Tex jacket, I assumed he was a boot. Since I was a "cool" NCO, I called him "buddy" throughout our short conversation—not understanding why he looked so constipated. For some reason, he didn't correct me for not addressing him as an officer.

Ross and I were ecstatic that someone in power had finally put their foot down on Reed, but we were wrong. Despite all we had been promised, Reed was still a team leader. We told Lt. Chittick that the boots all professed that they had no respect for Reed and would not follow him, but Lt. Chittick said that he didn't have enough to post him. He had bluffed when he said that he had a drawer full of counseling sheets; despite all of his threats, Squeak had never counseled Reed formally. What's more, neither Squeak, Gunny Brouillet or First Sergeant Young were following up on their promises to bust Reed down.

After several hints of decreasing subtlety, I finally demanded to know if Reed was getting busted down or punished. I was told that it had been too long since the incidents and, since there was no paper trail, nothing was happening. I kicked myself for not counseling Reed in writing for each incident. In Iraq, I had asked Squeak what I needed to do to charge Reed. Squeak told me that the apparatus did not exist to charge Reed in Iraq, but we could do it as soon as we got home.

I was still angry at Reed, but that wasn't my only reason for wanting to see him pay. The junior Marines had worked their asses off in Iraq and here was an NCO who was an embarrassment to his section and his Corps, who had acted like a child at best and a maniac at worst, and he had gotten off scot-free. Why shouldn't they do the same when they went back to Iraq?

A few days later, I was called in to First Sergeant Young's office and told to go to parade rest. He told me I was getting a Page 11 for the porn incident, which had happened six months earlier. I couldn't believe that he didn't have anything better to do. Ryan and Lopez received Page 11s as well, yet Reed was still wearing his corporal's stripes.

If I had even been sent to a real Corporal's Course or Sergeant's Course, like I had requested, I would have known the proper procedure for charging Marines. Instead, I had to question the company clerks and indifferent staff NCOs to learn the process. Writing the charge sheet was no small effort, since Reed had done so much. By the time I was done, his charge sheet was ten pages long. I charged him with 11 separate infractions of the Uniform Code of Military Justice, including assault, disobedience, disrespect and malingering. I had wanted to get him for "Conduct Unbecoming an NCO", but I found out that didn't exist as an expressly stated crime. The news that I was trying to charge Reed burned through the company and people who I barely knew or didn't even like me were coming up to me and giving me words of encouragement.

A few days after I turned in the charge sheet, I was summoned to First Sergeant Young's office. He waved me in and made a production of reading the charges. When he was done, he looked me in the eye and said that what he had read made him disgusted...with me. I knew he would try to turn it around on me. When he asked me why I didn't do this sooner, I told him that Gunny Brouillet and Squeak had told me that they couldn't bust anyone down until we got back to Cali. The first sergeant said that wasn't true; that Acosta and Cortez had been prosecuted while we were at the train station. I reminded him that they were charged only after the camp was up and running; Reed left shortly after we got there. When he said that too much time had gone by, I reminded him that Reed had been gone for most of the past six months. I had just received a Pg.11 from him for charges that were just as old. Every point he brought up, I had a counter-point, but I could tell that no matter what I said, he would not pursue the charges. He glanced back over the charge sheet, shaking his head and saying that if he had known about these incidents as they happened, he would have busted Reed down for each individual charge and Reed would be a private. It was impossible that he did not know of any of the incidents, especially the fight with Bodine, which occurred in front of the entire company five minutes after he gave Reed his "final warning."

I took solace in the fact that, if I could use my remaining leave and get my school cut, I only had 23 work days left in the Corps. People scoffed at my plan, but it gave me great hope.

When Gunny Linton and Gunny Brouillet retired, The Goose took over as company gunny and I became the acting platoon sergeant. My wife had serious medical problems that had her going in-and-out of the hospital, so I became my son's primary care-giver. To my amazement and eternal gratitude, The Goose and First Sergeant Young were extremely amenable, allowing me to come in late and leave early so I could put my son in day care. Though this book may seem like nothing but a litany of complaints, whenever I had a family problem (of which I had many) the staff NCOs and officers never hesitated to give me as much help as possible, always going far beyond what they were required to do. I had friends in other companies in similar situations, whose chains-of-command were nowhere near as sympathetic, who ended up going UA or shuttling their kids off to live with relatives.

With my unheard-of 9-to-5 schedule, I missed the busiest times for platoon sergeants—morning and evening formation. When I rolled in at 9:00AM, I would get the word from Ross or Rodgar or Monty—whoever was there that day. I tried to be the kind of platoon sergeant who would actually follow-up on things and take care of my Marines, but just keeping track of where all 54 Marines in the platoon were at any given moment was almost a full-time job. Keeping their cover stories straight was even harder. When Monty and Keller said, "We're going to Dental and then to the Education Center on Mainside," I knew that meant, "We will be gone all day, God knows where, but we'll call before evening formation."

After getting permission to come in late and leave early every day, I entered a realm of scandalousness the likes of which the Marine Corps has never seen. Throughout the "work" day, as acting platoon sergeant, I could make almost any excuse to get out of classes or formations. I would chill in Ross' room as we "went over the training schedule" which was remarkably similar to watching "Dawson's Creek" on cable TV. Like when I got into "Buffy, the Vampire Slayer" after I returned from Oki, my entire work day came to revolve around watching back-to-back episodes of "The Creek." Being that I was in my mid-twenties when it originally aired, I missed out on the lyrical beauty of the show, which revolves around a small town in North Carolina where half of the people are gay and the straight kids spend all of their time talking about sex instead of having it. In every episode, Dawson would almost get laid before his "morals" would stop him, as Ross succinctly put it.

The "Damn Dawson River" kids spoke in insanely-long compound sentences, that were pretentiously filled with words that would make an English Lit grad student bang his head against a wall. Anytime a character went for more than three sentences without letting the other person interject, we would yell "Speech!" Each episode had at least one word that no normal human being ever uses, let alone a high school kid. As a joke, Ross and I would use the Dawson's Creek Word of the Day while speaking to the platoon in formation, purposefully using it incorrectly, though few people noticed. When Ross nonchalantly told the platoon that they had a five-mile run the next day and that it "would be some intrusive shit", Jolly cocked his head to the side like a dog who had been given a command that he didn't understand, looking at the others to see if they heard the same thing.

After two weeks of successfully avoiding anything that resembled actual work, Ross and I started to scare ourselves. We had taken skating into uncharted territory and we were just asking to get caught. We both agreed that we had set some kind of record and that we should be proud, but we needed to buckle down before we got thrown in the brig.

After I gained my weight back during post-deployment leave, I kept working out daily. The only thing the Marine Corps really splurges on are their gyms. Once I got the morning platoon sergeant business out of the way, I would go to work out.

"Hey Showers, I'm going to the gym. Be back in an hour."

"Who said you could go?"

"I did."

"Damn, must be nice to be platoon sergeant."

"It is…Now go sweep my catwalks."

I had adopted a slow, incremental workout plan that, after several months, was showing some dividends. I was in better shape than I had ever been; even in Oki. I still couldn't fight, but I was strong enough that, when we wrestled, I could just grab my opponent and keep him from pinning me, which was as close as I ever came to winning.

Rohr had been hitting the weights hard as well and it showed. Though of average height and build, his arms would fill his rolled-up cammie sleeves, which Silva had told me was the ultimate goal for every Marine weightlifter. We had never patched things up like Kennel and I, had but we had never had as much of a blow-up either. There was just a lingering animosity, which was even stranger since we were both best friends with Ross.

Since some of the diggies that joined us in Samawah went on the Kuwait working party right after they got to Golf, I barely knew their names. When I heard one kid talking about the war, I made fun of him for not knowing what he was talking about, confusing him for another diggie that came after the war. Later that day, I realized my mistake and when the kid came into my office, I apologized profusely, which seemed to surprise him.

If we weren't doing anything important, I would let people go home, as long as they had a half-way decent excuse. After lunch, Ryan came up to me, looking frantic. He told me that he needed to drive his wife to the airport in LA, since her flight was leaving in an hour. He gave me a convoluted story about a friend of his wife renting a car to drive her to the airport, but the friend needed a ride back when she returned the car at the airport. I told him he could come up with a better story than that, but he insisted it was true. I threw my hands up and told him to just go. After that, any time Ryan spoke to me I said, "Let me guess, your wife's flying to Paris in forty-five minutes, right?"

RodriguezHool, a.k.a. Rodhool, was still such a boot that he would go to parade rest while walking if you called his name. He was getting married to a Mexican national and was having problems with the voluminous paperwork. Lt. Chittick denied his leave request, saying that the Martial Arts course took priority. Denying leave had been a major bone of contention throughout my enlistment. Every Active-Duty service member is entitled to 30 days of paid leave a year. Unless you're deployed, you're supposed to be able to take it whenever you want it, but in 2/5 we were only allowed to go during battalion-designated leave times. In Kuwait, we brought this up to Sgt. Maj. Davis during one of his NCO bitch sessions and he seemed legitimately surprised. He told us that it was our right to take leave any time it was reasonable to do so. He said that when we got back to Cali, we should alert him if anyone tried to deny our leave requests.

In all of the dozens of pushing matches and scuffles I saw in the grunts, I only knew one person who got seriously injured. Picas was the loudest of loudmouths and he got on almost everyone's nerves. He broke the rules by having a girl in the barracks after midnight and when Scott challenged him on it, they got into a shouting match. After it was broken up, Scott cornered Picas in his bathroom and beat him bloody.

The next morning, the two of them stood outside the First Sergeant's hatch, waiting to be charged. As happens so often, after fighting bitterly they were already back to being friends and were chatting amiably, even though Picas' lip was ripped almost in half. I liked Scott, he was always dependable and enthusiastic, but he needed to be seriously punished for what he did to Picas. Even though Picas was annoying as hell, he was a good kid and didn't deserve what happened to him. They each ended up with the same punishment—a Pg. 11 and some finger-wagging. Once again, the way Marines were disciplined was arbitrary and unfair. Having a woman in the barracks got the same punishment as assault. Seven month-old charges against Reed for endangering his squad were thrown out, but charges for looking at porn that were just as old, were approved for Ryan, Lopez and myself.

Every time I went to the company office, I felt like I was back in Iraq. I knew that the Marine Corps had a small budget, but our office made it look like it had no budget. None of the chairs matched; every piece of furniture was at least twenty years old. The Goose was quite proud of himself when he found a large piece of wood by the gas chamber and got the police sergeant to make it into a meeting table. We were having weekly piss tests that were administered in the company office and spills were frequent, so the whole office was a bio-hazard.

We had Martial Arts Training scheduled for the week before Christmas leave and it came down that no one could miss it for any reason. If they would have told us that earlier it would not have been a problem, but since we didn't find out until two weeks before Christmas, many people had made plans for that week. RodHool's leave was eventually approved, but Crozier was denied permission to go to his brother's wedding, since Lt. Chittick didn't think that was a good enough reason. Reed gave the lame excuse that he needed a week to drive to Michigan safely, so he wanted that week off as well. He told the LT that he would call his congressman if he was not granted the leave. Eventually, everyone got leave that week if they wanted it, good reason or not.

Chiariello was his usual sarcastic self, but he starting taking things too far. I had always worried that being too friendly with him would cause problems and it did. Whenever I saw him, I would say, "Hey, it's Bridgey McBridge. Crossed any you-know-whats lately?" While chatting casually with him at the armory, he called me by my last name. I gave him a terse warning, which he seemed to acknowledge. A few days later though, when Ross and I were talking to him, he turned to Ross and said, "Watch this…hey, *Meyer.*" When I exploded at him, he put his hands up, saying he was just joking. Once could be a mistake, but twice was him testing me. I asked Ross if I was being too harsh. He told me that Chiariello had been hitting the bottle hard since we got back, showing up to work drunk and pissing everyone off after-hours. I decided I would charge him if he did it again.

Heading to the libbo formation on Friday, I passed Chiariello, who was standing with Headquarters Platoon. I heard someone behind me call out my last name and laugh. I whirled around and Chiariello pointed at Wall and said that he did it. I was angry enough to consider rushing over and tackling Chiariello, but I didn't want to cause a scene. I'd deal with him on Monday.

I spent the entire weekend weighing my options, which varied from letting it go since I was so close to getting out, charging him or beating him up. Letting it go wouldn't work, since I needed to defend my rank. Since I was in the best shape of my life and Chiariello was in horrible shape from constant drinking, it wouldn't be a fair fight. I didn't want to be one of those Marines who threw away years of comradery and loyalty over one disagreement. It hurt me to know that I had to charge him, seeing how much time we had spent together in Iraq, but I had to do it.

On Monday, I went to the armory and told him to report outside. He walked out, looking bothered and I told him to go to parade rest.

"Are you serious?"

"Do I look serious?"

He put his hands behind his back and I read him his charge sheet. He tried to interrupt, but I told him to be quiet. He looked pissed and asked me if we could talk man-to-man, instead of lance-to-sergeant. I didn't want to be accused of hiding behind my rank, so I allowed it.

"Look, I really was just messing with you before, but when you yelled at me that time that Cpl. Ross was here, I realized you didn't think it was funny. Wall was the one who yelled your name, I swear to God. I've already got the XO looking to charge me because the counts are messed up in the armory. I really don't need more trouble."

I looked Chiariello in the eye. He was a hustler by nature—hell, that was why I liked him—but I thought that he was telling the truth. He hadn't spoken to me for three days after I put him on a working party in Iraq, so I guessed he would never want to speak to me again.

"Alright, man, I'll ask Wall. You're a scandalous fuck, but I think you're for real. Look, even you have to admit that you were pressing your luck. I didn't start this. I don't give a fuck about rank, personally, but there's things that I can do with it to help good Marines. If I allow smart-asses to de-value my rank in public, than why should someone in authority listen to me when I go to bat for guys like Crozier or RodHool?"

I made sure that we shook hands before I left, whatever good that did. Wall corroborated Chiariello's story, saying that he thought it would be funny to get me mad at him since he didn't think I'd go this far. I told him that he almost got Chiariello charged.

Carpenter was living in the barracks by then, awaiting a psych discharge. While in the company office, our new XO asked me if I knew Carpenter; I told him I wished I didn't, but I did. He told me that Carpenter was not allowed to handle weapons anymore. Carpenter was actually acting more normal now that he was under close supervision and away from his wife, but he was still an idiot and late or absent for everything. He had developed a weird penchant for buying cars he couldn't afford, selling them back to the dealership two weeks later and then buying another one. It was a testament to the power of credit since Carpenter's wife was still siphoning his bank account every payday, which she was still legally entitled to do until their divorce was final.

Speaking of cars, Ryan relayed a funny story from before the war. Carpenter had gotten his first car from one of the rip-off joints in Oceanside that charge dumb privates and lances 20% interest. While getting a ride to work, Ryan was sweating profusely.

"Damn, Carpenter, turn on the AC. I'm dying in here."

"I don't think this car has AC."

"Carpenter, I'm looking right at the controls. I know it has AC."

"I don't think so."

"What do you think those little wavy lines and the letters 'AC' mean?"

"Well…"

Ryan flipped the switch and a cool blast of air filled the car.

"You see, Carpenter? You had AC the whole time."

"Well, yeah, but I thought you meant the kind of AC like they have in a house."

"Princess" Jen knew that she still had all the rights of a military wife and she didn't hesitate to call the first sergeant any time she had a problem. After Carpenter told me that she had not shown up to any of her court dates for the drug charges, I tried to report her and get her arrested, but no one cared. There seemed to be a disconnect between the military and civilian justice systems. She told First Sergeant Young that she had lost her ID and needed a replacement to get on a flight the next day, so I was tasked with making sure it happened. After they had gotten into a domestic dispute, Carpenter was only allowed to come near her with an NCO escort. It galled me that when this lying, cheating, drug-addicted fugitive called the company office, I had to re-arrange my day around her. She refused to speak with Carpenter, so I had to talk to her. When she changed her story, telling me that she needed the ID that day, I told her to cut the crap. I would have Carpenter at the ID center the next morning, and if she wasn't there, she wasn't getting a second chance.

The next morning, she surprised me by actually being at the ID center early, having been dropped off by her new boyfriend, a druggie Marine. From 100 meters away, you might say she was good-looking, but the closer you got, the more she looked like a squat version of Courtney Love at her most crackish. I stood between them until I got sick of the whole sad situation and walked off. Carpenter deserved a lot of bad things, but no one deserved that bitch.

In mid-December, a new staff sergeant took over as platoon sergeant. SSgt. Bartlett had been in for eleven years and was just coming off a three-year stint in MSG. Unlike SSgt. Sikes—who came back to the grunts with a humble attitude, worked hard and earned our respect—SSgt. Bartlett came with the same attitude as Captain Kenney. He had no regard for our war experience and no trust for the NCOs. He marched the platoon the two blocks to the chow hall like a bunch of recruits, even those of us who weren't going to eat there. He then gave a ten-minute brief on how long we had to eat and where we should re-form at the barracks, which was beyond insulting.

I told him that I only had fifteen work days left in the Corps and that I needed to start checking-out, but he insisted that I go to all of the martial arts training and conduct my checking-out procedures during my lunch break. Only after I explained to him point-by-point each thing I needed to do and how long it would take did he allow me to skip an hour of martial arts each day. I got to polish up on my blood chokes and hip throws, which would certainly help me ease myself back into the civilian world.

Since Lopez had taken the Martial Arts Instructor Course in Kuwait, he led us in the day's bayonet training. The animosity toward him had died down, but it still flared up from time to time. As always, people did not want to take orders from someone of the same rank; many of the others joked around and ignored Lopez, who got angry and yelled at them. I asked Lopez if I could interject, since he was in charge, and I spoke to the Marines. I told them that, yes, the few Iraqis who actually did fight us were bitches, but Iraqis weren't the only people we might fight. I mentioned the troubles in North Korea and reminded them how fiercely they had fought the last time they tangled with America. Arab jihadists vary between cowardly and inept, but every victory the Marine Corps has won over Asians has been paid for in blood.

Lopez was only evaluating one Marine at a time, so I suggested that he start three lines. Since Showers and Miller were grey belts, I told them to help Lopez evaluate. They both whined and tried to beg off, so I had to pull rank and order them to help. We were short-timers, but we still had to contribute.

Since we didn't have our weapons with us, we used sticks as guns. I laughed as I looked over and saw Jesse making a working bow and arrow out of the thin sticks. Wherever we went, Jesse was always fashioning crude, silly weapons out of scrap wood and sticks. I told him he would be perfect for a show like "Survivor."

I joked that even if he won the million dollars, he would probably still want to stay on the island.

Breaking the Marines into smaller groups kept them busy, so they griped less, but they didn't stop giving Lopez static. Afterwards, while Lopez was away, I called the junior machinegunners to the side, dismissing Arellano and Carpenter. I asked them why they weren't supporting Lopez and they gave me a laundry list of complaints, all of which were minor gripes that came from living too close to each other in the barracks. I told them that if they still had any problems with him from the investigation, they needed to drop it. They needed to show a united front, like my seniors had, and not bicker in front of their boots, like we had under the Reed administration. That seemed to get their attention, but Fielder again brought up another minor problem he had with Lopez. I told them that this wasn't an order—I would be gone in a few weeks—it was just friendly advice. If they held on to their petty differences, they would look like fools in front of their boots—as Reed had done to us.

Wall continued to be a bad influence on Showers. Though Wall had finagled his way into HQ Platoon, where they actually got some work out of him, he still spent an inordinate amount of the work day in Showers' room. Wall had discovered a little-known Marine Corps program in which Marines who tested at less than an eight-grade level of comprehension could attend a month-long adult education course on Mainside. Wall didn't care about his education—he really didn't give a damn about anything—he just wanted to get out of sweeping and manning phones for a month and he wanted his good buddy Showers to join him. Wall and Showers went to get tested and, when the results came back, Wall had a third-grade education and Showers had a fifth since they had both purposefully tried to do badly. I told Wall he should be embarrassed to be a grown man with a 3rd-grade comprehension level, but he didn't care. He had cheesed out of the war because he was "allergic to leather." Showers had more physical problems than Wall, yet he had fought at The Bridge.

After Wall left, I took Showers aside. I told him that he had done a major repair job on his rep during the war and he shouldn't let himself be led down the garden path by Wall. Wall didn't give a fuck, but I knew Showers had his pride and I challenged him on his low scores. At first, he said he had done bad on purpose; then he said he hadn't; then he said he had, but only on one part. He told me he really was concerned about his education, so I asked him if he had ever gone to the base library that was three miles away. He got mad and refused to answer. I told him that I wasn't going to narc on him, just don't lie to me and say he cared about anything else than getting out of working parties for a month. He finally admitted that and I left. I made a conscious decision to spend more time hanging out with Showers to counter-act the negative influence of Wall.

By the end of the week, our morale was at an all-time low. The year had been a wringer and at the end, we seemed to have nothing to show for it—no respect from our superiors, no involvement in deciding our own training, no trust to do something as simple as walk to chow. I had been counting the days until I got out, but I wasn't alone. Slater had picked up sergeant meritoriously and he couldn't wait to get out. Ditto, all-stars like Tardif, Martinez and Budzynski. No one was getting out of the Corps because of the combat—getting shot at was part of the job—but being under attack by our own leaders in an atmosphere of condescension was more than almost anyone could stand.

My last time on duty would be on New Year's Eve, but since I wasn't a partier or a drinker, I didn't mind. SSgt. Bartlett threw a hissy fit when he found out that he had it on the same day, stomping out of the company office. I showed up early on the 31st, expecting only a few problems from lonely drunk Marines. I was paired with a boot lieutenant who had just come to the battalion.

Though most people had to pull duty every month or so, I only pulled it a few times during my entire enlistment. Being married helped, since they could never grab me to replace someone who was sick or UA, like they did to Keller on dozens of occasions. Having a last name that started with "M" helped even more. Whenever they made the roster, they would start at "A" and fill the roster before they got to "L". The next month, they would always start with "N" or "P".

It got cold in the duty office, which was an unheated storage room. When I was told that they needed someone to pick up a Marine from the airport, I jumped at the chance. Better a heated government van than shivering in that closet like Oliver Twist. A boot who had gone UA shortly after we returned from Iraq had turned himself in to authorities in Hawaii, which was a smart move. The government paid for him to fly back to Cali. Unfortunately, the van had no gas and the key to refill it didn't work, so I paid to fill the tank. It would get me out of that freezing room for several hours and I could sleep as the other guy drove. As usual, the word got completely messed-up and we were sent to San Diego before we found out that the kid had already landed at LAX. I got perverse enjoyment out of wearing my cammies at the airport and seeing the mixed looks of awe and fear in the eyes of the civilians.

When I got back, the boot-tenant was making a big deal about a staff sergeant who had not shown up for duty. The staff sergeant had gone to the hospital that morning and gotten a light-duty chit for extreme flu symptoms, but the lieutenant thought he was scamming and called him at home, ordering him to report to work. I told the kid that if the staff sergeant had a light-duty chit, then he was allowed to stay at home. A career staff NCO isn't going to risk being UA just so he can fake sick and party. Nonetheless, the officer kept calling the man's home until his wife refused to put him through to her husband. The lieutenant told the wife that her husband would be charged with being UA if he did not see proof that he was really sick. Not fifteen minutes later, the wife showed up in a red rage and proceeded to yell at the lieutenant like he was a little kid. She told him that she was disgusted with this chain-of-command's lack of respect for their Marines and their families. She said that she couldn't wait until they got to her husband's next unit; that she had never dealt with something like this in twelve years as a Marine wife. She thrust the light-duty chit in his face and stormed out in a huff. I had to sit on my hands to keep from applauding.

The BC showed up and tried to speak with us, which was usually awkward and fake in a politician-kissing-a-baby way, but this time he seemed sincere. I thought about how much we had hated this man in Iraq; how I had wished for his death on almost a daily basis, yet here he seemed wise and fatherly. He asked me if I was re-enlisting and I told him about my school cut. He said that the paperwork for my school cut had not crossed his desk, which was no surprise to me. All through December, I had been in and out of First Sergeant Young's office, trying to get him to approve my school cut paperwork. The paperwork had to go all the way up to the commanding general of the base, but I couldn't get it past the first sergeant's desk. He had no idea how to complete the paperwork, but he wouldn't admit it. Every time I submitted my package, he would circle a half-dozen needed corrections. When I would fix them and turn the package back in, he would find six more.

Though First Sergeant Young couldn't be bothered to get my school cut paperwork done, he had ample time and energy to make sure that I got another Pg.11 for the porn incident that was issued by Sprinkles, even though I had already been punished for the exact same "offense" by First Sergeant Young a month earlier.

Returning from leave, I resolved to use Request Mast to get my school cut moved forward. Fortunately, First Sergeant Young was leaving that week, having finagled himself a non-hiking job back in the Air Wing. When we got back from Iraq, he started taking leave every time we had a hike. He went to his buddies at Miramar, trying to get someone to pull strings so he could get out of the grunts. He must have had some juice because he got orders to leave Golf Company half-way through his three-year stint. Captain Kenney supposedly chewed him out for going behind his back, but I'm sure he was glad that First Sergeant Young was leaving. Though First Sergeant Young had followed Captain Hammond around wherever he went, I almost never saw him near Captain Kenney, which many people interpreted as a racial thing on First Sergeant Young's part.

We all groaned when we heard that the new first sergeant would also be from the air wing, but we ended up being pleasantly surprised. Almost immediately, First Sergeant Jackson made a good impression. He didn't look down on grunts like First Sergeant Young had and he actually had a sense of humor. Being over six foot tall also meant that he was blessedly free of Little Man's Syndrome. I spoke to him about my problems with getting my school cut approved and he cocked an eyebrow when I told him that I was trying to get out in less than a month. When I explained that the delay was not my fault, he said that he would check into it. He made no promises, but somehow I knew that he would get things done.

The day before I went on two weeks' leave, I received a bomb shell—Lt. Sprincin had given me an adverse fit-rep, the worst rating I could get. When I got to see the five-page report, I got sick to my stomach. The porn incident was mentioned on every page, sometimes several times, while my combat experience was only mentioned once. He accused me of not properly leading patrols in Samawah, when everyone knew that I was solely the driver on every patrol. Nowhere was it mentioned that I constantly accumulated more billets until I topped out with five. Nowhere was it mentioned that I had two people in my squad with severe mental problems. Just as I was stepping out of the Marine Corps, Sprinkles gave me a nice kick in the balls as a good-bye present. There were so many things wrong with his report that it wasn't even funny. Sprincin had never once counseled me on any of my supposed deficiencies, which was supposedly the reason that Reed's charges had all been thrown out. Sprinkles wrote the Fit/Rep four months late, and never had me sign it, which was required.

When I told Ross and some close friends about it, they shook their heads in disgust at Sprinkles and told me to ignore it since I was almost out. I went to someone who hated me to see if Sprinkles' accusations had any merit. When I told Squeak what Sprincin had said, he thought I was joking. Squeak corroborated that I had been made a driver because I was the only person with a humvee driver's license, not because of any supposed deficiency. Sprinkle's report was so egregious and inaccurate that even Squeak told me he would go to bat for me, which shocked the hell out of me.

I told First Sergeant Jackson how wrong the Fit/Rep was and asked him what I could do. While at first he seemed wary—what person wouldn't say those charges were false?—when he read my rebuttal, he seemed to get on my side. He told me that if everything I said was true, than I had a pretty good chance, but he didn't say what my "chance" was. I found out that Sprincin's accusations, since they came from an officer, would remain in my record no matter what. All I could do was get my rebuttal put in my record right next to the report. Sprincin was free to libel me in a set of records that would follow me the rest of my life.

Sprincin's own words damned him more than I ever could. After we returned from post-deployment leave, Sprincin left to become the XO of the Weapons Company, which was fine with us. He was universally hated in the platoon and if you didn't hate him yet, you hadn't met him. After his final formation with the platoon, he called us together informally and gave a little speech. He told us that after he had time to reflect, he felt that he had wronged us. He told us that whenever he spoke of us to fellow officers, he always under-sold our abilities and over-estimated our deficiencies. That attitude was reflected exactly in my report. After he finished the speech, I was one of the few people who stayed afterward and shook his hand. I didn't like him, but we had served together in war and I thought we were supposed to be a band of brothers.

Between the time he left Golf and the time I found out about the Fit-Rep, I noticed odd behavior from Sprinkles. There was a short hallway between the Golf and Weapons Company barracks and whenever I came around the corner and made eye contact with him, he would jump a little or look nervous. When I saluted him and gave a friendly greeting, he would seem surprised and embarrassed.

Not only did I have to rebut Sprinkles' report, I also had to rebut Captain Kenney's report which backed Sprincin's. For the period covered—March through September of 2003—Captain Kenney only knew me as a sergeant who had five billets and then went on leave, so I wondered why he would have such a bad impression of me, besides the fact that he was backing a fellow officer. Lt. Chittick wanted me to vent to him. When I asked him why Captain Kenney corroborated Sprincin, Lt. Chittick told me that Captain Kenney had a very simple view of Marines. You were either someone he could use or you were totally useless. He said Captain Kenney had a bad opinion of me because I had family problems that kept me from PTing in the morning. My family problems hadn't kept me out of the war that he watched on CNN.

The Goose called me into First Sergeant Jackson's office, which had become my second home lately, and told me to give him a run-down of all of the things Reed had done. They wanted to burn Reed for some reason. I hoped that they had finally come to their senses, but I sensed an ulterior motive. I went and got my charge sheet and let First Sergeant Jackson read it. He laughed while reading it; even I had to admit that if you didn't know Reed and didn't have to deal with him, his exploits could be quite entertaining. Every time I called home, my friends would ask for more Reed stories. First Sergeant Jackson dismissed me and I hung around the company office, waiting to ask The Goose what had incited this. It turned out that the great crime Reed had committed was supposedly making a smart comment under his breath while an officer was talking during a brief. Fucking perfect. Reed endangers his whole squad during the war and dishonors the Corps on multiple occasions, and no one cares, but when he slightly offends an officer in peacetime, they want to hang him by the short hairs.

Predictably, they didn't follow up on charging Reed, sufficing to let Gunny Linton chew him out, which surprised me since I thought Gunny had retired months earlier. Nevertheless, by this time, Reed was effectively neutered. He finally seemed to have realized that he didn't have a friend in the company and, while he didn't act normal, he didn't act like himself, which was an improvement. The boots realized that his rank was a joke now and they mocked him openly. Rager and Chiariello had started riding bulls in amateur matches on the weekends and Rager was sore the next Monday. When he fell back on a PT run, Reed told Rager that he should drop the rodeo and work out more.

"You know what, Reed? I got a better truck than you, a better-looking girl than you and I own my own house; so I think I'm doing pretty damn good. Why don't you shut up?"

After another PT session turned into a near-mutiny, SSgt. Bartlett called Weapons Platoon into a room for a heart-to-heart. Bartlett was running the platoon into the dirt every day and bragging about himself constantly. When he started threatening people for little things like laughing during PT, guys like Jones and Jesse started mouthing off, tired of his condescension. Jesse told Bartlett that people didn't like him because he was always bragging about himself, adding that, "No one likes a Reed." Everyone laughed while Reed sat there silently.

When I went on leave, my school cut was still very much in doubt. There was battalion-wide ignorance of how the school cut program worked and I found out that none of the half-dozen applicants in the battalion had been approved, even ones that had put their paperwork through months earlier. One Marine from Weapons Company was told his school cut was in-the-bag, so he had paid for the semester and gotten an apartment before he found out that his still paperwork was still hung up at battalion. Luckily, his chain-of-command was cool enough to give him off-the-record leave until his school cut got approved.

On the Thursday before I was due back from leave, I got a message from First Sergeant Jackson. I thought my leave was being canked or they were trying to foist duty onto me, like they had the previous week. When I called him back, he told me that he had gotten my school cut approved, but they were missing the paperwork that proved I went to the mandatory TEMP/TAP class. When I told him it was in my glove box, he said that if I wanted to get out of the Corps, I needed to get it to Division HQ before the end of the week.

The next Monday, First Sergeant Jackson told me how he had gotten my school cut approved so quickly. Realizing that all of the school cut packages were being held up at the battalion level, he simply avoided the middle man. He jumped the chain-of-command all the way to division HQ, called in some favors and got it done. There had been a long drought, but it looked like Golf Company finally had a real first sergeant on-board.

I had five days to check-out, a process that usually takes two to three weeks. The biggest obstacle was the final physical, so I went to get that out of the way first. I took my first hearing test since boot camp, and though I had a slight loss of hearing, it was nothing compared to the massive hearing loss most grunts experienced since they were too cool to wear ear plugs during training. I had been dreading the final physical because I had heard that anyone older than 30 had to "get their oil checked." I asked my buddy Doc Cox if that was true and he said he'd check. I told him if it was true, I would keeping re-enlisting until I died in combat at the age of eighty-two. When I went for my final physical though, all they did was check my blood pressure and send me to get interviewed by the MO, so I could get a final chance to claim any service-related ailments or disabilities. After dreading the finger in the ass for so long, I was almost disappointed when I didn't get it.

I still had almost fifty places scattered all over the base that I had to check-out of. In addition, I had to tie up some loose ends. I asked First Sergeant Jackson if he could get me my promotion warrant to sergeant, and though it bugged him that I waited until the last minute, he came through for me yet again. I also needed to add the "Plus-Up" to my GI Bill, which I had put off for years. The Plus-Up program had come into fruition when I was a boot, but my seniors had explained it so poorly that it seemed like a horrible idea. With the regular GI Bill, after you invest $100 a month for the first year, you rate about $900 a month for 36 months of school. Chuck had told me that if I paid an additional $600 to the G.I. Bill, I would get extra months added onto the end of the 36-month period, but no extra money per month. Texas had a program where all vets who enlisted there got free schooling after they exhausted their GI Bill, so it would be a waste to add months on to the end. In TEMP/TAP though, I learned how great a program Plus-Up actually was. For an additional $600, I would get an extra $200 per month, which ended adding $7200 to my $32,000 of GI Bill money.

After three days of checking-out, I had completed everything but the final gear turn-in, which I thought would be easy. Wrong. Supply was now run by civilian contractors as a for-profit business and they were complete pricks. All of the gear had to be laundered and any damage had to be repaired. No consideration was given for the fact that our gear had just been through a war. They made people sew up bullet holes and I knew one guy whose pack was not accepted by Supply because it had been damaged by an RPG. They refused to accept my flak jacket since it had small flecks of tar on it. They weren't just being pricks; profit was their ulterior motive. They had the power to declare any piece of gear "unserviceable" and then profit by selling the government a replacement. After waiting in line all morning, I had to go back to Mateo and try and clean tar off of my flak.

Supply was run by a mid-forties, ex-army guy with an earring who was despised by everyone on base. Not only was he lazy and rude, but he would try to order Marines around like he was in their chain-of-command, even making gullible lances clean up the parking lot and take out his trash. I assumed I could simply let them dock my paycheck to pay for my missing gear, but it wasn't that simple. Any missing gear, even a missing grommet for a pack strap, had to have a Missing Gear Statement signed by the Battalion Commander before it could be crossed off your account. When I told the guy that this was the last thing that was holding up me getting out of the Marine Corps, he told me to follow him outside. When we got outside, he looked around and then leaned in close.

"Do you have a big mouth?

I could see where this was going.

"No."

"That's good. Look, you slip a twenty into one of your black gloves and I'll sign off that you're good to go on all the little shit you're missing."

"Does that count the flak?"

"Shit no…I'm risking my job just hooking you up like this."

"I'll keep that in mind."

The small pieces of gear I was missing weren't even worth twenty dollars, but besides a missing green glove, none of the other pieces of gear were sold on base. The smallest pieces had to be ordered on-line, which could postpone my departure for another week. I'd keep him open as an option, but I hated the guy so much that I didn't want to give him the satisfaction of scamming me like he had so many others. Luckily, Cortez was willing to switch flaks in trade for a fleece that I didn't want since I thought that some of Monty's pee got on it when he spilled his piss bottle back at the LSA.

With the big-ticket item taken care of, I started walking down the catwalk, knocking on doors and offering to buy extra gear from people. I went to Miller from Third to call in a favor. A few months earlier, when my wife was in the hospital and I only had $200 in the bank, he asked to borrow $50, promising to pay me back the next day. Though I could barely feed my son at the time, I loaned him the money because I thought I could trust him. For the next three months, he had one lame excuse after another. It wasn't the money so much as the fact that someone I thought was my friend was trying to welsh on me. It was a bad way to go out on what I thought was a good friendship. I told him if he hooked me up with some of the gear I needed, I'd call it even.

The last piece I needed was a magazine pouch, but no one had one. I got a lead that Scott had an extra, but he was at lunch. My new school cut-adjusted EAS was on Sunday, but I could get out that day if I got everything done. It was Friday afternoon and it was looking unlikely that I would be able to turn in my missing gear and get my separation papers from PAC before the end of the day. When Scott finally came back from lunch, he told me that he didn't have an extra mag pouch, but he thought Miozza did. It turned out that Scott was wrong, but Miozza still hooked me up, taking a mag pouch off of his flak and giving it to me free of charge. I told him he just gave me my ticket to freedom.

I got signed off at Supply and my check-out sheet was almost complete. I went to Captain Kenney to get signed out of the company. To my shock, he wished me luck and told me to make sure to come back before I left, so he would know that everything went well. Yeah right. I hustled up to PAC to get the hell out of there, but after the usual interminable wait, I got some bad news. I still had several more forms to get signed at battalion and it was too late in the day.

I returned on Monday, got the forms signed and went straight to PAC. I was then told that they had to type up my separation orders, which wouldn't be ready until Wednesday.

"Fine. Fuck it. More pay."

"Actually, you were officially out of the Marines yesterday. You're not getting paid anymore."

"I'm not getting paid? Then why am I in uniform?"

"Damn if I know. Next!"

I returned on Wednesday and waited in line for hours next to Taylor, the guy from Echo Company with the "soapy water." Rank doesn't mean shit when you're getting out in an hour, so the lances were pricks, but I didn't want to yell at them for fear of them fucking with my paperwork even more. I got my DD214 in quintuplicate and was told to hand in my ID.

"Am I a civilian now?" I asked in a hopeful, little kid voice.

"Yep," he said as he turned around. Another piece of paperwork for him, but a milestone for me. I had someone take a picture of me with my separation papers in front of the check-out desk and then I stepped outside, in a daze.

I walked to my car and drove out through the camp, feeling like an escaped convict. When I stopped at the gas station by the gate, I saw some of the guys from my battalion heading out to the field. I wanted to wave good-bye and have them share in my excitement, but I decided against it. I was not one of them anymore. I drove out the gate, turned left at the highway, and drove south along the coast.

The End

978-0-595-35076-6
0-595-35076-3

Made in the USA